SAMNIUM AND THE SAMNITES

SAMNIUM AND THE SAMNITES

BY

E.T.SALMON

McMaster University, Hamilton, Ontario

CAMBRIDGE
AT THE UNIVERSITY PRESS
1967

CAMBRIDGE UNIVERSITY PRESS
Cambridge, New York, Melbourne, Madrid, Cape Town, Singapore,
São Paulo, Delhi, Dubai, Tokyo

Cambridge University Press
The Edinburgh Building, Cambridge CB2 8RU, UK

Published in the United States of America by Cambridge University Press, New York

www.cambridge.org
Information on this title: www.cambridge.org/9780521135726

First published 1967
This digitally printed version 2010

A catalogue record for this publication is available from the British Library

Library of Congress Catalogue Card Number: 67–10781

ISBN 978-0-521-06185-8 Hardback
ISBN 978-0-521-13572-6 Paperback

Additional resources for this publication at www.cambridge.org/9780521135726

CONTENTS

MAPS

*Map 5 is available as a download from www.cambridge.org/9780521135726

PLATES

Between pages 416–417

PREFACE

More than half a century has elapsed since Wilamowitz remarked that a study of the Italic peoples was badly needed. This is still true, even though such works as Syme's *Roman Revolution*, Sherwin-White's *Roman Citizenship* and Toynbee's *Hannibal's Legacy*, to mention only books in English and by no means all of them, have shed much light on many aspects of non-Roman Italy. Of the Italic peoples the Samnites are the ones who appear prominently in every account of Roman expansion in Italy. Indeed they have inspired some of Livy's finest writing and have evoked generous tribute from him, largely, I suspect, because the period of their greatness was for him *aetas qua nulla virtutum feracior fuit*, the heroic age of Rome. Yet no attempt has ever been made to describe these fiercest opponents of republican Rome from their own point of view. It is in an effort to remedy this deficiency that this book has been written. The present state of the evidence makes it a modest aspiration, but I hope that it may contribute to the growing activities in the Italic field.

The documentation, though necessarily heavy at times, is, of course, far from exhaustive. Allusion to modern writers has been severely limited, especially in chapters 5–10, where reference to the learned literature would have been overwhelming. Additional bibliographical information can be found in Broughton's *Magistrates of the Roman Republic*. Dates throughout are B.C. unless otherwise stated.

My obligations for material assistance and moral encouragement are numerous. An Overseas Award from the Canadian Department of External Affairs and Grants from the Humanities Research Council of Canada, from the Nuffield Foundation and from McMaster University have aided both peregrination and publication. The long and repeated sojourns in Samnium have been invaluable.

I am deeply indebted to friends for advice and counsel. Dr Lily Ross Taylor, of Bryn Mawr, often shared her vigorous and erudite enthusiasm about things Italic. Dr Franco Bonacina, of the Centro Didattico in Rome, placed his intimate knowledge of the Italian countryside always at my disposal. Drs T. R. S. Broughton, of the University of North Carolina, H. H. Scullard, of King's College, London, and A. H. McDonald, of Clare College, Cambridge, and the late Professors A. D. Nock and J. Whatmough of Harvard, willingly agreed to read some of the chapters in MS: they are, of course, in no way responsible for the errors that remain, but thanks to them the errors are fewer than they would otherwise have been. Dr Franz Stoessl, of the University of Graz, Dr Paolo Sommella, of the Istituto di Topografia Antica in Rome, General Domenico Ludovico, of the Italian Air Force, and my colleague Dr J. A. S. Evans, of the McMaster Department of History, responded with alacrity, whether it was information or photographs that were being sought.

An especial debt of gratitude is owed to the Soprintendenza alle Antichità degli Abruzzi e del Molise. Its director, Dr Valerio Cianfarani, guide and master of all who study Samnium, gave generously of his time and expert knowledge amid the excavations of Saepinum and amid the Italic treasures at Chieti. Dr Adriano La Regina has been unstinting with aid of exceptional usefulness both in conversation and in correspondence. My regret that these scholars' views on Bovianum Vetus became known to me only after my own work had already reached the printer (see p. 13) is tempered by the comforting reflexion that I am in their well-informed company in assigning Pietrabbondante to the Pentri and not, with Mommsen, to the Caraceni.

The readiness with which the Museo Nazionale at Chieti made available many of the photographs for the plates is gratefully acknowledged. So is the kindness of the staffs of many other museums —at Ancona, Aquila, Capua, Naples, Paestum, Santa Maria Capua Vetere, Sulmona. I well remember the good offices of Drs Nicola del Cioppo at Baranella, Renato Brancaforte at Campobasso, Angelo Viti at Isernia, Dante Marrocco at Piedimonte d'Alife and, outside Italy, the authorities of the British Museum, the Louvre and the Bibliothèque Nationale. I owe particular gratitude to the directors and librarians of the Institute of Classical Studies in London and the British School and American Academy in Rome.

In my own university I am in the debt of many. Its librarians showed both skill and speed in procuring rare and recondite materials via inter-library loan; its photographic unit gave efficient and punctual assistance in the preparation of illustrations; and Miss Jean Montgomery patiently transmuted much-emended calligraphy into the clarity of the type-written word.

Finally, I am grateful to the Syndics of the Cambridge University Press for providing very efficient and keen-eyed editorial and production teams whose vigilance has kept blemishes to a minimum.

Hamilton, Ontario E. T. SALMON
February 1967

CHAPTER I

THE SOURCES

Of all the tribes and nations with whom the Romans found themselves obliged to dispute the supremacy of Italy none were more formidable than the Samnites of Samnium. They were the stalwart possessors of a larger territory and of a more determined temperament than any other people in the peninsula. They were numerous enough and spirited enough to refuse to submit tamely to Rome, and the military and political opposition that they put up against her was of the toughest.[1] It is a commonplace that they, and they alone, were the really redoubtable rivals of Rome for the hegemony of peninsular Italy, and they came within measurable distance of winning it. For half a century and more, from 343 to 290, they engaged her in the three successive conflicts known as the Samnite Wars, and they renewed the struggle with her whenever opportunity offered in the course of the two centuries that followed: the war upon which the name of King Pyrrhus of Epirus has been bestowed might with equal propriety be called a Fourth Samnite War, as indeed Livy implies and Orosius positively states;[2] Hannibal, too, found some solace and support amongst the Samnite tribes; and in the first century the last great uprising of the Italians against Roman despotism once again found the Samnites in arms, characteristically displaying greater tenacity and a more resolute will to resist than any of the other insurgents.

In view of the notable role of this people it is surprising that they have attracted, relatively speaking, so little attention. No version of Roman history can possibly fail to give them a good deal of space. But this is invariably done within the Roman frame of reference, and not as an independent study, although they are worthy of investigation for themselves. The narrowness of the margin between victory and defeat for them is in itself a challenging subject of inquiry. Yet they have seldom any received thorough or searching attention. No

[1] Even after the Romans had celebrated twenty-four triumphs over them (Florus 1.11.8), the Samnites were still prepared to renew their resistance whenever they got the chance.

[2] Livy 23.42.2; Orosius 3.8.1; 3.22.12.

full-length, comprehensive monograph on the Samnites has ever appeared.[1] And this is the more remarkable seeing that, though remote, they are not mere creatures of legend, but are very much alive in a period that has been intensively scrutinized. It is a compact tale that begins with their sudden appearance as allies of Rome in 354 and ends with their massacre at the Colline Gate in 82, and, if not fully within the light of history, its outlines are firm and many of its details certain.[2] The Samnites are mentioned by name by Greek authors of the early fourth century, but only casually.[3] The surviving ancient accounts of Roman history are concerned almost exclusively with the Romans. The people whom the Romans defeated receive only incidental attention; they are mentioned only when they are considered relevant to the Roman story. Münzer has drawn attention to the narrow-mindedness of the accounts: 'Things are viewed from one specific aspect only. In the matter of relations between Rome and the outside world all views except the Roman were suppressed...'[4]

Dionysius of Halicarnassus, it is true, is one writer who is quite catholic, and he inserts into his narrative erudite excursuses about the various Italic peoples whom the Romans encountered.[5] But, for the period of Roman dealings with the Samnites, his *Roman Antiquities* (Books 15–20) are extant only in scanty fragments.[6]

The story of early Rome was itself told in the form of a fixed and inviolate tradition, some of which was already known to Greek writers of the fourth century, or earlier,[7] and the firm framework of

[1] B. Kaiser's *Untersuchungen zur Geschichte der Samniten* (Progr. Pforta, 1907) never got beyond volume I.

[2] It is precisely in the period of the Samnite Wars that Roman history acquires an aspect of vital reality. Certainly from the fourth century on Rome must have had historical records of a sort; Greek writers of that time would hardly have described an unlettered settlement as an 'Hellenic city' (Heraclides Ponticus *ap.* Plut. *Cam.* 22. 2.; cf. Demetrius Poliorcetes *ap.* Strabo 5. 3. 5, p. 232).

[3] Philistus *ap.* Steph. Byz. s.vv. 'Mystia', 'Tyrseta'; Ps. Scylax, *Periplus*, 15.

[4] *Römische Adelsfamilien*, p. 46, cf. p. 66; also see such passages as Livy 33. 20. 13; 41. 25. 8.

[5] Strabo also bestows more than a passing glance on non-Roman peoples, but primarily with the eye of a geographer.

[6] He was verbose and rhetorical and one wonders how trustworthy his information would have been, had more of it survived. His figure of 15,000 for the Roman dead at Heraclea hardly inspires confidence: he must have known that Hieronymus of Cardia, a contemporary of the battle, gave the number as 7,000 (Plut. *Pyrrh.* 17. 4).

[7] Thucydides' contemporary, Antiochus of Syracuse, referred to Rome (Dion. Hal. 1. 73. 4); Aristotle alluded to the sack of the city by the Celts (Plut. *Cam.* 22. 3); and Theopompus at least mentioned Rome (fr. 317 Jacoby). See further Dion. Hal. 1. 72 and E. Wikén, *Die Kunde der Hellenen, passim.*

which was rendered canonical by Fabius Pictor in the third. It derived ultimately from the bare and unadorned records of the Roman pontiffs (*tabulae pontificum*)[1] which were gathered together and expanded in the second century in the collection known as the *Annales Maximi*; and the individual historian felt it his duty not to depart from this established outline, but rather to produce a literary creation within it.[2] His not to embark on the task of painstaking research to confirm or radically modify the accepted version.[3] One result of this is that the appearances of the Samnites in ancient literature are haphazard and sporadic. The only occasion on which they receive even a semblance of continuous treatment is during their wars with Rome, and even these are described exclusively from the viewpoint of the Roman victors. Nor was this the result of accident. Fabius Pictor had set out deliberately to justify the ways of Rome to men. He sought to replace any and all conceptions of the history of Italy, which Greek writers had been spreading, with securely pro-Roman versions.[4] Duris of Samos, Hieronymus of Cardia, Philistus and Callias of Syracuse, Lycus of Rhegium and

[1] Every sacerdotal college seems to have preserved its *fasti* (*CIL*, I. 1976–2010). Those of the pontiffs were very ancient (Dion. Hal. 3. 36; cf. 5. 1) and some of them escaped the Gallic sack, so Livy implies (6. 1. 10 and even 6. 1. 2). A famous emendation of *de leg.* I. 2. 6 makes Cicero describe these records of the pontiffs as 'jejune'; Cicero, however, is referring to their style rather than their content. In fact the *tabulae* contained a good deal of information: they mentioned grain shortages and eclipses of the sun and moon, according to Cato (Aul. Gell. 2. 28. 6; cf. Dion. Hal. 1. 74), and probably much more, if the length of the *Annales Maximi* means anything. (The *Annales* were in eighty books; in other words their compass exceeded Livy's (see Cic. *de orat.* 2. 52; Festus, p. 113 L.; Macrob. 3. 2. 17; Serv. *ad Aen.* 1. 373; cf. Livy 1. 31, 32, 60 and especially Sempronius Asellio, fr. 2 P.).) Presumably those *tabulae pontificum* which were compiled during the Samnite Wars (that is, after the Gallic sack of Rome) survived intact into historiographical times; and from at least the Pyrrhic War onwards they were drawn up in firm chronological outline (Pliny, *N.H.* 11. 186). The information contained in the priestly records could be supplemented from popular ballads and folklore, to which a number of ancient authors allude (Varro *ap.* Nonius, p. 77; Livy 2. 61. 9; Hor. *Odes*, 4. 15. 29–32; Dion. Hal. 1. 79. 10; 8. 62. 3; Val. Max. 2. 1. 10; Plut. *Numa*, 5. 3).

[2] The *Annales Maximi* were anything but skimpy (see preceding note). They must have been padded with much fictitious material. Of the two items positively known to have been recounted by them, one is an obvious falsification (it is a line of poetry which purported to be a popular Latin verse, but was in fact a mere translation from Hesiod: Aul. Gell. 4. 5. 6). The other is probably trustworthy: it is an eclipse of the sun (5 June, *c.* 350 A.U.C.) recorded by Ennius, who had obtained it from the records of the pontiffs (Cic. *de re pub.* 1. 25). Ennius, however, like Cato (fr. 77P.), used the pontificial records before they were edited, and contaminated, as *Annales Maximi*. To identify the fictitious additions to the *Annales Maximi* is not easy: but one such is almost certainly the Camillus saga, which is certainly later than Fabius Pictor (M. Sordi, *I Rapporti Romano-Ceriti*, p. 46).

[3] The traditional version seems to be confirmed by the scanty surviving fragments from Greek writers.

[4] See especially M. Gelzer in *Hermes*, LXVIII (1933), 129–66.

Timaeus of Tauromenium between them may have had more than a little to say, and not all of it unfavourable, about the Samnites, while largely ignoring the Romans.[1] Pictor remedied this only too successfully.

The seventh to the tenth books of Livy are the principal source for the three Samnite Wars, and it is usually admitted that the account they contain rests upon a basis of solid fact. At the core of Livy's narrative, and deriving ultimately no doubt from the priestly records,[2] are the lists of Roman consuls, and these lists seem to be reasonably trustworthy.

Admittedly Livy's annalistic predecessors were only too prone to rely on the statements and records of careers which, according to Pliny, filled the archives of the great Roman houses and which, according to Cicero, Livy and Plutarch, were themselves replete with exaggerations and distortions, if not unblushing lies.[3] The generals who fought the battles sometimes composed their memoirs, and there is no reason to believe that in doing so they were either modest or scrupulous.[4] Nor should it be forgotten that Roman statesmen and generals sometimes also had their own personal poets and panegyrists to laud their exploits.[5] Even more numerous, glib and plausible were later members of a *gens* who were determined to parade its glories. The Flavii evidently had their own archives, the Carvilii their own family historian. If the Postumii had A. Postu-

[1] They could hardly have avoided mentioning the Samnites when they described the activities of Tarentum's assorted mercenary captains (Pliny, *N.H.* 3. 98; Plut. *Ag.* 3; Lycus, fr. 1. 2 (in Mueller, *FHG*, II, 371)). Theopompus, we know, paid little attention to the Romans (Pliny, *N.H.* 3.57). Hieronymus, however, did not ignore them (Dion. Hal. 1. 6. 1).

[2] It is usually impossible, however, to say which items in the narrative go back to the *tabulae pontificum* and which are culled from family or other records. Ti. Coruncanius, cos. 280, was one hero who certainly appeared in the priestly records (Cic. *Brutus*, 14. 55). We have no precise details about C. Tuditanus' *Libri Magistratuum* (Macrob. 1. 13. 21) or the *Libri Lintei* which Licinius Macer used (Livy 4. 1. 2; 4. 20. 8; 4. 23. 2; cf. Dion. Hal. 11. 62. 3; R. M. Ogilvie in *J.R.S.* XLVIII (1958), 40–56).

[3] Pliny, *N.H.* 35.7; Cic. *Brutus*, 16.62; Livy 8.40; Plut. *Numa*, 1 (citing a certain Clodius). One wonders whether the great plebeian houses, once they obtained political equality, did not concoct family records so as not to be outshone by their patrician rivals.

[4] Ap. Claudius Caecus, the celebrated censor of 312, was a man of letters according to Cicero (*Tusc. Disp.* 4. 1. 4), and he evidently recorded his Samnite War exploits: he vowed a Temple to Bellona then (Livy 10. 19. 17), and we know that this temple was adorned with shields lauding the achievements of Claudii (Pliny, *N.H.* 35. 12; the reference must be to 312, not to 495). Later generals who described their own operations (in letters, it must be admitted) were Scipio Africanus (at Nova Carthago: Polyb. 10. 9. 3) and Scipio Nasica (at Pydna: Plut. *Aem. Paul.* 15. 3).

[5] The case of Fulvius Nobilior and Ennius immediately springs to mind.

mius Albinus to glorify their name, the Valerii had Valerius Antias.[1] The Cornelii, with no fewer than six of the twenty-three known republican *pontifices maximi*,[2] were in a good position to tamper with the priestly records; and so too, probably, were the Papirii, early redactors apparently of the *Annales Maximi*.[3]

A welter of conflicting claims was spawned, with the various *gentes* either fabricating wholly imaginary exploits or seeking to seize the credit for achievements other than their own or belittling the claims of others. The rivalry between Fabii and Cornelii Scipiones is notorious, and for good measure the Fabii were also jealous of the Carvilii, and the Cornelii Scipiones of the Fulvii.[4] The Claudii and the Postumii were obviously targets for denigration by other aristocratic houses and, to judge from what Livy says, the Volumnii too had some annalists for them and some against.[5] It was always possible for a historian to stake out a claim for his own clan by simply inventing a promagistracy or some other special office in which a member of the family could be said to have particularly distinguished himself.[6]

Fortunately it seems to have been much less easy to invent consulships, and as a result the lists of consuls, and even of triumphs, do not appear to have been vitiated to the same wholesale degree.[7] It is true that they often fail to reveal which of the two consuls was responsible for any given action, so that it was easy for a tendentious annalist to invent or exploit the illness of one consul in order to

[1] Livy 8. 22. 2; 8. 37. 8; Val. Max. 8. 1. 7; Plut. *Rom. Qu.* 54, 59; Polyb. 39. 1. 4; Pliny, *N.H.* 11. 186.

[2] See Broughton, *MRR*, vol. 1, *ad ann.* 431, 332, 304, 221, 150, 141.

[3] See Dion. Hal. 3. 36. 4; A. Schwegler, *Röm. Gesch.* 1, 24 f.; F. Münzer in *R.E.* XVIII (1949), s.v. 'Papirius, nos. 1–5', cols. 1005 f.

[4] Livy 10. 17. 11 f. (=296); 10. 22. 1 f. (=295); 23. 22. 8 (=216); 28. 45. 2 (=205). Three Fabii in succession served as *pontifex maximus*; their terms of office covered almost the whole period of the Samnite Wars. Thus they were ideally placed to falsify records.

[5] See, e.g., Livy 9. 42. 3; 10. 15. 2; 10. 18. 7; 10. 19. 2 f.; 10. 23. 4; 10. 30. 7; and cf. *CIL*, 1², Elog. x, p. 192. The misfortune of the Postumii in being associated with Roman setbacks later in the Republic, e.g. in the Litanian forest (Polyb. 3. 118. 6; Livy 23. 24. 6; Front. 1. 6. 4), in the Jugurthine War (Sallust, *Jug.* 38) and in the Social War (Livy, *Epitt.* 72, 75), reinforced the unfavourable view of them that the Caudine Forks disaster had produced.

[6] During the period of the First and Second Samnite Wars, the Triumphal Fasti reflect only three dictatorships, whereas Livy records almost thirty (F. Cornelius, *Untersuchungen*, p. 36).

[7] For the period of the Samnite Wars, for instance, the iterated consulships usually occur after a reasonable interval and seem not implausible. (Before 343 they often happened at very short intervals; but perhaps that was inevitable when consuls were obtained from the small handful of patrician houses.)

ply the other with honours.[1] Under the circumstances Cato's refusal to name any commanders at all is understandable,[2] and so is Livy's honest bewilderment as to which commander should get the credit for certain victories.[3] Nevertheless the Consular and Triumphal Fasti are a well relatively pure and undefiled, and a large degree of credibility can be accorded them.[4]

The records of the foundations of colonies and the dedications of temples by the Romans are another reasonably trustworthy source of information. They seem to be generally accurate, and this is a matter of some importance, since it provides a yardstick for measuring the progress of Roman arms: temples were often vowed and colonies planted as the result of Roman victories.

Evidently then, Livy has preserved many grains of historical truth. He has, however, also mixed in a lot of fictional chaff. Apart from his own eagerness to embroider the tale and to convert what might have been a sober narrative into a heroic saga,[5] he has reproduced many of the wilder flights of fancy of his predecessors. Roman historians could never resist the temptation to magnify the exploits of either their nation or their family or both. This was true of the earliest of them as well as of the latest, of Fabius Pictor as well as of Valerius Antias.[6]

There were admittedly differences in degree. The earlier the writer the more likely he was to keep within bounds and to place some curbs on an unbridled patriotic imagination. Fabius Pictor and his near contemporaries, while far from truthful, seem to have

[1] Examples of consuls getting sick are L. Furius Camillus in 325 (Livy 8. 29. 8), P. Decius Mus in 312 (Livy 9. 29. 3), T. Manlius Torquatus in 299 (he died: Livy 10. 11. 1), L. Postumius Megellus in 294 (Livy 10. 32. 3).

[2] Pliny, *N.H.* 8. 11. Yet one might wonder whether Cato was not chiefly responsible for many of the legends that clustered around such great plebeian heroes as M'. Curius Dentatus and C. Fabricius Luscinus, both of whom he much admired (Cic. *Cato Maior*, 15. 15; *de re pub.* 3. 28. 40; Plut. *Cato Maior*, 2).

[3] Sometimes Livy's dilemma probably reflects not so much family rivalries as the Struggle between the Orders: the same victory was claimed for either the patrician or the plebeian consul, according to the annalist's predilection.

[4] The Younger Annalists did not know the *Fasti* in their present form, for which Varro's researches seem in large measure responsible. They might have given a soberer account of events had they been familiar with his scholarly reconstruction.

[5] Livy's attitude can be judged from his own words (10. 31. 15): *quinam sit ille quem pigeat longinquitatis bellorum scribendo legendoque quae gerentes non fatigaverint?* The tedium could be relieved by adding picturesque details, especially as the period of the Samnite Wars was the truly great age of Roman history anyhow: *illa aetate qua nulla virtutum feracior fuit* (9. 16. 9).

[6] See the remarks of A. Alföldi, *Early Rome and the Latins*, pp. 123–75.

written episodically and in relatively small compass and therefore provided themselves with only limited scope for fiction on the wholesale scale: they were *non exornatores rerum sed tantummodo narratores*.[1] Manifestly the elaboration of their accounts must have been less than was that of the year-by-year version of the so-called Older Annalists, such as Calpurnius Piso and Cassius Hemina,[2] of the age of the Gracchi. Yet even the latter were models of sobriety in comparison with the writers of Sulla's time a generation or two later, the notorious Younger Annalists, such as Valerius Antias and Claudius Quadrigarius.[3] Some of these wrote at such inordinate length as to allow themselves unlimited space in which to exaggerate or excogitate almost at will individual episodes for their favourites (although it should be added that by Cicero's day excessively long-winded exaggerations were no longer fashionable). Livy's use of, and dependence upon, the Younger Annalists is so universally recognized as to need no further demonstration;[4] and the consequences of this for his presentation of the Samnite Wars are worth pondering.

The writers of the Sullan period were contemporaries of the Social and the immediately succeeding Civil War and were so close to these crucial conflicts that their outlook could hardly fail to be coloured by them. In their own lifetime these writers had seen the Samnites make peace on their own terms in the Social War and, in the Civil, come within an ace of victory at the Colline Gate. Inevitably they interpreted the Samnite Wars of over two centuries earlier in the light of these stirring events. They were certain that both Romans and Samnites realized, from the moment of their first

[1] See Cic. *de orat.* 2. 54. Livy cites Fabius Pictor at 8. 30. 9 and 10. 37. 14, but this is no guarantee that he used him directly.

[2] Fabius Pictor is not usually reckoned an Older Annalist even though there is no absolute proof that he did not use the annalistic method. Livy never mentions Cassius Hemina, but does cite Calpurnius Piso (9. 44. 3; 10. 9. 12). The latter was also used by Diodorus, to judge from his failure to record any happening in the Varronian Year 307 (which year was omitted by Piso: Livy 9. 44. 3). At least one of the Older Annalists, Cn. Gellius, seems to have written carelessly and at great length (Dion. Hal. 6. 11. 2; 7. 1. 4).

[3] The *Annales* of Calpurnius Piso were 'written baldly' (*exiliter scriptos*): Cic. *Brutus*, 27. 106.

[4] Not that he actually names them much in his account of the Samnite Wars: Aelius Tubero (10. 9. 10), Claudius Quadrigarius (8. 19. 3; 9. 5. 2; 10. 37. 13), Licinius Macer (7. 9. 4; 9. 38. 16; 9. 46. 4; 10. 9. 10). But he frequently cites *quidam auctores*, by which it is generally agreed that Valerius Antias is usually meant. For good measure Tubero also seems to have used Antias. See A. Klotz, *Livius und seine Vorgänger*, pp. 201–97; R. M. Ogilvie, *Commentary on Livy i–v*, p. 5.

encounter, that the mastery of Italy was the prize of their contention and that they were therefore engaged on a struggle of titanic sweep and grandeur.[1] Under the circumstances the Younger Annalists were bound to describe the Samnite Wars in terms of a grand Roman epic. And for this they had a plethora of models ready to hand, Greek as well as Latin: *nec id tamen ex illa erudita Graecorum copia sed ex librariolis Latinis.*[2] If they felt no need to tamper much with the traditional framework, they could nevertheless give free rein to their inventive genius or imitative inclination for individual details within that framework.[3] To imagine or repeat Roman victories[4] and to suppress or gloze over Roman defeats was their standard, indeed their automatic, practice; and they enlivened their narrative by embroidering most events, real or fictitious, with picturesque, prolix and preposterous details. The remoteness of the period they were depicting and the tenacious conservatism of Roman aristocratic nomenclature greatly aided and abetted such forays into creative writing.

Nor did the Younger Annalists let their fancy roam merely over their own countrymen. They were liable to resort to the same practice, in reverse so to speak, when making their casual and cursory comments about the peoples whom Rome was uninterruptedly defeating. If the repeated use of the same name through generations of a Roman family made it possible to attribute to one of its ancient members exploits that more properly belonged to one of his descendants, it might seem fully justifiable to adopt the same procedure for the Samnites. If Samnite achievements in the Social and Civil Wars have influenced the interpretation which the Younger Annalists gave of the earlier Samnite Wars, one wonders whether their description of details in the latter also is not tricked out with episodes and personages from the former. It has, for instance, often been remarked that the Samnite worthies of the

[1] The Samnite Wars are viewed in this light by Cicero (*de off.* 1. 38), Livy (8. 23. 9; 10. 16. 7), Diodorus (19. 101. 7; 20. 80. 3), Dionysius of Halicarnassus (17/18. 3), and Appian (*Samn.* 4. 1. 5).

[2] Cic. *de leg.* 1. 2. 7 (on Licinius Macer).

[3] *Concessum est rhetoribus ementiri in historiis ut aliquid dicere possint argutius*: Cic. *Brutus*, 11. 42 (perhaps, however, Cicero is being ironical). Hellenistic historians could supply material with which Roman writers of the late first century might embellish what they had to say about the Samnite Wars: e.g. the comparison of Fabricius with Aristides (Cic. *de off.* 3. 87), the death of Aulius Cerretanus (Livy 9. 22. 7–10; cf. Diod. 17. 20, 21, 34), the excursus on possible Roman rivals to Alexander the Great (Livy 9. 17 f.).

[4] Note the allusion to *falsi triumphi* in Cic. *Brutus*, 16. 62.

fourth and early third centuries bear names remarkably like those of the Samnite leaders of the nineties and eighties, and some scholars go so far as to pronounce the earlier group fictitious anticipations of the later.[1] Such methods can, of course, be overdone. To deny the existence of Gavius Pontius in 321, simply because a Pontius Telesinus led the Samnite forces in 82,[2] is to carry scepticism to unjustified lengths.[3] The Churchill of the eighteenth century is not less real because a Churchill led Britain in the twentieth.[4]

Even so, it is a fact that the Younger Annalists, whether they were treating of either Romans or Samnites in the fourth and third centuries, were only too likely to be untrustworthy, and unfortunately much of what they wrote is reflected in the pages of Livy. Although well aware of their unreliability, he seems nevertheless to have relied upon them very heavily: perhaps he shared the Elder Pliny's conviction that there was no book so bad as to be entirely worthless.[5] In places his own narrative supplies needed correctives, as for the Caudine Peace in 321–316 or the Roman defeat at Lautulae in 315. In fact painstaking perusal of Livy is far from fruitless: from the information that he supplies a consistent account can often be pieced together that carries conviction.

There are a few other authors besides Livy who supply some information about the three Samnite Wars, but they need to be used with the same care and caution as he does. Indeed some of them, like Eutropius and Orosius, are merely epitomizing him, while at least one of them, Florus, improves on Livy, deliberately resorting to various rhetorical tricks in order to make his essentially Livian account still more arresting.[6] The slim scraps of information in

[1] Papius Brutulus of 323 (8. 39. 12) surely must be concocted from Papius Mutilus of Social War fame.

[2] Pontius Telesinus, the general in the Civil War in 82, claimed descent from the Second Samnite War hero, Gavius Pontius (Schol. Bern. *ad* Lucan 2. 137, p. 59). Pontii certainly lived at Telesia (*ILS*, 6510), and some ancient writers actually give Gavius Pontius the *cognomen* Telesinus (Eutrop. 10. 17. 2; Ampelius 20. 10; 28. 2; Auct. *de vir. ill.* 30. 1).

[3] The Roman disaster at the Caudine Forks was no fiction. Apart altogether from the improbability that Roman historians would have invented (or publicized) such a tale, the political ruin that ensued for the families of the disgraced consuls vouches for its reliability (after 321 the plebeian Veturii disappear for ever from the Consular Fasti and a Postumius Albinus does not reappear in them until 242). Admittedly this does not prove that Pontius was the victorious Samnite general; but it is significant that Pontius was one Samnite of whose personality the Romans had a very clear conception (cf., for example, Cic. *de off.* 2. 75).

[4] On family genealogies, see Cic. *Orator*, 34. 120; Corn. Nep. *Atticus*, 19. 1 f.

[5] Pliny, *Epp.* 3. 5. 10.

[6] See P. Zancan, *Floro e Livio, passim.*

Dionysius of Halicarnassus, Cassius Dio and Appian, the isolated incidents mentioned by the Elder Pliny, Frontinus and the author of the *De Viris Illustribus*, and the material strewn haphazardly through a number of Plutarch's *Lives* are similar in character to the matter found in Livy: they are all only too likely to have had the Younger Annalists as their place of origin.

The same is probably also true of the meagre notices in Diodorus despite the widely held belief that these derive from an older source. Diodorus completely ignores the First Samnite War and the opening eight years of the Second, although this is no proof that he knew nothing of them:[1] he is always capricious in selecting events for mention, even when recording the history of his own native Sicily.[2] Furthermore Diodorus is not extant for the Third Samnite War. So that it is only for the last fourteen years of the Second War that Diodorus is really useful. For twelve of these fourteen years he supplies succinct reports of the operations, which often differ from or supplement what Livy records and have had varying degrees of importance attached to them. The bareness of Diodorus' narrative has led many scholars to think that he is reproducing a version from the Older Annalists of the Gracchan age or from the discursive senatorial historians who preceded them:[3] Niebuhr and Mommsen actually went so far as to suggest that Fabius Pictor himself was the source.[4] Therefore it is often suggested that Diodorus is a more trustworthy authority for the Samnite Wars than any other ancient writer.

The grounds for this view are neither obvious nor convincing. It is true that Diodorus has used a chronological system that differs from Livy's (whose in turn was not the same as Varro's); but there is no reason to regard it as either better or older.[5] Nor is the threadbare nature of his Roman entries any guarantee that they derive from a single source or a particularly ancient one.[6] In fact Diodorus

[1] He obviously knew about the first eight years of the Second Samnite War, which included the hardly negligible Caudine Forks episode (19. 10. 1).

[2] Presumably he chose events that he thought would be most interesting to Greek readers.

[3] See, for example, A. Schwegler, *Röm. Gesch.* 2. 22. f.

[4] B. G. Niebuhr, *Röm. Gesch.* II, 192; T. Mommsen, *Röm. Chron.* pp. 125 f., and *Röm. Forsch.* II, 221–96; Diodorus' source seems to have included the so-called Dictator Years: A. Klotz in *Rhein. Mus.* LXXXVI (1937), 207.

[5] See G. Costa in *Atene e Roma*, XII (1909), 185–9 and more recently and more soberly G. Perl, *Diodors römische Jahrzählung*, p. 161.

[6] He might, of course, include material from the earliest Roman historians: but then so does Livy.

himself reveals that he used a variety of earlier authorities, and Latin ones at that.[1] It seems certain that they included at least one of the Older Annalists (Calpurnius Piso),[2] but it may be surmised that they included Younger Annalists as well.[3]

For the sporadic appearances of the Samnites after the three Samnite Wars we are dependent on scraps of information from several sources. Their role in the Pyrrhic War has to be pieced together from occasional notices in various epitomes of Livy or Dio, or else from scattered allusions in Plutarch, whose information is valuable since it goes back ultimately to Timaeus, an interested contemporary of the events. Some account of the Samnites' behaviour in the Second Punic War can be gleaned from Polybius and Livy. But Polybius, as usual, does not seem at all concerned to waste any sympathy on a non-Roman people; and what Livy has to say is at best incidental to his main narrative: it is desultory and summary when dealing with the Samnites' contribution to Hannibal's defeat, biased and inaccurate when describing their aid and comfort to the Punic enemy. Silius Italicus is much more generous towards them, until Cannae at least, but his fantasies can hardly be regarded as serious history.

After 200 the Samnites go virtually unnoticed for over a century. Then they suddenly reappear to play a major role in the Social and Civil Wars at the beginning of the first century. Unfortunately the ancient sources for these two crucial struggles are sketchy and scanty. The account of the Marsic War in Greek which Lucullus, an active participant, composed has not survived; nor has the work of the contemporary and highly regarded Sisenna. The fullest surviving account is in Appian, but it is a very uneven one. Even so, it is important and would be of still greater interest if it could be shown to derive from an Italic author. A recent attempt to demonstrate this, however, has not commanded assent,[4] and most students of the period will admit that even in Appian we get less trustworthy

[1] Diod. 1. 4. 4; cf., too, 11. 53. 6. His practice of calling south-eastern Italy Apulia (19. 65. 7) as well as Iapygia (14. 117. 1; 20. 35. 2; 20. 80. 1) may well be due to his use of more than one source. His name for the Samnites, Σαμνῖται (16. 45. 8; 19. 10. 1; 19. 65. 7, etc.), likewise indicates a Latin source.

[2] Calpurnius Piso omitted the Varronian year 307 (Livy 9. 44. 3); Diodorus (20. 45. 1) records no events in Roman history for this year.

[3] His mistaken account of the behaviour of Fregellae in the Second Samnite War (19. 101. 15) is due to the events at that town in 125.

[4] E. Gabba, *Appiano e la Storia delle Guerre Civili* (Florence, 1956). But there is no doubt that Appian's source was interested in and well informed about the Italian question.

information about the Samnites than the prominence of the part they played in the second decade of the first century deserves. The heavy dependence of the tradition concerning the first twenty years of the last century upon the mendacious *Memoirs* of Sulla, hardly the man to do justice to Samnites, may account for this.

After 82 the Samnites, to all intents and purposes, disappear from history. They make their exit with the same abruptness as, almost three centuries earlier, they had made their entrance.

Clearly we are but ill-supplied with ancient written material about this far from negligible people, and until recently archaeology has not contributed much in the way of material remains to remedy the deficiency. One might have hoped that discoveries would be made to supplement the few hints about the Samnites which Vergil lets drop in the second half of the *Aeneid*. In fact the harvest has been small. Some pre-Roman inscriptions have been found, enough certainly to confirm the assertion of the ancient writers that the Samnites spoke Oscan and to shed some flickering light on their political and religious practices. The number of such documents from Samnium proper, while not large, luckily includes the Agnone tablet, one of the longest of surviving Oscan inscriptions.

Investigation of Samnite sites has not been extensive. During the past century and a quarter more than one beginning has been made on the excavation of the settlement near Pietrabbondante, without much detailed or scientific publication of the finds, however; and at the beginning of this century Aufidena was carefully explored and promptly reported. Apart from this, little has been done except on a small scale by local and sometimes misguided enthusiasts.

The failure to conduct fully equipped and generously supported archaeological expeditions into Samnium is in striking contrast to the splendid activity so common elsewhere in Italy. Probably it is to be attributed to the fact that Samnium does, after all, belong to the south, and until recently the south was a very neglected part of Italy. Nevertheless it is somewhat surprising in view of the many sites there which, to judge from the polygonal remains that adorn them, would be archaeologically rewarding.[1] Their explora-

[1] For example: Capracotta, Carovilli, Castellone, Faicchio, Isernia, Monte Acero, Monte Cila, S. Nicola, Terravecchia, Treglia. It is only fair to add that in this matter, as in so much else, successive Italian governments since the Second World War have tried to make up, in some measure at least, for past remissness. The *mezzogiorno* is neglected no

tion would be sure to reveal many aspects of the life of the Italic people that more than any other put Rome on her mettle and bludgeoned her into greatness.

longer and of recent years its antiquities have attracted increasing attention. The most notable work there, it is true, has been done on a Roman site, imperial Saepinum; but there has been some exploration of Samnite Saepinum (mod. *Terravecchia*) in the mountains above it, and before many more years elapse we can confidently expect archaeological investigation to be vigorously and methodically pursued at other sites.

After the present work was already in the printer's hands, there appeared an important and valuable article by A. La Regina on recent finds (especially inscriptions) in Samnium and above all at Pietrabbondante (see *Rheinisches Museum*, CIX (1966), 260–85). The new evidence reveals that a better spelling for *Caraceni* would be *Carricini* (cf. the *Carecini* of Tacitus, *Hist.* 4. 5) and that their settlement Cluviae is more probably to be sought close to Casoli, in other words due west of Vasto (as proposed in this book: below, p. 26). Victoria can now be shown to have been one of the personified abstractions worshipped by Samnites (see below, p. 152). Several additional references to a *meddix tuticus* have been unearthed, but none to a pair of *meddices* (cf. below, p. 86). In this book it is assumed throughout, for the sake of convenience of nomenclature, that Pietrabbondante is the site of Bovianum Vetus. The scholars who have excavated at Pietrabbondante, however, argue strongly that there was probably no such place as Bovianum Vetus, in any case not at Pietrabbondante. There is no archaeological evidence there of a settlement, such as a *colonia*, that continued its existence into imperial times. One thing seems clear: Pietrabbondante is in the territory of the Pentri, as argued in this book (see below, p. 45).

CHAPTER 2

THE LAND

Samnium was the landlocked plateau in the centre of Southern Italy bounded, on the north, by the River Sangro and the lands of the Marsi and Paeligni; on the south, by the River Ofanto and the lands of the Lucani; on the east, by the plain of Apulia and the lands of the Frentani; and, on the west, by the plain of Campania and the lands of the Aurunci, Sidicini and Latini.[1]

Its grey, limestone mountains are its predominant feature;[2] and although by no means insuperable they certainly hinder traffic,[3] this being especially true of those on the western border. The mountains are chiefly responsible for the physical and cultural isolation that has characterized Samnium throughout the ages. In Samnium the Apennines are hardly a straightforward and continuous chain. In fact they seem to be scarcely a mountain range in the regular sense of the term at all, but rather a tangled labyrinth of massifs, spurs and re-entrants, varying in length, breadth and orientation, and interspersed with upland valleys often terminating in culs-de-sac.

Their haphazard pattern is sporadically emphasized by the grandeur of eye-catching masses, which are exceptional even for that rugged terrain. In the north rise the precipitous slopes of the Maiella, next to the Gran Sasso the loftiest section of the Apennines, a clump of peaks whose summits rise 8,000 feet and more: its heights, snowclad for most of the year, form a towering watershed between the valleys of the Rivers Sangro (anc. *Sagrus*) and Pescara (anc. *Aternus*). Standing out conspicuously in southern Samnium are the dome-shaped contours of the Monte Taburno (*c.* 4,000 feet at its highest point), of which the Mons Tifata overlooking Capua is a

[1] It corresponds approximately to the modern 'provinces' of Avellino, Benevento and Campobasso in the regions known as the Abruzzi, Molise and Sannio. For ancient accounts of Samnium, see Strabo 5. 4. 3, p. 242; 5. 4. 11f., pp. 249 f.; Pliny, *N.H.* 3. 63, 64, 70, 103, 105; Ptol. 3. 1. 7, 15, 56–9.

[2] About 65 per cent of its whole area is mountainous, and the remaining 35 per cent is very hilly.

[3] H. Nissen, *Italische Landeskunde*, 1, 384.

westward extension beyond the River Isclero.[1] Still further south, the Monti Irpini, while comparatively low (under 4,000 feet for the most part), are nevertheless sharply distinguishable and are intricate enough to offer a picturesque obstacle to any easy thoroughfare.[2] On the western boundary of Samnium a great natural bastion stands guard, the rugged hump of the Montagna del Matese (anc. *Mons Tifernus*),[3] over thirty miles long and fifteen miles wide, with a karstic lake on its summit and a high point, Monte Miletto, soaring over 6,700 feet. This massif can be kept within view almost all the way to the Adriatic. It dominates the broad valley of the River Volturno (anc. *Volturnus*)[4] and separates it from the narrow valley of the River Tammaro (anc. *Tamarus*) further east. Like the Monte Taburno, the Montagna del Matese has a westward extension on the other (western) side of the Volturno, the Monti Trebulani,[5] featured by Monte Maggiore (3,450 feet).

Each of these mountain clumps could serve as a refuge of last resort for one or other of the tribes of Samnium: the Maiella for the Caraceni, the Monti Irpini for the homonymous people, the Monte Taburno for the Caudini, and the Montagna del Matese for the Pentri.[6]

There is no comparable, clearly defined massif on the east of Samnium, where, consequently, the country seems somewhat

[1] The maps in K. J. Beloch, *Campanien*², and J. Heurgon, *Capoue préromaine*, show the Mons Taburnus as different from the *Monte Taburno* of today: in this they must be in error. The ancient name of the *Isclero* is unknown.

[2] Their lower altitude probably accounts for the greater ease with which invaders can overrun Hirpinian territory as compared with other parts of Samnium. In the Social War Sulla actually eliminated the more distant Hirpini before the Pentri had been subdued. Nevertheless such peaks as the sanctuary-crowned Monte Partenio (*c.* 4,800 feet) and the even loftier Monte Terminio (almost 6,000 feet) in the extreme south-west of Samnium are so high that from them it is possible to see the Maiella in the extreme north-east despite the intervening mountains. Another spectacular mountain in the south of Samnium is Horace's Mons Vultur, but like Vesuvius it is a separate volcanic upthrust (of some 3,500 feet) and not part of the Apennines. On the other hand the peaks of Cervialto and Marzano, respectively just over and just under 6,000 feet, are part of the limestone chain: they serve to separate the lands of the Hirpini quite clearly from those of the Lucani.

[3] For the Mons Tifernus see Livy 10. 30 etc. and perhaps Polybius 3. 100. 2 (emending Λίβυρνον: but see S. Weinstock in *R.E.* VI A (1936), s.v. 'Tibur', col. 818).

[4] At Venafrum the valley of the Volturnus is over five miles wide.

[5] The ancient name of the Monti Trebulani is unknown, unless it is to be sought in the emendation of 'Eribianon' of Polybius (3. 92. 1) to 'Trebianon'. Evidently the Mons Callicula of Livy (22. 15. 3; 22. 16. 5) was an outlying spur of the Monti Trebulani (G. De Sanctis, *Stor. dei Romani*, III, 2, 124; F. W. Walbank, *Commentary on Polybius*, I, 427).

[6] Zonaras 8. 6. 1 describes the Samnites as putting a massif to this kind of use in 277. Which one it was is unknown, Zonaras' name for it (the Cranite mountains) being otherwise unrecorded.

easier of access. Nevertheless eastern Samnium, too, has its limestone barrier. The Daunian mountains rise line after line in serried sequence something like the waves of the sea. Springing up, at times quite abruptly, from a coastal plain which occasionally narrows almost to nothingness, is an uninterrupted panorama of whale-backed mountains averaging 2,000 feet or more in height.

Fretting their way amid this maze of mountains and fertilizing the intermontane basins are a number of pebbly and usually scanty streams. The Apennines, unlike the Alps, do not attain the altitude of permanent snow and therefore cannot give birth to rivers of considerable volume or to systems of inland waterways. They do, however, feed a large number of rills, brooks and creeks in Samnium. All of these, apart from the Volturno and its tributaries, flow into the Adriatic. At certain periods in winter, when flash floods are likely to occur, raging torrents may fill their rocky beds. In summer, however, most of them meander along in serpentine trickles amid the gravel.[1]

In the north, as already noted, is the Sangro. Corresponding to it on the south is the Ofanto (anc. *Aufidus*), which takes its rise on Monte Calvello near S. Angelo dei Lombardi, hardly more than twenty miles from the Tyrrhenian coast and yet somehow, to the surprise of Polybius and later historians, manages to wind its way through the Apennines and flow right across Southern Italy into the Adriatic. Between the Sangro and the Ofanto and flowing roughly parallel with them are, from north to south, the Trigno (anc. *Trinius*), the Biferno (anc. *Tifernus*), the Fortore (anc. *Frento*),[2] the Celone (anc. *Aquilo*), the Cervaro (anc. *Cerbalus*),[3] and the Carapelle (ancient name unknown: it is called the Calaggio in its upper reaches). On the west, disemboguing into the Tyrrhenian Sea is the storied Volturno, which for much of its course flows through Samnite territory.[4] It has, indeed, been called 'the Samnite

[1] The Ofanto, for example, the most considerable stream in Southern Italy, carries 2,000 or more cubic yards of water per second in some seasons; yet in late summer it may carry as little as 2 cubic yards or less.

[2] The name *Frento* (whence presumably Frentani) occurs only in Pliny, *N.H.* 3. 103, where however there is a variant reading *Fertur* (whence presumably the modern name Fortore).

[3] *Cerbalus*, like *Frento*, occurs only in Pliny, *N.H.* 3. 103. Its valley, dominated by the town of Aequum Tuticum, was evidently an important channel of communications.

[4] The Volturno winds in a series of bends, each of which encloses a small plain and was dominated by one or more Samnite strongholds: viz. Venafrum, Rufrae, Allifae, Cubulteria successively, as one moves downstream.

stream',[1] a title that might more appropriately be applied to one of its tributaries, the not inconsiderable Calore (anc. *Calor*), the only river of consequence that belongs wholly to Samnium.[2] Likewise in the west is the Liri (anc. *Liris*) and its tributaries: at one time Samnite territory stretched right up to its left (eastern) bank.

These streams, uncertain and unreliable though practically all of them are, provide Samnium with water enough for its pastoral and agricultural livelihood. But there is not much else in the way of economic activity in the country, since the mountains lack the mineral resources to support industrial enterprise.

Some of the mountain valleys and rolling uplands are surprisingly fertile, such as the one around Bovianum Pentrorum.[3] And there are some lush, if limited, meadows along the banks of the streams: the Sangro in spring, for instance, is delightfully verdant. The forests, too, are deserving of notice. More than one ancient writer comments on the trees that in those days clothed the mountains of Samnium,[4] and these woods by checking the run-off of water must have helped to prevent floods and to keep some covering of soil on the limestone ridges.[5] Undoubtedly they made for better agricultural conditions in the uplands. Since antiquity, however, there has been considerable deforestation due to excessive grazing.[6] This began at least as early as the second century, and since then much priceless soil has been washed away.[7] Many a mountain slope that was once covered with trees has become a stone-strewn scree or at best can show little but scrub, garique and aromatic herbs.[8]

Even in antiquity many of the mountains were bare, or at most

[1] H. Nissen, *Ital. Landeskunde*, II, 777.

[2] In its upper reaches it is dominated by Allifae, then flows through Beneventum and is controlled by Telesia at the point where it joins the Volturnus.

[3] The configuration of the Bovianum valley is such, however, that the sun enters it obliquely for the most part.

[4] See Livy 7. 34. 1; 9. 2. 7; Sil. Ital. 8. 564; Plut. *Pyrrhus*, 25. 3; cf. H. Nissen, *Ital. Landeskunde*, I, 175.

[5] G. East, *Historical Geography of Europe*, p. 10.

[6] T. Frank in *Camb. Anc. Hist.* VIII (1930), 336.

[7] Cf. the description of desiccated Attica in Plato, *Critias*, 111 B–D: 'only the bones of the wasted body still remain...all the richer and softer parts have fallen away; and the bare skeleton of the land is left'.

[8] Recently reafforestation projects have begun to restore the woods to Samnium. They are about 40 per cent beech and 25 per cent oak, the latter mainly at lower levels. At the higher levels conifers naturally predominate. Chestnuts are comparatively rare: they find the limestone uncongenial.

covered with only a very thin layer of fertile earth,[1] to conserve which the slopes were sometimes precariously terraced. This, however, was a laborious business in an earthquake-racked land whose hillsides are unstable and erodable.[2]

Thus, Samnium is picturesque but physically difficult. Moreover its climate is bracing to the point of harshness.[3] The altitude and the isolation from the sea combine to make the winters as wild and as rigorous as anywhere in Italy,[4] and they may last for months on end: in some regions snow may lie on the ground for a third of the year.[5] The summers, on the other hand, are hot and parched, and periods of drought are not uncommon, especially in the eastern parts of Samnium. Measured in inches, the rainfall seems adequate enough, but much of it is precipitated in the form of sharp, torrential and destructive showers.

Even if conditions were better in antiquity, Samnium could have been no bountiful provider. Much of the land was unpromising and could be worked only with difficulty, although, as in other parts of Italy, farming was practised at surprising heights above sea level. A remarkably large proportion of the soil was worked, and some of it very intensively.[6] Indeed there was probably a good deal of overcropping of farms which were for the most part small. Even this, of course, did not enable the Samnite uplands to produce three or four crops a year in the manner of Campania. Besides, much of the higher ground could not be cultivated at all and was suitable only as summer pasturage for sheep and goats.

Samnium was a rugged nurse of rugged men, but even the toughest tillers of the soil could not make its gullies, slopes and valleys support a population of more than a certain density. Whenever that density was attained and exceeded, as it periodically was, large-scale emigration inevitably ensued, and adjacent fertile regions were then exposed to the terror of assault from the high-

[1] Even this 'fertile' layer is often not particularly good soil.

[2] Pliny, *N.H.* 3. 106, noted the frequency of landslides.

[3] Anyone who has felt the *paesano* whistle across the Monte Taburno into the Valle Caudina will have few illusions about how harsh a Samnite winter can be.

[4] Horace, *Odes*, I. 28. 26, who had good reason to know, mentions the lashing of the forests of Samnium by the biting winds.

[5] After a severe winter spring can be late in coming and sharp frosts are not uncommon even then. A climate such as this makes olive-growing and viticulture uncommonly difficult in many regions.

[6] The chief crop was cereals. This is still true, although some variety has been introduced in modern times in the form of horticulture and more extensive market-gardening.

lands.[1] The Samnites were uncomfortable neighbours: they enjoyed a reputation for continuous aggression. They could raid with both assurance and impunity, since reprisals against their own mountain fastnesses were neither easy nor rewarding.

The rivers and mountains dictate the approaches to Samnium. On the north, access is possible around the Fucine Lake. East of the Fucine basin routes were found through the mountains, in the absence of convenient rivers, in what is today the National Park of the Abruzzi.[2] West of the Fucine Lake one can follow the narrow gorge (Val Roveto) along which the Upper Liris threads its way south-eastwards through the country of the Marsi, and thus reach Sora, the point where the river emerges into the more open country of the Volsci and makes a big bend towards the west. It is at Sora that the reaches of the Middle Liris begin: here passage between Latium and Samnium is reasonably easy. Indeed this is the one place where one can proceed directly from Latium into Samnium. Clearly Sora, controlling so sensitive a region, is a very strategic site. Fregellae,[3] further downstream, is also an important nodal position: it dominates communications between Latium, Samnium and Campania.

On the south, there is a route into the undulating country of the Hirpini from the tortuous ravines of Lucania past the foothills of Mount Vultur and across the Ofanto. It is controlled by Venusia, the key to the whole valley of the Upper Ofanto, strongly placed on a ridge surrounded on all sides except the south by escarpments. Further west, secondary routes into Samnium from Lucania[4] can be easily blocked at Compsa.

On the east, one enters Samnium by following the courses of various rivers upstream. These were the *diversa itinera* by which refugees from Hannibal's defeat of the Romans at Herdoniae in 210 made their way to Marcellus in Samnium.[5] One of them, that by the

[1] Cf. Livy 7. 30. 12.

[2] The ancients in fact seem normally to have used the route via Scanno (*CIL*, IX, p. 291; L. Mariani in *Monumenti Antichi*, X (1901), 266), although they also knew the lofty but easier route further east in Paelignian country across the Piano delle Cinque Miglia.

[3] Fregellae was only twenty-four hours from Rome, if one travelled energetically and uninterruptedly (Livy 26. 9. 6).

[4] These gullies, near Monte Postiglione (= anc. *Mons Alburnus*) and the confluence of the Rivers Bianco and Tanagro, were called, appropriately enough, Nares Lucanae.

[5] Livy 27. 1. 15.

valley of the Fortore, has always been little better than a boulder-strewn ravine. The others have had roads along them from ancient times, although the frequent landslides make them very difficult to maintain. When Horace used the one along the Carapelle valley in 37 he found that it provided relatively easy passage between Southern Samnium and Apulia.[1] The one via the valley of the Cervaro is more difficult: it is indeed followed by the modern railway and a national highway, but has to negotiate a narrow defile above Bovino (anc. *Vibinum*). The valley of the Ofanto was the easiest and carried the most traffic. These river valley routes, however, lead only into Southern Samnium and the Hirpinian town of Aeclanum.[2] The approach to Northern Samnium from the east has to be by way of Luceria: its hill dominates the region where the Samnite mountains meet the Apulian plains and has always been a key site.[3]

In the west, one can enter Samnium from Campania by way of the Volturnus valley, past Venafrum,[4] the stronghold of Aesernia and the northern tip of the Matese massif. Another route, leading directly to the great communications centre of Beneventum (Samnite *Malventum*), is via the Valle di Maddaloni between the Mons Tifata and Monte Longano; this route continues along the valley of the Calor, but it was flanked all the way on both sides by Samnite territory and strong points.[5] Yet another route from Campania to Samnium is along the south side of the Mons Taburnus, an approach dominated by the fortress of Saticula in the valley of the Isclero.

From very early times the drovers' trails provided relatively easy communication across Samnium. The ubiquitous mountains sometimes make these rough tracks circuitous, but they must have been serviceable roads. Their surfaces were the natural rock and could support wheeled and even heavy traffic. The most famous of them traversed Samnium from north to south, and it was along it that Hannibal passed through Samnium more than once without undue difficulty. In other words, even in pre-Roman days, there was a

[1] Easy, at least, until the rains came to make the going difficult (*Satires*, I. 5. 95).

[2] A. von Hofmann, *Land Italien und seine Geschichte*, p. 342. Aeclanum must have been the next most important communications centre to Beneventum amongst the Hirpini.

[3] Diodorus, 19. 72. 9.

[4] Venafrum can be reached from the Liris as well as from the Volturnus valley (by way of Fregellae and the saddle called Annunziata Lunga).

[5] Nola controls the point where this route joins the Campanian plain.

fairly complex, if somewhat primitive, system of communications, which Roman engineers as usual exploited to the full, when they later developed the great arterial highways. These Roman roads, constructed originally to serve military ends, tended to go up hill and down dale, sometimes ignoring the local needs of Samnium. Nevertheless they seem to have linked up the principal urban centres.

The Via Appia of the third and second centuries traversed all Samnium, passing through Beneventum, Aeclanum and Venusia, although traces of it are hard to find beyond the first-named city. Another highway that seems to have gone right across Samnium was also quite early, even though the surviving epigraphic evidence for it dates from imperial times.[1] The road started north of Samnium and crossed the Sangro to Aufidena in the territory of the Caraceni by a bridge that existed already in republican times.[2] From Aufidena it passed through the Rionero gap and went on to Bovianum in the territory of the Pentri and Beneventum in the territory of the Hirpini: from there apparently it proceeded to the Adriatic. This might be the Via Minucia which, so Cicero, Horace and Strabo seem to say, ran across Samnium.[3] Also it might be the road by which Horace and his companions reached the Adriatic from Beneventum in 37.[4] There was also another road running east from Beneventum: it went slightly north through Aequum Tuticum and in A.D. 109 was made into the Via Traiana.[5] It is impossible to say

[1] Vol. IX of the *CIL* is particularly informative on the roads in Samnium.

[2] *CIL*, IX, 2802.

[3] The road from Aufidena via the Rionero Gap and Aesernia to Bovianum (= the modern state highway No. 17) is today sometimes colloquially called Via Nazionale dei Pentri. The Via Minucia has not been certainly identified. As it could take a traveller at least part of the way between Alba Fucens and Aecae (Cic. *ad Att.* 9. 6. 1), it may have been the road which can still be traced between Corfinium and Aequum Tuticum. It undoubtedly went to Brundisium (Hor. *Epp.* 1. 18. 20) and if the 'Minoice' of Strabo (6. 3. 7, p. 282) has been correctly emended, it went there from Beneventum. Perhaps it came down from the Paeligni country, crossed the Caraceni, following a famous drover trail through the Pentri to Beneventum, and thence via the Hirpini to Apulia (V. Cianfarani, *Guida delle Antichità di Sepino*, p. 53). Its builder may have been Q. Minucius Rufus, possibly sometime between 125 and 120 (F. Münzer in *R.E.* XV (1939), s.v. 'Minucius, no. 56', col. 1964). Or could it have been a popular name applied to a road over which M. Minucius Rufus, co-dictator with Fabius Cunctator in 217, travelled? Cf. the so-called Route Napoleon in France.

[4] Horace, *Sat.* 1. 5. 71–97.

[5] For the date, see R. Gardner and T. Ashby in *P.B.S.R.* VIII (1917), 104, and, for a recently discovered milestone from it, see N. Degrassi in *Studi Annibalici* (1964), p. 88. V. A. Sirago (in *L'Antiquité Classique*, XXVII (1958), 21) identifies the Via Minucia with the Via Traiana: but this is not justified on the ancient evidence.

whether the Via Aurelia Aeclanensis (of Marcus Aurelius' day?) was also a Roman rebuilding of an ancient Samnite road owing to our total ignorance about it: we do not even know its route.[1] About the Via Herculia, however, which linked Aequum Tuticum on the Via Traiana with Beleianum near Mons Vultur on the Via Appia in late imperial times, one can speak with greater assurance. It must have been following an ancient path: even its name may be quite early, since it was the practice of the southern Italians to name roads after Hercules long before the Christian era.[2]

Clearly discernible remains of other roads still survive. Allifae, for example, was a regular communications centre. From it one road, perhaps the earliest known mountain road in Southern Italy,[3] ran across the forbidding Montagna del Matese; and the route followed by its paved Roman successor can still be traced, even if with difficulty. Other roads from Allifae led (*a*) via Telesia to Beneventum, (*b*) across the Volturno to Teanum Sidicinum, and (*c*) via Rufrae to Venafrum.

An even more important communications centre than Allifae was Aesernia, the key to Northern Samnium, the fortress which controls the gap around the northern end of the Montagna del Matese. From Aesernia roads led to Venafrum and the olive groves of the Liris valley, to Atina and the iron ore of the Meta mountains, to Aufidena and the Sangro valley, and to Bovianum and the Pentrian country.

The nodal point of greatest consequence of all, however, was Beneventum—in Samnite times, no less than in Roman, medieval and modern.[4] As already noted, it lay on Samnium's great north road (Via Minucia?) and also on the later Via Appia and Via Traiana. Roads radiated from it in every direction: across the comparatively low watershed of the Hirpinian country to Apulia and, in the opposite direction, along the valley of the Sabbato (anc. *Sabatus*?)[5]

[1] Built apparently under Hadrian and Antoninus Pius (*CIL*, III, 1456). It may have been the road from Herdoniae to Aeclanum (*CIL*, IX, 1156), although this latter seems normally to have been called Via Herdonitana (G. Alvisi in *Arch. Classica*, XIV (1962), 157).

[2] Near modern Melfi. For roads named after Hercules, see [Arist.] *de mir. ausc.* 97 (93).

[3] A. Maiuri in *Not. d. Scavi* (1929), p. 34; D. Marrocco, *Antica Alife*, p. 32.

[4] In Northern Samnium there was nothing to compare with it as a focus, not even Aesernia.

[5] The name *Sabatus* does not occur in ancient literature. However, the people who lived in its valley are called Sabatini (Livy 26. 33 f.), and the modern name *Sabbato* has come down through medieval times. Hence there can be no real doubt as to what the river was called in antiquity.

to Abellinum. All roads may lead to Rome: in Samnium they certainly all led to Beneventum.

It is clear that the routes into, across and out of Samnium could be controlled by a comparatively small number of strong-points, a fact that did not elude the Romans. But the difficult nature of the terrain and the fighting qualities of its inhabitants combined to keep Samnium independent for many years. It took the Romans over three-quarters of a century to clamp an iron vice upon the country by the establishment of Latin Colonies at Cales (334), Fregellae (328), Luceria (314), Saticula (313), Interamna Lirenas (312), Sora (303), Venusia (291), Beneventum (268) and Aesernia (263).

The boundaries of Samnium, as of any other country, varied at different times in its history.[1] No ancient writer has left a precise and accurate description of them. Ancient men of letters seldom regarded such geographical details as a suitable subject for their talents: *impeditum opus et facundiae minime capax*.[2] General descriptions of Samnium have been left by Strabo and Pliny, to whose accounts details can be added from Ptolemy and others. But these were written after Augustus' reorganization of Italy, and may not be relevant for the fourth century.[3] Samnium had been split and dismembered long before Augustus, and one consequence was that what had originally been the compact area of Samnium was distributed over several of the Augustan 'regions'. The land of the Caudini (Western Samnium) was in Region I ('Latium and Campania'); the land of the Hirpini (Southern Samnium) for the most part was in Region II ('Apulia'); and the land of the Caraceni and Pentri (Northern Samnium) for the most part was in Region IV ('Samnium').[4] Strabo and Pliny, especially Pliny, whose whole

[1] More than once Strabo (5. 4. 11, p. 249; 6. 1. 2, p. 254) insists on the difficulty of defining the boundaries precisely.

[2] Pomponius Mela, *praef.* Generally an ancient writer on geography preferred to compile a *periplus* rather than describe a hinterland (K. J. Beloch in *Mem. dei Lincei*, ser. 3, x (1882), 429 f.).

[3] They did of course use some pre-Augustan sources, Strabo particularly. They also relied heavily on their personal knowledge of the regions they were describing.

[4] The numbers, but not the names, of the regions were official. See especially R. Thomsen, *The Italic Regions*. On pp. 17 f. he carefully analyses the method followed by Pliny in the third book of his *Natural History*. Pliny (*N.H.* 3. 46) says that his starting point was Augustus' *discriptio Italiae*; but he cites many other authorities. He takes each of the eleven Augustan regions in turn, and first names all the towns on its coast in succession,

description is based on the Augustan division of Italy,[1] are only too likely to assign to other districts places which in an earlier day had formed part of Samnium: the 'Samnium' of Region IV was a very truncated version of the Samnium of the fourth century. Strabo makes this clear to his readers by occasionally inserting a short historical comment or excursus. Pliny, however, is not similarly informative.[2]

For the present study it is desirable to establish as nearly as possible the boundaries of Samnium in the mid-fourth century. The chorographic writers are of some help, but often reliance has to be placed on inferences drawn from the course of events and from what Vergil or Silius Italicus seems to preserve of Cato's account of Italic peoples,[3] or above all on details casually let drop by writers like Livy and Diodorus. The latter pair, unfortunately, are not the most trustworthy of guides. Livy's notions about the geography of Italy sometimes border on the grotesque and Diodorus' reliability can be gauged from the fact that he is prone to regard any Roman operation against Samnites as taking place in or near Apulia.[4]

whether they were municipally organized or not. He then lists in alphabetical order towns in the interior of the region, naming however only those that were municipally organized and especially singling out those that were styled *coloniae*. But Pliny decided to list these interior towns, not only according to their Augustan region, but also according to their original tribal affiliation; and the boundaries of the Augustan regions did not correspond with the old tribal boundaries but cut across them. In trying to reconcile ancient tribal divisions with Augustan regional divisions Pliny became very confused and made numerous errors. This is particularly true of his account of Region II, which embraced large areas which had once belonged to Samnium.

Mela gives little more than an account of coastal towns, and for this probably uses the same source as Pliny did (viz. a *periplus* compiled by Varro). Ptolemy for the most part lists towns according to their ancient tribes: but he is not free from errors. Strabo also adheres to the tribal principle in the main. He is the most useful of the chorographers for the present study, possibly because he is a historian turned geographer. His source, apart from his own knowledge and observation, is not always certain. He made extensive use of Polybius, Poseidonius and Artemidorus and his sources undoubtedly included a Latin chorographer (6. 3. 10, p. 285). For all his excellence, Strabo unfortunately is not completely free from mistakes. See, further, W. Aly, *Strabo's Geographica*, IV, 261 f.

[1] Unlike Pliny, Strabo did not make Augustus' *discriptio Italiae* the framework for his account of Italy. Both these writers were also historians, but their historical writings have not survived. In their surviving remarks on Samnium there is far more material of a historical nature in Strabo than in Pliny.

[2] Pliny's geographical description of Italy in his Book 3 is very confused. Sometimes he locates places in the wrong Augustan region, his account of Region II being particularly jumbled. Thus he assigns Ficolea, Fidenae and Nomentum to Region IV (*N.H.* 3. 107), whereas all three of them belonged to Latium in Region I and indeed to that part of it furthest removed from Samnium.

[3] It is probable that Silius, at least, did not use Cato directly.

[4] Diodorus, for example, seems to place Lautulae in Apulia: 19. 72. 7 f.

Map 1. The Samnites and their neighbours *c.* 350.

On the north, the River Sangro for much of its course was the extreme limit of Samnite territory. Uncertainty exists, however, at the north-east and the north-west. In the north-east Cluviae, whatever its status in later times, seems to have been a part of Samnium in the fourth century. This town was situated north of Monte Pallano near the point where the borders of the Marrucini, Frentani and Samnites came together, and its assignation to Samnium strengthens the conjecture that the frontier between Samnium and Frentani lay about twenty miles from the Adriatic coast and ran parallel with it. On the north-west, Samnite territory in the fourth century encompassed the lofty (*c.* 7,000 feet) mountain mass known as the Meta. The Samnite fortress of Cominium, whose name is preserved by the Val di Comino, lay well to the west of the Meta, near modern Alvito, and during the fourth century Samnium expanded to include territory all the way to the River Liris: Atina, Casinum, Arpinum, Fregellae and Interamna Lirenas (and presumably Venafrum and Aquinum) were Samnite towns in that period.[1]

On the south, the Ofanto was the same kind of natural boundary as the Sangro was on the north. But in the fourth century Samnium stretched well beyond it and included both Venusia[2] and, further west, Compsa[3] (but not apparently either Silvium, south-east of Venusia, or Eburum, south-west of Compsa).[4]

On the east, Teanum Apulum, Arpi and Canusium were outside Samnium. Luceria, on the other hand, should very probably be assigned to it. On its first certain appearance in history this town was under Samnite control. Perhaps the frontier here ran from Luceria

[1] See Livy 9. 28. 6; 10. 39. 5 for Atina; Varro, *L.L.* 7. 29 for Casinum; Livy 9. 44. 16, and Diodorus 20. 90. 4 for Arpinum; Livy 8. 23. 6 (and many other passages) for Fregellae. Interamna is first mentioned in 312, when the Romans established a Latin Colony there (Livy 9. 28. 8; Diodorus 19. 105. 5). Venafrum is not recorded in literature before the Social War, but some third-century coins which have been assigned to it with a high degree of probability indicate that it was Oscan-speaking (Vetter, p. 135). Aquinum makes its first appearance in history in the Second Punic War (Livy 26. 9. 3; Sil. Ital. 8. 403).

[2] By Horace's day Venusia no longer had any military importance and no one really cared whether a Venusine was *Lucanus an Apulus*. But Horace himself makes it clear that it was a Samnite town when it received its Latin Colony in 291 (*pulsis*...*Sabellis*: *Sat.* 2. 1. 36).

[3] Compsa is explicitly described as Hirpinian by Livy 23. 1. 1 and Pliny, *N.H.* 3. 105.

[4] Silvium (mod. *Gravina*) was temporarily captured by the Samnites in the Second Samnite War (see below, p. 247). Pliny, *N.H.* 3. 98, is the only ancient writer to mention Eburum or Eburi (mod. *Eboli*), and he insists that it was in Lucania (yet it lay north of the R. Silarus).

to Venusia, bending to the west of Aecae, Vibinum and Ausculum: the coinage issues of the latter suggest that it at least must have been independent.

On the west, the boundary ran across the Monti Trebulani separating Sidicine Teanum and Auruncan Cales on the one side and the Samnite towns of Rufrae, Trebula and Cubulteria on the other.[1] Further south, in Campania proper, Saticula and Caudium were clearly in Samnium, while Calatia,[2] Suessula, Nola and Abella are described as if they were outside it. The situation still further south in Campania is uncertain. The view that in the fourth century the homoglot Alfaterni of Nuceria and its neighbouring towns were a part of Samnium does not seem very likely. Their action in signing an agreement with the Samnites in 316 shows that they were sometimes ready to make common cause with the latter, but it implies no less clearly that they were not then included in the Samnite League.[3]

Even without the Alfaterni, however, the Samnites were a formidable people when they first appeared in history in 354. In all they controlled at least 6,000 square miles of territory, the largest political unit in Italy at that time.[4] How populous they were it is impossible to say: modern estimates are little better than sheer guesses. There is every reason to believe, however, that in the mid-fourth century their population as well as their territory was bigger than that of any other contemporary state or league in peninsular Italy.[5]

[1] For Rufrae, see Vergil, *Aen.* 7. 739; Livy 8. 25. 4 calls it Rufrium. Its site is marked today by *S. Felice a Rufo* alongside of the town of *Presenzano*. Trebula (for which see Livy 23. 39. 6) is the modern *Treglia*. It is the town which has given its name to this mountain massif, and is usually called Trebula Balliensis to distinguish it from other towns of the same name: Trebula Mutuesca (mod. *Monteleone*), Trebula Suffenas (near mod. *Ciciliano*), and the Trebula *in Caracenis* (near mod. *Quadri*). The name Cubulteria is established by epigraphic evidence (*CIL*, x, 4620; Livy 23. 39. 6; 24. 20. 5 calls it Compulteria). The site is marked by the church of *S. Maria di Covultere* near *Alvignano*.

[2] Calatia (mod. *Le Galazze*) in Campania is often confused palaeographically with Caiatia (mod. *Caiazzo*) in Samnium. It apparently was a member of the Campanian League which Capua headed.

[3] Livy (8. 23. 1) similarly implies that Oscan-speaking Nola, the key to Central Campania, was not a member of the Samnite League.

[4] Corresponding to rather more than 15,000 square kilometres.

[5] It is worth noting, however, that at the end of the nineteenth century the population there was slightly denser than the average for Italy as a whole (T. Fischer, *La Penisola Italiana*, p. 291).

CHAPTER 3

THE PEOPLE

During the period of the Roman republic the region described in the preceding chapter seems to have been called *Safinim* by its inhabitants.[1] Their name for themselves must have been **Safineis* or something similar.[2] In the Latin language, which avoided intervocalic *-f-*, *Safinim* by assimilation became *Samnium*; and from this the Romans obtained the toponymic *Samnites* for its inhabitants. In Greek the people are called *Saunitai*, cognate with *Samnites*, and their territory *Saunitis*.[3] The story that the Greeks fashioned these names from *saunion*, meaning 'javelin', is a crude and transparent piece of popular etymology.[4]

Ancient tradition was unanimous in regarding the Samnites as immigrants into Samnium, their predecessors there being the Opici.[5] The Opici (Osci) gave their name to the language (Oscan)

[1] The name occurs on an inscription from Pietrabbondante and on a coin issued by the Social War insurgents (Vetter, pp. 108, 139), and it is usually regarded as a nominative singular (so, e.g., in W. Schulze, *Latein. Eigennamen*, p. 478, n. 10). For the suggestion that it may be a genitive plural, see E. A. Sydenham, *Rom. Rep. Coinage*, no. 639, p. 94.

[2] The form *Safineis* does not occur, but the *gentilicium* Safinius does, and in an Oscan-speaking district (Cic. *pro Cluentio*, 25, 68).

[3] *Saunitis* is the form found in Ps. Scylax 15; Polyb. 3. 91. 9; Strabo 5. 4. 3 and 13, pp. 242 and 251.

[4] Festus, pp. 436, 437 L. There are similar tales that the name Falerii is derived from *falarica* (Festus, pp. 206, 210 L.) and Cures from *cureis* (Dion. Hal. 2. 48. 4). Mommsen, *Unterital. Dial.* p. 293, derived the words 'Safines' and 'Sabines' from *sapinus* (= 'pine-tree'), which would make them dwellers in the pine forests. Cf. Peucetii (from πευκή?).

[5] Opici, Obsci, Osci are identical. Strabo (5. 4. 3, p. 242) distinguishes Opici and Osci (Obsci), but is in error: Opici was the regular Greek name and Obsci (Osci) the form it took in Latin. (Some modern scholars for the sake of convenience call the pre-Sabellian inhabitants of Campania Opici, reserving the name Osci for the people that resulted when these Opici fused with the Sabellians who came into Campania later: G. Devoto in *Enciclop. Italiana*, s.v. 'Oschi'.) The origin of the name Opici is uncertain. It has been variously derived from:

(i) a place-name (the Opici are the people from Opi, a town in the Abruzzi: E. Vetter in *R.E.* XVIII (1942), s.v. 'Osci', col. 1545);

(ii) a divinity (the Opici are the servants of Ops: G. Verrecchia in *Samnium*, XXV (1952), 124; M. G. Bruno in *Rend. Ist. Lomb.* XCVI (1962), 430);

(iii) an occupation (*opus* = 'field work': the Opici are farmers: A. Sogliano in *Rend. Acc. Lincei*, ser. 5, XXI (1912), 209; G. Devoto in *Enc. Ital.* s.v. 'Oschi'. Cf. *Terra di Lavoro*, the immemorial name of their principal habitat);

(iv) an adjective (*obscus* = 'sacred' in Oscan, according to Festus, pp. 204, 205; the Opici are *sacrati*).

For the Opici as predecessors of the Samnites, see Strabo 5. 4. 12, p. 250. For the Ausones (i.e. Osci) as predecessors of the Hirpini, see Festus, p. 16 L. See, too, below, p. 37, n. 6.

spoken by the Samnites in the fifth century and later; but, apart from this, very little is known about them other than that ancient opinion insisted that at one time they had occupied a very large part of Southern Italy.[1] In that case their territory must have shrunk considerably by the fourth century, since they seem to be the same people as the Ausones,[2] who under the rhotacized name of Aurunci appear then in the pages of Livy as a small people confined to the narrow buffer zone between the Rivers Liris and Volturnus in the Latium–Campania border region.[3]

It is probable that the language of the Opici resembled that of the Samnites,[4] and that they were an earlier group of related immigrants who had made their way into Southern Italy.[5] The aboriginals they found there are unknown. Sergi called them 'Mediterraneans',[6] but such a resort to *ignotum per ignotius* is more misleading than enlightening, since it might be taken to imply that the neolithic inhabitants of Italy were all of one race and stock.[7] It can be presumed in any event that the aboriginals of Samnium, whoever they were, remained a substratum in the population and that the people subsequently identified as Opici established themselves on these prehistoric inhabitants in the days before the earliest Samnites.

The ancients believed that the Samnites migrated into Samnium

[1] Thuc. 6. 2. 4; Diod. 5. 7. 5; Dion. Hal. 1. 72. 3; cf. K. J. Beloch, *Campanien*[2], pp. 3 f.; J. Heurgon, *Capoue préromaine*, p. 50. Consider, too, the implication of *Ausonia* as a name for Italy.

[2] Antiochus (*fl.* 420) of Syracuse identified Ausones and Osci (Strabo 5. 4. 3, p. 242; cf., too, Arist. *Pol.* 4 (7). 10. 5 (1329 b)).

[3] The tale that Rome defeated Aurunci near Aricia in the fifth century (Livy 2. 26. 4 f.; Dion. Hal. 6. 32. 3) is probably due to confusion of Suessa Pometia with Suessa Aurunca. For the identity of Aurunci and Ausones, see Servius, *ad Aen.* 7. 727; cf. Livy 9. 25. It is true that Livy distinguishes the two peoples (8. 15 and 16), but if there was any distinction it was political, not ethnic.

[4] E. Vetter in *R.E.* XVIII (1942), s.v. 'Osci', col. 1547. If a coin bearing the legend MAKDIIS were correctly identified as Auruncan (Brit. Museum, *Catalogue of the Greek Coins*: Italy, p. 75), the case would be established. Almost certainly, however, the coin is not Auruncan (Vetter, p. 133). On the other hand Mamercus, a typically Oscan name, was in common use in the far south long before Samnites or Lucani got there (see W. A. Oldfather in *R.E.* XIV (1930), s.v. 'Mamerkos, no. 1', col. 950): this suggests that the 'Opican' language was very like Oscan: see, too, A. J. Toynbee, *Hannibal's Legacy*, I, 94.

[5] At least their religion, in so far as it can be appraised, did not differ much from that of the Samnites (R. M. Peterson, *Cults of Campania*, p. 4).

[6] *Italia: le Origini*, p. 130.

[7] E. Pulgram, *The Tongues of Italy*, p. 106, shows how neolithic Italy must have been inhabited by peoples of widely different origins. There is, however, no evidence for striking physiological differences. Literature and archaeology alike suggest that the Samnites were typical caucasoid Europeans.

from the country of the Sabines, they being descendants of these latter.[1] According to one version this meant that the Samnites were ultimately Greeks, since there was a tale that the Sabines were of Spartan origin.[2] The lack of Graecisms in the Oscan speech of the Samnites makes nonsense of this latter story, which arose partly from the resemblance of their rough and warlike manner of living to that of the Spartans, partly from a Tarentine attempt to flatter them, and partly from the tradition of a Tarentine colony in Oscan-speaking Italy.[3] Even more absurd is the fairy tale that the Sabines, and hence the Samnites, were descended from the Persians.[4]

The alleged descent of the Samnites from the Sabines cannot be simply dismissed off-hand. Nomenclature makes it reasonably certain that the two peoples were related. *Safinim*, *Sabinus*, *Sabellus* and *Samnis* (the latter from *Samnitis* by syncope)[5] are etymologically connected. They all have as their initial syllable the Indo-European root *sabh-*, which can also be seen perhaps in the name of the god Sabus, the eponymous divinity of the Sabines according to Cato.[6] The root *sabh-* became *sab-* in the Latinian dialects and *saf-* in the Osco-Umbrian.[7] *Sabini*, the name by which the Romans called the nearest speakers of an Oscan-type language, is thus the Latin form of **Safineis*.

This does not mean, however, that in historical times the Romans ever confused Sabines and Samnites, any more than other nations have ever mistaken the English of Britain for the Angles of Jutland.

[1] Dion. Hal. 2. 49. 4; Strabo 5. 4. 12, p. 250; Plut. *Numa*, 1. 3; cf. Justin 20. 1. 4.

[2] This is reminiscent of the persistent tradition that Diomede founded many places in Southern Italy, including such Samnite towns as Aequum Tuticum and Beneventum (Servius, *ad Aen.* 8. 9).

[3] Like the Spartans the Samnites defended their settlements with the sturdy right arms of their men rather than with walls (Livy 10. 45. 12; cf. Plut. *Romulus*, 16. 1). Justin (23. 1. 7) says that the Lucani, Sabellian kinsmen of the Samnites, educated their boys in the Spartan manner.

[4] Servius, *ad Aen.* 8. 638, quoting Hyginus. The story is a mere variant of the other, since it derives from the fable that the Persians were identical with the Lacedaemonians (Arrian 5. 4. 5).

[5] G. Perl, *Diodors röm. Jahrzählung*, p. 82.

[6] Dion. Hal. 2. 49. 2. The difference in the length of the initial syllable (*Săbus*, but *Săbinus*) does not necessarily invalidate the argument. Cf. *Āsia*, *Ăsia*. Some argue that Samnium was originally **Sab-nio-m*, 'the land of the god **Sabo*': H. Philipp in *R.E.* 1 A (1920), s.v. 'Sabini', col. 1571. On Sabus see Sil. Ital. 8. 420–3.

[7] Note that only the aspirated *-b-* became *-f-* in Oscan. The unaspirated Indo-European intervocalic labial remained *-b-*, in Oscan no less than in Latin. Thus we get Oscan *trííbom* 'house', cognate with Latin *trabem* 'beam' (both accusative singular).

Beloch's assumption that the Romans did not know the word *Samnites* until they learned it from the Greeks late in the third century is highly unlikely. He suggests that before then the Romans had regularly called the inhabitants of Samnium *Sabini* or possibly *Sabelli*, the result being that Roman writers of a later age when describing events earlier than 250 were only too likely to confuse Samnites with Sabines.[1] It is true that the earliest extant occurrence of the Greek word *Saunitai* antedates by a century or more the first surviving mention of *Samnites* or *Samnium* in Latin.[2] Moreover *Saunitai* was no doubt the source of *Saunitis*, the Greek name for Samnium. But it is very difficult to see how *Saunitai* could be the origin of Latin *Samnites* or how *Samnium* could be derived from *Samnites*. The exact reverse is far more likely: *Samnites* is obviously formed from *Samnium*, the assimilated Latin form of Oscan *Safinim*.[3]

Accordingly Beloch's theory that the ancient historians, and pre-eminently Livy, spoke of Samnites when they meant Sabines, especially in their accounts of the Third Samnite War (but curiously enough not in the earlier two struggles), falls to the ground. In fact ancient writers differentiate the two peoples unmistakably.

To recognize that Sabines and Samnites were distinct and were never mistaken for one another is not to deny their relationship. Admittedly the Sabines cannot be proved to have been originally Oscan-speaking, but such scanty remains of their own language as their early romanization has permitted to survive do seem to display some Oscan characteristics.[4] Accordingly both Sabines and Samnites can be reckoned 'Italic' peoples, in other words peoples who spoke a variety of Indo-European that is first securely attested in Italy, but not elsewhere, in the Iron Age, about the year 600. This, of course, is not to say that the Samnites were descended from the Sabines. The story that they were is probably nothing more than antiquarian fiction, rendered plausible by the common ancestry which both peoples could claim in a very dim and distant past and

[1] K. J. Beloch, *Römische Geschichte*, pp. 427 f.

[2] *Saunitai* apparently occurred in the eleventh book of Philistus (see Steph. Byz. s.v. 'Tyrseta') and certainly *c.* 350 in Ps. Scyl. *Periplus*, 11, 15 (emending Δαυνῖται). The first occurrence of *Samnium* in Latin is on the sarcophagus of the consul for 298, L. Cornelius Scipio Barbatus (but the inscription is much later than the sarcophagus). In view of the greater antiquity of Greek literature, it would be surprising if it did not mention *Saunitai* before Latin literature recorded *Samnites*.

[3] For the use of the name *Samnites* in the fourth century, see E. Wikén, *Die Kunde der Hellenen*, pp. 109, 120.

[4] See Vetter, pp. 158–63.

rendered popular by the indefatigable Varro, who was only too eager to publicize and exaggerate the role which his Sabine compatriots had played in history.[1]

The adjective *Sabellus* sheds little light on the relationship of the two peoples. In extant Latin *Sabellus* is not a synonym for *Sabinus*, nor a derivative from it. The diminutive from *Sabinus* would be **Sabillus*, not *Sabellus*.[2] Whatever its morphological history there is fortunately no doubt about the meaning of the word. According to Varro, Strabo and Pliny, *Sabellus* signifies 'Samnite',[3] and in a number of passages it can have this and no other meaning.[4] Even in texts where ambiguity is possible, the meaning 'Samnite' is not excluded. Beloch's guess that the word was in common use before and during the third century is unconvincing. *Sabellus* in fact is not demonstrably older than the age of Varro.[5] It was in his day, the period of the Social War, that need was felt for some generic term to describe all of the distinct and physically separated peoples who spoke Oscan. It was no longer possible to call them all simply by the blanket term 'Samnites',[6] since this name had acquired pejorative associations and moreover had the precise and definite meaning of 'inhabitants of Samnium'. To lessen the possibility of misunderstanding Roman antiquarians brought into vogue the term *Sabelli*,

[1] Varro (*L.L.* 7. 28) obviously thought that the Sabine and Samnite languages were related; and, even though he probably could not speak either tongue, he must have had some grounds for his opinion.

[2] Strabo 5. 4. 12, p. 250, obviously distinguishes Sabines and Samnites, even though he thinks that *Sabellus* was derived from *Sabinus*. On the form **Sabillus*, see H. Philipp in *R.E.* I A (1920), s.v. 'Sabini', col. 1571. It has been suggested that *Sabellus* originally meant 'servant of Sabus' (W. Schulze, *Latein. Eigennamen*, p. 481, n. 8); but there can be no certainty about this.

[3] Serv. *ad Georg.* 2. 168; Strabo 5. 4. 12, p. 250; Pliny, *N.H.* 3. 107. Note how for Silius Italicus the *Sabelli* are hurlers of the javelin (*saunion*), in other words *Saunitai* (Samnites): 4. 221.

[4] For example, Hor. *Sat.* 1. 9. 29 (the *Sabella anus* cannot have been Sabine); *Sat.* 2. 1. 36 (the *Sabelli* dwelt near Venusia); Livy 8. 1. 17 (the *Sabellus ager* is Samnium); Livy 10. 19. 20 (the *cohortes Sabellicae* are Samnite units). Clearly, whatever its origin, *Sabellus* is not a variant of *Sabinus*. When ancient writers meant 'Sabine', they used the word *Sabinus* (this is true of the poets as well as the prose-writers, *Sabinus* and *Sabellus* being metrically identical).

[5] H. Philipp in *R.E.* I A (1920), s.v. 'Sabini', col. 1570.

[6] Strabo applies the name *Samnites* to Frentani (5. 4. 2, p. 241), Campani (5. 4. 3, p. 242), Lucani (5. 4. 8, p. 247), Bruttii (6. 1. 3, p. 254) and other neighbouring peoples (6. 1. 4, p. 255), as well as to the inhabitants of Samnium. Livy (4. 52. 6) also calls the Campani Samnites, and Diodorus frequently describes Campanian mercenaries by that name. Admittedly the Apuli are nowhere called Samnites: it is from the legends on their coins that we know them to have been Oscan-speaking. It is not difficult to see how at the time of the Social War the Romans would feel the need of some term to distinguish other Sabellians from the Samnites.

meaning 'Oscan-speakers'. In the same way, in modern times, the term 'English' usually has reference to the inhabitants of England; today it is no longer used generically for 'speakers of English'. For the latter the expression 'Anglo-Saxon' has become quite common.

Today scholars no longer equate *Sabellus* and *Sabinus*. They do, however, apply the word *Sabellus* to the small peoples of Central Italy who spoke Oscan-type dialects. Although not demonstrably in conformity with ancient usage, this practice has in fact become so widespread as to be normal; and as practically all writers on republican Italy today employ *Sabellus* in this sense, and, as some generic term for the 'oscanizing' peoples is needed, the present study will not depart radically from the current fashion.[1] It will use 'Sabellic' for the speakers of Oscan-type dialects (Paeligni, Vestini, Marrucini, Marsi)[2] and 'Sabellian' for the speakers of Oscan proper (Samnites, Frentani, Sidicini, Campanians,[3] Lucani, Apuli, Bruttii, Mamertini). To avoid misunderstanding, however, 'Samnites' will not be used as a generic expression, even though the ancient writers often used it in that way. In this study, whenever the word 'Samnite' occurs, it means 'inhabitants of Samnium', the Sabellians *par excellence.*

Indo-European, under which all Latinian and Osco-Umbrian languages can be subsumed as 'Italic',[4] is generally admitted to have been brought into Italy in the Bronze Age, if not earlier, by immigrants from beyond the peninsula.[5] As the 'Italic' languages

[1] Cf. G. Devoto, *Gli Antichi Italici*², p. 114: 'Per indicare le popolazioni dell'Appennino centrale esso (= *Sabellus*) ha giustificazione non storica, ma soltanto pratica.' See, too, the remarks of J. Whatmough, *Prae-Italic Dialects*, II, 226.

[2] The 'Sabellic' character of Vestinian and Marsic cannot be established beyond all possibility of doubt. But both peoples formed part of the 'Sabellic' League with Paeligni and Marrucini, and seem to have shared in the common harbour at the mouth of the Aternus (at the city now known as *Pescara*). Juvenal (14. 181) certainly regarded the Vestini as Sabellic.

[3] It is necessary to distinguish the generic term Campanians (= inhabitants of Campania generally) from the specific appellation Campani (= the people who made up the league headed by Capua).

[4] Italian scholars (e.g. G. Devoto, *Gli Antichi Italici*², *passim*) are inclined to restrict the term 'Italic' to the speakers of Osco-Umbrian: i.e. to the peoples living east of the so-called Rome–Rimini line. This view seems unduly restrictive: J. Whatmough in *Language*, XXIX (1953), 190.

[5] It is impossible to say with certainty whence, when or on how many separate occasions these immigrants came, what their numbers were, what divisions existed or developed among them, or why dialects of theirs ultimately came to prevail. Perhaps Oscan triumphed because its speakers had a well-organized social system of a patriarchal kind and were mingling with 'aboriginals' who lacked really strong communities.

fall into two main groups, it has been argued that this presupposes two large-scale prehistoric mass invasions, the first carried out by 'Latinians' and the second by 'Osco-Umbrians', perhaps as much as one thousand years later. There is no positive evidence to substantiate this theory, and its proponents are at variance concerning the route which the mass assaults followed. The usual view brings the invaders down from the north across the Alps;[1] some recent opinion envisages them as coming from the east by way of the Adriatic.[2]

If it is true that speakers of Indo-European had been on Italian soil since Chalcolithic times, or earlier, then the communities that centuries later were using Latinian and Osco-Umbrian dialects could be the result of persistent infiltration by groups of Indo-European-speaking pastoral warrior nomads who already in the prehistoric period had mingled, no doubt violently, with the 'aboriginals' into whose midst they had penetrated.[3] In other words, the communities that in historical times used Latinian or Osco-Umbrian languages could have grown, developed and acquired their separate tribal identities over the centuries in Italy itself. Pallottino suggests that it was by some such process as this that the Etruscan nation came into being, and that it could equally well have been the case for the communities that spoke 'Italic' tongues.[4]

The 'Osco-Umbrian' peoples, therefore, who included both Samnites and Sabines, had evolved from the fusion of unidentifiable 'aboriginals' with infiltrating 'Indo-Europeans', and it may be further conjectured that they were evolving precisely during the centuries when the so-called 'Apenninic' culture flourished.[5] By 600 distinct and separate Oscan–Umbrian tribes had come into being; and, by 500 if not earlier, the people known to history as the

[1] This, the view of F. von Duhn (*Italische Gräberkunde*, vol. 1) and earlier scholars, is the commonly held one (see, e.g., G. Devoto in *Enc. Ital.* s.v. 'Sanniti', p. 741). Proponents of it usually bring the immigrants across the Alps (M. G. Delfino, *Serta Eusebiana*, p. 32) and make the cremating 'Latinians' keep west of the Rome–Rimini line and the inhuming 'Osco-Umbrians' east of it.

[2] M. Pallottino, *The Etruscans* (Penguin Books, 1955), pp. 38 f. He does not concur in the over-simplified view that the invaders came in only one or two migrations. One consequence of this theory is the implication that the Sabines descended from the Samnites rather than the other way round (M. G. Bruno in *Rend. Ist. Lomb.* XCVI (1962), 622). From Dion. Hal. 2. 49. 1 one might possibly infer that the Umbri were displaced Sabines.

[3] The rite of the Sacred Spring (for which see below, p. 35) proves them to have been pastoral: they sacrificed animals, not first-fruits. 'Originally war was nothing but a struggle for pasture grounds' (A. Hitler, *Table Talk*, 10 Oct. 1944).

[4] M. Pallottino, *Etruscologia*³, pp. 33 f., 51 f.

[5] U. Rellini seems to have coined the expression 'Apenninic Culture'. In general, see S. M. Puglisi, *La Civiltà Appenninica* (1959).

Samnites must have been clearly identifiable and in undisputed possession of Samnium.[1] Even by then, however, the process of tribal formation and consolidation was not at an end, and Sabellian peoples continued to be born almost within the full light of history.[2]

The manner in which individual Sabellian tribes came into being can be visualized to some extent from the tradition preserved by ancient writers that a religious ritual, the Sacred Spring (*Ver Sacrum*), caused the speakers of Oscan to push ever further along the Apennines with periodical descents into the plains on either side. As Sabellian expansion was still going on in historical times, the ancient writers could hardly have been mistaken about this, its cardinal feature. The *Ver Sacrum*, in other words, is not to be dismissed as a mere aetiological fiction designed to explain why Sabines were sometimes called *Sacrani*.[3] For that matter it was not confined to Sabellian Italy.[4] Livy suggests that the Celts of Cisalpine Gaul had a very similar practice;[5] and he actually gives details of a Sacred Spring to which the Romans had recourse as a result of the crisis brought on by Hannibal's invasion of Italy.[6] The Roman *Ver Sacrum* was a much less drastic affair than the Sabellian variety, but its irrefutable historicity is a guarantee of the non-fictional character of the latter. Fully historical also is the Sacred Spring vowed in the last century B.C. by the insurgents of the Social War, all of whom were either Sabellian or of Sabellian origin.[7]

The Sabellian *Ver Sacrum* is described by Strabo and others.[8] In order to win a battle, avert a peril, or end a natural calamity such as famine or plague, the Sabellians would promise to sacrifice to Mamers everything that was born in the following spring.[9] The children born then, however, were not literally immolated. They were allowed to grow up, but as *sacrati*:[10] in other words, they were consecrated to the god; and on reaching adulthood they were obliged to leave their tribe and seek fresh woods and pastures new

[1] They seem to have gained control of Aufidena some time between 700 and 600: J. Heurgon, *Capoue préromaine*, pp. 84 f., following Mariani.

[2] See below, p. 37.

[3] Festus, pp. 424, 425 L.; Servius, *ad Aen.* 7. 796.

[4] Dion. Hal. 1. 16. 1; 1. 24. 4; 2. 1. 2.

[5] 5. 34. 3 f.

[6] 22. 9–10; 33. 44. 1; 34. 44. 1.

[7] Sisenna, fr. 99, 102 P.

[8] Strabo 5. 4. 12, p. 250, and see below, p. 36, n. 7.

[9] For Mamers as the divinity involved, see J. Heurgon in *Latomus*, VI (1957), 6 f. (Strabo *loc. cit.* says that it was everything born that year and not just in the spring that was devoted to the god; Dion. Hal. 1. 16. 4 seems to say the same.)

[10] The terms *sacrati* and *Sacrani* seem synonymous: the latter appears to be applied only to Sabines.

under the guidance of an animal that was sacred to the divinity. The path-finding animal might be a bull, a wolf, a woodpecker, a bear, or possibly a stag;[1] and the emigrating band settled on the spot they thought the animal indicated.

Those who emigrated in this way must have been typical warrior-herdsmen of the sort found elsewhere: Alföldi has recently described how settlers of their type established themselves in Latium.[2] Nor is the path-finding animal unparalleled: it is known from other communities of Indo-European speech.[3] The remote origin of the practice might perhaps be sought in some ceremony connected with the seasonal migration of flocks.[4] It may well be the case that an actual animal was not involved and that the emigrants marched out under a banner upon which the animal was emblazoned.[5] In any case, it is obvious that the real motive for any Sacred Spring was overpopulation.[6]

Some of the sacred springs of the Sabellians and all of those of the Sabellic and Umbrian peoples, assuming that these latter also had the practice, occurred in prehistoric times. No authentic details survive concerning the arrival in their respective habitats of Picentes, Frentani, Sidicini and Apuli (Sabellians), Vestini, Paeligni, Marrucini and Marsi (Sabellic), Umbri, Volsci, Aequi, and Hernici (Umbrians?).[7]

[1] A bull led the Samnites, wolves the Hirpini and Lucani (Strabo 5. 4. 12, p. 250; Festus, p. 93 L.; Servius, *ad Aen.* 11. 785). The Picentes were guided by a woodpecker, a bird celebrated for its augural qualities (Pliny, *N.H.* 10. 40; Strabo 5. 4. 2, p. 240; Festus, p. 235 L. The name of the Praetuttii—from Oscan *touto* 'the people'—proves that there were Sabellians among the Picentes). The Ursentini of Pliny (*N.H.* 3. 98) had presumably been conducted by a bear. The suggestion of H. Rix (in *Beiträge zur Namenforschung*, VI (1955), 14 f.) that the Frentani are named after the Illyrian word for 'stag' is unconvincing; but the Oscan *gentilicium* Cervidius suggests that a stag could be a path-finder. Both wolf and woodpecker are prominent in the foundation saga of Rome (Ovid, *Fasti*, 3. 54), and the bull unquestionably was closely associated with Mars (G. Hermansen, *Studien über Mars, passim*).

[2] *Early Rome and the Latins* (1965), pp. 5 f.

[3] Cf. E. Pais, *Storia di Roma*³, I, 262 f.

[4] S. M. Puglisi, *Civiltà Appenninica*, p. 97.

[5] A bronze rooster found during the excavation of Pietrabbondante might be of this type, a military emblem resembling the Roman eagle.

[6] Varro, *R.R.* 3. 16. 29 (*propter multitudinem liberorum*). Cf., too, Dion. Hal. 1. 16. 2, where Aborigines means Sabines.

[7] Picentes: Pliny, *N.H.* 3. 110 (see also above, note 1); Frentani: Strabo 5. 4. 2, p. 241; Sidicini: Strabo 5. 4. 3, p. 242; Apuli: the legends on their coins; Vestini: Juvenal 14. 180; Paeligni: Ovid, *Fasti*, 3. 95; Marrucini: Verg. *Aen.* 7. 750 (cf. Cato, fr. 53 P.); Marsi: Serv. *ad Aen.* 7. 684, and Juv. 3. 169. There is little evidence for the speakers of Umbrian dialects. The Hernici (if they spoke a variety of Umbrian: their name looks Oscan) may be Sabellic in origin (Anagnia was, according to Serv. *ad Aen.* 7. 684 (cf. Festus, p. 100 L.); but this may merely mean that Marsi once occupied the site). For the possibly Sabellian character of the Aequi, see Vetter, p. 163.

In Southern Italy the Sabellian movement affected the Greek colonial settlements (*inter alia*, it caused the Greeks to establish colonies at Thurii (443) and Heraclea (432)), and it is consequently reflected in Italiote historical records.[1] These are not very detailed or invariably trustworthy, but must be correct in their suggestion that there was a movement of population of some magnitude and some duration.[2] It may have been in full swing at the time of the Roman monarchy, which, as Pareti suggests,[3] could have been the period when the Samnite, as well as the Roman, nation was consolidating itself. The tradition was that the first *sacrati* to settle in Samnium had been led by a certain Comius Castronius and a bull to Bovianum (presumably Bovianum Vetus), which became the cradle of their nation.[4] But it was probably many long years before they had any firm political organization.[5] *Tantae molis erat Sabellam condere gentem.*

For other parts of Southern Italy the Greek sources actually purport to provide some dates. At the beginning of the fifth century much of the region was under Greek, and some of it under Etruscan, political and cultural domination. Shortly after 500, however, the Italiote settlements began to grow weak through internecine strife and other factors, and simultaneously Etruscan power in Campania collapsed. The speakers of Oscan seized their chance and poured out of the overpopulated mountains of Samnium. The emigrating bands did not settle as closed social units, and no doubt the further they got away from Samnium the smaller the proportion they became of the population.[6] Their dilution, however, did not prevent them from imposing their Oscan language upon all of Southern Italy except the Sallentine peninsula and certain coastal districts which remained under Greek control.

Lucania, apart from a few Italiote settlements, was completely

[1] See, for example, Diod. 5. 7; 12. 31; 14. 91; 16. 15.

[2] For folk upheavals in sixth-century Italy, see J. Heurgon, *Capoue préromaine*, pp. 82 f. One need not, however, accept Cato's notion that the starting point of the whole Sabellian diffusion was Testruna, a Sabine village (Dion. Hal. 2. 49. 2).

[3] *Storia di Roma*, I, 102. The earliest graves at Aufidena belong to the seventh century. The earliest polygonal walls at Allifae can hardly antedate 600.

[4] Strabo 5. 4. 12, p. 250; Festus, p. 436 L. Comius is not a common Oscan praenomen, although it is found in an Oscan inscription (Vetter, no. 148; from the same place as the celebrated Agnone Tablet).

[5] A. Sogliano in *Rend. Accad. Lincei.* ser. 5, XXI (1912), 213.

[6] In the far south their predecessors were Chones or Oenotri rather than Opici, according to Strabo 6. 1. 1–4, pp. 252–4.

under Sabellian control by *c.* 435,[1] and its conquerors, the Lucani of history, had spilled over into the 'toe' of Italy and oscanized large parts of it as well. In 356, according to Greek tradition,[2] the slaves of the Lucani in the far south rebelled, seized Terina, Hipponium, Thurii and many other cities[3] and established themselves as an independent Sabellian nation in the Ager Bruttius (or Bruttium, as modern scholars conveniently call it).[4] They were subsequently known as Bruttii, that being allegedly the expression for 'rebellious slaves' in the local dialect.[5]

The Sabellians had not expanded only towards the deep south. They had also moved westward into Campania. They were there at least as early as 471, Cato's year for the 'foundation' of Capua.[6] Not that Capua was actually founded in that year: it was, as Velleius (himself a Sabellian) insists, much older. Nor did it come under Sabellian control in 471. But the nation of the Campani may well have been born in that year, a nation that as a result of its closer association with the Greeks was much more cultivated and sophisticated and incomparably wealthier than the parent stock it had left behind in the highlands and was soon in many ways markedly different from it.

The usual view is that Capua fell to the Sabellians in 445. This, however, is to misinterpret a passage in Diodorus,[7] who in fact nowhere records the Sabellian seizure of the town. What Diodorus says is that in 445 the Campani emerged as a distinct and separate nation (at or near Capua, to judge from their name), and this means that their beginnings are to be sought somewhat earlier, perhaps in 471. As time went on, more and more of them took up

[1] Presumably they were responsible for the failure of the refounded Sybaris, 453 (Diod. 11. 90; 12. 10).

[2] Diod. 16. 15; Justin 23. 1. 13; Aul. Gell. 10. 3. 19; Festus, p. 31 L.

[3] See Diod. 12. 22. 1.

[4] Yet Consentia could be regarded as Lucanian as late as 327 (Livy 8. 24. 4).

[5] Steph. Byz. s.v. 'Brettios' quotes Antiochus as saying that the name was already in existence in 452; and see Strabo 6. 1. 4, p. 255. Yet *famel* seems to have been the Oscan word for slave: Festus, p. 77 L. Slav and 'slave' are an analogy from later Europe, but it may be suspected that in both cases the common noun derives from the proper rather than the other way round.

[6] Vell. Pat. 1. 7. 3–4. Cato, according to Velleius, said that Capua was founded by Etruscans some 260 years before the Romans captured it (in 211?): in other words, 471. It seems unlikely that Velleius has misquoted Cato, so that the latter must have made a mistake. Did he intend to say 260 years before the *Sabellians* captured it (*c.* 423)? This would make its foundation date 683, not an impossible figure.

[7] Diod. 12. 31. 1. His date, 438, is equivalent to Varronian 445.

residence in Capua itself. They are said to have become its sudden and undisputed masters by an act of treachery that made their name notorious. During a religious festival they fell upon its Etruscan overlords while they were asleep, massacred them, took their place and married their women. This occurred in 423.[1] In 421/420 Cumae in its turn fell to the Sabellians, many of its Greek inhabitants seeking and finding asylum at neighbouring Neapolis (*Naples*), which managed to preserve its independence thanks to timely assistance, first from Tarentum and later from Rome.[2]

From what has been said it is clear that the Sabellians were not a unitary nation, but were divided into a number of tribes. These tribes might differ from one another in customs and manners, as well as in political allegiance. According to Cato, their mutual animosities popularized their word 'to haggle' and led to its adoption into Latin as a neologism.[3] Various causes account for their fissiparousness: political immaturity and a consequent lack of centralized government, the haphazard timings of their separate migrations, their unequal degrees of exposure to external influences, the divisive effect of their mountain abodes, and not least the heterogeneity of the aboriginal populations amongst whom they settled and whose habits they absorbed. Obviously each of the Sabellian peoples of historical times was an amalgam of two or more ethnic elements from Italy

[1] Livy 4. 37. 1 (cf. 28. 28. 6); Strabo 5. 4. 3, p. 242. Sabellians allegedly seized other towns in the same treacherous way: Cumae (Strabo 5. 4. 4, p. 243), Metapontum (Strabo 6. 1. 5, p. 264), Messana (Polyb. 1. 7. 3; Dion. Hal. 15. 3), Rhegium (Diod. 23. 3) and Caulonia (Paus. 6. 3. 12; Strabo 6. 1. 10, p. 261) (the last two seizures were carried out by Rome's *legio Campana*, which is also said to have made attempts on Thurii: Livy, *Epit.* 12; Dion. Hal. 20. 4. 2; Pliny, *N.H.* 34. 32). The monotonous reiteration of the tale makes it very suspect. The ultimate origin for it was probably Timaeus' account of the Mamertine capture of Messana, an incident about which the Sabellians preserved a very different tradition. Their historian Alfius said that the Mamertini came to help the hard-pressed people of Messana and were invited to stay and form a single community with them, being given land for the purpose (Festus, p. 150 L.), an account that C. Cichorius is overhasty in rejecting as 'romantic fiction' (*Röm. Studien*, p. 60). The seizure of Rhegium by the *legio Campana* may not have been the black deed that later Roman tradition insisted: its real motive may have been to forestall contemplated Rhegine treachery. See F. Cassola, *I Gruppi Politici*, p. 171; A. J. Toynbee, *Hannibal's Legacy*, I, 101. The Etruscans, angry at the loss of Capua, no doubt aided the Greeks in spreading the legend of Sabellian perfidy, which seems to have become a commonplace in Etruscan tradition (a fresco depicting it was found in the François tomb at Vulci). The Romans, too, were more than content to publicize any tale to the discredit of Sabellians.

[2] Livy 4. 44. 12; cf. 8. 22. 5 f.; Diod. 12. 76. 4; Strabo 5. 4. 4, p. 243. The dates for the fall of Capua and Cumae (423 and 421 respectively) may well be accurate, since they probably derive from Timaeus.

[3] *natinari*: Festus, p. 166 L.

itself, and some of them may have contained an Illyrian strain as well.[1] Some scholars actually postulate, without being able to prove, a large Illyrian admixture in the Samnites.[2]

The earliest surviving references to Samnites are found in Greek writings of the fourth century. Philistus of Syracuse (*fl.* 370) alluded to them in his eleventh book as inhabiting towns named Tyrseta and Mystia.[3] More informative is the *Periplus* of *c.* 350, which used to be attributed to Scylax of Caryanda. According to it, on the west coast of Italy 'the Samnites adjoin the Campani and to sail past their territory takes half a day'; on the east coast, 'after the Iapyges and Mount Drium (= Garganus) there is the race of the Samnites who extend from the Tyrrhenian Sea to the Adriatic; to sail past their territory takes two days and a night'.[4] As the *Periplus* usually reckons a day's sail as about thirty miles,[5] Samnite territory on the west coast stretched fifteen miles (from the Surrentine Peninsula southwards to the River Silarus) and on the east coast seventy-five miles[6] (from the Mons Garganus northwards to the River Aternus). These are easily identified landmarks of the type one would have expected the Greek compiler of a mariners' manual to use.

When he says that the Samnites inhabited the solid block of territory running right across Italy between these two stretches of coast, he must be using *Samnites* with the generic meaning for which later the word *Sabelli* was coined.[7] It is true that elsewhere the *Periplus* singles out the Lucani and Campani by name; and because

[1] If it is true that the Messapic language has many Illyrian characteristics, then it is good proof that Illyrians did cross the Adriatic.

[2] For example, F. Altheim, *Gesch. latein. Sprache,* p. 268. The alleged origin of the Paeligni from Illyria (Festus, p. 248 L.) is too uncertain to be adduced as evidence; and the similarity between Samnite and Illyrian marriage customs is inconclusive (the Babylonians had the same custom: Strabo 5. 4. 12, p. 250; Herodotus 1. 196). On the other hand for possible Illyrianisms in the pre-Sabellian language of Lucania, see Vetter, no. 186.

[3] Steph. Byz. s.v. 'Mystia' and 'Tyrseta'. Philistus was probably using the name 'Samnites' in a generic sense. Mystia, at least, seems to have been in Bruttium (Pliny, *N.H.* 3. 95).

[4] Ps. Scylax, *Periplus,* 11, 15 (emending 'Daunitai' to 'Saunitai' and 'Orion' to 'Drion').

[5] On this reckoning, however, some of the resulting distances in the *Periplus* are absurd.

[6] Unless it be assumed that the same distance was covered in a night as in a day: in which case it would be ninety miles.

[7] Actually the text of the *Periplus* (at §15) says of the Samnites: 'In this people there are the following tongues and dialects: Laternii [Alfaterni?], Opici, Cramones [Caraceni? cf. Cranite mountains], Boreontinoi [Frentani?], and Peucetieis [Picentes?].' This passage is usually regarded as a gloss.

of this it is often argued that the document means Samnites in the specific sense and is therefore alluding to the Samnite League which certainly existed in Samnium at about that time. The compiler of the *Periplus*, however, had good reason to use the particular when referring to Lucani or Campani, and the generic when referring to other Sabellian peoples. He himself reveals that his information about the inhabitants of Italy was obtained from the Italiote Greeks, and as there were no Greek colonies in the region occupied by his 'Samnites' and, to judge from the archaeological evidence, no Greek trade either, he had had no opportunity to learn any details about it. Furthermore the political divisions among an apparently homogeneous people in the interior of Italy could have been of little interest either to him or to prospective users of his manual. Accordingly the *Periplus* is not describing either Samnium or the Samnite League; it is simply stating the ethnic fact: Sabellians (Alfaterni, Samnites, Apuli and Frentani) did extend from the Gulf of Salerno on the Tyrrhenian to the south-central coast of the Adriatic.[1] But the Sabellian peoples it is referring to were not all members of the Samnite League: had they been, the surviving ancient accounts of the Samnite Wars would be simply incomprehensible.[2]

The Samnite League, in fact, was an association of the tribes inhabiting Samnium, for there was more than one of them. Divisions were not only normal between the various Sabellian peoples but were also not uncommon even within the same Sabellian people. The Larinates, for example, were indistinguishable, yet politically separate, from the other Frentani. Similarly the Campanians were split up into Campani in the north, and Alfaterni in the south, with Nola, Abella[3] and other sovereign communities in between.

The tribes of Samnium proper are named, even if not very often, by the ancient writers. Four are mentioned, and they are all

[1] So B. Kaiser, *Untersuchungen*, I, 13; L. Pareti, *Storia di Roma*, I, 147. On the other hand K. J. Beloch, *Röm. Gesch.* p. 366, F. E. Adcock in *Camb. Anc. Hist.* VII (1928), 585, F. Altheim, *Geschichte lat. Sprache*, p. 266, and F. W. Walbank, *Commentary on Polybius*, I, 49, all think that the *Periplus* is describing the Samnite League. Yet nowhere else is there trustworthy evidence of the League stretching from sea to sea; indeed Livy (9. 13. 7) seems certain that it did not.

[2] Frentani, Apuli and Alfaterni, while sometimes hostile to Rome (Livy 8. 37. 3; 8. 40. 1; 9. 41. 2; Diod. 19. 67. 7; Appian, *B.C.* 1. 39. 175), were all at times on the side of Rome in the Samnite Wars (the Frentani valorously so: see Plut. *Pyrrhus*, 16. 10; Florus 1. 13. 7). It is to be noted that Polybius (2. 24. 12) classifies the Frentani with the Sabellic League in 225, rather than the Samnite.

[3] Nola and Abella were sometimes close associates, sometimes bitter enemies.

specifically recorded as opponents of Rome in the Samnite Wars.[1] They are the Caraceni, Pentri, Caudini, and Hirpini. If Samnium contained other tribes than these, their names have not survived.[2]

The spasmodic nature of the Sabellian folk movements and the varying personalities of those who led the successive sacred springs help to account for the tribal divisions. The retinue of a charismatic leader might grow into a distinct tribe, as with the Germans and Turks in historical times. How the four known Samnite tribes differed from one another the scanty surviving evidence fails to reveal. They all obviously had a strong sense of nationality and they were at least sufficiently akin to be able to group themselves without difficulty into the formidable Samnite League.

Like other leagues in early Italy, the Samnite League may have come into being in the first instance for sacral and religious purposes. But for the period for which records exist the really important end it served was military. We do not know when it was first organized. The absence of the Campani from it in historical times suggests that it did not exist when the Sabellians made themselves masters of Campania. And there is no hint in the ancient sources that the Campani had once belonged to it and subsequently broken away.[3] Consequently the emergence of the Campani as a distinct and separate people about the middle of the fifth century may well be the *terminus post quem* for the Samnite League. Before this, indeed, they may have had only the most rudimentary forms of political organization.

After the year 400 we hear of leagues among three Sabellian peoples, the Campani, Lucani and Samnites. The Campani, although mentioned by Diodorus as early as 445, could hardly have been organized in their league until after their seizure of Capua in

[1] Caraceni (Zon. 8. 5), Pentri (Livy 9. 31. 4; Dion. Hal. 17/18. 4. 4, 5. 1), Caudini (Vell. Pat. 2. 1. 5; Livy 23. 42. 1), Hirpini (Livy 23. 42. 1). Generally speaking it is only after the Pyrrhic War and the dissolution of the Samnite League that the tribes are separately named.

[2] Unless we are to see them in the curious names in Ps. Scylax, *Periplus*, 15 (see above, p. 40, n. 7).

[3] K. J. Beloch, *Röm. Gesch.* p. 404, postulates some such behaviour as this for the Frentani, who, he unconvincingly argues, were members of the Samnite League before, but not after, *c.* 350. The silence of the sources about any such behaviour by the Campani is the more noticeable since the Greek historians were sufficiently concerned about the near neighbours of the Italiote communities to describe the Bruttian defection from the Lucanian League.

423. The Lucanian League was certainly in existence by 390, since it had diplomatic dealings at about that time with the brother of Dionysius of Syracuse.[1] The Samnite League, to judge from the language of Livy and Diodorus, was already in existence by 354 when it signed a treaty with Rome. But the Campanian and Lucanian examples and the general Sabellian lack of political sophistication suggest that it could not have been very much older than that. Perhaps the treaty with Rome was the first major political action taken by the League.

Although the ancient literature does sporadically particularize the members of the League, it fails to localize them with any precision and in general gives very few details about any of them.

The Caraceni, the most northerly tribe, seem to have been the least populous: in fact they were so few that some scholars have denied their separate existence.[2] There is, however, evidence of their distinctive identity. Towns specifically identified as Caracenan are Aufidena and Cluviae.[3] The location of these places indicates that the Caraceni lived in the valley of the River Sagrus and the mountains overlooking it. Their name[4] may contain the same root as Celtic **carreg* 'rock' (cf. Eng. 'crag'), to which has been added the Latinian *-no* suffix. In other words the Caraceni, like the Hernici, were the men of the rocks.[5] The same *car-* root is also found in such names as Carseoli, Carsulae and Carsitani, and perhaps in Ceraunii, Cranite Mountains, and Cercolae.[6]

[1] Diod. 14. 102.

[2] So, for example, G. De Sanctis, *Stor. dei Rom.* I, 102, n. 61. Scholars have also denied that the Caudini (R. S. Conway, *Italic Dialects*, I, 169), or the Hirpini (C. P. Burger, *De Bello cum Samnitibus Secundo*, p. 27) were Samnites. There is general agreement that the Pentri were Samnites.

[3] Ptol. 3. 1. 58; Tac. *Hist.* 4. 5. Cluviae must have been north of Monte Pallano; it did not, however, belong to Voltinia, the Roman tribe in which many Caraceni were enrolled. If the Caretini Supernates and Infernates of Pliny, *N.H.* 3. 106, are Caraceni, then the location for the latter suggested in the text would be about right; and this would mean that Trebula (= mod. *Quadri* on the R. Sangro) was another of their towns (*CIL*, IX, p. 262).

[4] A. J. Toynbee, *Hannibal's Legacy*, I, 101, regards Caraceni as a homonym of *Coloecini* (a people of Illyria: Polyb. 5. 108. 8). This is unconvincing.

[5] Festus, p. 89 L.

[6] For Carsitani, see Macrob. 3. 18. 5. Cluverius, *Italia Antiqua*, p. 1194, derived *Caraceni* from Mt Caricius, a name known only from a faulty emendation of Zon. 8. 7 (with which cf. Dion. Hal. 20. 17). *Saraceno*, or something similar, is found not infrequently in Central Italy, even in regions which could hardly have had memories of unwelcome visits from Moslems: for example, the mountain overlooking *Pietrabbondante* (Bovianum Vetus) is called *Caraceno*, formerly *Seraceno*. Caraceno also occurs as a surname in the Abruzzi.

The difficulty of deciding where the divisions lay between the various Samnite tribes is especially great in the case of the Caraceni and their immediate neighbours, the Pentri. The name of the latter people shows the same root as Celtic *pen* 'summit', so that the Pentri are the highlanders.[1] They lived in the heart of Samnium, on and near the Montagna del Matese and in the valleys of the Rivers Trinius and Tifernus; and all the evidence indicates that they were strong and formidable, the backbone of the nation. There was a heavy concentration of them in the only open area of any size in Samnium outside of the Hirpinian country, the valley dominated by Bovianum[2] and Saepinum.[3] Other of their towns can perhaps be identified from the Roman tribal arrangements of later days, when the Samnites had all become Roman citizens. The Romans, when incorporating a people into their own citizen body, did not always respect the native tribal divisions of the incorporated,[4] but in the case of the Samnites they seem to have done so for the most part. The Caudini are shown by the tribal status of their towns to have been assigned to the Roman tribe Falerna.[5] Galeria, to which Abellinum and Compsa belonged, was evidently the Roman tribe of the Hirpini.[6] For the Caraceni and the Pentri, however, the picture is not so clear-cut. As a result of the Samnite Wars both tribes lost territory and population to Rome, but both were still technically independent of, even if allied with, Rome until after the Third War. After the Pyrrhic War, however, the remnants of the Caraceni seem to have been absorbed, some of them by the kindred and neighbouring Frentani,[7] but most of them by the Pentri, with whom thereafter, so it would appear, they formed a single tribal state. Pentri and Caraceni together were referred to at the time of the Social War simply as 'the Samnites'. (This expression did not include the Hirpini, who by then were regarded by the Romans as a separate

[1] This root can be seen in such names as Pennines, Apennines, Penta, Pentima, Pentoma. E. Vetter (in *Beitr. zur Namenforschung*, VI (1955), 243) sees in Pentri the same root as in Eng. 'penetrate' and suggests that they are 'the men of the interior'. This is very unconvincing.

[2] That is, Boiano, not Pietrabbondante.

[3] Saepinum also controlled the valley of the Tammaro and the route around the southern end of the Montagna del Matese.

[4] As Strabo (13. 4. 12, p. 628) emphasizes.

[5] Caudium, Telesia and apparently Caiatia all belonged to Falerna. There is no evidence for Cubulteria. Trebula Balliensis may have belonged to Pupinia.

[6] Aeclanum exceptionally was in Cornelia, perhaps as a reward for the loyalty which its 'free corps' under Magius' command displayed towards Rome in the Social War.

[7] The Caretini of Pliny, *N.H.* 3. 106, seem to have been *in Frentanis*.

people, or the Caudini, who had long since been annexed, town by town, into the Roman body politic.) As a result of the Social War, the 'Samnites' became Roman citizens and entered the tribe Voltinia, that tribe being thought appropriate for them presumably because it was already the tribe of Aufidena, the Caracenan town which had been taken by Rome *c.* 269. Voltinia is also the Roman tribe of Bovianum, Saepinum, Bovianum Vetus, Fagifulae and Ter(e)ventum.[1] Of these Bovianum was certainly Pentrian and the rest probably were: Bovianum Vetus at least, the putative 'metropolis' of Bovianum, undoubtedly belonged to 'Samnium' (*Safinim*) in the days when that name connoted 'the land of the Pentri'.[2] These latter-day 'Samnites' were all assigned by Augustus to his Region IV. Besides the above-named places, however, there were those other lands and settlements in Northern and Western Samnium which the 'Samnites' had lost much earlier as a result of the three Samnite Wars. These had been allotted to Teretina, the Roman tribe to which Allifae, Atina, Casinum and Venafrum belonged (about Aquilonia we have no information). Under Augustus' arrangements they were part of Region I, and for that reason the chorographers, especially Pliny, are likely to describe them as belonging to Campania. There is no certain way of telling whether in their Samnite days before 269 they had been Caracenan or Pentrian. Local antiquarians are confident that Allifae was Pentrian, and this is what its location would lead one to expect.[3] Casinum and Venafrum were probably Pentrian for the same reason, and also Atina since it shared their vicissitudes. Aesernia, too, may have been a Pentrian town; but its destiny made it very different from the others. It became a Latin Colony in 263, so that its ultimate Roman tribal affiliation (Tromentina) has not the same relevance.

The Caudini, named presumably after the town of which they made themselves masters as they consolidated their position along the edge of the Campanian plain, were the most westerly and therefore the most exposed of the Samnite tribes to the Greek influences

[1] There is epigraphic evidence for the form Terventum: see G. Mansuelli in *Samnium*, XXII (1949), 156.

[2] Mansuelli, *loc. cit.*, suggests that the River Trinius may have been the boundary between Caraceni and Pentri. Yet Bovianum Vetus seems Pentrian.

[3] It suffered at Hannibal's hands, which is what one would have expected of a Pentrian community (see Livy 22. 13, 17, 18; 26. 9; cf. Sil. Ital. 8. 535; 12. 526). This, however, would be inconclusive if by Hannibal's day the Caraceni were already absorbed into the Pentri.

emanating from Campania. This made them the most urbanized and the most easily fragmented of all the Samnites.[1] The Romans were able to break them up into a number of 'independent' municipal commonwealths, most of which were annexed by Rome within a relatively short time and ultimately formed part of Augustus' Region I. The towns of the Caudini included their 'capital' Caudium and the three settlements on and about the Monti Trebulani west of the Volturnus River, Caiatia, Trebula and Cubulteria.[2] Telesia, probable native town of the great Gavius Pontius, and Saticula, the Latin Colony of 313, were also presumably Caudine.[3] The Caudini lived among the mountains that ringed the plain of Campania (the Mons Taburnus and the Monti Trebulani) and in the valley of the River Isclero and the middle reaches of the Volturnus.[4]

The Hirpini were the most southerly of the Samnites, living in and about the valleys of the Rivers Aufidus, Calor and Sabatus.[5] They were separated from the Pentri to the north, perhaps by the River Tamarus, and from the Lucani to the south by the mountains Cervialto and Marzano. It may be suspected that they resembled the Lucani in some respects more than they did their fellow Samnites.[6] At any rate both they and the Lucani are said to be 'wolf men' (respectively from Oscan [*h*]*irpus* and Greek *lucos*, meaning 'wolf' in each case).[7] The Romans were apt to insist that the Hirpini were distinct from the other tribes of Samnium, and it is true that the Hirpini had their own foundation legend, although so did one and possibly all of the other tribes as well. Some scholars accept the Roman viewpoint and even make the Hirpini so distinct as to exclude them from the Samnite Wars and even from Samnium

[1] They are named by Polyb. 3. 91. 5 (emending 'Daunioi'), Livy 9. 12. 9; 23. 41. 13; 24. 20. 4; Vell. Pat. 2. 1. 5; Ptol. 3. 1. 58.

[2] No ancient writer positively identifies these towns as Caudine, although Livy (23. 14. 13) to all intents and purposes does so.

[3] Livy's account of the Caudine Forks affair suggests that Pontius, the Samnite hero, was a Caudine; and he seems to have come from Telesia. Saticula was certainly Samnite, and it is difficult to see what tribe it belonged to if not the Caudini.

[4] Gratius Faliscus, *Cyneget.* 509, regards the Mons Taburnus as Caudine.

[5] For a Samnite tribe the Hirpini are relatively well documented: *CIL*, IX, 136, 98; Polyb. 3. 91. 9; Cic. *de div.* 1. 79; *de leg. agr.* 3. 8; Livy 22. 13, 61; 23. 11, 37, 41, 43; 27. 15; *Epit.* 75; Strabo 5. 4. 12, p. 250; Vell. Pat. 2. 16, 68; Pliny, *N.H.* 3. 99, 102, 105; Sil. Ital. 8. 569; Appian, *B.C.* 1. 39, 51; Ptol. 3. 1. 62; Festus, p. 106 L.; Serv. *ad Aen.* 11. 785.

[6] For instance, in the relative rarity amongst them of names ending in *-iedius* or *-idius*.

[7] Festus, p. 98 L.; Serv. *ad Aen.* 11. 785. Pliny (*N.H.* 3. 71), however, derives Lucani from Lucius, the name of their leader. Their name shows the same root as Lucetius, the Oscan word for the bright sky (Serv. *ad Aen.* 4. 570).

altogether.[1] This is quite unjustified. Admittedly the Hirpini are not separately mentioned during Livy's description of the Samnite Wars; but neither are the Caraceni nor the Caudini. Even the Pentri are not singled out then more than once by Livy or twice by Dionysius. The reason for this failure by the ancient writers to differentiate the various Samnite tribes at that stage of their history is obvious. At that time the Samnite League was in being and acting unitedly, so that there was little reason for naming the tribes individually. Yet Livy says quite unequivocally that the Hirpini were a people of Samnium,[2] and he makes it clear that the Samnite Wars were fought in part on Hirpinian territory. For good measure he insists, later in his *History*, that the Hirpini had fought the Romans throughout the Samnite and Pyrrhic Wars.[3] From the time of the Second Punic War onwards, that is long after the dissolution of the Samnite League, the ancient writers do frequently mention the Hirpini as if they were a separate Sabellian people;[4] but, in doing so, they are merely reproducing the official Roman view. It was in the interest of Rome to promote particularism by fostering the notion that the various Samnite tribes, and even towns, were quite distinct from one another. The Romans converted the Caudini into a number of completely separate boroughs, and they may have tried to split up the Hirpini still further by establishing the Abellinates as 'independent'.[5] Ptolemy even distinguishes the Caraceni from the Samnites.[6] *Divide et impera* was the Roman practice, even if not demonstrably a Roman proverb. It was particularly easy to represent the Hirpini as a separate people, since after the Pyrrhic War they were physically sundered from their kinsmen as a result of Roman seizures of wide tracts of Samnium. Augustus later reinforced this official view by assigning them to Region II, whereas the Pentri and Caraceni were partly in Region IV and partly with the Caudini in Region I.

If, however, one has regard to the facts rather than to Roman

[1] So, for instance, C. P. Burger (see above, p. 43, n. 2).

[2] 23. 1 1; 24. 20. 3–5; 27. 1. 1; 27. 2. 4.

[3] 23. 42. 1–2.

[4] Commencing with Polyb. 3. 91. 9 (see above, p. 46, n. 5).

[5] Cf. H. Nissen, *Ital. Landeskunde*, II, 822 f. Ptol. 3. 1. 62 calls Abellinum Hirpinian, yet Augustus assigned at least some Abellinates to Region I (Pliny, *N.H.* 3. 105), whereas Hirpini in general were in Region II. The later constitutional arrangements of Abellinum may mean that it obtained Roman municipal status earlier than other Hirpinian communities: see F. Sartori, *Problemi di Storia Costituzionale Italiota*, p. 114, n. 26.

[6] 3. 1. 58.

propaganda, the case is clear. The behaviour of the Hirpini guarantees that they were Samnites of Samnium. Their participation in the Samnite and Pyrrhic Wars must be regarded as historical, since it is inconceivable that Samnium could have challenged Rome so dangerously and so often without the support of this large and populous tribe, which rivalled the Pentri in power.[1] Such action on their part is conclusive. Even Polybius, who was the first to record them as a separate people, regards them as part of the Samnites in his roster of Italian military strength in 225.[2]

Their chief towns were Abellinum, Aeclanum,[3] Beneventum (or Malventum as it was called when it belonged to them), Compsa and Trevicum, their loftiest town (*c.* 3,500 feet); to these we should probably add Aequum Tuticum, and perhaps Luceria and Venusia before they became Latin Colonies.

The pressure of population, which in the fifth century had caused the Samnites to spill out of their own lands into the plain of Campania or into the tangle of mountains further south, was still making itself felt in the fourth. By then, however, there were no lands left on which to create new Sabellian peoples: accordingly existing states simply annexed neighbouring territories to themselves. How the Samnite League apportioned its conquests amongst its four member tribes we can only conjecture, but annexations undoubtedly occurred:[4] the League was not content merely to stage hit-and-run raids for loot. The Samnites badly needed good grazing land for their livestock and they were especially attracted by the plains of Apulia, by the Volscian-held valley of the River Liris, and by the richest land of all, Campania. No doubt the neighbours of the Samnites assaulted them in reprisal,[5] but in violent exchanges of this kind the advantage lay with the men of the mountains, partly because their more pressing necessities made them tougher and more persistent and partly because, unlike their neighbours, they

[1] H. Nissen, *Ital. Landesk.* II, 804, regards the Hirpini as the most powerful of all the Samnite tribes.

[2] 2. 24. 10.

[3] Assuming, that is, that Aeclanum existed as early as the fourth century.

[4] Perhaps newly annexed lands became part of the tribe that was physically nearest: e.g. Venafrum would join the Pentri, Cubulteria the Caudini, Luceria the Hirpini and Cominium the Caraceni.

[5] The polygonal walls on Monte Cila above Allifae seem to have been built by the Samnites to contain assaults from Campania.

had not been drained of their fighting elements by the recruiting agents of Greek tyrants.[1]

Nevertheless the Samnites felt a need for strategic security against the menaces of Siceliote tyrants as well as an outlet for their surplus population, and this kept them in an expansive mood in the fourth century. They pushed east, towards Apulia, and evidently got control of Luceria:[2] if not actually Samnite, it was certainly friendly towards them in the early stages of the Second Samnite War.[3] To the west, towards Campania, they established themselves firmly on both banks of the middle and upper Volturnus:[4] Venafrum, Cubulteria, Trebula and Caiatia were all west of the river and all of them Samnite throughout the Samnite Wars.[5] In the north-west the Samnites were steadily drawing nearer to the Liris basin and its Volscian inhabitants: Atina and Casinum became Samnite towns.

This was bringing them dangerously close to Latium, where, by the middle of the fourth century, the Romans had achieved political predominance. These latter could hardly remain aloof in the face of the persistent Samnite advance towards the River Liris. Sooner or later a confrontation between Samnites and Romans was bound to occur.

[1] The Samnite mercenaries so frequently mentioned in Diodorus (e.g. in 13. 14, = 410) seem usually to have been Campanians. (The Carthaginians also employed them: an Italic cuirass has been found in Tunisia.)

[2] The name Luceria shows the same Oscan root as Lucetius, Lucani, etc.

[3] Its status in the First Samnite War is unknown.

[4] Allifae, which had ceased to be part of Samnium in the early fourth century, was reincorporated.

[5] In the south they had expanded across the Aufidus: Venusia was a Samnite town down to the closing days of the Third Samnite War.

CHAPTER 4

THE CULTURE

(a) EVERYDAY LIFE

The Samnites have bequeathed no literature to reveal their social, political and economic relationships, their military life, and their varying vicissitudes. But we have information gleaned from ancient authors, archaeological finds and what can be legitimately inferred from the known practices of the Sabellians in Campania and elsewhere.

Like any other area Samnium underwent a continuous and persistent development;[1] and, if its comparative remoteness and the conservative character of its inhabitants made the pace of change somewhat slow, the wars with Rome did something to accelerate it. Over the centuries the gradual transition from village life to a more urbanized type of culture brought inevitable consequences for the social structure, military technique, economic activity and ritual observances. We cannot document the changes in detail,[2] but it is clear that contact with the Romans had some influence on political concepts, the proximity of Campania on commercial life and cultural growth, and the example of the Greeks on religious beliefs.

Very few urban agglomerations of any size existed in pre-Roman Samnium. Its mountains could not rival the metalliferous hills of Etruria and foster the growth of cities like Tarquinii, Caere or Veii. In fact the Samnites may not even have had their own native word for 'city'. Theirs was a rustic society,[3] and some of their settlements may have been collections of shepherds' huts (Varro's *casae repentinae*) intended mainly for seasonal use.[4]

The demographic pattern this suggests is confirmed by the ancient writers who describe the Samnites as dwelling in hamlets.[5] Casual

[1] Cf. Livy 4. 4. 4: *quis dubitat quin in aeternum urbe condita, in immensum crescente nova imperia, sacerdotia, iura gentium hominumque instituantur?*

[2] Perhaps Samnite mountain communities developed in somewhat the same way as their counterparts in Greece (for a description of whose evolution see Plato, *Laws*, 3. 680 d).

[3] *Montani atque agrestes* (Livy 9. 13. 7). Studies of their language reinforce the impression of a peasant society (E. Vetter in *Glotta*, XXIV (1942), 215).

[4] Varro, *R.R.* 2. 10. 6.

[5] Livy 9. 13. 6; Strabo 5. 4. 11, p. 250; App. *Samn.* 4 (Festus, p. 502 L., says the same of related Sabellic peoples, and Plut. *Rom.* 16. 1 of the Sabines).

allusion to these is a feature of the surviving accounts of the Samnite Wars, and many of them make one, and only one, appearance in history.[1] The excavators of the necropolis at Aufidena discovered traces of not a few small settlements in its neighbourhood. To this day many ruins of unidentifiable sites exist in Samnium.[2]

There were, of course, some urban centres. Aesernia, Allifae, Cubulteria, Malventum, Saepinum, Telesia, Trebula Balliensis and a few other places seem to have been towns of at least some consequence in the days of an independent Samnium. Their size, however, was small. The circuit of the town walls at Aufidena was only about a mile, that of Samnite Saepinum slightly less; and excavations suggest that Pietrabb-ondante was not a large site. Of course, as Thucydides points out,[3] the length of the perimeter wall is not necessarily an accurate indication of the size of a town. Nevertheless the smallness of the areas occupied by the towns is some measure of their comparative unimportance in Samnite life. It is significant that only one of the Samnite tribes was named after a town: the Caudini. And if they were more urbanized than the other Samnites it was because they were more exposed to the Greek influences from neighbouring Campania.[4]

In the interior of Samnium, villages, whose walls barely extended to half a mile, were the rule.[5] Many of them were little more than fortified strong-points, perched on the mountain tops and conforming to the contours of the land: these settlements were born of strategic necessity.[6] Other villages sprawled athwart the drovers' trails and such other roads as existed in pre-Roman Samnium:

[1] On such ephemeral appearances see Polybius 3. 36. 3. The single record is likely to be in the pages of Livy, Diodorus, Strabo, Silius Italicus, Plutarch or Stephanus Byzantius. No doubt many of the places thus fleetingly mentioned were places of refuge into which the Samnites fled when Roman armies overran the *vici* on lower ground. Some localities which played a role in history only once have nevertheless become immortal, e.g. the Caudine Forks and the Mons Callicula.

[2] To give some examples: Agnone, Baselice, Campochiaro, Castel di Sangro, Castellone, Castelvetere sul Calore, Civitalba, Frosolone, Letino, Montefalcone, Quadrelle.

[3] Thucyd. 1. 10.

[4] Their settlements were also larger. Thus the walls of Trebula Balliensis extended some 2,500 metres.

[5] G. Colonna cites examples at Carovilli and elsewhere: *Archeologia Classica*, XIV (1960), 83.

[6] *praeruptis oppida saxis*: Verg. *Georg.* 2. 156 (*oppida* in this context is equivalent to *castella*: E. Kornemann in *R.E.* XVIII (1939), s.v. 'Oppidum', cols. 709 f.). The sites were chosen with a view to their defensive possibilities: *seclusae nationes locorum difficultate, quarum aliae se in erectos subtrahunt montes, aliae ripis lacu vallibus palude circumfunduntur* (Seneca, *Consol. ad Marc.* 18).

these had been brought into existence by the needs of a fairly simple agrarian economy and served as distribution centres and farm settlements; they were protected by palisades.[1]

After the Roman conquest the Samnites began to forsake their fortified eyries, either because compelled to do so by the Romans or because more settled conditions had arrived and life on more accessible sites was no longer perilous. Towns like Allifae, Bovianum and Saepinum descended to less elevated positions, Roman Saepinum being more than 1,300 feet lower than its Samnite predecessor. Their economic well-being profited in consequence,[2] while the Samnite towns that remained on the hilltops tended to dwindle into insignificance.

The Samnites were a nation of peasants and herdsmen and doubtless had communal grazing lands. But there are also indications that Samnium, like other parts of Italy,[3] contained large landed estates owned by a handful of dynastic families who enjoyed wealth, power and authority and for centuries were the leaders of the nation and the makers of its policy. There must have been servile and feudal aspects to a society which did not live under a city system of government but was organized in rural communities. The lower orders must have been economically dependent on the aristocrats.[4] Of actual slavery there does not seem to have been much.[5] The evidence of the ancient writers and the muster figures for 225 are conclusive on this point. Ancient literature often mentions the slaves and serfs of Etruria but makes no allusion to any in Samnium; and the 225 roster reveals the Etruscans and Sabines as being able together to mobilize no more than 54,000 men, whereas the Samnites by themselves could field 77,000.[6] The low figure for the Etruscans and

[1] An example is Hirpinian Aeclanum at the time of the Social War (App. *B.C.* 1. 51. 222).

[2] Nevertheless they did not prosper as much as a Roman foundation planted in Samnium such as Beneventum.

[3] In Picenum, for instance, the family of Pompey was the ruling house: Cass. Dio 33, fr. 107 B. See, especially, R. Syme, *Roman Revolution*, p. 83. The Oscan-speaking aristocrats may have supplied their Latin-speaking opposite numbers with certain customs, that of the *ius imaginum* for instance (a death mask has been found at Capua).

[4] The Samnites may have had something resembling the Roman system of *clientela* (K. Latte in *Gött. gelehrte Nachrichten*, 1 (1934), 69).

[5] Evidently there was some. The Oscan word for 'slave' is said to have been *famel* and there is a possible instance of it with this meaning in an inscription from Samnium (Vetter, no. 176; cf., too, no. 2). Latin *familia* is derived from Oscan *famel* by Festus, p. 77 L. The servant of Pontius, who met Sulla at Silvium on his return to Italy in 83, may be an example of a Samnite slave (Plut. *Sulla*, 27. 6).

[6] Polyb. 2. 24; cf. Strabo 5. 4. 12, p. 250.

the high one for the Samnites must be due respectively to the large number of non-combatant slaves or serfs in the one case and to their paucity in the other.

The average Samnite may not have been a slave, but he lived a life of toil and hardship, no doubt as the retainer of a local dynast. His rough and ready life had few comforts and no high cultural tradition. One aspect of this is the marked deterioration of Campanian civilization with the coming of the Sabellians.[1] Strabo regards Campania, Lucania and Bruttium as 'barbarized' by the arrival of the speakers of Oscan;[2] and, if he be regarded as a prejudiced Greek, there is the testimony of the Latin writers. For Vergil *Saticulus asper* epitomizes the Sabellians of Campania,[3] and according to Velleius, himself a Sabellian, *Cumanos Osca mutavit vicinia*.[4] Even the coins of Naples begin to show barbarization after 400.[5] The speakers of Oscan were in fact proverbial for their uncouth ways.[6]

Originally, as in all primitive agrarian communities, a Samnite was known by only one name. But in the historical period the Sabellians regularly used both *praenomen* and *gentilicium*. In other words a Samnite at birth, like a Roman, inherited a family name from, and was given a personal name by, his father.

Some of the *praenomina* are clearly numerals and remind one of such Roman names as Quintus and Sextus.[7] Their original purpose must have been to indicate the month of the year in which birth had taken place: Sepis (cf. the rare Latin *praenomen* Septimus), 'born in the seventh month'; Dekis (cf. Latin Decimus), 'born in the tenth month'.[8] Other *praenomina* are actually formed from the name of the month: Mamerkis (cf. Latin Marcus), 'born in March'.[9] With the passage of time these original meanings lost their significance and the names came to be used without reference to the month of birth. As at Rome, certain *praenomina* no doubt became traditional

[1] J. Heurgon, *Capoue préromaine*, p. 340.

[2] Strabo 6. 1. 2, p. 253.

[3] Vergil, *Aen.* 7. 729.

[4] Vell. 1. 4. 2.

[5] E. Lepore in *Parola del Passato*, VII (1952), 306–10.

[6] Pliny, *N.H.* 29. 14 (quoting Cato); Aul. Gell. 13. 9; cf. 2. 21; 11. 16; Lydus, *de mens.* 1. 13. For Cicero the meeting of a Sabellian town council resembled a scene in an Atellane farce (*ad fam.* 7. 1. 3). Strabo regards the Sabellian Frentani as 'beastly' people (5. 4. 2, p. 241).

[7] For which see H. Petersen in *Trans. Amer. Philol. Assn.* XCIII (1962), 347–54.

[8] See Vetter, nos. 5c, 6, 82, 86. No *praenomen* reflects a numeral higher than ten; so that the practice originated at a time when the year was divided into ten months. Samnite nomenclature, like Roman, throws some light on their calendar.

[9] Vetter, no. 197; Festus, p. 116 L.

in different families: a son, no matter when he was born, was likely to get the *praenomen* favoured by his family.[1]

The number of *gentilicia* in common use amongst the Sabellians was large. Those that end in *-idius*, *-edius*, or *-iedius* have been carefully studied by Schulten and seem to be more common among the Sabellic peoples than the Samnites proper.[2] Interesting specimens of them are those like Hirpidius and Ursidius, formed from the name of the *Ver Sacrum* animal. Most *gentilicia*, however, originated out of *praenomina* as patronymics and were formed by converting the genitive singular of the father's name into an adjective, usually by attaching the suffix *-ius*. Pontius is an example; and names like Decimius, Marcius, Nonius, Octavius, Quinctius and Sextius show that Latin nomenclature passed through a similar development.[3]

It is often asserted that in Oscan, as contrasted with Latin,[4] the same name might be used indifferently as either *praenomen* or *nomen*.[5] This is not confirmed, however, by the Oscan inscriptions. In them the personal name usually ends in *-is* (in the nominative singular), whereas the *gentilicium* has *-iís*. These obviously correspond to the Latin endings *-us* and *-ius* in such pairs as Marcus, Marcius and Sextus, Sextius.[6] It is, of course, possible that it was only a spelling convention to use *-is* for the personal name and *-iís* for the *nomen* and that there was no perceptible difference between the two suffixes in pronunciation. More probably, however, the modern belief in the interchangeability of Sabellian *praenomina* and *gentilicia* derives from the Roman habit of transliterating both the *-is* and the *-iís* suffix as *-ius*: thus the Oscan *praenomina* Dekis and Sepis appear in Latin as Decius and Seppius.[7]

1 Festus, p. 174 L., implies that the Otacilii had a predilection for the *praenomen* Numerius; but he should not be pressed to mean that a Samnite, like a Greek, was normally named after his grandfather, although an example of this is epigraphically attested at Sabellian Capua (Vetter, nos. 95, 96).

2 A. Schulten, 'Italische Namen und Stämme' in *Klio*, II (1902), 167–93, 440–65, and III (1903), 235–67 (especially 264–7).

3 English practice is shown by such surnames as Arthur, Charles, George, Henry, Leslie, etc., to be similar. In some instances the genitive (i.e. the patronymic) survives as the surname: e.g. Johns, Williams.

4 Latin, however, might have the same name as both *praenomen* and *gentilicium*. Junius occurs as a personal name in republican times (*ILS*, 8654).

5 See, for instance, D. O. Robson in *Amer. Journ. Philol.* LIX (1938), 302, and the articles in *R.E.*, s.vv. 'Herennius', 'Herius', 'Numerius', 'Novius', 'Ovius', 'Paccius', 'Vibius'.

6 See G. Bonfante, 'The Origin of the Latin Name-System' in *Mélanges Marouzeau*, pp. 41–59: he suggests that the Romans may have copied Osco-Umbrian usage.

7 Vetter, no. 16 (Dekis); Livy, *Epit.* 12 (Decius); Vetter, no. 82 (Sepis); Livy 26. 6. 13 (Seppius. Yet the Sabellian *gentilicium* of this was written Seppiís: Vetter, no. 16).

Sabellian usage in the matter of *cognomina* ('surnames' in the literal sense of the word) is uncertain. The Oscan inscriptions might suggest that the Samnites rarely used them, or at any rate rarely wrote them.[1] This, however, may be merely due to the antiquity of the documents. Latin inscriptions of the same period likewise rarely show *cognomina*. *Cognomina*, in fact, were not often written before the time of Sulla.[2] Yet in the case of Romans this certainly did not mean that *cognomina* were unknown, even though they may have been confined to the leading families. (It is, however, true that even after Sulla's day there were prominent Roman families, such as the Antonii, Fannii and Gabinii, which do not seem to have used them.[3])

In the matter of *cognomina* Samnite practice probably differed little from Roman. Some, presumably aristocratic, families certainly used them since both the Oscan inscriptions and the literary sources supply examples. Some of them, like Roman *cognomina* in the Fasti, may be fictitious. Samnite *cognomina* may of course be simply due to romanization, although it is curious in that case that the most convinced of Samnites, C. Papius Mutilus, used one.

Samnite usage also resembled Roman in yet another particular. A Samnite, like a Roman, was identified in official documents by means of a patronymic, his father's *praenomen* (generally, however, with the word for 'son'—*puklo* or its abbreviation—omitted).

Another point of similarity was that Samnite women, like Roman, seem to have been normally called by the feminine form of their father's *gentilicium*.[4]

Clearly Samnite society, like Roman, was patrilineal.

The bracing climate of Samnium[5] and the prevalence of sheep-herding there dictated the use of woollen clothing for the most part; and woollen remains were found in some Aufidena graves.

[1] G. De Sanctis, *Stor. dei Rom.* III, 2, 216, denies that they used *cognomina*.

[2] They begin to appear on Roman coins *c.* 140 and in Greek and Latin inscriptions *c.* 120. Presumably one reason for using *cognomina* was to enable outsiders to see their way through a maze of family relationships.

[3] Cf. R. Syme, 'Imperator Caesar: a Study in Nomenclature' in *Historia*, VII (1958), 172–88.

[4] Vetter, no 70. But note Paculla Annia, a Sabellian woman from Capua (Livy 39. 13. 9 = 186). Should this perhaps be Paculla Annii (sc. *filia*)?

[5] See Livy 10. 46. 1. *Rugosus frigore pagus* could describe a Samnite settlement as well as Mandela (Hor. *Epp.* 1. 18. 105). The Samnites evidently used coarse dark hoods to protect their heads from the cold: Juv. 3. 170.

The habit of marking female graves with spindles suggests that weaving was a major occupation of Samnite women: indeed women are shown busying themselves with wool in Sabellian tomb-paintings. Linen, also, was by no means unknown: apart from the references to a Linen Legion and a linen book in Livy,[1] remains of the textile were present in the tombs at Aufidena.

Fourth-century Sabellian tomb-paintings suggest that the speakers of Oscan favoured what looks like a *chiton* for the men and a long, white, sleeveless *peplos*[2] held high up by a band around the waist for the women: but these paintings depict the Sabellians of Campania and show Greek influence.[3] The plethora of *fibulae* in the graves does indicate, however, that the Samnites wore clothes that were loose and pinned and not much stitched or sewn: they must have been draped and folded rather than shaped and tailored.

Samnite graves, of both men and women alike, contain bronze and iron ornaments but not in profusion. The types vary, those shaped like a figure 8 being particularly popular. Gold and silver are almost never used, being foreign to Samnium and too expensive to import. In addition to plain rings, some of them of 'open' type, Samnite men wore armlets (often in pairs), some of them fairly thick and many of them spiral and ending in a snake's head.[4] A ring-collar, occasionally engraved with incised decoration and usually pierced with holes from which to suspend amulets and pendants of a common and ordinary kind, was also worn by the men.[5] Apparently it was put around the neck in boyhood and never subsequently removed. One is reminded of the practice of the Celts, although it must be emphasized that the Samnite ring-collar does not much resemble the Gallic torque. The most valuable and most valued item worn by a Samnite seems to have been his broad girdle: it was made of leather and often covered with bronze and provided with an ornamental metal clasp which had been imported from Italiote regions. Samnite women for their part wore rings, usually plain and sometimes large and heavy, anklets, bracelets, and necklaces of terracotta beads.[6] In addition the women wore a

[1] Livy 10. 38. 3–13.

[2] A comparatively narrow strip of embroidered material might hang down the front of the *peplos* or a rectangular cape, usually red, be worn over it.

[3] This would be especially true of the scenes that depict elaborately clothed women.

[4] They might be worn around the calf as well as around the biceps.

[5] In Northern Samnium at least.

[6] Amber beads were exceptional and the prerogative of the better off.

chain-ornament of the type called 'châtelaine'. Roughly rectangular in shape, it had a central section consisting of links of mail, along either side of which were a number of metal spirals; attached to its lower portion was a disk of metal, usually perforated. The châtelaines, like the ring-collars of the men, seem to have been of Picentine origin and often had amulets and pendants suspended from them.

South Italians in general seem to have had a fondness for ornament,[1] but the Samnites were too poor to indulge themselves very much. Samnite women could not only not afford ear-rings, but in some cases not even hairpins; and practical objects like *fibulae* or even eating-knives, decoratively attached to girdles, were used as much as possible by both sexes for bodily adornment. One or two graves at Allifae show a very little ivory, amber, coral, horn, enamel, bright glass and scarabs, as well as the tiniest amount of silver and electrum; but Allifae, on the borders of Campania, was quite exceptional in boasting of some wealth.

So far as is known monogamy was the rule amongst the Samnites. It is also safe to conjecture that down to the Social War endogamy was as normal amongst them as amongst certain other Italic peoples: according to Aulus Gellius certain classes among the Marsi chose to marry only Marsi until long after the Social War.[2] The famous case of the Otacilii, however, proves that Samnites could marry outside their nation. Probably not many of them did so. This at any rate seems to be the implication of their extraordinary physical homogeneity. Approximately fifteen hundred of their skeletons were examined at Aufidena, and almost without exception they were found to be of dolichocephalic individuals of medium height. No doubt after the Social War (91–87) intermarriage between Samnites and other Italians became increasingly common, and ultimately of course they were absorbed into the population of the peninsula as a whole. By then, however, their history as a separate people was over.

The description of Samnite marriages in Strabo presumably has reference to the days before they were assimilated by the Romans: 'It is said that the Samnites have a splendid law and one well

[1] The tomb-paintings show that the Sabellian women of Campania were very fond of jewellery, and they could afford a much more valuable kind than the maids of the mountains.

[2] Aulus Gellius 16. 11. 1.

calculated to produce excellence. For they are not allowed to bestow their daughters on the men they wish, but every year ten maidens and ten youths are selected, the best of their sex. And the best maiden is given to the best youth, the second to the second, and so on. If the youth who obtains the prize changes and turns out bad, they dishonour him and take away the woman that had been given him.'[1]

Strabo's account is confirmed by Nicolaus Damascenus.[2] According to him, however, the best youth took the girl of his choice, rather than the one adjudged the best (which, however, may be just another way of saying the same thing). Nicolaus' language is so nearly identical with Strabo's as to justify the conjecture that both versions derive from the same source. Strabo's own language might suggest that the story was idle hearsay, but the account, whether garbled or not, might rest on a basis of fact.

Neither Strabo nor Nicolaus reveals by what criterion a youth or maiden was adjudged the best. Frazer is confident that the question was settled by some kind of athletic contest.[3] This may have taken the form of a race, something with which anthropologists are familiar from many peoples and places; or, in view of Sabellian fondness for gladiatorial contests, brides may have been won by combat.

Neither of the ancient writers identifies the exact period when this type of marriage was in vogue or in which stratum of the Samnite population it was practised. The care with which both Strabo and Nicolaus parade ten as the annual number suggests that only a small section of the population of Samnium was involved. The ten youths and ten maidens of the Samnites remind one irresistibly of the nine youths and nine maidens of the Illyrians from whom, according to Pliny, the Messapic-speaking people of the heel of Italy were descended.[4]

Strabo's remarks about Samnite divorce are tantalizing. Exactly what he means by a husband who turned out bad is anything but clear. He may be thinking of a man who proved to be a coward or

[1] Strabo 5. 4. 12, p. 250.

[2] *Ap.* Stobaeus, *Florilegium*, 44. 41 (= Müller, *F.H.G.* III, 457).

[3] J. G. Frazer, *The Golden Bough*, II, 305.

[4] Pliny, *N.H.* 3. 102. That a marriage custom like the one Strabo records of the Samnites did in fact exist in Illyria is shown by the account of marriage among the Eneti (= Veneti?) in Herodotus (1. 196), who points out that the Assyrians also had a similar practice.

who had lost his estate or his caste. In any case the provision for dissolving a marriage implies a certain degree of social discipline, if not of class solidarity.[1]

Horace, who as a native from Venusia was in a position to know, implies that a Samnite wife enjoyed respect and exercised authority in the household: it was she who trained the children and she had a reputation for doing so with strictness.[2]

The tone of Samnite life was evidently healthy. It is an appropriate coincidence that Horace, the herald of Augustus' programme for rehabilitation of the family, and Papius, the instrument chosen by Augustus to implement it in A.D. 9, both came from Sabellian Italy.

One of the few glimpses we are given of how Samnites comported themselves in everyday life is supplied by Athenaeus.[3] According to him, the Italiote Greeks took over from the Samnites and Messapians the custom of having the hair, including the pubic hair, removed from their bodies in barber-shops in full view of passers-by.[4] The practice may offend modern notions of propriety, but hardly convicts the Samnites of indecency. It is true that in antiquity the 'Oscans' enjoyed a reputation for grossness and obscenity,[5] but this was simply due to a crude piece of popular etymology: *obscenus* from *Obscus* (*Oscus*). Even if those scholars are right who find scatology in some Oscan inscriptions,[6] there is no reason for thinking the Samnites more lewd than their fellow Italians. The moral atmosphere of a people should not be judged from its graffiti.

The pastimes of the Samnites undoubtedly included hunting, but it may be suspected more for food than for fun. Silius Italicus says

[1] No importance can be attached to the tale that a certain P. Cernius castrated a man named Pontius for seducing his wife (Val. Max. 6. 1. 13). In any case it is not certain that the principals in this story were Samnites, despite the name Pontius.

[2] Horace, *Odes*, 3. 6. 39–41. Their affection for children emerges clearly from the care that was lavished on children's graves at Aufidena.

[3] Athenaeus 12. 518b. His mention of Theopompus and Timaeus (12. 517 d) may mean that he is referring to the third century.

[4] Clearly a widely held belief that Samnites were bearded (see, for example, J. Heurgon, *Capoue préromaine*, p. 226) is unfounded. Admittedly lunate razors are not found in their graves, but they could have shaved with knives. Besides Athenaeus, there is the evidence of Sabellian tomb-paintings to show that they might be clean-shaven, especially after the time of Alexander the Great. See, too, *Bull. Arch. Napoletano*, N.S., II (1853/54), 30, fig. 5a and pl. 10 (a bearded civilian from Capua).

[5] Festus, p. 204 L.; cf. Quint. 6. 3. 47.

[6] See, for example, Vetter, no. 102.

that the Hirpini got their living from hunting,[1] and hunting scenes occur in the Sabellian tomb-paintings.

The Samnites also became very fond of the theatre, once they had been introduced to it. When Saepinum was rebuilt, the theatre was the finest structure in the town. But if the Atellane farces were what they preferred, we must assume that their taste was for broad humour and satirical invective rather than sophisticated discourse.

The fresco of the dancing girls from nearby Ruvo encourages one to believe that folk-dancing was another of their entertainments.

Yet another, and a much less innocent one, was the sport of the arena. Gladiatorial games were very popular with them. In fact it was probably from the Sabellians and not from the Etruscans that the murderous pastime was introduced to Rome in 264.[2] The word *lanista* may be Etruscan,[3] yet it is remarkable that there are no authentic representations of gladiatorial combats in Etruscan art before 250. And their absence is not due to mere squeamishness, since other scenes of brutality and terror are depicted. Yet amongst the Sabellians the savage sport is shown in all its gruesome reality in tomb-paintings of the early fourth century. It cannot be proved to have originated in Samnium, but it did make its appearance in Campania simultaneously with the Sabellians, to become a marked feature of Campanian life: even dinner parties were regaled with combats.[4] Campania was always the headquarters of the gladiatorial profession. Recruits were found and trained there; and it was there incidentally that gladiatorial revolts broke out. The amphitheatre at Pompeii is much older than any known at Rome, and the one at Capua served as model for the Colosseum. If the latter was the largest of all arenas, the two next biggest were both in Campania, at Capua and Puteoli respectively.[5] The sport was closely associated with Sabellians. Rome for long knew no other gladiators than the variety known as 'Samnites'. Other types were late arrivals, the 'Thracians' being an innovation of Sulla's and the 'Gauls' of Julius

[1] Sil. Ital. 8. 571; cf. 8. 564 and 13. 219 (hunting on the Mons Tifernus and Monti Trebulani).

[2] In 264 Junius Brutus gave a gladiatorial show in honour of his dead father (Livy, *Epit.* 16; Val. Max. 2. 4. 7; Serv. *ad Aen.* 3. 67) and is said to have got the idea from the Etruscans (Nicolaus Damascenus, fr. 78, in F. Jacoby, *Frag. Griech. Hist.* II A, 378): this is accepted by K. Schneider in *R.E.* Supptbd. III (1918), s.v. 'Gladiatores', col. 761.

[3] Isidore, *Or.* 10. 159; Ernout-Meillet, *Dict. Etym.* s.v.

[4] Strabo 5. 4. 13, p. 250; cf. Livy 9. 40. 17; Sil. Ital. 11. 51.

[5] External axes (in metres): Colosseum 188 × 156; Capua 167 × 137; Puteoli 149 × 116.

Caesar's.[1] Down to the first century 'gladiator' and 'Samnite' were synonymous terms, and many of the gladiators must have been quite literally Samnites. Indeed one of them became almost proverbial.[2]

Originally the combats may have taken place only at funerals[3] and were probably not fought *jusqu'à la mort*: in the Sabellian tomb-paintings a referee controls them and crowns the victor with a laurel wreath.[4] But, when the contests ceased to be part of a funeral rite,[5] they did not remain thus relatively innocuous. A painting found in 1954 shows a gladiator who is obviously mortally wounded. How the bloody entertainments were provided amongst the Samnites is not recorded: perhaps by the upper-class leaders, either privately or when holding public office. One way of getting the spectacles may have been to match prisoners-of-war in pairs and let them fight to the death with the victor saving his life.[6]

Even without the gladiatorial combats the death rate in Samnium was probably high. Theirs was a peasant society, existing at subsistence level and seeking medical cures by offering terracotta models of afflicted parts of the body to gods in the temples. From such a society one would expect a high birth rate and a short life expectancy. The land would fill up to the maximum number that it could barely support. Once this number was reached emigration, peaceful or otherwise, into neighbouring lands became necessary. Failing that, famine and epidemics presumably solved the problem.

When death came, the Samnite was buried, not burned.[7] The carefully excavated necropolis at Aufidena shows that the same inhumation rite was practised for centuries. Because of this it is

[1] The first mention of 'Thracians' is in Cic. *de prov. cons.* 9; cf. *Phil.* 6. 13; 7. 17; for 'Gauls' see G. Lafaye in Daremberg–Saglio, s.v. 'Gladiator', p. 1587.

[2] A son of Aesernia: Lucilius 1. 149–52 Marx; E. S. Ramage in *Amer. Journ. Phil.* LXXXI (1960), 70. The first person to have pictures made of gladiatorial shows and exhibited in public may have been a Sabellian: at any rate Pliny calls him C. Terentius Lucanus (*N.H.* 35. 52).

[3] But they are not shown amongst the funerary sports in Etruscan tomb-paintings.

[4] The paintings, however, show a profusion of blood.

[5] Strabo 5. 4. 13, p. 250; Sil. Ital. 11. 51; Athen. 12, p. 528 a.

[6] This is implied by Serv. *ad Aen.* 10. 519.

[7] The view that the Sabellians, being Indo-European, must originally have cremated their dead, but discarded the habit in the seventh century when they learned inhumation from the aboriginals amongst whom they settled, is not very probable. For the necropolis at Aufidena see L. Mariani in *Monumenti Antichi*, X (1901), 225–638, pls. VI–XV; G. De Petra in *Archivio Stor. Prov. Napoletane*, XXVI (1901), 325–42. Perhaps only the better classes got individual graves; the lower orders, as at Rome, may have been simply flung into pits, without much by way of funeral rites.

uncommonly difficult to date individual burials. Only rarely and at more sophisticated sites such as Allifae is there any imported material in the grave to help establish its date.[1]

Like certain other Italic peoples, and incidentally also like Mycenaean kings, the Samnites occasionally placed a grave or graves within a circle of upright stone slabs.[2] Usually however they did not.

At Aufidena the graves were lined, the earliest (seventh to fifth centuries) with wooden planks,[3] later ones with stones, and the most recent of all (fourth to third centuries) with tiles.[4] The bottom of many graves was covered with gravel for drainage.

On the floor of the grave lay the skeleton at full length, supine and with the head sometimes propped up.[5] When buried the corpse had worn clothing and jewellery. The grave also contained earthen and sometimes metal ware, most of it locally made.[6] The pottery was mostly rough *impasto* ware, and almost always included a large hand-made jar,[7] often with smaller earthenware pieces inside it, which served the needs of the deceased, and a bowl which, to judge from the remnants of food in some specimens, had been used at the funeral feast (*silicernium*).[8] The metal ware consisted of iron weapons (spears, short swords and daggers mostly)[9] and bronze or iron objects of everyday use (*fibulae*, knives, axes and 'symbolic razors').[10]

1 But even at Allifae only the early graves contain imports.

2 Perhaps all graves within the circle belonged to members of the same family or at least the same burial club. *Iovila* inscriptions show that at Capua a Sabellian *gens* buried its members in a clan circle.

3 The planks were fitted together without nails.

4 The tiles seem to conform to the Oscan standard of weight; yet they sometimes have Latin letters stamped on them.

5 A stone, a heap of earth, the jawbone of an ox, or an arm bent beneath was used to support the head. The legs were sometimes, but not always, crossed; one arm (rarely two) rested on the diaphragm or breast.

6 The pottery was often enclosed in its own stone compartment within the grave. It included very little imported ware (no Lucanian, Apulian, Gnathian or Greek vases, and only a little cheap South Italian ware, black 'Etrusco-Campanian' pottery, or *bucchero*: the kind of stuff Samnite herdsmen might have acquired on their annual southward treks to winter pastures).

7 The large jar usually had four (or two) handles or lugs and was of interesting design: bowls, cups and the like were inside it.

8 From these remnants it can be inferred that a species of thick gruel was a principal item of diet for Samnites. They also ate fruit, vegetables, calves' heads and other meat. *Iovila* inscriptions seem to allude to the *silicernium* at Sabellian Capua.

9 There were a few scabbards, maces, and bronze girdles, but Italic cuirasses (breast-plates with three disks) were extremely rare.

10 The 'symbolic razors' are not lunate but quadrilateral, and are probably not razors at all since they are found in female as well as male graves. Perhaps they were eating utensils. The axes may have served as weapons.

Stones, or, in the most recent burials, tiles, covered the grave, a relic this of the old Italic practice of heaping stones over the tomb. Inscribed markers (*stelae*), however, were not used. The only identifying mark was likely to be a spear on a man's grave and a spindle on a woman's.

The graves at Aufidena were dug by people living in an Iron-Age type of civilization. And they were not elaborate. These are probably the graves of the more well-to-do, yet signs of wealth are conspicuously absent: a very few of the fifteen hundred graves contained a metal rather than a terracotta bowl or had a covering consisting of a single stone instead of several; and one tomb quite exceptionally produced a tiny specimen of gold. But that was all. Even the soil in which the graves were dug was of the poorest, land suitable for no other purpose. And only the barest minimum of it was used: some graves were so narrow that the body had to be turned slightly on its side to make room for the objects buried with it and were so short that spears had to be broken before they could be interred.

Aufidena shows that the normal Sabellian practice was not to use funerary inscriptions. Those who settled outside Samnium occasionally failed to resist the example of their neighbours. The Sidicini of Teanum identified their dead with *stelae* in the third century,[1] and the closely related Paeligni in the first actually set up a gravestone inscribed with poetry in the Roman manner.[2] Oscan sepulchral inscriptions have also come to light in Lucania (at Anxia).[3] Yet in general Sabellians adhered tenaciously to unidentified inhumation, even in Campania where they were greatly exposed to Greek influence. It is true that about a score of Oscan inscriptions, the so-called *Iovilae*, have been found in Campania which are somehow connected with burials. The stones or tiles with rounded tops on which they are found may be tomb markers, but the inscriptions themselves seem more votive than sepulchral.[4] They give the name and date of interment of the deceased and occasional details about the burial rites: sacrifice of a piglet, staging of a banquet and the presence of public officials are specifically mentioned. Two of them

[1] E. Gabrici in *Monumenti Antichi*, XXI (1910).

[2] Vetter, no. 213: the 'Herentas' inscription. See, too, Vetter, no. 209.

[3] Vetter, nos. 73, 184, 203.

[4] For the *Iovilae* see J. Heurgon, *Les Inscriptions Osques dites Iúvilas*, especially p. 52; Vetter, pp. 70–1. The Oscan they use is not free from latinisms: one of them contains the Latin word *divinus* (Vetter, no. 80). Emblems on the stones (or tiles) are probably not heraldic crests, but are intended merely for decoration.

seem to imply that the dead person received a state funeral. Whether the *Iovilae* are votive or not, they are evidence only for Capua, since they are found nowhere else.

Chamber tombs decorated in the Etruscan manner with fresco paintings have been found at Allifae, but not in the interior of Samnium.

(*b*) THE ECONOMY

Roman writers, or writers who depend on the Roman tradition, allude not infrequently to Samnite wealth and riches.[1] Livy mentions the bountiful loot to be found in such Samnite towns as Bovianum, Murgantia, Romulea, Duronia and Saepinum. He also talks about whole Samnite armies outfitted with silver and gold. The Elder Pliny, more modestly even if not much more plausibly, dilates on Samnite stores of bronze, while other writers contribute their mite with the story of the incorruptible Fabricius, who nobly resisted fabulous offers of Samnite gold.[2]

No one will seriously believe that such gilded troops existed. The intention of the fanciful story is to enhance the achievement of the stern and simple Romans in humbling a people of far greater resources.[3] It is true that by raiding and plundering their neighbours the Samnites were able to enrich their own poor settlements, and apparently they did this not infrequently. In the days of their independence they provided for their economic needs, in some measure at least, by stealing from their neighbours rather than by trading with them. *Ad iniurias vicinorum prompti*, as Justin says of the Sabellian Bruttii.[4] Livy talks of the *nefarium latrocinium Samnitium* and in other passages he describes Samnite looting of Campania and the lands of the Aurunci. Dio gives a graphic account of a Caracenan fastness (*Castel di Sangro*?) piled high with booty resulting from brigandage.[5]

[1] Modern writers sometimes unthinkingly reiterate this: cf., for instance, R. Payne, *The Roman Triumph*, p. 44: 'from the Samnites the Romans learned the arts of opulence'.

[2] See Livy 9. 31. 5; 9. 40. 3; 10. 17. 4 and 9; 10. 39. 4; 10. 45. 14; Pliny, *N.H.* 34. 43; Florus 1. 13. 22; Aul. Gell. 1. 14. 1; Oros. 3. 22. 2. App. *Samn.* 4. 1 also talks about Samnite gold.

[3] It is also meant to emphasize Roman virtue which was proof against bribes; and it could help to illustrate the rhetorical maxim *fas est et ab hoste doceri*: Fabius Pictor solemnly asserted that it was from the Sabine ancestors of the Samnites that the Romans learned to appreciate wealth (Strabo 5. 1. 1, p. 228).

[4] Justin 23. 1. 3.

[5] Livy 7. 30. 12; 10. 20. 9; 10. 31. 2; Zon. 8. 7.

Samnite military enterprise may also have helped the Samnite economy in another way. Those Samnites who served abroad as mercenary soldiers contributed something to the material well-being of their homeland, just as do their modern descendants who emigrate to the New World and send back remittances.[1]

These facts, however, can hardly be taken to substantiate Livy's exaggerations. For that matter an attentive reading of Livy's text will sometimes supply its own corrective. Thus, he tells us that over two and a half million pounds of bronze accrued to the Roman treasury as booty from the Third Samnite War.[2] This must have been the stock of metal that formed the base for the first issue of Roman coins.[3] Yet it is Livy himself who reveals, in the same passage, that the bronze had not been simply pillaged from Samnite towns: it was realized from the sale of Samnite prisoners-of-war. It is likewise Livy who tells us that the Samnite towns stacked high with booty were really quite few in number.[4] Thus the effect of Samnite warfaring on the economic life of Samnium—and undoubtedly there was some—was haphazard, sporadic and short-lived.

The wealth that Samnium produced from the resources within its own borders was meagre indeed. Its limestone ranges were not rich with ores or lodes.[5] The one mineral recorded in them is obsidian, but it existed in such minute quantities that its extraction was not worth while.[6]

The economy of the Samnites, in fact, could have been neither complex nor diversified. They lacked raw materials for industries and, being landlocked, enjoyed practically no opportunity for any activities connected with the sea. Therefore, when not preying on their neighbours, they were obliged to obtain their living directly from the soil. They were a peasant people, *montani atque agrestes*,[7] living a hard and frugal existence: *rusticorum mascula militum / proles*

[1] Evidence for Sabellians serving as mercenaries is copious: see, for example, Polyb. 1. 7; 1. 69; 3. 29; Diod. Bk. 14 *passim* and elsewhere; and the remarks of J. Bayet, *L'Hercule romain*, pp. 84 f.

[2] Livy 10. 46. 5.

[3] R. Thomsen, *Early Roman Coinage*, I, 30; III, 258.

[4] Livy 10. 45. 14.

[5] Exploitation of the marble quarries at Cubulteria dates from imperial times (*CIL*, X, 4574) and of the bauxite of the Matese and Maiella mountain masses from the twentieth century.

[6] Curiously enough, this volcanic glass is called after a Samnite (a certain Obsidius), who however had become familiar with it in Ethiopia rather than in his native habitat (Pliny, *N.H.* 36. 196 f.).

[7] Livy 9. 13. 7.

Sabellis docta ligonibus / versare glebas.[1] In the days of their greatness even their aristocrats may have been essentially nothing more than well-to-do peasants, landed proprietors who directly supervised and themselves participated in the farming and stock-breeding operations on their fields, in the same way that their Roman opposite numbers did.[2]

The Samnites possessed no upland valleys as fruitful or as extensive as the one that the Paeligni tilled around Sulmo and Corfinium. There were, however, some fertile tracts where farming was both feasible and extensively practised, especially in Western Samnium. Ancient writers record the fertility of Allifae,[3] the palatable wine of Trebula Balliensis[4] and the magnificent olives of Venafrum and the Mons Taburnus.[5] The land of the Hirpini was a large producer of cereals and still is: it celebrates an annual agricultural festival at *Frigento* near ancient Aeclanum.[6] There were farming operations around Aufidena and along the middle Sagrus.[7] And if Marrucine Teate could produce some of the choicest figs,[8] neighbouring Eastern Samnium could not have been wholly unproductive. Sweet Sabellian cabbages enjoyed some renown, even though the fields that grew them are not described.[9] The Volturnus valley supplied raw materials for the unguents industry of Capua.[10]

Forestry products, too, must have been quite important in the economy.[11] This is still true even today when the mountains show the effect of their age-long deforestation. Molise and Eastern Campania boast some fine stands of timber.

All these agrarian pursuits must date from very early times. The excellent wine of Beneventum with its smoky flavour is recorded

[1] Horace, *Odes*, 3. 6. 37–9. (It is a Sabellian who is talking: *Epp.* 1. 16. 49; and he seems to imply that the Sabellians, as typical farmers, gave their name to a farming implement.)

[2] A veritable bourgeoisie did not emerge until after the imperialist conquests of the second century.

[3] Cic. *pro Planc.* 22; *de leg. agr.* 2. 66; Sil. Ital. 12. 526.

[4] Pliny, *N.H.* 14. 69. Already in the second century, if not earlier, Southern Italy was exporting much wine (O. Bohn in *Germania*, VII (1923), 8 f.; IX (1925), 78 f.).

[5] Cato, *de agric.* 146; Hor. *Odes*, 2. 6. 16; Strabo 5. 3. 10, p. 238; Verg. *Georg.* 2. 38; Pliny, *N.H.* 15. 8; Vib. Sequester 2, p. 38. The olives of Cominium were also famous: Pliny, *N.H.* 15. 20.

[6] On 15 August. Yields per acre are small, but total production is large.

[7] *Liber Colon*, pp. 259 f.

[8] Pliny, *N.H.* 15. 82.

[9] Pliny, *N.H.* 19. 141.

[10] H. Nissen, *Ital. Landesk.* II, 787.

[11] For the well-wooded character of Samnium in antiquity, see above, p. 17.

already in the fourth century, before ever the town had the name of Beneventum.[1] There is no need to assume that it was only as a result of the prosperity following upon the Punic Wars that the Samnite nation began to exploit its woodlands, took to viticulture and developed olive groves, orchards, market gardens and grain fields in the fertile valleys of the Volturnus, Calor, *Isclero* and Aufidus or in the open spaces around *Carpinone*, *Campobasso*, Bovianum, Saepinum, Beneventum, Abellinum, Terventum and *S. Agata di Puglia*.

In some districts, however, it was stock-raising rather than agriculture or forestry that was of chief importance.[2] This is especially true of the country of the Caraceni and Pentri, much of which is unsuitable for cultivation. Cattle-raising has been practised there from prehistoric times[3] and was certainly of great importance in the economy. That is shown not only by the path-finding steers of the Sacred Spring ritual and the existence of at least two towns named Bovianum, but also by allusions to cow-herding in the surviving literature.[4] Indeed cattle-raising must have been more important in antiquity than now, since many of the bare rocky hills which today do not provide even rough pasturage undoubtedly did so before their denudation. The Montagna del Matese was one region where dairy-farming was extensively practised.[5]

References to Samnite cavalry show that horses also were bred,[6] and we can confidently assume that Samnium likewise reared asses, mules, poultry, goats[7] and pigs,[8] even though fewer of these last than were raised in Cisalpine Gaul.

Above all, however, the Samnites were great breeders of sheep, which were valued for their milk products as well as for their wool.

[1] By Plato the Comic Poet (*ap.* Athen. 1, p. 31 E).

[2] Livy 9. 31. 7 and 16. To what extent there was antagonism between agricultural peasants and stockbreeders we do not know.

[3] S. M. Puglisi, *La Civiltà Appenninica*, pp. 31–41.

[4] Livy 24. 20. 4; Verg. *Aen.* 12. 715. For the characteristics of cattle-raising people, see P. Linton, *The Tree of Culture*, pp. 257 f.; the Samnites fit the description admirably.

[5] See H. Nissen, *Ital. Landesk.* II, 786. The Matese massif also has much agriculture: indeed it celebrates its cereal production in an annual festival (at *Letino* on 21 August).

[6] Polyb. 2. 24. 10; Livy 10. 14. 11; Strabo 5. 4. 12, p. 250; 6. 3. 9, p. 284.

[7] The Samnite commander in the fresco from the Esquiline (third to second century) wears a goatskin.

[8] Ultimately (in the fourth and fifth centuries A.D.) Samnium was a very important pig-breeding region: see, for example, *Theodos. Code* 14. 4. 3 and 4.

Admittedly when Justin[1] and Livy[2] imply that in the fourth century Sabellian men were normally shepherds, they may only be reflecting the state of affairs with which they were themselves familiar: by the late Republic the Romans had reduced the amount of agriculture in Samnium. Nevertheless sheepbreeding had always been common. In summer pastures were found there at surprising heights above sea level.[3] In the winter months the Samnites drove their animals long distances to grazing lands in the plains. This is the famous system of transhumance.[4] That oxen were also involved is proved by epigraphic evidence,[5] but first and foremost it was sheep that made the annual treks.[6] The *calles*, that is the drovers' trails which led across Samnium to and from the winter pastures, are mentioned both in ancient literature[7] and in inscriptions. They date from the Iron, if not the Bronze Age, Apulia being the chief but not the only destination.[8] Called *tratturi* in Italian, they still exist, although since World War II transhumance is swiftly disappearing.

It has been suggested that this method of stock-raising only assumed really large proportions after the Second Punic War, when the Roman state greatly increased its holdings of *ager publicus*.[9] Moreover Roman insistence on law and order throughout the peninsula made transhumance a more straightforward proposition than it had hitherto been besides encouraging huge capitalist enterprises of the kind to which Varro alludes.[10] Manifestly the system did take on increased importance from the second century onwards. But

[1] Justin 23. 1. 7.

[2] Livy 9. 2. 2 (the force of Livy's evidence is perhaps somewhat reduced by his describing a similar incident at Etruscan Rusellae: 10. 4. 6; 10. 5. 13. But the part of Samnium he is referring to in 9. 2. 2 still boasts drovers' trails).

[3] Capracotta, near which was found the Agnone tablet, is the loftiest town in peninsular Italy (and one of the loftiest anywhere).

[4] References to transhumance in ancient literature are frequent. See, for example, Cic. *pro Cluentio*, 59, 161; Varro, *R.R.* 2. 2. 10; 3. 17. 9; Livy 22. 14. 8; Sil. Ital. 7. 365. Cicero avers that, had Catiline succeeded in carrying out his plan to get control of the drovers' trails (*calles*), he would have been most difficult to suppress. In 59 the senate planned to stultify Caesar's consulship by making *silvae callesque* one of the consular *provinciae* for that year (Suet. *Iul.* 19. 2).

[5] *CIL*, I^2, 585.

[6] For a description of a flock moving along a drovers' trail see Verg. *Georg.* 3. 339–48; and for a pictorial representation of one see the relief at Sulmona reproduced by M. Rostovtzeff (in *Soc. Econ. Hist. Rom. Emp.*[2], p. 20).

[7] *CIL*, IX, 2438. Tac. *Ann.* 4. 27. 2 implies that the *calles* of Southern Italy were normally the *provincia* of a quaestor.

[8] There were grazing grounds around Metapontum and in Bruttium (Varro, *R.R.* 2. 9. 6; Livy 24. 20. 16).

[9] A. Grenier in *Mélanges d'arch. et d'hist.* XXV (1905), 293–328.

[10] *R.R.* 3. 1. 8.

archaeology has proved that prehistoric Samnium already had a pastoral economy.[1] Possibly some of the Samnite attempts at expansion and conquest are to be interpreted as efforts to obtain full and unhampered control over the trails. The Samnites, however, were not alone in using them. The Sabellic peoples of central Italy also practised transhumance.

A typical drovers' trail is over one hundred yards wide, and in the days before good roads it must have served as the main artery of communication. The most celebrated is the one that runs from the territory of the Pentri past Bovianum, Saepinum,[2] Beneventum, Aequum Tuticum and Gerunium to Apulia; it is the subject of the famous inscription from Saepinum of Marcus Aurelius' reign.[3] Other *tratturi* led down to the far south of Italy from the tribes in the central Apennines. Those from the country of the Vestini and Marrucini proceeded to Apulia by way of the Frentani and past the town of Larinum. Those from the Marsi and Paeligni also reach the neighbourhood of Larinum, but by way of Samnium. Larinum obviously was a veritable centre for a whole network of trails.[4] The Marsic *tratturo* starts near Opi, the place whose name is sometimes said to have provided the root element in the word 'Oscan', skirts the modern towns of Alfedena, Pescolanciano, Duronia, Molise, Roccaspromonte and Madonna della Neve, and thence heads eastwards. The Paelignian trail stretches from the Piano delle Cinquemiglia past Pietrabbondante and Trivento to the warmer south.

What tolls were exacted along the trails we do not know. The Lex Agraria of 111 seems to stipulate that during the actual passage en route to or from the grazing lands the herds are to be exempted from any charge for roadside pasture. But, even if it be assumed that this is merely the codification of an immemorial, traditional right, it has reference only to Roman land. The Roman government interested itself actively in any drovers' trails that traversed Roman public land: it might even assign them as a *provincia* to one of the

[1] For prehistoric transhumance on Mons Taburnus see A. Maiuri, *Passeggiate Campane*, p. 361. Over 60 per cent of the animal bones found on a Copper Age or Neolithic site in Hirpinian territory came from sheep (D. H. Trump in *Pap. Brit. Sch. Rome*, XVIII (1963), 1–32. See, too, App. *B.C.* I. 8. 33).

[2] In Roman Saepinum this *tratturo* formed the *decumanus* of the town: V. Cianfarani, *Guida delle Antichità di Sepino*, p. 53 (he identifies it with the Via Minucia, for which see above, p. 21).

[3] *CIL*, IX, 2438. On this inscription note the remarks of A. Passerini, *Le Coorti Pretorie*, pp. 251 f., and of F. Millar in *Journ. Rom. Stud.* LIII (1963), 31.

[4] See Cic. *pro Cluentio*, 198.

magistrates.[1] No detailed information survives about transit dues over the trails in non-Roman areas, although it is known that attempts to exploit and victimize the drovers were not unknown.[2]

As a result of Samnite, Pyrrhic and Hannibalic Wars the Roman state acquired large tracts of *ager publicus* in Southern Italy. That this increased pastoral activities relative to agricultural in Samnium is certain. The regions taken by Rome must have included some of the ancestral grazing lands of the Samnites,[3] and, even though it seems certain that Samnites were permitted to use Roman state lands, Roman ownership of these must have constituted a standing grievance, especially if the Samnites were now obliged to pay for the use of pastures which had earlier been freely at their disposal.[4]

Of native Samnite industry there could not have been much. Undoubtedly their textiles were mostly home-made, and mostly of wool woven by the women. A great centre of the wool trade was Luceria, the border town with Apulia.[5]

There must also have been some metal-using crafts and artisan activities, even if on a comparatively small scale.[6] No doubt the Samnites, like any other people, preferred to fashion their own military equipment so far as possible, importing the necessary raw materials. There were slight differences between their arms and those of their neighbours, the Samnite javelin for instance not being identical with the Picene.[7] This suggests that for obvious prudential reasons they made their own weapons.

There was also some manufacture of pottery. Simple black painted ware has been produced in the Abruzzi from the Iron Age if not earlier, and fragments of it have been found at Samnite Saepinum. Most Samnite pottery is crude *impasto* ware of very

[1] See H. F. Pelham in *Class. Rev.* x (1896), 7. From the time of Nero on, they appear to have been replaced by procurators under the general supervision of the *a rationibus* (Statius, *Silv.* 3. 3. 92).

[2] Cic. *pro Cluentio*, 161.

[3] Varro, *R.R.* 2. 1. 16.

[4] Naturally they would attempt to evade payment. The *multi pecuarii*, whom the plebeian aediles brought to trial in 196 and 193 (Livy 33. 42. 10; 35. 10. 11) presumably for failure to pay the *scriptura*, may not have been exclusively Roman citizens: some of them may conceivably have been Samnites.

[5] *CIL*, IX, 826; Hor. *Odes*, 3. 15. 14. For the Apulian wool trade generally see Strabo 6. 3. 9, p. 284.

[6] Venafrum made iron implements (Cato, *de agric.* 135; cf. *CIL*, x, 1, 4855) and Atina had iron foundries (Verg. *Aen.* 7. 630).

[7] G. Devoto, *Gli Antichi Italici*[2], p. 103.

mediocre quality.[1] Only the vases of some towns near Campania show any elegance, but there is nothing particularly Samnite about them. Saticula is no longer thought to have been a ceramic centre.[2] On the other hand, Telesia, like Saticula a Caudine town close to the border with Campania, does seem to have been one: its pottery belongs to the third and second centuries. The black variety is certainly not original Samnite ware: it is identical with the pottery produced at Cales, the town of the Aurunci which became a Latin Colony in 334, and there is every reason to believe that the factory at Telesia was simply a branch of the main centre of production at Cales.[3] The red variety is undistinguished *impasto* ware. Allifae also manufactured pottery of a very common sort. Evidently no native ceramics industry worthy of the name existed in Samnium.[4]

In such trade and commerce as there was—and there was certainly some since even rustic, inaccessible third-century Agnone worshipped Euclus (= Hermes, the god of trade)—the Samnites used the Oscan system of weights and measures: the pound weighed 273 grammes and the linear foot was 27·5 centimetres.[5] Until the Social War, however, the states of Samnium did not mint or issue coins of their own,[6] even though they must have been perfectly familiar with the idea of money and may have used the coins of neighbouring states. Some Samnite towns are indeed known to have issued their own coins; but they did so only when they did not officially belong to Samnium or form part of one of the Samnite tribal states. Thus, Allifae and Fistelia (if that was Samnite) struck silver coins in the

[1] G. Patroni, 'La ceramica antica nell'Italia meridionale', in *Atti Accad. Napoli*, XIX (1897), 37–130.

[2] The so-called Saticulan pottery was entirely Greek and not Samnite at all (R. M. Cook, *Greek Painted Pottery*, p. 328). See further, below, p. 132.

[3] Much of the 'Calenian' ware was manufactured elsewhere than at Cales: see R. Pagenstecher, *Die calenische Reliefkeramik*.

[4] Crude pottery replaced Attic and Italiote ware in the burials in Campania after the Sabellians' arrival there (E. Lepore in *Parola del Passato*, VII (1952), 306).

[5] So T. Frank, *Econ. Survey of Anc. Rome*, I, 422 and W. Becher in *R.E.* XIX (1938), s.v. 'Pfund', col. 1474. Doubts have been expressed whether there was a separate and distinct Oscan pound (R. Thomsen, *Early Roman Coinage*, II, 26).

[6] T. Mommsen, *Röm. Münzwesen*, pp. 118–20. Fourth-century silver coins with the legend ΣΑΥΝΙΤΑΝ (written retrograde) do not come from Samnium: perhaps they were minted at Tarentum as a compliment to the Samnites (B. V. Head, *Historia Numorum*², p. 27). The coins found at *Campobasso* and bearing the legend ΠΕΡΙΒΟΛΩΝ ΠΙΤΑΝΑΤΑΝ are also probably Tarentine: they seem to belong to Pitanatae, the 'Laconian colony' which Tarentum planted near 'the Samnites' (Strabo 5. 4. 12, p. 250). The Lucani and Bruttii, but not the Samnites, are said to have minted coins while Pyrrhus was in Italy (Diod. 22. 8. 1).

fourth century, and Aquilonia, Cubulteria and possibly Venafrum, Caiatia and Telesia issued bronze coins in the third.[1]

The legends on the silver from Allifae and Fistelia are more often Greek than Oscan: this in itself is enough to show that these are coins of Campania rather than of Samnium. The helmeted head of Minerva on the obverse indicates the same thing: it is a type found on the more or less contemporary issues of Neapolis, Hyria (pre-Sabellian Nola?), Nola and other Campanian towns. Clearly the didrachms of Allifae and Fistelia were intended for trading with, and circulation in, Campania rather than the highlands. The Allifae silver belongs to the period (*c.* 350 and earlier) when the Sabellians, after expanding into Campania and cutting their ties with their fellows in Samnium, had consolidated their control over the various urban centres, including Allifae, in their new homeland.[2] Later in the fourth century the Samnites of Samnium began to do what this earlier wave of Oscan-speakers had done: namely expand towards Campania. They evidently succeeded in getting possession of the Volturnus border region, including Allifae, and in reannexing it to Samnium. They were then stopped from going further by the Romans in the First Samnite War (343–341). But the return of Allifae to Samnium brought its coinage operations to an end: no later issues from there are known.[3]

The certain coins of Aquilonia and Cubulteria and the more doubtful ones of Venafrum, Caiatia and Telesia[4] are later and of

[1] The old view that Samnite Compsa issued coins in the third century has been discarded. Coins with the legend COSANO belong to Cosa, the Latin Colony founded in Etruria in 273.

[2] Surviving polygonal defences above Allifae could be those erected by the Samnites against Campanian enemies operating out of that town. The graves at Allifae that show evidence of some wealth (F. von Duhn, *Ital. Gräberkunde*, I, 611 f.) belong to the period when Allifae formed part of Campania rather than Samnium.

[3] The vicissitudes of Fistelia may have paralleled those of Allifae, although our ignorance about its exact location renders certainty impossible. Its coins are usually found with, are similar in type to, and apparently date from the same period as, those of Allifae. Fistelia therefore was probably somewhere near Allifae in the Volturnus valley. Even so, the experiences of the two were probably different. Fistelia was issuing coins *c.* 300 to judge from its coin legends (see below, p. 117, n. 4). This suggests that unlike Allifae it did not revert to Samnium. Most of its surviving coins, however, were found there (at *Campobasso*, Telesia and Aesernia).

[4] There are two coins with legends which seem to indicate Venafrum. Whether Telesia and Caiatia are to be added to this list of towns is uncertain. One coin has the legend TEDIS or TELIS; there is no proof that it comes from Telesia. The only evidence for a coin with Oscan legend from Caiatia is an assertion by Garucci (no such coin exists today). Caiatia undoubtedly issued coins with Latin legends. See Vetter, pp. 134 f.

bronze and of a different order.[1] They can no more be regarded as officially Samnite than can those of Aesernia and Beneventum which, despite the Oscan letters they occasionally display, were officially the coins of Latin communities.[2] The coins of Aquilonia and the rest belong to the third century after these towns had been forcibly divorced from Samnium and established as autonomous communities by the Romans.[3] The coins thought to come from Venafrum, Caiatia and Telesia have a head of Minerva on the obverse and a cock with eight-point star on the reverse; the coins of Aquilonia show a similar obverse, but a different reverse.[4] These types are also found on bronze coins of identical weight from nearby Aquinum, Cales, Suessa Aurunca and Teanum Sidicinum. The coins of Cubulteria resemble those of contemporary Naples in type and even show the same mint-mark (the Greek letters IΣ). Coins from Aesernia, Cales, Suessa Aurunca and Teanum Sidicinum also show this mint-mark.[5] Thus, it seems clear from the coins that the quondam Samnite towns, presumably with Roman permission if not encouragement, had formed a close monetary league with the towns immediately west of Samnium. In other words, they no longer belonged to Samnium: on the contrary, they had turned their backs on it, for trading purposes anyway.[6]

When the Social War (91–87) broke out, the insurgent allies of Rome issued their own coins, some with Latin, others with Oscan legends. These coins were intended to rival the Roman *denarius*, none of them being of bronze. Like the Roman *denarius*, they were of silver; and they were of the same weight and size and in some instances displayed the same types.[7] Some of them have an oath

[1] Their legends, although written in Oscan, show the -NO- suffix of the so-called 'Romano-Campanian' series and are probably close to the latter in date (in other words, third century) (R. Thomsen, *Early Roman Coinage*, III, 158).

[2] There is no evidence that Malventum minted coins before it became Beneventum in 268. The bronze coin with the legend MALIES or MAIIES is not from there (B. V. Head, *Hist. Num.*², p. 28; R. S. Conway, *Italic Dialects*, I, 152).

[3] B. V. Head, *Historia Numorum*², p. 27.

[4] The implication is that Aquilonia was in north-west Samnium, which is also what is suggested by the find-spots of its very rare coins, Pietrabbondante and Campobasso. Hence, although Vetter (p. 137) and some historians (e.g. K. J. Beloch, *Röm. Gesch.* p. 447) seek Aquilonia at Lacedonia in the far south of Samnium, most numismatists do not (A. Sambon, *Monnaies antiques de l'Italie*, p. 109).

[5] On these coins see J. Heurgon, *Capoue préromaine*, pp. 230 f. [6] See below, pp. 254, 278.

[7] All insurgent issues, apart from a single gold coin, are *denarii*: larger or smaller denominations than this were apparently not minted. It is possible that, like the original issue of Roman *denarii* of over a century earlier, the coins were struck as pay for the soldiers. See E. A. Sydenham, *Roman Republican Coinage*, pp. 89–95; A. Voirol in *Schweizer Münzblätter* (1953/1954), pp. 64 ff.

scene on the reverse which shows two (and sometimes four, six or even eight) warriors swearing allegiance over a sacrificial piglet (*caesa porca*).[1] This is unabashed imitation of Roman issues.[2] The oath scene first appeared on the earliest Roman gold coins (of 216?);[3] thereafter it had been reproduced on some silver issues and most significantly on the coins of the moneyers Gaius Sulpicius and Tiberius Veturius which appeared in 93/92 just before the Social War broke out.[4] The scene suited insurgent propaganda admirably. As originally used by the Romans it had been intended to underline an alliance between Romans and Allies; its reappearance on Roman coins of the nineties was probably to remind the Italians that they owed loyalty to Rome. Insurgent use of the scene is a pointed retort: it is not only an allusion to the more truly federal character of their own movement but also a sarcastic reminder of the way Rome had exploited and abused her alliances. Other insurgent coins show the Dioscuri; and this too was a common Roman type. Thus there cannot be the slightest doubt that the insurgent coins were intended to challenge and, so far as possible, supplant those of Rome.[5] The rebels were deliberately coining in silver on the Roman standard, thus invading one right which Rome had most jealously guarded for herself.[6] The insurgent issues bore the name *Italia* (Latin) or *Vitelio* (Oscan) instead of *Roma*, in order of course to contrast the confederate nature of their organization with thc domination practised by Rome. Propaganda is no less evident in some of the other insurgent coin types, those for instance which show an Italian (Samnite?) bull goring or trampling a Roman wolf.

What is more difficult to decide is which of these insurgent coins were specifically Samnite.[7] The coins with Oscan legends must have been intended for use in the southern wing of the rebel con-

[1] The expression is Vergil's (*Aen.* 8. 641; cf. 12. 170).

[2] E. Babelon, *Monnaies de la rép. romaine*, I, 74.

[3] For the date see R. Thomsen, *Early Roman Coinage*, II, 284.

[4] R. Thomsen, *op. cit.* II, 256, n. 96; H. A. Grueber, *B.M.C.* II, 281 f.

[5] The 'Confederate money' issued by the South in the American Civil War was essentially similar.

[6] A. Pagani in *Riv. Ital. di Numismatica*, ser. 4, IV (1944/47), 10; A. Voirol in *Schweizer Münzblätter* (1953/1954), p. 64.

[7] Those with the head of Mamers instead of a female divinity (Italia?, Diana?, Bellona?) and those which show a standing warrior with a spear in his right hand and a bull reclining at his feet may be Samnite. These coins are, however, inscribed with the name *Vitelio*.

federacy where the Samnite, C. Papius Mutilus, was commander-in-chief: many of them are actually inscribed with his name, some of them even showing his title as well (*embratur*, Latin *imperator*).[1] But the southern wing comprised more than Samnites (Pentri and Hirpini): it also included Lucani, Apuli, Campanians and the Latin Colony of Venusia, so that the coins with Oscan legends were not necessarily Samnite. Moreover the Oscan and Latin coins of the insurgents were undoubtedly interchangeable: one issue even has *Italia* in Latin on one side and *Papius* in Oscan on the other. Clearly the Oscan coins were intended to circulate in the Latin or northern wing of the confederacy as well as in the Oscan-speaking districts.[2] In other words, the Oscan coins, or most of them at least, must be coins of the insurgent confederacy as a whole and not just of its Samnite component. Exactly where they were minted it is impossible to say with certainty, but it would be logical for coins of the confederacy as a whole, whether they bore Latin or Oscan legends, to be struck at the town whose name they so eagerly display, Italia, the insurgent capital (really Paelignian Corfinium). Later when the insurgent capital was moved from Corfinium, first to Bovianum and subsequently to Aesernia, the mint presumably was also transferred.

The Oscan issues, however, include one with the proud legend *Safinim* (the Oscan word for *Samnium*). This seems unequivocal: the coin must be specifically Samnite, belonging to the period when, after all the northern and most of the southern rebels had collapsed (89/88), the Samnites were left to carry on the fight virtually alone. By then 'Samnium' had replaced 'Italia'. It is true that the Lucani also remained in arms at that time, but they were physically separated from the Samnites owing to surrenders of intervening insurgents' districts. By then Aesernia had replaced Bovianum as the insurgent capital, and presumably the Safinim issue was minted there.[3]

It is likewise to this late period of the war that we are to date the only known gold piece of the insurgents. Only one specimen survives, and it was clearly intended to win the favour and if possible the

[1] In contrast only one coin survives bearing the name of Poppaedius Silo. Yet he is described as the heart and soul of the revolt.

[2] One coin survives with the name of the Samnite commander-in-chief, Papius Mutilus, written on it in Latin.

[3] The crude and uninscribed coins issued towards the war's end might also be Samnite. The date seems established by the fact that there are no insurgent issues imitative of Roman coins minted after 88.

help of Mithridates, King of Pontus, in the fight against Rome. The coin is almost identical in type with those of Amisus, the principal city in Mithridates' kingdom. Its excellent workmanship, which is in striking contrast with the poor and at times barbarous appearance of late rebel coins in general, suggests that it may even have been minted at Amisus, perhaps as one of a very small and limited issue. The moneyer under whose authority it appeared is named in impeccable Oscan script on the coin: Minius (or Minatus) Iegius son of Minius (or Minatus). It seems reasonable to conjecture that, no matter where it was actually minted, it was a specifically Samnite coin, just like the Safinim issue.

With it the numismatic history of Samnium comes to an end. It is clear that purely Samnite issues were confined to one or two years at the most, between 89 and 87, and they were minted under extraordinary circumstances for very special occasions. They hardly affect the generalization that Samnite tribal states did not issue coins.

The failure of the Samnite tribal states to use coins of their own minting before 90 and the relative infrequency of coin finds of any kind, Samnite or otherwise, in Samnium suggests that the Samnites did much of their trading under a system of barter or by resort to weighed bullion.[1] It is notable that Carthage, one of the great trading states of antiquity, made extraordinarily little use of coins for a very long time; and it is well known that Roman coinage did not begin until after 300.[2]

There are, however, reasons besides the absence of coinage for concluding that Samnium was an economic backwater. It was an isolated land whose most valuable and practically only resource was its stock of hardy and comparatively abundant manpower. Its objects of trade were few and limited. Imports of significance are not commonly found there, and the few that have turned up did not have far to travel: they came from the immediately contiguous areas of Italy. Excavations at Aufidena disgorged a few trifles from Apulia and Tarentum, but nothing of demonstrable overseas provenance. It is true that some transmarine objects had found their way into Allifae in the fifth century at the time when that town was

[1] In other words, the Samnites may have had something similar to Roman *aes rude*.

[2] It began, interestingly enough, as a result of the Samnite Wars. See above, p. 65.

an integral part of Hellenized and Etruscanized Campania, but the stream had dried up again in the late fourth century, by which time Allifae had been reincorporated into Samnium.

The overwhelming majority of Samnites were not men of commerce, although their fondness for Hercules, a divinity closely associated with trade and the protection of profit,[1] might have induced them to become such, had favourable conditions presented themselves. Certainly the Sabellians in Campania showed a flair for business.[2] Those of Samnium, however, remained rustics living more or less directly from the soil.[3] It is significant that the Romans found that it was often more effective to make war on them by devastating their fields and destroying their villages than by assaulting their towns.[4] Their fields unfortunately were anything but the best in Italy: Pyrrhus noted the wealth of the farmlands under Roman control and the poverty of the land of his own Italic allies.[5]

The living which the Samnite way of life provided was a frugal one, devoid of luxuries of any kind: its austerity indeed became a by-word.[6] Actually the material poverty of the Samnites' culture is one of the reasons for the scarcity of tangible evidence concerning them. Theirs was a typical subsistence economy in which each *pagus* had to rely largely on its own resources for the basic necessities of life, food, clothing and materials for housing.

It is hardly surprising that these deprived mountain-dwellers should be consistently represented as covetous of neighbouring and better lands. They represent a permanent fact in the economic life of Italy: the urge to forsake the picturesque but unproductive mountains of the south for more fertile regions.[7]

(*c*) GOVERNMENT

The Samnite tribal states developed out of peasant societies. *Fera quaedam sodalitas et plane pastoricia atque agrestis...quorum coitio illa silvestris ante est instituta quam humanitas atque leges.*[8] The transition from

[1] G. De Sanctis, *Stor. dei Romani*, II², 502; IV, 2, 260; K. Latte, *Röm. Religionsgeschichte*, p. 215.

[2] Cato, *de agric.* 135; Plautus, *Rudens*, 631; *Pseudolus*, 146.

[3] Cf. Horace's description of the Aufidus as *agrestium regnator populorum* (*Odes*, 3. 30. 10f.).

[4] Livy 10. 17. 2.

[5] Dio, fr. 40. 27.

[6] Juvenal 3. 169.

[7] They might almost be regarded as ancient forerunners of the nineteenth- and twentieth-century emigrants to the New World.

[8] Cic. *pro Caelio*, 26: Cicero is talking about the *germani Luperci*, whose name however is identical with Hirpini.

barbarism to civilization could have occurred in the manner envisaged by Plato for primitive mountaineer societies.[1] But all we know concerning the way the Samnites organized themselves derives from casual allusions in the literary sources and Oscan documents. The literary sources, however, are Roman or Roman-inspired, while the Oscan documents with one or two exceptions date from the period when the Sabellians were already under Roman domination; and, as we have been recently reminded, 'Rome was the great centre of political innovation in Italy'.[2] Consequently it is by no means easy to decide what institution is genuinely Samnite and what is mere imitation of something Roman.[3]

Most of the Oscan documents come from towns in Campania; the merest handful were found in Samnium proper. And, manifestly, what is true of the urbanized Campanians, who were under strong Roman influence from at least 338, can hardly be invariably true of the tribally organized Samnites, who resisted romanization right down to 87.[4]

One thing is certain: the city-state as a unit of government did not exist among the Samnites. The political and administrative unit of the Sabellians generally and of the Samnites especially was not the *municipium*, but the *touto*. This word is said to have the same meaning as Latin *populus*, but probably has no exact equivalent.[5] It is found in the name of the Samnite town Aequum Tuticum, which may mean that that was the place where at one time assemblies of the Samnites were held.[6]

The *touto* was the unit that possessed corporate existence and it

[1] Plato, *Laws*, 3. 679–81.

[2] A. D. Momigliano in *J.R.S.* LIII (1963), 114.

[3] This is true even of Pompeii, for which we have more material than for any other Sabellian community (except possibly Capua) (F. Sartori, *Problemi di Storia Costituzionale Italiota*, p. 74). Nomenclature is not a certain criterion (F. P. Garofalo in *Rend. dei Linc.* ser. 5, XII (1903), 61): an institution with a Roman name may not be Roman in origin. Further uncertainty arises from the fact that the surviving scraps of information come from widely separated and perhaps widely differing parts of Italy.

[4] It is usually assumed that local differences among the Sabellians were minor; but this must be accepted with caution. Even the individual tribes composing the Samnite League may have differed somewhat from one another in their constitutional arrangements. Nevertheless the political picture seems to have been broadly similar wherever Sabellian tribal states existed.

[5] It may survive in the name of the Praetuttii (Praetuttiani): 'those living outside the state' (i.e. the subjugated): H. Rix in *Beiträge zur Namenforschungen*, VI (1955), 20–6.

[6] D. Petroccia in *Samnium*, XXXVI (1963), 55–88 (who probably exaggerates the size and consequence of Aequum Tuticum).

was evidently larger than the average *civitas*.[1] Of the *civitas* itself, with its distinctive individuality and civil constitution, there is no sign amongst the Samnites.[2] It is true that, when the Romans took the Caudini out of Samnium, they were able to organize them into separate civic communities; but, even after this, rump Samnium does not appear to have known what Isidore calls the *dignitas civitatis*.[3] The Samnites did not think in terms of a city-state with its *territorium* included, so to speak, within the urban centre. Their conception was of a territorial area in which urban agglomerations were more or less incidental, although they might be used as centres from which to conduct the business of the tribe. The Samnites had certainly passed beyond the stage of mere rudimentary village organization; but there is no trace of any true municipal organization of an elaborate communal kind amongst them. The Samnites were in that pre-urban stage in which the tribal community formed the basis of political organization.[4] Right down to the days of the Social War they do not appear to have had any genuine boroughs at all.

Their sub-tribal entity was the immemorial Italic institution, the *pagus*;[5] and traces of their *pagus*-arrangements survived into Roman times. The unmistakably Oscan character of such a name as *pagus Meflanus* (listed in the alimentary tables of the *Ligures Baebiani et Corneliani*)[6] shows that it goes back to the *touto* of the Hirpini. At Beneventum Roman territorial divisions in imperial days cut right across the old *pagus* boundaries: the *pagus Aequanus* was assigned partly to the *colonia* at Beneventum and partly to the *colonia* of the Ligures Baebiani.[7] At Capua the old *pagi Tifatinus* and *Herculaneus* were reactivated when the Romans obliterated political life there

[1] G. Camporeale in *Atti. Accad. Toscana* (1956), p. 97.

[2] Livy 8. 23. 6 uses the expression *civitas Samnitium*; but by this he clearly means the *nomen Sabellicum*.

[3] Isidor. 15. 2. 11.

[4] This is equally true of the related Paeligni and Marsi, who likewise lived in *vici* (Festus, p. 502 L.). For such peoples the tribe was the state, not a subdivision of it (as it was for the Romans).

[5] The evidence is abundant: e.g. *ILS*, 932, 5609, 6302, 6350, 6509, 6532, 6550; Degrassi, *ILLRP*, II, 1271 c; cf. Livy 31. 30. 6. See, further, E. Kornemann in *R.E.* XVIII (1942), s.v. 'Pagus', cols. 2318–39; S. Mazzarino in *Historia*, VI (1957), 98–122. One of the most important functions that local officials performed was the *lustratio pagi* (Ovid, *Fasti*, I. 667; Tib. 2. 1. 17; *CIL*, IX, 1618). It may be of some significance that Horace, the Sabellian poet, seems to be particularly conscious of the *pagus* (*Odes*, 2. 13. 4; *Epp.* I. 18. 105). *Pago* survives as a place-name in modern Italy.

[6] *ILS*, 6509.

[7] *Ibid.*

in 211.[1] Each *touto* contained a number of *pagi*,[2] but how the larger organization developed out of the smaller we do not know.[3] The *pagus* was an administrative sub-unit, the smallest such amongst the Italic peoples, but it was not a town: it was a district of variable size usually larger than a *fundus*, but smaller than a *territorium*,[4] and might itself contain one or more settlements, either unwalled but stockaded villages (*vici*) where the country was flat,[5] or walled citadels of refuge (*oppida*, *castella*) where the country was mountainous.[6] Neither *vici* nor *oppida* seem to have had any political life of their own: they were not the administrative sub-units. The *pagi* were.

The *pagus* was a semi-independent country district, concerned with social, agricultural and especially religious matters, and it may also have been through it that military levies were raised. It provided for the needs of government at the purely local level, and to that end could own communal property, including buildings. The members of a *pagus* could meet in an assembly, and there pass by-laws and elect the *pagus* officials: *pagi scita* and *pagi decreta* are known and likewise the Roman names of the officials (rarely *aedilis pagi*, usually *magister pagi*).[7] A *pagus* could also have its own council (*delecti pagi*).[8] How many *pagi* comprised a *touto* and what their mutual ties and relations were it is impossible to say.

When, however, a number of *pagi* agreed to cooperate closely a *touto* was born. And once it came into being it could evidently command the fierce loyalty of those who professed allegiance to it. In their native mountain habitats the Samnites had a strong sense of tribal solidarity (in other words, loyalty to their *touto*), and they gave expression to this in resounding feats of arms.

[1] *CIL*, IX, 1455. Indeed the *pagus Herculaneus* in many ways came to resemble a *municipium* (M. W. Frederiksen in *Pap. Brit. Sch. Rome*, XIV (1959), 90 f.).

[2] *ILS*, 5642 (the Paeligni); Caesar, *B.G.* 1. 37; 4. 1 (the hundred *pagi* of the Suebi).

[3] Some idea might be gleaned from Strabo 8. 3. 2, p. 336, who describes how Peloponnesian villages developed into cities.

[4] A. Schulten in *Philologus*, LIII (1894), 634. Originally the Romans may have thought of the *pagus* as a region that could field 1,000 men.

[5] Livy 9. 13. 6; 10. 17. 2; cf. App. *B.C.* 1. 51. 222; *Samn.* 4. The expression κώμη ἀτείχιστος is a cliché of ancient literature. For some account of a people living in *vici*, see Strabo 4. 1. 11, p. 186 (the Allobroges).

[6] Livy 10. 18. 8. For some account of a people living in a *castellum*, see *ILS*, 5946 (the Langenses Viturii near Genua).

[7] *ILS*, 5614, 6302, 6303; *CIL*, IX, 726, 3137, 3138; Pliny, *N.H.* 2. 28. Festus, p. 502 L., implies that the Roman *magister vici* developed out of a *pagus* official.

[8] *CIL*, IX, 726 (Larinum).

Livy refers to the *populi Samnitium*.[1] Presumably each of these *populi* was a *touto*. Their number probably varied at different times. During the recorded history of the Samnites we hear of the four to which allusion has already been made: the Caraceni, Caudini, Hirpini and Pentri. Strabo implies that each of these tribes was a political entity in itself[2] and Livy confirms this for the last three (he never mentions the Caraceni separately).[3] It seems safe to infer that each of these four tribes made up a *touto*, but we cannot say how, or if, they differed from one another in their constitutional and political practices.

Presumably each had a locality which, while itself a submunicipal unit, served as the 'capital' (the *caput gentis*, so to speak), the centre of administration for the whole *touto*. Oscan inscriptions mentioning a *meddix tuticus*, the highest official in a Samnite state, indicate that Bovianum was the capital for the Pentri, and Livy confirms this.[4] There was, however, also a *meddix tuticus* at Pietrabbondante,[5] which may mean that the Pentri had no firmly fixed capital and that it differed at various times. For an ancient tribal state to have more than one administrative centre is by no means unparalleled: the Durotriges of Gaul had two and the Parisii of Britain no fewer than four.[6]

The capitals of the other three Samnite tribes are largely a matter of guesswork. Its name suggests that at one time Aequum Tuticum of the Hirpini served as some sort of political meeting-place, but it never seems to have been a place of much consequence. Malventum, on the other hand, must always have been important and it is inconceivable that it was not the Hirpinian capital in its pre-Roman days. After 268, when it became the Latin Colony of Beneventum, the roles played by Compsa and Aeclanum suggest that one of them might have replaced it as the administrative town,

[1] Livy 9. 22. 2.

[2] Strabo 6. 1. 2, p. 254.

[3] See above, p. 42, n. 1.

[4] Vetter, nos. 159, 160; Livy 9. 31. 4.

[5] Vetter, nos. 148, 150, 151, 153. For this reason Pietrabbondante has often been regarded as a separate capital—of the Caraceni (T. Mommsen, *Unterital. Dialekte*, p. 173; *CIL*, IX, pp. 239, 257; J. Jung, *Grundriss der Geographie von Italien*[2], p. 43). But the inscriptions recording a *meddix tuticus* there belong to the period when there was no longer a separate tribal state of the Caraceni: see below, p. 290.

[6] A. L. F. Rivet, *Town and Country in Roman Britain*, p. 157; I. A. Richmond, *Roman Britain*, p. 79. Cf., too, Pliny, *N.H.* 3. 37: *Vocontiorum civitatis foederatae duo capita Vasio et Lucus Augusti.* In a tribal state the *touto* was wherever the men happened to be.

unless indeed the Hirpini too had more than one and used them both.[1]

For the Caudini it is surely as certain as anything can be that eponymous Caudium must have served as capital in pre-Roman times.

The Caraceni presumably used Aufidena as their chief centre.[2] The smallness of the tribe makes it probable that this was the only settlement they had bigger than a village, and it is significant that once it was annexed by Rome *c.* 268 the Caraceni seem to have disappeared as a separate tribe.[3]

Each *touto* was a republic, not a kingdom. Possibly, like the Romans and other peoples of early Italy, the Samnites had had kings at one time but if so it was in so remote a past that they had forgotten their title: Oscan had no word for 'king'. By historical times, certainly, the Samnites shared the normal Italic repugnance for the institution of monarchy.[4]

A Sabellian state was not only republican: it was also 'democratic'. This was true of the Bruttii, the Lucani and of Nola and Abella in Campania (and indeed of the Campani in general); and Livy evidently thought of the Samnites in the same light: he describes them as openly and loudly critical of their magistrates.[5] Individual Sabellians reflected the democratic temper of their communities: examples that spring to mind are 'Hamilcar', the Samnite, a democratic leader in Carthage in the second century[6] and Blossius

[1] Livy 23. 1. 1. implies Compsa, but modern scholars seem to prefer Aeclanum (*CIL*, IX, 98). Livy does not mention Aeclanum in the Samnite Wars, and H. Nissen, *Ital. Landesk.* II, 817, is doubtful whether it existed then. Dion. Hal. evidently thought that it did: see Steph. Byz. v.s. 'Aecalon'.

[2] An inscription from Aufidena (Vetter, no. 141) has been emended to read *m.t.* (i.e. *meddíss tovtíks*): G. Balzano in *Not. d. Sc.* (1932), pp. 128–9. Yet the *m.* is quite uncertain and the *t.* visible only to the eye of faith (E. Vetter in *Glotta*, XXIX (1942), 223, who however prints the inscription in its emended form in his *Handbuch*). If the emendation is right, it presumably means that the office of *meddix tuticus* was allowed to continue even after Rome annexed Aufidena *c.* 268. Aufidena was definitely a Caracenan town (Ptol. 3. 1. 58).

[3] See below, p. 290.

[4] Cf. Livy 5. 1. 3; R. Bloch in *Rev. Etudes Lat.* XXXVII (1959), 122; M. G. Delfino in *Serta Eusebiana*, p. 76. Oros. 3. 22. 10 must be in error in providing the Samnites with a king. Note how the Marrucini, when they wished to say 'queen', were obliged to borrow the Latin word (Vetter, no. 218).

[5] Livy 8. 27. 8; 10. 13. 3; 23. 2–4; Diod. 19. 10; Strabo 6. 1. 3, p. 254. Oscanized Naples was democratic until 326, when it acquired an oligarchic (pro-Roman) government (F. De Martino in *Parola del Passato*, VII (1952), 338 f.).

[6] Appian, *Pun.* 68; S. Gsell, *Hist. anc. de l'Afrique du Nord*, III, 323.

of Cumae, of about the same time, who seems to have taught the Gracchi any democratic notions they fostered.[1] Precisely what the ancient writers meant by 'democratic' in this context is nowhere made very explicit.[2] For Polybius democracy seems to have meant the absence of tyranny, a federal system in which all members have equal rights, and a system in which the government is elected and controlled by 'the people', but in which the 'good and substantial' citizens have a greater share in expressing and formulating 'the will of the people' than has the common crowd.[3] In actual practice, the Samnite states were not very democratic in the modern sense of the word.[4] In Samnium, as in the less developed parts of Italy generally, dynastic families with large estates commanded the allegiance of whole regions. Amongst the Hirpini the Magii *c.* 90 could enrol an entire army.[5] These local aristocracies monopolized political power probably because only the wealthiest could afford to be office-holders. Livy avers that the *primores* amongst the Samnites in the days of their independence were the *nobilitas*.[6] Elsewhere he reveals that the commander of Samnite forces in 217, the Pentrian Numerius Decimius, was the foremost man in wealth and lineage of all Samnium.[7] In yet another passage he says that the accession to the headship of the Sabellian state of Capua in 211 of a certain *Seppius Loesius, loco obscuro tenuique fortuna ortus*, bordered on the incredible.[8] The two last examples both date from the period of Roman supremacy. But Livy could equally talk about a *vir nobilis potensque* even in 323; and he alludes to the power of Samnite

[1] Cic. *Lael.* 37; Val. Max. 4. 7. 1; Plut. *Ti. Grac.* 8. 17; D. R. Dudley in *J.R.S.* XXXI (1941), 94 f.; E. Gabba in *Athenaeum*, XXIX (1951), 258. The name Blossius is very Sabellian: Marius Blossius was *praetor Campanus* in 216 (Livy 23. 7. 8); Blossius occurs on an Oscan inscription from Capua (Vetter, no. 81); and Cic. *de leg. agr.* 2. 93 regards the Blossii as an ancient and haughty Sabellian family.

[2] See Arist. *Pol.* 5. 3; 6. 5; cf. A. H. M. Jones, *The Greek City*, p. 166.

[3] Polyb. 6. 43. 1 implies that this view of democracy was the traditional one. See K. von Fritz, *The Theory of the Mixed Constitution*, p. 7.

[4] As the Romans regularly favoured oligarchy and as the Samnites regularly opposed the Romans, they were inevitably bound to be regarded as democratic.

[5] Velleius 2. 16. 2.

[6] Livy 10. 38. 12 (in a passage that is highly suspect). Verrius Flaccus, the Augustan antiquarian, likewise referred to a *princeps* of the Samnite nation (a certain Sthenius Mettius): Festus, p. 150 L.

[7] Livy 22. 24. 12 (the casual way the reference to Decimius is introduced guarantees its trustworthiness).

[8] Livy 26. 6. 13 f. Loesius was probably described in these derogatory terms since he opposed the Romans (at Rome a *novus homo* who was anything but a pauper could be described as *humili atque obscuro loco natus*: Cic. *II Verr.* 2. 5. 181). Loesius was a well-known name at Capua: it was even attached to one of the months (Vetter, no. 74).

aristocrats in 293;[1] so that, long before Roman partisan interference, political power amongst the Samnites was wielded by the aristocrats.[2] As in early Rome, a handful of families or clans supplied the leaders for centuries. It has often been remarked that the Samnite leaders of the Social War period bear names remarkably similar to those of the leaders in the great Samnite Wars of the fourth and third centuries: Statius Gellius (towards the close of the Second Samnite War) and Gellius Egnatius (the hero of Sentinum) suggest another Statius and Marius Egnatius, who were both prominent in the Social War;[3] a Pontius appears prominently in the fourth century and in the first;[4] and, though less convincingly, so does a Papius.[5]

There is no indication that the Samnite masses were dissatisfied because a comparatively small group thus perpetuated its own power. A clique imposed by the Romans, such as the senate at Capua, was bound to be hated by the commons; but the lower orders may have willingly acquiesced in the rule of families who traditionally had always been their leaders.

The small ruling class maintained its power through the office of the meddix, which accordingly merits close investigation.

The word *meddix* occurs in Oscan inscriptions in the form *meddíss*.[6] It does not occur in Latin inscriptions, where the Latin title *praetor*

[1] Livy 8. 39. 12; 10. 41. 11.

[2] The well-to-do minority usually exercised power (cf. Strabo 1. 1. 22 f., p. 13). Only they could afford it, since local office not only was unremunerated but also probably had to be bought (M. W. Frederiksen, *op. cit.* on p. 80, n. 1: the *aragetud multasíkud* of Vetter, no. 116, may not be *argento multaticio*, as usually interpreted (*CIL*, I, 181), but *summa honoraria*). The Romans ensured that their favourites amongst the self-styled best people got into power (we even know the name of the family they installed at Compsa in the third century when the Hirpini were still nominally independent). As early as the fourth century pro-Roman aristocrats were to be found amongst the Aurunci and Paeligni (Livy 9. 25. 4; Diod. 20. 90. 3). At Nola in 216 they did not hesitate to execute seventy commoners in order to support the *primores* (Livy 23. 17. 1 f.; cf. Plut. *Marc.* 10. 2). Of course not every aristocrat was pro-Roman. Those at Privernum vehemently opposed Rome (Livy 8. 20 f.).

[3] The Egnatii were merchants at Delos and bankers in Asia and evidently were a wealthy family (J. Hatzfeld, *Les trafiquants italiens*, p. 244, n. 1).

[4] Gavius Pontius and Pontius Telesinus respectively. Similarly in Sabellian Capua the name of the leading man was Calavius in 321 and also in 216 (Livy 9. 7. 2; 23. 2. 2).

[5] Nevertheless the Papii were an old dynastic family in Samnium (F. Münzer in *R.E.* XVIII (1949), s.v. 'Papius, no. 12', cols. 1078 f. In general see G. De Sanctis, *Per la Scienza dell'Antichità*, pp. 207 f.).

[6] The form *medís* also occurs (Vetter, no. 223) and might be preferable since *meddíss* can be plural as well as singular. The spelling *meddíss* is undoubtedly the normal one.

is regularly substituted for it.[1] Ancient authors also usually refer to a *meddix* as *praetor* or στρατηγός;[2] but they do sometimes use the word *meddix* itself.[3]

Meddix was an old Italic title used by all the other Sabellian and Sabellic peoples and by the related Volsci as well.[4] It is generally agreed that it is cognate with Latin *iudex*.[5] According to Festus, *meddix* was a generic term equivalent in meaning to Latin *magistratus*.[6] It could, however, be made specific by the addition of a qualifying adjective. The chief *meddix*, the head of the state, was called *meddix tuticus* (*meddíss tovtíks*), the adjective clearly being formed from *touto*.

Ennius' and Livy's definition of the title as *summus* is confirmed by the Oscan inscriptions.[7] The *meddix tuticus* had full unfettered authority in his *touto*. Unlike other officials he is not described as acting only on the authority of a council, although he was expected to consult one;[8] and it was made clear that the other officials were subordinate to him. In addition to supervising the workings of the law he was the military leader of the state[9] and had a role, originally no doubt the chief role, in its official religion.[10] He summoned and presided over meetings of council and assembly and supervised state finances. As an eponymous magistrate his office was an annual one.[11] He seems, however, to have been eligible for immediate re-election: this was certainly the case at Capua and amongst the Sabellian insurgents in the Social War.[12]

[1] *CIL*, IX, 689, 690, 698. *Meddix* was probably translated as *praetor* since at the time that the Romans first became aware of the Sabellian office their own corresponding official was called *praetor*, the title consul not yet having been taken into use.

[2] Livy 8. 39. 13; 23. 7. 8; 24. 47. 7; Diod. 22. 13. 2, 5.

[3] Ennius 8. 298 Vahlen (= fr. 173 Valmaggi); Livy 23. 2. 3; 23. 35. 13; 24. 19. 2; 26. 6. 13; Festus, p. 110 L.

[4] Vetter, nos. 8, 13, 14, 15, 71, 81–6, 88, 91, 107, 115, 116 (Campanians); 192 (Lucani); 196 (Mamertini); 212, 216 (Paeligni); 223 (Marsi); 219 (Marrucini); 226 (Aequiculi). There is no surviving evidence from the Frentani or Vestini, but their commanders in the Social War are significantly called *praetors*. The Sabines and Umbrians, however, did not use the title *meddix*: they preferred *maro* (an Etruscan title?).

[5] G. Camporeale in *Atti Accad. Toscana* (1956), p. 97.

[6] Festus, p. 110 L. In the Tabula Bantina (Vetter, no. 2) the word *meddix* has the generalized meaning of 'magistracy'.

[7] Especially the *Iovilae* (Vetter, nos. 75–94). Ennius' evidence is particularly valuable since he himself spoke Oscan. His words are: *summus ibi capitur meddix, occiditur alter.*

[8] Livy 8. 39. 12; A. Rosenberg, *Staat der alten Italiker*, p. 104.

[9] Livy 8. 23. 2; 23. 35. 13; 24. 19. 2.

[10] Vetter, nos. 86, 88; Livy 23. 35. 13. A. Bernardi in *Athenaeum*, XVI (1938), 239–74, suggests that at Velitrae the *meddices* were nothing but religious officials: this is unconvincing.

[11] Vetter, nos. 14, 71, 149.

[12] Livy 23. 2. 3; 24. 19. 2; 26. 6. 13. Re-election, however, was probably not very common, since it would complicate dating under a system which used an annual eponymous magistrate.

In wielding supreme authority the *meddix tuticus* obviously resembled the Roman consul.[1] Unlike the latter, however, he does not appear to have had a colleague on equal terms with himself. It has been convincingly argued that the native *meddix tuticus* was originally a single official.[2] In Samnium, so far as we know, this was the case at all times.[3] The earliest occurrence of the word *meddix*, on a helmet from Lucania, refers to a single official.[4] At Capua, before Rome suppressed its local government in 211, there was one *meddix tuticus Campanus*.[5] At Mamertine Messana Diodorus reveals that, prior to 265, that is before coming within the Roman sphere of influence, Messana had only one supreme chief official.[6]

Unquestionably pairs of *meddices* existed. They appear on inscriptions from Mamertine Messana, Volscian Velitrae, Campanian Nola and Paelignian Corfinium.[7] The typically Oscan adjective *tuticus*, however, is not used with any of these pairs, and the influence of the Roman collegial system could explain them all.[8] The pair at Messana are the result of close Mamertine relations with Rome after 265. The proximity of Velitrae to Rome made Roman influence there inescapable: indeed by the third century, the date of the inscription concerned, it was quite marked.[9] An inscription that

[1] So Festus, p. 404 L. (who also likens the *meddix* to the Carthaginian *sufes*). J. Heurgon, *Capoue préromaine*, pp. 234 f., compares him rather to the Latin dictator: but see G. Camporeale in *Atti Accad. Toscana* (1956), p. 97.

[2] S. Weinstock in *R.E.* xv (1931), s.v. 'meddix', cols. 26 f.; cf. *Klio*, xxiv (1931), 229, 242, 246. Livy 23. 2. 3; 23. 7. 8; 23. 35. 13; 24. 19. 2; 26. 6. 13, 17 clearly implies that the *meddix Campanus* served without a colleague.

[3] On a document from there containing two names the title is attached to only one of them (Vetter, no. 160).

[4] Vetter, no. 192.

[5] *meddís tovtíks Kapuans* (Vetter, no. 88; cf. no. 86). Comparable are *meddix Pompeianus* (*medíss pompaians*: Vetter, no. 8), *meddix Nolanus* (*meddíss novlans*: Vetter, no. 1). Where there was no risk of ambiguity *meddix* alone was used (Vetter, no. 192).

[6] Diod. 23. 13. 2–8.

[7] Vetter, nos. 196, 222, 115, 212. Their presence seems highly probable also at Paelignian Superaequum, Marrucine Teate, Marsic Vicus Supinus and Campanian Cumae (Vetter, nos. 216, 219, 228 c; *CIL*, x, 3685, 3698). F. Sartori, *Problemi di Storia Costituzionale Italiota*, pp. 41, 69, 74, 77, 157 f. (cf. E. Manni, *Per la Storia dei Municipii*, pp. 131 f., 148 f.), regards also the *duoviri* in Roman Campania as survivals of pairs of *meddices*. This however conflicts with his own view (pp. 27, 69) that a pair of *meddices* had unequal powers and ignores the fact that newly constituted *municipia* owed their duoviral constitution to Augustus (see A. Degrassi, *Scritti Vari di Antichità*, I, 185–92). For that matter towns in Samnium with *duoviri* had not been civic commonwealths in their Samnite days. See, too, A. Degrassi, *op. cit.* pp. 153 f.

[8] F. P. Garofalo in *Rend. dei Lincei*, ser. 5, XII (1903), 64; H. Rudolph, *Stadt und Staat im röm. Italien*, pp. 90 f., 207 f.; A. von Blumenthal in *Die Welt als Geschichte*, II (1936), 15 f.

[9] By then it was part of the Roman state.

alludes to one of the pair at Nola contains the Latin neologisms *senatus* and *quaestor*.[1] The two at Corfinium are named in a document which uses the Latin script and includes a Latin verb superficially oscanized.[2]

Besides its chief magistrate a Sabellian state also had lower officials. A *Iovila* inscription from pre-211 self-governing Capua seems to mention a *meddix minor*[3] and another may contain the Oscan equivalent of *cum meddix quisquis minor est aderit*.[4] Ennius and Livy also reveal the existence of magistrates below the *meddix tuticus*.[5]

Every *pagus* in a *touto* may well have had its own *meddix*:[6] he would be subordinate to the *meddix tuticus*. *Meddices* who are not *tutici* are also securely documented: there were *meddices decentarii* (*meddíss degetasios*) at Campanian Nola[7] and *meddices atici* (*medix aticus* [*sic*]) at Paelignian Corfinium.[8] The Nolan *meddix decentarius* was the exact equivalent of the *quaestor* at Abella, who in his turn strikingly resembles the *quaestor* at Pompeii and at Bantia: in neither of these two places was he the chief official. The *quaestor* apparently could act only on the authority of the council; unlike the

[1] Vetter, no. 1.

[2] Vetter, no. 212: *locatin* for *locaverunt*.

[3] Vetter, no. 88 B: *medik. minive* (the interpretation *meddix minor* is highly dubious: Vetter thinks *minive* is two words, without interpunct: *mi(nius) nive(llius)*, the name of the *meddix* concerned). See further A. Rosenberg, *Staat der alten Italiker*, pp. 15–28; G. Devoto, *Gli Antichi Italici*², p. 259; S. Mazzarino, *Dalla Monarchia allo Stato Repubblicano*, pp. 171 f.; F. Sartori, *Problemi di Storia Costituzionale Italiota*, p. 25; A. Bernardi in *Athenaeum*, XXIV (1946), 97.

[4] Vetter, no. 87, reading *pon medd(íkom) pís m(íní)veṛeṛ ad(f)ust*, the suggestion of J. Heurgon, *Etude sur les inscriptions osques*, p. 89. In view of the complete uncertainty about the key word *miniverer*, it is impossible to attach much importance to this inscription (even though Heurgon's proposed reading has won influential support: e.g. G. Bottiglioni, *Manuale dei Dialetti Italici*, p. 220). Hence one can be rightly sceptical of the notion that Sabellian magistrates were usually pairs, with one member superior to the other.

[5] Ennius has *summus meddix, alter meddix*, which implies that there were at least three. Livy 7. 31. 11; 8. 23. 2; 10. 13. 2 mentions *magistratus* of the Samnites (which could, it is true, mean only the *meddices tutici*). If Heurgon's emendation of Vetter, no. 87, is sound, then any *meddix*, whether *tuticus* or not, could officially witness the *Iovila* ceremonies.

[6] G. De Sanctis, *Storia dei Romani*, III, 2, 216, n. 17. The *meddix* mentioned in a document found at Molise (Vetter, no. 156) could be of this type (R. S. Conway, *Italic Dialects*, I, 181, however, sees him as the *meddix* from neighbouring Bovianum).

[7] Vetter, nos. 1, 115, 116: Oscan *deketasio*—or *degetasio*—could become *decentarius* in Latin by rhotacism. See R. S. Conway, *Italic Dialects*, p. 612.

[8] Vetter, no. 212, which may belong to the age of Sulla. F. Sartori, *Prob. di Stor. Cost. Ital.*, pp. 23 f. and F. P. Garfalo in *Rend. dei Lincei*, ser. 5, XII (1903), 77, suggest that the *atici* may be the same as the *tutici*. The view of Vetter *ad loc.* that the adjective might have the same sense as English 'acting' (i.e. acting *meddix*) seems implausible. The view that the pairs did not enjoy equal powers (G. Camporeale in *Atti Accad. Tosc.* (1956), p. 51) derives from an over-ready acceptance of the view that there were two *meddices tutici*, one of whom was inferior to the other.

meddix tuticus, he could not use his own discretion. Moreover the *quaestor*—and the same is true of the *meddix decentarius*—was not a single official; contrary to a common belief, he and his fellows presumably formed a college. The *meddices decentarii* at Nola were evidently financial officers.[1] Presumably they had been created when the administration grew larger and more complex, and they relieved the *meddix tuticus* of duties that had once been his. The functions of the *meddix aticus* at Corfinium strongly resemble those of the *meddix decentarius* at Nola, so that he too perhaps is to be equated with the *quaestor*.[2] The title at Nola may mean that the official there was chiefly concerned with funds derived from tithing: he certainly controlled what appears to be the equivalent of the Roman *pecunia multaticia* which was managed at Rome by the quaestor. The title of the *meddix aticus* seems vaguer: perhaps he supervised all types of public revenue.

The names of all other lesser Sabellian officials, where known, seem to be with one possible exception clearly Roman.[3] This, however, is no proof of Rudolph's theory that Rome was responsible for practically all the magistracies in Italy.[4] A Roman title does not prove Roman origin. The Tsars of the Slavs hardly descended from the Caesars of the Romans. The Sabellians adopted Roman names for some of their native institutions simply because Roman nomenclature was better adapted to specialization of function than Oscan.[5] In some instances the institution as well as the name was derived from Rome: the *aídil*, for instance, does not look like the native officer of a *touto*. But this is not inevitably or invariably true of all the other minor officials.

[1] For V. Pisani, *Lingue dell'Italia*, p. 66, they are the receivers of fines (cf. Greek δέκομαι). At Pompeii and Bantia the *quaestor* was in charge of *pecunia multaticia* (Vetter, nos. 12, 2), and the *meddix decentarius* was equivalent to the *quaestor* (Vetter, no. 1). According to Varro *ap.* Aul. Gell. 11. 1. 5, *multa* was a 'Sabine' word in use down to his own day. Cf. *CIL*, 1, 181: *quaistores aire moltaticod dederont.* The earliest mention of the *meddices decentarii* is on the Cippus Abellanus (Vetter, no. 1) of *c.* 165.

[2] A. von Blumenthal in *Indogerm. Forsch.* XLVIII (1930), 246. Some scholars equate the *meddix aticus*, less convincingly, with the aedile: V. Pisani, *Lingue dell'Italia*, p. 112; M. Hofmann in *R.E.* XVIII (1942), s.v. 'Paeligni', col. 2248. In the Iguvine Tables there is a similar adjective (*ahtus*), which however is used to indicate the oracular power of a god (J. W. Poultney, *Bronze Tables of Iguvium*, pp. 174 f.).

[3] The one possible exception is the *kenzstur*, and he too might well be of Roman origin (see below, p. 90).

[4] H. Rudolph, *Stadt und Staat im römischen Italien*, *passim* and especially 66–80.

[5] A legal document such as the Cippus Abellanus (Vetter, no. 1) shows that the Sabellians found it convenient to use Latin technical expressions.

Some of the officials are epigraphically attested only at Lucanian Bantia *c.* 100,[1] which was hardly a typical Sabellian community.[2] Nevertheless some of the 'Roman' titles may have been adopted by Sabellians everywhere and for that reason all that are mentioned anywhere in the Oscan inscriptions are here listed:

aidilis[3] (Oscan *aídil*, where intervocal *f* might have been expected). Found at Aufidena (which was under the strongest Roman influence since 269) and at Pompeii (where he was certainly inferior to the *meddix*).

censor[4] (Oscan *kenzstur*). Found at Pietrabbondante, Histonium, Bantia and Antinum.

legatus[5] (Oscan *lígat*). Found at Nola and Abella.

praefectus[6] (Oscan *praefucus*). Found at Bantia.

praetor[6] (Oscan *praetur*). Found at Bantia (where he obviously is the official known earlier as *meddix tuticus*).

promagistratus[6] (Oscan *prumeddix*). Found at Bantia.

quaestor[7] (Oscan *kvaísstur*, where the labial *p-* might have been expected instead of the labiovelar *kv-*). Found at Abella, Pompeii (which evidently had a pair of them), Bantia, Potentia, and Vicus Supinus.

quattuorvir[8] (Oscan *IIII-nerum*). Found at Pompeii and possibly at Aufidena.

tribunus plebis[9] (Oscan *tr. pl.*). Found at Bantia, Teanum Sidicinum, and the oscanized Latin Colony of Venusia.

triumvir[6] (Oscan *trium nerum*). Found at Bantia.

These obviously Roman titles, in some instances at least, may have been applied to genuinely native offices: the *kvaísstur* and the

[1] The date is uncertain but is probably after that of the Latin inscription on the other side of the plaque; the Latin inscription is not much earlier than 100 (H. S. Jones in *J.R.S.* XVI (1926), 171; E. Y. Yarnold in *Amer. Journ. Phil.* LXXVIII (1957), 163–72). The Tabula Bantina could be as late as the age of Sulla (E. Schönbauer in *Anzeiger österr. Akad. der Wissenschaften*, no. 10 (1955), 131–53; cf. Johnson, Coleman-Norton and Bourne, *Ancient Roman Statutes*, p. 20).

[2] Bantia may have been politically separate from the other Lucani as early as the third century. By the first century, thanks perhaps to the proximity of the Via Appia, it had become much latinized: *inter alia*, its *meddix tuticus* had acquired the title *praetur*.

[3] Vetter, nos. 8, 9, 10, 143. Clearly *aídil* is no Sabellian title; nor is *kvaísstur* (see n. 7, below).

[4] Vetter, nos. 2, 149, 168, 223. In Oscan the best spelling for the title appears to be *kenzstur* (G. Camporeale, *Atti Accad. Toscana* (1956), pp. 86 f.).

[5] Vetter, no. 1; cf. Livy 41. 8. 6–12.

[6] Vetter, no. 2. The view of E. Schönbauer (*op. cit.*, see n. 1, above) that the *praefucus* was a Roman official analogous to the *praefectus Capuam Cumas* is unconvincing: under certain circumstances other Bantian officials could fine the *praefucus*. Perhaps he resembled the *praefectus* at Salpensa and was the *praetor*'s deputy.

[7] Vetter, nos. 1, 2, 11, 12, 16, 17, 18, 19, 180, 181, 228 d.

[8] Vetter, nos. 29, 30, 141.

[9] Vetter, no. 2; *ILS*, 6298; *CIL*, IX, 438; X, 4797. At Bantia no one could be tribune if he had already held some other office.

lígat, for instance, seem to have functions for which Roman influence is not responsible. On the other hand some of the offices, as well as the titles, seem to be direct imitation of Rome: the Oscan *tr. pl.*, for instance, does not look very Sabellian (although curiously enough he may have had some counter-influence on the Roman plebeian tribunate: at Bantia his power of veto was carefully circumscribed, and possibly it was from this that Sulla got his idea of limiting the tribune's power). Most controversial is the *kenzstur*. There are those who argue that this is a native title as well as a native office, so that in this instance the Romans might be the borrowers. The presence of the *-t-* in the title is said to be the decisive factor: it is argued that it would never have been inserted if the noun *censor* had been borrowed, so that it must be a native element. This, however, is not convincing. The suffix *-tur* could have been used through analogy with *kvaísstur* and *praetur*;[1] and it is to be noted that amongst the Frentani the *-t-* does not occur, the pair of censors at Histonium being called *kenzsur*.[2] It seems more likely that the Sabellians got the name from the Romans, and perhaps the office as well, since all ancient sources regard the censorship as a distinctively Roman magistracy.[3] At Bantia the *censtur*'s office has become the terminal point of the hierarchy just as the censorship was at Rome.

One thing, at least, seems certain: by adopting Roman titles for their secondary officials, the Sabellians took much of the load off the term *meddix*, which henceforth could be used without qualifying adjective to mean *meddix tuticus*.[4]

[1] M. G. Delfino in *Serta Eusebiana*, pp. 45, 65, as against J. Heurgon, *Capoue prérom.* p. 236; J. W. Poultney, *Bronze Tables of Iguvium*, p. 8; G. Camporeale in *Atti Accad. Toscana* (1956), pp. 86–91. The suffix of *embratur* (which was certainly formed from Latin *imperator*) supplies yet another analogy.

[2] Vetter, no. 168. Among the Marsi, on the other hand, the official was called *cetur* (Vetter, no. 223).

[3] It has been argued (by A. Rosenberg, *Staat der alten Italiker*, pp. 31 f. and G. Devoto, *Gli Antichi Italici*², p. 263) that the *kenzstur*'s appearance amongst the mountaineer and relatively unromanized Sabellians (Samnites, Frentani, Lucani: Vetter, nos. 149, 168, 2) bespeaks a non-Roman origin for him. Yet Bantia was heavily romanized when it had censors (presumably there was a pair of them, at any rate more than one); and romanized Campania had them too (the cognomen *Censorinus* appears in a document from Capua: Vetter, no. 81). Censors at Suessula, Abellinum, Thurii and elsewhere could be due to Roman colonization. For the censorship as a distinctively Roman magistracy, see J. Suolahti, *Roman Censors*, p. 21. Amongst the Samnites, Frentani and Marsi the *kenzstur* was somehow involved when buildings were being dedicated: perhaps he was one of the regular magistrates who assumed the title *kenzstur* for the performance of certain specific duties, although his status at Bantia renders this improbable.

[4] Vetter, nos. 156, 223.

Like the Romans and Etruscans the Sabellians presumably had an official hierarchy. At Bantia, at about the time of the Social War, there was a definite *cursus honorum*, the prescribed order of offices being quaestor (originally *meddix decentarius*?), praetor (originally *meddix tuticus*) and censor, with biennial intervals between the offices: five years had to elapse before an office could be repeated. Although this *cursus* seems much more rigid than its counterpart in Rome at that time, it may be suspected that Bantia adopted it as a result of Roman influence, if not pressure. Contemporary Beneventum, which closely imitated Roman institutions, had the same *cursus*;[1] and contemporary Halaesa, a *civitas foederata* in Sicily, was 'advised' by Rome in this regard.[2]

We can only speculate about symbols of authority and other trappings of office.[3] The suggestion that an ancient stone throne still visible in the Piazzetta San Rocco at Cerce Maggiore near Saepinum served a Samnite *meddix* in the same way that a *sella curulis* served the Roman consul is unconvincing: the ivory *sella curulis* was totally unlike the stone relic at Cerce.[4] For that matter Cerce probably did not have a *meddix*: in antiquity it could only have been a small fortified *oppidum*.

Presumably the Samnites elected their officials: their close kinsmen, the Lucani, certainly elected their praetor[5] and Sabellian communities which were municipally organized, for example the Campanian towns, or Bantia, had both a council and an assembly[6] which exercised elective functions. The unurbanized, tribally organized *touto* of the Sabellic Marrucini also had an assembly.[7] In Samnium there exists at Trebula Balliensis an area that probably served as a meeting-place for the assembly of the Caudini;[8] and amongst the Hirpini the name of the town Aequum Tuticum obviously means Forum Publicum. That the topography of Samnium

[1] *ILS*, 6492.

[2] Cic. *II Verr.* 2. 49. 122.

[3] Some of the oath-scene coins of the Social War insurgents show a spear stuck upright in the ground: could this be magisterial insignia? Cf. Festus, p. 55 L.: *hasta summa armorum et imperii est*. There is no evidence that the Samnites used the *lituus* (*quod clarissimum est insigne auguratus*: Cic. *de div.* 1. 17. 30; cf. L. Banti, *Il Mondo degli Etruschi*, pls. 37 and 52).

[4] For the Cerce throne see *Samnium*, xxx (1957), 33.

[5] Livy, 25. 16. 6.

[6] At Bantia forty apparently formed a quorum.

[7] Vetter, no. 218.

[8] A. Maiuri in *Not. d. Sc.* (1930), p. 218.

was no obstacle to gatherings is seen during the Social War when the Italici held meetings of a council and also apparently of an assembly,[1] at Corfinium and elsewhere. It can then be surmised that each Samnite tribe had both a council and an assembly, which met periodically at some centre, presumably at the summons and under the presidency of the *meddix tuticus*. Livy took it for granted that there were such gatherings.[2] It is not easy, however, to discover the Oscan names for the two bodies, such words as *senatus* and *comono* being Latin neologisms.[3]

Sabellian Pompeii had an institution called *kombennio-*.[4] Although mentioned in a formula which at Abella, Nola and Bantia is applied to the *senatus* and although discharging functions like those of a *senatus* elsewhere,[5] this was evidently not a council but an assembly of the citizens. In a 'democratic' community the role it played could very well have been discharged by a primary assembly; and the etymological correspondence between Pompeian *kombennio-*, Bantian *comono*, Iguvine *kumno-* and Roman *conventus* and *contio* indicates that in fact we are here dealing with a meeting of the people,[6] summoned by the properly empowered *meddix*.

Besides the *kombennio-*, however, we also hear of a *komparakio-* at Pompeii. Like the *kombennio-* it was a group of some kind. It is sometimes claimed that the *komparakio-* was the more restrictive body of the two and therefore was probably the council.[7] The grounds for this opinion are not very evident. In the only inscription in which the *komparakio-* is unmistakably, even if fragmentarily, recorded and, for that matter, also in the inscription where the word is wholly restored, the language and formula used are identical

[1] H. D. Meyer in *Historia*, VII (1958), 78 f.

[2] Livy 8. 39. 10; 10. 12. 2; 23. 2, 14, 15, 16, 39, 43; 24. 13. 8; cf. Dio 15, fr. 57, 30 and 34; Zon. 9. 2. 11.

[3] Vetter, nos. 1, 2. *Comono* resembles Latin *comitia* also in being a neuter plural. The word *senatus* has also been plausibly restored in an Oscan inscription recently found in Lucania (G. O. Onorato in *Rend. Accad. Napol.*, N.S., XXVIII (1953), 339).

[4] Vetter, nos. 11, 12, 18. The full form of the nominative is not recorded.

[5] For example, it supervised expenditures by the quaestor.

[6] Livy's word for such an assembly of Samnites is *coetus* (9. 10. 8). An assembly of a mere *pagus* can hardly be meant.

[7] Vetter, nos. 17, 19. The inscriptions are fragmentary, but the restoration seems certain, in no. 17 at least, in view of *comparascuster* in the Tabula Bantina (Vetter, no. 2). The full spelling might be *komparakiof*: cf. the *tribarakiuf* of the Cippus Abellanus (Vetter, no. 1). The *kombennio-* is usually regarded as the primary assembly (A. Sogliano, *Pompeii Preromana*, pp. 156 f.; M. W. Frederiksen in *Pap. Brit. Sch. Rome*, XIV (1959), 93. Cf. G. Devoto in *Enciclopedia Italiana*, s.v. 'Oschi', p. 653).

with those which in other inscriptions are applied to the *kombennio-*. *Komparakio-* and *kombennio-* therefore must be two different names for the same thing. In other words Pompeii, unlike Rome, did not have two different assemblies.[1] At Rome it was the various ways of organizing the people in groups for voting purposes that was responsible for a plurality of assemblies, whereas Sabellian communities do not seem to have been organized in this way. There is no trace of voting by groups at Bantia, and, if that heavily romanized community did not have the practice, it is unlikely that other Sabellian states had it either. Assuming that a Sabellian state had only one assembly and that it was to it that the word *komparakio-* as well as the word *kombennio-* referred, we must conclude that the Oscan word for 'council' has not survived.[2] We can either imitate Livy and the Sabellians themselves and call it by the Latin name *senatus* or we can use the English name for the institution.[3]

There is no epigraphic evidence to show how a Samnite council was recruited. Livy's references to the senate at Capua imply that when the Second Punic War broke out the members of that body had been appointed by a magistrate. But this evidently was not normal, to judge by the seething hostility of the Capuan plebs and from the way that Pacuvius Calavius, the people's leader and *meddix tuticus* of Capua, solved the crisis between senate and plebs by proposing that the hated senators be replaced by new ones, chosen by popular election.[4] The action of the Capuan plebs on this occasion cannot be taken as conclusive evidence for an Oscan tradition of an elective council; but it does reinforce the strong probability that the Samnite tribal councils were formed by democratic election.

The functions of the council must have been advisory and probouleutic; but, in addition, it may have wielded very considerable powers, like the Roman senate, greater powers perhaps than

[1] Iguvium and possibly Bantia had two: G. Camporeale in *Atti Acad. Tosc.* (1956), p. 75.

[2] One would have expected a word derived from *casnar* (= 'old' in Oscan: Varro, *L.L.* 7. 29; Quint. 1. 5. 8; Festus, p. 41 L.; Vetter, no. 214). Perhaps it was something resembling Marsic *casontonia* (Vetter, no. 228 a).

[3] Livy sometimes uses expressions akin to the English: *concilium Samnitium* (7. 31. 11), *publicum consilium* (8. 39. 10; 23. 2. 4). Elsewhere he uses the term *senatus* (23. 3. 5; 23. 35. 2; 26. 16. 6).

[4] Livy 23. 2–4; see F. Buecheler in *Rhein. Mus.* XXXII (1877), 490. The reference here may be to the diet of the Capuan League and not merely to the senate of Capua itself (assuming that there were two separate bodies).

in theory it was supposed to possess.[1] A Sabellian senate undoubtedly had the right to appoint legati: it did so at Nola and at Abella after deciding where a temple should be built; and presumably it did so in Samnium after deciding to protest to Rome about the way Samnites were being permitted and perhaps even encouraged to leave Samnium.

Something is also known about the function of a Sabellian assembly. Besides the right to elect officials and possibly council members, it must also have had legislative powers, like those of the *touto* of the Marrucini in the third century,[2] and judicial powers, like those of the assembly at Bantia in the second and first.[3]

The Sabellians also had a political and/or military organization called the *vere(h)ia*.[4] It existed amongst the Sabellians of Campania and the Frentani, and so probably amongst the Samnites as well. It may have been a youth organization, the youths being the 'gate-wardens' (Oscan *vero* = Latin *porta*).[5] This organization played an important part in the military life of the state and, like the *iuventus* at Rome,[6] was almost certainly an aristocratic institution. At Sabellian Pompeii the so-called Small Palaestra, an elegant gymnasium in which *ephebi* could train and take exercise, was clearly intended for the *jeunesse dorée*; and amongst the probably related Aurunci there was a youth organization drawn from the classes and not from the masses.

The constitution of a Sabellian state could be described as 'mixed', the *meddix tuticus* supplying the monarchical element, the council the aristocratic, and the *kombennio-* (or *komparakio-*) the democratic. Not that Polybius discusses the Sabellians in his remarks on the mixed constitution; but then in Italy he had eyes only for

[1] Livy 8. 39. 10–14 obviously thought that it could sit in a judicial capacity, exercise complete control over a Samnite's person and property and subordinate the *meddix* to itself. (But this passage in Livy is very untrustworthy: it is the one that describes a fictitious episode that was invented to justify Rome's alleged double-dealing over the Caudine Forks disaster.) Livy 41. 8. 6 describes a *legatio* which had probably been sent out by a Samnite senate.

[2] Vetter, no. 218.

[3] Vetter, no. 2.

[4] Its functions were political and military rather than athletic and sporting (G. O. Onorato in *Rend. Acc. Lincei*, ser. 8, VI (1951), 260 f.).

[5] Vetter, nos. 11, 87, 108. V. Pisani, *Lingue dell'Italia*, p. 58, is very sceptical of it.

[6] M. Della Corte, *Juventus*, *passim*. For the youth organization amongst the Aurunci, see Livy 9. 25.

the Romans. It is perhaps not being unduly fanciful to suggest that their constitutional arrangements may have helped to foster the tale that the Sabellians were of Lacedaemonian descent, since the Spartans were the people with a mixed constitution *par excellence.*

Down to the third century, the four tribes of Samnium were joined together in an association called *civitas Samnitium* by Livy.[1] The term Samnite League seems justified, on the analogy of the Latin League about whose organization in the fourth century Cincius, an antiquarian of Augustus' day, supplies a little information.[2]

It is usually assumed that the ties binding the Samnite League were quite loose, the chief basis for this opinion being the Sabellian lack of cohesiveness in general.[3] The Frentani, for instance, more usually threw in their lot with their Sabellic than with their Sabellian neighbours, the Samnites. The Lucani only made common cause with the Samnites occasionally and were often at daggers drawn with them. The Bruttii broke away from the Lucani and the Larinates away from the Frentani. And there was fierce hostility between the Sabellians of Samnium and those of Campania. Moreover what we know of other leagues in early Italy, such as the Etruscan and the Latin, suggests that individual league-members could go to war with one another. The Samnite tribes may often have quarrelled among themselves,[4] and it would be strange indeed if agricultural communities did not come to blows with pastoral. Such internal disagreements between the Samnite confederates encouraged the Romans to attempt to split the Hirpini from the Pentri and the Caudini from both and even from one another.

Samnite disunity can, however, easily be exaggerated. If Samnites, Lucani and Bruttii failed to form a political union, it may have been due in large part to differing racial strains. The common language (whose dialectal variations were really quite minor) should not be taken as proof of ethnic identity. The non-Sabellian element in the ethnic make-up of Lucani and Bruttii was larger than in

[1] Livy 8. 23. 6.

[2] Festus, p. 276 L. This Cincius must not be confused with the historian Cincius Alimentus (A. Alföldi, *Early Rome and the Latins*, p. 119).

[3] Note how in 180 Cumae dissociated itself from the Oscan-speaking districts of Campania by requesting permission to make Latin its official language (Livy 40. 42. 13).

[4] There are hints that a tribe could go to war by itself: Livy 10. 14. 9; 10. 38. 2; Diod. 19. 72. 5.

that of any tribe in Samnium. This disunifying factor would reinforce the instinct for particularism that prevailed in early Italy[1] and that is exemplified by the Frentani and Campanians, who are not markedly different from the inhabitants of Samnium in their racial stock, yet rarely act in unison with them. The lowland Campanians, if not the Frentani, had diverged from their backward highland origin to a more advanced form of culture and this made them reject their rustic kinsmen. Undue importance should not be attached to the later separation of Hirpini from Pentri and of Caudini from both. Judicious annexations of territory enabled Rome to split the Samnite tribes apart and then to exploit their physical separation from one another. All history demonstrates the ability of great powers to sow dissension among the peoples within their sphere of influence.

Nevertheless the Samnites were imbued with national consciousness,[2] and Roman attempts to balkanize them were never fully successful. When convinced that they were threatened from without or that some enterprise undertaken in common would benefit them all, the Samnites sank their internal differences and presented a united front to the outside world. It is significant that, as late as the first century when the Social War broke out to test the sentiments of the peoples of Italy, the Hirpini ranged themselves unhesitatingly by the side of the Pentri against Rome, despite the very intensive romanization to which they had been exposed during the preceding century and a half.

In the fourth and early third centuries, when the Samnites were truly independent, the Samnite League did have unmistakably a strong sense of union. It was not held together merely by one tribe dominating all the others. The tribes are represented as united in their determination to oppose Rome to the desperate end, one indication of this being the almost total failure of the ancient authors to distinguish one tribe from another, or even to name them individually, in the accounts of the Samnite Wars. Furthermore there is no record of Rome being able to play off one tribe against another. She was able to win (Sabellian) Campani, Frentani, Apuli and even Lucani to her side; but there is no known instance of a member of the Samnite League making common cause with her against the

[1] See the excellent remarks of A. Bernardi in *Athenaeum*, XX (1942), 102.

[2] For their pride in their nation see Granius Licinianus, p. 20 F.

other Samnites.[1] The particularism that existed in Samnium as elsewhere in Italy did not alter the fact that the Samnite League represented a beginning towards political unity.

The association of Samnite tribes at the very least took the form of a permanent military alliance, what the Greeks called a *symmachy*, although unlike some Greek *symmachies* it does not seem to have had a *hegemon* to dragoon the other members. Essentially it was an everlasting league for the purpose of making war on outsiders and promoting other common objects, the first of which was the winning of divine favour: Livy is obviously right in suggesting that sacral as well as military ties kept the Samnites together.[2]

The Samnite League was no full-fledged *Bundesstaat*, or federal union: it was a *Staatenbund*, or confederation.[3] Its four constituent members were virtually independent states, whose range of agreed common activities was probably narrow. Perhaps there was some kind of *sympolity*, and, although we do not hear of a popular assembly for the whole League, it is significant that the federal-type alliance of Italic states in the Social War does seem to have had an assembly. The Samnite League undoubtedly had a council or Diet, to which ancient authors often allude and the purpose of which was to direct common policy. Livy suggests that the *meddices* were expected to consult it,[4] and both he and Dionysius of Halicarnassus mention the representatives (*magistratus*, *probouloi*) sent to it by the Samnite communities.[5] But the number from each tribe, the method of their selection, and their tenure of the office are alike unknown. It would be indeed surprising if they were not the *principes Samnitium*.[6] Presumably the Diet of the Samnite League, as of the Latin, met once a year, and more often if need be, possibly in a *circus*, to use Livy's word.[7] It may, however, have met in various places, coming

[1] In the Second Punic War Rome did induce the Pentri to stand by her against the other Samnites, who joined Hannibal. But by then there was no longer a Samnite League.

[2] Livy 10. 38; Dion. Hal. 17/18. 2. 3.

[3] Macedonia was organized along similar lines during the last twenty years of its 'independence'. Perhaps the Romans modelled post-Pydna Macedonia with its four separate republics on the Samnite League.

[4] Livy 7. 13. 11; 8. 39. 10 f.; 10. 12. 2. In 9. 3. 9 he very similarly represents Gavius Pontius in 321 as having a council to consult.

[5] Livy 7. 13. 11; 8. 23. 2; Dion. Hal. 15. 7. 4; 15. 8. 1; 17. 1. 4; cf. App. *B.C.* 1. 51. 224.

[6] Cf. A. Alföldi, *Early Rome and the Latins*, p. 37.

[7] The council of the Hernici met in the *Circus Maritimus* (Livy 9. 42. 12), a large, elliptical, man-made hollow some 2½ miles south of Anagnia (M. Cagiano de Azevedo in *Studi in Onore di Calderini e Paribeni*, III, 334). The meeting of the Latini was an *agora* according to Dion. Hal. 5. 61. 1.

together wherever it was most convenient for the immediate purpose.

The exact functions of the Diet are a matter for speculation. As a diplomatic body with real powers in time of war, it must have helped to frame the foreign policy of the League as a whole and decided strategy. Certainly in view of what Livy tells us and of what took place later at Corfinium in the Social War, it seems likely that, once hostilities broke out, the Diet directed the war effort. It is improbable that its four constituent tribes had legal, penal and law-enforcement systems in common or that its Diet had the duty of supervising industry, commerce and the promotion of trade. It is more than likely that the League really came to life only at times of immediate common danger. But in the Italy of the fourth and early third centuries such occasions were very frequent,[1] and when they occurred the Samnite tribes were prepared mutually to make concessions for their common good.

When war threatened, the League appointed a commander-in-chief.[2] In this it was behaving like other Sabellian leagues.[3] The Lucani, for instance, adopted unity of military command whenever it was urgently needed and appointed a former *meddix* as commander-in-chief: they had been doing this, says Strabo, from very early times.[4] There is thus some justification for regarding the Samnite League as in essence the formalization of an ancient Sabellian practice. The title borne by this commander is uncertain. Beloch argued that it was *meddix tuticus*,[5] but this view seems to run counter to the documentary, literary and etymological evidence. The Oscan

[1] Note the words of Dion. Hal. 17/18. 2. 3.

[2] Livy 9. 1. 2.

[3] The Sabellic League also had the practice: at any rate Paeligni and Marrucini served under a common commander at Pydna (Plut. *Aem. Paul.* 20).

[4] Strabo 6. 1. 3, p. 254; cf. Livy 25. 16. 6.

[5] K. J. Beloch, *Campanien*[2], pp. 11, 315; *Röm. Gesch.* p. 387. Beloch argued that the name of the *meddix tuticus* at Capua in 214, Cn. Magius Atellanus, proves him to have been from Atella and not from Capua itself: in other words, he must be a federal official of the League. The argument is not cogent. Even if the cognomen is used, as Beloch suggests, to show that Magius was from Atella and not merely to distinguish him from the famous Magius family of Capua which subsequently moved to Aeclanum (Velleius 2. 16. 2), it does not prove Beloch's point: if an immigrant from Tusculum could be consul at Rome in the fourth century (Pliny, *N.H.* 7. 136), why could not an immigrant from Atella be *meddix* at Capua in the third? For that matter Atellanus may not mean that Magius came from Atella (L. R. Taylor, *Voting Districts of the Roman Republic*, p. 180; E. Badian in *Historia*, VI (1957), 334 f.). Beloch's view is usually rejected (G. Devoto in *Encic. Italiana*, s.v. 'Sanniti', pp. 741 f.; L. Pareti, *Storia di Roma*, I, 611).

inscriptions do not leave the impression that the *meddix tuticus* is a federal official and that an undefined *meddix* is the official of an individual state. The literary authors may not have known what the generalissimo's title was, but they evidently knew what it was not. It was not *meddix* or *meddix tuticus*. If it had been, they would have said so. Livy sometimes calls him *dux*, sometimes *imperator*; Strabo calls him *basileus*; Festus uses the word *princeps*.[1] Etymology may not be fully conclusive; but clearly a *meddix tuticus* is the *meddix* of a single *touto*, not the *meddix* of a league of several.

It emerges from Strabo that the commander-in-chief was appointed for one campaign. Livy's language is more ambiguous and could mean that he was appointed for one year. He did not share the office with a colleague but was in sole command, and for this reason he seems to some scholars to resemble the dictator of the Latins.[2] Also he was eligible for reappointment: at any rate, Papius Mutilus was appointed more than once in the Social War.

Although the Samnite League lacked well-organized centralization, the importance it assumed in time of war proves that it was not simply a lifeless aggregate of parts. Within it it contained the seeds of federalism. The Sabellians seem to have had a bent for this, a kind of instinctive impulse towards combination.[3] This is not surprising. Greek example suggests that federal unions were more likely to emerge among peoples who were politically backward and who had not established flourishing, self-governing, municipal commonwealths. The Sabellians in general, and particularly the Samnites, were not living in a state of advanced political development: their political organisms were seldom urban. But even amongst the most advanced of the Sabellians there is an example of what appears to be a full-fledged federal union. Capua, Atella, Calatia and 'Velecha'[4] are shown by the identity of their coins to have enjoyed full 'sympolity' during a few years of the Second Punic War when they were in revolt from Rome. Perhaps no other Sabellian grouping was so tightly knit as this one; but we hear of a League headed by Nuceria Alfaterna in Southern Campania, and

[1] Livy 9. 1. 2; 9. 22. 11; 10. 19. 14; 10. 29. 16; Strabo 6. 1. 3, p. 254; Festus, p. 150 L.; A. Rosenberg, *Staat der alten Italiker*, p. 17. The Samnite commander-in-chief in the Social War is proved by coin legends to have been called *imperator* (Osc. *embratur*).

[2] T. Mommsen, *Röm. Staatsrecht*, II, 1, 169; J. Heurgon, *Capoue préromaine*, p. 236.

[3] F. P. Garofalo in *Rend. Accad. Lincei*, ser. 5, XII (1903), 67.

[4] Velecha may be the town of the Sabatini (for whom see Livy 26. 33. 12; 26. 34. 6).

we know that the relations of Nola and Abella in Central Campania were sometimes extraordinarily close.[1] Mention should also be made of the insurgents in the Social War, all of whom were either Sabellian or Sabellic (i.e. near-Sabellian). They banded themselves into a confederacy. Scepticism about its completely federal nature may well be justified, yet it was obviously something more than a mere military alliance. The name Italia, which its coins show it to have adopted, its common capital and senate at Corfinium, and the assembly which it periodically summoned and which presupposes a common citizenship for all its members, indicate an attempt to organize Italy along federal lines.

Evidently the political outlook of the speakers of Oscan differed from that of the speakers of Latin.[2] An institution like the Latin League, it is true, prevents us from denying to the speakers of Latin all conception of a wider union. Usually, however, they seem to have favoured the small sovereign unit, and it is worth emphasizing that when the Romans organized Italy it was not on a federal pattern: the Roman practice was to make a separate, bilateral alliance with each state individually.[3] The political instincts of the speakers of Oscan, on the other hand, were federative: Sabellians, Samnites, Sabellic tribes were all prone to form leagues.

Thus, there seems to have been a fundamental difference of viewpoint between Romans and Samnites, although we have no means of knowing to what extent the Sabellians rationalized the matter. If the Romans failed to produce any political philosopher apart from the notable, but solitary, exception of Cicero, it is unlikely that the Sabellians ever had anyone to speculate in writing on the nature of the state. But Cicero himself includes the Samnites among the nations capable of political thought.[4]

Possibly Sabellian statecraft would never have been capable of devising a system for linking a number of separate communities into a union that was cohesive, tightly close and truly indivisible. Or possibly the Sabellian temperament would never have been able to submit to the discipline required of political innovators. In the

[1] Perhaps this is the reason why Justin regards them both as 'Chalcidian' colonies (20. 1. 13).

[2] This has recently been splendidly emphasized by A. J. Toynbee, *Hannibal's Legacy*, 1, 84–280, who sees the Samnite Wars largely in terms of a struggle between the municipal idea represented by Rome and the tribal concept represented by Samnium.

[3] The federative principle was absent from the Roman organization of Italy (P. Fraccaro, *Opuscula*, 1, 104).

[4] Cic. *de re pub.* 3. 4. 7.

event the Sabellians did not get the chance to impose their ideas. It was the people with strong central organization, not the people with a federal outlook, that won the great struggle for the hegemony of Italy. Nevertheless one cannot help but wonder what the subsequent political history of Italy might have been, had the Sabellian principle of a league of equal states prevailed over the Roman practice of *divide et impera*.

(*d*) THE ARMY

The army of the Samnites, like those of the early Celts or Germans, must have consisted originally of bands of men, each led by its own leader who demanded and received allegiance from the individual warriors in his band.[1] The battle waged by the Fabian clan at the River Cremera in 477 shows that the military system of early Rome was also of this type. It was probably the Samnite Wars that forced Romans and Samnites alike to realize that this method of conducting their military affairs was inadequate. Certainly by the time of the Third Samnite War, if not earlier, the Samnites had fully developed and carefully organized tribal armies. These seem to have differed but little from the Roman army. Livy obviously thought that a Samnite army in column of route looked like a Roman one.[2] Nor does he hesitate to talk about Samnite 'legions',[3] and he receives some confirmation from the fact that once the Romans had Sabellians within their 'confederacy' they were able to organize a *legio Campana*, complete with attached Oscan-speaking Sidicine auxiliaries, without much difficulty.[4] A Samnite army had cohorts, of 400 men according to Livy, and it fought in maniples. Its officers included military tribunes.[5]

Samnite cavalry is not described in detail by ancient writers, but it enjoyed a high reputation,[6] somewhat surprisingly since Samnium is not cavalry country.

[1] K. Latte in *Gött. gelehrte Nachrichten*, I (1934), 68. [2] Livy 10. 35. 18.

[3] Livy 8. 30. 11. He may merely be using Roman terminology for the sake of clarity, but it is highly probable that the Samnites had formations that resembled Roman legions and that may even have been called such. The Sabellic Marsi had 'legions' (Vetter, no. 228a, possibly a fourth-century document), and so did the Sabellian Campani (Vetter, no. 6, admittedly a latinized document). Livy 8. 24. 2 attributes legions to the Lucani and Bruttii no less than to the Samnites.

[4] Livy, *Epitt.* 12, 15; Dion. Hal. 20. 4.

[5] Livy 9. 43. 17; 10. 40. 6; Diod. 23. 2; Livy 10. 20. 15.

[6] Livy 8. 38. 5; 8. 39. 3; 9. 27. 5; 10. 20. 13; 10. 41. 11; Dion. Hal. 20. 1. 3; Plut. *Pyrr.* 13. Livy 9. 22. 4 implies that it was influenced by Tarentine cavalry (for which see Diod. 19. 29, 39; P. Wuilleumier, *Tarente*, p. 666): G. P. Carratelli in *Parola del Passato*, VII (1952), 257.

Samnite tactics are mentioned only incidentally. Their military successes in a mountainous terrain confirm what Cicero implies: that they used a flexible and open order of fighting, instead of relying upon a close-packed phalanx.[1] Livy's picture of a kind of Samnite equivalent to the Theban Sacred Band, clad in white linen and stationed on the right wing, might indeed suggest a phalanx;[2] but it occurs in the description of a fictitious incident and may itself be a quite imaginary detail inspired by the Samnite performance at the Colline Gate in 82. According to Frontinus and Livy the shock of the Samnites' initial charge was very difficult to withstand.[3] These doughty highlanders must have penetrated all the way to the *triarii* and brought the Romans close to disaster more than once.[4]

We are better informed about their military equipment than about their military organization and methods, since both ancient literature and archaeology have something to say on the subject. The literature must be read with caution. According to Livy[5] the Samnites in 309 fielded two 'armies' which were resplendent in gold and silver respectively. Their shields were broad at the top to protect chest and shoulders and tapered towards the bottom to make them more manageable. Besides this, the troops wore what Livy calls a 'sponge' to protect the breast, a single greave to cover the left leg (the right leg remaining bare), and helmets with crests to make them appear taller. The gold-shielded outfit had multi-coloured tunics, while the silver-shielded wore tunics of white linen; and some texts of Livy add that the gold-shielded group had gilded scabbards, golden baldrics and gold-caparisoned horses, and the silver-shielded one silver scabbards and baldrics.

This entire account can be dismissed at once as fanciful. It does not correspond with the material evidence found by the archaeologists.[6] Livy himself admits that he is describing novel, and not normal, Samnite gear, something for a special occasion.[7] And the special occasion, as it happens, is fictitious: the operations assigned by Livy

[1] Cic. *de orat.* 2. 80. 325.

[2] Livy 9. 40. 9: he says that they usually concentrated their main strength on the right wing. Yet at Ausculum and Sentinum they were on the left (Dion. Hal. 20. 1; Livy 10. 27. 10). At the Colline Gate it *was* their right wing that performed bes t(see below, p. 386).

[3] Front. *Strat.* 2. 1. 8; Livy 10. 28. 3.

[4] See Livy 8. 8. 11: *rem ad triarios rediisse.*

[5] Livy 9. 40. 1–4; cf. Florus 1. 11. 7.

[6] P. Couissin in *Rev. Arch.* ser. 5, XXXII (1930), 260.

[7] Livy 9. 40. 1: *ut acies sua fulgeret* novis *armorum insignibus.*

to 309 really belong to 293, under which year indeed he repeats some of the above details (two forces, one of them a Linen Legion; opulent arms; crested helmets).[1] But the details, whether given under 309 or under 293, are untrustworthy. Combat troops do not carry gold- or silver-plated shields into battle,[2] and even if they did Samnium could never have afforded to outfit two whole armies with such shields together with matching scabbards, baldrics and saddle-cloths.[3] On the other hand, elaborate ceremonial dress is to be found in all armies. The Romans certainly had such apparel, and Livy might well have had in mind the gilded standards and silver-plated shields carried by Roman soldiers at great state funerals, Sulla's for instance.[4] He clothed his Samnites in silver and gold since the more valuable the metal, the greater the glory and prestige accruing to their Roman conquerors.

Livy's abnormal shape for the Samnites' shields is no more convincing than the abnormal materials of which they were made. It is clear enough what the shields are. They are sawn-off Italic *scuta* of the traditional elliptical type. Shields truncated in this manner were used by the 'Samnites' of the gladiatorial arena, who could afford to have the tops of their shields cut away, since their faces were well protected by the visors on their helmets, so that they did not need the upper part of the shield.[5] But Samnite warriors, unlike 'Samnite' gladiators, did not have visored headpieces and would not have left their faces exposed by carrying shields that had been trimmed down to a straight horizontal line at the top, not even as a unique experiment.[6] Livy is describing the shields, not of Samnite soldiers but of the gladiators known as 'Samnites'.

[1] Livy 10. 38. 2–13.

[2] It is of course possible that the shields were painted to look like gold or silver.

[3] Livy 9. 40. 5 himself admits that such equipment really represented booty for the victor rather than armour for the wearer, a remark clearly inspired by the tradition that the Romans obtained metal for votive statues and other religious paraphernalia from captured Samnite equipment (Livy 10. 29. 14; Pliny, *N.H.* 34. 43). Extravagantly clad forces are a rhetorical commonplace of the Hellenistic world (Polyb. 5. 79; 31. 3; Livy 37. 40; Diod. 17. 57; 19. 28; Justin 12. 7. 5; Curtius 4. 13. 17; 8. 5. 4; Plut. *Sulla,* 16) and no doubt individuals of exceptional wealth or significance did go into battle arrayed like Solomon in all his glory: King Bituit of the Arverni late in the second century is an instance (Florus 1. 37. 5. Cf., too, the *cinctus Gabinus* of the Roman general intent on 'devoting' himself: Livy 5. 46. 2; Serv. *ad Aen.* 7. 612).

[4] C. Vermeule in *J.R.S.* L (1960), 8–11; App. *B.C.* 1. 106. 498.

[5] Q.F. Maule–H. R. W. Smith, *Votive Religion at Caere*, p. 59.

[6] G. Devoto, *Gli Antichi Italici*², p. 204, suggests that these special shields were used only once, as an experiment at Aquilonia in 293.

The single greave is equally unauthentic. It is true that Vergil and Silius Italicus give Livy support of a kind by saying respectively that the Hernici went into battle with only one foot shod and the Sabini with only one greave.[1] Moreover representations of Italic soldiers wearing only one greave have come to light, the purpose of it being presumably to prevent the shin from being chafed by the rim of the shield. There is one from Amiternum at Sulmona and another of *c.* 100 at Aquila showing two men in combat. But these are pretty obviously gladiators, and gladiators are not infrequently depicted with a single greave. One is shown on an inscription from Beneventum, another in a recently published Sabellian tomb-painting; a marble fragment in Berlin shows more than one, and a stele from Ephesus, also in Berlin, has one incised on it.[2] It is highly unlikely that Samnite soldiers in the field were outfitted in exactly the same way as gladiators in the arena.

The 'sponge', like the special shield, also seems to belong more to the arena than to the battlefield. The guess[3] that it was originally a pad worn by the Italic warrior beneath a metal disk that protected his chest and subsequently came by metonymy to mean the metal disk itself will not recommend itself to anyone who recalls that the scale corslet worn by gladiators in the arena was also called a 'sponge'.[4] Representations of such gladiators have survived from antiquity.[5] Few, however, will believe that the ordinary Samnite soldier wore such armour. If any possessed it, it could have been only the well-to-do, just as in the Roman army of the second century.[6]

Crested helms have been archaeologically verified as Italic military headgear. But it was a sign of special distinction to wear them.[7] That probably is why Livy describes the élite force as having them.

Livy's linen tunics are much more normal. Pliny and Festus

[1] Verg. *Aen.* 7. 689 (cf. Thucyd. 3. 22. 2; Macrob. 5. 18. 5); Sil. Ital. 8. 419.

[2] *CIL*, IX, 1671; *Amer. Journ. Arch.* LXII (1958), pl. 114; L. Pareti, *Storia di Roma*, III, 687 f.

[3] F. Weege in *Jahrb. des deut. arch. Inst.* XXIV (1909), 148, who adduces Aristotle, *Hist. Anim.* 5. 16; cf. Thucyd. 4. 34; Pliny, *N.H.* 8. 192. D. Ludovico, *Dove Italia Nacque*, p. 3, suggests that Latin *spongia* might be an attempt to reproduce an Oscan word: according to him, *spogna* means 'fennel' (whose folded stalks might suggest mail armour) in one of the Abruzzi dialects of modern Italian.

[4] Tert. *de spect.* 25.

[5] See *Cambr. Anc. Hist.*, vol. of plates 4, 91 (*a*)—a relief in Munich.

[6] Polyb. 6. 23. 15.

[7] Livy 10. 38. 12.

join him in recording the tradition that on at least one occasion the Samnites fielded a *legio linteata*.[1] Under the year 309 Livy implies that the name arose from the fact that the soldiers were clad in linen, a not uncommon ancient practice.[2] Under the year 293, however, he derives it from the fact that the recruits for the force had been enrolled in a huge compound covered over with linen, his description of which may owe something to Polybius' account of a Roman camp.[3] Neither of Livy's suggestions is really adequate. Nevertheless linen tunics, either plain or particoloured,[4] are authentic Samnite equipment. They actually appear as soldiers' apparel in Sabellian tomb- and vase-paintings.

It will be seen that much of Livy's account of Samnite military equipment is untrustworthy. Livy's motive is aetiological: his aim is to explain the origin of certain pieces of gladiatorial gear.[5] To this end he has drawn on his own imagination, on rhetorical commonplaces, and on Polybius' description of the outfit of second-century Roman *hastati*. Admittedly Polybius' *scutum*, which is normal Roman, may not have contributed much to Livy's description of the truncated Samnite variety, but the single greave, coat of mail and crested helmet all seem to be taken with little change from Polybius.[6]

For Samnite combat weapons we must turn elsewhere than to Livy. There was a tradition that the Samnites used both the hurling spear (*pilum*) and the long ribbed shield (*scutum*) and that it was in fact from them that the Romans obtained these weapons.[7] The most explicit version of this tale occurs in the so-called Ineditum Vaticanum, a fragment in Greek whose unknown (second-century?) author

[1] Pliny, *N.H.* 34. 43; Festus, p. 102 L.

[2] Homer (*Il.* 2. 830) describes Amphios as λινοθώρηξ; the Argives are linen-corsleted goads of war (*Anth. Pal.* 14. 73. 4); Faliscan troops were clad in linen (Sil. Ital. 4. 223); Tolumnius of Veii wore a linen tunic when Cornelius Cossus won the *spolia opima* from him (Livy 4. 20. 7); Hannibal's troops at Cannae were clothed in linen (Livy 22. 46. 6).

[3] Livy 10. 38; cf. Polyb. 6. 31. 10. It is possible that Livy realized that troops clad in linen were too normal to be singled out as a Linen Legion and consequently felt that a different explanation was needed.

[4] The *tunicae versicolores* of Livy 9. 40. 3; cf., too, Livy 22. 46. 6.

[5] He himself admits this (9. 40. 17). It is curious, however, that he mentions only crested helms and not helms with feathers, since the 'Samnite' gladiators undoubtedly wore the latter (Varro, *L.L.* 5. 142).

[6] Polybius 6. 23.

[7] Hence *pilum* is sometimes called a Sabellian weapon (Verg. *Aen.* 7. 665). Similarly Sil. Ital. 4. 221 talks of the *iaculator Sabellus*.

resembles Diodorus as to both style and source.[1] But Ineditum Vaticanum is not alone in believing that it was thanks to the Samnites that the Romans substituted the hurling spear (*pilum*) for the thrusting (*hasta*) and the long shield (*scutum*) for the round (*clipeus*). Sallust even suggests that by his day this opinion was generally held.[2] If it was, Livy did not share it. He not only omits to mention this Roman borrowing from the Samnites, but by implication denies it. He dates the Roman adoption of the *scutum* either to the reign of Servius Tullius, which seems rather fanciful, or, contradicting himself, to *c.* 400, soon after pay for military service was introduced at Rome, which might not be at all fanciful.[3] In either case Livy was of the opinion that the Romans adopted this equipment long before they ever clashed with Samnites.

Several ancient authors support him in suggesting that the Romans were already using the *scutum* before the Samnite Wars, although it is doubtful how far their evidence ought to be pressed: they may have been merely indifferent to antiquarian accuracy.[4]

The way that the story of the Romans' borrowing military notions from the enemy appears in Ineditum Vaticanum should make us wary. According to this source, a Roman envoy demonstrated Roman morale and confidence to the Carthaginians on the eve of the First Punic War by pointing out that it was the regular practice of his countrymen to copy the special skills of others and then surpass their teachers at their own game. Thus, they adopted *clipeus* and *hasta* from the Etruscans and soon worsted them in their

[1] First published by H. von Arnim in *Hermes*, XXVII (1892), 118–30. The analogous passage in Diodorus is 23. 2; cf., also, Dio, fr. 43. 8 (= Zon. 8. 9. 1).

[2] Sallust, *Cat.* 51 (where *arma* = *scuta* and *tela* = *pila*: A. Reinach in *Rev. Arch.* X (1907), 125 f., 226 f., 243 f.). Other ancient authors support Sallust: Clement, *Stromat.* 1. 16. 75; Eusebius, *Praeparatio*, 10. 6; Symmachus, *Ep.* 3. 11. See, too, Athen. 6, pp. 273 f.: he attributes only the *scutum* to the Samnites, reckoning the *pilum* as of Spanish origin. See E. Meyer in *Abhand. Berl. Akad.* (1923), no. 3, pp. 19–31. The story could easily have grown out of the fact that in the time of Marius a new type of training was introduced for Roman soldiers, modelled on that of 'Samnite' gladiators: Front. *Strat.* 4. 7. 5.

[3] Livy 1. 43. 4; 8. 8. 3. P. Couissin, *Les armes romaines*, pp. 224 f., accepts Livy's view that the *pilum* was not obtained from the Samnites.

[4] Diod. 14. 116. 6; 20. 1. 5 (Diodorus 23. 2 may resemble Ineditum Vaticanum, but he does not actually name the Samnites: he merely says that the *scutum* which the Romans substituted for the *clipeus* was very unlike the rectangular *scutum* they had used in prehistoric times); Dion. Hal. 13. 8. 2; Plut. *Camillus*, 40. 4; *Romulus*, 21; and Polyaenus 8. 7. 2. Moreover Plutarch makes it clear that he for one is not writing without regard for antiquarian details: he says that the Romans were already using the *scutum* in the eighth century (having got it from the Sabines) and he recounts an anecdote of 377 that would make no sense if the Romans had not been then equipped with the *scutum* instead of the *clipeus*.

own phalanx tactics; they took the *scutum* and *pilum* (and also cavalry tactics) from the Samnites and promptly defeated these latter; they learned siege operations from the Greeks, presumably those of Tarentum and Rhegium, and soon outstripped them; they would similarly acquire the art of naval warfare from the Carthaginians and would not be long in besting them at it. This passage is pure rhetoric of the sort that finds its pithiest expression in the oft-repeated commonplace *fas est et ab hoste doceri.*[1] The appearance of this particular piece of boasting in the pages of other historians of Rome does not make it any more trustworthy.[2] Roman willingness to learn from the enemy was a traditional article of Roman pride,[3] and the way that it is set forth in Ineditum Vaticanum is too neatly symmetrical and schematic to be at all plausible.

In any case the matter is put beyond doubt by the archaeological evidence, which reveals that the *scutum* was in general, even though not exclusive, use among the various Italic peoples well before ever Romans and Samnites came to blows about the middle of the fourth century.[4] It had been used in some parts of Italy from prehistoric times.

The evidence for the *pilum* is more shadowy, and the old argument as to where the Romans got this weapon, and when, is still unsettled, although it seems fairly certain that they did not get it from the Samnites.[5] On *a priori* grounds the rhetoric that brings the *pilum* to Rome from Samnium is no more likely to be accurate than that which similarly attributes the *scutum* to the Samnites. In fact *pilum* and *scutum*, and manipular tactics, too, for that matter, seem to hang together. They are all aspects of the same military reform: manipular tactics postulate the use of *pilum* and *scutum*, and vice versa. Hence it is probable that the Romans adopted all of them simultaneously, at the beginning of the fourth century and, as Livy and Plutarch suggest, possibly at the instigation of Camillus.[6]

[1] Ovid, *Metam.* 4. 428; cf. Polyb. 6. 25. 11. [2] Diod. 23. 2; Zon. 8. 9. 1.

[3] For that matter, as A. J. Toynbee, *Hannibal's Legacy*, 1, 518, remarks, 'States have often reformed their military organisation after they have suffered disastrous defeats'.

[4] P. Couissin, *Les armes romaines*, pp. 240–7.

[5] In view of the fact that *Samnites* was thought to derive from *saunion* (Festus, p. 437 L.), it is not surprising that they should be credited with the *pilum*.

[6] The disasters to the Fabii at the Cremera and to the Romans in general at the Allia had demonstrated the advisability of their exchanging phalanx tactics for manipular which required *pilum* and *scutum*. Note that the modification of the *pilum* in Marian times was accompanied by some change in the shield and in tactics (Plut. *Marius*, 25. 1; Festus, p. 274 L., 149 L., 238 L.).

The archaeological evidence makes it certain that in the days of their true independence the Samnites were typically Italic in their military equipment as in so much else.

The graves at Aufidena contained comparatively little military equipment, probably because the Samnites had to import most of the metal needed for their weapons and were therefore reluctant to bury them in any quantity with the dead. Helmets, shields and greaves did not turn up in the tombs at all, and breastplates only with the utmost rarity. On the other hand, sculptured representations of Sabellian warriors have survived. Sabellian tomb-paintings and South Italian vases also depict fighting men, some of them indubitably Samnites, and their equipment.[1] Thus some idea of what a Samnite soldier looked like in the days of his nation's greatness becomes possible.[2]

His close-fitting helmet was often adorned with crest or horns[3] (especially, one suspects, if he were an officer). It might also have sockets on either side, in which one, two and sometimes more eagle feathers were set upright.[4] These *aigrettes* were a widespread Italic practice, known to Romans as well as Samnites, and they are frequently represented in paintings, on coins and in sculpture.[5] Literary allusions to them suggest that they symbolized the warrior's identification with the war god, Mars.[6] Not every soldier wore them, however. The Sabellian tomb-paintings show helmeted warriors fighting, some with and some without the *aigrettes*. A bronze helmet from Larinum labelled Samnite tapers towards the crown and is surmounted by a boss, but has no provision for feathers.[7] It may be that

[1] Roman lamps also show Italic military equipment occasionally. So do the coins of the Social War insurgents, although unfortunately not in any detail. A coin from Larinum, however, clearly shows a Samnite-type helmet (A. Sambon, *Monnaies antiques de l'Italie*, p. 121). For a picture of a Sabellian fighting man, see *Corpus Vasorum Antiquorum*: Italia, fasc. II: Museo Campano, pl. 23. 3.

[2] But the picture cannot be regarded as completely certain. The tomb- and vase-paintings are sometimes earlier than the Samnite Wars; nor can we assume that the Campanian Sabellians which they depict looked exactly like the men of Samnium: the rosters in Verg. *Aen.* 7 and in Sil. Ital. Book 8 suggest that the various Italic peoples had differing accoutrements.

[3] Horned helmets are by no means exclusively Celtic (Q. F. Maule–H. R. W. Smith, *Votive Religion at Caere*, p. 48). The horns indicated that the Sabellian soldier was fighting under the emblem of Mamers (with whom the bull was closely associated).

[4] An Italic helmet in the Louvre has holes for five feathers.

[5] Polyb. 6. 23. 12 f.; cf. Prop. 4. 10. 20. The Sabines did not use the *aigrettes* according to Sil. Ital. 8. 419. They were usually white, but sometimes black.

[6] Verg. *Aen.* 6. 779; Val. Max. 1. 8. 6.

[7] The *conus implumis* of Sil. Ital. 8. 419? It can be seen in the Museum at Campobasso.

they were officers' insignia: certainly M. Fannius, the Samnite (?) commander in the fresco from the Esquiline of *c.* 200, wears them, whereas some of his men do not. On the whole, however, it seems more probable that they are decorations, won for bravery on the field of battle.[1]

The Samnite soldier's tunic, of linen or possibly leather, was short-sleeved and abbreviated, barely reaching to the loins, where it ends sometimes in a kind of apron. Around his waist he wore a broad leather belt covered with bronze and furnished with elaborate clasps. These belts were sometimes of fine workmanship and were evidently greatly valued.[2] The prominence with which they are paraded as trophies in the tomb- and vase-paintings suggests that they had symbolic significance as well as practical usefulness. (Archaeological evidence reveals that young boys had such belts and this supports the theory that they were more than mere military equipment.) Loss of the belt may have been tantamount to losing one's liberty. This might explain why at Caudium the defeated Romans were allowed to retain only their tunics, and why the Romans were so eager to treat the Samnites in the same way.

To protect the torso, and especially the heart, the Samnites used a circular disk about 7½ inches in diameter and sometimes decorated with an animal. The Warrior of Capestrano shows that originally a single disk[3] was worn on the breast with another to match it on the back. Later, additional protection was given by placing a second disk alongside it;[4] and by the fourth century if not earlier a third disk had been added below the other two. The three disks could be combined into a single piece of protective armour roughly triangular in shape, and when two such trefoils were hinged together at the shoulders and under the armpits a cuirass was formed. Specimens of this *corazza Italica* have been found in Samnium, and they are also represented on bronze statuettes and in Sabellian tomb-paintings.[5] Probably not every Samnite soldier had

[1] *pinnas quas insigniti milites in galeis habere solent* (Varro, *L.L.* 5. 142).

[2] A few were found at Aufidena. One has also been discovered at Ielsi (M. Della Corte in *Not. d. Sc.* (1926), p. 441).

[3] καρδιοφύλαξ; Polyb. 6. 23. 14.

[4] A specimen of this type is in the Louvre.

[5] Italic cuirasses have turned up in Central Europe and in Africa (J. Heurgon, *Capoue préromaine*, p. 424, n. 6; V. Pârvan, *Getica*, pp. 433 f. and pl. xx). The cheek-pieces of some helmets in the museum at Ancona, said to be Gallic, are miniature replicas of the trefoil cuirass. The decorative Roman *phalerae* probably evolved from the disks (E. Meyer, *Kleine Schriften*, II, 239).

one: many had to be content with the single disk and the inadequate protection it afforded.

In the paintings the Samnite shield is deeply convex, usually round, but sometimes oval.[1] But there is evidence that, like other Italic peoples, the Samnites also used the long elliptical *scutum*.[2] It was bisected by a vertical rib with a boss in the middle. Apparently the shield proper was not made of metal; like the Lucani and the troops of Spartacus the Samnites seem to have made their shields of osiers covered with sheeps' hides.[3]

The Samnite soldier covered his legs with greaves, not one but two, reaching to the knees. The evidence for this is abundant: the Louvre statuette, Sabellian tomb-paintings, the Esquiline fresco.[4]

For offensive weapons the Samnite had lances (normally for thrusting), a species of small javelin (represented in the tomb-paintings: possibly it is the *aclys* of Vergil),[5] long daggers with hilts ending in a knob, and less frequently short, two-edged stabbing swords. A few maces have also been found, but, despite Silius Italicus and Vergil, it cannot be proved beyond all doubt that Sabellians ever used battle-axes or curved swords.[6]

One is left with the impression, not of Livy's refulgent 'enemy' troops at Aquilonia, but of a Samnite army unencumbered by much defensive armour and well equipped for strong and flexible action, an army that deserved its reputation for military prowess.[7]

[1] The round shield may be due to the snobbish predilection of Italic artists for the *clipeus* (which, at Rome anyway, was the shield of the highest class). Sometimes the *scutum* does win the approval of the artist (*scutati* are shown defeating *clipeati* on Calene cups: R. Pagenstecher, *Die calenische Relief-Keramik*, pl. 16, 135 *a*), but generally the *clipeus* is preferred.

[2] This is not well attested archaeologically but Dion. Hal. 20. 1. 5 has no doubts whatever on the matter and the Samnite commander of the Esquiline fresco has one.

[3] Note how Carvilius could not use captured Samnite shields for his great bronze statue (Pliny, *N.H.* 34. 43). Apparently only the rim of the shield was of metal (Plut. *Cam.* 40. 4). Florus (3. 20. 6) describes how Spartacus' troops made shields out of osiers and sheeps' hides; and Servius (*ad Aen.* 7. 632, quoting Sallust) says that the Sabellian Lucani made their shields that way too.

[4] But he may not always have covered his feet. Many Sabellian soldiers are depicted with bare feet, whether as an artistic convention or because they often were in fact without footwear.

[5] Verg. *Aen.* 7. 730.

[6] Verg. *Aen.* 7. 732; Sil. Ital. 8. 550, 582 (who, however, is avowedly describing Campanian equipment, which he evidently thought of as differing from Samnite). A curved sword appears on a *patella* found on the territory of the Sabellic Marrucini (P. Couissin, *Les armes romaines*, p. 261).

[7] *durati usu armorum* (Livy 7. 29. 5); *Samnis belliger* (Sil. Ital. 10. 314). Cf., too, Cato, *de agric.*, *prooemium: ex agricolis et viri fortissimi et milites strenuissimi gignuntur.*

Whether it equally deserved its reputation for ruthlessness is much more debatable. Roman condemnation of the savagery of the Samnites in murdering their captives in cold blood and in massacring those of their own recruits who recoiled from a stern military oath[1] comes oddly from a people who, according to Livy, slaughtered all the adult males in a Samnite town and decimated its own troops for alleged cowardice.[2]

No doubt there were ugly stains on the Samnites' record. As late as the last century B.C. they put defenceless prisoners to death more than once,[3] and in an earlier age some Sabellians were not above mutilating the enemy dead.[4] That they were any worse in this regard than their Roman foes will not, however, be very apparent to anyone who contemplates the behaviour of Cornelius Sulla or who remembers Livy's gruesome picture of Roman battle practices: *gladio Hispaniensi detruncata corpora, bracchiis cum umero abscissis, aut tota cervice desecta divisa a corpore capita patentiaque viscera et foeditatem aliam vulnerum.*[5] Nor should it be forgotten that the Roman writers who complacently glorify Rome's extermination of the Aurunci are obliged to record the humanity of Gavius Pontius in sparing the surrendered Roman invaders of the Caudine Forks.[6]

It is possible that the unenviable Sabellian reputation for treacherous barbarism was largely due to the perfidy with which the Campani are said to have made themselves masters of Capua in 423,[7] an atrocity which, the Roman writers insist, so far from being isolated was repeated time and again.[8] That there is gross exaggeration in this picture of the speakers of Oscan seems certain. After the *furor Sabellicus* at Capua it was unlikely that other cities would have been so trusting as to open their gates to 'Samnites'. Perhaps the latter are merely being traduced by their Roman enemies, who

[1] Livy 9. 12. 8; 9. 43. 1; 10. 38. 11.

[2] Livy 9. 31. 8; 2. 59. 10 f.

[3] The incidents at Venafrum and Nola in the Social War. See below, p. 358.

[4] The body of Alexander of Epirus was subjected to indignities by the Lucani: see Livy 8. 24. 14 f.; and cf. L. A. Holland in *Amer. Journ. Arch.* LX (1956), 246.

[5] Livy 31. 34. 4 f.

[6] With Livy 9. 25. 9 (*nullus modus caedibus fuit deletaque Ausona gens*, etc.) contrast such a passage as the one Appian, *Samn.* 4, puts into the mouth of Gavius Pontius.

[7] For alleged Samnite treachery see Livy 7. 29; 7. 30; 8. 24. 6: *ut pleraque eius generis ingenia sunt cum fortuna mutabilem gerentes fidem.* For their perfidious behaviour at Capua see above, p. 39.

[8] The incidents are recorded by writers in the Roman tradition who depend ultimately on Greek sources, Timaeus' account of the Sabellian seizure of Messana probably being the origin of all of them. The Sabellians gave a very different account of how they came to that town. See above, p. 39, n. 1.

were not above doing precisely what they condemned the Samnites for doing.[1] In any case, even if the Campanian outrage at Capua in 423 is securely historical, it was not perpetrated by the Samnite army, but by colonists who had been admitted to a share in the city.

(*e*) LANGUAGE

The language of the Samnites was the one that modern scholars, following ancient example,[2] have agreed to call Oscan after their alleged predecessors in Southern Italy.[3] In historical times it was no mere local vernacular. It was a distinct and separate language, with a fairly strict orthography, in official use over a very large part of Italy. The Roman writers certainly regarded it in this light, quite justifiably, since in the fourth century and for long thereafter it was spoken over a much wider area and was normally written with much greater care than contemporary Latin.[4]

In the fourth century Oscan was spoken virtually everywhere in Southern Italy below the Rivers Liris and Sangro except in the heel and in the Greek colonies on the litoral. In the third and second centuries it jumped the straits of Messina and was carried by the Mamertini into the north-eastern corner of Sicily as well. And even this does not tell the whole story, since the Oscan dialects must also be taken into account. In the regions south of the Rivers Liris and Sangro the dialectal variations were negligible.[5] There were indeed some differences between the Oscan of Samnites, Frentani and Campanians on the one hand and the Oscan of Lucani and Bruttii

[1] Livy 7. 38. 5 (plot to seize Capua); 8. 16. 10 (capture of Cales).

[2] Plato, *Ep.* 8. 353e; Ennius *ap.* Aul. Gell. 17. 17. 1; Varro, *L.L.* 5. 131; Livy 10. 20. 8; Festus, p. 150 L. (and many other passages).

[3] The name might have been given to the language of the Samnites who invaded the Opici in the same way that the name Hittite, which originally belonged to an aboriginal population of Anatolia, has been applied to the Indo-European language of the invaders of that land. Another possibility is that the Samnite invaders were so small a conquering minority that they were assimilated by the Opici and lost their linguistic identity (cf. the fate of the Bulgarians in Thrace or the Normans in England): had that been the case, it would have been understandable and reasonable that the tongue spoken by the Samnites in historical times should be called Oscan. A third, and perhaps more probable, possibility is that the language of the invading Samnites resembled that of the invaded Opici: see above, p. 29.

[4] The Sabellians, in fact, seem to have taught the Romans much about correct orthography.

[5] That is, so long as Oscan remained unaffected by Latin. As romanization spread, dialects developed: by 100 the Oscan spoken at Bantia in Lucania was a heavily palatalized variety full of latinisms (for its Messapic substratum, see E. Vetter in *R.E.* Suppt., bd. VI (1935), col. 306).

on the other, but they were not very striking.[1] The languages spoken in Central Italy, however, are another story. They are dialects of Oscan,[2] but they display an almost exaggerated degree of particularism. Paeligni could almost certainly have understood Samnites, without interpreters and without difficulty, whereas Vestini and Marrucini probably could not, even though the scanty remains of their languages palpably resemble Oscan. The Marsi, too, seem to have spoken an Oscan-type dialect, and possibly so did the Sabini and the Aequi in the days before their latinization.[3] It is the Oscan character of their languages that has induced modern scholars to describe the Paeligni, Vestini and Marrucini (and usually the Marsi as well) as 'Sabellic', although the ancients applied the word *Sabellus* to the speakers of authentic Oscan further south.[4]

In general Oscan grammar resembles Latin. The systems of declensions and conjugations in the two languages are very similar, gender, voice, mood and tense being used in the same way. In syntax also the two languages correspond quite closely. It is in phonology, morphology and orthography that they differ, at times quite sharply. This is clearly seen not only in the inflectional endings (Osc. *profatted*, Lat. *probavit*), but also in such features as: the labialization in Oscan of the Indo-European guttural velar (Osc. *pis*, Lat. *quis*), the substitution in Oscan of *d* for final *t* (Osc. *deded*, Lat. *dedit*), the smaller degree of rhotacism in Oscan (Osc. *fakinss*, Lat. *facinora*),[5] the more complete transformation of Indo-European *bh* to *f* in Oscan (Osc. *tifei*, Lat. *tibi*),[6] the preference in Oscan for the fricative cluster *ft* (Osc. *scriftas*, Lat. *scriptae*), and the tendency for short vowels to disappear in Oscan through syncope (Osc. *embratur*, Lat. *imperator*).

[1] About the Oscan of the Apuli no certain pronouncement is possible: it has survived only in coin legends.

[2] They are called Northern Oscan by R. S. Conway, *The Italic Dialects*, pp. 233–66.

[3] Festus, p. 204 L., also links Volscian with Oscan; but the only surviving inscription in it (Vetter, no. 222) indicates that it was closer to Umbrian.

[4] The longest and best-known documents are, *in Oscan*: the Agnone tablet (Vetter, no. 147), the Vibia Imprecation (Vetter, no. 6), the Cippus Abellanus (Vetter, no. 1), and the Tabula Bantina (Vetter, no. 2); *in Oscan-type dialects*: the Marrucine Tabula Rapinensis (Vetter, no. 218) and the Paelignian Herentas inscription (Vetter, no. 213).

[5] Oscan did reach the stage where in some words *s* has become *z*.

[6] See above, p. 30 (the remarks on **Safineis* and *Sabini*).

For the above examples words which markedly resemble one another in the two languages have been deliberately chosen. It is more normal, however, for the two vocabularies to look very unlike (examples: Osc. *tanginod*, Lat. *sententiā*; Osc. *puf*, Lat. *ubi*; Osc. *veru*, Lat. *portam*). Oscan, in fact, has the appearance of being almost aggressively distinct from Latin, closely related though the two languages are.

The large area over which it was spoken is a measure of the consequence attaching to the Oscan language. Yet for all its importance Oscan does not seem to have been reduced to writing until comparatively late. At the time of the big Sabellian expansion in the fifth century, which brought about the consolidation of the Samnite nation and the emergence of the Lucani as a separate people, the speakers of Oscan evidently knew not the art of writing. Had they known it, then assuredly in later times all of them would have been using the same alphabet, whereas in fact their scripts varied.

Seeing that the art of writing was already known and practised in the sixth and fifth centuries in the area occupied by the Vestini in historical times, it is surprising that the nearby speakers of Oscan were unfamiliar with it or at any rate had not taken it into use by 450. Yet they evidently had not done so. It was only after the Sabellians had established themselves in Campania in the late fifth century and had encountered the superior culture of the Greeks and Etruscans that they began to express themselves by means of the written word.[1]

After their arrival in Campania the Sabellians appropriated the alphabet of the Etruscans, modified it to their own phonetic requirements while retaining the Etruscan practice of reading from right to left, and thus made Oscan a written as well as a spoken language. Such was the origin of the native Oscan alphabet.[2]

The date for the Sabellian adoption of writing is confirmed by the peculiarities of this native alphabet. The Etruscan alphabet is generally agreed to have been obtained from the Western Greek one

[1] By then they had long since 'frozen' their burial rite: hence the absence of funerary inscriptions in Oscan.

[2] M. Lejeune in *Rev. Etudes Latines*, XXXV (1957), 88–105; cf. R. von Planta, *Gramm. der osk. umbr. Dialekte*, I, 42.

used by the Chalcidian colonists at Cumae. But just as the Etruscans, in order to obtain a more suitable vehicle for the sounds of their language, had found it expedient to make some changes in an alphabet which surviving *abecedaria*[1] prove to have been originally adopted in its entirety, *c.* 650 or earlier, so did the Sabellians in their turn find it necessary to modify what they acquired from the Etruscans.

By the late fifth century the Etruscans had discovered that they could manage efficiently with an alphabet of only twenty letters, since their language on balance had fewer sounds than that of the Western Greeks. The Etruscans were thus able to drop, add or juggle letters. By the end of the fifth century they had discarded the letter O, for which they had no use; and for their own sound *f* they had added the letter 8.[2] Besides this they had also rearranged the letters for the various stops. Etruscan had only one series of the latter: namely the unvoiced consonants *p*, *t* and *k*.[3] It lacked the voiced equivalents *b*, *d* and *g*. This meant that the Etruscans could either jettison the Greek letters for the latter three or employ them differently. What they did was to discard B, use D with the same value that it had in the Megarian alphabet[4] and attach the sign C[5] to their own voiceless occlusive *k*. As the Sabellian alphabet also uses these letters with the same values, it must have been created after the introduction of these changes by the Etruscans. This fact helps to date the native Oscan alphabet securely to the last quarter of the fifth century or later.[6]

The Sabellians, unlike the Etruscans, did have the sounds *o*, *b*, *d* and *g*, but, by the time they took to writing, the Etruscan alphabet

[1] From Cerveteri, Colle, Formello, Leprignano, Marsigliana d'Albegna, Narce, Viterbo (see L. Banti, *Il Mondo degli Etrusci*, p. 25). For an Etruscan *abecedarium* from Campania see F. Weege, *Vasculorum Campanorum Inscriptiones Italicae*, 1–3.

[2] Hitherto they had represented the sound *f* by the letters *vh* or *hv*. The origin of the sign 8, which was also used in Lydian, is uncertain: see Sommer in *S B Bay. Acad. Wiss.* (1930/31), and G. Pugliese-Carratelli in *Parola del Passato*, xv (1960), 60. It is found on *abecedaria* of the fifth century and later from Bomarzo, Chiusi and Nola.

[3] It also had the corresponding voiceless aspirates *ph*, *th* and *ch*, the origin, so it is commonly believed, of the *gorgia toscana* in Italian.

[4] Namely to represent the sound *r*, the symbol for which in Western Greek writing is usually P, but sometimes R.

[5] This was the Western Greek letter for the voiced *g* (hence its use in the regular abbreviations for the Latin *praenomina* Gaius and Gnaeus).

[6] There is no specimen of written Oscan earlier than the fourth century (M. Lejeune, *Rev. Etudes Lat.* xxxv (1957), 89, 92): but the alphabet could, of course, have been created long before the date of the earliest surviving document. Even so, the native Oscan alphabet cannot be much older than 350 (J. Beloch, *Campanien*², p. 4).

no longer had the letters for them.[1] For *o* they took the symbol which the Etruscans used for their sound *x* (𐌙),[2] but ultimately modified it slightly by changing the upright stroke between the arms to a diacritical mark thus: 𐌙̇.[3] For *b* and *g* they used the letters B and C which stood for these sounds in the Western Greek alphabet.[4] This obliged them to find another symbol for their voiceless velar *c*: they chose the Greek letter K, which suited well. The voiced plosive *d* was more difficult. As noted above, by the late fifth century the Etruscans had already assigned the Western Greek symbol for this sound D to their own liquid consonant *r*; and the Sabellians faithfully followed the Etruscans in this, so that in the native Oscan alphabet the sound *r* is written as a D. Consequently they had to find some other letter for the dental *d*. They adopted R, the letter which in the alphabet of Greek Cumae stood for the liquid *r*. Thus in the native Oscan alphabet the letters D and R exactly interchanged the values which they bore in most Greek alphabets and which they still bear in ours.

Another symbol which the Sabellians took from the Western Greek alphabet was Ͱ. The Greeks used this as an aspirate; but the Sabellians already had the Etruscan symbol 𐌇 for that.[5] They used Ͱ for a sound of their own, a mid-high front vowel corresponding to *į*, which originated from either *i* or *e* and was approximately midway between them in sound.[6]

As a result of Sabellian modifications of the Etruscan system of

[1] Etruscan, of course, had some sounds not found in Oscan, namely those represented by the symbols ⊗, φ, χ, ⋈. The Sabellians could presumably have retained these symbols and used them with different values: but they did not do so. Perhaps they wished to avoid confusion so far as possible.

[2] 𐌙 appears on the very early and as yet undeciphered inscription from Novilara in Picenum, seemingly to represent the sound *o* (J. Whatmough, *Prae-Italic Dialects*, II, 521).

[3] This letter and also Ͱ, the other letter with a diacritical mark, are absent from the earliest *Iovila* inscriptions. Hence they were probably not devised until 300 or later. They may have suggested the use of the diacritical mark to Sp. Carvilius at Rome *c.* 234 (Plut. *Quaest. Rom.* 59; see *Trans. Amer. Phil. Assoc.* XXX (1899), 24–41): he added it to the symbol C to distinguish the voiced velar from the voiceless; and thus the letter G was born. (The earliest example of the letter G seems to be in the Tabula Rapinensis (see Vetter, no. 218).)

[4] By putting C to this use they were undoing what the Etruscans had done. For the way the peoples of Italy obtained from Greek alphabets the symbols that were lacking in Etruscan, see M. Lejeune in *Rev. Et. Lat.* XXXV (1957), 92, 103 f.

[5] The use of the aspirate in Oscan suggests that the Arrius of *Catullus* 84 may have been a Sabellian.

[6] They also used Ͱ as the second letter in diphthongs: *aí*, etc., and in the combination —*ií* (= *ī* apparently). The Emperor Claudius later used it for the sound midway between *i* and *u* when he attempted to reform the Roman alphabet.

writing, the native Oscan alphabet came to have twenty-one letters, one more than the developed Etruscan alphabet.[1]

𐌀	𐌁	𐌂	𐌃	𐌄	𐌅	𐌆	𐌇	𐌉	𐌊	𐌋	𐌌	𐌍	𐌐	𐌓	𐌔	𐌕	𐌖	𐌚	𐌝	𐌞
a	*b*	*g*	*d*	*e*	*v*	*z*	*h*	*i*	*k*	*l*	*m*	*n*	*p*	*r*	*s*	*t*	*u*	*f*	*í*	*o*

Generally speaking, both the writing and the spelling in the alphabet are meticulous.[2] Indeed for a period in the second century the Sabellians attempted to distinguish a long vowel in the initial syllable of a word by reduplicating it.[3] The practice did not last, but it indicates that Sabellian writing was anything but slapdash.

The native Oscan alphabet manifestly was devised, not only at a time when the Etruscans had already discarded the letters O and B and had substituted D for R, but also at a time when the Sabellians were in close enough physical contact with the Western Greeks to be quite familiar with their letters for the sounds *b*, *g* and *h*. In other words the Oscan alphabet can hardly be earlier than the end of the fifth century, and is almost certainly later. This dating is confirmed by the legends on the coins of Allifae and Fistelia, which were at first written in Greek characters and only became Oscan later in the fourth century.[4] It is also consistent with the view that the Sabellians began to read and write only after their arrival in Campania and indeed after they had already begun their expansion into Lucania.[5]

Clearly much thought and care went into the perfecting of this so-called native Oscan alphabet, but no single individual was credited with its invention. At any rate no one has named the Sabellian Cadmus or Demaratus for us. There can, however, be very

[1] The order of the letters is established by fragments of Sabellian *abecedaria* found at Pompeii (see Vetter, no. 69). In Oscan writing, which was read *sinistrorsum* like Etruscan, the letters have a back-to-front appearance: see, for example, Plate 12. On the alphabet see G. Devoto, *Gli Antichi Italici*[2], pp. 158 f.; A. C. Moorhouse, *Triumph of the Alphabet*, 132 f.

[2] One word is separated from another by a single interpunct (double interpuncts occur only in the earliest documents). Unlike Etruscan, Oscan did not separate syllables by means of interpuncts. Sometimes the diacritical marks of 𐌞 and 𐌝 got omitted, but usually not.

[3] This practice, however, was not adopted at Capua, the town that has yielded so many of the surviving Oscan inscriptions.

[4] Actually it is a coin from Fistelia that shows the earliest example of the letter 𐌞 (Vetter, p. 136). This suggests that Fistelia belonged to Campania, not Samnium (see above, p. 72).

[5] Note also that the proposed date does not contradict the statement of Livy (9. 3. 4 f.) that the Samnites were familiar with writing in 321.

little doubt that it was devised by the Sabellians of Campania, from whom numerous commercial and other contacts quickly took it to the Samnites of Samnium and to the Frentani on the Adriatic coast.[1] The Samnites continued to use it for as long as they spoke Oscan. But it made no headway north of the Sagrus or south of the Aufidus.

The other speakers of Oscan (the Lucani, Bruttii and Mamertini) used a Greek script.[2] This was not because they had little business with the Campanians (which would be incredible), but because they had such close relations with their Greek neighbours: Ennius in fact averred that the Bruttii were bilingual, speaking Greek as well as Oscan, and Horace says the same of the Apuli of Canusium.[3]

The Sabellic peoples of Central Italy also, so far as we know, never adopted the native Oscan alphabet for their Oscan-type dialects. They regularly used the script which the Romans allegedly learned from King Evander, even the oldest Paelignian inscription being in Latin letters. This is perhaps what one might have expected of peoples who normally preferred to cooperate with the Romans than with the Samnites.[4]

There have been instances of peoples who while still in a preliterate stage of development succeeded in producing and maintaining a fairly advanced culture and even in preserving a literature, in the form of an oral tradition.[5] But it is writing that enables a society to develop a specialized economy beyond the household type, capable of supporting the complexities of civilized life, and it is hardly surprising that the Sabellians should have adopted it once they arrived in an area where it was commonly known and prac-

[1] Proof of such contacts is the *devotio* from Campania (Cumae?) which curses Decius Herius of Saepinum (Vetter, p. 35).

[2] The Greek alphabet used in a few documents of the Lucani, Bruttii and Mamertini differs only slightly from the western Ionic one. (The use of η and ω where one might have expected ε and ο represents an attempt to reproduce the open quality of the relevant Oscan sounds: I. Fischer in *Studii Clasice*, IV (1962), 11.) Later, after the Romans had established their supremacy, the Lucani, Bruttii and Mamertini abandoned Greek characters for Latin: The Tabula Bantina of *c.* 100, for instance, the longest surviving Oscan document, is in the Roman alphabet. The failure of the Lucani, Bruttii and Mamertini to use the Oscan alphabet means that the latter was devised after these peoples had established themselves in their historical habitats.

[3] Festus, p. 31 L.; Hor. *Sat.* I. 10. 30.

[4] As in modern Yugoslavia, the historical vicissitudes of a tribe decided which alphabet it would use.

[5] The epics of Yugoslavia (and possibly those of Homer) were preserved by oral tradition. It will also be remembered that the North American Indians were able to negotiate diplomatic agreements in their preliterate days.

tised. They did not, however, all become literate overnight and it is not easy to trace the progress of literacy amongst them.

The only references to Samnite writing in Livy are to a document of religious character and to correspondence that passed between the illustrious Gavius Pontius and his father, and these can probably be dismissed as apocryphal. Still less is to be said about Samnite literature. In fact it is far from certain that there was any.[1]

There is excellent proof of the vitality of the Oscan language in the 'comedies of Atella' (*fabulae Atellanae*), which became and remained so popular at Rome that a contest in reciting scenes from them was still staged there in Oscan even in Augustus' day.[2] Something is known about these rather crude farces. Like the Italian Pulcinella or our own Punch and Judy shows, they always featured the same stock characters, four in number: Bucco the Braggart, Dossennus the Hunchback, Maccus the Glutton and Pappus the Dotard. The players wore masks, and gross personalities and spicy conundrums seem to have punctuated the dialogue. Livy in a famous chapter tells us that they were brought from the Oscan areas to Rome well after the time of Livius Andronicus (*fl.* 240). At Rome they were performed by youthful amateurs, not by professional actors, and for many years they were nothing more than extemporaneous improvisations.[3]

[1] It has often been suggested that there was a flourishing Oscan literature: see, for instance, T. Mommsen, *Unterital. Dialekte*, pp. 101, 117; *CIL*, x, p. 124; H. Nissen, *Ital. Landesk.* I, 538; E. Vetter in *R.E.* XVIII (1942), s.v. 'Osci', col. 1549; L. Pareti, *Storia di Roma*, I, 474. But it seems very improbable. Not only have no Oscan literary texts survived, but also no ancient writers refer to Sabellian literary activity in the way that Livy (9. 36. 3) and the Emperor Claudius (*ILS*, 212) do to Etruscan; and, so far as is known, Sabellian contact with the Greek world did not flush any literary figure in the manner that Roman contact with Tarentum, once it occurred, promptly produced a Livius Andronicus.

[2] Strabo 5. 3. 6, p. 233.

[3] Livy 7. 2. 12. The Atellanae were a *levissima apud vulgum oblectatio* (Tac. *Ann.* 4. 14) and did not appear in writing until relatively late (after 150: C. Cichorius, *Röm. Studien*, pp. 82 f.). The best-known writers of them are L. Pomponius Bononiensis (Hieron. *ad an.* 89) and a certain Novius (Cic. *de orat.* 2. 279), who so far from being identical with Naevius is actually later than Pomponius (see Vell. 2. 9. 5). They may have been named after Atella simply because they purported to give scenes of Sabellian life (the Sabellians being chosen because of their reputation for uncouthness). But perhaps they were no more representative of Sabellian life than a minstrel show is of Negro life in the U.S.A. Actually the four stock characters seem to have had different names in Sabellian Italy: there Dossennus was Manducus (Varro, *L.L.* 7. 95), Pappus was Casnar (Varro, *L.L.* 7. 29), and either Bucco or Maccus was Messius (Hor. *Sat.* 1. 5. 52; cf. Varro, *L.L.* 7. 96). The masks that were worn strengthened their Sabellian connexion, since one word for masks is *oscilla*, popularly derived from Osci (Serv. *ad Georg.* 2. 389). (Actually both the mask and the normal name for it (*persona*) were obtained from the Etruscans, who had a masked demon, Phersu (J. Heurgon, *Capoue prérom.* p. 434).)

It is most improbable that the Sabellians knew the Atellane farce until after they had reached Campania. Naevius is said to have produced a farce at Rome in the late third century, which by coincidence may have resembled the later Atellanae.[1] Certainly the Atellane farces proper cannot be shown to be any older than this.[2] The association with Atella and the Etruscan-type name of one of the characters (Dossennus) and the Greek names of two of the others (Maccus and Pappus) show that it was the Campanians who were responsible for these comedies.[3] They must have been greatly influenced by, if indeed they did not derive their inspiration from, the Italiote *phlyakes*.[4]

The earliest use the Samnites had for writing was not for Atellanae but for official purposes, and it is reasonable to assume that from 354 onwards their dealings with the Romans were regularly recorded in writing. Treaties could be written on the skins of animals, as Rome's treaty with Gabii was, or perhaps inscribed on pillars in temples, as was the Sabine practice.[5]

Nevertheless the percentage of literate Samnites in the fourth century must have been very small. Probably only a handful of priests and official scribes knew how to write. Even at Rome, where an alphabet had been devised much earlier and used for epigraphical purposes as early as the sixth or fifth century,[6] writing was still a *res nova inter rudes artium homines*; few Romans could read and write before 300.[7]

It is true that Nearchus of Tarentum, writing *c.* 209, represented

[1] Festus, p. 238 L. For Naevius' date see Aul. Gell. 17–21 (quoting Varro).

[2] Their heyday at Rome was the age of Sulla: D. Romano, *Atellana Fabula*, p. 40.

[3] The use of the mask (*persona*) suggests the same thing. The Campanians learned of Phersu from the Etruscans of Capua. Phersu, it is true, appears in funeral rites, but the association of comedy with death is very old (J. Heurgon, *Capoue préromaine*, pp. 434 f.). The Atellanae originally may have been staged at funeral games (if so, they may not antedate 173, the earliest known date for plays at a funeral: Livy 41. 28. 11).

[4] P. Frassinetti, *Fabula Atellana*, p. 38. What have been often taken for scenes from the Atellanae (see *Not. d. Scavi* (1936), p. 58, fig. 5; M. Bieber, *History of Greek and Roman Theatre*, p. 297), are probably representations of *phlyakes*: on the other hand, Horace, *Sat.* 1. 5. 51–70, may give us some idea of what an improvised Atellana was like. The *phlyakes* were clearly older than the Atellanae: scenes from them are pictured on Italiote vases of the fourth century.

[5] Dion. Hal. 4. 58. 4; 3. 33. 1.

[6] The inscription under the *lapis niger* in the Roman forum.

[7] Livy 1. 7. 8; cf. 6. 1. 2. Elsewhere (9. 36. 3), Livy says that Roman boys were instructed in Etruscan letters before 300 in the same way that they were instructed in Greek letters after 100. If this is not a fairy tale, it can have reference only to boys of aristocratic birth.

Pontius, father of the great Samnite hero of 321, as a man of studious and literary tastes. Nearchus, if Cicero quotes him accurately, depicted Pontius *père* as discoursing gravely on philosophic, presumably Pythagorean, themes with such intellectual giants as Plato of Athens and Archytas of Tarentum.[1] This, however, is hardly evidence that by the fourth century the Samnites were more advanced in matters intellectual and cultural than the Romans.[2] It is an isolated anecdote of dubious authenticity. Pontius was an aristocrat of the Caudini, living close to Hellenic influences. Such a person might have acquired some taste for literature, but it by no means follows that his ruder fellows, the Samnites in general, had done so. Indeed such archaeological evidence as there is from the heart of Samnium reveals quite clearly that contacts between it and the Greek world were anything but common. The alleged meeting of Pontius with Plato and Archytas is just barely possible on chronological grounds, provided that we assign it to 349; and it is not entirely out of character, since Plato himself bears witness to his friendly relations with Archytas.[3] Even so, the story could well have been invented by Tarentine sources at a time when the Tarentines were anxious to flatter the Samnites. The tale merely confirms that as a result of the Caudine Forks affair a fairy-tale atmosphere had grown up around the Pontii: they had become figures of legend, a legend which depicted Pontius senior as a kind of Nestor or venerable Timoleon who could naturally be expected to expatiate on Pythagorean themes, since some of Pythagoras' ideas grew out of Italic practices.[4]

[1] Cic. *Cato Major*, 12. 41 (Cicero may have got the story from Cato's *Origines*). See, too, Cic. *de re pub.* 1. 16 and Plut. *Pyrrhus*, 20. 4 (who suggests that the Samnites were interested in Epicurean philosophy).

[2] F. Altheim, *Hist. of Roman Religion*, p. 279, suggests that 'Greek culture was widely extended among the nobles of Samnium', but this is very unconvincing.

[3] It is, however, chronologically implausible. Nearchus would have been ten or less when he heard the story from his elders of eighty or over; moreover Plato's friendship with Archytas belongs to 367–361 rather than 349 (Plato, *Epist.* 7. 338 c, 339 d). See F. Münzer in *Hermes*, XL (1905), 53; E. Pais, *Storia di Roma*³, I, p. 88, n. 1.

[4] Strabo 5. 4. 12, p. 250. G. Pugliese Carratelli (in *Parola del Passato*, VII (1952), 256) finds a kernel of truth in the story. It will also be remembered that, according to Diogenes Laertius (8. 14), Romans, Lucani, Messapii and Picentini came to listen to the words of Pythagoras (with which cf. Cic. *Tusc. Disp.* 4. 1). Laertius may not be very reliable however (he is probably not quoting Aristoxenus of Tarentum (*fl.* 4th cent.)); in any case he does not include Samnites in Pythagoras' audience. Incidentally apocryphal anecdotes were as likely to be told of Archytas as of the Pontii (J. A. Philip in *Phoenix*, XVII (1963), 255). There seems to have been a literary convention to represent soldier heroes as deeply interested in philosophy: the bluff old Roman Fabricius is so depicted (Cic. *Cato Maior*, 13. 43).

On the whole it seems most unlikely that there could have been a Samnite literary public in the fourth century.

The third century witnessed greater development. The Romans began to inscribe their tombstones and to show an interest in writing; and the Agnone tablet proves that the Samnites, too, began to make greater use of writing, especially for religious purposes. It has even been suggested that there were schools where Sabellian scribes were taught how to master the art.[1] The painstaking punctiliousness[2] in spelling, word separation and general aspect of so many Oscan documents certainly indicates careful training.[3] Nevertheless the Samnite reading public in the third century B.C. could not have been large, since even the much more advanced Sabellians of Campania were not more than rudimentarily literate by the middle of the next century.[4] Samnite literary writers cannot be shown to have existed at all.

The second and first centuries witnessed a slow spread of literacy, and this coincided with the consolidation of Roman political supremacy in Italy and with the beginnings of a Roman interest in creative writing. The result was a tendency for the emerging literature of the peninsula to be in the language of its masters. Italians with a bent for writing preferred Latin to their own vernaculars. Those whose mother tongue was Greek are the exceptions to prove the rule, while Naevius, Ennius, Plautus, Caecilius Statius and Pacuvius are the examples to demonstrate it. The Latin-using Italian writers, however, do not include any Samnites.[5] The failure of Samnium even in later days to produce notable literary figures is

[1] A. von Blumental in *Die Welt als Geschichte*, II (1936), 18 f.; E. Vetter in *R.E.* XVIII (1942), s.v. 'Osci', cols. 1554 f.; M. Lejeune in *Rev. Ét. Latines*, XXXV (1957), 104.

[2] Some Oscan inscriptions, of course, are carelessly written. This is particularly true of the imprecation tablets. The earliest documents, also, sometimes suggest that the writer was fumbling.

[3] Perhaps the Samnites began to keep historical records in the third century: Livy (10. 38. 6) suggests that they had some then, and so did the Latini and the Sabini (Livy 8. 10. 8; Dion. Hal. 2. 49; cf. Pliny, *N.H.* 18. 6; Aul. Gell. 7. 7). Such records would have been as jejune as the priestly records of contemporary Rome.

[4] E. Pulgram in *Amer. Journ. Phil.* LXXXI (1960), 16. It was only in the third century that literacy began to be at all common even amongst the Greeks (J. A. Davison in *Phoenix*, XVI (1962), 229 f.); and at Rome the overwhelming majority of the people were then still illiterate. Yet Rome had adopted writing long before Samnium.

[5] Unless D. O. Robson (in *Amer. Journ. Phil.* LIX (1938), 301–8) is right in conjecturing that Caecilius Statius was not an Insubrian, but a Samnite settled in Cisalpine Gaul. Cato (*de agric.* 151. 1) quotes a Minius Percennius, whose name is clearly Sabellian; but he came from Campanian Nola and evidently used Latin. Lucilius also came from an Oscan-speaking district; but his own mother tongue was probably Latin.

strong presumptive evidence that it was a region with few, if any, literary traditions.[1]

In fact, apart from the *fabulae Atellanae*, there is no certain and unmistakable allusion anywhere to an Oscan literature.[2] Ennius' famous remark that he possessed three hearts since he knew how to speak Greek, Oscan and Latin is irrelevant in this connexion.[3] Ennius himself came from Rudiae, where the language was Messapic:[4] in other words, for him Oscan was just as much an acquired language as Greek or Latin. But he did not learn it because of its literature or other cultural refinements. He did not learn even Latin for that reason: in his day Latin had little literature to speak of.[5] Ennius' *lingua culta* was Greek. He learned Latin because it was supremely useful to know the language of the masters of Italy, and Oscan for an equally pragmatic reason: in his day it was the language of everyday use throughout Southern Italy. But the practical and the cultural are not necessarily identical, and it is noteworthy that, whereas Ennius turned his knowledge of Latin to literary account, he did nothing of the sort with Oscan, so far as we know.[6]

By the first century literacy must have been common not only at Rome, but also amongst the Sabellians.[7] By then, however, the supremacy of Latin had been placed beyond the reach of challenge by its adoption after the Social War as the official language everywhere in peninsular Italy.

There were, it is true, the 'Oscan comedies', as Cicero calls them, to show that Oscan was still widespread and lively and that

[1] It is to be noted that Horace, who went to school in a Sabellian district under a strict Sabellian master, studied Latin and Greek literature, not Oscan (*Epp.* 2. 1. 50–75).

[2] The notion that the Romans obtained the trochaic tetrameter from the speakers of Oscan (F. Altheim in *Glotta*, XIX (1931), 24–48) seems absurd. The metrical funerary inscription in Paelignian, the so-called Herentas inscription (Vetter, no. 213), imitates Roman practice rather than the other way round.

[3] Aul. Gell. 17. 17. 1.

[4] See O. Haas, *Messapische Studien*, p. 15. (The name Ennius itself could however be Oscan.)

[5] Literature only came to Rome *pinnato gradu* after the Second Punic War.

[6] Latin poets did not normally write in a second language. Ovid is a unique exception (N. I. Herescu in *Ovidiana*, p. 404). For bilingualism in antiquity see T. J. Haarhoff, *Stranger at the Gate*[2], pp. 319–26.

[7] It was then that Rome got its first library of consequence, that of Lucullus (F. G. Kenyon, *Books and Readers in Anc. Greece and Rome*[2], p. 79), and that Pompeii became plastered with signs in Oscan which rank and file soldiers were expected to be able to read (this at least is one interpretation of the so-called *eituns* inscriptions: Vetter, nos. 23–8).

the Sabellian public was still avid for ephemeral reviews filled with caustic personal allusions.[1] But otherwise Latin was the literary medium.

The Empire produced some writers of Sabellian origin but none of them, with the exception of Velleius Paterculus, demonstrably from Samnium.[2] Horace, although unsure as to which Sabellian people he belonged to, was confident that he was no Samnite.[3] His contemporary, the shadowy Alfius Flavus, whose name is Oscan and who wrote a sympathetic version of the Sabellian seizure of Messana, seems to have been more at home in Campania than in the highlands.[4] About the origin of Petronius in the reign of Nero nothing is known: his name could be Oscan and his *Satiricon* proves him to have been familiar with Southern Italy.[5] Papinius Statius in the reign of Domitian was clearly of Sabellian stock; but he came from Naples.[6] Only Velleius Paterculus can be shown to have come from Samnium. He came from the Hirpinian country.[7] But his compendium of Roman history is not only no literary masterpiece: it is also not discernibly Samnite in tone. Its obsequious and dishonest adulation of Tiberius, and even of Sejanus, is far removed from the proud and independent Samnite spirit of an earlier day. In fact, to judge from Velleius' summary of late republican literature,[8] his literary horizon did not extend beyond Latin into any of

[1] Cic. *ad fam.* 7. 1–3. His 'Oscan comedies' are Atellanae. That the Samnites liked the theatre is shown by the care with which a stone theatre was constructed at Pietrabbondante (probably in the first century and before ever a stone theatre was built at Rome). A. Maiuri, *Passeggiate Campane*, p. 386, envisages liturgical performances in this theatre, a view evoked by the graceful architecture and lofty site which excavation has confirmed. But no doubt the inhabitants of the settlement went to see the antics of Dossennus and his masked companions as well.

[2] Samnium had its literary dabblers of course. M. Pomponius Bassulus, who held the highest local office at Aeclanum in Trajan's day, amused himself by writing some comedies and translating others from Menander. His widow had some of his verses inscribed in a very un-Samnite way on his tombstone. They are nothing more than sententious doggerel: *ILS*, 2953.

[3] *Lucanus an Apulus*: *Sat.* 2. 1. 34.

[4] Festus, p. 150 L.; C. Cichorius, *Röm. Studien*, pp. 58–67. His name may be Alfius Flavius: in any case it is Oscan (Livy 23. 53. 12). But there is nothing to show that he wrote in that tongue (E. Pais, *Storia di Roma*³, 1, 97). He obviously knew the Lucrine Lake district very well: he described the gambols of an amiable dolphin there, which may not be as incredible as they sound in view of the recent career of the dolphin Ogopono in New Zealand. See Pliny, *N.H.* 9. 25; Ovid, *ex Ponto*, 4. 16. 23; Seneca, *Controv.* 1. 7. 22, 3 exc. 7.

[5] But with its coastal cities rather than with the highlands of Samnium.

[6] Stat. *Silvae*, 3. 5. 81.

[7] Velleius 2. 16. 2.

[8] R. Syme, *Roman Revolution*, p. 488; Velleius 2. 9.

the other Italic languages. He is a completely assimilated minor Roman writer of the silver age of Latin literature.

It is obviously impossible to make confident pronouncements about Samnite writing or to estimate what effect the Samnites had on Latin literary traditions and practices. But one thing the Romans may have owed to the Sabellians: their development of lampooning satire. *Satira quidem tota nostra est*, and it may have had its origin in Sabellian districts.[1] At the very least it derived strength and reinforcement from there. If satire originated from rustic dramatic improvisations, it may have owed a good deal to Southern Italy. Even the *phlyakes*, the coarse dramatic skits of the Italiotes which, as we have seen, probably influenced the Atellane farces, may have been heavily indebted to the ironical approach to life of the natives in whose midst the Greek immigrants had settled. The Atellane farces themselves evidently contained much that was satiric. Gnaeus Naevius, from Sabellian Campania according to the usual account, so annoyed the Metelli by his sarcastic references to them, that he himself was hounded into exile and the proverbial expression *superbia Campana* was fastened on the Latin language.[2] Gaius Lucilius, the father of Roman satire, came from Suessa Aurunca, a Latin Colony in an Oscan-speaking district. Horace makes the Samnite Messius Cicirrus ('Game-cock') try to outdo Sarmentus Scurra ('Buffoon') in an exchange of abusive personalities.[3] Horace himself was a Sabellian,[4] and it is to be noted that his earliest essays in verse were of the trenchant kind: it was only after he had become securely established in Maecenas' circle in Rome that his writing began to display a more urbane and kindlier tone,[5] and even then there were occasional relapses. The Sabellians may also have helped the Romans to the habit of discovering contemporary and satiric allusions in revivals of old plays.[6] The literary forbears of Pasquino

[1] Quint. 10. 1. 93. All the early writers of satire came from Oscan-speaking districts. Cf. P. Lejay, *Œuvres d'Horace: Satires*, p. lxxxi.

[2] Aul. Gell. 1. 24; cf. Cic. *de leg. agr.* 2. 33. The traditional story, it must be admitted, is very suspect: see H. B. Mattingly in *Historia*, IX (1960), 414–39. For Naevius' Campanian origin see H. T. Rowell in *Mem. Amer. Acad. Rome*, XIX (1949), 18–30. See, too, E. V. Marmorale, *Naevius Poeta*[2], *passim*.

[3] Hor. *Sat.* 1. 5. 51–70.

[4] For Horace's Sabellian origin see V. A. Sirago in *L'Antiquité Classique*, XXVII (1958), 13–30. He calls himself *Sabellus*: *Epp.* 1. 16. 49.

[5] Hor. *Epp.* 1. 19. 23 f.

[6] Cicero describes how quick Roman audiences were to find covert reflexions on contemporary politics in the dialogue of old plays (*pro Sestio*, 55. 118; *Phil.* 1. 15. 36; *ad Att.* 2. 19. 3; 16. 2. 3).

and Marforio should almost certainly be sought in antiquity; perhaps the search for them could be narrowed to the speakers of Oscan.

(*f*) ART AND ARCHITECTURE

The earliest forms of art in Samnium are those of an Iron Age culture which in the seventh century was still young in that region of Italy.[1] It was also very persistent: the local products,[2] impasto ware,[3] bronze and iron ornaments and weapons,[4] continued to be made almost without change in the two succeeding centuries, during which the Samnites were consolidating their tribal states. It is characteristic of this time that no significant influences from outside were really assimilated. A few foreign objects had indeed made their way into Samnium from an early date, at first from Picenum and Apulia[5] and later from Italiote and Etruscan centres in Magna Graecia and Campania; and in the Samnite necropolises these imported objects are seen side by side with the native products.[6] But with very few exceptions the latter are unaffected by the extraneous designs and forms.[7]

From about 400 on the assimilation of Greek influences becomes increasingly obvious. The development is not consistent, however, and the archaeological finds are so sporadic and scanty that any generalization would be rash, particularly in the absence of literature and inscriptions. Despite these limitations, to record and summarily

[1] The Iron Age culture seems to have begun in peninsular Italy in the ninth century and to have spread to Samnium in the eighth (M. Pallottino, *The Etruscans*, pp. 32–8).

[2] For these see pp. 56, 71, 108–10.

[3] Occasionally vases of handsome shape are found, such as the cup with high lunate handle from Melizzano, if that be Samnite (M. Rotili, *L'Arte nel Sannio*, p. 13). But usually the pottery is very plain, relieved if at all only by engraved decoration of a very simple kind (L. Mariani, 'Aufidena', in *Monumenti Antichi*, x (1901), 275). A centre for the manufacture of such crude ware was Allifae, right down to the days of Horace (*Sat.* 2. 8. 39).

[4] Designs of late Iron Age type (a fantastic quadruped with its head and tail in the shape of a bird's head) decorate the pectoral disks. Traces of orientalizing influences from across the Adriatic can also be discerned. The bronze ornaments are much less crude than the impasto vases (L. Mariani, *op. cit.* pp. 299, 353–6).

[5] G. Devoto, *Gli Antichi Italici*², p. 196. Some of the objects were probably brought back by shepherds who had accompanied the flocks on their annual migrations to Apulia. At Saepinum even a Messapic fibula has been found (G. Ambrosetti in *Arch. Class.* x (1958), 16).

[6] The imports consist of inexpensive Etrusco-Campanian vases and a few *bucchero* and Italiote pieces. Bronze vessels, possibly of Greek manufacture, are rare (L. Mariani, *op. cit.* pp. 276–95).

[7] The wealthier Samnite tombs at Allifae and Suessula show Iron Age furnishings similar to those at Aufidena.

describe the works of art and the architecture helps to illustrate the cultural aspects and currents. Fortunately, too, the much richer finds from Campania and Lucania shed illuminating evidence on the archaeological material in Samnium itself. Throughout Sabellian Italy the predominant phenomenon is that the Greek models lose their essential qualities and acquire a rustic, harsh and expressive individuality which is Italic. This can be seen in terracotta, stone and bronze pieces.

In Samnium proper figurative art is very rare before the end of the fifth century.[1] But to about that time there has been assigned a piece of sculpture that appears to be an isolated example of indigenous work free from any Greek and Etruscan influences. This is the terracotta head from Triflisco in the museum at Santa Maria di Capua Vetere.[2] It was found in 1955 by pure chance at a depth of 20 feet during dredging operations on the right bank of the Volturnus at Triflisco, near the sites of Caudine Telesia and Caiatia. It is a life-size head of a garlanded and bearded man, and the uneven firing suggests that it was produced by primitive methods. The face, flattened to the point of seeming two dimensional, is meant to be seen only from the front. Its dominating features are the large rigid eyes and neat high arches of the eyebrows joined at the top of the straight nose. The lack of a sense of volume and the graphic rendering appear to be typically Italic. The beard is made of small bits of terracotta, irregularly arranged and intended to suggest tight curls: they are covered with thin incised lines which blend into the cheeks.[3] Napoli, the first to study the head carefully, directs attention to the effect of abstraction produced by the geometric disposition of the upper part of the face and the total absence of Greek structural character or any other classical values. Their absence from what was surely a work of some endeavour points to a period before Hellenic influence had begun to manifest itself in Samnium. Napoli tentatively suggests the late fifth or early fourth century, in other words the

[1] 'Samnium', 'Samnite' and 'Sabellian' are not found in the index of G. M. A. Richter's *Ancient Italy*; nor are any Samnite towns apart from Beneventum (and it only for Trajan's Arch).

[2] M. A. Napoli, 'Testa di divinità sannitica da Triflisco', in *Parola del Passato*, XI (1956), 381–91. Triflisco is at the southern end of the Monti Trebulani.

[3] Care for detail is seen also in the eyes: the iris is a pellet of terracotta with a hole in the middle, the eyelashes and eyebrows are hatcheted with small incised lines and the contours about the eyes are raised. The ears, on the other hand, are very perfunctorily done, obviously because the face is intended to be viewed from the front.

period when the Samnites were consolidating their grip on Campania. The Triflisco head may be that of a divinity.[1] If it is and if it belongs to a cult-statue, it is a remarkably early specimen.[2]

Terracotta, as readers of Pliny will remember,[3] continued long in use. An example is the statue of a goddess, just under life size, which is now at Vienna and is proved by its Doric *chiton*, helmet and aegis to be an Athena.[4] It was found in the eighteenth century amid the vestigial ruins of its temple at Roccaspromonte near Bovianum and is thought to be a copy of early fifth-century Attic work, stiffened by schematic features of Italic type. The Oscan inscription on its supporting base was destroyed at the time of its discovery, but fortunately not before it was copied down, perhaps inaccurately. This inscription may be later than the statue itself since it shows a degree of latinization compatible with the late second or early first century, at which time Greek gods had long been at home in Samnium. The Roccaspromonte statue is the earliest known image of Athena from a hill town of the interior.[5]

A probable counterpart to this Athena was a statue of Mefitis whose base has been found at Hirpinian Aeclanum. The fragment of a marble head was found near the base, and it has been suggested, rather implausibly, that this belonged to a Roman copy of the original terracotta piece.[6]

Very little stone statuary survives from Samnium. In 1959 a damaged limestone head was discovered, or rather rediscovered, at

[1] The laurel wreath which it appears to be wearing suggests that it may be.

[2] The Triflisco head seems a unique example of a type of Samnite art. Napoli stresses the difficulty of finding comparisons to it, unless one takes refuge in 'confronti impossibili'. One such 'impossible comparison' might be with the head of a figure on a Nolan amphora, now in Manchester and attributed to the Berlin painter (R. M. Cook, *Greek Painted Pottery*, fig. 37 A): but the similarities, although startling at first glance, are essentially superficial.

[3] Pliny, *N.H.* 34. 34. He is confirmed by Sabellian Capua, where much terracotta has been found. There are many representations of the *kourotrophos* from the town's Hellenistic phase, some of them very gracefully composed despite their rustic Italian qualities.

[4] S. Mirone in *Aréthuse*, 1 (1923/24), 141–50, pls. xxii, xxiii. He proposes an Italo-Etruscan origin for it.

[5] Vetter, no. 158; cf. V. Pisani, *Lingue dell'Italia*, no. 38. If this statue was not made in Samnium, it may have got there as war loot. Such looting was common enough: cf. the probably apocryphal story in Ps. Plut. *Parall. Min.* 37, of a certain Fabius Fabricianus who purloined a statue of Aphrodite Nicephoros—from Samnium actually.

[6] I. Sgobbo in *Not. d. Scavi* (1930), p. 406; Vetter, no. 162. The dedication, interestingly enough, was made by a female member of the celebrated gens Magia, from which Velleius Paterculus derived his origin.

Pietrabbondante and is now housed in the museum at Chieti. As in the Triflisco head the eyes are fixed in a frontal stare, and the expression is striking. Crudely worked without grace, style or sophistication of any kind, the head looks primitive and is probably older than the third century. A third-century date might make it contemporary with another head, it too from Pietrabbondante (so it is said) but of a very different order, being a skilfully fashioned portrait in bronze (see Plates 9(*b*), 10(*a*)). Both heads in their different ways are examples of Italic realism; but the limestone one is 'popular' and in no sense 'official' and its simplicity contrasts sharply with the Hellenistic refinements of the bronze specimen.

Other stone sculpture is too worn or too late to reveal much about Samnite art.[1] The relief on the end face of the polygonal retaining wall of the theatre at Pietrabbondante is too poorly preserved to be certainly identifiable: presumably it is an Atlas. The two helmeted warriors in low relief on one side of a plinth in the museum at Isernia may well be Roman rather than Samnite: the great circular trumpets which they are blowing seem to be of Roman design.[2] Isernia can also boast of having yielded the celebrated low relief, now in Paris, of a traveller with a mule paying his bill at an inn for board, bed and *puella*. It is a genre scene of a sort to confirm what Horace has to say about the accommodating disposition of hotel maids in Samnium in Roman times.[3]

[1] The museum at Chieti contains some small stone pieces from Samnium: two statuettes of women and two of horsemen (one of the horsemen from Trivento, but the others apparently from Agnone). These, however, are very fragmentary. Also at Chieti is a stone centaur which used to stand in the public gardens at Boiano; but both its date and its provenance are uncertain. Stone sculpture from other parts of Sabellian Italy includes the third-century metope of local stone depicting the punishment of Ixion: it was found at Pompeii in 1953 and seems 'primitive' (G. M. A. Richter, *Ancient Italy*, pp. 30 f.). The head in high relief which once adorned the Porta Nolana at Pompeii (see Vetter, no. 14) must have resembled the still existing head of Hercules on the Porta di Boiano at Roman Saepinum. Far more interesting are the hundred and more tufa statues, many of them life-size, in the Museo Campano at Capua (A. Adriani, *Il Museo Campano: sculture in tufo*). They were all found in the Fondo Patturelli sanctuary on the eastern outskirts of Capua and are crudely carved representations of the *kourotrophos*, a woman clad in a long heavy *chiton* solidly seated on a *thronos* and holding one, two or even a dozen swaddled infants on her lap. They all look much alike regardless of age: some belong to pre-Sabellian times (H. Koch in *Mitt. des arch. Inst.: röm. Abt.* XXII (1907), 14), others to Roman (J. Heurgon, *Capoue préromaine*, pp. 334 f.).

[2] It has been suggested that they form part of a Samnite 'triumph': C. Drago in *Samnium*, VI (1933), 58. This is unconvincing: there is a popular and unofficial air about them.

[3] *CIL*, IX, 2689; Baumeister, *Denkmäler des klass. Altertums*, I, fig. 2373; T. Kleberg, *Hotels, restaurants et cabarets*, p. 154, fig. 7. Cf. Hor. *Sat.* I. 5. 82–5.

Objects in bronze from Samnium are more abundant than those in stone.[1] The earliest of them probably is the small statue of a Samnite warrior acquired by the Louvre in 1859.[2] It looks earlier than the Samnite warriors in fourth-century Campanian tomb-paintings, and the Louvre lists it as belonging to the fifth century. But like other pieces from Samnium it may be later than it looks.[3] The statuette is 11½ inches high and represents a soldier, or perhaps the god Mamers, standing in full armour. He wears the short-sleeved tunic (apparently of leather), the three-disk cuirass and the broad belt of the Samnites and greaves which cover both legs. The shield and lances he once carried are lost, and the helmet he wears lacks both the crest and the Italic twin feathers, although the groove and sockets for these are clearly discernible. The figure is treated with a hard simplicity. The shoulders are crudely attached, but in a way which intensifies the impression of strength; the big hands, bare feet and heavy thighs are offset by the narrow long waist; and the grim gaunt face has typical Italic features: a low forehead and large prominent eyes. The back is as arresting as the front. The harshness of line is very similar to that 'which long persists in the Peloponnese, especially in the inner districts', as seen for example in the bronze from Dodona now in Berlin.[4]

Among the later bronzes from Samnium pride of place belongs to the life-size head now in the Cabinet des Médailles of the Bibliothèque Nationale in Paris, formerly described as 'Tête d'un chef de guerre', from Pietrabbondante.[5] Recent investigation suggests that it more probably came from a village near Terventum[6] and there is no specific indication that it is the head of a soldier. It is 11 inches high. The heavy type of bronze, the treatment of the hair and of the harsh planes about the forehead and firmly closed mouth seem Italic. So does the general squareness of the head. But

[1] Bronze-casting was later in being developed (Pliny, *N.H.* 35. 153).

[2] It is said to have been found in Sicily. It could have been taken there by a South Italian mercenary. See Plate 11 (*a*).

[3] G. M. A. Richter, *Ancient Italy*, p. 5, implies that it is very early, even though 'its awkward pose, thickset proportions and primitive features have little in common with Greek archaic art'.

[4] J. D. Beazley in *Cambr. Anc. Hist.* IV, 593. See, too, Vol. of plates I, 360 c (= the Dodona bronze, which belongs to the sixth century and is much earlier than the Louvre warrior. Dodona is a region and an environment much like Samnium).

[5] See Plate 10 (*a*). There is no way of knowing whether this head was made in Samnium or imported there.

[6] G. Colonna in *Studi Etruschi*, XXV (1957), 567–9.

the execution of the piece owes much to Hellenistic techniques, in the carefully studied, sometimes excessive, particulars and in a general quality that is close to that of Hellenistic portraiture. Assuming that the third-century date assigned to it is correct, the 'Bovianum' head marks an exceptionally swift development of the cultural pace in Samnium, if only because of its presence among the Pentri at that time.[1]

Some late bronzes from the nineteenth-century excavations at Pietrabbondante, which were perhaps made by local artisans and which are now in the Musée du Cinquantenaire at Brussels, display varying combinations of Greek and Italic elements.[2] A horse, resembling the spirited breed of Campania, is a particularly nice *phaleratus*[3] with a delightfully realistic expression. A bare-headed, bare-legged and well-proportioned Italic warrior, clad in a very short tunic, moving jauntily forward, proclaims his origin by the grip of his left hand, which once held a lance: he, too, looks earlier than he is and the bronze is somewhat inexpertly cast.[4] The same is true of the statuette of a thick-necked, heavily clad peasant woman, whose crudely shaped right hand once held a *patera* in a gesture of worship. A privately owned four-inch statuette of a girl dressed in a long *chiton*, she too depicted, quite realistically, in an act of worship, is also worth mentioning: it comes from Frigento, near the famed Vallis Amsanctus, in Hirpinian country, but in style and workmanship reminds one of the Pietrabbondante pieces. They probably all belong to the second or first century, and are popular art of a perennial kind.[5]

One cannot, of course, be sure that the statuettes found in Samnium were actually made there. It is reasonable to suppose that some of them were imported, above all from Etruria, the one region of Italy where bronze was relatively plentiful in antiquity. Etruria undoubtedly mass-produced figurines and exported them in quan-

[1] The 'Bovianum' head has often been associated with the much-discussed 'Brutus' in the Capitoline Museum. But, as J. M. C. Toynbee has recently reminded us (in *J.R.S.* LV (1965), 285), some scholars think that the 'Brutus' might even be a Renaissance copy of a Greek work.

[2] They are depicted in S. Reinach, *Répertoire de la statuaire grecque et romaine*, II, p. 534, no. 1; II, p. 652, no. 11; III, p. 59, no. 4. See, too, G. Q. Giglioli in *Arch. Class.* IV (1952), 174–87, plates XL and XLI.

[3] That is, wearing a necklace of linked disks (military emblems?).

[4] He can be compared with the bronze statuette of a youth found near Allifae, which can be seen in the museum at Piedimonte d'Alife (*Not. d. Sc.* (1929), pp. 35 f.).

[5] G. Q. Giglioli in *Arch. Class.* IV (1952), pl. xliv.

tity.[1] But other places besides Etruria unquestionably manufactured such objects, Capua for instance, where the Cipii, a Sabellian family, were particularly prominent in bronze-making.[2] The popularity and profusion of small bronzes in Samnium suggest that it too produced them *en masse*; it may even have been the home of itinerant bronze casters.[3]

One bronze figurine, that was almost certainly locally made, is a two-faced Janus, which was found at Luceria.[4] Everything points to its being the work of the Oscan-speaking element in that Latin Colony: it is crudely cast, and the artisan, who evidently knew not Janus, seems to have tried without much success to copy the image of the divinity which appeared on Roman coins.

Of all the bronze idoletti in Samnium, however, the most common, appropriately enough, are warriors. They are late derivations from Greek work of the fifth and fourth centuries and represent some of them Mamers Promachos, but most of them Hercules. Local museums in the Abruzzi, at Campobasso, Sulmona and elsewhere, contain many specimens.[5] They are normally about six inches high and show the warrior wearing a crested helmet, with a spear or club in his right hand and a lion-skin or cloak over his bent left arm.[6] They have not been catalogued or classified properly, Fogolari's corpus of bronzes being far from complete.[7]

For painting we must look elsewhere than Samnium.

The frescoes that have been found in Sabellian tombs are briefly discussed in an appendix: see below, pp. 140–3.

The art of the vase-painter was apparently unknown. The old belief that red-figure ware was produced in quantity in Samnium, and specifically at Caudine Saticula, has now been exploded. The Saticulan pottery, bell craters mostly, is 'a myth. The vases found

[1] Pliny, *N.H.* 34. 34. It is said that one of the attractions of Volsinii for the Romans was its two thousand or more bronze statues.

[2] M. W. Frederiksen in *Pap. Brit. Sch. Rome*, XIV (1959), 109.

[3] The collection of bronzes at Paestum is evidence for schools of bronze-casters in Southern Italy.

[4] U. Scerrato in *Archeologia Classica*, VII (1955), 192 f. and pl. lxxix.

[5] Examples have been found at Barrea and Alfedena (L. Mariani in *Mon. Antichi*, X (1901), 260) and no fewer than five at Saepinum (*Not. d. Sc.* (1926), pp. 249 f.): the latter seem to be of Roman age however. See Plate 11 (*b*).

[6] The figure is usually full or three-quarters front, turning to the right. Sometimes it seems muscle-bound, but more often has very broad shoulders and elongated limbs.

[7] G. Fogolari in *Studi Etruschi*, XXI (1950/51) and succeeding issues.

there may all be assigned to other definite fabrics and many of them are Attic of the fourth century.'[1]

Despite repeated destruction at Roman and later hands remains of Samnite architecture still survive. Built to guard against invasion, the polygonal fortifications on the mountain heights of Samnium are its earliest considerable monuments. *Murus erant montes*, and no doubt the Samnites exploited the natural defences to the full; but they also strengthened them with their own man-made obstacles, constructed in the so-called 'Cyclopean' style.[2] Unquarried, or at best roughly quarried, limestone boulders of moderate size were placed one on top of the other without cement and kept in place by their own weight.[3]

Despite their limitations these walls may have served as prototypes for the more skilfully fashioned polygonals that mark the course of Roman expansion. Perhaps the Sabellians were responsible for spreading the use of polygonal construction in Italy. Of the many specimens that survive there the overwhelming majority are found in regions that either were peopled by, or had come under strong influence of, the speakers of Oscan or Oscan-type dialects.[4] It is rare, if not non-existent, in Northern Italy, in pre-Roman Etruria, and in Magna Graecia. The Romans also do not seem to have been

[1] A. D. Trendall, *Paestan Pottery*, p. 108. Pottery of quality from Sabellian Italy was made in Campania, at places like Abella and Cumae (J. Heurgon, *Capoue préromaine*, pp. 418 f.). Some of the vase-paintings provide a commentary on Sabellian life: they depict convivial symposia or Samnite warriors fully accoutred (see, for example, the vase from Caivano in *Corpus Vasorum Antiquorum*: Italia, fasc. 1 (= Museo Campano), 1935: pl. 18, nos. 2 and 3).

Paestum also provides a commentary on Sabellian activities with its 'superb series of farcical representations on the Phlyax vases' (J. D. Beazley in *Camb. Anc. Hist.* v, 444). These burlesque and parody the great heroic attitudes of epic and mythology: even the Etruscan masked demon reappears, no longer terrifying but merely ridiculous. These spontaneous creations were not without effect on the Atellane farces (see above, p. 120), but it is doubtful to what extent Sabellian craftsmen were responsible for them: the known phlyax potters all seem to be Greek (A. D. Trendall, *op. cit. passim*).

[2] Propertius 4. 4. 13. At Alfedena, Alife, Faicchio and elsewhere the walls may go back to the sixth century, or even the seventh.

[3] G. Lugli, *La Tecnica Edilizia Romana*, I, 100–3, classifies polygonals in four types according to their degree of sophistication. Style I ('Cyclopean') is frequently found in Samnium (Allifae, Aufidena, *Faicchio*, Saepinum); and so is Style II (Aesernia, *Pietrabbondante*, Calatia, *Castel di Sangro*, Trebula Balliensis). Style III is rare (the theatre at *Pietrabbondante* being the chief example). Style IV is not represented in Samnium.

[4] *Baselice, Campochiaro, Frosolone, Montefalcone* are some of the little-known places where polygonal remains exist. For some account of Samnite walls see A. Maiuri in *Not. d. Sc.* (1926), pp. 250 f. (Saepinum); (1928), pp. 450 f. (Allifae); (1929), pp. 207 f. (*Faicchio* and *Monte Acero*); (1930), pp. 214 f. (Trebula, *Castellone*).

familiar with it until they established close contacts with the Samnites: the 'Servian Wall', built before their earliest official dealings with Samnium, was in ashlar masonry (*opus quadratum*). Shortly after 354 the Romans were using polygonal construction and if they learned the method from the Samnites they promptly improved upon it to develop Lugli's 'third style', in which the faces of the blocks are dressed smooth, the joints carefully fitted together, and triangular stones used to fill the spaces between larger ones.[1]

The Samnites often built their 'Cyclopean' walls to barricade strategic mountain passes and the routes into Samnium, in somewhat the same way that the Phocians had blocked the defile at Thermopylae in early times.[2] The ruins of such fortifications are imposing evidence for the concerted efforts of the Samnite tribes. The great polygonal perimeters on Monte Acero and Monte Monaco, which were connected by a bridge over the River Titernus, at the southern end of the Matese massif, could not possibly have been built by one or two villages alone.[3]

Naturally the Samnites also protected their mountain settlements with 'Cyclopean' masonry, sometimes entire hill-tops being encircled with ring-walls, despite the immense amount of labour involved. Examples can be seen at Aufidena and many other sites.[4] That the settlements were founded and fortified with solemn formalities may well be doubted, even though the Samnites were not unfamiliar with the idea of a precisely defined boundary. Their sacred grove near Agnone seems to have had its precinct definitively marked; and the wording of the Cippus Abellanus suggests that the Sabellians of Campania may have been familiar with the notion of the ceremonial furrow.[5] In Campania, however, the Sabellians were bound to become acquainted with the *Etrusca disciplina*.[6] The

[1] The more sophisticated Roman polygonal walls, which were often backed by an *agger*, were intended to resist siege (as Hannibal discovered to his cost). They were used especially for the spectacular fortifications of the Latin and Citizen Colonies (Norba, Cosa, Pyrgi, etc.) which date from 338 (E. T. Salmon in *Phoenix*, VII (1953), 94 f.).

[2] Herodotus 7. 215.

[3] The polygonal substructure of the bridge survives: the original superstructure does not (probably it was of wood) (A. Maiuri in *Not. d. Sc.* (1929), pp. 211 f.).

[4] See A. De Nino, *Archeologia Leggendaria*, p. 35; Marion E. Blake, *Ancient Roman Construction in Italy*, I, 85 f.

[5] The word *uruvo* in the inscription seems to mean 'ceremonial furrow': cf. Oscan *urvat* (= 'surrounds' according to Festus, p. 514 L.) and Latin *urvum* (= 'tail of the plough' that made the ceremonial furrow). See Vetter, no. 1; E. Pulgram in *Amer. Journ. Philol.* LXXXI (1960), 25–9; M. G. Delfino, *Serta Eusebiana*, p. 50.

[6] Cf. Varro, *L.L.* 5. 143; Festus, p. 358 L. Etruscan *limitatio*, however, was more a method for subdividing fields than for planning towns.

ruder Samnites of the highlands had little contact with Etruscans and no notion of civic commonwealths. Their settlements were spontaneous affairs and they were fortified as necessity would seem to dictate. The vaguely trapezoidal shape of the enceinte at Samnite Saepinum (*Terravecchia*) suggests that it merely followed the contours of the hill on which it was perched,[1] and from this one may infer that Samnite settlements did not display an orderly, planned appearance. Probably they consisted of clusters of buildings crowded together, their outward aspect reflecting their haphazard growth. Without regular shape or plan they continued the tradition of the Bronze Age,[2] and Livy's picture of early Rome as a crowded irregular settlement could apply to any Samnite town.[3]

The ring walls might be both massive and lofty: at Saepinum they are ten feet thick and at Allifae thirty feet high. Yet Livy's repeated descriptions of Samnite *oppida* falling to the Romans without undue difficulty indicate that the walls were not impregnable.[4] Their very roughness and crudity may have helped assailants to scale them. For that matter they were not intended to withstand sieges. Normally built near the crest of a hill without towers or bastions or, presumably, battlements, they seem to have served principally as rallying points where the defenders could regroup. Like the Spartans, the Samnites put more trust in the arms of their men than in blocks of limestone.[5]

Usually there was more than one circuit. At Aufidena and on the acropolis at Trebula Balliensis there appear to have been three. At Saepinum there were two, and these were only about three and a half yards apart: Samnite Pompeii similarly had two, presumably coeval, curtains, in its case about six yards apart.[6]

The gates in the wall were usually more heavily fortified towards the left, so as to force the attackers to approach with their right, unshielded side towards the wall, in the manner recommended by Vitruvius.[7] Saepinum and Trebula each had three gates, the classical number for an Italic *urbs iusta*.[8]

[1] G. Colonna in *Archeologia Classica*, XIV (1962), 97.

[2] As seen in such settlements as Passo di Corvo (Apulia) or Promontorio del Milazzese and Isola di Salina (Lipari Islands).

[3] *Forma urbis occupatae magis quam divisae similis*: Livy 5. 55. 5. Cf. Verg. *Georg.* 2. 532: *hanc olim veteres vitam coluere Sabini.*

[4] See, for example, Livy 10. 44. 1.

[5] *Non enim muris magis se Samnites quam armis ac viris moenia tutabantur*: Livy 10. 45. 12.

[6] A. Maiuri in *Mon. Antichi*, XXXIII (1929), 265 f.

[7] Vitruvius 1. 5. [8] Servius, *ad Aen.* 1. 422; G. Lugli, *Tecnica Edilizia Romana*, I, 86.

The only site to give us even a vague idea of the lay-out of a typical Samnite town is Samnite Saepinum, which dates from 300 and earlier. Its partial excavation permits the following tentative conclusions.

Piazzas, where they existed, presumably were not square in the Greek manner, but either irregular or rectangular, the latter being the *consuetudo Italica* according to Vitruvius.[1] Roads meeting at right angles were not unknown in early times, but true axial symmetry (*symmetriarum rationes*) belongs to the days of Roman supremacy.[2] The section of Pompeii dating from the period of earliest Sabellian settlement was not town-planned in the regular sense of the word.[3] The neatly gridded town of *decumani* and narrower *cardines* that impresses all visitors dates from the later period when the Sabellians had learned about Hellenistic town planning from the Greeks of Campania.

We can say little about Samnite public buildings. No certainly identified specimen of a Samnite council chamber or other government structure survives.[4] Amphitheatres and baths belong to the Roman period, and we do not know where the Samnites staged their gladiatorial games in earlier days.[5] It is safe to assume that their buildings were made of simple local materials, not of costly imported marble and the like, and lacked monumentality. Perhaps their principal public edifices were temples and theatres, and of these fortunately specimens do survive.

From the third century on, if not earlier, roofed temples began to supplement and supplant the groves and open-air precincts as Samnite places of worship. Often situated in carefully cleared spaces, they stood on high *podia* approached by a flight of steps, with a deep vestibule at the front and none at the rear end. The broad *cella* was invariably single, not tripartite as so often in Etruria and Latium. The wooden superstructure was protected against the weather with fictile revetments and the tiled saddle-roof, adorned with antefixes and acroteria, overhung the wall by a wide margin.

Examples of temple *podia* still exist in Samnium proper. Remains

[1] Vitruvius 5. 1. 1, 7; 5. 11. 1; 6. 7. 1.

[2] Vitruvius 6. 3. 11; A. Boethius, *Golden House of Nero*, p. 36.

[3] M. Rostovtzeff, *History of the Ancient World*, II, 55.

[4] Livy 7. 31. 11 thought that the Samnites had a *curia*.

[5] They were held alfresco, to judge from the Sabellian tomb-paintings.

have been unearthed at several places: at Quadri, at Schiavi d'Abruzzo, at S. Giovanni in Galdo, and above all at Pietrabbondante. In actual fact at the last-named place excavation has lately laid bare a sacred precinct on the eastern slope of Monte Caraceno with buildings symmetrically arranged in terraces: in addition to the well-known theatre and small temple another and larger temple now stands revealed.[1]

These structures are not without some ornate features: a Samnite *podium*, for instance, was likely to have both a moulded base and a decorative cornice. Such departures from simplicity were the result of Hellenistic influence which had reached Samnium from Campania: for architectural inspiration, as for the art of writing, the Samnites looked thither rather than to Latium. Thus, the larger temple at Pietrabbondante reminds one of the altar in the Fondo Patturelli at Capua, while the smaller temple is suggestive of the tufa monuments of 'Samnite' (= second-century) Pompeii, with which indeed it might well be contemporary.

This is not to say that influences from Latium failed to penetrate Samnium. There were, after all, Latin Colonies established there. At Isernia one can still see incorporated in the cathedral the *podium* of a temple built, presumably in the third century, by the Latin Colony of Aesernia. The moulding on this *podium* is of the type to be seen on Altars XI and XII in the recently discovered sanctuary at Lavinium.[2]

At least some Samnite temples lay on an east–west axis, but not enough remains above the *podium* of any of them to make confident reconstruction of a complete specimen possible.[3] The small temple at Pietrabbondante[4] seems to have had a *cella* and narrow *prodomos*,

[1] G. De Petra, *Giorn. Scav. Pomp.*, N.S., II, 117 f.; R. Delbrück in *Mitteilungen des arch. Inst.: röm. Abteil.* XVIII (1903), 154–8; A. Maiuri in *Not. d. Sc.* (1913), p. 456; A. La Regina in *Ulisse*, IX (1966), 122 f. For the conjunction of temple with theatre (as for example at Gabii), see J. A. Hanson, *Roman Theater-Temples* (Princeton, 1959), p. 30.

[2] F. Castagnoli in *Bull. Comunale*, LXXVII (1959/60), 145 f. See Plate 8.

[3] The excavators of 1857/58 found what seemed to be fragments of the entablature near the small temple at Pietrabbondante. They were adorned with triglyphs and lions' heads (M. Ruggiero, *Scavi di Antichità nelle Province di Terraferma dal 1743 al 1876*, pp. 643 f.). Some unfluted column drums nearby may not have belonged to the temple, although unfluted columns (with four-faced Ionic capitals) are known from elsewhere in Samnium (I. Sgobbo in *Not. d. Sc.* (1930), p. 408).

[4] Its original excavators thought that it was dedicated to Mars, but of this there is no proof. Nor does the fact that at Rome Apollo had a temple next to a theatre (Livy 40. 51. 3; cf. *Res Gestae Divi Augusti*, IV, 22; *CIL*, I², pp. 215, 252) mean that the shrine of Pietrabbondante belonged to him. The original excavators thought that they had found

but no portico (unless, as has been suggested,[1] one was subsequently added).

Finds at Ielsi, Alvignano (= *Cubulteria*) and elsewhere in Samnium, as well as at Cumae and Capua (Mons Tifata, Fondo Patturelli), show that Sabellian temples of the fourth and third centuries had the terracotta revetments normal to Italic sanctuaries.[2] The development of terracotta manufacture in Campania, where Capua had been most prominent in the sixth and fifth centuries for its abundant production, richness and variety of style, suffered an interruption with the coming of the Sabellians.[3] But the decorative art revived to some extent towards the end of the fourth century and later in the period corresponding to the Hellenistic phase at Capua and the period to which the terracotta revetments of Sabellian temples belong.[4] In the early, archaic phase the antefixes had blossomed with delightful varieties of heads wreathed in semicircles of leaves and startling apotropaic Gorgons. These same motives were continued in the Hellenistic phase, even though less expressively, together with palmettes and much else of the older repertory. Fragments of these architectonic ornaments can be seen in the museums at Capua, Campobasso and Piedimonte d'Alife.

The Hellenization of the architecture of Samnium which is suggested by the alleged alterations to the Italic temple at Pietrabbondante can also be seen in the remains of the theatre which stands some 55 metres to the south of it. The theatre has a number of features similar to those found in the two theatres at Pompeii: indeed these latter can be better interpreted in the light of the uncomplicated example from Pietrabbondante, which seems to be entirely free of later additions and alterations. The *cavea*, built into the slope of the hillside, is supported by well-joined polygonal masonry whose blocks have been cut and smoothed with

traces of the base that supported the cult image alongside the north wall, it being placed there, according to them, to enable the worshipper to face it and simultaneously see the east (= the rising sun): cf. Vitruv. 4. 5. 1 and Serv. *ad Aen.* 12. 172. There is, however, no trace of such a statue base now, although there is masonry along the north wall which looks like material from the theatre strewn at random (cf. R. Delbrück, *loc. cit.* above, p. 137, n. 1).

[1] A. Maiuri, *loc. cit.* above, p. 137, n. 1.

[2] Such temples must have presented a gay appearance (G. De Sanctis, *Storia dei Romani*, I, 421). But there is no evidence for Samnite acroteria as magnificent as the Etruscan ones.

[3] J. Heurgon, *Capoue préromaine*, p. 361.

[4] This is true also at Venafrum (G. Verrecchia in *Samnium*, XXXIII (1960), 41).

care.[1] Within this autochthonous framework the theatre is Hellenistic in plan and detail. The three front rows form a beautiful semicircle to which rounded flights of steps from each side of the *orchestra* give easy access. Above these first three rows the *diazoma* is paved with well-cut slabs of limestone, and the upper rows of the *cavea* (two of which survive)[2] are divided into five *cunei* by six short flights of steps. The *parodoi* had no *tribunalia* over them and there was no *crypta*. The elegant and well-preserved seats of the three front rows are of polished stone with shaped, slightly inclined backs: they were the *proedria* for *meddices* and similar dignitaries. On the end faces of the walls of the *parodoi* there are figures in relief (Atlases).[3] The straight *proskenion* wall has traces of engaged columns, between which light, movable panels must have been used, as in other Hellenistic stage settings.

The large theatre at Pompeii, first built at the end of the third century, before it acquired later Roman additions, had a plan very similar to this one at Pietrabbondante, being equally without a *crypta* or *tribunalia* over the *parodoi* and with the same Hellenistic *proskenion*. Both theatres are older, perhaps much older, than the earliest stone theatre in Rome.[4] The later, small theatre at Pompeii, the so-called Odeon, also resembles the one at Pietrabbondante: it too has what appear to be Atlases at the end of the *parodoi* and has small semicircular stairs giving access to the front rows of the *cavea*. In one notable respect Pietrabbondante differed from, and had the advantage over, Pompeii: its theatre was in bright, hard limestone instead of dull tufa.

Any attempt to reconstruct the *scaena* at Pietrabbondante is out of the question, but it is natural to envisage it as having the same neat elegance as the rows of the *proedria*. And beyond it is the magnificent landscape. Built at well over 3,000 feet the theatre is the loftiest in Italy. It throws an unusually bright light on what must

[1] One reached the *cavea* at Pietrabbondante from the large temple on the terrace above it by means of an opening through the outer retaining wall.

[2] Perhaps there were never more than two. Cf. Juvenal 3. 172 f.: *ipsa dierum festorum herboso colitur si quando theatro*.

[3] The reliefs are 'old acquaintances from Greece and Sicily' according to A. Maiuri, *Passeggiate Campane*, p. 385.

[4] Lugli's 'last century B.C.' as the date for the Pietrabbondante theatre (*Tecnica Edil. Romana*, II, pl. XXIII, 4) seems late: G. Bloch–J. Carpopino, *Hist. rom.*^{3}, II, I, 375, assign it to the mid-second century; and R. Delbrück, *op. cit.* (above, p. 137, n. 1), p. 158, regards it as slightly older than the small theatre at Pompeii.

have been the state of civilization among the Samnites during the last days of their 'independence'. It and the axially aligned, adjoining temples are a complex of buildings that together must have made up a sanctuary. Evidently for the Samnites, as for other Italic peoples, theatrical performances could have a religious aspect.

Samnite houses inevitably reflected Samnite poverty.[1] Livy suggests that they were only too likely to be very flimsy.[2] The masses must have lived in simple, crude, presumably one-roomed affairs, for which the Latin words *mapalia* or *tuguria* would probably be appropriate. The Aufidena graves testify to the austerity of Samnite dwellings. The coarse and unpretentious pottery and eating utensils found in them came from very simple cottages. It seems probable that many Samnite houses were of a temporary, makeshift character suited to the needs of herdsmen who moved their quarters along with their flocks. Even the houses of Samnite notables could have contained but few amenities.[3] They are not likely to have been superior to those of their Roman opposite numbers, which as late as the early second century, to judge from the little we know about them, afforded only the barest minimum of comfort.

Appendix: Note on the Sabellian tomb-paintings

The Sabellian tomb-paintings are the most remarkable manifestation of art among the Oscan-speaking peoples.[4] They have not been described above since they have not been found in Samnium itself except for the few that have been unearthed at Allifae, and these might belong to the time when that town was not technically part of Samnium. A brief discussion of them is necessary, however, since their genre scenes shed light on Samnite life and character.

[1] The Oscan word for house (*triíbom*: cf. Latin *trabem*, 'beam') suggests that Samnite houses were made of wood, which is what one would have expected in a peasant society (E. Vetter in *Glotta*, XXIX (1942), 215). There is archaeological confirmation of this in Sabellian Campania (F. von Duhn, *Italische Gräberkunde*, I, 541 f.).

[2] Livy 10. 44. 1. Some of the houses in Sabellian Campania were, of course, anything but flimsy: the Houses of the Faun, of Pansa and of Sallust at Pompeii, like the Samnite House at Herculaneum, were elegant and even elaborate. But although they belong to the 'Samnite Period' (= second century), they are not relevant for Samnium. The House of the Surgeon at Pompeii may be more revealing. It was originally built in the fourth or third century, and its rectangular plan and simple *atrium* may reflect the sobriety of contemporary Samnite well-to-do houses at places such as Bovianum and Malventum. See, too, E. Gjerstad in *Gnomon*, XXVI (1954), 135 f.

[3] *nihil splendidum, nihil ornatum fuit praeter ipsos* (Cic. *Paradoxa*, 5. 2. 38).

[4] They can be seen in the museums at Naples and Paestum. Those formerly housed in the Museo Campano at Capua were destroyed during World War II.

On reaching Campania the Sabellians discovered the world of Greek and Etruscan civilization and adopted the fashion of the frescoed Etruscan chamber tombs.[1] Their paintings have been found not only in Campania proper, at Capua, Cumae and Abella, but also on its outskirts, at Allifae in Samnium and at Paestum and Albanella in Lucania.

The themes are largely Greek, of the type found on Greek vases, the technique Etruscan.[2] The scenes are painted on a whitish coat of plaster applied to the slabs of porous local stone, tufa or travertine, with which the tomb is lined. The lower part of the walls is a painted dado, often bordered on its upper edge with a spiral hook pattern.[3] The actual scenes are above this dado, and another border, of meanders and rosettes (or of mere straight lines with sometimes a row of olive leaves between them), forms a cornice at the top of the wall. Painted Ionic columns, symbolic of the tomb, often separate one scene from the next and the shorter walls sometimes display a picture of the deceased surmounted by a kind of triangular gable which is decorated with a palmette or garland and pomegranates.

The earliest of these paintings, variously assigned to the end of the fifth or the beginning of the fourth century, were found at Paestum in the Tomb of the Warrior and are now in the Naples Museum.[4] On one of the long walls two mounted horsemen face each other on either side of the much damaged figure of a cupbearer. On the succeeding short wall there is a funerary table laden with great vases and a pomegranate, a still life suggestive of ritual. The other long wall shows a young girl offering a cup to warriors, two of whom advance towards her on foot: these wear the helmet with aigrettes, the tunic, belt and cuirass of the Samnites. The first warrior carries a staff with the spoils of an enemy, which also look Samnite; the second grasps an upright lance with his left hand and rests the other on a standing oval shield. Behind him there is a third warrior who is mounted and followed by a servant on foot. The design of these figures is neat and sure; they are well-spaced in a clear and coherent sequence. The Greek element, perhaps a Greek hand, are manifest.[5] The

[1] There is, however, only one Etruscan tomb-painting from Campania which antedates the arrival of the Sabellians there: it was found at Capua. See P. J. Riis, *An Introduction to Etruscan Art*, plate 18, no. 26.

[2] The technique, however, also owes something to the Greeks, especially in the colouring (P. C. Sestieri in *Riv. Istit. Arch. e Storia dell'Arte*, V/VI (1956/57), 100).

[3] The spiral hook border was a universal fashion: it appears in the Tomb of the Shields at Tarquinii, in the Bellerophon mosaic at Olynthus and almost everywhere in Campania and Lucania.

[4] It is reproduced in part in A. Maiuri, *Roman Painting*, p. 16, and in M. A. Napoli, *Pittura Antica in Italia*, p. 9.

[5] The third-century fresco from the Esquiline now in the Capitoline Museum, which depicts scenes from the Samnite (?) wars in superimposed tiers, is sometimes compared with this painting from Paestum. But the latter, apart from its greater artistic merit, derives from Attic prototypes, whereas the Esquiline fragment shows the influence of the Hellenistic narrative style.

details of Samnite armour would have contented Livy. Even more impressive in this last regard, however, was the painting, no longer extant, of the horseman from Capua, resplendent in full panoply.[1]

Gradually the native element asserts itself, far more successfully than in the Etruscan tomb-paintings according to Weege,[2] even though the repertory of Etruria is much more rich and varied.

By the end of the fourth century the Sabellian newcomers have developed their own style and their paintings have begun to acquire a somewhat rustic and lively quality. In those from Paestum a stock theme is the chariot race, in which the most successfully done of all the components are often the horses, the famous local breed (*Campanus sonipes*), drawn with a racy freedom even in paintings which are otherwise inferior. Another very recurrent theme is the gladiatorial combat, an excellent example of it being in the tomb Laghetto X, discovered in 1954. These themes become increasingly stereotyped and inferior.[3]

From Albanella, near Paestum, comes an important slab belonging to a fourth-century tomb. On it a charming, graceful girl carries offertory vases. The dark red dress on the light background recalls the Athenian lekythoi of a century earlier, but the figure, successfully grown to a larger size, looks South Italian.[4]

The fresco of the matron and her attendant from Cumae, now in the Naples Museum, is the best example of the popular style prevailing in Campania.[5] The robust matron, seated on a *thronos*, glances complacently at herself in a mirror: her large neck and face are drawn with continuous lines worthy of Picasso. She looks like a local type and can fairly be described not as Greek, but as 'Osco-Samnite'. A girl, richly dressed[6] like her mistress in a red and white *chiton*, stands beside her with a *calathos* and a small scent-jar in her hands. As in other paintings, red pomegranates float about, decorative symbols of resurrection from the world of the dead. But it is the charms of the present that the painting extols, of florid, third-century Campania. The matron's robe, although its decorative patterns have been long familiar in the Greek world, has taken on an Oscan aspect and exhibits the particular, striking quality

[1] See Plate 10(*b*).

[2] F. Weege in *Jahrb. deutsch. arch. Inst.* XXIV (1909), 131. His dating for the paintings still seems valid, but his classification of their themes is over-rigid: it overlooks the ambiguity that pervades some of the scenes where the worlds of the living and the dead continuously merge into one another, something that may be connected with the Orphic beliefs that were so prevalent in Campania (see C. Albizzati in *Diss. della Pont. Accad.*, ser. 2, XIV (1920), 177–90; J. Heurgon, *Capoue préromaine*, pp. 426 f.).

[3] A scene from the Laghetto X tomb is conveniently reproduced in Napoli, *op. cit.* (above, p. 141, n. 4), p. 10. For the standardization of the chariot-racing and gladiatorial themes see Sestieri, *op. cit.* (above, p. 141, n. 2), p. 98.

[4] She is reproduced in Maiuri, *op. cit.* (above, p. 141, n. 4), p. 19.

[5] Reproduced in Maiuri, *op. cit.* p. 22.

[6] Cf. the *versicolores* of Livy 9. 40. 3 and the gay colours of Plautus, *Pseud.* 145 f.

of a national costume. Despite Greek detail, the classical prototypes are far removed from this fresco and there is no attempt to imitate them. The picture is a local scene described in the vernacular of the region.[1]

(*g*) RELIGION

For information about Samnite religion we depend on what few items appear incidentally in ancient authors, on what is revealed by the Oscan inscriptions,[2] and on what can be inferred by analogy from Italic practices in general.

In the Latin authors an incidental mention is more trustworthy than a passage written consciously for effect. The inscriptions can almost invariably be relied upon. The ones known as *Iovilae* supply much interesting information about the Sabellian calendar, festivals, sacrifices and official nature of the cults. But they all come from a sanctuary at Capua that goes back to pre-Sabellian times, and presumably reflect non-Sabellian contamination.[3] In fact, most Oscan inscriptions belong to the period when the native Samnite civilization had been long exposed to Greek, Etruscan and Roman influences. Fortunately one of them, the Agnone tablet, deals with Samnite cults and it happens to be not only the longest, but probably also the oldest, inscription from Samnium proper. Its value can hardly be overestimated, not least because it strengthens the impression left by the *Iovilae*.

To the literary and epigraphical material one can add what is suggested by a study of, and comparison with, the beliefs and cults of other Italic peoples, among whom there undoubtedly was a community of religious ideas.[4] There were, however, also differences, even between the various Sabellian peoples according to Strabo.[5] Some cults which were of great local importance, such as those of Vulcan, Janus and Saturn at Rome, were not widely spread

[1] Some scholars see in the robust matron from Cumae a forerunner of the principal figure in the Dionysiac fresco at the Villa dei Misteri (A. Maiuri, *op. cit.* pp. 23, 52; cf. E. Strong in *Camb. Anc. Hist.* IX, 823, and Vol. of plates IV, 76*b*). Apart, however, from superficial coincidences, there is no essential resemblance between the neo-classical Domina from Pompeii and the Sabellian Matrona from Cumae.

[2] Most of them from Capua and some of them earlier than 211, when Capua ceased to be Oscan-speaking (officially at least).

[3] J. Heurgon, *Etude sur les inscriptions osques de Capoue dites Iúvilas* (Paris, 1942). The alleged *Iovila* from Cumae is not a *Iovila* at all.

[4] K. Latte, *Römische Religionsgeschichte*, p. 4; S. Mazzarino, *Dalla Monarchia allo Stato Repubblicano*, pp. 76 f.

[5] 6. 1. 2, p. 254.

elsewhere.[1] Nevertheless general Italic similarities make analogies possible and illuminating.

It was the Etruscans, not the Samnites, that Livy described as *gens ante omnes alias eo magis dedita religionibus quod excellerent arte colendi eas*.[2] Yet religion played a role of some consequence in the affairs of the Samnites also. For them all life and action was associated with and the result of divine action. Just as fear of the gods promoted the cohesion of the Roman state,[3] so too religion was one of the bonds which held the Samnite League together. It would be wide of the mark to suggest that all Samnites everywhere subscribed to the same body of doctrine, but it is evident that the Samnite tribes had some *sacra* in common.[4] During the Samnite Wars they are described as enrolling whole armies with binding rituals. Another point that stresses their deep sense of religion is their evident respect for the religious practices and beliefs of the peoples they conquered, at Cumae for instance.[5] Note, too, that, after large-scale Samnite immigration into Fregellae, a cult centre in that Latin Colony acquired such fame that it was permitted to survive the Roman destruction of the town in 125.[6]

In their attitude towards the supernatural they no doubt resembled their putative ancestors, the Sabines, who according to Cato were descended from the god Sabus[7] and were so renowned for their scrupulous religious observances that their name was derived, significantly even though fancifully, from the Greek verb 'to worship'.[8] The Sabines were the religious folk *par excellence*. According to Varro,[9] it was from them that the Romans obtained many of their divinities,

[1] Although Latin Colonies might be instrumental in spreading the cults of these deities into Samnium: coins show that Vulcanus was worshipped at Aesernia, and a statuette of Janus has been found at Luceria. If Vulcan really was the god of earthquake, one might have expected his worship to be widespread in Samnium, the land of seismic disturbances. Saturn seems to have been of Etruscan origin.

[2] 5. 1. 6. Yet the real *contemptor divom* in Vergil's *Aeneid* is an Etruscan (Mezentius).

[3] According, at any rate, to Polybius 6. 56. 7.

[4] The Sabellic League, composed of their cousins the Marsi, Marrucini, Paeligni and Vestini, had *sacra* in common in the third century (see M. Hofmann in *R.E.* XVIII (1942), s.v. 'Paeligni', col. 2246). One thinks, too, of the Latin-speaking peoples.

[5] Greek cults persisted at Cumae for centuries after the Sabellians had become masters of the place: Strabo 5. 4. 4, p. 243.

[6] Strabo 5. 3. 10, p. 237 (cf. pp. 233, 238).

[7] Dion. Hal. 2. 49. 2; cf. Sil. Ital. 8. 422 f.; Serv. *ad Aen.* 8. 638.

[8] Festus, p. 456 L.; cf. Pliny, *N.H.* 3. 108.

[9] *L.L.* 5. 73.

including the Di Novensides, whatever they were;[1] and traditionally it was a Sabine, King Numa, who fashioned the religion of early Rome. No doubt Varro[2] has exaggerated the number of gods supplied to the Romans by his ancestors.[3] Even so, the Sabines' reputation for *pietas* shows that their influence on Roman religious development could hardly have been negligible.

The ancient writers do not reveal any religious differences between Samnites and Sabines, presumably because there were no differences to record: the argument from silence here seems valid. Their name suggests that the Samnites, too, were devoted to Sabus, and, like the Sabines, they were greatly concerned to win divine favour.[4] The Sacred Spring testifies to the seriousness with which they discharged religious obligations. For a pastoral and agricultural people to dedicate everything born in a certain spring to a god is an extreme act of dedication, and, even if we assume that they sometimes resorted to casuistry to lessen the impact of the incredible sacrifice (as the Romans evidently did on the only recorded occasion when they celebrated a *Ver Sacrum*),[5] the great Sabellian expansion suggests that, with them, the Sacred Spring was certainly not just a mere formality in which they did little more than make a token offering.

The Sabine influence on Roman cults implies similarity between the latter and those of the Samnites. In any case the affinity had older and deeper roots. All the Italic peoples had certain religious beliefs in common. Livy undoubtedly thought that this was so: he represents the Romans as celebrating a Sacred Spring[6] and the Samnites as having fetials.[7] Nor is this just an instance of Livy in the manner of Plautus attributing Roman customs to a non-Roman

[1] No doubt they are the same as the Di Novensiles of Livy 8. 9. 6 (even though there is no absolute proof that Latin *novensiles* = Sabine *novensides*, a form epigraphically attested from the Marsic region (Vetter, no. 225)).

[2] The same is true no doubt also of Cato, another eminent Sabine.

[3] *L.L.* 5. 66. He identifies Dius Fidius, for example, with Sabine Semo Sancus. Yet Dius Fidius may have been a purely Roman god who was exported to other Italic peoples (Jupiter appears as Fisos or Fisovios in Umbria: *Tab. Iguv.* Ia15; VIb15). See J. Collart, *Varron grammairien latin*, pp. 229–43. Varro automatically regarded any cult that was fostered on the Quirinal (the hill with Sabine associations) as Sabine: note, for example, his remarks on the worship of Salus: *L.L.* 5. 74.

[4] Livy 8. 39. 10.

[5] For the tricks to which the Romans resorted on this occasion, see A. D. Nock in *Harv. Theol. Rev.* XXXII (1939), 83–96; J. Heurgon in *Latomus*, XXVI (1957), 40–50.

[6] Livy 22. 10; Festus, p. 519 L., explicitly says that the Sacred Spring was an Italic custom. The Etruscans are said to have known the practice (Serv. *ad Aen.* 7. 697). Was it originally Sabellian?

[7] Livy 8. 39. 4; cf. 9. 1–12; cf. Dion. Hal. 15. 7. 6; App. *Samn.* 4. 1.

people in order to enliven his picture of them, since a fetial seems to be represented on some oath-scene coins of the insurgents in the Social War. In fact the peoples of Italy, including the Samnites, took fetials for granted:[1] the Romans did not have to concern themselves with possible modifications of their fetial practices until they clashed with extra-Italian peoples in the third century.[2]

Livy also represents the Lex Sacrata, which in one of its aspects stipulated that whoever violated it might be 'devoted' to some deity, possibly together with his family and property, as common to both Romans and Samnites, and to other Italians as well. Altheim, indeed, insists that it originated with the Sabellians and reached the Romans from them.[3] More probably it was an idea that was widespread throughout early Italy, at any rate in the primitive form of it which bound a group of men together for a military or semi-military undertaking:[4] the Etruscans knew it and so did the Ligurians.[5]

Devotio is another example. It was not an idea 'almost peculiar to the Romans'.[6] Livy indeed had to explain it at some length to his Roman readers.[7] It was an Italic institution.[8] It is significant that any Roman seeking to consummate it had to invoke the Di Novensides, as well as the great gods of Rome. It is true that we are nowhere explicitly told that the Samnites ever resorted to *devotio*; but at least Papirius Cursor in the pages of Livy describes the soldiery of their

[1] They were popularly, even if erroneously, believed to have been invented by the Aequi (Livy 1. 32. 5).

[2] Serv. Dan. *ad Aen.* 9. 52; cf. Ovid, *Fasti*, 6. 205 f.; Walbank–McDonald in *J.R.S.* XXVII (1937), 193.

[3] See his *Lex Sacrata* 11 f., where the relevant ancient literature is cited. The Samnites must have passed a *lex sacrata* when they formed their 'Linen Legion'. Livy (10. 38. 3–13) does not use the expression on that occasion, but Pliny (*N.H.* 34. 43) does, and even Livy (10. 38. 12) mentions the *sacrata nobilitas*. For the Roman *lex sacrata*, see Livy 7. 41. 4 (= 342); and, for one of a different type in the late Republic, see Cic. *pro Sest.* 7. 16; cf. K. von Fritz, *Studies Presented to D. M. Robinson*, II (1953), 897.

[4] G. Niccolini in *Historia*, II (1928), 4; K. Latte in *Gött. gelehrte Nachrichten*, I (1934), 69 and in *Studies Presented to D. M. Robinson*, II (1953), 897.

[5] Livy 9. 39. 5; 36. 38. 1. Livy (4. 26. 3) also refers to a *lex sacrata* among the Aequi and Volsci in 431. He clearly regarded the Sabellian capture of Capua in 423 as an occasion when a Lex Sacrata was invoked (Livy 10. 38. 6; cf. 4. 44. 12; Diod. 12. 76. 4; Strabo 5. 4. 4, p. 243).

[6] The description of it given by W. Warde Fowler, *Religious Experience of the Roman People*, p. 206.

[7] 8. 10. 11–14. This, however, may not be very significant: by Livy's day many archaic practices needed explanation, especially as the Augustan regime encouraged their revival. Thus Livy (4. 20. 5–11) similarly explained the *spolia opima*.

[8] A. Bouché-Leclercq in Daremberg–Saglio, II, 114, 117. Dio, fr. 40. 38 (= Zon. 8. 5), suggests that in cases of *devotio* the enemy were, so to speak, in the know.

Linen Legion as *devotus*.[1] Incidentally the story of Codrus suggests that the practice was also known outside of Italy.[2]

Polylatry is another feature of Samnite religion that stamps it as Italic. The Samnites, like other Italians, used the same spot for the simultaneous worship of two or more gods. Their gods were not isolated, so to speak, in the privacy of their individual temples as were those of the Greeks. Nor were numerous divinities housed in one place simply because they all discharged the same functions. On the contrary, Italic gods were highly specialized.[3] The minutely diversified activities of Roman gods were a subject of mockery for St Augustine. He could have been equally satirical at the expense of the Samnites, as the Agnone tablet shows.

No less Italic was the kourotrophic aspect of Samnite religion. Admittedly it was the Campani and their predecessors who were responsible for the statues of a mothering goddess with swaddled infants on her lap, found in such abundance at Fondo Patturelli on the eastern outskirts of Capua. But Amma and a divinity that seems to be Mater Matuta who were worshipped at Agnone prove that Samnium too had its *kourotrophoi*. The mothering goddess may not be nursing the infants.[4] She may be protecting them from, or curing them of, illness, since amongst the Italic peoples religion also had a therapeutic role to play, at the popular level anyway. Throughout early Italy, including Samnium, there were local shrines where devotees made anatomical dedications in terracotta in the hope of miraculous cures, usually from goddesses. The very un-Greek habit of fashioning models of the afflicted parts of the body in terracotta and dedicating them was very widespread;[5] and votive deposits of this kind have been found in Samnium.

Obviously the primitive religion of the Samnites did not differ markedly from that of other Italic peoples; and it may be con-

[1] Livy 10. 39. 16; and cf. G. Devoto, *Gli Antichi Italici*², p. 283.

[2] L. A. Holland in *Amer. Journ. Arch.* LX (1956), 243–7, and A. Boethius in *Eranos*, LIV (1956), 202–10 make the interesting suggestion that the Warrior of Capestrano, now at Chieti, represents an Italic soldier who was devoted but survived (see Livy 8. 10. 11–14). Fragments of a female statue found nearby tell against the theory.

[3] See K. Latte in *Archiv für Religionswissenschaft*, XXIV (1926/7), 244–58.

[4] Evidence from Chianciano suggests that she may be Mater Matuta, 'a fostering goddess of children, born or coming to birth': Maule-Smith, *Votive Religion at Caere*, p. 86.

[5] Greek medicine was decidedly more scientific than this. For some account of votive therapeutic terracottas in Samnium, see A. Rocco in *Samnium*, XXIV (1951), 133–6: he finds them crude, but with an expressive vivacity.

jectured that the whole Roman conception of *ius gentium* with its religious overtones largely evolved out of a stock of ideas and customs which were not the monopoly of any one single people of early Italy, but were held in common by them all. The ultimate kinship of the various Italic peoples will account for this basic similarity in their religions.[1]

It is evident that several strands were intertwined in the religion of the Samnites.[2] The 'Mediterranean' elements underlying the Indo-European and later Greek and Etruscan influences are only a few of the ingredients of Samnite religion. It is compounded of animism, with its accessories of fetishism and magic, of anthropomorphism and personification of abstractions. The animal pathfinder of a *Ver Sacrum* even suggests a possible trace of theriomorphism.[3]

It might seem reasonable to argue that there was a regular progression of ideas in the course of which an animistic conception of vague and shadowy spirits ultimately gave way to an anthropomorphic notion of firm and definite deities.[4] Dionysius of Halicarnassus suggests that something of the sort occurred on the Capitoline Hill at Rome and Tacitus' comment on the Germans will spring to mind: *ceterum nec cohibere parietibus deos neque in ullam humani oris speciem assimulare...arbitrantur.*[5] But, while neat and to outward seeming logical, such a tidy development is mostly imaginary. From their earliest days the Samnites had clearly defined gods as well as half-gods and *numina*, but these latter did not invariably antedate the former. The exact degree of anthropomorphism in their religion, before Greek and other influences permeated it, cannot be deter-

[1] See the remarks of A. Boethius, *The Golden House of Nero*, p. 23.

[2] A. von Blumenthal in *Die Welt als Geschichte*, II (1936), 20.

[3] In Italy, Faunus looks like a theriomorphic relic. See, too, A. Stenico in *Athenaeum*, XXV (1947), 55–79; and also J. Heurgon on the 'Mediterranean rat-god' in *Nouvelle Klio*, III (1959), 105–9. Totemism cannot be proved for peninsular Italy (F. Altheim, 'Italia', in *Studi e Materiali di Storia delle Religioni*, X (1934), 125–55), although there are scholars who regard the animal path-finder as a totem (G. De Sanctis, *Storia dei Romani*, IV, 2, 220). The wolf priests amongst the Romans and Sabines (*Luperci*, Pliny, *N.H.* 7. 19) need not imply theriomorphism (or were they goat priests? See M. Durante in *Par. del Pass.* XIII (1958), 412–17).

[4] It is an anthropological commonplace that in primitive societies cults and festivals, essentially apotropaic in character, are established long before the idea of a god is developed. But as M. P. Nilsson points out, in *Harv. Theol. Rev.* XLII (1949), 73, the historical evidence shows that animism does not necessarily precede deism.

[5] Dion. Hal. 3. 69. 4; Tac. *Germ.* 9. 4.

mined; unquestionably there was always some. Belief in specific individual gods is not incompatible with an animistic attitude.[1]

The Samnites, as an agrarian Italic people, visualized their world as filled with mysterious powers or spirits of whom they stood in nervous awe and with whom it was essential to establish right relations. These *numina* were not necessarily genderless and kinless,[2] although the conception of some of them was pretty vague. They may not have been envisaged in human form; their name, number and sex sometimes seem uncertain.[3] They were thought to dwell in particular localities or to exercise certain functional powers: indeed, in so far as they were gods of pure function, they may have amounted to little more than mere acts of divine will.[4] Many of them, however, were visualized as human in appearance and as goddesses rather than gods, and veneration paid to them was not mere crude nature worship: the Samnites did not simply identify the multitude of spirits with the forces of nature.[5]

Whether these spirits were kindly or malign, their goodwill had to be won and their enmity averted. In the house, the powers immanent in such crucial spots as the door, the hearth and the pantry, and in the field the spirits of boundary, hilltop, cavern,[6] grove,[7]

[1] Or even with an attitude still more primitive (see R. B. Marett, *The Threshold of Religion*[3], *passim*). Varro, according to Aug. *de civ. Dei*, 7. 17, said that the Roman gods were a mixture: *di certi, di incerti, di selecti.*

[2] Maule-Smith, *Votive Religion at Caere*, p. 73.

[3] The epicene and anonymous nature of some Italic divinities is responsible for such formulae as *sei deo sei deivae sacrum*; *si deus, si dea es*; *sive mas, sive femina* (*ILS*, 4015; *CIL*, I[2], 801; VI, 110; Cato, *de agric.* 13. 9).

[4] A god conceived of as an act is very old and very widespread in Italy: *Numini Iovi* (*CIL*, VIII, 9195) means Jupiter in his quality of act (F. Altheim, *History of Roman Religion*, p. 195).

[5] G. Wissowa, *Rel. und Kultus der Römer*[2], p. 315: his view is disputed by C. Koch, who cites Festus, p. 22 L. s.v. 'Aureliam familiam', but not very convincingly (see his *Gestirnverehrung in Italien* (1933) and *Römische Jupiter* (1937)).

[6] An example is the Grotta di Ciccio Felice (on Marsic territory): A. M. Radmilli in *Riv. di Scienze Preistoriche*, XI (1956), 31–52. Cf. *Fasti Archeologici*, XII (1959), 191–2.

[7] Oak-groves were especially the scene of cult (for the Celts as well as Italici: cf. Livy I. 10. 5). It may have been the fondness of the woodpecker for oak-trees that caused the Sabellians to hold this bird in such exaggerated esteem. Oak groves were and are numerous in Samnium: in ancient times a name such as Tifata (= *iliceta* according to Festus, p. 503 L.; more probably it means a hill-top covered with holm-oaks: J. Heurgon, *Capoue préromaine*, p. 315) and in modern times a name such as Cerce (from *quercus*?) tell their own story. Amongst the Umbrians Mars Grabovius is the 'oak-god'; cf. too Verg. *Aen.* 8. 351–2:

hoc nemus, hunc (inquit) frondoso vertice collem,
(quis deus, incertum est) habitat deus.

spring,[1] stream and burial-place, had to be kept favourable. The most famous spirit-haunted place in Samnium was the valley of Amsanctus, of which Vergil has left a vivid, but largely imaginary, description.[2] The noxious exhalations emanating from its pool of cold but seething water are awesome even to the modern visitor.[3] Upon the temperamental powers that controlled such places often depended a man's life and prosperity and the fertility and well-being of his crops and flocks. One was personally and even urgently concerned with them.

The most rudimentary type of these beliefs is fetishism and traces of something akin to it have been found amongst the Samnites.[4] This may explain why the tusks of the Calydonian boar were carefully kept at Beneventum for centuries.[5]

Fear of polluting and contaminating elements or actions and ensuing taboos and purifying ceremonies were normal in early Italy.[6] Invasion of one's territory automatically brought contamination; and it has even been suggested that the Italic ceremony of sending a surrendered enemy under the yoke, as at the Caudine Forks, was ultimately based on the idea that the passage beneath the cross-piece would keep those who had been defeated and who were a source of dangerous contagion completely separate from the land and people they had attacked.[7] To circumvent the effect of maleficent places dedications were made to the spirits inhabiting them. Areas of mephitic exhalation especially were *loca sacra*, and there were many such places of miasma in Samnium:[8] there was one near Aequum Tuticum and perhaps another near Aeclanum, besides the famous one at Vallis Amsanctus.

[1] *nullus enim fons non sacer* (Serv. *ad Aen.* 7. 84; cf. Sen. *Ep.* 41. 3). Cf. the worship of Lymphae and Imbres in the grove at Agnone. See below, p. 160.

[2] *Aeneid* 7. 563–72; cf. Cic. *Div.* 1. 36; Pliny, *N.H.* 2. 208; Claud. *de raptu Pros.* 2. 350. On mephitic areas, see Pliny, *N.H.* 31. 27 (from Varro); Vitruv. 8. 3. 17; Serv. *ad Aen.* 11. 785. For evidence of Mefitis-worship in the Amsanctus region, see Vetter, no. 162.

[3] The intervocal *-f-* indicates that Mefitis was Sabellian. There is no proof, however, that Mefitis-worship came to Rome from Samnium. If it did, it happened early, since there was a temple and grove sacred to this deity on the Esquiline as early as the third century (Varro, *L.L.* 5. 49; Festus, p. 476 L.).

[4] For the dynamistic (or orendistic) conception of nature, see H. Wagenvoort, *Roman Dynamism*, p. 75.

[5] Procop. 5. 15. 8.

[6] The taboo on iron was observed by the Romans and by the Volsci, near kinsmen of the Samnites. Leather was another material often viewed with misgiving. On taboos, see Pliny, *N.H.* 28. 78; J. G. Frazer, *The Golden Bough*, I, 172–8; W. Warde Fowler, *Rel. Experience of the Roman People*, pp. 27–40.

[7] Warde Fowler, *Religious Experience of the Roman People*, p. 217.

[8] I. Sgobbo in *Not. d. Scavi* (1930), p. 404. See Plate 4 (*b*).

Ritual purification was widely practised.[1] The altar halts prescribed at Agnone must have been, to some extent at least, for purposes of lustration, just as at Iguvium in Umbria. Other peoples of early Italy officially celebrated a *lustratio populi* and the Samnites must have done so too. Presumably each Samnite *pagus* undertook the lustration ceremonies in an *ambarvalia* type of procession.[2]

On the lower level of ordinary life the Samnites resorted to charms and other apotropaic devices.[3] Horace, himself a Sabellian, alludes to *Sabella carmina* (i.e. spells).[4] Doubtless they were chanted at harvest festivals and marriages, by peasants with red-stained faces exhibiting the liveliness and licentiousness normal in rural Italy.[5] These rudimentary practices are nearer to magic than religion, and they were widespread in Samnium. The amulets and talismans from Aufidena as well as many anatomical ex-votos bespeak reliance on imitative magic. Oscan imprecation tablets (*tabulae devotionum*)[6] have been unearthed, so far indeed only in Campania,[7] but they surely must have been in vogue in Samnium as well.[8] Then, too, even though the Samnites probably had little to do with Etruscan *haruspices*,[9] they certainly were not above trying to divine the future: witness the *anus Sabella* with her prophetic urn in Horace.[10] Like their Sabine 'ancestors' they also sought omens from the flight of birds.[11] This perhaps hardly qualifies as superstition: to informed country dwellers the behaviour of birds is always revealing. But on the whole Livy's description of the Samnites as *operati superstitionibus* seems justified.[12]

[1] Tab. Iguv. VI b, VII a and b; Cato, *de agric.* 141. Such purification ceremonies usually took place in the spring.

[2] For the *lustratio pagi*, see G. Wissowa, *Rel. und Kultus der Römer*², p. 143, n. 2.

[3] Pliny, *N.H.* 28. 19.

[4] *Epodes*, 17. 28.

[5] The practice of painting the face ritually red was widespread throughout the Mediterranean (C. H. Gordon, *Before the Bible*, pp. 136, 231. In Italy, see Tib. 2. 1. 55; Verg. *Ecl.* 6. 22; 10. 27 (and Serv. *ad locc.*); Pliny, *N.H.* 33. 111).

[6] G. Wissowa, *Rel. und Kultus der Römer*², p. 384. For the title *devotio*, see A. Audollent in *Mélanges Boissier*, pp. 39–43.

[7] The most famous specimen is that of Vibia from Capua (Vetter, no. 6).

[8] This is not to say that a Samnite state officially countenanced magic. Presumably it was the simple rustics who were most addicted to it, just as amongst the Romans it was the *rustica plebs* that was chiefly responsible for introducing superstitious practices flagrantly at variance with the *ritus Romanus* and the *patrius mos* (Livy 25. 1. 8).

[9] Haruspicy was not an Italic practice; some varieties of it were unknown, even at Rome, in King Pyrrhus' day (Pliny, *N.H.* 11. 186).

[10] *Satires*, 1. 9. 29. Cf., too, the episode of Sulla and Pontius' prophetic servant (Plut. *Sulla*, 26). Diodorus (22. 13. 2) describes an instance of Etruscan-type divination among the Sabellian Mamertini.

[11] Cf. Cic. *de div.* 2. 80; *de re pub.* 2. 26.

[12] Livy 10. 39. 2.

The Romans applied the term *numina* to the vague and impersonal powers, from the time of Augustus onwards at any rate.[1] What the Samnites called them we do not know. Nor do we know whether they distinguished immanent spirits from the more functional ones: the Romans gave names of a substantival type to the former (e.g. Robigus) and names of an adjectival type to the latter (e.g. Portunus).[2]

On the whole it seems probable that the animistic strand in the Samnite religious tradition was more a feature of the informal worship practised in private life and household cults than of any consistent religious systems such as are found in the public cults fostered by the state.

At a higher level of religious concept are the so-called personified abstractions.[3] The Romans displayed a marked propensity to deify moral powers or virtues (for example *Virtus*) and the objects of emotions or blessings (for example *Spes*). Other Italic peoples had the same habit:[4] the Sabines worshipped *Nerio* (= *Virtus*) and the Samnites *Mefitis*;[5] and it is a moot point who originated it. Devoto argues that the Romans borrowed from the Sabellians,[6] and it is a fact that the earliest recorded Roman temples for deities of this sort belong to the period of the Samnite Wars: *Salus c.* 302 and *Victoria c.* 300.[7] On the other hand, at Capua, *Spes*, *Fides* and *Fortuna* do not seem to have gained prominence until the Romans were in complete and firm control.[8] Probably the practice came quite naturally to any people for whom multinuminism was normal, so that any Italic

[1] See A. Grenier in *Latomus*, VI (1947), 297–308: but not everyone will accept his ideas about *numina* developing into full-fledged gods.

[2] At least, according to Warde Fowler, *Religious Experience of the Roman People*, pp. 117 f.

[3] Cic. *de leg.* 2. 11. 28; Pliny, *N.H.* 2. 14; Juv. 1. 115 f.; H. L. Axtell, *Deification of Abstract Ideas.*

[4] Vetter, nos. 29, 182 (both from Oscan-speaking Italy).

[5] G. Devoto, *Gli Antichi Italici*², p. 238, connects Mefitis with Sabine Mefula and suggests that she was originally a goddess of inebriation and vertigo. But he seems over-ready to find personified abstractions: he regards Herentas as one (229 f.).

[6] *Gli Antichi Italici*², p. 233. J. Hellegouarc'h, *Le vocabulaire latin*, p. 26, suggests that the borrowing may have been in the reverse direction. In a way the goddess Roma is an example of a deified abstraction and the Sabellians and Sabellic insurgents of the Social War were not above imitating her by deifying Italia.

[7] See Livy 9. 31. 10; 9. 43. 25; 10. 1. 9.

[8] M. W. Frederiksen in *P.B.S.R.* XIV (1959), 89 (rejecting G. Wissowa, *Rel. und Kultus der Römer*², p. 260). *Spes*, however, seems not to have been worshipped at Rome before the First Punic War (Tac. *Ann.* 2. 49). Livy (10. 14. 8), however, implies Samnite worship of *Fortuna*.

people was prone to it.[1] Certainly there was no dearth of abstract deities at Umbrian Iguvium.

The household, even more than the individual, might be regarded as the logical starting point of religious cult, since the latter would have the preservation of the family as its chief object; and the three big events in the household were birth, marriage and death.

Among the divinities who assisted at a Samnite birth were evidently some of those who appear at Agnone. They have been identified as equivalent to Latin *genetrix*, *obstetrix* and *nutrix* or simply as 'the goddess of happy childbirth'.[2] The maieutic Lucina is of course ubiquitous in Italy in one form or another.[3]

At weddings there probably were religious ceremonies to promote fertility and to bring good fortune. A death was the occasion of solemn functions. Not that the Samnites shared the excessive Etruscan preoccupation for the fate of the dead. They did not give them elaborate and solidly built tombs. But the Sabellian tomb-paintings do suggest that they shared the general South Italian interest in the after-life; and they eased the journey of the dead to this underworld by inhuming them with care and ceremony. At Aufidena the burial rites included some form of purification and a funerary meal. The tomb paintings from Sabellian Campania indicate that for notables there were also funeral games, including gladiatorial combats.

Whether there was any worship of the dead once they had been commended to the chthonic deities is debatable. The Di Manes suggest that the Romans revered at least the dead members of their household, and perhaps not illogically,[4] since the individual Genius is set free by death and can therefore become quite properly an object of worship. At Sabellian Capua the *Iovilae* suggest an ancestor cult.

[1] There is no need to accept the suggestion of S. Weinstock, in *Harv. Theol. Rev.* L (1957), 211–47, that it was Hellenistic ideas of world dominion that influenced the Romans to deify Victoria. See also above, p. 12, n. 1.

[2] See below, pp. 159–61. Doubtless there were purificatory rites, featured possibly by the use of vervain. (See Pliny, *N.H.* 15. 119, who may however be letting his fancy run away with him.)

[3] From birth the individual Samnite male may have had his 'Genius' and the Samnite female her 'Juno' (presumably under some other name, since they may have become acquainted with Juno only in comparatively late times).

[4] The Romans were also prone to give divine honours to founders of cities and patriarchs after death. Romulus, for example, became Quirinus and Latinus was identified with Jupiter Latiaris.

So does the frequent identification of Lares with Manes.[1] At the very least it is safe to say that the Samnites felt great concern for their dead ancestors and held them in the highest honour. Lares-worship undoubtedly flourished among them as among all the other inhabitants of Italy, including the slaves.[2] The South Italians on Delos in the second century, who included many Sabellians, worshipped their Lares;[3] and in the first century the *Sabellus poeta* gives us the very Italic picture of Phidyle.[4] Perhaps, too, Ovid's picture of the household gods attending the family meals was inspired by Italic practice:[5]

> *ante focos olim scamnis considere longis*
> *mos erat, et mensae credere adesse deos.*[6]

The rituals of individual and family life were more of the nature of propitiation than of worship and had to be performed very meticulously. A *numen*, unlike a god with human attributes, was not susceptible to a personal appeal: he could not be reasoned with or expected to show any indulgence for a flaw or shortcoming.[7] The Samnite worshipper dared not leave a loophole for misapprehension by a power that might be legalistically demanding. Hence, like the early Romans, the Samnites were *in dis immortalibus animadvertendis castissimi cautissimique.*[8] Their household cults must have been a matter of daily preoccupation for them.

Much of what is known about Roman field cults is applicable in all probability to the Samnite, about which detailed information is sparse. The Samnites would be especially meticulous in celebrating such cults,[9] and there were many agrarian divinities, as well as

[1] For the Lares as dead ancestors, see S. Weinstock in *J.R.S.* L (1960), 116; and note Festus, p. 108 L. (*Lares animae putabantur esse hominum redactae in numerum deorum*); p. 273 L. (*deorum inferorum quos vocant Lares*); Varro, *L.L.* 9. 61 (*videmus enim Maniam matrem Larum dici*).

[2] As the word seems Etruscan, this is perhaps rather surprising.

[3] *Inscriptions de Délos*, 1760 f.; M. Bulard, *La religion domestique dans la colonie Italienne de Délos, passim.*

[4] Horace, *Odes*, 3. 23; cf. *Epp.* 1. 16. 49: for the Italic character of the Phidyle ode, see T. Plüss in *Neue Jahrb.* II (1899), 501, and F. A. Sullivan in *Class. Phil.* LV (1960), 111. Similar pictures are to be found in Plautus, *Aulul.* 23 f.; Cato, *de agric.* 143. 2; Tib. 1. 3–33 f.

[5] Gods present at meals are not a very Roman idea (A. D. Nock in *Harv. Theol. Rev.* XXXVII (1944), 169).

[6] Ovid, *Fasti*, 6. 305 f.

[7] A. D. Nock in *Harv. Theol. Rev.* XXXII (1938), 83–96.

[8] Aul. Gell. 2. 28. 2.

[9] Cato, *de agric.* 5. 1 f.: *feriae serventur...rem divinam nisi Compitalibus in conpito aut in foco ne faciat.*

vaguer *numina*, to bear in mind. The divinities they are known to have worshipped include Vesuna, the harvest goddess known from many parts of Italy,[1] as well as the teeming agricultural pantheon from Agnone.

Associated with the field cults were the festivals of the agricultural and pastoral year, featured by ceremonies of ritual purification. To make many certain pronouncements about these is difficult owing to the uncertainty surrounding the Samnite calendar.

Samnite nomenclature suggests that the Samnites, like the Romans, originally had a ten-month year.[2] Plutarch indeed says that the Sabines had the same months in the year as the Romans,[3] which may mean that the Samnites did also. Not that that tells us the Samnite names for all the months. In fact we know the names of only six of them.

Although not listed by Ovid as one of the Italic peoples who dedicated a month to Mars,[4] the Samnites undoubtedly had one named after Mamers. There are numerous allusions to it at Sabellian Capua and it is vouched for by the *praenomen* Mamercus.[5] That it was for the Samnites the first month in the year, just as it was for the Romans, down to 153, is not explicitly stated, and Ovid avers that the month named after Mars might vary from one Italic people to another.[6] Nevertheless it probably was the same for Romans and Samnites. A Sacred Spring, since it was dedicated to Mamers, was presumably celebrated in the month that bore his name, and that month obviously coincided with our and the Roman month of March. A further indication is that, among the Sabellians as among the Romans, intercalation of extra days (which ought to be done at year's end) took place immediately before the month of March.[7]

Festus says that the Oscan name for May was Maesius and this is

[1] The *Iovilae* reveal that there was a festival called Vesulliae, which presumably honoured Vesuna: see Vetter, nos. 78, 80, 81 (from Capua) and 150 (from Pietrabbondante). She was also worshipped by the Umbrians (*Tab. Iguv.* IV, 3, etc.), Marsi (Vetter, no. 223), Marrucini (Vetter, no. 228 b), and Etrusci (G. Wissowa, *Rel. und Kultus der Römer*[2], p. 199). The name Verulae suggests that she was also known to the Hernici.

[2] For the Oscan calendar, see J. Whatmough in *Harv. Stud. Class. Phil.* XLII (1931), 157–79; J. Heurgon, *Capoue préromaine*, p. 389; Vetter, pp. 69–70. Van Johnson, in *Amer. Journ. Phil.* LXXXIV (1963), 28–35, argues that the Italic year was originally one of four months. If so, it was in prehistoric times and has little relevance for the present study.

[3] *Romulus*, 21, *Numa*, 18–19.

[4] *Fasti*, 3. 87 f.

[5] Vetter, nos. 79, 84, 85, 86, 92. For Mamercus, Vetter, nos. 119, 197.

[6] In fact amongst the Sabines and Paeligni (the peoples whom the Samnites might be expected most likely to resemble) the month named after Mars was the fourth, according to Ovid.

[7] For Sabellian intercalation, Vetter, nos. 84, 85.

confirmed by the existence of the *praenomen* Maius and the *gentilicium* Magius.[1]

Ovid may imply that only Latins and not Sabellians had a month named after Juno.[2] If this is true and not just a piece of popular folklore, then June may have been called the Falernian month, or something similar, in Oscan. There seems to have been a month by that name at Capua, and it may be the month with the most daylight, since the name Falernian has been connected with the Etruscan word *falado* meaning 'sky'.[3]

Both the Sabini and the Vestini had a month named after Flora; and as the Samnites undoubtedly worshipped her it is natural to think that they also dedicated a month to her. Her festival at Rome was one of the *feriae conceptivae* and hence movable: it was usually celebrated about the end of April or beginning of May. But May certainly was not her month among the Sabellians. It may have been July, as apparently it was among the Vestini.[4]

The Romans originally called August Sextilis: and the *praenomen* Sextus and the *gentilicium* Sextius have reference to this month. The Sabellian name for it seems to have been Sehsimber or something similar.[5]

There was also a Sabellian month named after Loesius, although we can say little about it other than that it was a month that witnessed much purification. Loesius appears as the name of a *meddix tuticus* at Capua in 211, but that it was also the name of a divinity there is no evidence. It has been thought to be an Etruscan word; and Pisani suggests that the Loesian month may be 'the month in which the furrows are traced', which might make it October; others, however, refer it to February.[6]

Unfortunately there is little information as to which were the *dies religiosi* in these Oscan months.[7] The Sabellians, or at any rate

[1] Festus, p. 121 L.; Vetter, nos. 1, 96, 100, 149; Velleius 2. 16. 2.

[2] *Fasti*, 6. 59–62. [3] Vetter, nos. 82, 83. For *falado*, see Festus, p. 78 L.

[4] *ILS*, 4906; *CIL*, I^2, 756; IX, 3513; Vetter, no. 227; Varro, *L.L.* 6. 25; Pliny, *N.H.* 18. 286; H. J. Rose in *OCD*, s.v. 'Flora'; V. Pisani, *Lingue dell'Italia*, p. 116.

[5] Vetter, no. 25.

[6] J. Heurgon, *Etude sur les inscriptions osques*, p. 82; Vetter, no. 74; A. Pisani, *Lingue dell'Italia*, p. 76. W. Schulze, *Lat. Eigennamen*, pp. 184, 486, regards the name as Etruscan. Moreover it may be the name of a festival rather than a month: Vetter, p. 72.

[7] Such days are referred to in the Oscan word *fisiais* (cf. Latin *feriae*): Vetter, nos. 74 and 81c. J. Whatmough, in *Harv. Stud. Class. Phil.* XLII (1931), 170, unconvincingly thinks the Oscan word refers to a Fisian month (= February). G. Devoto (in *Enc. Ital.* s.v. 'Oschi', pp. 653 f.) unconvincingly thinks it must refer to a god called Fisu (Latin *Fidius*?).

those of them who had come under strong Roman influence at Capua, had a day which they called the Ides. Like its Roman counterpart it seems to have belonged especially to Jupiter.[1] Then there was the day on which the festival of Diana-Hecate was celebrated: this was the thirteenth of August everywhere in Italy, if Statius is to be believed,[2] one Ides that was not Jupiter's. Otherwise our ignorance is pretty complete.

Whatever the dates of the Samnite festivals, they were probably celebrated with 'games' of various kinds, with *ludi taurei* perhaps to promote fertility,[3] and almost certainly with ritual dramas, mimes and the like.[4]

A very valuable document for the agricultural (and indeed other) aspects of Samnite religion is the *Tabula Agnonensis*, a perfectly preserved bronze tablet measuring 6½ inches by 11, now in the British Museum. It is inscribed in Oscan on both sides, the letters being clearly and deeply incised. It is provided with a carrying handle. If this document belongs to *c.* 250, as the form of its letters and other criteria make probable, we have in it the means of making some appraisal of Samnite religion from its own witness before the Second Punic War helped to change the religious outlook along with a lot else in early Italy.[5]

The Agnone tablet identifies the divinities who had altars[6] in

[1] F. Altheim, *History of Roman Religion*, pp. 164–7 (very speculative).

[2] *Silvae*, 3. 1. 59 f.

[3] Their Sabine 'ancestors' celebrated *ludi taurei* (Festus, pp. 478 f. L.; Livy 39. 22; *CIL*, XIV Supp. 4511; Serv. *ad Aen.* 2. 140). So did the Romans (A. Piganiol, *Recherches sur les jeux romains*, p. 148, n. 7).

[4] For Samnite fondness for theatrical representations, see above, pp. 60, 124.

[5] First published by F. S. Cremonese in *Boll. dell'Istit. di Corrispondenza Arch.* x (1848), 140–7. It was actually found closer to Capracotta than to Agnone, but it is commonly known as the Agnone tablet and will be so called here. For a recent discussion of it, see G. Camporeale in *Archivio Glottologico Italiano*, XLII (1963), 161–5 (with bibliography). The view that the tablet betrays a Campanian, rather than a Samnite, origin (F. Altheim, *Terra Mater*, p. 152) does not recommend itself to me. See Plate 12.

[6] Oscan *statif* probably means a 'halt' in front of an altar (Latin *statio*), not 'statue' as used to be believed: V. Pisani in *Arch. Glott. Ital.* XXVII (1935), 161. At Iguvium there were 'halts' for lustration. (One thinks of the fourteen stations of the Roman Catholic Via Crucis.) We can only guess at the appearance of the altars. At Larino one can see a cylindrically shaped piece of masonry which is said to be a Sabellian altar. But the recently discovered altars at Lavinium may be a more accurate guide: they are featured by mouldings by no means unknown in Oscan-speaking Italy. For an illustrated description of them, see F. Castagnoli in *Bullettino della Commissione Archeologica Comunale*, LXXVII (1960), 145–72 + pls. 1, 2. It is also possible that the altars at Agnone were merely piled sods in the primitive fashion of early Italy. Serv. *ad Aen.* 12. 119 says that even after stone altars had become common it was customary to put a sod on top.

or near a carefully delimited *hortus* where the tablet must have been prominently displayed: the iron chain by which it was suspended, on a tree presumably,[1] still survives in part. The 'garden' was one of the sacred groves which were so plentiful in early Italy and which have bequeathed such names as Luco (*lucus*) and Nemi (*nemus*) to modern Italy.[2] It must have closely resembled the one at Fondo Patturelli on the eastern outskirts of Capua, which was also under Sabellian control for centuries, was likewise dedicated to a divinity of complex nature and also had many altars (thirteen as against fifteen at Agnone). Quite recently another polylatrous precinct of this kind has been found near Rome, at Lavinium, where thirteen altars, not all of them dedicated to the same deity, are still *in situ*.[3]

The grove at Agnone was sacred to Kerres and, so the Oscan text seems to say, was maintained by worshippers offering tithes. Inside the grove sacred processions were held, presumably at certain well-known seasons and with the worshippers moving widdershins, as they did in so many religious processions in early Italy.[4] During the processions halts (for lustration purposes?) were made at the altars of each of fifteen divinities.[5] At each of two annual festivals[6] (or less probably every second year, the interpretation of the Oscan text being uncertain)[7] a fire was kindled and offerings made on a sacrificial altar. Ceremonies were also held outside the grove proper, apparently on the occasion of a festival to Flora, when ritual halts were made in honour of four deities,[8] only two of whom had altars inside the grove.

The grove must have been situated somewhere near the spot on the Monte del Cerro between Capracotta and Agnone in the territory

[1] Cf. Pliny, *N.H.* 16. 237: *vetustior autem urbe in Vaticano ilex, in qua titulus aereus litteris Etruscis religione arborem iam tum dignam fuisse significat.*

[2] The most famous such grove is the Nemus Dianae near Aricia. One very near, if not actually in, Samnium was at Luceria (*ILS*, 4912; *CIL*, IX, 782; Bruns, p. 283; Johnson, Coleman-Norton and Bourne, *Ancient Roman Statutes*, p. 20). The Trojans found Evander sacrificing in such a grove when they reached the site of Rome (Verg. *Aen.* 8. 104).

[3] The polylatrous one at Pisaurum is also well known (*CIL*, I², 167–80), but the *cippi* there are apparently not altars. The Lavinium site might give some idea of what the one at Agnone looked like.

[4] A lustral procession is depicted moving counter-clockwise on Trajan's Column (E. Strong, *Cultura Romana*, fig. 99); but Solinus, p. 195, mentions a clockwise lustral procession.

[5] Nos. 1–15 on the list in the text.

[6] G. Giacomelli in *Studi Etruschi*, XXIV (1955/56), 341.

[7] It has been suggested (not very plausibly) that the engraver may have misspelt a key word (F. Bechtel in *Hermes*, LVII (1922), 160).

[8] Nos. 2, 6, 16 and 17 on the list in the text. It is not made clear in the case of these four that the halts are at altars.

of the Caraceni, where the tablet was found over one hundred years ago, an area at that time still suggestively called Uorte (= Orto? Latin *hortus*, the *horz* of the tablet).

In all, seventeen divinities are named on the Agnone tablet counting the two aspects of Jupiter separately, and this congestion is dramatic proof of the polylatrous tendencies of the Samnites. But the Latin names of the σύνναοι θεοί who shared this open-air sanctuary are in some cases far from certain. The following are their names, listed in their order on the tablet and where possible in Latin form.

(1) Vezkeí: neither a certain nominative form for this Oscan dative nor a generally accepted Latin equivalent for the name seem possible.[1]
(2) Euclus, either with or without the epithet *Pater*: he was worshipped outside as well as inside the grove.[2]
(3) Kerres (Ceres?).
(4) Filia Cerealis.[3]
(5) Inter-Stita.[4]
(6) Amma Cerealis (Mater? Nutrix?): she was worshipped outside as well as inside the grove.[5]

[1] 'Vezkeí' has been variously identified as Lucina (?) (J. Whatmough in *OCD*, s.v. 'Religion Italic'), as the national god of the Aurunci (F. Altheim, *Terra Mater*, p. 155, and J. Heurgon, *Capoue préromaine*, p. 333), as an aspect of Venus (V. Pisani, *Lingue dell'Italia*, p. 93), and, more convincingly, as a divinity of the revolving year (Renard-Schilling, *Hommages à Jean Bayet*, p. 39).

[2] Euclus is Mercury (Hesychius, s.v. 'Eukolos'), here in his chthonic aspect as the *psychopompos*, according to F. Altheim, *Terra Mater*, p. 148. Mercury is sometimes closely associated with Ceres: e.g. on the occasion of the *lectisternium* in 217 (Livy 22. 10. 9).

[3] In Oscan *futreí kerriaí*; *futreí* is the word for *filia* (F. Thurneysen in *Glotta*, XXI (1932), 7). As divine genealogies were normally absent from Italic religion, there must be Greek influence here. Amongst the Paeligni the daughter of Ceres is actually named as Persepona (Vetter, no. 213).

[4] Inter-Stita (Oscan *anter-statai*) might be the midwife who (in Oscan) stands 'between' when delivering the offspring, whereas (in Latin) she stands 'opposite' (whence *obstetrix*): in Oscan the name is clearly written as two words. The name suggests Marsic *Stata Mater* (Vetter, no. 226; cf. Cic. *de leg.* 2. 28), one of whose functions was apparently to put out fires; Umbrian *Praestota* (J. W. Poultney, *Bronze Tables of Iguvium*, p. 277), an epithet of Mars in his protective capacity; or the Roman *Lares Praestites*, the guardians of the whole community whose festival was celebrated on 1 May. Pisani, *Lingue dell'Italia*, p. 93, suggests that Interstita is the middle deity of a triad. There is, however, no evidence of triads in Samnium, despite Sabellian polylatrous tendencies.

[5] Amma is evidently a colloquial word, something like 'mama': cf. Isid. *Etym.* 12. 7. 42: *strix vulgo amma dicitur ab amando parvulos unde et lac praebere fertur nascentibus*. It must mean *nutrix* or something similar (Vetter, no. 147; H. Le Bonniec, *Le culte de Cérès à Rome*, p. 41). Hesychius, s.v. 'Ammas', equates her with Demeter, which is not seriously at variance with this. The daughter of Ceres, the midwife, and the nurse are logical associates of Ceres. F. Altheim, *Terra Mater*, pp. 92–108, less convincingly seeks an association with Anna Perenna.

(7) Lymphae Cereales.[1]

(8) Liganacdix Intera, either with or without the adjective *Cerealis*: *liganacdix* might be *legifera* or *liknophoros*.[2]

(9) Imbres, either with or without the adjective *Cereales*.

(10) Matae, either with or without the adjective *Cereales* (Mater Matuta?).[3]

(11) Jupiter Juventus.[4]

(12) Jupiter Rigator, either with or without the adjective *pius*.[5]

(13) Hercules Cerealis.[6]

(14) Patana Pistia (Panda?).[7]

[1] Oscan *diumpaís*, where initial *d-* is equivalent to Latin *l-* (cf. *dacruma*, *lacrima*). The interpretation *Lymphae* therefore seems highly probable: in Greek Nymphae, the deities of river sources (F. Heichelheim in *R.E.* XVII (1937), s.v. 'Nymphai', col. 1581).

[2] Oscan *entraí* is presumably Latin *Intera*. A. von Blumenthal, *Rh. Mus.* LXXXV (1936), 65, equates Oscan *entraí* with Greek ἐνέρτερα, i.e. 'chthonia'. The equation *liganacdix* = *legifera*, as suggested by Thurneysen, is today widely accepted (Vetter, p. 106; Le Bonniec, *op. cit.* p. 42). But is not *liganacdix* more likely to be an Oscan attempt to reproduce Greek *liknophoros*, with the voiced plosive *g* replacing the occlusive consonant *k* and with anaptysis? (The habit of anaptysis, prevalent in Sabellian Campania, spread into Samnium.) 'Displayer of the winnowing fan' was an epithet of Dionysus well known in Italy: it is applied, for instance, to Bacchic initiates in an inscription from Tusculum (see Vogliano-Cumont in *Amer. Journ. Arch.* XXXVII (1933), 215 f., and M. P. Nilsson in *Harv. Theol. Rev.* XLVI (1956), 177 f.). (Vetter, p. 106, accepting the equation *liganacdix* = *legifera*, argues that Intera is placed between Lymphae and Imbres precisely because she is *legifera* and it is important that the crops get their water in a regular and orderly fashion. This is ingenious, but far-fetched.)

[3] F. Altheim, *Hist. of Roman Rel.* pp. 163, 186, connects *Matae* with Latin *Manes*. But more probably the word should be related to Mater Matuta, an Italic goddess worshipped by many Italic peoples: Aurunci, Latini, Sidicini, Volsci and probably Samnites (it is generally agreed that she is the deity referred to in an Oscan inscription from Macchia di Valfortore (Vetter, no. 175), which is near Larinum but was perhaps in Samnium). Mater Matuta was concerned with childbirth and nursing and with the ensuring of a supply of dew to the crops.

[4] Oscan *diovei verehasioí* seems clearly to be Latin *Iuppiter Iuventus* (*CIL*, IX, 5574; XI, 3245). Vetter, p. 104, prefers the interpretation Jupiter Vergarius, an otherwise unknown deity who presided over the changing seasons.

[5] Oscan *diovei regaturei* probably is not Jupiter Rector, but Jupiter Rigator, the god who brings water (so Vetter, p. 107).

[6] Hercules was sometimes closely associated with Ceres at Rome (see F. Altheim, *Terra Mater*, pp. 152 f.): she and he had a joint festival there on 21 December (Macrob. 3. 11. 10). J. Bayet, *Orig. de l'Hercule rom.* p. 121, plausibly suggests that at Agnone Hercules is 'Héraclès fécondant'.

[7] Cf. Arnob. 4. 428: *et quod Tito Tatio, Capitolium ut capiat collem, viam condere atque aperire permissum est, dea Panda est appellata vel Pantica.* Panda and Ceres, if not identical (Varro *ap.* Aul. Gell. 13. 23. 4), were certainly closely related (Nonius Marcellus 1. 6L.). The name is not formed from Greek πίστις (Latin *Fidius*), but from πετάννυμι (= Arnobius' *aperire*): E. C. Evans, *Cults of the Sabine Territory*, pp. 180–2. Clearly we are here dealing with an agricultural deity, possibly the one that makes the husks open wide so that the grains of cereal come out easily in the threshing (E. Schwyzer in *Rhein. Mus.* LXXXIV (1935), 97–119). A. von Blumenthal (in *Rhein. Mus.* LXXXV (1936), 66) less plausibly regards Patana Pistia as a goddess of childbirth: his view is that Oscan *patanaí* is really Greek πότνια, and he relates Oscan *piístiaí* to Latin *quies* (cf. Festus, p. 306 L.: *quietalis ab antiquis dicebatur Orcus*).

(15) Diva Genita.[1]
(16) Perna Cerealis, who was worshipped only outside the grove proper.[2]
(17) Flora Cerealis, who was worshipped only outside the grove proper.[3]

Even with the most sober of interpretations, these names give a striking sense of vitality and youth. Some of them, Jupiter, Hercules, Flora, and, if correctly identified, the Lymphae, Imbres, Mater Matuta and Panda, are no strangers. Others, such as 'Vezkeí' and Inter-Stita, are as mysterious as some of the deities in the Iguvine Tables. The striking and notable feature of the Agnone tablet is the importance attached to Kerres. Not only does the 'garden' belong to Kerres,[4] but the majority of the gods who have altars there are described by an adjective formed from this name: Schwyzer even suggests that this would be the case with all of them, had space on the tablet allowed.[5] Pairs of divinities, where one seems to be in a state of dependence upon the other, are very common in early Italy. Often the pair consists of a male and a female, without any discernible conjugal relationship however. Janus Junonius is a well-known example from Rome, and Varro could adduce at least eight other instances from there.[6] The Umbrians had Çerfus Martius and the Campanians Venus Iovia.[7] The exact reason for the seeming subordination of one god to the other is hard to fathom. Latte suggests that originally it was in order to stress a special aspect of a god's power or will.[8] On the Agnone tablet the adjective *Cerealis* is given to many of the divinities since they are performing a Kerres-like function, generating and fostering life and vegetation and providing, sometimes as elaborately as nature herself, the nourishing elements

[1] Perhaps to be identified with the Genita Mana of Pliny, *N.H.* 29. 58; Plutarch, *Rom. Quest.* 52. Cf., too, Latin *genetrix.*

[2] Perhaps the goddess of happy childbirth (S. Weinstock in *R.E.* XIX (1937), s.v. 'Perna', col. 873). F. Altheim, *Terra Mater*, pp. 92–108, also relates her to Anna Perenna.

[3] Flora is a very Italic deity, specifically Sabellian according to F. Altheim, *Hist. of Roman Religion*, p. 137. (Bayet, *Orig. Herc. Rom.* p. 312, regards her as Sabine.) She acquired some Greek trappings (Varro, *L.L.* 7. 45; Henzen, *Acta Fratrum Arvalium*, p. 146).

[4] J. Whatmough, in *Language*, III (1927), 106, erroneously makes Hercules the chief deity at Agnone.

[5] *Rhein. Mus.* LXXXIV (1935), 109: this, however, hardly seems likely.

[6] *ap.* Aul. Gell. 13. 23. 2.

[7] Tab. Iguv. I b 28; VI b 58; *CIL*, X, 3776.

[8] *Archiv Rel. Wiss.* XXIV (1926), 244 f. J. Heurgon, *Capoue préromaine*, pp. 386 f., points out that the relationship was likely to become genealogical or matrimonial once the Italici had become influenced by the *interpretatio Graeca.*

of life.[1] That should not be taken to mean that for the Samnites Kerres was the supreme divinity.[2] Jupiter was that[3] and he is present twice, and it is to be noted that he neither needs nor gets the Cerealis appellation. Nevertheless Kerres is at the very centre and core of the religious exercises in the grove; and it is an interesting coincidence that the tablet should have been found on Monte del Cerro and should have been made of bronze, a metal prominently featured in rituals relating to Ceres.[4] Kerres is a relatively well-known Italic divinity, not one of the numinous type, who was worshipped by the Paeligni,[5] Marrucini[6] and Umbri[7] amongst others. The name Kerres even occurs in Latin inscriptions, and Cerus was mentioned in the Salian hymn.[8]

Whether Kerres is to be identified with Roman Ceres is a moot point.[9] In some ways the two deities are dissimilar, and the Romans at least thought that the rites of Ceres were Greek, not Italic, in origin:[10] and certainly the triad Ceres–Liber–Libera seems to have reached Rome from Greek Sicily by way of Campania.[11] Nevertheless the Paeligni seem to have regarded Kerres and Ceres as one and the same, and there are other indications to support this. The avenging Ceres of the celebrated Oscan curse tablet from Capua, the so-called Imprecation of Vibia, looks very much like Kerres;[12] and Roman Ceres, like Samnite Kerres, had many other deities closely associated

[1] *Grabovius* is similarly added to the names of some of the gods at Iguvium. C. Koch, *Der röm. Jupiter*, pp. 60 f., unconvincingly argues this means that the Italic peoples did not think of their gods as kinless and that we should reject Warde Fowler's view that it was the Greeks who introduced the notion of divine relationships (see *Rel. Exp. of the Rom. People*, pp. 148–58).

[2] R. Pettazzoni in *Studi e Mat. di Storia delle Religioni*, XIX (1946), 142–56.

[3] For Jupiter as the *regnator omnium deus*, to use the expression of Tacitus (*Germ.* 39. 5), see below, p. 166.

[4] Velleius I. 4. I.

[5] Vetter, no. 213 (where *Cerfum* has reference to Ceres).

[6] Vetter, no. 218 (= the Tabula Rapinensis, now in Berlin). In this document, thought to be contemporary with the Agnone tablet, Kerres is again closely linked with Jupiter and is clearly female, strongly resembling Juno.

[7] Poultney, *op. cit.* pp. 166, 276–88 (where Çerfus seems to be male and is associated with Mars rather than Jupiter).

[8] See, for example, *ILS*, 2963; *CIL*, I², 43, 445; XI, 6708; Varro, *L.L.* 7. 26; Festus, p. 109 L.

[9] The association of Kerres with Jupiter and Hercules at Agnone reminds one of the *kourotrophos* at Fondo Patturelli and of Hera Argeia at Foce del Sele and might suggest identification with some aspect of Juno (cf. above, n. 6). There cannot be any connexion between Kerres and *cerrus*, the Latin word for a species of oak-tree: this type of oak was unknown in most of Italy (Pliny, *N.H.* 16. 17).

[10] Cic. *pro Balbo*, 56; Val. Max. I. I. I.

[11] I. S. Ryberg, *Arch. Record of Rome VII–II century*, pp. 154 f.

[12] Vetter, no. 6, where Ceres is 'Arentike' (= avenging? Cf. Hesychius, s.v. 'Arantisin').

with her: at Rome at the beginning of seed time the flamen Cerealis invoked no fewer than twelve other gods.[1] On the whole only the most determined sceptic will insist that there is no connexion.[2]

Ceres–Kerres represents the supreme creative force (*a creando dicta*),[3] the deity that presided over the generative powers of nature and whose *numen* got food out of the ground,[4] the goddess who in primitive Rome was the beneficiary from punishments inflicted on peccant individuals.[5] The Agnone tablet proves that Kerres can also safely be reckoned among the *di patrii* of the Samnites.[6] This is probably also true of some of the other gods at Agnone: 'Vezkeí', Inter-Stita, Intera and above all Jupiter.

The reason for keeping Perna and Flora, both *Cereales*, outside the grove has not been satisfactorily explained. It has been suggested that Flora's name on the tablet looks like an oscanized borrowing from Latin and that she owes her presence at Agnone—and likewise her exclusion from the actual grove there—to Roman influence;[7] others, however, regard Flora as a goddess who reached Rome from the Sabellians, and Varro certainly claims her as Sabine.[8] Flora was unquestionably a very important divinity, particularly so when in association with Ceres (Kerres). They complemented one another neatly and between them ensured the food supply for man, Kerres (Ceres) being the generative force and Flora the power that fosters and protects the blossoms.[9] This close association of Flora with Kerres assured her a special position at Agnone: she was important enough there to have her own festival.[10]

[1] Serv. Dan. *ad Georg.* 1. 21.

[2] G. De Sanctis, *Stor. dei Romani*, IV, 2, 243.

[3] Serv. *ad Georg.* 1. 7. If Ceres is related to *creare*, then in effect *cerealis* = *genialis* (J. Whatmough in *OCD*, s.v. 'Religion, Italic'). Perhaps Ceres is also related to the verb *crescere*.

[4] *a gerendis fructibus*: Cic. *de nat. deorum*, 2. 67; 3. 52; cf. Varro, *L.L.* 5. 64. *Nutrit rura Ceres*: Hor. *Od.* 4. 5. 18.

[5] Pliny, *N.H.* 18. 12; Plut. *Rom.* 22. 3. There is, however, no way of proving that at Agnone Kerres is female.

[6] Or should one use the Roman expression *di indigetes*? (for whom see S. Weinstock in *JRS*, L (1960), 117).

[7] M. G. Delfino in *Serta Eusebiana* (Genova, 1958), p. 54. Flora was certainly a very ancient deity at Rome: at one time she had her own flamen there, according to Varro, *L.L.* 7. 45.

[8] F. Altheim, *Hist. Rom. Religion*, p. 137; Varro, *L.L.* 5. 74.

[9] Cf. August, *de civ. Dei*, 4. 8: Proserpina (i.e. *filia Cerealis*) presides over *frumentis germinantibus*, Flora over *florentibus fructibus*. See, too, Pliny, *N.H.* 18, 286.

[10] Flora was undoubtedly popular with Sabellians (see Vetter, nos. 21 (from Pompeii), 183 (from Lucania)), as well as with Romans (Cic. *II Verr.* 5. 36). According to Cornutus *ad* Juvenal 6. 249, *Flora erat apud antiquos ministra Cereris*.

Other divinities at Agnone also obviously have functions bearing directly on farming operations: Lymphae, Imbres, Matae, Jupiter Rigator, Patana Pistia; and they seem to have highly specialized functions. If the identifications are correct, the Matae ensure that the crops get the dew they need, while Patana Pistia's function is to get the husks open cleanly so that the grains come away easily in the threshing. The resemblance to Rome is striking. There, too, if Varro is to be believed,[1] the agricultural gods acquired very specialized functions, each presiding over some detail of the farmer's work.[2]

Clearly the religious exercises in the grove at Agnone were those of a community living close to the soil. The worshippers were peasants concerned to win the favour of the ancestral gods of the Italian countryside. *Fortunatus et ille deos qui novit agrestes.*[3] Only a few of these gods, such as the Lymphae and Imbres, seem to be primitive and animistic in character. Thus, Agnone was not a completely unsophisticated rustic community. It had come under some external influences, probably under Roman and certainly under Greek, since its gods included the palpably Hellenic Euclus (= Hermes, the god of trade) and another for whom the Oscan equivalent of a Greek compound adjective had been excogitated. By the middle of the third century neither the Samnites nor their religion were exclusively agrarian.[4]

Many of the divinities at Agnone are fully developed gods: Jupiter, for instance, and Kerres. So far as we can see, the Samnites had had such divinities from their earliest days.[5] Mythology, it is true, with its cosmogony, celestial marriages and genealogies,[6] was as foreign

[1] Or, more accurately, Augustine quoting Varro (*de civ. Dei*, 4. 8). Augustine is obviously mocking, and even burlesquing, the Roman gods.

[2] Serv. *ad Georg.* 1. 21: *nomina haec numinum inveniuntur, id est in libris pontificalibus qui et nomina deorum et rationes ipsorum nominum contineant, quae etiam Varro dicit.* It is probable that Varro was himself responsible for some of the religious atomism to which he draws attention.

[3] Verg. *Georg.* 2. 493.

[4] Of course at Agnone Euclus–Hermes could be the chthonic *psychopompos* and thus very much connected with the soil. But, as Mommsen points out (*Unterital. Dial.* p. 133), even Kerres was not exclusively agricultural.

[5] Their spiritual horizons, like those of the Romans, were by no means bounded by a world of vague, impersonal powers (H. J. Rose in *Mnem.* ser. 4, III (1950), 281–7; G. De Sanctis, *Storia dei Romani*, IV, 2, 125; J. Bayet, *Histoire politique et psychologique de la religion romaine, passim*).

[6] Despite the Filia Cerealis of the Agnone tablet or the 'Sons of Jupiter' (Dioscuri) from the Paelignian country (Vetter, no. 202). There is no list of Samnite divinities recorded in literature as there is of Etruscan (the list compiled by Martianus Capella in the fifth century A.D.).

to the native Samnite religion as to the native Roman. The Samnites' religion was not one handed down from poets and philosophers, as the Roman *pontifex maximus* Mucius Scaevola might have put it.[1] But it was a religion organized in accordance with nature and therefore appropriate for a people with a long tradition, and their anthropomorphic divinities had complete and individual personalities and performed recognized and well-defined functions.

The origin, the number, and the universality of such full-fledged gods are very uncertain. Jupiter, certainly, was of immemorial antiquity and the Samnites' worship of him antedated their arrival in Italy. Most of their other gods they got to know only after establishing themselves in Samnium. Kerres for instance may have sprung quite literally from the soil of Italy: inscriptions from the Paeligni suggest that she had a chthonic aspect.[2]

Some of the Samnite gods must have been worshipped only in certain areas,[3] possibly only in certain families,[4] since it was normal in early Italy for a divinity to be settled in, and to belong to, one spot. The *pagus* organization undoubtedly contributed to this pattern, since a *pagus* was in some respects a religious entity which had its own specific acts of worship peculiar to it. And we can envisage a Samnite dynastic family as standing in a special relationship with a certain god from the fact that we can document something of the sort at Rome, Iguvium and Capua. The Vesullii, for instance, may have been in a very preferred position with the goddess Vesuna.[5] Even Jupiter in certain of his aspects seems to have become almost parochial. Many of the local divinities, to judge from the preponderance of goddesses at Agnone and from the disproportionate number of goddesses in terracotta votive deposits, were envisaged as female, possibly because in very early Italy kinship was determined through the women. The cults of some of these local divinities may

[1] See August. *de civ. Dei*, 4. 27 and 31, quoting Scaevola and Varro.

[2] Vetter, nos. 204, 205, 207. Italic chthonic deities seem more often to be female than male.

[3] Note how at Capua in 94 it was the *pagus Herculaneus* that celebrated the Terminalia (*ILS*, 6302; *CIL*, I^2, 682; x, 3772).

[4] At Rome the Fabii had their own *sacra* on the Quirinal (Wissowa, *Rel. und Kultur der Römer*[2], pp. 33, n. 32; 433, n. 1), and along with the Potitii and Pinarii they enjoyed the particular favour of Hercules (Livy 5. 46. 2; A. D. Momigliano in *J.R.S.* LIII (1963), 117). The Valerii were especially connected with Vica Pota (Livy 2. 7. 12; Ascon. p. 13 Cl.; Plut. *Public.* 10. 4). At Iguvium Hondus Iovius seems to have been partial to certain select clans (Tab. Iguv. II a 21).

[5] J. Heurgon, *Capoue préromaine*, p. 390. The *gens Vesullia* seems to be confined to Oscan-speaking Italy.

have shown some tendency to spread once the art of writing came into common use, since invocation of the objects of worship would become increasingly formalized and the formulae could be more easily disseminated through the written word. But Sabine Vacuna and Volscian Declona show that local deities sometimes remained such.[1]

Transcending the local divinities were the universal gods worshipped everywhere in Samnium, and among all Sabellians and most Italici.

There is no doubt that Jupiter, the great sky and weather god, was, as Livy implies,[2] the chief native divinity of the Samnites. According to Servius, the Oscan name for him was Lucetius (the aspect of him which the Salii invoked at Rome), but this name does not occur on the Oscan documents.[3] They lead one to believe that he bore a name in Oscan remarkably similar to the one he bore in Latin, and it is fairly obvious that Oscan Iovilo is a diminutive formed from the name Jove.[4] The importance of Jupiter in Campania seems to increase after the Sabellians arrived there. Like the Romans, they regarded the Ides as the day that particularly belonged to him: the *Iovilae* make that clear. It is also possible that the Sabellians sometimes celebrated a five-day festival in his honour.[5] There is abundant evidence for Jupiter-worship throughout Oscan-speaking Italy. At Agnone there were the two manifestations of him already mentioned, Jupiter Juventus and Jupiter Rigator. At Capua there was Jupiter Tifatinus and Jupiter Compagus, and further south we encounter Jupiter Vesuvius. At Cumae and other places in Campania a group or fellowship worshipped Jupiter Flagius. Hirpinian Compsa had Jupiter Vicilinus. Some of these titles are strange and presumably

[1] For Vacuna, see C. Koch in *R.E.* VII A (1948), s.v. 'Vacuna', col. 2041, with the literature there cited. For Declona, see Vetter, no. 222.

[2] Livy 10. 38. 3: Jupiter was the chief deity at Fondo Patturelli (J. Heurgon, *Capoue préromaine*, p. 363), and as we have seen was not subordinate to Kerres at Agnone.

[3] Serv. *ad Aen.* 4. 570; cf. Festus, p. 102 L.; Macrob. I. 15. 14; Wissowa, *Rel. und Kultus der Römer*², p. 114. The initial syllable of the name is very widespread: it can be seen in Lucina, Luceria, Lucania (and its eponymous hero Lucius (Pliny, *N.H.* 3. 71)), and Lucullanus (the name of a *pagus* at Beneventum: *CIL*, IX, 1618). There are two instances, both very late, of Juno being called Lucetia (Mart. Cap. 2. 149; Myth. Vat. 3. 4).

[4] But the *Iovilae* do not say that the dedication is being made to him, or to any other god for that matter (Vetter, no. 94, is quite exceptional).

[5] A festival called *pomperias* appears in the Oscan documents. It seems equivalent to Umbrian *pumpedias*, and may owe its name to its duration for five days. For increased importance of Jupiter once the Sabellians reached Campania, see J. Heurgon, *Capoue préromaine*, pp. 362 f.

result from assimilations with purely local divinities; and it may be that an epithet such as Vicilinus (= 'fellow-villager'?) indicates a purely local aspect of the god.[1] Nevertheless that worship of him among the Samnites was universal is certain.[2]

Jupiter's partner Juno on the other hand may have been originally a stranger to Samnium. The Sabellians, of course, encountered her once they reached Campania: Juno Gaura, for instance, was worshipped at Capua.[3] But it may have been the Romans who took her into the highlands.[4]

A god to whom the Samnites paid particular devotion was Mars or, to give him their name for him, Mamers.[5] It was usually to Mamers that a Sabellian Sacred Spring was dedicated.[6] Hence we must suppose that he had his own official cult.[7] As already noted, one of the Oscan months was named after him. And the Sabellian and Sabellic tribes showed a distinct tendency to name themselves also after him: witness the Mamertini, Marsi and Marrucini (the latter two being mere variants of the same name, according to Cato).[8] The popularity in Samnium of the name Herius may also stem from

[1] Jupiter Compagus: *ILS*, 6302; Mommsen in *CIL*, I, p. 159, and X, p. 367. Jupiter Vesuvius: *CIL*, X, 3806. Jupiter Flagius (= *Jupiter Flazzus* or *Flazius* of Puteoli? *CIL*, X, 1571): Vetter, nos. 85, 108; J. Heurgon, *Etude sur les inscriptions osques*, p. 85. If his name is connected with *flagrare* and hence with *fulgere*, he may be identical with Jupiter Fulgor whose festival at Rome fell on 7 October. Whatmough's identification of him with Jupiter Liber (*Class. Quart.* XVI [1922], 185) is unconvincing. Jupiter Vicilinus: Livy 22. 44. 8. Is Vicilinus related to *vicus*? (Dwellers in a *castellum* were called *castellani* (*ILS*, 5946).) In addition, Jupiter Milichius appears at Pompeii (Vetter, no. 8) and Jupiter Sequundanus was worshipped by South Italians on Delos (*Inscr. de Delos*, 1754).

[2] Casagiove, a village near Capua, presumably preserves in its name the record of a temple to Jupiter. There is similarly a village near Capua called *Casacellula* or *Casacerere*, which is interesting in view of the status of Kerres among the Samnites.

[3] *CIL*, X, 3783 (of 71 B.C.).

[4] W. F. Otto in *Philologus*, LXIV (1905), 161–73. In Samnium the Latin Colonies, significantly, seem to have been the centres of her worship: Aesernia (*CIL*, IX, 2630) and Beneventum (*ILS*, 3110; *CIL*, I^2, 396; IX, 1547, 2110, 2111).

[5] Vetter, no. 164. Mars was pan-Italic (W. Schulze, *Lat. Eigennamen*, p. 464) and was important throughout Italy: in the tutelary triad at Rome (Jupiter, Mars and Quirinus) he outnumbers Jupiter two to one.

[6] J. Heurgon in *Latomus*, XXVI (1957), 5–51; W. Eisenhut in *R.E.* XV A (1955), s.v. 'Ver Sacrum', col. 917. The *sacrati*, who settled at Messana, are said to have been dedicated to Apollo (Festus, p. 150 L.; cf. Vetter, no. 196). Yet they are called Mamertini. Mamertine coins showing Apollo do not begin to appear until 220 (M. Särström, *Study in the Coinage of the Mamertines*, p. 138).

[7] This may have involved the use of temple serfs. The kindred Frentani had a large number of such Martiales as the result of 'religious ordinances of great antiquity' (Cic. *pro. Cluentio*, 43).

[8] Cato *ap.* Priscian IX, p. 871 (= fr. 18 Jordan). But the derivation from the god's name was disputed in antiquity: Cn. Gellius derived the name Marsi from Marsyas (Peter, *H.R.R.* I^2 (1914), 149 fr. 7, 150 fr. 9).

the cult of Mamers, whose companion was Her(i)es.[1] When a Samnite, or other Italic, warrior wore the aigrettes in his helmet it was apparently with the hope of identifying himself with Mamers.[2] He has been aptly called the national Italic god. Varro's claim[3] that he was Sabine in origin can be dismissed; but whether he was in the first instance a god of war or of agriculture is uncertain.[4] His vernal character and his aspect as a fecundating power and protector of the fields, harvest and cattle were suited to either role.[5] He had undoubtedly accumulated functions connected with agriculture.[6] Mamers was the god who personified the activities of youth and as such was endowed with vigour and the ability to fight as well as to avert evil. Perhaps it was due to the Samnites that his warlike aspect came to predominate.

The goddess Diana was the female counterpart of Mars, and martial attributes (she seems identical with Bellona) would endear her also to the Samnites. Despite Altheim, she is an old Italic divinity whose worship goes back to a remote antiquity, and she had chthonic and kourotrophic as well as warlike aspects. As Diana Tifatina, the goddess of the holm-oak grove, she was lavishly worshipped by the Sabellians of Capua, and it is unlikely that they had been unfamiliar with her until they reached Campania.[7]

A native deity common to all the Italic peoples was the Earth Goddess. She was worshipped quite certainly by the Marrucini[8] and possibly under the name Famel (cf. Semele) by the Paeligni,[9] both

[1] Festus, p. 89 L.; Aul. Gell. 13. 23. 2.

[2] Verg. *Aen.* 6. 779; Val. Max. I. 8. 6; H. J. Rose in *J.R.S.* XXXVII (1947), 184.

[3] *L.L.* 5. 73; cf. Dion. Hal. 2. 48.

[4] For the evidence see Marbach in *R.E.* XIV^2 (1930), s.v. 'Mars', cols. 1934–7.

[5] For his vernal character and fecundating power, see Lucret. I. 31–40 and H. Wagenvoort in *Mededelingen der koninlijke Nederlandse Akademie van Wetenschappen*, XIII (1951), 163–99. For him as a protector of fields, etc., see Cato, *de agric.* 83 (Mars Sylvanus); cf. Dion. Hal. 4. 22. I.

[6] Cato, *de agric.* 141.

[7] For the antiquity and various aspects of Diana see Cato *ap.* Priscian 4, p. 129; 7, p. 337; Festus, p. 128 L.; A. E. Gordon, *Cults of Aricia*, pp. 7 f., and *Trans. Amer. Philol. Ass.* LXIII (1932), 177; J. Heurgon, *Capoue préromaine*, pp. 303–13, and *Rev. Et. Lat.* XXV (1947), 236–49; H. Mattingly in *Proc. African Class. Assns.* I (1958), 26 (her Bellona aspect, which inspired Pontius' servant to prophecy: Plut. *Sulla*, 27. 6); A. Alföldi in *Amer. Journ. Arch.* LXIV (1960), 141; A. D. Momigliano in *J.R.S.* LIII (1963), 107. Although her identification with Artemis at Rome is not reported until 187 (Livy 39. 2. 8), F. Altheim (*Griech. Götter in alten Rom*, pp. 93 f.) is unconvincing in thinking her a late arrival. For her temple on the Mons Tifata (= today's basilica of *San Angelo in Formis*) see Festus, p. 503 L., and cf. G. De Sanctis, *Stor. dei Rom.* IV, 2, 159, n. 126: J. Beloch, *Campanien*^{2}, p. 362, thinks that it was a federal sanctuary, which would certainly be in keeping with her character. Her name may be similar to, but is unconnected with, Janus (A. K. Michels in *Phoenix*, XII (1958), 36 f.).

[8] E. Galli in *Studi Etruschi*, XIII (1939), 232–48.

[9] Vetter, no. 209, with the commentary in V. Pisani, *Lingue dell'Italia*, p. 109. But *famel* could be the Oscan word for slave: above, p. 52, n. 5.

of which peoples were neighbours and kindred of the Samnites; so that even if there is no positive evidence for a Tellus-cult among the Samnites it can quite safely be postulated. The palm-trees and pomegranates, typical fertility and resurrection symbols, that appear in Sabellian tomb-paintings point to the same conclusion.[1]

The inscription *anagtiaí diíviaí* on a gold ring from Aesernia shows that Angitia, a goddess of healing and security, belonged to the Samnites as well as to the Marsi and others, even if her most celebrated shrine was on Marsic soil.[2]

A nation of herdsmen could also be expected to have shepherd gods analogous to the Roman Faunus and Silvanus, and in fact the Fatui, who are to be identified with Fauni, are epigraphically attested among the Hirpini.[3]

Feronia, a *kourotrophos* and goddess of wild creatures as well as the patroness of slaves and freedmen, was worshipped throughout agricultural Italy. As she was believed to have originated among the supposed ancestors of the Samnites,[4] she must have been reckoned one of their native divinities.

The same conjecture can be made about Sancus, the god of sowing, who as the father of the eponymous god Sabus (according to some versions at least) was even more authentically Sabine.[5]

It would be surprising, too, if the same were not also true of Picus, popularly even if erroneously regarded as the eponym of a Sabellian people; of Lucina or her equivalent, the Italic goddess of childbirth; and of Luna and of Terminus, both of whom were widely known in Central Italy.[6]

[1] Possibly the Samnites' inhumation rite does also: see Dietrich, *Mutter Erde*, p. 66. It is not always easy to distinguish the Earth Goddess from 'a personification of Italia' (E. Strong in *J.R.S.* XXVII (1937), 114–26).

[2] One of her functions was to cure snakebite (but that does not make the proposed etymology Angitia from *anguis* trustworthy). Anaptysis (which was very common amongst the Sabellians of Campania) is responsible for the form of her name at Aesernia. Amongst the Paeligni, interestingly enough, she gets the epithet Cerealis. See Vetter, nos. 204–8, 211.

[3] Vetter, no. 165. Cf. Serv. *ad Aen.* 8. 314.

[4] This version of her origin, although accepted by Dion. Hal. 2. 49. 5, is from Varro (*L.L.* 5. 74) and very suspect. She may have been Faliscan (M. G. Bruno in *Rend. Istit. Lombardo*, XCV (1961), 534). For her kourotrophic aspect, see Bloch-Foti in *Revue de Philol.* XXVII (1953), 76, n. 3.

[5] Dion. Hal. 2. 49. 2.

[6] The comparative method, however, has its limitations, as the case of Janus shows. He seems almost exclusively Roman, even though he was regarded as the oldest god in all Italy (Herodian 1. 16. 1). He was evidently a stranger to Samnium until the Latin colonists brought him to Luceria in 314: a small statuette of him from there is nothing but a crude copy of his likeness on Roman coins (U. Scerrato in *Archeologia Classica*, VII (1955), 192–4 and pl. LXXIX).

The Agnone tablet shows that the Samnite religion embraced Greek as well as native Italic gods. Some of the foreign divinities may have been brought in quite deliberately.[1] It was from Tarentum that Greek ideas came into the heart of Italy.[2] Members of the Olympic community were sometimes either wholly or partly assimilated to native divinities. Such syncretism had begun even before the fifth-century Sabellian expansion into Campania, and (so it has been argued)[3] even before Rome had undergone much Hellenization. If it is true that Greek deities reached Rome via various Italic peoples, the preliterate Samnites could hardly have been the intermediaries. Indeed most people will believe that a city which less than three-quarters of a century after its destruction by the Celts in 387 could be described by a Greek contemporary as 'Greek'[4] needed at most only Etruscans, and perhaps not even them, to introduce it to Hellenic ways and practices. The *abundantissimus amnis* which brought Greek culture to Rome was the Tiber itself, not the Calor.[5]

An early importation, but from Croton (where there seems to have been a very ancient Rhodian settlement) rather than Tarentum, was Hercules. His altar in the Forum Boarium at Rome is on the route followed by the Luperci, in other words on the very boundary of the Palatine settlement. His cult became widespread in early Italy and he acquired many purely Italic traits.[6] The Etruscans adopted

[1] During the Samnite Wars the Romans sought the aid of gods other than their own: they imported Aesculapius in 293 (the incident is abundantly documented: e.g. Livy 10. 47. 7). The Samnites may have done something similar. There was also the venerable Italic practice of abducting the enemy's god (*evocatio*) (see Livy 5. 21 and 22), to which the Samnites may likewise have had recourse.

[2] Tarentum had been a centre of Greek influence long before the Spartan colony was established there. Already in Achaean times there was a Hellenic (Rhodian?) colony at Scoglio del Tonno, now a reef of islets at the western tip of the harbour but in those days a promontory (Lord William Taylour, *Mycenaean Pottery in Italy*, pp. 81–137). See, too, P. Wuilleumier, *Tarente*, pp. 663 f. Livy 39. 8–14 tells us that it was a Greek priest who spread the Bacchanalian rites.

[3] F. Altheim, *Terra Mater*, pp. 1–20.

[4] See Heraclides Ponticus *ap.* Plut. *Camillus*, 22. 3. Heraclides, impressed perhaps by Rome's dealings with Naples in 327/326, may have exaggerated somewhat: he was prone to purvey childish stories (Cic. *de nat. deorum*, 1. 13). Dion. Hal. *passim* also stresses the Hellenic character of Rome, and he too could be exaggerating (H. Hill in *J.R.S.* LI (1961), 88–93). But Demetrius Poliorcetes said the same thing (Strabo 5. 3. 5, p. 232). The evidence is cumulative.

[5] Cic. *de re pub.* 2. 19. 34. The Romans, however, did not need even the Etruscans to introduce them to Castor and Pollux: these deities reached Latium directly from Magna Graecia in the sixth century (F. Castagnoli in *Studi e Mater. di St. delle Religioni*, XXX (1959), 109; S. Weinstock in *J.R.S.* L (1960), 112–18).

[6] [Arist.], *de mirabilibus auscultationibus*, 97; Dion. Hal. 1. 40. 6; Wilamowitz, *Heracles*², I, 25; G. De Sanctis, *Stor. dei Romani*, IV, 2, 262; J. Toutain in *Rev. Etudes Latines*, VI (1928), 200 f. From his appearance at Agnone, he seems to have been more than a demigod to

him with enthusiasm and so did the Samnites. No doubt they approved of his *virtus*; at Agnone it is his fecundating power that predominates. He remained popular with them throughout their history.[1]

The Samnites likewise adopted Pollux and Castor. These stalwarts of Spartan Tarentum had no Samnite centre of worship as important as Tusculum, but they had a temple in Sabellian Capua and appeared on the coins of Luceria (in Samnite territory, even if a Latin Colony) already in the third century. Later they were to appear on the coins of the Social War insurgents.[2]

The Nymphae were other early arrivals: and they, too, found a welcome among the Samnites, being included amongst the divinities at Agnone.[3]

Apollo, the particular protector of pastoral communities and in his solar aspect the supreme dispenser of agricultural wealth,[4] was bound to be one of the greatest gods. He seems to be closely associated with Mars and might possibly be a legacy from the Samnites' more remote past.[5] On the whole, however, the probabilities are that he was a Greek importation into the Italic world, possibly from Cumae. At Rome he seems quite unimportant before the Second Punic War:[6] the Sibylline books had indeed acquired great consequence before

the Samnites, and it may have been they who helped to popularize his *martial* aspect at Rome (J. Bayet, *Les origines de l'Hercule romain*, pp. 291, 325–32; R. M. Peterson, *The Cults of Campania*, p. 23). It is to be noted that Rome marked her victory in the Second Punic War by dedicating a huge statue to Hercules on the Capitol (see below, p. 272, n. 4). Did this result from an *evocatio* of a martial Hercules? Prior to 312 the cult of Hercules at Rome seems to have been the private concern of the Potitii and the Pinarii (Bayet, *op. cit.* pp. 241 f.; Wissowa, *op. cit.* p. 274).

[1] *CIL*, IX, 2322; A. Rocco in *Samnium*, XXV (1952), 53–5. An important Sabellian shrine to Hercules lay on the boundary between Nola and Abella (E. Pulgram in *Amer. Journ. Phil.* LXXXI (1960), 16–29). The magnificent sanctuary on the Monte Morrone in Paelignian country was also apparently dedicated to him. For Sabellian worship of Hercules, see Vetter, nos. 1, 148, 216, 217, 220.

[2] The Dioscuri certainly had a temple at Capua (R. M. Peterson, *The Cults of Campania*, p. 343; J. Heurgon, *Capoue préromaine*, p. 123) and they were also favourites of the Paeligni (Vetter, no. 202) and the Marsi (Vetter, no. 224). Their appearance on insurgent coins in the Social War may, of course, be merely due to the fact that these coins are imitations of Roman issues.

[3] After their appearance at Agnone, the Nymphae are not documented again in Samnium until quite late (*CIL*, IX, 2163, from Caudium). See H. Herter in *R.E.* XVII (1937), s.v. 'Nymphai', col. 1569.

[4] C. Koch, *Gestirnverehrung im alten Italien, passim*. The title *Lycaeus* suggests some relationship with Mars' animal, the wolf. There was undoubtedly close association between Mars and Apollo: see Roscher's *Lexikon der Mythologie*, s.v. 'Mars'.

[5] G. Devoto, *Gli Antichi Italici*², pp. 47 f., feels sure only of Jupiter as a survival from their pre-Italian days. For his connexion with Mars, see Roscher, *Lexikon*, s.v. 'Mars'.

[6] G. De Sanctis, *Storia dei Romani*, IV, 2, 184–91.

then, but they may not originally have been connected with his cult. In any event, whenever he arrived, he became very popular in Oscan-speaking Italy. Festus implies that he was known throughout Samnium as early as the third century, and epigraphy lends some support to the story that he was the chief deity of the Mamertini at Messana.[1] Campania can still boast of a village called Casapulla, which presumably occupies the site of one of his temples;[2] and he was one of the principal deities worshipped by the Italian, and largely Sabellian, community on Delos in the second century.

Hermes, the *kriophoros* (or *moschophoros*?), was another god who recommended himself to a nation of herdsmen. Roman experience suggests that he was a relative late-comer, but we have already seen him as Euclus at Agnone in the third century. His cult evidently spread through Sabellian Italy, since the Frentani put him on their coins. The Samnites evidently knew him in various aspects, since a second-century tomb-painting from the oscanized Latin Colony of Aesernia shows him in his role of *psychopompos*.[3]

Dionysus came to enjoy an enormous vogue in Southern Italy. As he was already well known in Cumae by the fifth century[4] and was already by then being depicted on 'Saticulan' vases, he was adopted early; and there was a native Italic deity to whom he could be conveniently assimilated, called Liber in Latin and Loufir in Oscan.[5] His cult seems to have had an especial appeal for female worshippers (it will be remembered that its most zealous proselytizers at Rome were Sabellian priestesses),[6] but the Samnites must always have been hospitably inclined to a god so closely connected with the soil. After the Second Punic War the mystic-cult of Dionysus–Bacchus became widely popular in Southern Italy.[7]

[1] Festus, p. 150 L.; Vetter, no. 196. See C. Cichorius, *Römische Studien*, p. 60.

[2] And his temple at Pompeii dates from the 'Samnite period': Vetter, no. 18. The temple at Pietrabbondante probably was also dedicated to him. Reject, however, the curious theory of V. D'Amico, *Religione e Lingua dei Sanniti* (Campobasso, 1952), *passim*, that Apollo was the chief god of the Samnites.

[3] Reproduced in M. A. Napoli, *Pittura Antica in Italia*, p. 15.

[4] F. Cumont, *Les rel. orient. dans le paganisme rom.*[4], p. 197. Livy (39. 8. 3), however, implies that the Romans at least acquired him from Etruria. A 'Samnite' Dionysiac sanctuary has been discovered just outside Pompeii (A. Maiuri, *Pompei* (Itinerario)[5], p. 102).

[5] Vetter, nos. 170, 209. For the assimilation of Dionysus, see A. Bruhl, *Liber Pater*, *passim*.

[6] Livy 39. 13. 9; 39. 17. 6; F. Altheim, *Hist. Rom. Religion*, pp. 293, 310.

[7] But the debaucheries and excesses which according to Livy (39. 8–14) then featured it are not in keeping with what is known of Samnite family life.

Other immigrant deities besides Dionysus had little difficulty in finding more or less suitable Italic equivalents. Demeter, whose name can be restored with some confidence on a fragmentary Oscan inscription, came to be identified, ultimately even if imperfectly, with Kerres.[1] Aphrodite could be equated with Herentas–Venus.[2] Some of the characteristics of Ares could be attributed to Mamers.[3] Athena became identified with the (originally Faliscan?) Minerva, got her head on to the coins of Aesernia, Allifae, Aquilonia, Telesia and Venafrum, and acquired an important shrine at Luceria, the oscanized Latin Colony: she was even honoured in a Latin inscription set up on the island of Rhodes by a speaker of Oscan.[4] The Sabellians seem to have found in the Vibiae something equivalent to the Erinyes.[5]

In most cases the assimilation was far from complete, and some of the imported gods were never identified at all with native ones. *Nolle deos mutari veterem formam.*[6] Nevertheless they did not as a rule remain entirely unaffected by their new environment: like Hercules, they lost some of their Greek aspect and acquired an Italic one. By way of compensation native gods for whom no Greek name could be found, Flora for instance, might acquire some Greek trappings.

After 425 the speakers of Oscan were firmly established in Campania and were there exposed to the influence not only of Greece, but also of Etruria the *genetrix et mater superstitionis*.[7] But the *interpretatio Etrusca* does not seem to have had as much appeal as the Greek. Despite the polylatrous tendency of the Samnites there is no

[1] Vetter, no. 175. See J. Bayet in *Rev. Belge de Philologie et d'Histoire*, XXIX (1951), 5–32, 341–66.

[2] The Italic stem *her-* implies creative power and Herentas was associated with vegetable growing (cf. Festus, p. 51 L.; J. Heurgon, *Capoue préromaine*, p. 289; G. Wissowa, *Rel. und Kultus*², p. 385; M. Lejeune in *Hommages à Jean Bayet*, pp. 383–400). The original character of Herentas is very uncertain. Perhaps she was at first a fertility goddess rather than a personification of desire.

[3] G. Hermansen, *Studien über den italischen und römischen Mars*, pp. 15–18.

[4] Verg. *Aen.* 7. 805 makes Camilla, the Volscian (i.e. the near-Sabellian) maid, disclaim any use for Minerva-worship. Yet Minerva was certainly worshipped by Sabellians from early in the third century (A. Degrassi, *ILLRP*, I, no. 245; Vetter, nos. 27, 76, 80, 192, 203) and probably by Samnites in the late second or early first century (Vetter, no. 158, where the acephalous *tanas* probably refers to Athena: the suggestion that *frunter* contains a god's name is unconvincing). Minerva's head also appears on coins and *Iovila* inscriptions from Sabellian Italy. For the shrine at Luceria see Strabo 6. 1. 4, p. 264, and for the Rhodes inscription *CIL*, I, 2, 404. Bronze figurines showing her complete with aegis have been found in some quantity in Central Italy (see G. Q. Giglioli in *Arch. Classica*, IV (1952), pl. XL, XLV, XLVI, XLVII). Varro (*L.L.* 5. 74), of course, claims her as Sabine.

[5] Vetter, no. 6.

[6] Tac. *Hist.* 4. 53.

[7] Arnob. 7. 26. Cf. Livy 5. 1. 6: (*Etrusci*) *gens ante omnes alias...dedita religionibus.*

evidence for an authentic example of an Etruscan-type triad. Even in Cumae the introduction of such a triad apparently had to await the coming of the Romans.[1] The orgiastic practices of the Etruscans also were not adopted in Samnium, and their monster-filled eschatology found little favour there. The partly theriomorphic Tuchulcha did not become a Samnite divinity, although a demon is occasionally shown as the companion of the dead on their last journey in Campanian tomb-paintings.[2] Even Samnite addiction to divination and magic remained seemingly unaffected by Etruscan practices.[3]

Their tomb-paintings reveal that the Sabellians of Campania were acquainted with Greek notions of divinity and the after-life already by 400, if not earlier. It was after that date, however, that Hellenization made extensive headway.[4] The third century was the period when Greek influences asserted themselves in full spate, because of the activities of King Pyrrhus, the Sicilian operations in the First Punic War, and Ptolemaic commercial and political enterprises, but above all because of the Second Punic War crisis,[5] which

[1] This was also the case at Pompeii: A. K. Lake in *Mem. Amer. Acad. Rome*, XII (1935), 134. Despite Maule-Smith, *Votive Religion at Caere*, p. 45, triads were an Etruscan idea: L. Banti in *Studi Etruschi*, XVII (1943), 187–224; J. Bayet, *Hist. pol. et psych. de la rel. romaine*, p. 119. The Sabellian temple at Cumae, with the still unpublished Oscan inscription behind its south wall, had to be enlarged to accommodate a Roman triad: M. W. Frederiksen in *P.B.S.R.* XIV (1959), 89. The triad of Jupiter Flagius–Damusa–Vesuna postulated by G. Devoto for Sabellian Campania (in *Enc. Ital.* s.v. 'Oschi', pp. 653 f.) depends upon a forced interpretation of the relevant inscriptions (Vetter, nos. 85, 106).

[2] M. S. Bertarelli in *Fasti Arch.* XII (1959), 186, no. 2871. On Etruscan eschatology, see A. D. Nock in *Amer. Journ. Phil.* LXXII (1951), 73 (rev. of Grenier).

[3] V. Pisani, *Lingue dell'Italia*, p. 99, and G. Bottiglioni, *Manuale dei Dialetti Italici*, p. 206, suggest that the Samnites had *fulguriatores*. But their only evidence is the word *frunter* in Vetter, no. 158: they seek a relationship between this word and the word *frontac* on the Etruscan bilingual from Pesaro. It is a mere guess that these two words are somehow connected. In any case the Etruscan one may be only a name (A. Degrassi, *I.L.L.R.P.* II, no. 791), and in that case it is not easy to see why the Oscan one should mean *fulguriator*. Diodorus 20. 26. 4 mentions a town in Samnium called Ceraunilia, which suggests thunderbolts (like those that descended on the Iapygii? see Athen. 12, p. 523): this, however, is far from saying that the Samnites had any knowledge of the Etruscan *libri fulgurales*.

[4] There was some Hellenization in the fourth century (F. Sartori in *Rev. Stor. Ital.* LXXII (1960), 9), although for the most part 'the new Hellenization of Italy (comes) after the Pyrrhic War' (M. Rostovtzeff, *Soc. and Econ. Hist. Hell. World*, III, 1415, n. 198). Apollo, Hermes, Demeter, Dionysus and the Dioscuri had reached Rome by 484, but thereafter no more Greek cults were imported until Aesculapius was brought during the Third Samnite War (G. Wissowa, *Rel. und Kultus*², pp. 268, 293, 297, 304). For the influence of Pyrrhus, see J. Gagé in *Rev. hist. des religions*, CXLV (1954), CXLVI (1954) and CXLVII (1955): his combinations are often far-fetched, however.

[5] Livy (25. 40. 2) says, with some exaggeration, that it was the Roman capture of Syracuse in 212 that started Italian admiration for Greek accomplishments.

helped to foster foreign cults in Rome and in Italy generally. The Samnites, however, seem to have been selective. They did not adopt every Greek divinity and, despite their predilection for polylatry, do not seem to have taken to that typically Hellenistic institution, the pantheistic cult. The Romans may have introduced Greek cults as a means for circumventing a ban on political associations.[1] Perhaps the Samnites, too, adopted those foreign gods whose worship was most conducive to the formation of political groups disguised as devotees.[2] In any event 'the new Hellenization of Italy' went gradually forward: the Agnone tablet is conclusive evidence of it.

After the third century, during the long years of the Samnites' association with Rome, Hellenic-type conceptions and practices made ever greater inroads on native usages. A plethora of statuettes of Hercules, found and in many cases probably made in Samnium, are Hellenic in style and suggest that by the second century the Greek influence was much stronger than it had been when the cult of Hercules had first been introduced centuries earlier.

By the late second century the application of Greek mythology to Italic gods (the *interpretatio Graeca*) must have brought about some change in the Samnite view of divinity, since by 100 few if any of the native deities could have remained completely unchanged. Moreover, by then Roman as well as Greek influences had made themselves felt, neither the Samnites' innate conservatism nor their anti-Roman sentiments enabling them entirely to escape the stream of ideas emanating from the city on the Tiber. For that matter the Romans sometimes ordered their Allies in Italy to participate in Roman festivals of thanksgiving and to suppress cults and rituals of which they disapproved.[3] The so-called Oath of Philippus illustrates the spread of Roman notions. In it the Samnites and other Italic insurgents of 91 swore to be eternally grateful to M. Livius Drusus and to Rome once they obtained Roman citizenship. Diodorus purports to reproduce the oath verbatim; but the order in which the gods are invoked and other considerations prove that his version cannot be authentic. The significant thing, however, is that whoever fashioned the document took it for granted that the Samnites

[1] A. Alföldi in *Studi e Materiali di Storia delle Religioni*, XXXII (1961), 36.

[2] Or are we to say of the Samnites what Dion. Hal. (2. 18. 2) said of Romulus? πάντα τὰ τοιαῦτα ὁμοίως κατεστήσατο τοῖς κρατίστοις τῶν παρ' Ἕλλησι νομίμων.

[3] In 181, for instance (Livy 40. 19. 5).

and their associates would be quite familiar with typically Roman gods,[1] Jupiter Capitolinus, for instance.

When the Oscan civilization received its *coup de grâce* at the Colline Gate in 82, a religious *koiné* became possible for Italy, and the Olympic religion then came to predominate among the Samnites.[2] But, despite the attenuation of the native Samnite religious tradition, some primitive practices must have lingered on in the rural districts, and, although the Romans did not hesitate to interfere with the religious life of the peoples of Italy, when it suited their interests to do so, they did not in practice often seek to suppress forcibly native cult observances. Rudolph, who argues that whenever Rome incorporated Italian communities she suppressed their original civic institutions and replaced them with others of her own devising, admits that she did not do this with their religious institutions.[3] And one remembers the treatment of the rebellious Hernici in 306: Rome allowed them no native officials, with the significant exception of officials in charge of sacred rites.[4] Indeed Rome sometimes officially encouraged what Festus calls the *municipalia sacra*, at Lanuvium for instance.[5] Consequently there must have been religious survivals in rural Italy. Perhaps such present-day ceremonies as the snake festival at (Paelignian) Cocullo and the Ceri festival at (Umbrian) Gubbio, with their essentially pagan overtones, derive ultimately from the worship of Angitia and Kerres.[6]

The evidence at our disposal deals with the externals of the Samnite religion. Little is known about its spiritual content. The adjective *pius*, which has contractual implications,[7] is applied to Jupiter on the Agnone tablet, and this suggests that the Samnites approached their gods in the bargaining spirit of *do ut des*. The

[1] Ὅρκος Φιλίππου, the title it bears in the MS, should probably be emended to Ὅρκος Φιλίας (O. Hirschfeld, *Kleine Schriften*, pp. 288 f.). Although probably a forgery (H. J. Rose in *Harv. Theol. Rev.* xxx (1937), 165–81), it could be contemporary with the Social War, having originated perhaps from circles that had come under Hellenistic influences and were eager for Roman citizenship (E. Gabba in *Athenaeum*, xxxii (1954), 111, n. 2). See further, below, p. 338, n. 3.

[2] Cf. Livy 8. 11. 1: *omnis divini humanique moris memoria abolevit nova peregrinaque omnia priscis ac patriis praeferendo.*

[3] H. Rudolph, *Stadt und Staat im römischen Italien*, pp. 30 f. and elsewhere.

[4] Livy 9. 43. 24.

[5] Festus, p. 146 L.; Livy 8. 14. 2.

[6] T. Ashby, *Some Italian Scenes and Festivals*, pp. 109–22 (Cocullo); H. M. Bower, *Elevation and Procession of the Ceri at Gubbio*, pp. 19–140; I. Rosenzweig, *Ritual and Cults of pre-Roman Iguvium*; and R. S. Conway, *Ancient Italy and Modern Religion*, pp. 1–10 (Gubbio).

[7] H. J. Rose, *Anc. Roman Religion*, p. 17; J. Hellegouarc'h, *Le vocabulaire latin*, p. 276.

Sacred Spring also illustrates their adherence to the principle of the *votum*. The idea of the *quid pro quo* predominated. No doubt the Samnites discharged their vows punctiliously. They help to prove the truth of Varro's assertion that in Italy religion was always dominated by interest.

Gradually their spontaneous awe at the spirit-filled world around them must have given place to a growing rationalism. The knowledge of writing and the spread of Greek ideas may have brought some systematized formality into Samnite cult practices, but in the process some vitality was drained away. Livy's *doctrina deos spernens*[1] encompasses more than just the Romans.

Even so, Samnium remained prevailingly peasant country where a *diligentior ritus patrii custodia*[2] prevailed. Ovid suggests that even at the very end of the first century the rustic *pagus* was still the centre of an active religious life.[3] He of course had his own Paelignian homeland in mind, but his picture was true also of the Sabellians of Campania,[4] and it must also have been true of the neighbouring, closely related Samnites. The *lustratio finium* carried out by the *pagus Lucullanus* on the territory of Beneventum[5] looks very much like a survival from the pre-Roman and pre-Latin days of that town. Paganism in the literal sense of the word was never completely eradicated in Samnium.

State cults with an institutional character undoubtedly existed among the Samnites. They could have no more envisaged a religion distinct from the state or a state distinct from its religion than any other people of early Italy. Each tribe presumably had its own particular *sacra*, divine patrons and organized apparatus of state worship. This is proved for the Sabellian Campani by the *Iovila* inscriptions and we get a further glimpse of the organized religion of the Campani in Livy: *Campanis omnibus statum sacrificium ad Hamas erat*.[6] The Oscan inscriptions support Livy in implying that the magistrates played an official part in the religious life of a Sabellian state.[7]

[1] Livy 10. 40. 10.
[2] Velleius 1. 4. 2.
[3] *Fasti*, 1. 669–74.
[4] M. W. Frederiksen, *P.B.S.R.* XIV (1959), 85; *ILS*, 6302 (the *pagus Herculaneus* and the Terminalia); *CIL*, 1, 2, 674, 677–83, 687, 688.
[5] *ILS*, 6507.
[6] Livy 23. 35. 3. Hamae lay three miles north-east of Cumae (*Not. d. Sc.* (1885), p. 81; J. Heurgon, *Capoue préromaine*, pp. 382–4).
[7] Livy 23. 35. 13; Vetter, nos. 86, 88A.

Whether in Hellenic fashion a Samnite tribe sought to procure the *pax deorum* by means of *lectisternia* and fasts, except when ordered to do so by Rome, it is impossible to say.[1] Certainly offerings of cakes and beverages featured in their rituals just as they did in those of other Italic peoples, and their cults were unquestionably celebrated with sacrifices: the Sacred Spring proves this spectacularly. The animals with which they sought to placate their divinities included those normally offered to the gods by primitive peoples who get their living from the soil: viz. sheep and oxen, the most valuable property such communities possess. The animal, however, for which we have documentary evidence is the pig, the victim in many primitive Italic cults.[2] The *Iovilae* show that a pig was at least sometimes sacrificed at the funeral of a Sabellian at Capua. It was also the animal that helped solemnly to formalize the Caudine Peace.[3] A *porca caesa* likewise appears on the coins of insurgents of the Social War, who included Samnites. In their prehistoric past the Samnites may also have had recourse to human sacrifices: it is implicit in the rite of the Sacred Spring, in which even in later times the 'sacrificed' children were veiled (or possibly blindfolded),[4] in other words dedicated; and it may be implicit in the gladiatorial games of which the Sabellians were so fond (Varro at least thought that these were commutations of human sacrifice).[5] Florus roundly accuses them of human sacrifice in historical times (but the parallel passage of Livy reveals that this is the occasion when Samnite soldiers who showed reluctance to swear to fight to the death were slaughtered on the spot).[6] The Romans, who prided themselves on their emancipation from what Cicero calls the *immanem ac barbaram consuetudinem hominum immolandorum*,[7] did not get rid of it entirely. And Roman human sacrifices were not always of foreigners as they were in 226.[8] As late as imperial times, according to Pliny and others,

[1] See Livy 40. 19. 4–5. *Epulae publicae* were conducted by Sabellians in Campania, significantly under a Greek name (Vetter, nos. 76, 81, 84, 86, 88).

[2] Varro, *R.R.* 2. 4. 9; Festus, p. 274 L.; Vetter, p. 69; cf. Polyb. 2. 15. 3. The pig was the animal sacrificed to Juno and, we may suspect, to Kerres (Serv. *ad Aen.* 8. 84; cf. Cato, *de agric.* 139; Hor. *Epp.* 2. 1. 143).

[3] Cic. *de inv.* 2. 30. 91. Treaties negotiated by fetials were solemnized *porca caesa* (Suet. *Claudius*, 25. 5).

[4] Festus, p. 520 L.

[5] See Serv. *ad Aen.* 3. 67.

[6] Florus 1. 11. 9; Livy 10. 38. 3–13.

[7] *Pro Font.* 31; cf. Caes. *B.G.* 6. 16.

[8] The sacrifice of foreigners in 226 and 216 (for which see Livy 22. 57. 6; Oros. 4. 13. 3; Plut. *Marc.* 3. 6; *Rom. Qu.* 83; Dio, fr. 48 M.) may have been an exercise in sympathetic magic, an attempt to annihilate hostile nations symbolically.

the Romans occasionally offered human beings to their gods.[1] The Samnites might well have done so earlier. *Tantum religio potuit suadere malorum.*[2]

Besides the rites and festivals celebrated by the individual tribes, there must have been others that belonged to the Samnite League as a whole. The Sabellian Campani had a federal shrine at Hamae, just north of Cumae, and the Sabellic League had federal *sacra.*[3] The Samnites, who included the 'federal' Diana among their divinities, also had such institutions, according to Livy. In fact the Samnite League could conceivably have originated as a religious association. Its sacred gathering-place is unknown. Excavations at Pietrabbondante have disclosed a religious centre of some importance,[4] but it cannot be shown to have served the Samnite League in the same way that Volsinii did the Etruscan League or Aricia the Latin.

Both literary and documentary sources indicate that the *meddices*, including specifically the *meddix tuticus* and apparently the *kenzstur*, played a part in the religious life of the state:[5] they were officially present at certain ceremonies to ensure that all details of ritual were properly performed. There must also have been official priests and other functionaries to supervise and regulate the state festivals, to insert the intercalary period as required, to define the limits of sanctuaries, to keep records and to adapt the religious life of their states to the changed conditions brought about by Roman supremacy.[6] These priests later probably formed the basis for Augustus' system of *seviri Augustales.*[7] The Samnites presumably also had priestesses: at any rate, their close kinsmen the Campani certainly did.[8]

[1] Pliny, *N.H.* 28. 12; Suet. *Aug.* 15; Dio 43. 24; 48. 14; 48. 48; S.H.A. *Aurelian*, 20; Tert. *Apol.* 9. 5.

[2] Lucretius I. 101.

[3] For Diana as a 'federal' divinity: Livy I. 45. 2; Dion. Hal. 4. 25. 3; cf. Thuc. 3. 104. 3.

[4] G. De Sanctis, *Storia dei Romani*, I, 103; H. Nissen, *Ital. Landesk.* II, 787.

[5] Livy 23. 35. 13; Diod. 22. 13. 2–8; Vetter, nos. 86, 88A. Similarly amongst the Sabines two of the *octoviri* may have been specifically charged with religious functions (A. Rosenberg, *Staat der alter Italiker*, pp. 40–6).

[6] The Museo Nazionale at Naples houses a fresco painting, purportedly of a Sabellian priest, of *c.* 400.

[7] M. W. Frederiksen (in *P.B.S.R.* XIV (1959), 83 f., 93) points out that right down to the end of the Republic Capua had religious officials called *magistri* who *inter alia* supervised the *fanum Dianae Tifatinae.*

[8] Livy 39. 13. 9; so did the related Paeligni: Vetter, no. 213.

There is no evidence for priestly castes among the Samnites, unless we regard the apocryphal Ovius Paccius as a member of one. More probably the priesthoods were monopolized by their *primores*, but we do not know whether, like their Roman counterparts, the Samnite pontiffs made unscrupulous use of religious ritual to serve their own political ends.[1]

There may also have been priestly brotherhoods, such as the Atiedii at Iguvium or the Arvales at Rome. Perhaps it was such a brotherhood that celebrated the rites at Agnone.

The official priesthood would naturally have to concern itself with state shrines and their contents. Forest groves no doubt long remained the ordinary meeting-places of Samnite worshippers: the spirit immanent in grove or cavern requires no temple. Similarly at Rome open-air sanctuaries existed before temples: it is known, for instance, that an *ara Dianae* preceded the Temple of Diana on the Aventine.[2] By the time, however, that the recorded history of the Samnites begins, temples as well as open-air shrines must have been in use.[3] The Samnite Wars brought on a most feverish period of temple building in Rome. Their effect on Samnium must have been similar. Livy alludes casually to one of the Samnite temples: it was dedicated to Jupiter Vicilinus in Hirpinian Compsa.[4] Remains of several can be seen at Pietrabbondante. Most Samnite temples, it may be suspected, were built during the period when the Samnites were under Roman domination; but it is safe to assume that the Samnites built far fewer temples than their Roman overlords. As members of the Roman 'confederacy' they supplied soldiers to help Rome win

[1] According to Polybius (6. 56. 6 f.), the Roman *nobiles* did not prostitute religious practices to serve political ends in pre-Gracchan days. But the Roman *patres* evidently did (in 215, for example, they were able to get the election of two plebeian consuls declared void on the ground that *id deis cordi non esse*: Livy 23. 31. 9). Livy (9. 11. 12) does not hesitate to talk about *ludibria religionum*—precisely in the period of the Samnite Wars. See, further, Cic. *de legibus*, 2. 12. 30–1; L. R. Taylor, *Roman Politics*, pp. 76–97.

[2] At Aufidena an open-air sanctuary surrounded by a simple portico was found, with a shrine at its centre (V. D'Amico in *Not. d. Sc.* (1902), pp. 516–25), a kind of half-way house from open grove to roofed temple. For the Aventine open-air sanctuary, see *ILS*, 4907. *Haec fuere numinum templa*, as Pliny (*N.H.* 12. 3) says of trees.

[3] A temple existed already in the sixth century in the sacred area of S. Omobono in Rome; and temples were bound to attract cult statues and paraphernalia of Greek origin, such as *lectisternia*.

[4] Such a temple might have been directly under the charge of the *pagus* in which it was situated (Frederiksen in *P.B.S.R.* XIV (1959), 90). The Cippus Abellanus (Vetter, no. 1) suggests that temples might have treasuries attached to them, as at Rome.

her empire, but the material profits from the Mediterranean conquests were used for monumental edifices on Roman soil rather than on Samnite.[1]

Cult images and temples were not necessarily inseparable notions. The temple of Vesta at Rome was famed for not having a cult-statue,[2] and the image of Diana Nemorensis stood in its grove at Aricia long before it was housed in a temple.[3] The ancient writers believed that the Romans for long observed an aniconic severity, regarding the famous terracotta statue of Jupiter on the Capitol or the wooden statue of Diana on the Aventine as the oldest statue in Rome.[4] But crude statues found at Castelgandolfo (i.e. Alba Longa) imply that from the earliest beginnings of their nation the Romans must have known about cult images, and the Warrior of Capestrano suggests that an Italic people, even one that was not in direct contact with Greek settlements, could be expected to be familiar with them too as early as 500.[5] The Triflisco head, if correctly identified as that of a Samnite divinity, means that already by 400 the Samnites had begun to make statues of their gods. It is true that, contrary to what used to be believed, the Agnone tablet does not refer to statues, but only to altars. Even so, by the third century the idea of fashioning a god in the image of man must have been very familiar to the Samnites. Soon after that there came the diffusion of mass-produced small bronzes of Hercules and Mars.

1 For Roman monopolization of the profits of empire, see E. Badian, *Foreign Clientelae*, p. 151. But even on Roman soil itself temples may not have been very numerous. At Ostia the earliest surviving remains of temples seem to date from the last century B.C. And before the Pyrrhic War the temples were quite simple (Pliny, *N.H.* 16. 36; Obsequens 8).

2 Ovid, *Fasti*, 6. 295.

3 This cult image (which may be represented on a coin issued by P. Accoleius in 43) possibly was as old as the sixth century (A. Alföldi in *Gymnasium*, LXVII (1960), 193 f., and *Amer. Journ. Arch.* LXIV (1960), 143).

4 Varro *ap.* August. *de civ. Dei*, 4. 31; Ovid, *Fasti*, 1. 201; Pliny, *N.H.* 35. 157. The statue of Diana was frankly admitted to be copied from Massiliote sculpture (Strabo 4. 1. 5, p. 180). When Pliny, *N.H.* 34. 15, says that the oldest statue at Rome belonged to the period of Spurius Cassius, he probably means the oldest statue still surviving in his day.

5 'The theology of Greek archaic art' was affecting Central Italy quite powerfully in the sixth century (Maule-Smith, *Votive Religion at Caere*, p. 70). It is incorrect to imply that the Warrior of Capestrano is entirely free of Greek influence (*contra* G. M. A. Richter, *Ancient Italy*, pp. 5 f., 31).

Appendix: Note on Livy's reference to Samnite writing

The most detailed reference to Samnite writing in Livy concerns an alleged book of religious ritual. Livy asserts[1] that, on the eve of particularly important Samnite military enterprise—he specifically mentions the move against Capua in 423—a priest performed a special sacrifice, to Jupiter, so it is implied, in accordance with directions read out of an old linen book. After the sacrifice, the troops were compelled to take a most dreadful oath to follow their commanders unflinchingly and to kill anyone who was seen to flee. Those who refused to take the oath were beheaded then and there among the slaughtered sacrificial victims.

Such a ceremony took place before the Battle of Aquilonia in 293, when the men were formed into two groups: a special force (the Linen Legion) and another force which was larger in numbers and not inferior in equipment and valour. On this occasion the functioning priest was a certain aged Ovius Paccius: the solemn if gruesome affair, in which the tens of thousands of participants[2] vaguely suggest ancient equivalents of Japanese Kamikaze,[3] took place in the middle of a military camp, the nobles among the Samnites taking the oath in a linen-covered enclosure some 200 feet square.[4]

The description of the enclosure seems to derive from the description of a Roman camp in Polybius.[5] Nevertheless Livy's account is not to be summarily rejected in its entirety as merely the figment of an annalist's imagination. The Samnite *corps d'élite*, the *legio linteata*,[6] seems genuine enough. At any rate there was a firm tradition about it: the Elder Pliny and Festus, no less than Livy, both allude to it,[7] and the language used by the three authors is sufficiently different to make it probable that the versions are independent. Livy himself was so impressed by this special Samnite force that he introduced it into his narrative more than once. He had given it a prominent role in the operations of the Varronian

[1] Livy 10. 38. 3–13.

[2] Exactly how many thousands is rather uncertain: Livy (10. 38. 12) allots 16,000 men to the special force, 20,000 to the other force (10. 38. 13); but he had given their combined total as some 40,000 (10. 38. 4).

[3] There is also some resemblance to the Theban Sacred Band and, even more significantly, to the *coniuratio* of the Fabii before the Cremera operation.

[4] That is, the equivalent of 4 *versus*. (A *versus* was a unit of measurement for land in Sabellian Campania which was 100 feet (presumably Oscan feet of 27·6 cm.) square: Varro, *R.R.* 1. 10. 1.)

[5] Polyb. 6. 27–32 (especially 31. 10).

[6] Livy's expression (10. 38. 12): the Samnites may have used the word *legio* or something very like it: see Vetter, no. 6.

[7] Pliny, *N.H.* 34. 43; Festus, p. 102 L. And there may be an echo of it in Sil. Ital. 4. 223, who stations 'linen-clad' Faliscans alongside of Sabellians. Cf., too, Florus 1. 11. 7 (who derives from Livy).

year 309; and he gave additional details about it for those of 293.[1] This is some measure of the impact made by the 'Linen Legion' on the historiographical record of the Samnite Wars. Thus it seems unlikely that this tale of a Samnite special force is a complete fiction. Just as recurrent in Livy and seemingly just as genuine is the statement that a religious ritual took place in a Samnite camp. It clearly concerns the whole Samnite army and hence the Samnite League.

In great conflicts it is not unusual for one side to put an élite formation in the field and for the other side to preserve a record of the fact. This, however, is far from saying that we should therefore unhesitatingly accept all of the details which Livy gives concerning the outfitting and the preparation of the Samnite special force. In fact the details he supplies are highly unconvincing. He gives his description of the special force's weapons and accoutrements under the year 309 rather than 293, and it includes the palpable absurdity of having the Linen Legion outfitted with silver equipment including shields inlaid with the metal.[2]

Equally untrustworthy are the details he gives for the induction ceremonies in 293. And this is not surprising, since a Roman historian could hardly have known what went on at a secret ceremony in the Samnite camp shortly before a battle. There were neither Roman witnesses to view the scene nor Samnite historians to record it; and, as the incident did not occur in the vicinity of a Greek settlement, Livy's account cannot derive from some Hellenic source. Livy himself insists that everybody present had been sworn to secrecy about what he saw and heard,[3] and his suggestion that the Roman commander learned all that occurred from Samnite deserters and then left a record of it in writing is hardly convincing.[4] The jejune notices, which were all that were kept in Rome by way of historical records at the beginning of the third century, could conceivably have contained an allusion to a special Samnite force; but few will believe that they also included a minutely detailed account of the religious ceremonies with which deserters said the force had been assembled.

To these general considerations we can add others of a more specific nature. The notion of the 16,000 warriors of the Linen Legion being sworn in one at a time is preposterous. The ten Samnite nobles, who according to Livy first administered the oath individually to ten others, and the succeeding teams of ten would have needed many hours, working

[1] In 309 as well as in 293 the Samnites had two forces (the one in tunics of many colours having equipment of gold: Livy 9. 40. 3). In 293 one of the forces is called a *legio sacrata* (10. 38. 12): there was also a *legio sacrata* involved *c.* 309, albeit an Etruscan one (9. 39. 5). Livy himself hints very broadly that the details of 309 more properly belong to 293 (10. 38. 1–2).

[2] Livy 9. 40. 1–4.

[3] 10. 38. 9.

[4] 10. 40. 1, 6.

swiftly and uninterruptedly, to perform such a task, even supposing that it took only one minute to induct each man. In fact Livy's account of the Samnite muster is simply a fanciful mixture of Roman procedures as described by Polybius.[1]

Another highly suspect feature of Livy's narrative is the item about the Samnite priest following directions for the sacrifice that were read out from an old linen book. Everything about this is suspicious. In the first place, the names borne by the priest are simply too good to be true. They are so typically Oscan as to be downright unconvincing. Even a casual perusal of the surviving documentary material reveals that the names Ovius and Paccius were in the most common use wherever and whenever Oscan was spoken.[2] They are the names which would automatically occur to a Roman writer who wished to label a Samnite. One might compare the way that to an Englishman a Scot is invariably Jock and an Irishman Pat. Secondly, a Roman writer inventing a Samnite priest would inevitably provide him with the necessary appurtenance of a sacred book containing the relevant ritual. For it was a common Roman procedure to have liturgical formulae read aloud.[3] Other peoples of Italy had the same practice, the Etruscans for instance,[4] who may have taught it to the Romans, and possibly the Sabellians.[5] Even so, this is clearly the sort of stock-in-trade that a Roman might be expected to include when describing a religious ceremony whether real or imaginary.[6] Thirdly, the book itself is made of linen, a detail added no doubt to contribute verisimilitude. But this, too, could be nothing more than a rather clumsy invention requiring no great effort of the imagination, least of all from a Roman writer. Linen books of a religious character, although not necessarily containing liturgical formulae, were commonplace in ancient Italy. The most famous specimens were the Sibylline books (of whose alleged provenance from a Sabellian area Livy was well aware). But many others can be cited: the *Libri Lintei magistratuum*, which Licinius Macer and Aelius Tubero claimed to have consulted in the Temple of Juno Moneta on the Capitol; the mummy wrappings with their Etruscan text which are now in the museum at Zagreb; the linen 'corslet' inscribed with an account of Cornelius Cossus' winning of the *spolia opima*; and the

[1] Polybius 6. 20 and 24.

[2] Ovius: Vetter, nos. 18, 26, 178, 195, 224; *ILS*, 5880; *CIL*, I^2, 1700; Livy 9. 26. 7. Paccius: Vetter, nos. 6, 54d, 72e, 73, 87, 142, 158, 163, 174, 203, 204, 210, 223.

[3] See, for example, Livy 39. 18. 3 and cf. the remarks of A. D. Nock in *Gnomon*, XXVI (1954), 420 f. (reviewing Leipoldt–Morenz).

[4] *Libri Etrusci* were celebrated (Lucr. 6. 381 f.; Cic. *de div.* 1. 20. 47; C. Thulin, *Die etruskische Disziplin*, III).

[5] An initiate was introduced into the Bacchanalian rites to the accompaniment of sacred formulae read aloud by a priest (Livy 39. 18. 3).

[6] Sometimes the Romans behaved like the Greeks and refused to permit the writing out of religious formulae (Festus, p. 14 L.; Dion. Hal. 2. 72. 2); the Celts were adamant in refusing (Caes. *B.G.* 6. 14).

linen rolls which were kept at Anagnia in the time of Marcus Aurelius.[1] A Roman writer describing a Samnite priest was almost inevitably bound to provide him with a linen book: it was a kind of conventional stage prop. Livy implies that it existed before ever the Sabellians reached Campania: it apparently laid down the procedures which they observed when effecting their stealthy seizure of Capua in 423.[2] Yet, all the evidence indicates that, before their expansion into Campania, the Sabellians were still in their preliterate stage: they had no books at all, sacred or otherwise. Livy's ancient book of Samnite ritual, like the priest who obtains directions from it, is almost certainly a fiction modelled on the *rituales libri* of the Etruscans.[3] It certainly cannot be adduced as evidence that the religion of the Samnites was 'revealed' in carefully preserved sacred writings.

What Livy or his source appears to have done is to take the authentic fact of a special Samnite force (possibly of the sort that implemented a Sacred Spring) and embellish it with rhetorical details in order to impress his readers with a scene that is at once dramatic and macabre: such elaborating details as the induction ceremonies, the linen book and the recitation of liturgical formulae were taken from Roman practice. Even the episode in which the oath is administered to the Samnite warriors, apart from its bloodcurdling features, recalls what took place in a Roman legion on the occasion of the swearing of the *sacramentum*. It is merely a more savage version of a standard Roman procedure with which Livy was perfectly familiar.[4]

The one non-Roman item in the whole business is the gory detail of the reluctant recruits being immediately massacred and spattering the other soldiers and the altars with their blood (*nefando sacro mixta hominum pecudumque caede respersus; respersae fando nefandoque sanguine arae*); and this gruesome touch is nothing but sensationalism which Livy inserted in order to make a vivid and horrendous impression.[5] It is the purple patch

[1] Livy 4. 7. 12; 4. 13. 7; 4. 20. 7, 8; Fronto, *Epp.* 4. 4. To these examples we can add the inscribed rolls held by Etruscans reclining on sarcophagus lids, like the famous one at Tarquinia: these are almost certainly sculptured representations of linen rolls (J. Heurgon, *La vie quotidienne chez les Etrusques*, p. 275).

[2] Livy manifestly envisages this linen book as the Samnite equivalent to the Roman *annales maximi*: viz. a priestly record of events in earlier years. And it is, of course, reasonable to assume that, once the Samnites took to writing, their priests kept some record of important events just as the Roman pontiffs did.

[3] Festus, p. 358 L.

[4] In Livy's lifetime the methods of recruitment and induction were in part, at least, those that had been in vogue much earlier (R. E. Smith, *Service in the Post-Marian Roman Army*, pp. 45–58). See Dion. Hal. 10. 18; Festus, p. 250 L.; Macrob. 3. 75; and above all Polyb. 6. 19–21, where the language is very similar to that used by Livy in his account of the Samnites in 293. The conjectures of V. Basanoff (in *Latomus*, IX (1950), 265, 272) on Livy's description of the Samnite mobilization in 293 are not convincing.

[5] See Livy 10. 39. 16; 10. 41. 3. But even this sanguinary detail is not completely un-Roman, since a Roman soldier who violated his *sacramentum* could be despatched without more ado. The gory aspect of the Samnite muster was probably suggested to

that helps his narrative to grip his readers in awed fascination. We can hardly cite it, as Warde Fowler does, as evidence that the sprinkling of blood, normally conspicuous by its absence from Roman ritual, was nevertheless a prominent feature of Samnite.[1]

In view of all this, even though we may accept as trustworthy the implication that Samnite religious practices resembled those of the Romans, we must also reluctantly conclude that Livy's version of the way the Samnites got together a special force for the Battle of Aquilonia really throws no light whatever on their religious beliefs. The picturesque embroidery is all a figment of the imagination, either Livy's own or his source's.

Livy by the tale that the Catilinarian conspirators bound themselves by fearful oaths and drank the blood of a slain, perhaps of a sacrificed, man (Sall. *Cat.* 22; Minucius Felix 30. 5). There were also some other famous blood-spatterings in the last century which may have contributed their mite. In 80 C. Papius Mutilus, proscribed by Sulla and repudiated by his wife, stabbed himself at her door, *et sanguine suo fores uxoris respersit* (Livy, *Epit.* 89). In 55 the blood-soaked garments of Pompey caused his wife Julia to have a miscarriage (Val. Max. 4. 6. 4; Plut. *Pomp.* 53. 3; cf. Dio 39. 32. 3). *C.* 49 Antony's wife Fulvia was spattered with blood at Brundisium (Cic. *Phil.* 3. 4; cf. 3. 10; 5. 22; 13. 18).

[1] W. Warde Fowler, *Rel. Exp. of Rom. People*, pp. 196, 331.

CHAPTER 5

THE FIRST SAMNITE WAR

The Samnites of Samnium begin their recorded history in 354[1] when they signed a treaty with Rome.[2] Precisely which Samnites these were is not explicitly stated, but both Livy and Diodorus obviously think of them as the Samnite League, a view which the sequel would appear to confirm. The dealings of Rome do not seem to have been confined to just one or other of the Samnite tribes, but to have embraced them all. Nor is there any record of the League being formed after this date.

If this treaty be accepted as historical—and there is no obvious reason why it should not be—[3] two questions at once arise: why was it signed and what were its terms?

It has often been suggested that the Romans and Samnites were induced to sign the treaty by their common fear of the Celts. The Celtic sack of Rome occurred over thirty years earlier; but there had been at least one and quite possibly several Gallic incursions into peninsular Italy since then, and the victims of the Celts must have included speakers of Oscan as well as speakers of Latin. Nor could it be comfortably assumed that the raids were a thing of the past. As a matter of fact, reports of serious and alarming Gallic invasions continued to be heard for long after 354,[4] and one wonders whether the Samnites may not have helped the Romans to repel the Gauls in 349.[5] On the whole, then, the view that Romans

[1] There is an earlier reference to them in the tale that the Fabii adopted the *praenomen* Numerius when the survivor of their massacre at the blockhouse on the Cremera in 477 married the daughter of Otacilius from Samnium (Festus, p. 174 L.; Auct. *de praenom.* 6. The story reminds one of Cleisthenes of Sicyon and his daughter). But this story can hardly be older than the third century, which is when the Fabii began using the *praenomen* Numerius (F. Münzer in *R.E.* VI (1909), s.v. 'Fabius (27), (163), (171)', cols. 1747, 1881, 1885), and it may even have been invented by Cincius Alimentus in the second (J. Pinsent in *Phoenix*, XVIII (1964), 28).

[2] Livy 7. 19. 4; Diod. 16. 45. 8 (= 350, by his system of chronology).

[3] Its historicity can hardly be doubted: it is vouched for, *inter alia*, by the implication in the Rome–Carthage treaties that Rome had signed agreements with peoples beyond Latium. Some scholars, while accepting it, argue it was only the Samnites living in the vicinity of the Liris who signed it (H. Philipp in *R.E.* I A (1930), s.v. 'Samnites', col. 2143). But see B. Kaiser, *Untersuchungen*, I, 31.

[4] Mommsen's remarks on the Gallic assaults (*Röm. Forschungen*, II, 364–81) are still valuable.

[5] Polyb. 2. 18. 4–9; Livy 7. 25–6; Dion. Hal. 15. 1; Aul. Gell. 9–11.

Map 2. The Liris–Volturnus region.

and Samnites, both of them potential targets of Gallic attack, signed a defensive treaty against them is reasonable enough.

Tumultus Gallici, however, are not the entire explanation. There were other peoples than Celts spurring Romans and Samnites on to an *entente*. The activities of Italiote and Siceliote Greeks, while dangerous to both, were particularly menacing to the Samnites;[1] and the Etruscans were an especial cause of preoccupation to the Romans.[2] Nor was this all. To concern for their present security both sides added vigilance for their future prosperity.

In the years immediately preceding 354 both Romans and Samnites had been extending the radius of their influence. In the fifth century the Romans, with the cooperation of their allies, the Latins and Hernici, had repelled the various assailants of Latium: Etruscans, Sabines, Aequi, Volsci. In the fourth century they were busy rolling back the last-named, the most persistent and stubborn of all the non-Latin-speaking intruders. The Samnites, for their part, had been using the device of the Sacred Spring from time immemorial to relieve the pressure of population on their own poor land by pouring into the lands of their neighbours. Thus, they had spilled out into Picenum, the Frentani country, Northern Apulia, Lucania and Campania. In the fourth century their target was the area to the west of Samnium, where the valley of the River Liris beckoned. Here the attraction was twofold. The Liris valley could serve as an outlet for their surplus population and, besides this, it could provide them with badly needed economic resources. This is particularly true of the Middle Liris, that stretch of the river which extends from its confluence with the Lacerno just above Sora[3] to its confluence with the Rapido at Interamna.[4] The valley of the Middle Liris was not only good agricultural land: it was also an area of some mineral wealth. Its dominating feature is the picturesque and imposing mountain massif now known as the

[1] Dionysius of Syracuse (*qui multas Italiae civitates subegerat*: Justin 23. 1. 2) may have had Gallic mercenaries operating out of Apulia (M. Sordi, *I Rapporti Romano-Ceriti*, pp. 153–65; cf. Justin 20. 5. 4).

[2] From 387 to 358 Rome's relations with Etruscans (and especially with Caere) were generally friendly. From 358 on they became hostile (Livy 7. 15).

[3] Above Sora the valley of the Liris was Marsic territory (Livy 4. 45. 7, emending 'Antium' to 'Antinum'). From Sora it is possible to reach the Sagrus and Samnium by way of the Lacerno.

[4] Below the junction of Liris and Rapido (or Gari as it is here called) was Auruncan territory.

Monte della Meta.[1] Today the mineral deposits there are too meagre to be exploited commercially, although they continued to be extracted until only a few years ago.[2] In prehistoric times, however, the riches of the Meta were by no means negligible: its copper and, more particularly, its iron deposits were extensively worked by the inhabitants of early Italy.[3] The Etruscans may have been exploiting these deposits already in the sixth century, in the days of their expansion south of the Tiber. When the Etruscans were pushed back into Etruria proper in the fifth century, the Samnites, whose own mountains entirely lacked metal-bearing ores, followed in the track of their retreat. By one hundred years later they had penetrated deeply into the Meta region and by the middle of the fourth century they were firmly established in a fortress well to the west of it, named Cominium.[4] For them the Meta constituted a region of the highest importance.

By the middle of the fourth century, however, the tentacles of the Romans were also stretching towards the Middle Liris, across the country of their allies, the Hernici.[5] Proof of their progress was the creation in 358 of the new citizen tribe, Poblilia, in the valley of the River Trerus, on territory that separated the western Volsci on the coast of Latium from their kinsmen, the northern and eastern Volsci in the valley of the Middle Liris. Simultaneously (358) the Romans had re-established that superiority relative to the Latins which the assault of the Celts had so gravely impaired.[6] According to Livy, contemporary opinion in Italy expected the Romans to subjugate all the smaller peoples living between Rome and Campania.[7]

[1] The Meta forms one of the peaks of the mountain group known as Le Mainarde. Others are the Cornacchia, Petroso, and Cavallo.

[2] G. Colasanti, *Cercatori di Ferro, passim.* Iron pyrites are still sometimes found in the River Melfa.

[3] There was even some silver and, in the Valle di Canneto along the Upper Melfa, some copper (J. Heurgon, *Capoue préromaine*, p. 21). The mineral deposits of the Meta region account for the importance of Atina in early Italy (Verg. *Aen.* 7. 630). Atina was still a *praefectura plena virorum fortissimorum sic ut nulla tota Italia frequentior dici possit* in the days of Cicero (*pro Plancio*, 8. 21). Even today it still has iron foundries. Nearby Venafrum also worked the iron from the Meta: it manufactured farming utensils *c.* 200 (Cato, *de agric.* 135; cf. *CIL*, x, 1, 4855).

[4] The Val di Cómino has preserved the name down through medieval times. Cominium is perhaps to be sought immediately west of Alvito: M. Jacobelli, *Bull. Com.* LXXI (1943–5), Appendice 18. Oscan inscriptions have been found in the vicinity, at Barrea (Vetter, nos. 143, 145).

[5] The district known as La Ciociaria.

[6] Livy 7. 12. 7; cf. Polyb. 1. 6. 4; 2. 18. 5.

[7] Livy 7. 30. 8.

By the mid-fourth century, then, the valley of the Middle Liris was rapidly becoming the mecca towards which two powerful peoples were inflexibly headed. It was, it is true, still held then by the Volsci, but the Volsci were manifestly in retreat: *ferocior ad rebellandum quam ad bellandum gens*.[1] Their strength was in decline, and the real question was who was to replace them as masters of the river valley.

It is against this background that the Roman–Samnite treaty of 354 is to be set. The two parties must have signed it, not merely in order to give one another moral and material support against marauding Celts and others, but also to assure each other about their respective intentions and above all in order to arrive at an understanding about the future of the valley of the Middle Liris, seeing that the Volsci would soon cease to form an effective buffer there.

The ancient writers are unanimous in insisting that the first clash between Romans and Samnites was to decide which of them should control Campania. But it is worth noting that, before the first clash ever occurred, the two peoples had already had dealings; and these derived not from their potential rivalry in Campania, but from their simultaneous expansion towards the Middle Liris, the Romans approaching it along the valley of the Trerus and the Samnites along the valley of Cicero's natal stream, the Fibrenus.

For both sides the Middle Liris was a sensitive area. It was the river that was intimately involved in the great fight for supremacy in Italy. Complete Roman control of it would threaten Samnite mining operations in the Meta; complete Samnite control of it would point a dagger at the heart of Latium. Agreement could allay mutual apprehensions at a time when both nations, having gone through their periods of formation and consolidation, were ready for fresh adventures.[2]

A treaty, then, was drawn up in 354. Livy and Diodorus merely say that it was signed;[3] they do not give details about its terms in the way that Polybius does for the treaties Rome signed with

[1] Livy 7. 27. 7.

[2] Livy (7. 19. 4) depicts the Samnites as seeking the treaty out of the respect they felt for Roman military might. But it is also possible that the Romans were seeking to reassure the Samnites about the implications of the reactivated Romano-Latin alliance of 358 (E. T. Salmon in *Phoenix*, VII (1953), 131 f.).

[3] Their dry and matter-of-fact way of reporting it suggests that they simply took the item over as it stood from some official and presumably ancient record.

Carthage.[1] As Samnite society was then primitive and not tightly organized the treaty could have provided only for what was obvious, uncomplicated and easily enforceable. Obviously it was an agreement between two equal, high contracting powers, analogous to the instrument which Rome signed with Carthage at about the same time (in 348 actually). No matter what the narratives of Livy and Dionysius of Halicarnassus may imply,[2] it could hardly have resembled the *foedera* which in later times disguised subordination under the appearance of alliance and linked the various peoples of Italy to Rome in a kind of military confederacy, obliging them to accept and assist her military leadership. The developed Roman theory of various types of treaty (*foedus aequum*, *foedus iniquum*, *societas*, *societas et amicitia*, *amicitia*) had not emerged so early. Livy does, it is true, interpret the treaty to mean that the Samnites became the *socii et amici* of the Romans;[3] but they can no more have been such than were the contemporary Carthaginians.[4] This instrument of 354 is the first treaty that Rome signed with any Italian state outside Latium,[5] and it could not have subordinated one of the signatories to the other. The ancient writers make it clear that it was not imposed by a victor on the vanquished. There can be no doubt whatever that it was what later would have been called a *foedus aequum*.[6]

It can quite safely be assumed that the treaty was, or at any rate purported to be, defensive in character, since that was the only type of treaty that the fetials countenanced, and both Romans and Samnites used fetials for their international diplomacy. But, however defensive in its wording, it must in fact have been an agreement to divide the Volscian territory in the region of the Middle Liris into spheres of interest; and it must have defined in clear and precise language the line that neither side was to transgress. The idea of a

[1] It could not have contained anything comparable to the 'fine print' of many modern contracts; and perhaps the Roman tradition failed to preserve any of its terms, since they might have revealed too candidly the extent of Roman duplicity in 343. Regrettably the treaty is not discussed in H. Bengtson, *Staatsverträge des Altertums*, vol. II.

[2] Livy 7. 30. 4; Dion. Hal. 15. 6. 8.

[3] Livy 7. 31. 2.

[4] Livy 7. 27. 2, of course, regards the Carthaginians also as *socii et amici*. Cf., too, Dion. Hal. 17. 2. 2.

[5] Unless M. Sordi (*I Rapporti Romano-Ceriti*, pp. 36, 69 f.) is right in postulating treaties with Caere and other Etruscan states *c.* 386.

[6] Livy actually uses the word *aequus* (9. 4. 4, = 321). Note how Justin 43. 5. 10 (= Pompeius Trogus) describes the Rome–Massilia treaty of 386 as a *foedus aequum*. The expression *foedus iniquum*, of course, is not used by ancient writers even though the Romans often put into practice the idea that it represented.

demarcation line was, of course, in common use among the Hellenistic states, but that is not to say that it was an un-Roman concept. The early treaties between Rome and Carthage undoubtedly defined the spheres of interest of the high contracting parties, and the Samnite treaty must have done so too.[1] The problem is to identify the dividing line. No ancient writer describes it for us unequivocally and in so many words, but there is clear evidence that it was the Liris itself, the right bank of the middle reaches of the river being the eastern limit of the Roman zone and the left bank the western limit of the Samnite.[2] The choice of a river as the line had the obvious advantage of making any breach of it patent and undeniable; it was the sort of line that in later times the Romans often used to delimit an area.[3] In the years immediately after 354 both Romans and Samnites advanced to the Middle Liris but did not cross it.

That Romans and Samnites should have agreed thus to divide the Middle Liris valley rather than fight over it is not surprising. Each side had other preoccupations: the Samnites with Italiotes and Siceliotes, the Romans with recalcitrant Latins and Hernici. Neither side was itching to fall out with the other, since they were fairly evenly matched. For, although the Samnites controlled by far the largest territory of any people in peninsular Italy at that moment and probably the largest population as well, the strength of Rome was far from negligible: she, too, by now controlled much territory and much population.[4] Had either side insisted on becoming the exclusive heirs of the Volsci along the Middle Liris war was inevitable, and the outcome of war was unpredictable. It seemed far better to agree to share the prospective Volscian legacy jointly.

The bargain appears to have been kept: the First Samnite War interrupted it, but only temporarily. In the quarter of a century

[1] C. P. Burger, *Neue Forschungen*, II, 11. Possibly the treaty also guaranteed legal protection to Samnite visitors to Rome (such as Otacilius?): the 386 treaty with Massilia, the 348 one with Carthage, and, if Miss Sordi is right, the 386 one with Caere, may all have contained such a clause (Polyb. 3. 24. 13).

[2] A. Bernardi in *Athenaeum*, XX (1942), 23.

[3] In medieval times the Liris was the southern boundary of the Papal States.

[4] Rome was certainly the biggest city: the description of Capua as 'almost as big' (Florus 1. 11. 6) is probably an exaggeration. The 'Servian' wall, exactly contemporaneous with the Romano-Samnite treaty, had a perimeter of almost seven miles (G. Lugli in *Historia*, VII (1933), 7; Castagnoli–Cechelli–Giovannoni, *Topografia e Urbanistica di Roma*, pp. 19, 66). A. Afzelius, *Römische Eroberung Italiens*, pp. 138–43, suggests that the Samnites controlled 21,595 square kilometres of territory and 650,000 inhabitants and the Romans only some 6,095 square kilometres and 317,400 inhabitants (but he admits that his figures include areas that were not in fact part of Samnium).

after 354 Rome obtained control of Sora,[1] Satricum,[2] Fabrateria[3] and Luca,[4] all of them Volscian and all of them, so far as we know, west of the river. Livy makes it clear that the Samnites were kept informed and raised no objections.[5] Similarly the Romans acquiesced without protest when the Samnites took Interamna,[6] Casinum,[7] Arpinum[8] (and presumably Aquinum),[9] and destroyed Fregellae,[10] two of which were certainly Volscian towns and all of which were east of the river.[11] As a result of this joint expansion Roman and Samnite spheres of interest became contiguous in the Liris basin.[12] But it was not as a result of this particular physical contact that the two powers came to blows.

Conflict arose between them over an area on which they had not reached prior agreement.[13] Northern Campania became the bone of contention: it was a fertile and populous region, and neither side could afford to let the other get control of it.[14] No doubt they could have agreed to partition it in the same way that they had done the Middle Liris valley. They did not do so, however, probably because there did not seem to be any particular urgency. In the mid-fourth century the valley of the Volturnus, unlike the valley of the Liris, was not obviously becoming a power vacuum: the

[1] Livy 7. 28. 6. Sora was exclusively west of the river in antiquity. There is no need to reject (with K. J. Beloch, *Röm. Gesch.* p. 368) the notice of its capture by Ser. Sulpicius Rufus in 345: the Temple of Juno Moneta was vowed that same year and would appear to pinpoint the event (Sulpicius' victory is not reflected in Triumph. Fasti, possibly because there was no set battlepiece). A Sulpicius is also said to have taken it in 314 (Livy 9. 24 f.).

[2] Satricum (for which see further, below, pp. 229–34) was probably located at mod. Boville Ernica or possibly Monte San Giovanni.

[3] Fabrateria is to be sought at S. Sozio, alongside Ceccano.

[4] Luca is recorded again by Livy in 294 (10. 33. 1) and in 216 (22. 42. 4). It was located somewhere near Ceccano, perhaps at Villa S. Stefano (traditionally a very ancient town) or more probably at Castro dei Volsci (where polygonals still survive).

[5] Livy 8. 19. 1.

[6] That Interamna became Samnite is suggested by Sil. Ital. 8. 402 (emending *Larinatum* to *Lirenatum*).

[7] Varro, *L.L.* 7. 29.

[8] Livy 9. 44. 16; Diod. 20. 90. 4. Arpinum was certainly once Volscian (Juv. 8. 245; Sil. Ital. 8. 404; Plut. *Cic.* 1).

[9] Aquinum is not recorded until the Second Punic War.

[10] Like Arpinum, Fregellae is recorded as formerly Volscian (Livy 8. 22. 2; 8. 23. 6; Dion. Hal. 15. 8. 4).

[11] Despite Livy 8. 6. 8, these Samnite conquests probably all took place before 340 (L. Pareti, *Storia di Roma*, I, 577).

[12] Livy 8. 20. 12.

[13] Livy 7. 32. 3; 8. 23. 8; Dion. Hal. 15. 3. 2. Florus (1. 11. 1–7) suggests that the Samnite Wars were almost exclusively a struggle for Campania.

[14] For the Romans it meant a source of grain, and Rome was susceptible to famine (Livy 4. 52. 5–6).

Campani were by no means in decline.[1] Moreover Roman interests had not yet reached the valley of the Volturnus. When the crisis came over Campania, it seems to have taken both Romans and Samnites alike by surprise.

Ancient tradition insists that it was some eleven years after the signing of the Roman–Samnite treaty that armed conflict broke out between the two powers. *Eo anno adversus Samnites gentem opibus armisque validam orta arma.*[2] This is the so-called First Samnite War. But, although a number of ancient writers refer to it, only one gives details about either it or the circumstances leading up to it: namely Livy, and he was writing some three and a half centuries after the event. This is what Livy says:[3]

In 343 the Samnites made a threatening move against the Sidicini (an Oscan-speaking people living in and around the town of Teanum on the western borders of Samnium).[4] In alarm, the Sidicini invoked the aid of the neighbouring Campani, who were likewise Oscan-speaking and lived in Northern Campania, forming a league headed by Capua, next to Rome the *urbs maxima opulentissimaque Italiae*.[5] When the Campani agreed to help the Sidicini, the Samnites, who had long coveted Campania's fertile fields, shifted their hostility to them, seized the ridge on the eastern border of Campania which ends in the Mons Tifata overlooking Capua, and then routed Campanian forces on level ground near the city. It was now the turn of the Campani to become alarmed, and they invoked the aid of Rome. The Roman Senate at first refused to take any action prejudicial to the Samnites, with whom they had so recently signed a treaty. But when the Campani thereupon surrendered themselves and placed themselves abjectly and unreservedly under the protection

[1] Reject Livy 7. 29. 5; 7. 32. 7; 7. 38. 5. See, too, Cic. *In Pison.* 11. 25; Polyb. 7. 1.

[2] Livy 7. 29. 1. Since its signing the treaty had served Rome well: it had left her free to deal with the Etruscans, who became hostile at about the time the treaty was signed.

[3] The chief sources for the First Samnite War are Ox. Pap. 1. 12, p. 27, col. III (which assigns it to 340/339); Tr. Fasti *ad an.* 343; Cic. *de div.* 1. 24. 51; Dion. Hal. 15. 3. 2; Front. *Strat.* 1. 5. 14; 4. 5. 9; App. *Samn.* 1; Auct. *de vir. ill.* 26, and above all Livy 7. 29–8. 2.

[4] Livy (7. 29. 4), anxious to justify Roman infraction of the treaty of 354, insists that the Samnite aggression against the Sidicini was unprovoked. Elsewhere, however, he regards the Sidicini as troublemakers (8. 17. 3). Their city was strongly placed at the junction of five important roads.

[5] Livy 7. 31. 1. The League, which Capua headed, included Casilinum, Calatia and Atella (Livy 9. 28. 6; Diod. 19. 101. 3) and perhaps Puteoli, Volturnum, Liternum and the Sabatini (whoever they were) (K. J. Beloch, *Röm. Gesch.* p. 387). Cumae, Suessula, Acerrae, Nola, Abella and above all Naples were evidently not members of it.

of the Romans, the Senate directed the Samnites not to molest people who had by this action become Roman citizens. The Samnites rejected this ultimatum, and hostilities with the Romans inevitably ensued.

Both of the consuls for 343 took the field. M. Valerius Corvus, *maximus ea tempestate imperator,*[1] met the Samnites first and after a hard fight managed to rout them near the Mons Gaurus in Campania.[2] But the other consul, A. Cornelius Cossus, attempting to invade Samnium, marched into an ambush near the Samnite stronghold of Saticula and was saved from disaster and enabled to win a victory only by the tactical skill and personal bravery of one of his military tribunes, P. Decius Mus.[3] A short time later, Valerius Corvus defeated Samnite troops again, this time near Suessula. This brought the campaigning for 343 to an end, and the Romans left a garrison in Campania for the winter months.

In 342 Livy reports no fighting between Romans and Samnites.[4] One consul, Q. Servilius Ahala, stayed in Rome. The other, C. Marcius Rutilus, went to Campania to assume command of the garrison that had wintered there. Discovering that this garrison was planning to seize Capua by treachery,[5] Marcius Rutilus got rid of its ringleaders. But some of his troops mutinied near Tarracina, seized a position in the Alban Hills and made T. Quinctius (the consul of 354?) act as their leader. To deal with this situation M. Valerius Corvus, the consul of 343, was named dictator, with L. Aemilius Mamercinus as his master of the horse; and, as many of the mutineers were veterans of Valerius Corvus' victories of the previous year and consequently well disposed towards him, he managed to bring them under control. Nevertheless redress of plebeian grievances was one result of the mutiny.[6]

In 341 L. Aemilius Mamercinus, the master of the horse in 342, became consul and invaded Samnium, while his colleague C.

[1] Livy 8. 16. 4.

[2] At least so Livy 7. 32. 3 seems to say: but there are variant readings to *Mons Gaurus*. Auct. *de vir ill.* 26 assigns the Gaurus victory to P. Decius Mus.

[3] Decius' exploit is also alluded to by Pliny, *N.H.* 22. 9 (in a passage where Ennius seems to be the source: cf. Pliny, *N.H.* 7. 101. Perhaps the poet invented the tale about Decius).

[4] Lacking other military activity to report, Livy (7. 38. 1) records under the year 342 a Latin move against the Paeligni which in fact occurred in the Latin War two years later (see below, p. 207).

[5] They proposed to use the method made notorious by the Sabellians at Capua (Livy 7. 38. 5).

[6] For the mutiny, see also Dion. Hal. 15. 3; App. *Samn.* 1–2.

Plautius Venno (or Venox) stopped a hostile move of the Volsci near Privernum. The Samnites, instead of sending troops against Mamercinus, sent envoys, and shortly afterwards peace was signed between Romans and Samnites. The Samnites renounced their interest in the Campani, the Romans renounced theirs in the Sidicini, and the treaty of 354 was renewed.[1]

Since the days of Niebuhr, if not earlier, this account of the First Samnite War has evoked incredulity. And not without reason: it contains absurdities that are blatant and that in part are contradicted by later events. What we are told about Capua, for instance, throughout the remainder of the fourth and most of the third centuries makes it certain that Livy's tale of the Campani meekly agreeing to become a Roman protectorate in 343 is an exculpatory anticipation of the events of 211 when Capua, after its revolt to Hannibal and subsequent capture by Rome, was treated harshly in the manner reserved for unconditionally surrendered enemies. It can be taken as certain that in 343 the Campani became, not the *dediticii* of Rome, but the *socii*, in the manner of the contemporary Latins and Hernici. The status of *dediticii* was invented for them by patriotic Roman annalists anxious to mitigate Roman duplicity towards the Samnites in 343 and Roman severity towards the Campani in 211.

Livy's account of the details of the fighting in the First Samnite War is no more trustworthy than his description of its antecedents. He himself admits that the early chroniclers of Rome knew nothing about some of them;[2] some of them undoubtedly derive from the notorious Valerius Antias of the first century, Livy's principal source for this part of his narrative,[3] so that any episode in which a Valerius appears may possibly be fictitious. Similarity with incidents of later history is also a ground for suspicion; and there is more than a little of this. The First Samnite War begins like the Second, with a Cornelius attempting to invade Samnium from Campania.[4] The tale of the trap into which the Romans march near Saticula in 343 reads remarkably like an earlier, if less disgraceful, version of the Caudine Forks affair of 321. Details for the roles of Cornelius and Decius in it seem to be obtained from the parts played by a

[1] Livy 8. 1. 8; 8. 2. 3.

[2] *Adeo nihil...inter antiquos rerum auctores constat* (Livy 7. 24. 7 (= 342)).

[3] J. Heurgon, *Capoue préromaine*, p. 163. Antias, however, may not have been the only one to exaggerate the role of the Valerii in Roman history: the *gens* Valeria had its own historians, culminating in Valerius Messalla (Pliny, *N.H.* 35. 8).

[4] Livy 8. 23. 13.

later Cornelius and a later Decius, in 306 and 297 respectively.[1] Valerius Corvus' victories at Mons Gaurus and Suessula in 343, outside the area of the Campani,[2] seem to anticipate Roman operations against Hannibal in these same districts in 215; and one may well wonder how the Mons Gaurus, which is close to Cumae but far from Capua and Samnium, could have come into the picture at all in the First Samnite War (although both it and Suessula conceivably were the scene of operations after 341 in the Latin War when Rome proceeded to annex the districts south of the Campani). One may also justly make merry at Livy's figures for Samnite casualties in the year 343: 'dreadful massacre' at Mons Gaurus;[3] 30,000 killed thanks to Decius;[4] under 40,000 killed, but 40,000 shields and 170 standards captured at Suessula.[5] These absurd statistics derive almost certainly from the egregious Valerius Antias.

The events recorded for 342 also fail to carry complete conviction. The plebeian mutiny, near the territory of the Aurunci, which a Marcus Valerius brought under control in 342, finds its parallel in the plebeian discontent which was stilled, likewise near the territory of the Aurunci and likewise by a Marcus Valerius, in 335.[6]

The year 341 can also boast of something with its parallel in later history: in 341 C. Plautius and L. Aemilius Mamercinus were consuls and the Volsci caused trouble at Privernum; in 329 Plautius and Mamercinus were likewise consuls and were likewise reported as having to conduct operations near Privernum. In this instance, it is true, the earlier year seems the more appropriate one for the events described.[7] Even so, there can be little doubt that Beloch is

[1] Livy 9. 43. 8; 10. 14. 21. The account of Decius' derring-do also owes something to the career of the tribune Caedicius in 258 (see Cato, fr. 83; Livy, *Epit.* 17). On the other hand J. Heurgon, *Capoue préromaine*, p. 272, points out that the exploit attributed to Decius might explain his *cognomen*, which like other animal *cognomina* is certainly curious (cf. Macrob. 1. 6. 28). Heurgon's further conjecture (in *Nouvelle Clio*, III (1951), 105–9), connecting the name *Mus* with that of a rat-god, seems fanciful. Nor is it probable that Decius was of a Campanian family (as is suggested by F. Münzer, *Röm. Adelsfamilien*, p. 37; J. Heurgon, *Capoue préromaine*, p. 272; and A. J. Toynbee, *Hannibal's Legacy*, I, 339 f.). Admittedly there was an Oscan *praenomen Dekis* and a Latin *gentilicium Decius*: but the grounds for equating the two are not very obvious.

[2] Livy (7. 38. 4); and their conduct in the Second Punic War indicate that Suessula and Cumae were not members of the Capuan League.

[3] Livy 7. 33. 13.

[4] Livy 7. 36. 13.

[5] Livy 7. 37. 15–16.

[6] Livy 8. 15 and 16.

[7] In fact the Privernate War is also variously referred to 357 (Tr. Fasti *ad an.*; Dion. Hal. 14. 23) and 329 (Livy 8. 19–21). The version that assigns it to 341 seems the most plausible. Livy probably recorded fighting in 329 because it was inconceivable to him that a colony could be established at Tarracina without conflict (8. 21. 11).

right in regarding the Roman invasion of Samnium in 341, which curiously involved no fighting, as the invention of some annalist: its aim was to bring the war to a close on an appropriate note.[1]

Thus Mommsen's view that no certain pronouncements can be made about the details of the First Samnite War seems sound. Some scholars go even further than this and, impressed by the lack of authentic details and by the *volte face* of Latins, Campani and Samnites in 340, deny that the war ever took place at all.[2] This, however, is carrying scepticism too far, and leaves too much unexplained.

In the first place, the account of the war's outbreak is so unflattering to the Romans that it is inconceivable that their own historians would have invented it or would have preserved a record of it, if somebody else's historians had done so. Livy[3] obviously finds it just as embarrassing to justify the behaviour of the Romans in 343 (when they welshed on their 354 treaty with the Samnites in order to support Capua) as in 219 (when they welshed on their Ebro treaty with the Carthaginians in order to support Saguntum).

Secondly, it is obvious that, immediately after the period to which the First Samnite War is assigned, Rome had acquired interests in Campania. It is very improbable that the Samnites would have acquiesced in Roman penetration into such a key area without some show of resistance.

Thirdly, the failure of the Romans to elect any censors between 351 and 340 may well be due to the incidence of a Samnite war. Also the election of two patricians, instead of the normal one patrician and one plebeian, to the consulships of 343 may mean that there was some kind of crisis in that year.[4]

Fourthly, there is the evidence of the Elder Pliny. He asserts that, in response to a directive from the Delphic oracle, the Romans during the course of a Samnite war erected statues to Pythagoras as the wisest and to Alcibiades as the bravest of the Greeks.[5] Pliny's

[1] K. J. Beloch, *Röm. Gesch.* p. 371.

[2] So, for example, F. E. Adcock in *Cambr. Anc. Hist.* VII (1928), 588. Adcock thinks that the war of 343 was in fact the Latin War; but he can find no certain hostilities until 340.

[3] Livy 7. 31 and 32.

[4] J. Suolahti, *The Roman Censors*, p. 204.

[5] Pliny, *N.H.* 34. 26. The Romans may have chosen Pythagoras as the wisest in order to ingratiate themselves with the Italiotes of Magna Graecia (A. Alföldi, *Early Rome and the Latins*, p. 346). On the statue of Pythagoras, see G. Becatti in *Boll. d'Arte*, XXXIV (1949), 97, 110; and, for Rome's earliest contacts with the Greeks, W. Hoffman, *Rom und die griechische Welt im vierten Jahrhundert*, pp. 17 f.

statement is supported by Plutarch,[1] but the best proof of its reliability is that the statues stood in the Comitium at Rome right down to Sulla's day. Pliny's unspecified Samnite war must be the First, since by the time of the later ones Alexander the Great rather than Alcibiades (who did not enjoy lasting fame with the Romans)[2] would surely have been selected as the bravest of the Greeks.

Fifthly, there is the treaty which Carthage signed with Rome in 348 and which is securely historical. This treaty guarantees a certain degree of trustworthiness to the story that the Carthaginians sent their Roman friends a golden crown to commemorate their victory in the First Samnite War.[3]

Finally, the *cognomen* of the Roman consul for 341 is worth noting. The last element in the name of L. Aemilius Mamercinus is Oscan.[4] This, however, does not mean that he was of Sabellian origin since, until the second century at any rate, it was normal for an Italic *cognomen* to denote, not a Roman's origin from, but some special relation with, an Italic people. In the case of Aemilius, it may be that he did receive the peace mission from the speakers of Oscan at the end of the First Samnite War, as Livy says he did,[5] was styled Mamercinus in consequence, and was the first member of his *gens* to bear this *cognomen*.

The First Samnite War can then be regarded as historical. The fact that Diodorus does not mention it is irrelevant. He himself admits that he was capricious in choosing which events of Roman history to record,[6] and indeed in Books 17 and 18 he ignores Italy completely. Quite possibly the war came about more or less by accident.[7] The Romans at least could not have been anxious to commit themselves to a theatre of operations with which their lines

[1] Plut. *Numa*, 8. 10.

[2] It was the anti-Syracusan policy of Alcibiades which made him popular in fourth-century Rome, the enemy of Dionysius (A. Alföldi, *loc. cit.*); but his fame did not last long (Livy 28. 41. 17). Alexander's repute reached Rome very early. His companion Cleitarchus claimed that a Roman delegation called on Alexander *c.* 325 (Pliny, *N.H.* 3. 57). Alexander's complaints about Antiate pirates (Strabo 5. 3. 5, p. 232) must have brought him to the notice of the Romans.

[3] Livy 7. 38. 2 (= 342). Cf. R. Meiggs, *Ostia*, p. 23.

[4] Livy (8. 1. 1) calls him Mamercus. The form *Mamercinus* could be an anachronism, since it displays the typically Latinian -NO- suffix, which might well have come into vogue later than 340.

[5] Livy 8. 1. 7.

[6] Diod. 19. 10. 1.

[7] E. Badian, *For. Client.* p. 21, however, argues that the Romans deliberately provoked it 'to confront their lukewarm allies with the Samnite danger'. If so, the lukewarm allies were singularly unimpressed, to judge from their behaviour in 340.

of communication were precarious.[1] It was the Samnite move against Teanum that started the train of events, and Teanum, which is near the reaches of the Lower Liris, may not have been explicitly covered by the Roman–Samnite treaty of 354, which seems to have dealt only with the middle stretch of the river. The town was on the Samnite side of the river, and the Samnites presumably counted on Roman inaction when they moved against it. After all, the Romans had not hesitated to attack the Aurunci when advancing their sphere of influence to the right bank;[2] so why should the Samnites hesitate to do likewise to the Sidicini when pushing theirs forward to the left bank? This probably was the line of reasoning of the Samnites, and that they were justified in it is indicated by Roman indifference to the fate of the Sidicini once the war was over.[3] It was the involvement of the Campani that brought the Romans into the dispute, and the Samnites had had no reason to anticipate that their action against Teanum was going to affect the Campani or even if it did that this would drag the Romans in. *Belli causa extrinsecus venit, non orta inter ipsos est.*[4]

About the most that can be said concerning the actual fighting is that the Fasti Triumphales, which are usually trustworthy elsewhere, are probably sound in recording a Roman victory over the Samnites in 343. Where the consuls achieved this, however, is very uncertain: perhaps on level ground somewhere near Capua, since in 343 the Romans were much more likely to have been successful against the Samnites on level ground than in a mountainous terrain. As Livy pictures the people of Capua streaming out to congratulate the Roman victors,[5] the battle may have occurred on the very outskirts of Capua, perhaps near the shrine of Juno Gaura,[6] which Livy or his source confused with the Mons Gaurus near Cumae.[7] There is no need to believe that this was an overwhelming defeat for the Samnites, despite Livy's tale of a panic-stricken rout.[8] Even Livy admits that the Samnites fought stubbornly and that nightfall ended the action; and in the accounts of the Samnite Wars a report of darkness intervening is usually tantamount to an admission that

[1] The communications of the Romans with Campania remained extremely tenuous until they established Latin Colonies at Cales (334) and Fregellae (328).

[2] See Livy 7. 28. 3–6 (= 345).

[3] Livy 8. 2. 3.

[4] Livy 7. 29. 3.

[5] Livy 7. 33. 8.

[6] On Juno Gaura, see *ILS*, 6303 (of 71 B.C.). Cf. J. Heurgon, *Capoue préromaine*, pp. 377 f.; K. Meister, *Lateinisch–griechische Eigennamen*, I, 48.

[7] Monte Barbaro, overlooking Lake Avernus.

[8] Livy 7. 33. 17.

the Romans had nothing or at most very little to brag about.[1] Possibly this was the only engagement of consequence in the First Samnite War, despite the ancient tradition that there were three such.[2] Certainly the war was no life-and-death struggle. After the one notable action, it dragged on desultorily for a while and then came to an end. The Romans were ready to make peace once the immediate threat to Campania was past, and the Samnites for their part were also willing to halt hostilities since the Tarentine mercenary, Archidamus of Sparta, had arrived to threaten their rear.[3]

Although no mighty cataclysm the First Samnite War was of major significance in Roman history. It did not reduce the Samnites to impotence or bring them under Roman domination. They did not become members of the so-called Roman 'confederacy': indeed that organization was still in the future. Livy says that at the war's end the Samnites simply renewed their treaty with the Romans, and he evidently means on the same terms as in 354.[4] In other words, both sides agreed to continue their division of the Middle Liris region (and in fact they did so). Livy, however, also makes it clear that the two parties agreed to divide between themselves the peoples who were responsible for engendering the short-lived conflict:[5] the Samnites recognized the Campani as belonging to the Roman sphere and the Romans recognized that the Sidicini were in the Samnite (these terms too were kept). Clearly it was a negotiated peace. Nevertheless it was to have a lasting and, for the Samnites, fatal consequence. It had redressed the balance between them and the Romans permanently and irreversibly in favour of the latter. Overnight the territory and population under Roman control had increased to a size that rivalled Samnium. Henceforth, in any future struggle the Samnites might count for a little while on such strength as Teanum possessed, but the Romans had gained far more; they would be able to add the resources of Northern Campania to those that they already controlled. It is true that their use of these Campanian resources would be subject to checks and interruptions, and it is true that

[1] Cf. Dion. Hal. 16. 3. 1; P. Binneboessel, *Untersuchungen über Quellen und Geschichte des zweiten Samniterkrieges*, p. 106.

[2] Dion. Hal. 15. 3. 2 supports Livy in this.

[3] Archidamus may have landed in 343. He died on the same day as the Battle of Chaeronea, 338 (Theophr. fr. 259, 260; Diod. 16. 83. 3; Plut. *Cam.* 19; P. Lévêque, *Pyrrhos*, p. 266).

[4] Livy 8. 2. 1.

[5] Livy 8. 3. 8.

much hard fighting and many long years were to elapse before the Samnites bowed to the inevitable. But the seeds of the inevitable were sown in the First Samnite War, when the situation of the Samnites relative to the Romans shifted for the worse—demographically, materially and strategically.

The Roman decision to support the Campani in 343 appears in the pages of Livy as a sudden and precipitate one. One may well doubt, however, that it was quite as hasty or as unpondered as Livy implies. It was certainly a dangerous decision, given the extent of Samnium and its population: Rome ran a considerable risk when she agreed to back the Campani. It turned out, however, to be a major decision of the utmost importance, since it inaugurated for Rome an imperial career that was to lead her ineluctably into the deep south and ultimately, even if not foreseeably, to the hegemony of the Italian peninsula and to world dominion. This makes it likely that the decision was anything but haphazard. There must have been an influential group at Rome, who had given the matter careful thought and who well before 343 had made up their minds that expansion southward was the correct policy for Rome to pursue, should a favourable opportunity ever arise. But the ancient writers do not name the statesman, or statesmen, who decided in 343 that the occasion had now presented itself, almost like a bolt from the blue, even though fraught with considerable risk. According to Livy,[1] it was the Roman Senate that made the fateful decision: but presumably the Senate made it at the urging of some group.

It is tempting to argue that a new dynamic element had been brought into the governing class of the Roman state by the Licinio-Sextian legislation of 367/366 and that it was the plebeians, newly admitted to the highest office, who must have been responsible for the southward drive.[2] This, however, may merely be an example of *post hoc, ergo propter hoc*, and Fraccaro may well be right in insisting that, generally speaking, plebeian statesmen were more interested in the north-east than in the south-east: their axis of advance was along the line of the later Via Flaminia rather than that of the later Via Appia.[3]

Examination of the Fasti Consulares reveals that the Licinio-

[1] Livy 7. 31. 8. [2] T. Frank in *Camb. Anc. Hist.* VII (1928), 671.

[3] P. Fraccaro, *Opuscula*, I, 109. M. Sordi, *I Rapporti Romano-Ceriti*, pp. 75 f., insists that the plebeians, who won a share in political power in 366, were more interested in an understanding with the Etruscans than with the southern peoples. The words of Livy 8. 29. 5 are worth noting.

Sextian legislation could not have laid it down that, starting with 366, one of the consuls must always be a plebeian.[1] It merely stated that one of them *might* be. To use Livy's word, the consulship had simply become *promiscuus*.[2] Now it happens that in each of the first eleven years after the legislation (that is, from 366 to 356 inclusive) one of the consuls *was* a plebeian. Nevertheless the so-called Struggle between the Orders was evidently anything but over: the patricians had not renounced their desire to monopolize political power.[3] That was shown in 355 when they succeeded in getting members of their order into both consulships. They managed to repeat the feat in 354 and again in 353. For a few years the patricians were evidently in control of the apparatus of the Roman state.

Once the patricians were again in charge of it, the Roman state signed a treaty with the Samnites (354), which, as we have seen, proclaimed the policy of expanding at least as far south as the River Liris. The stage for it had been set by the reconciliation with the Latins in 358 for which patricians seem to have been chiefly responsible.[4] This, too, of course, might be nothing more than a case of *post hoc, ergo propter hoc*.

For the next nine years after 353, except in 351, 349 and 345,[5] one patrician and one plebeian consul were the rule. Then in 343 both consuls were once again patrician, and it is to be noted that this was the year when the decision to bring Capua and her league into the Roman orbit was adopted.[6] Once again, nothing more than coincidence may be involved.

The story, however, does not end even there. Livy insists that the plebeians were violently opposed to the First Samnite War, and other ancient writers imply the same thing. Indeed in 342 the Roman army staged a mutiny in order to extort additional concessions from the patricians, and it was apparently then that the law was passed stipulating that henceforth one consul must, and

[1] K. von Fritz in *Historia*, I (1950), 3 f.

[2] Livy 7. 21. 1; 7. 32. 14.

[3] See, for example, Livy 7. 17. 10–13 (= 355); 7. 21. 1 (= 352); 7. 22. 1, 10 (= 351); 7. 24. 11 and 7. 25. 1 (= 349/348). The mediocre performance of Genucius against the Hernici in 362 may have helped to discredit plebeian consulships.

[4] M. Sordi, *I Rapporti Romano-Ceriti*, p. 77 f., has convincingly argued that it was patricians who were instrumental in bringing the Latin treaty back to life in 358.

[5] In 351 the Romans signed a forty-year treaty with the South Etruscans (Livy 7. 22. 5), one object of which may have been to free their hands for activities in Southern Italy. In 349 the patrician masters of the state began negotiations which led to a treaty with Carthage in 348 (Livy 7. 27. 2; Diod. 16. 69. 1; Polyb. 3. 24. 5): this treaty implies at least some Roman interest in the south.

[6] A treaty with Falerii in this very year (Livy 7. 38. 1) facilitated the southern policy.

both might, be plebeian,[1] and from then on one patrician and one plebeian become in fact the rule until 172, when both were plebeian. There is however one pair of consuls after 342 who might both more properly be considered patrician: viz. Sp. Postumius Albinus and T. Veturius Calvinus, consuls in 334 (and again in 321).[2] Technically they probably did not infringe the law of 342, since the branch of the Veturii to which Calvinus belonged had presumably 'gone over' to the *plebs*.[3] But it was precisely in 334, when both consuls, whatever they were *de iure*, were *de facto* patrician, that another major decision affecting southward expansion was made. That was the year when the Romans, according to Velleius Paterculus, penetrated into the south even beyond Capua and her league by annexing Suessula and Cumae:[4] as a precaution against any attempt by the Samnites to prevent the operation, they established a Latin Colony at Cales facing Samnite-controlled Teanum.[5]

Coincidence oft-repeated ceases to be fortuitous. It is overwhelmingly probable that expansion southward was sponsored by a patrician group.[6] Perhaps no Roman statesman, whether patrician or plebeian, could have ignored the threat to the Campani in 343 or have resisted the temptation to seize the opportunity for bringing them into Rome's orbit. And there are indications that, whatever the attitude of the plebeian rank and file, some plebeian notables supported the policy: e.g. C. Marcius Rutilus and Q. Publilius Philo.[7] But the fact remains that it was under patrician direction, and evidently with some plebeian opposition, that the big decisions for a forward southern policy were made. Plebeian notables were more concerned at this time to establish their prescriptive right to one of the consulships than to interest themselves in foreign adventures.

[1] The Leges Genuciae (Livy 7. 42. 2). One consequence was that in the Samnite Wars a man normally obtained a second consulship, if at all, only ten years after his first. Before 343 a second consulship was likely to follow hard on the heels of a first, since the size of the group from whom consuls were chosen was so small.

[2] In 321 the disaster occurred at the Caudine Forks. Did this discredit patrician pairs for ever? Ap. Claudius Caecus failed in both his later attempts to have only patrician consuls (Cic. *Brutus*, 55; Livy 10. 15. 7–11).

[3] Mommsen, *Röm. Forschungen*, I, 120. But see G. Forni in *Athenaeum*, XXXI (1953), 229, who denies such a *transitio*.

[4] The *partique Samnitium* of Velleius (1. 14. 3); cf. Livy 8. 16. 13 f. (= 338).

[5] Strabo 5. 4. 11, p. 249. The decision to send the colony was taken in 335 (Livy 8. 16. 13 f.); the colony was actually sent in 334 (Vell. Pat. 1. 14. 3).

[6] It was patricians above all who had prepared the way for it by reactivating the treaty with the Latins in 358 (M. Sordi, *I Rapporti Romano-Ceriti*, pp. 77 f.).

[7] 'Manager of Rome's Campanian policy' (F. E. Adcock in *Camb. Anc. Hist.* VII, 593).

The patrician pair of consuls who were in office in 343 when the risk of war with the Samnites was accepted rather than let slip the chance of winning a southern domain were M. Valerius Corvus and A. Cornelius Cossus; and Livy seems to make Valerius the spokesman for the policy.[1] That does not necessarily mean that the Valerii and Cornelii were the exclusive framers of it. The role of the Valerii, at least, has almost certainly been exaggerated by Valerius Antias.[2] The Aemilii and Papirii (and no doubt others) probably had a say in the matter.[3]

The motive of the advocates of southern expansion, it has been recently suggested, was an economic one. Hitherto Rome had been an agrarian state with her interests confined to Latium. But in the fourth century her horizon expanded to include the world of trade, commerce and industry beyond, and influential members of her governing class wished to avail themselves of the wider opportunities that seemed to be beckoning.[4] This is quite plausible, although as thus stated it may be somewhat oversimplified. Concern for the security of the state must always have been a weighty consideration.

Once the First Samnite War was over, both the Samnites and Rome sought to make the peace terms good, but, when they set about consolidating the territories to which they had staked their respective claims, they at once encountered resistance.

The small peoples between Latium and Campania resented being bandied about between the two giants.[5] The Aurunci[6] and some of the Volsci took to arms rather than submit to Rome, and the Sidicini and the rest of the Volsci similarly defied the Samnites. The Hernici, so far as is known, made no move; but the Latins and Campani, alarmed at the growing preponderance of Rome, did not

[1] Livy 7. 32.

[2] Especially when their exploits are performed in or near Antium: as, for example, in Livy 7. 27 and 7. 40.

[3] J. Heurgon, *Capoue préromaine*, pp. 252–9, regards the Aemilii as Samnitophiles. This seems highly unlikely. An Aemilius was credited with the annexation of Privernum (Livy 8. 20 f.) and the Aemilii seem to have been political allies of Publilius Philo (F. Münzer, *Röm. Adelsfamilien*, p. 36). It was a Papirius who proposed that Acerrae be annexed with *civitas sine suffragio* in 332 (Livy 8. 17. 12).

[4] See E. S. Stavely in *Historia*, VIII (1959), 410–33; F. Cassola, *I Gruppi Politici Romani*, pp. 26–68, 101–51.

[5] It is difficult to accept E. Badian's picture of Rome (*Foreign Clientelae*, p. 30) as a 'courageous Latin state [which] seemed the champion of the small peoples against the aggressive Samnite Confederacy'.

[6] For the hostility of the Aurunci, see Triumph. Fasti *ad an.* 340 and Livy 8. 15. 2. The crucial battle was fought on their territory.

hesitate to support the Aurunci, Volsci and Sidicini. These alignments, rather than a Latin demand for one of the consulships and for half the places in the Roman Senate,[1] led to the conflict traditionally known as the Latin War of 340–338.[2] In it Romans and Samnites made common cause. This may seem surprising behaviour from such recent enemies, but history can provide parallels. The Romans were not going to take the chance of letting the Samnites reduce the Campani for them. The Samnites, for their part, may have argued (mistakenly in the event) that a strong Latin–Campanian–Sidicine–Volscian–Auruncan combination would be more dangerous to them than the kind of Latium that they hoped would emerge from the Latin War: viz. a Latium that was restless and disgruntled under a precarious Roman leadership.

It is almost as difficult to reach certainty about the details of the Latin War as of the First Samnite War, even though it, unlike the earlier conflict, is reflected in the pages of Diodorus. At least one point is clear: the Samnites cooperated with the Romans in the conflict. Although physically separated from one another by the Latins and their associates, the two large powers succeeded in joining forces. In 340 the Roman consuls led an army due east into the territory of the Marsi and Paeligni,[3] who were induced by either threats or persuasion to permit their transit,[4] and from there reached the Samnites, presumably by way of Aufidena and Aesernia. In an evident attempt to foil this manœuvre, the Latins sent an expedition against the Paeligni, but they failed to stop it.[5] The

[1] In attributing these demands to the Latins, Livy (8. 4 and 5) is anticipating the antecedents of the Social War.

[2] The principal sources are Ox. Pap. I. 12, p. 27, col. III (who dates it 339–336); Livy 8. 3–14; Diod. 16. 90. 2; Dion. Hal. 15. 4; Val. Max. I. 7. 3; 6. 4. I; Auct. *de vir. ill.* 26. 4; 28. 4. See, too, above, Map I, p. 25.

[3] Their aim undoubtedly was to split the Campani from the Latini. The route they used is uncertain. Hostile Tibur blocked the way due east (the later Via Valeria). Hence they reached the vicinity of the Fucine lake either via the Liris valley or via the line of the Via Salaria. Dion. Hal. (15. 4. I) suggests that they used the route of the later Via Appia to reach Campania, which seems out of the question, although it is worth noting that, later at any rate, there was a cross road from the Via Appia to the Via Salaria (*CIL*, IX, 4321): see F. Barreca in *Bull. del Museo della Civiltà Romana*, XVIII (1956), 18 f.

[4] Neither Marsi not Paeligni were *socii et amici* of Rome at this stage: Livy 8. 29. 1–6 (= 326).

[5] F. E. Adcock must be right in regarding the Latin move against the Paeligni as an incident in the Latin War (*Camb. Anc. Hist.* VII, 549). Livy (7. 38. I) lists it under the year 342, but the casual and jejune way he does so suggests that he is merely reproducing some ancient record, which some Younger Annalist may have managed to insert into the tradition at the wrong place. Presumably the Latins moved via Tibur.

Romans and Samnites effected their junction and then came down the valley of the Volturnus River. They met and heavily defeated the Latins and their associates in a battle in which the Romans are said to have lost one of their consuls, P. Decius Mus,[1] and the Samnites to have given a good account of themselves.[2]

The ancient writers agree that this battle was fought at the foot of a mountain not far from Capua.[3] According to Livy and others, the actual site was close to a place called Veseris, which seems to be identical with the Auruncan place-name Vescia.[4] Diodorus, on the other hand, places the battle near Suessa.[5] The two versions are not seriously at variance, since Vescia and Suessa could not have been far apart. As a matter of fact Livy, too, records an engagement, which must have been fought near Suessa, since it occurred 'between Minturnae and Sinuessa' (at an otherwise unknown locality called Trifanum).[6] He confusedly regards this as a second encounter. Obviously there was only one battle,[7] and it must have taken place near the foot of the Rocca Monfina, like Mt Vesuvius an extinct volcano at that time.[8] We can agree to call it the Battle of Suessa.[9]

The Latin War thus resembles the First Samnite in witnessing only one major action. As a result of the Battle of Suessa the alliance of Latins, Campani, Aurunci, Volsci and Sidicini fell apart,[10] and the Romans and Samnites could now proceed to deal with their recalcitrant smaller neighbours one by one.

[1] P. Decius Mus is the hero of 343. That he lost his life by *devotio* seems improbable: the story that he did is an anticipation of his son's self-sacrifice at Sentinum in 295 (see below, p. 267). Perhaps Valerius Antias has been at work here, since the pontifex maximus alleged to have supervised the ceremonial in connexion with the *devotio* of 340 is a Valerius.

[2] One version said that, like the Spartans at Marathon, the Samnites procrastinated and arrived too late for the battle (Dion. Hal. 15. 4. 3). Even Livy could not bring himself to believe this libel (8. 11. 2; cf. 8. 10. 7).

[3] Livy 8. 6. 8: here he locates it at Vesuvius (cf. Val. Max. 1. 7. 3), probably by mistake since elsewhere the name is given as Veseris (see below, n. 8). Dion. Hal. 15. 4. 2–5 could think of only one mountain near Capua: viz. Mons Tifata.

[4] Cicero, *de off.* 3. 3. 112; *de fin.* 1. 7. 23; Livy 8. 8. 19; 10. 28. 15; Val. Max. 6. 4. 1; Auct. *de vir. ill.* 26. 4 (who calls Veseris a river). Vescia (8. 11. 5) may have been a town: mention is usually made, however, of Ager Vescinus.

[5] Diod. 16. 90. 2.

[6] Trifanum (Livy 8. 11. 11) may have been a cult centre for the three Auruncan towns, Suessa, Cales and Minturnae.

[7] As J. Clason, *Röm. Gesch.* II, 237, noted long ago.

[8] If Veseris is the Rocca Monfina, confusion with Vesuvius is understandable: not only were the names very similar, but also both mountains at that time were extinct volcanoes. Both have erupted since, Vesuvius often and Rocca Monfina in the sixth century A.D.

[9] Not the Battle of Sinuessa as A. Klotz, *Livius und seine Vorgänger*, p. 23, would have it, emending Diodorus' Suessa. See above, Map 2, p. 188.

[10] Livy 8. 11. 11; 8. 15. 2; Triumph. Fasti *ad an.* 340.

The Romans went to work methodically. *Nec quievere antequam expugnando aut in deditionem accipiendo singulas urbes Latium omne subegere.*[1] It may, as Livy says, have taken them several years to stamp out every pocket of resistance throughout the region which they envisaged as their sphere of interest, but by 332[2] all of Latium (including Tibur and Praeneste) and all of Northern Campania (including Cumae, Suessula and Acerrae) had been brought under their control.

It seems unlikely that the Samnites needed several years to establish their supremacy over the smaller area to which they laid claim. Livy, not being concerned to record their history, did not feel it necessary to pay much attention to their part in the mopping-up operations after their joint victory with the Romans in the Battle of Suessa. Presumably it did not take them much time to deprive the Sidicini of their independence.[3] Modern scholars, it is true, have suggested that the Sidicini were brought, not under Samnite domination, but under Roman,[4] the argument being that had this not been the case their town of Teanum would have been recorded as playing some role in the Second Samnite War, whereas in fact Teanum is not mentioned until the Third Samnite War (when it casually appears at the beginning of hostilities, seemingly as an ally of Rome).[5] Such an argument from silence is hardly valid (it could be applied equally well to Aesernia, which surely must have been Samnite throughout the first three wars between Rome and the Samnites), and it flatly contradicts Livy, who states quite positively[6] that the Sidicini were not brought into the Roman sphere but on the contrary maintained their hostility to it.[7] There is, in fact, no reason to believe that the Samnites failed to carry out their original intention of subjugating the Sidicini, especially now that the

[1] Livy 8. 13. 8.

[2] In which year Acerrae was annexed (Livy 8. 17. 12; Velleius 1. 14. 4).

[3] See Livy 8. 2. 5.

[4] The Triumph. Fasti *ad an.* 340 record a victory over the Sidicini: but in this the Romans may have been helping their Samnite allies.

[5] Livy 10. 14. 4. See G. De Sanctis, *Stor. dei Romani*, II, 270; K. J. Beloch, *Röm. Ges.* p. 370.

[6] Livy 8. 2. 3–6; 8. 15–17.

[7] Livy records Sidicine hostility to Rome in order to justify the colonization of Cales. That the Sidicini wiped out a city of the Aurunci in 337 when C. Sulpicius and P. Aelius were consuls (Livy 8. 15) is fiction: it was the Romans who wiped out the Aurunci in 314 when C. Sulpicius and Poetelius were consuls (Livy 9. 25). That the Sulpician *gens* reduced the Aurunci seems established by the thrice-repeated tales of their activities against them—in 345, 337 and 314.

Romans had given it their blessing. In other words the Samnites imposed their will on the Sidicini, and Teanum came effectively under their control.

It is universally recognized that the settlement imposed by Rome after the Latin War had momentous effects on her subsequent history. It also had far-reaching implications for the future of the Samnites. Essentially what the Romans did was to confiscate some land from the defeated Latins, Volsci, Campani and Aurunci and distribute it either in viritane allotments or to the Roman Citizen Colonies at Ostia and Antium. Much more important was the complete change which they brought about in the political complexion of an enlarged Latium. They incorporated many of the Latin-speaking communities into their own state, apparently conferring the full Roman citizenship upon them;[1] but they made some of them Latin Colonies (Signia, Norba, Ardea, Circeii, Setia); and some they made 'allied' towns (Tibur, Praeneste, Cora and possibly Laurentum).[2] The peoples that did not speak Latin (Volsci, Aurunci, Campani) were also incorporated into the Roman state, but not in the same way, either because their ethnic make-up or their distance from Rome made direct domination of them difficult, if not impossible. They were given a status which had been devised some time earlier for the city of Caere in Southern Etruria: they were made *cives sine suffragio*.[3] In effect they thus became Roman subjects: they still enjoyed local administrative autonomy, but they had ceased to decide their own policies or control their own destinies. The Campani had defeated the Samnites but, like the horse that with man's help conquered the stag in Horace's fable,[4] they had a master for ever after.

As a result of these arrangements the territory of the Roman state by 332 stretched continuously from the Ciminian Mountains well north of Rome to the slopes of Vesuvius well south of Capua.[5]

[1] *Civitas sine suffragio* was never used for Latin-speakers (P. Fraccaro, *Opuscula*, I, 107). Originally it may have been a mark of Roman honour and esteem for individuals, but when given to whole communities it had come to denote inferior status long before the Second Punic War (see Livy 9. 16. 2 (Satricum, 319); 9. 43. 24 (Anagnia, 306); M. Sordi, *I Rapporti Romano-Ceriti*, pp. 110 f.).

[2] The Hernici also remained as 'allies': they had not joined the Latins in the war against Rome.

[3] *Civitas sine suffragio* cannot be proved for the Aurunci but seems altogether probable: they had participated in the Latin War, at least in its opening phases.

[4] Hor. *Epp.* I. 10. 34–8.

[5] Suessula and Acerrae were the southern limits of Roman territory in 332.

But this block of territory, although unbroken,[1] was not everywhere safe and secure. It was wider at its two extremities than in the middle: the region of the Auruncan Mountains, near Fundi and Formiae, constituted a narrow waist. It is true that the Citizen and Latin Colonies named above defended both the coastal and the interior boundaries of the block of territory.[2] But the tenuousness of Roman communications through it was emphasized by the long detour which the Romans had been obliged to make by way of the Marsi and Paeligni in the Latin War.[3] There were in fact only two routes. There was the inland route which followed the valleys of the Rivers Trerus and Liris and was essentially the route of the later Via Latina:[4] this route was flanked on the east by Hernican and other non-Roman (i.e. potentially hostile) territory virtually all the way from Rome to Capua. Then there was the coastal route which, after crossing the Pomptine Marshes, ran south of the Volscian and Auruncan Mountains, and was essentially the route of the later Via Appia: this passed through Roman territory all the way,[5] but it could easily be cut by a thrust towards the Tyrrhenian Sea from either Teanum or the Middle Liris valley, in both of which places the Samnites were now established.

The Romans, concerned about the weakness of these communications, not unnaturally strengthened them as much as they could. Thereby they ran the risk of Samnite resentment, if not active hostility, but the First Samnite and Latin Wars had swung the balance of power in their favour. Hence it was a risk that they were prepared to accept. To neutralize Teanum they confronted it with a Latin Colony at neighbouring Cales in 334.[6] It is probable that Cales had previously been Auruncan rather than

[1] It had enclaves of 'allied' territory inside it: e.g. Cora, Laurentum (?) and possibly Formiae and Fundi (their *civitas sine suffragio* (Livy 8. 14. 10) may have been a prerogative enjoyed individually by their burghers if they visited Rome).

[2] The number of Colonies was soon increased with the addition of Cales (334), Tarracina (329), and Fregellae (328).

[3] For the importance of communications with Campania, see Livy 7. 30. 7 and M. A. Levi, *La Politica Imperiale di Roma*, pp. 36 f.

[4] It has been suggested that the Via Latina was built as early as 334 (T. Ashby, *Roman Campagna in Classical Times*, p. 153). This seems unlikely since the Samnites at that time controlled Casinum, Aquinum, Teanum.

[5] Unless Formiae and Fundi, as suggested above (n. 1), were technically 'allies'.

[6] Teanum and Cales are separated only by the River Savone and the low Rocchetta watershed. Ancient writers (apart from Silius Ital. 8. 511) usually regard Cales as Auruncan (reject the notion of K. J. Beloch, *Röm. Gesch.* p. 388, that it was Sidicine).

Sidicinan territory, so that technically the Romans may not have been guilty of infringing their treaty with the Samnites. Even so, the Samnites must have regarded the colonization of Cales as an unfriendly act.

In the Middle Liris region the Romans showed still less regard for Samnite susceptibilities. There in 328 they planted a Latin Colony at Fregellae, a strategic position controlling (*a*) a Liris crossing, (*b*) the Trerus valley road (later Via Latina), and (*c*) the easy way over the Auruncan Mountains to the Tyrrhenian Sea.[1] This was more than an unfriendly act: it constituted a *casus belli*,[2] since Fregellae was on the left, or Samnite, bank of the Liris.

Samnite countermoves, of course, had not been lacking, but the Samnites needed to tread warily since Alexander of Epirus, the Molossian *condottiere* who had succeeded Archidamus of Sparta in the service of Tarentum,[3] was holding a dagger at their back and had an understanding with Rome.[4] Accordingly the Samnites had to content themselves with a diplomatic offensive. To contain what appeared to them excessive Roman expansion in Northern Campania, they sought to extend their own influence in Central and Southern Campania, and not without success. The Alfaterni of Southern Campania, to judge from the later behaviour of Nuceria, their chief town, concluded an *entente* with them, and evidently so did Oscan-speaking Nola, which controlled the entrance into Central Campania from Samnium.[5] In predominantly Greek-speaking Naples a pro-Samnite faction came into existence, composed no doubt of elements disquieted by what the Romans had done in Northern Campania: as a result Naples became a bicultural city.[6]

By 327 the situation had become explosive. Alexander of Epirus,

[1] The colony at Fregellae (Livy 8. 22. 2) dominated a very strategic zone (G. W. L. Nicholson, *The Canadians in Italy, 1943–45*, pp. 394–426). For the Liris crossing there, see Livy 8. 22. 2.

[2] Livy 8. 23. 6; Dion. Hal. 15. 8. 4; 15. 10. 1; App. *Samn.* 1. 4.

[3] Alexander reached Italy *c.* 334 (T. Frank in *Cambr. Anc. Hist.* VII, 640) or later (P. Lévêque, *Pyrrhos*, p. 266): the 340 of Livy 8. 3. 6 is an error.

[4] Livy 8. 17. 9; Justin 12. 2. 12. It may have been their treaty with Alexander that forbade the Romans to sail beyond the Lacinian headland. Rome had also freed her hands in the north by signing a treaty with the Gauls: Polyb. 2. 18. 9; cf. Livy 8. 17. 7; 8. 20. 5.

[5] Nola was the 'New Town': it probably replaced Hyria, a town whose coins have survived. The territory of Nola abutted on that of Naples (Cic. *de off.* 1. 10. 33; Dion. Hal. 15. 5).

[6] For Naples as a mixed Graeco-Sabellian city, see Strabo 5. 4. 7, p. 246.

the factor making for restraint, had lost his life in battle against the Lucani at Pandosia *c.* 330;[1] the Samnites violently resented the Latin Colony at Fregellae; the Romans ominously noted Samnite headway in Central and Southern Campania. The stage was thus set for the Second Samnite War.

[1] For the date see Aeschines, *In Ctes.* 242; Arrian 3. 6. 7; G. F. Unger, *SB Münch. Akad.* (1876), p. 572. Orosius (3. 11. 12) says that 'Samnites' (i.e. Sabellians) killed Alexander. Livy (8. 24. 1) remarks that Alexander's death freed the Samnites to take up the Roman challenge at Fregellae.

CHAPTER 6

THE SECOND SAMNITE WAR

By common consent the Second Samnite War was the greatest of all the Samnites' struggles with Rome. Even without its interlude of uneasy peace it lasted longer than any of the other wars and it certainly demanded remarkable sacrifices from both sides. Furthermore, if it was not featured by any battle quite as decisive as that at Sentinum in the Third War, it was the most decisive of all the wars in its ultimate results, since it paved the way for Roman supremacy in peninsular Italy. Whether or not the two sides were consciously aware of it at the time, they were in fact fighting for the primacy of the Saturnian land. The writers of the Augustan age were convinced that they were fully conscious of this.[1] Livy, for example, makes Samnite spokesmen say at the war's outbreak: *Samnis Romanusne imperio Italiam regat decernamus.*[2] But the Augustan authors were writing after the Social and Civil Wars, by which time it was abundantly clear to all that the struggle in the fourth century had been to decide whether Italy should be Roman or Sabellian; and Livy, at least, depended heavily on annalists of the Sullan period whose view of the Samnite Wars was coloured by the way the Samnites had fought Roman domination to the bitter end in their own lifetime. Nevertheless it may be true that, even as early as the Second Samnite War, the two peoples had an instinctive and possibly a conscious inkling that peninsular hegemony was the prize for which they were contending.

Whoever seeks to narrate the Second Samnite War is faced with the difficulty of describing a contest which, while in a sense within the full light of history,[3] is remote enough to lack authentic primary sources. *Nec quisquam aequalis temporibus illis scriptor exstat.*[4] Details concerning the war have indeed survived, but from the pens of men who lived long after the events they recount and who are

[1] See, for example, Diod. 19. 72. 3; 37. 2. 22.

[2] Livy 8. 23. 9.

[3] Now for the first time flesh-and-blood figures, authentic human personalities, emerge in Roman history.

[4] Livy 8. 40. 5.

often unreliable.[1] When to this we add that only the Roman version of the war has survived, it is obvious that we cannot hope to get a picture of it that is accurate and true in all particulars. Even a general view of the course of the struggle cannot be obtained with any degree of ease, owing to the preference of the ancients for recording it year by year. Their annual lists of incidents, sometimes irrelevant and occasionally repetitious, frequently fictitious and nearly always confusing, make it difficult to see the wood for the trees. Nevertheless, if due allowance be made for the known prejudices and practices of Livy and Diodorus, some reconstruction of the main outlines of the war may become possible.

The Second Samnite War, as Thucydides said of the Peloponnesian War, had an underlying cause and a more immediate *casus belli*. The underlying cause was the disposition, inevitable in the case of dynamic nations like the Romans and Samnites which had not yet reached a stage of decline, to expand. A clash of interests was only too likely to occur sooner or later, and both sides had resorted to diplomatic activity in preparation for it. On the whole, one is left with the impression that the Romans had been more successful than the Samnites between 338 and 328 in extending the range of their influence, since in addition to enlarging their own territory they had, temporarily at any rate, and perhaps precariously, managed to encircle the Samnites by reaching an agreement with Alexander of Epirus. Livy even claims that, by the time hostilities came, they had also concluded alliances with Lucani and Apuli;[2] but in this he is quite certainly mistaken. In fact he himself admits as much a few pages later, when he reports that the Lucani repudiated their treaty and that the Apuli were enemies rather than allies.[3] One may conjecture that his description of these peoples as allies in 326 arose from his mistaking the inhabitants of Luca in the Liris valley for the inhabitants of Lucania, and, once convinced that the inhabitants of Lucania had become allies of Rome, he assumed that the inhabitants of nearby Apulia had done so too, an assumption that provided him with a convenient, if false, explanation for the ineptitude that brought the Romans to disaster at the Caudine Forks in 321. But, even though the story of the Lucanian and Apulian

[1] 'The most corrupt part of Livy is his account of the Second Samnite War' (B. G. Niebuhr, *Röm. Gesch.* III, 94).

[2] Livy 8. 25. 3; 8. 27. 2.

[3] Livy 8. 27. 6–10; 8. 29. 1; 8. 37. 3, 4.

alliances is false, it is still true that in the decade before the war Roman diplomacy aimed at containing the Samnites.

No doubt the Samnites attempted something similar. Later events make it probable that they sought alliances in Etruria and Umbria on the other side of Rome. If so, there is no record that their quest was successful before the outbreak of war. Perhaps their reputation as barbarous, unscrupulous and rapacious neighbours worked to their disadvantage.[1] On the other hand, it is possible that, if their own account of the period had survived, it might reveal that they were more successful in strengthening their situation than Livy could bring himself to admit.[2]

Mutual attempts at encirclement impressed both sides with the strategic importance of Central Italy, and as a consequence the Sabellic peoples dwelling there were not allowed to remain aloof from the conflict.

The ancient sources make it clear that the Romans were responsible for the actual *casus belli* by their despatch of a Latin Colony to Fregellae.[3] Needless to say, they do not admit this in so many words. They talk virtuously, if vaguely, about Samnite perfidy, provocation and preparation.[4] This, however, will deceive nobody; as we have seen, there must have been a group at Rome with a dynamic southern policy, and this group could now plead its case with even greater insistence and vigour. The annexation of Northern Campania, a region with industrial enterprises and commercial connexions, must have had a revolutionary effect on the economy of the Roman state. Almost overnight Rome had acquired trading, manufacturing and maritime interests, which the advocates of expansion in the south could point to whenever their policy was

[1] Their reputation as allies was also bad (Livy 8. 27. 10): they obliged their associates to give hostages and admit Samnite garrisons. (Of course, Roman behaviour was often similar.)

[2] Evidently it was at Samnite prodding that the Privernates gave Rome so much trouble *c.* 329. The Samnites also tried to stir nearby Fundi and Formiae into anti-Roman activity (Livy 8. 19. 4; 8. 20. 7; 8. 23. 2). A. Afzelius, *Römische Eroberung Italiens*, p. 162, argues that the Samnites might also have reached an understanding with Tarentum, stipulating that the Tarentines would bring no new *condottiere* to Italy, while the Samnites kept the Lucani from attacking Tarentum. (But Tarentum did welcome another *condottiere* in 314, if only for the briefest time.)

[3] See above, p. 212. The colonization of Cales (334) was an additional offence, and possibly even the colonization of Tarracina (329), although one would have thought that this latter town was far enough away to be unobjectionable.

[4] Livy 8. 22. 2–10; 8. 23. 6–7; 8. 39. 10. The words Livy (9. 11. 7) makes Pontius say to the Romans seem apposite: *semper aliquam fraudi speciem iuris imponitis.*

challenged. After 341 patricians, originally responsible for the southward drive, were still regarded by Livy,[1] and presumably by his sources, as particularly prominent in promoting it. It was they who were chiefly criticized when the policy came to grief in 321 and again in 315. Nevertheless they certainly did not lack for support from prominent plebeians. By 326 the plebeian right to one of the consulships was firmly established: plebeian notables were thus no longer preoccupied with domestic politics and more and more they made their voice heard in foreign policy. The Second Samnite War was not won only by patrician heroes, such as L. Papirius Cursor and Q. Fabius Rullianus.[2] Plebeian aristocrats carried an equal share of the military burden,[3] and their participation in the policy-making must have been on a similar scale. Some of these plebeians are positively identified for us by Livy: Q. Publilius Philo, C. Junius Brutus Bubulcus, C. Maenius, P. Decius Mus. Indeed it appears that the Second Samnite War was the formative period of the exclusive patricio-plebeian 'nobility' of the Roman Republic. It was as a result of their joint ordeals and endeavours in this arduous struggle that the two orders were cemented together, so to speak, in a proud and select aristocracy. At the outbreak of the First Samnite War in 343, the plebeian leaders' demand that one of the two consulships should always be theirs was still being determinedly resisted. By the end of the Second Samnite War in 304[4] this demand had long been taken for granted[5] and a closed 'nobility' had been formed that was so united that its members, patricians and plebeians alike, went into mourning when an upstart outsider of servile origin like Cn. Flavius was elected curule aedile over two 'noble' plebeians.[6]

Against Roman moves in the south the Samnites now (328/327) actively retaliated, and Livy, whose failure to identify the authors of

[1] Livy 9. 26. 10, 16.

[2] Papirius Cursor and Fabius Rullianus were the Roman leaders *par excellence* at this time (A. Heuss, *Röm. Gesch.* p. 57).

[3] As Livy (10. 7. 8) puts it on a later occasion (300): *non plus spei fore senatui populoque Romano in patriciis quam in plebeiis ducibus*. It is, of course, also true that some of the plebeian generals received severe setbacks in the field: e.g. Publilius Philo in 315 and Marcius Rutilus in 310 (see below, pp. 234, 245).

[4] At the outset of hostilities the patricians frustrated the attempt of the plebeians to get a plebeian named as dictator (Livy 8. 23. 13–17, = 327).

[5] Except possibly by recalcitrants such as Ap. Claudius Caecus: Livy 10. 6–8; 10. 15. 8.

[6] Livy 9. 46; Pliny, *N.H.* 33. 17.

the Roman policy of expansion at this time was presumably due to his reluctance to admit Roman aggression, displays no similar reticence in the case of the Samnites. He names a certain Papius Brutulus as the Samnite villain in the piece.[1] Scepticism is justified. The name and the fate of its bearer sound like those of Papius Mutilus, the Samnite hero of the Social War (91–87),[2] and may well be concoctions. Livy does not bring it into his narrative until 322, when he records a Samnite peace offer that was certainly abortive and no less certainly fictitious: it is there that he seizes the opportunity for branding Papius Brutulus as the warmonger.

In any case, whether incited thereto by the otherwise unknown Papius Brutulus or not, the Samnites intervened at Naples. They saw to it that the faction favourable to themselves got control of Palaeopolis, the part of the city that was its original core,[3] and through their protégés they became the virtual masters of Naples.[4] In 327, 4,000 Samnites, together with 2,000 other Sabellians from pro-Samnite Nola, arrived in Palaeopolis to guarantee continued tenure of power by the pro-Samnite faction. This was a manifest threat to Capua and the Ager Falernus, where Roman settlers were now established.[5]

Faced with this affront the Romans did not hesitate. They at once despatched to Campania the whole of their then armed establishment: two legions, commanded by the consuls for 327, L. Cornelius Lentulus and Q. Publilius Philo, the latter of whom at least had proved his mettle as a consular commander twelve years earlier during the Latin War. Their object was not merely to protect Capua, but if possible to bring the Parthenopean city of Naples also under Roman control. This show of force proved persuasive. The regime in Palaeopolis, indignant by now at the misbehaviour of the Sabellian troops,[6] decided to change sides. The Samnite garrison

[1] Livy 8. 39. 12–15; 9. 1. 6. Dio, fr. 36. 9, calls him Papirius instead of Papius and Zonaras 7. 26 Rutulus instead of Brutulus.

[2] Papius Mutilus committed suicide (Livy, *Epit.* 89); so did Papius Brutulus according to Livy 8. 39. 14.

[3] Palaeopolis is to be identified with Pizzofalcone in modern Naples (see *Parola del Passato*, VII (1952), 250, 269 f.). This was separate from Neapolis proper (Livy 8. 22. 5) and was peopled by the *incolae veteres* (Livy 4. 37. 1). There was similarly a Palaeopolis at Panormus (Polyb. 1. 38. 9) and at Emporiae (Livy 34. 9. 1; Strabo 3. 4. 8, p. 160).

[4] Dion. Hal. 15. 5. 5; 15. 6. 3.

[5] Livy 8. 11. 3; 8. 23. 1. Rivalry and mutual suspicion between Naples and Capua were normal (Livy 8. 22. 7; Dion. Hal. 15. 5. 1).

[6] An Oscan-speaking garrison was bound to be described as a sinister menace (see above, p. 39).

was tricked into departing, and during its absence the demarchs[1] Charilaus and Nymphius admitted a detachment of Publilius Philo's troops under the command of a military tribune named L. Quinctius. A screening operation by Philo's colleague Cornelius Lentulus, allegedly in the Volturnus valley opposite Callifae, Allifae and Rufrae,[2] prevented any aid being sent from Samnium, and by the end of 326 the pro-Samnite faction had been suppressed at Palaeopolis and Naples brought firmly within the Roman sphere of influence with a very favourable and, as it turned out, very enduring treaty of alliance.[3] The price, of course, was war with Samnium, and the formality of declaring this duly occurred in the same year (326).

Such were the beginnings of the Second Samnite War and the chief share of the blame for its outbreak at this particular juncture clearly belongs to the Romans. Livy even admits that the consul L. Cornelius Lentulus was on Samnite soil before ever the war had officially begun.[4]

The first five years of hostilities, 326–322, to use the traditional Varronian dating, witnessed no sensational event or even large-scale operation. Diodorus has nothing whatever to say about these years. Livy gives a year-by-year account,[5] which is featured by a plethora of words and a paucity of facts.

In 326 he says that Callifae, Allifae and Rufrae came under the power of the Romans, who also devastated wide areas of Samnium. The item concerning the ravaging of Samnium is too vague to be

[1] According to Livy 8. 25. 9 they were *principes civitatis*. Not all scholars agree that this means that they were demarchs (see G. P. Carrattelli in *Par. del Pass.* VII (1952), 260, and E. Siena in *Studi Romani*, IV (1958), 519). Both names appear Greek and were undoubtedly used in that part of Italy: Charilaus appears on coins from Naples (Sambon, *Monnaies de l'Italie*, I, no. 469) and Nympsius (*sic*) on inscriptions from there and from Ischia (*IG*, XIV, 726, 894). It was also a Nympsius from Naples who commanded Dionysius' Campanian mercenaries (Diod. 16. 18. 1). Nympsius was a Sabellian (and at Naples Greeks and Sabellians shared power: Strabo 5. 4. 7, p. 246). Livy's Nymphius might also have been a Sabellian, one of the 'Samnites' who according to one version betrayed Naples to the Romans (Livy 8. 26. 6).

[2] Livy 8. 25. 4. Callifae, if not a mere doublet for Allifae, might be the modern *Calvisi*: Mommsen (*CIL*, X, p. 444) ingeniously conjectured Caiatia for Livy's Callifae. Allifae lay near the modern *Piedimonte d'Alife* (D. Marrocco, *Antica Alife*, pp. 18 f.). For Rufrae, see above, p. 27, n. 1. How Cornelius could have got past the Samnite-held Monti Trebulani to capture these towns it is not easy to see.

[3] In 90 Naples was reluctant to exchange its status of favoured ally to that of *municipium* with Roman citizenship (Cic. *Pro Balbo*, 8. 21): *urbis eximia semper fuit in Romanos fides* (Velleius 1. 4. 2). See, too, Strabo 5. 4. 7, p. 246. That Philo celebrated a 'triumph' for his success seems reasonably certain, the doubts of K. J. Beloch (*Röm. Gesch.* p. 392) notwithstanding.

[4] Livy 8. 23. 13; 8. 26. 1; cf. Dion. Hal. 15. 10. 2.

[5] Livy 8. 25–40.

enlightening, and if Livy means that the three towns named were captured, one may be justifiably sceptical since by Livy's own admission Allifae was still in Samnite hands years later.[1]

In 325, besides reporting an attack by the Roman consul D. Junius Brutus on the Vestini which more probably belongs to 317 and the consulship of C. Junius Brutus,[2] Livy says that the other Roman consul, L. Furius Camillus, invaded Samnium, but under 'doubtful auspices',[3] so that the Romans found it necessary to appoint a dictator, whose most notable exploit was to quarrel violently with his master of the horse.[4] This must mean that there were no outstanding Roman successes to report and probably not even any operations of moment.

324 is one of the so-called 'dictator years' and therefore not separately recorded by Livy. This does not mean, however, that it is something completely fictitious. It corresponded, if not to one of our calendar years, at least to part of one and therefore may have witnessed some action;[5] and what Livy says of the activity of the dictator, L. Papirius Cursor, and his master of the horse, Q. Fabius Rullianus, clearly belongs to 324 as much as to 325. According to him, Papirius Cursor defeated the enemy 'in Samnium',[6] while Fabius Rullianus was reported by his later clansman Fabius Pictor (but significantly not by some other writers)[7] as winning a victory at a place called Imbrinium, which is never heard of otherwise, slaying 20,000 Samnites in the process.[8] Yet simultaneously the Samnites were still full of fight: they were unimpressed by Papirius Cursor and won a skirmish, and it was either they or some other alarm that shortly created a panic in Rome. Besides

[1] Livy 9. 38. 1 (= 310): it might be argued that the Samnites had recovered it at the Caudine Peace.

[2] According to Livy 8. 29. 11–14 Junius Brutus stormed two otherwise unknown Vestinian towns, Cutina (which suggests Aquae Cutiliae *in Sabinis* west of the Vestini) and Cingilia (which suggests Cingulum *in Piceno* east of the Vestini). For the conjecture that Junius Brutus' activities belong to 317 rather than to 325, see K. J. Beloch, *Röm. Gesch.* p. 404. The Junii Bruti were past masters at falsifying the records (A. Alföldi, *Early Rome and the Latins*, p. 114).

[3] Livy 8. 30. 1.

[4] This quarrel is narrated by Livy at great length: he devotes to it approximately one-third of the fifteen chapters he uses to describe the period 326–322 (8. 30. 11–8. 35. 12). His account owes much to what was related of the quarrel between Fabius Maximus and Minucius in 217 (for which see Livy 22. 14. 27–9).

[5] So M. Sordi, *I Rapporti Romano-Ceriti*, p. 154, n. 3.

[6] Livy 8. 36. 8–9.

[7] Livy 8. 30. 7–9.

[8] Livy 8. 30. 3–7. 30,000 is the more usual conventional number for Samnite slain in the first two wars.

this, Roman forces withdrew from Samnium.[1] All of this means that border raids by both sides were the rule in 324. One of these, perhaps at Imbrinium wherever that was, may have been successful enough to justify the triumph recorded for Papirius Cursor in the Fasti.[2]

The year 323 is admitted by Livy to have been free of any serious military operations. According to him, the Samnites were granted a year's truce, which they failed to observe.[3] His further assertion that the Samnites had humbly sought for peace and been arrogantly refused is rhetorical nonsense.[4] It is, however, just barely possible that the Romans were content to let the fighting with the Samnites lapse for a while since hostilities were threatening in Apulia.[5]

In 322 there is also vague mention of activity in Apulia,[6] but in general Livy devotes rather more attention to the war with the Samnites. It now emerged from its doldrums, but evidently not on a large scale, since according to Livy neither of the consuls celebrated a triumph. (This does not stop Livy from ascribing deeds of derring-do to M. Fabius Ambustus, which he had presumably found in the pages of Fabius Pictor.) Livy says that the only person to celebrate a triumph in 322 was the dictator A. Cornelius Cossus; but as he was named dictator in order to celebrate games in the praetor's absence, it may be doubted whether he conquered any Samnites.[7] Livy reveals that in such encounters as there were in 322 the Samnites were not exactly disgraced. Significantly enough, nightfall intervened to end one of them.[8] The Fasti and other sources record triumphs for both the consuls of this year, Q. Fabius Rullianus and L. Fulvius Curvus;[9] but it may well be doubted whether the Samnites suffered

[1] Livy 8. 35. 10, 11; 8. 36. 1, 12; 8. 37. 6.

[2] Triumph. Fasti *ad an.* 324; Livy 8. 37; Auct. *de vir. ill.* 31. 4. Note the suspicious coincidence that another Papirius celebrated a triumph on exactly the same day almost one hundred years later (Triumph. Fasti *ad an.* 231).

[3] Livy 8. 37.

[4] Livy 8. 36. 11; 8. 37. 2. Cf. Dio, fr. 36. 10; Zon. 7. 26.

[5] Livy 8. 27. 3. Any Roman moves in Apulia in 323 when C. Sulpicius Longus was consul are anticipations of the operations there in 314, when C. Sulpicius Longus was likewise consul.

[6] Livy 8. 40. 1; Auct. *de vir. ill.* 32.

[7] See Livy 8. 39, 40. The exploits attributed to Fabius Ambustus may be a Fabian invention (cf. Livy 8. 40. 4; 22. 31. 11); those invented for Cornelius Cossus compensate for his indifferent performance in the First Samnite War (see above, p. 196).

[8] Livy 8. 38.

[9] Auct. *de vir. ill.* 32 makes Fabius Rullianus (whom he calls Rutilius) triumph *de Apulis et Nucerinis* (meaning *Lucerinis*). Pliny, *N.H.* 7. 136, records a more startling triumph for this year: this was the year when the same man (L. Fulvius Curvus of Tusculum) first fought Rome as an enemy and later led her army to victory and celebrated a triumph.

a really heavy defeat, even though Fabius Rullianus may have scored some kind of success. After all, he must have acquired his great military reputation somewhere.[1] There is every reason to be sceptical of Livy's tale that in 322 the Samnites desperately begged for peace, even going to the length of forcing their chief warmonger, Papius Brutulus, to commit suicide, but were haughtily rebuffed. This tale was invented to show how Nemesis overtakes Arrogance: the disaster which struck the Romans in the very next year is specifically related to Roman arrogance in this by Livy.[2] It is, then, safe to surmise that 322 was yet another year of border warfare.

Inconclusive skirmishes and frontier raids were, then, the order of the day during the first five years of hostilities. They seem to have been carried out by comparatively small bodies of men.[3] The consuls, each apparently commanding one legion in this period, acted independently of one another, so Livy implies; and sometimes forces other than consular were put in the field (under a dictator's command), a type of strategy permitting speedy strikes at several points simultaneously. The Samnite effort no doubt closely resembled the Roman.

Unfortunately information as to where the operations took place during these five years is almost entirely lacking. It is improbable that any of them were staged on the littoral, even though later in the war both sides did experiment with naval activity. In general sea-borne operations were few and minor in the Second Samnite War.[4] It was the fighting on land that mattered. Where to localize it, however, in the first five years is difficult to determine. Livy as often as not merely places it 'in Samnium'.

[1] Fabius Rullianus' career is difficult to reconstruct. Auct. *de vir. ill.* 32 agrees with the Triumph. Fasti that he celebrated three triumphs (apparently in 322, 309 and 295).

[2] Livy 9. 1. 4–11. Cf. Dio, fr. 36. 10; Zon. 7. 26.

[3] Diod. 19. 10. 1 hints that that is why he did not bother to record them. The Fasti record triumphs in 326, 324 and 322. That in 326 is probably genuine because of the success at Naples; that in 324 belongs to a dictator year and is automatically suspect; even Livy (8. 40. 1) is doubtful of those in 322.

[4] For naval activity in the Second Samnite War, see Livy 9. 38. 2, 3; App. *Samn.* 7; Dio, fr. 39. 4. It was apparently during it that the Romans for the first time kept a fleet in being: in 311 they appointed *duoviri navales* to equip a fleet and keep it in repair (Livy 9. 30. 4); in 310 they staged a seaborne raid on Nuceria Alfaterna (Livy 9. 38. 2) and throughout they must have used the Greeks of Naples as *socii navales* (the role of Naples after 326 is not recorded). There was also some Samnite naval activity: the Samnite garrison was enticed out of Palaeopolis in 326 by the prospect of being able to stage naval raids on Roman territory (Livy 8. 26. 1) and the Romans sent a Latin Colony to Pontia in 312 (Livy 9. 28. 7) to render this sort of thing impossible.

It could hardly have taken place in Apulia. There is vague mention of operations there in 323 and again in 322, but one may doubt whether any actually occurred, since Livy admits that there were none worth mentioning in the former year and is himself sceptical that there were any at all in the latter.[1] It is a safe conjecture that Apulia is dragged into the accounts of this stage of the war in order to condone the Roman strategy that ended in disaster at the Caudine Forks in 321. Roman writers could plead that it was eagerness to rush to the help of allies in Apulia that led the Romans headlong into the ambush at the Forks. The truth is that, as Livy insists, the Romans had enemies, not allies, in Apulia in 321.[2] At that time Luceria was hostile to Rome, and it remained hostile until captured and colonized in 315/314.

Modern scholars usually regard Northern Campania as the principal theatre of operations during the first five years,[3] although the evidence for this is negligible. Livy, it is true, makes a Samnite spokesman say at the war's outbreak that the conflict would have to be waged in Campania, and in the first year of hostilities he records the suspect item that the Romans captured towns in the Volturnus valley: otherwise not a word about Campania until 321.[4] Had it played a significant role in the opening years one would have expected to read of raids from the Caudine settlements on the Monti Trebulani (Trebula Balliensis, Cubulteria and Caiatia) into the Falernian and Vescine districts,[5] which is what happened later in the Second and throughout the Third Samnite War. Perhaps the Samnites in the early stages of the Second War were hoping for defections of Campani and Aurunci from Rome and for that reason abstained from turning their lands into battlefields.

On the whole the probabilities are that at the start the Liris valley was, as Dionysius of Halicarnassus implies,[6] the principal theatre of operations. For both sides it was an even more sensitive area than Northern Campania, since from it the Romans could

[1] Livy 8. 37. 6.

[2] Livy 8. 37. 4–5; 9. 12. 9–10. Likewise Auct. *de vir. ill.* 32 records a triumph *de Apulis* in 322.

[3] So, for instance, C. P. Burger, *Der Kampf zwischen Rom und Samnium*, pp. 22 f.; G. De Sanctis, *Storia dei Romani*, II, 290 f.; P. Ducati, *L'Italia Antica*, p. 340.

[4] *Campus Campanus in quo concurrendum est* (Livy 8. 23. 8). See, too, 8. 25. 4, and above, p. 219, n. 2.

[5] The Ager Falernus centred on Forum Popilii (mod. *Carinola*?) in Northern Campania; the Ager Vescinus was the adjoining Auruncan territory.

[6] Dion. Hal. 15. 10. 2.

strike at Samnium most directly and most swiftly and from it the Samnites might hope to penetrate into Latium, the real core of Roman strength.[1] There is, in fact, some positive evidence for war activity in the Liris valley. Appian records that between 326 and 321 the Samnites and Romans came to blows at Fregellae.[2] The Roman success at Imbrinium recorded by Livy, if not completely fictitious, may also have occurred in the Liris valley. Livy does not say where Imbrinium was, but he does reveal that, although on Samnite territory, it was within a day's journey of Rome and that a force in its vicinity could screen an army marching eastward across Italy along the line of the later Via Valeria. This description will not fit a town in Northern Campania, but it is just barely applicable to one east of the river in the Liris valley, where, incidentally, a place-name ending in *-inium* is anything but strange (cf. Cominium).[3]

A war that had been caused by Roman encroachment in the Liris valley might very well have been fought there, initially at any rate. Neither side, however, damaged the other very effectively there, and certainly neither side scored a clean break-through.

In order to end this five-year deadlock the Roman consuls for 321, T. Veturius Calvinus and Sp. Postumius Albinus, decided on a change in strategy. They agreed to pool their two armies and invade Samnium,[4] not from the Liris valley, but from Campania. But, although men of southern vision,[5] they were not men of military experience, and disaster ensued. Livy suggests that their object was to march right across the entire breadth of enemy territory to relieve beleaguered Luceria, but this is a military absurdity.[6] Even Veturius and Postumius must have realized that. Their aim must have been the much more limited, although even so not exactly

[1] Moreover had they ever succeeded in establishing themselves firmly on both banks of the Liris, Campania would have been completely at their mercy.

[2] App. *Samn.* 4. 1.

[3] See Livy 8. 29. 7–9; 8. 30. 4; 8. 33. 3, for Imbrinium. It is the only topographical detail supplied by Livy for 325–322, and it is mentioned in a dictator year (or Livy's equivalent thereof). Yet Imbrinium does not look like an invention (C. P. Burger, *Kampf zwischen Rom und Samnium*, p. 22).

[4] Cornelius Cossus' setback near Saticula in 343 (if it is not fiction) illustrated the danger of trying to push into Samnium with only one legion.

[5] Their earlier consulship (334) had been featured by the colonization of Cales.

[6] Yet G. De Sanctis, *Stor. dei Romani*, II, 308, and F. E. Adcock in *Camb. Anc. Hist.* VII, 599, accept it. C. P. Burger, *Kampf zw. Rom und Samnium*, p. 24, more cautiously says that the consuls were attempting a border raid. Actually Luceria was not even a friend, much less a beleaguered ally, of Rome at this time: above, p. 223, n. 2.

modest, one of knocking the Caudini out of the war and then advancing on Malventum, the 'capital' of the Hirpini: such blows might induce the Samnite League to sue for peace.

Accordingly each of the consuls for 321 brought his legion to Calatia.[1] From there they planned to advance round the south side of the Mons Taburnus towards the Caudini. But they did not advance very far. That year, the Samnite League had a generalissimo of exceptional competence, Gavius Pontius.[2] Obviously well informed about the Roman concentration and its intention, he disposed his men carefully on the ridges lining a defile on the Roman axis of advance and barricaded the narrow exit from the defile, the end towards Caudium, with a road block of trees and boulders. Once both Roman legions were inside the defile, he obstructed the narrow entrance to it as well, the end towards Calatia. After some days of unavailing attempts by the ambushed Romans to fight their way out, the consuls felt that they had no option but to surrender.[3]

This is the disaster of the Caudine Forks, one of the most celebrated in the annals of the Roman Republic, and also one of the most elusive. Exactly where it took place has long been a matter of debate. The site is obviously to be sought between Calatia and Caudium, but the precise location is uncertain. Traditionally the defile is identified with the valley between *Santa Maria a Vico* and *Arpaia*, where there is a locality significantly known from medieval times or earlier as *Fórchia*. Some scholars, however, regard this defile as either too small to accommodate the 12,000–16,000 men involved, or too exposed to make Pontius' surprise at all plausible, or too unlike Livy's description of the Forks. These objections are formidable. The other choices for the scene of the disaster, however, seem open to even graver objections: the *Moiano–Airola* valley, besides being no larger, was dominated by Saticula, in 321 a Samnite fortress which the Romans would never have dared to ignore; the *Arpaia–*

[1] Calatia is the modern *Le Galazze*. Mommsen (*CIL*, x, p. 444) emends Calatia to Caiatia (= mod. *Caiazzo*), but this seems impossible. Even Livy nowhere claims that Caiatia was in Roman hands before 321.

[2] For Pontius, see Livy 9. 10. 2; 9. 10. 6; 9. 12. 9. Presumably he was a Caudine, but apparently not from Caudium itself, since his family was domiciled quite some distance from the Caudine Forks (Livy 9. 3, 4, 5, 9). Livy's epitomators (Eutrop. 10. 17. 2; Auct. *de vir. ill.* 30. 1) boldly describe Pontius as coming from Telesia, which was undoubtedly the native town of later Pontii (*ILS*, 6510), including apparently one who claimed descent from the present hero (see above, p. 9, n. 2).

[3] There was evidently heavy fighting (Ox. Pap. *ad an.* 320/319; Cic. *Cato Maior*, 12. 41; *de off.* 3. 30. 109; App. *Samn.* 4. 2; Dio, fr. 36. 9–14; Zon. 7. 26).

Montesarchio–Sferracavallo valley is undoubtedly large enough (if anything it is too large), but its general topography is quite unsuitable for the kind of trap the Samnites are said to have sprung. On the whole, therefore, the traditional identification seems the most likely.[1]

With the surrendered consular armies in their power the Samnites announced the terms on which they would make peace.[2] Their demands were conceded, and the consuls signed for Rome. The terms stipulated that the Romans withdraw from Samnite territory, abandon the Latin Colonies which they had established on the borders of Samnium,[3] and abide by the treaty which they had signed with the Samnites in 354 and renewed in 341. They had to hand over 600 *equites* as hostages for their scrupulous observance of these provisions.

Once the peace treaty was signed the lives of the Roman troops were spared. They were disarmed, sent under the yoke clad only in their tunics and allowed to go, free but humiliated.

Whether the Caudine Peace took the form of a treaty (*foedus*) or, as Livy insists, of a less formal agreement (*sponsio*), guaranteed

[1] So A. Maiuri, *Passeggiate Campane*, p. 350. For all their fame, this is the only appearance of the Caudine Forks in history. The name is variously given as *Furculae Caudinae* (Livy 9. 2. 6), *Furcae Caudinae* (Lucan 2. 137), and *Caudinae Fauces* (Sil. Ital. 8. 566). The exact significance of *furculae* or *furcae* in this context is uncertain. The numbers of men involved have been grossly exaggerated: 40,000 (Dion. Hal. 16. 3) or 50,000 (App. *Samn.* 4. 2). G. De Sanctis, *Stor. dei Romani*, II, 305, more reasonably conjectures 18,000; but even this seems an overestimate. The following identifications are in some cases certain and in all cases plausible: not *Arienzo*, but *Santa Maria a Vico*, twelve miles from Capua, is the *primae angustiae* of Livy (9. 2. 8): its name preserves the Vicus Novanensis (= Ad Novas) of the Itineraries. *Arpaia* is the *aliae angustiae*, the *saltus artior impeditiorque* of Livy (9. 2. 8–9), and is perhaps the 'Forks' proper (note the proximity of *Fórchia*). Aerial photographs reveal how suitable are *Monte Tairano* and *Monte Vorrano*, which flank—on north and south respectively—the *campus* (Livy 9. 2. 7) between these two towns, for concealed and well-fortified strong points (see Plate 3). The *campus* itself is, as Livy (9. 2. 7) says, *satis patens* and *herbidus*, even if not exactly *aquosus*.

H. Nissen (in *Rhein. Mus.* XXV (1870), 1–65) argued strongly for the Arpaia–Montesarchio–Sferracavallo valley. This seems impossible: the Samnites would not have had the men to encircle it in strength, its eastern exit at Sferracavallo is open and easy and simply cannot be described as *angustiae*, and it contains Caudium itself (*Montesarchio*), which the silence of Livy implies to have been outside the defile. In fact, Nissen's proposed identification simply does not harmonize with any of the details given by Livy, topographical or other. The suggestion of E. Pais (*Storia di Roma*³, V, 502) that the 'Forks' are to be sought in the valley of the Isclero below Sant'Agata dei Goti makes no strategic sense: Sant'Agata almost certainly was Saticula (see Livy 23. 14. 13), and in 321 Saticula was a Samnite stronghold.

[2] The Romans asked for terms (Livy 9. 4. 2), just as Metellus did almost two and a half centuries later (Sallust, *Hist.* 1. 28 M. [= 87]).

[3] Samnite territory would include Teanum Sidicinum (assuming, as seems probable, that the Romans had taken it). The Latin Colonies on the borders of Samnium are Fregellae and Cales.

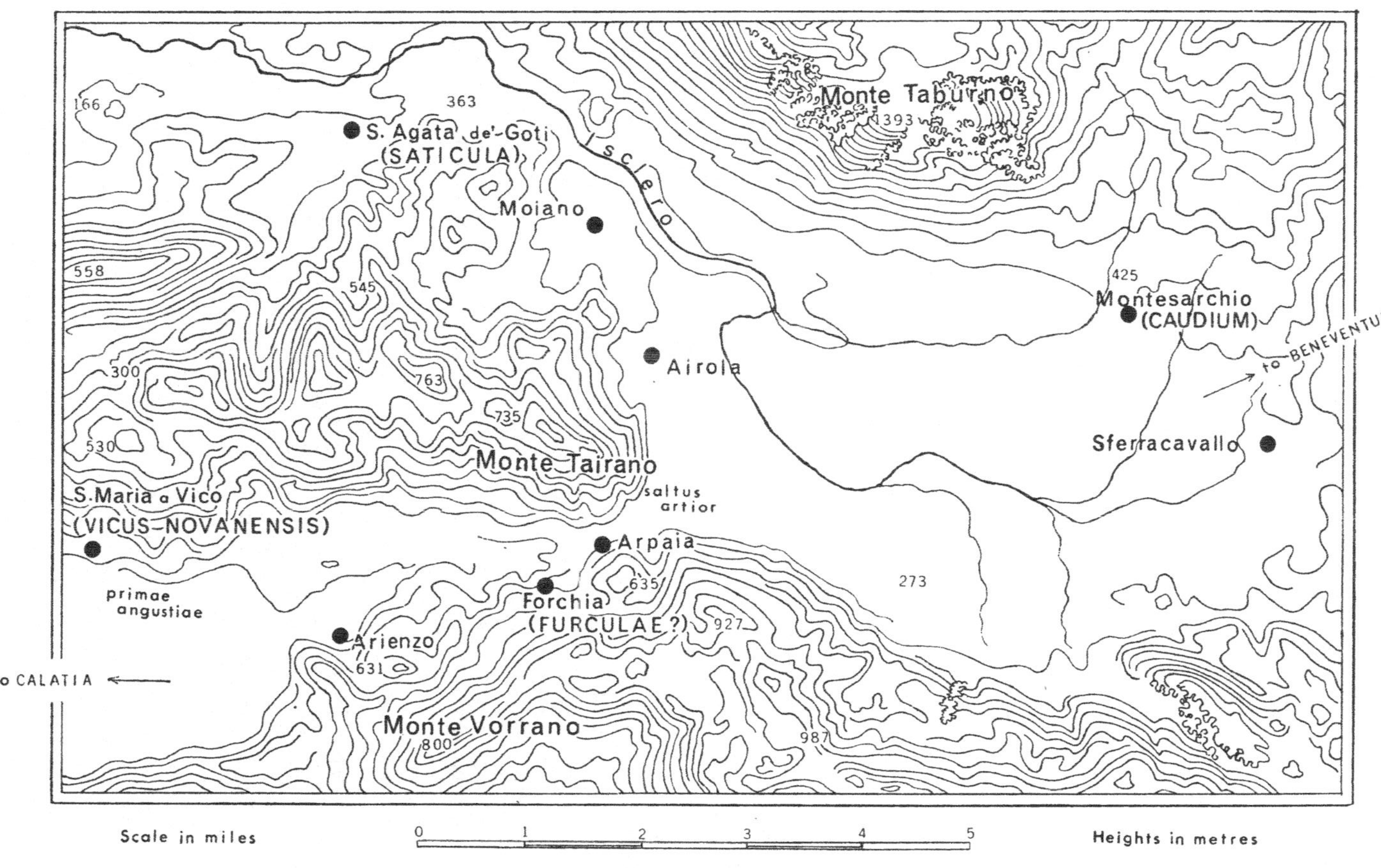

Map 3. The Caudine Forks.

by the word of honour of the consuls and other high-ranking Roman officers present, is largely irrelevant. The essential point is that the peace did come into effect and fighting ceased.[1] But it suited the vanity of the Romans of a later age to insist that, smarting under the indignity, the Roman Senate rejected the peace on the ground that Postumius and Veturius had exceeded their authority in concluding it and immediately resumed hostilities by sending the consuls for 320 on an expedition of revenge, which retrieved the national honour with brilliant, but barren, successes deep inside Samnium. This is obvious, chauvinist fiction, which may have been suggested by the notorious incident in Spain in the second half of the second century, when the Roman government did repudiate an agreement pledged and signed by a defeated Roman general. Even Livy concedes that it was doubtful which Samnite general was defeated in 320 and which Roman general ought to get the credit; for good measure he admits elsewhere that the Caudine Peace came into force and that it was only in 316 that the war broke out afresh.[2]

The Caudine Peace, then, was not repudiated. It lasted for five years, that is, almost as long as the interval between the Second and Third Samnite Wars. Careful examination of what Livy and Diodorus say[3] about this quinquennium reveals that Romans and Samnites were not then at war.[4] There being very little of a military nature to record, Livy fills up most of his account of the period with

[1] For an example of a *sponsio* in the Second Samnite War, see Livy 9. 41. 20 (the agreement with Ocriculum in 308). Livy (9. 5. 4), Dion. Hal. (16. 5. 1) and App. (*Samn.* 4. 6) all claim to know the names of the Roman officers who swore to the *sponsio*. These, however, are historically worthless; they include *legati legionum*, a type of officer that was not even in existence in 321 (Mommsen, *Röm. Staatsrecht*, II, 700 f.). Cicero evidently believed that a *foedus* was signed (*de invent.* 2. 30. 91; cf., too, the coins of the Veturian *gens* which depict the *foedus*, and Claudius Quadrigarius *ap.* Livy 9. 5. 2). If a copy of the instrument was preserved at Rome, it was because it was implemented. In fact Livy 9. 1. 1 admits that the Caudine Peace took effect; and that presumably is how the Romans recovered their 600 equestrian hostages.

[2] For the alleged Roman repudiation of the Caudine Peace, see Livy 9. 15. 9; 9. 16. 11; 25. 6. 12; Dion. Hal. 16. 3; Florus 1. 16 (with rhetorical elaboration); Eutrop. 2. 9; Dio, fr. 36. 21–4; Zon. 7. 26; Auct. *de vir. ill.* 30; Orosius 3. 15; Triumph. Fasti *ad an.* 319. See Livy 9. 21. 2 for the admission that hostilities were in fact not resumed until 316. For ancient comparisons of the Caudine Forks with Mancinus in Spain, see Cic. *de off.* 3. 109; Vell. Pat. 2. 1. 15; Plut. *Ti. Gracch.* 7. 2; App. *Hisp.* 83; Florus 2. 18. 7.

[3] The first mention of the Second Samnite War in Diodorus is under the Varronian year 318 (19. 10. 1–2).

[4] Diodorus records Roman activity in Apulia in 318 and 316. Livy records no Roman actions against Samnites other than the fictitious revenge expedition after the Caudine Forks disaster.

rhetorical irrelevancies: prolix apologiae by the defeated Postumius and the victorious Pontius and a long-winded essay on Alexander the Great's ability to rival Rome. This does not make the task of reconstructing the history of these years any easier; but an account not devoid of plausibility is possible.[1]

The supposed revenge expedition of the consuls in 320 bristles with absurdities. Papirius Cursor's troops, just as if Rome did not already have trouble enough, gratuitously attack the Apuli, recover all the standards, weapons and hostages lost at Caudium, and send 7,000 Samnites, possibly even including Pontius himself, under the yoke with one tunic apiece. Publilius Philo's troops charge like the Light Brigade, non-stop, all the way from Campania to Apulia across the entire width of Samnium.[2] Livy styles all of this a *subita mutatio rerum*.[3] It is more than sudden: it is utterly incredible. But the fiction is also explicable. Livy is clearly anticipating the activity of Papirius Cursor and Publilius Philo five years later. As the most experienced generals of their day they were the ones to whom the Romans turned in times of trouble.[4] The crisis caused by the Caudine disaster of 321 led to their election as consuls for 320, and the crisis caused by the resumption of hostilities in 316 was to lead to their election as consuls for 315. Livy, however, interchanges their roles in the two years. He sends them into the field in 320; and, as we shall see, keeps them in Rome in 315. The exact reverse was the case. It was in 315 that they went forth to engage the enemy: in 320 they stayed in Rome to defend it in case the victors of Caudium should advance into Latium.[5]

Livy says further that, while they were conducting their expedition of revenge, Satricum revolted from Rome and Fregellae was taken by the Samnites. Now it is probable enough that Rome's Caudine disaster encouraged Satricum, a Volscian town in the Liris valley,

[1] See Livy 9. 7–21; Diod. 19. 10. 1; 19. 65. 7. For the prolix digression on Alexander the Great, see P. Treves, *Il Mito di Alessandro e la Roma d'Augusto* (Milan–Naples, 1953).

[2] See Livy 9. 12. 9–9. 15. 11. The capture of Pontius is recorded again over a quarter of a century later in 292 (Livy, *Epit.* 11). The absurdity of the charge across Samnium can be measured from Livy's statement (25. 15. 1) that even after the Via Appia was built it was a big day's march to get to Beneventum from Capua. To go in a day from Cales to Suessula (through easier country than Samnium) was reckoned extraordinary (Livy 24. 13. 9).

[3] Livy 9. 15. 8.

[4] *quod nulli ea tempestate duces clariores essent* (Livy 9. 7. 15).

[5] See especially Livy 9. 12–14; 9. 22. 1. His account of 320 shows that in 315 Cursor must have gone to Apulia and Philo to Campania.

resentful of its annexation by Rome with *civitas sine suffragio*, to rebel; and no doubt some of its Volscian neighbours followed its example: but, as will be seen below, this almost certainly did not happen in 320.[1] Nor did Fregellae revolt, or get captured by the Samnites; it was surrendered to them (presumably in this year 320) in fulfilment of the Caudine Peace terms.

In 319 Livy records the recovery of Satricum and the subjugation of the otherwise unknown Ferentani. The customary view, that these latter are the same as the Frentani, the Samnites' Sabellian neighbours on the Adriatic coast, while palaeographically possible, is *a priori* improbable: during the Caudine Peace Rome would not have dared to post her forces far away from Latium and to provoke the Samnites by armed activities along their eastern frontiers. The Ferentani, therefore, must be the same people as the Forentani, whom Pliny places in Augustus' Region I ('Campania and Latium') and who later (in 280) supplied a cavalry troop to the Roman army that faced Pyrrhus at Heraclea. Theirs must have been one of the Volscian communities in the Liris valley to join Satricum in its revolt from Rome, a revolt which is almost certainly later than the date assigned to it by Livy. At any rate the Roman reconquest of Satricum, and of the Ferentani too presumably, seems more likely to belong to 315 when Q. Aulius Cerretanus was master of the horse than to 319 when he was consul.[2]

[1] For Satricum see Livy 9. 12. 5; 9. 16. 2 and for its site in the Liris valley Cic. *ad Q. Fr.* 3. 1. 4, and above, p. 194, n. 2. For the alleged Samnite capture of Fregellae, see Livy 9. 12. 6–8: forgetting that, Livy (9. 28. 3) reports its capture (or at least the capture of *arx Fregellana*) again in 313. No doubt Cales and Teanum Sidicinum were also given up by the Romans in 320. There were surprisingly few revolts after Caudium: neither the Campani nor the Aequi rebelled (Livy 9. 7; 9. 45. 5; Dio, fr. 36. 15). Nor are the Aurunci described as having done so.

[2] For the Frentani (or Ferentani as Cicero's text at *pro Cluentio* 97 calls them) as enemies of Rome, presumably at some time other than 319, see App. *B.C.* 1. 39. 175. For the Forentani in Region I, see Pliny, *N.H.* 3. 64 (Pliny is, of course, capable of attributing a community to the wrong region). Livy's references to Volsci at Ferentinum (4. 51. 7; 4. 56. 6) may perhaps more properly belong to this community than to the Hernican town to which he obviously assigns them. For the Forentani who fought Pyrrhus, see Jordanes, *Rom.* 154; they may be the Volsci listed by Dion. Hal. 20. 1. 2–3. When Diodorus 19. 65. 7 records the Roman capture of Ferente in 316, he may unwittingly mean the community of the Ferentani (he places Ferente in Apulia: but he is prone to localize any Samnite War activity there). If the Ferentani were subjugated in 316, Livy's date of 319 for the event gets some explanation: an Aemilius commanded in both years (as consul in 319, as dictator in 316). The recovery of Satricum is associated by Livy not only with the name of Aulius but also with the capture of Luceria (9. 16. 11); and this belongs to 315 (see below, p. 238), when Papirius Cursor was consul. (Oros. 3. 15. 10 agrees that Satricum fell in his consulship, although Orosius has the wrong consulship in mind.)

In 318 and 317, by Livy's own admission, a truce prevailed between Romans and Samnites. For these two years he records that two new tribes of Roman citizens were created, the Oufentina near the Middle Liris and the Falerna in Northern Campania, a notice that is certainly authentic. He also says that a Roman army was sent against Apuli and Lucani, a notice that is just as certainly false. Rome still did not feel sufficiently secure to denude her frontier with Samnium of troops and send them far away to the distant south. Nor would she have recklessly added to the list of her enemies at that time by attacking Apuli and Lucani. Furthermore Livy's account of these alleged southern operations is too odd to be convincing. He says that Rome conquered Teanum Apulum and Canusium in 318 and Teate, Forentum and Lucanian Nerulum in 317. Thus he has failed to realize, first, that Teanum Apulum and Teate are one and the same, and, secondly, that at this juncture it was beyond the bounds of possibility for a Roman force to get to Nerulum (in the most distant part of Lucania, near Thurii) or even to Forentum (south of Venusia). Livy in fact is here attributing to C. Junius Brutus, *cos.* 317, the operations of a later C. Junius Brutus, *cos.* 277, who *was* active around Forentum and Nerulum. The consul of 317 was almost certainly busy elsewhere, trying to restore Rome's authority among the Vestini in Central Italy. The Lucani against whom the Romans moved during the Caudine Peace must have been the inhabitants of Luca in the Liris valley, who are to be numbered like the Ferentani amongst the Volsci joining Satricum in its revolt.[1]

The dealings that the Romans had with the Apuli in 318/317 must have been of a diplomatic nature, even though it suited their martial pride to claim later that they had brought the Apuli over by force of arms rather than by negotiation. They signed alliances with various Apulian communities in order to pose the Samnites with a possible threat to their rear: with Arpi, the most important one, with Teanum Apulum, with Canusium, and with some others unnamed.[2]

[1] See Livy 9. 20, and Diod. 19. 10; and for the sites of Forentum and Nerulum: Hor. *Odes*, 3. 4. 16; Suet. *Aug.* 2 and 4; *CIL*, 1^2, 638; K. J. Beloch, *Röm. Gesch.* pp. 402, 465.

[2] The Samnites coveted the grazing lands of Arpi (Varro, *R.R.* 2. 1. 16; 2. 2. 9) and it had constructed massive walls against them (Strabo 6. 3. 9, p. 283). It is not surprising that it would agree to an alliance with Rome.

In 316, according to Livy (and Diodorus supports him), the Romans were involved in operations against rebellious Volsci. This notice is trustworthy enough. The Volsci, already rendered restive by the Roman setback at Caudium, were further provoked in 318 when Roman citizens were settled in the Liris valley and assigned to the new tribe Oufentina. Resentful at this intrusion, Satricum, Luca, the Ferentani and perhaps others revolted, probably with Samnite encouragement. The Romans decided to crush this threat to their vulnerable Liris frontier, and sent a strong force against Satricum. They were taking a risk in despatching an army into a zone about which the Samnites were extremely sensitive, but they doubtless hoped that their new Apulian alliances, with their implied threat of two-front war, would restrain the Samnites. As a further precaution they appointed a dictator. But, as Livy says, the Samnites now had a pretext for renewing open hostilities: they promptly sent help to Satricum and also moved against Plistica, another (and pro-Roman) settlement in the Liris valley. The Second Samnite War had been resumed.[1]

This review suggests that during the Caudine Peace Rome's main aim was to repair broken fences. It was probably now that it was decided to enlarge each consular army to two legions[2] and to field additional forces as circumstances dictated. Somehow new legions were enrolled and fitted out. There is no need to believe that, if they were fitted out with *pilum* and *scutum*, the Romans learned the use of these weapons from the Samnites. But it may well be that, during the Caudine Peace, Roman troops did undergo more intensive training in manipular tactics, employing smaller and more mobile units like those of the Samnites.

Rome's search for allies during the Caudine Peace may have been helped by the truculence of the Samnites in Apulia, where they evidently dominated Luceria.[3] Some Apuli argued that, if they were not going to be allowed to remain neutral in any case, the 'friend-

[1] Livy 9. 21 and 22; Diod. 19. 72. 3–4. The Roman dictator in 316 was L. Aemilius Mamercinus, who had brought the First Samnite War to an end (see above, p. 200). I have shown elsewhere (in *Trans. Amer. Phil. Assn.* LXXXVII (1957), 99–104) that there is confusion between the names Satricum and Saticula in the years 316 and 315.

[2] The enlargement of consular armies to two legions each may have come a little later: it was in 311 that the number of military tribunes was increased (Livy 9. 30. 3). It was probably the increase in size of the consular armies that caused Diodorus in his notices of the Second Samnite War to record the consuls as acting jointly: for him two legions meant two consuls.

[3] Livy 9. 12. 9.

ship' of the more distant Romans was the lesser of two evils,[1] and that explains why Arpi, Teanum and Canusium reached their understandings with Rome. Incidentally Rome had at once sought to consolidate her communications with these new allies. In 317 C. Junius Brutus secured the route across Central Italy by subduing the Vestini.[2]

The Samnites, for their part, could not have been idle during the Caudine Peace. Undoubtedly they strengthened their hold on the left bank of the Liris and, quite clearly, they lent support to anti-Roman movements on the right bank.[3] They likewise improved their position in Central and Southern Campania. When hostilities were resumed in 316 Nola seems to have been under their control, and Nuceria Alfaterna, head of a league which may have included Stabiae, Pompeii and Herculaneum, was also firmly on their side.[4] In addition, later developments suggest that between 321 and 316 the Samnites had been matching the Roman diplomatic effort in Apulia with one of their own in Etruria.

The war now entered on a new phase, a phase for which jejune notices in Diodorus supplement the narrative of Livy, so that more details are recorded for the last ten years of the struggle than for the first ten.[5]

Both sides braced themselves for the effort that was clearly going to be needed in 315. The Samnites evidently concentrated their forces for a heavy blow in the west. The Romans elected as their consuls for 315 the experienced L. Papirius Cursor and Q. Publilius Philo, the same pair that had been elected to cope with the Caudine crisis five years earlier. As we have already seen, Livy has exactly reversed the roles played by these consuls in 320 and in 315 respectively. In 320 they must have stayed in Rome; and, since Livy himself soon reveals that there were Roman armies (the consular

[1] Cf. Livy 9. 13. 6: *omnia pacata Samnitium magis iniuriis et odio quam beneficio ullo populi Romani.* The Romans no doubt used Romanophil elements in Apulia; they certainly did elsewhere: at Sora (Livy 9. 24. 3), amongst the Aurunci (Livy 9. 25. 6), at Narnia (Livy 10. 10. 1).

[2] See above, p. 220. Reject the fanciful notion of C. P. Burger, *Der Kampf zwischen Rom und Samnium*, p. 45, that Rome maintained communications with Apulia by way of the Hirpini.

[3] Just as in 327 they had urged other Volsci (Privernum, Fundi, Formiae) to rise against Rome: see above, p. 216, n. 2.

[4] Livy 9. 41. 2 f. even seems to regard it as part of Samnium.

[5] Diodorus begins to list events in the Second Samnite War in the Varronian year 318 (19. 10. 1): but he records none for 317 or 307.

ones apparently) in both Apulia and Campania in 315, the inference is ineluctable: in 315 L. Papirius Cursor went to Apulia to attack the Samnites at Luceria and Q. Publilius Philo went to Campania to attack the Samnites at Saticula. Simultaneously another Roman force, under Q. Fabius Rullianus, continued to press the attack on Satricum and the Volscian rebels in the Liris valley. This no doubt was a logical consequence of the policy of southward expansion, but, as the sequel quickly showed, it was a dangerous dispersal of Roman strength.

In Apulia, Papirius Cursor, supported presumably by Rome's new Apulian allies, laid siege to Samnite-controlled Luceria; and in the Liris valley Fabius Rullianus recovered Satricum.[1] But in Campania something went wrong. A Samnite force either defeated or eluded Publilius Philo and began to move towards Latium: its commander, whom our Roman sources do not identify, must have been an officer of unusual competence, Gavius Pontius himself perhaps.[2] The Roman dictator Fabius Rullianus was the only Roman commander near enough to take measures of defence. His task now, no easy one, was to save Latium if he could. He decided to cover the inland route (Via Latina) himself, while his master of the horse Aulius Cerretanus protected the coastal one (the later Via Appia) by posting his forces near Tarracina.[3] Meanwhile the unnamed Samnite commander came steadily on. The Latin Colonies had been evacuated and no longer barred his way, and he reached the site of Fregellae without undue delay. There he was faced with the choice of continuing on to Rome along the Trerus valley or of wheeling to the left and splitting Roman territory asunder at its

[1] Oros. 3. 15. 10 attributes this feat to Papirius Cursor, possibly because of his confused recollection of the earlier rivalry between Papirius and Fabius. The Ferentani may have been already reduced to obedience in the preceding year (see Diod. 19. 65. 7, capture of 'Ferente'). The recovery of Satricum and the capture of Luceria belong to the same year (Livy 9. 16. 11; Triumph. Fasti *ad an.* 319).

[2] The Roman setback may have occurred near Saticula. This would account for the confusion between Satricum and Saticula referred to above (p. 232, n. 1). When there was both a reverse (at Saticula) and a rebellion (at Satricum) to record, the temptation for the Roman tradition to conflate the two and claim a victory (preferably at the town of the enemy: viz. Saticula) proved irresistible. If Gavius Pontius was the Samnite commander responsible, the failure of our (Roman) sources to name him can be easily explained: according to them he had been captured during the revenge expedition of 320.

[3] Lautulae must have lain near mod. *Itri* (L. Pareti, *Storia di Roma*, I, 700): see Livy 7. 39. 7; 22. 15. 11, and H. Nissen, *Italische Landeskunde*, I, 328; II, 642. Strategic justification for the Roman troop dispositions is supplied by Cic. *ad Att.* 8. 113. 1 and *ad Fam.* 7. 23. 3. Diod. 19. 72. 7–8 seems to think that Lautulae was in Apulia.

narrowest point by marching across the col between the Ausonian and the Auruncan Mountains. He chose the latter course, and this brought him up against the forces of Aulius Cerretanus at Lautulae, the narrow defile near Tarracina that controls the coastal road and has been aptly styled the Thermopylae separating Central from Southern Italy. The inexperienced Roman levies were no match for their hardy opponents and went down to shattering defeat. Aulius himself fell, and the verdict of the Caudine Forks seemed confirmed.[1]

Roman territory had now been split asunder. The southern portion, inhabited by citizens without the franchise, was either persuaded or coerced by the Samnites to renounce allegiance to Rome: Aurunci and Campani rebelled. The northern portion (*Latium Vetus*), inhabited by citizens with full rights, lay exposed to the depredation of the enemy, and it was probably now that the Samnites advanced with fire and sword as far as Ardea.[2]

Meanwhile Rullianus, and presumably the authorities in Rome itself, were trying desperately to protect the various approaches to the city. They evidently succeeded in doing so, but at the cost of weakening the Roman forces in the Liris valley. There the Samnites stormed across the river to capture Sora and other places. To complete the discomfiture of the Romans, pro-Samnite factions began to gain strength amongst the Sabellic tribes of Central Italy, which lay athwart the lines of communication of the Roman forces in Apulia. Samnite success had reached its high-water mark.[3]

The Roman drive to the south had run into appalling difficulties

[1] In 9. 22 and 23 Livy prefers to regard Lautulae as a drawn battle ended by nightfall: he makes Aulius fall at Satricum (9. 22. 9; above, p. 230, n. 2) and he records a fictitious victory by Fabius Rullianus to offset Lautulae (9. 23. 7–17). In other passages (9. 23. 5; 9. 25. 2, 5) Livy agrees with Diod. 19. 72. 7–8 that Lautulae was a Roman defeat.

[2] See, especially, Diod. 19. 76. 1. Strabo (5. 3. 5, p. 232; 5. 4. 11, p. 249) describes how the victorious Samnites overran Latium: Ardea never recovered from the blow and dwindled into an insignificant village (A. Boethius, *Atti del Quinto Congresso di Studi Romani*, II (1940), 235). Presumably it was now that Amyclae near Lautulae was destroyed by 'serpents' (Greek ὄφεις: i.e. Opici, Osci): Pliny, *N.H.* 3. 59; Serv. *ad Aen.* 10. 504. Roman treatment of some towns, when they were recovered, was so mild as to make it certain that they had not rebelled spontaneously but had been dragooned by the Samnites. It is clear that Capua, Calatia and Atella, the principal towns of the Campani, were amongst those that were induced to renounce their allegiance to Rome.

[3] For the Liris valley developments, see Livy 9. 21. 6; 9. 22. 11; 9. 23. 2; Diod. 19. 72. 3. Both authors suggest that the Roman setbacks there occurred before Lautulae; in addition Livy wrongly describes Sora as a colony then.

and many a Roman 'noble' must have been asking himself whether it was worth while. It is clear that by now a powerful group in the Senate had had enough of it with its attendant military risks. This, however, was no time for recrimination. For the moment all Roman efforts had to be bent towards the task of restoring the situation; but, once the most pressing peril was past, it would be possible to demand a reckoning from the authors of Rome's misfortune. To cope with the emergency the Romans, not surprisingly, had recourse to the dictatorship. Successful commanders of an earlier day were appointed to that office in each of the next three years: C. Maenius in 314, C. Poetelius Libo and, as an added precaution, Q. Fabius Rullianus in 313, and C. Sulpicius Longus in 312.[1]

Our sources and the sources known to our sources are more than usually confused in their accounts of the achievements of the generals who retrieved the situation for Rome. But careful examination of the ancient texts makes it possible to extract a coherent picture, and possibly to give credit where credit is due, with some degree of plausibility.

Lautulae did not prove to be a second Caudium. This time the Romans had not lost two consular armies in the critical battle. This time, too, thanks to the careful reorganization of their armed forces during the Caudine Peace, they had trained reserves available. Instead of recalling the army that was besieging Luceria, which would in any event have arrived too late to affect the issue, they rushed reinforcements into Latium to halt the widespread Samnite devastations.

Fortunately for the Romans, no hostile move was made at this stage by the Etruscans, who before Lautulae may have been prudently appraising Roman strength before committing themselves and after Lautulae may have concluded that, for the time being at any rate, the Samnites hardly needed help from anybody.

As a matter of fact this was the very moment when the Samnites would have welcomed support in the north, since they found themselves suddenly confronted with distraction in the south. Once again a mercenary captain arrived from across the Adriatic to

[1] Maenius had defeated the Latins in 338; Poetelius had been thrice consul—in 360, 346 and 326, unless the dictator of 313 was this man's son (see Broughton, *MRR*, I, p. 146); Longus proved his mettle in 314. Fabius Rullianus is one of the great heroes of the Second Samnite War: yet one wonders whether the story of his co-dictatorship in 313 is not a Fabian fiction which may have been suggested by the co-dictatorship of Fabius Maximus and Minucius in 217.

divert their attention. Acrotatus, son of the King of Sparta, invited by Syracusan exiles and others to come to Sicily to drive out the tyrant Agathocles, responded with alacrity. En route he stopped at Tarentum in 314, and this disturbed the Samnites. It is true that his sojourn in Italy turned out to be of the briefest; but the Samnites could not anticipate that. All they knew was that on his way west he had interfered forcefully in the affairs of Illyricum; and he might do the same thing in Italy. His strength was not enormous, but neither could it be totally ignored, especially when there was a Roman army in Apulia presumably willing to cooperate with him. For the critical period of the struggle between Romans and Samnites the latter were just sufficiently preoccupied about what was going on to the south of them as not to be able to give their undivided attention to operations in Latium. This must have been a factor helping to promote the recovery of the Romans. In the very year that Acrotatus landed in the south they pulled off a victory in the west that proved to be crucial. While the experienced C. Maenius as dictator directed affairs in Rome, the two consuls took the calculated risk of committing both their armies, possibly as many as four legions, to a set battlepiece, perhaps against the anonymous Samnite hero and his conquering army; and they won the day. This removed the threat in Latium and Campania. Clearly it was an action of vital importance, since it seriously impaired Samnite military power in the west. The architect of victory, according to Livy, who is supported by the Fasti Triumphales, was the consul, the competent and experienced C. Sulpicius Longus. The scene of the victory was most probably Tarracina. Diodorus' text seems to name that town, and the Tarracina area is entirely suitable. Livy's site for the battle, somewhere near Caudium, is a military absurdity: no Roman force could have penetrated that far across rebel and enemy territory after Lautulae. Livy's figure for Samnite casualties is equally absurd, the regular (and ridiculous) 30,000 killed.[1] Still more preposterous is Livy's story that as a result of the victory the Romans went on to besiege Bovianum. This town, as the 'capital' of the Pentri, the most powerful of the Samnite tribes, was always the ultimate Roman objective and hence is regularly named whenever the Roman

[1] For Acrotatus' landing at Tarentum, see Diod. 19. 70. 8. For the battle see Livy 9. 27 and Diod. 19. 76. 2 (emending περὶ Κίναν πόλιν). Niese's *Pinna* (*Grundriss Röm. Gesch.*[4], p. 67), Beloch's *Apulia* (*Röm. Gesch.* p. 406), or Pais' *Cyme* (*Stor. di Roma*[3], v, 36) as the site of the encounter seem unsuitable. Diodorus' figure for Samnites killed is 10,000.

writers wish to be more than usually sensational: its capture is reported no less than three times. But it is quite out of the question for the Romans to have advanced as far as Bovianum in 313 and have then passed the winter there. Livy is simply bemused by his own fantasy of a revenge expedition after Lautulae analogous to the fictitious one after the Caudine Forks. It is to be noted that even Livy admits that the Roman siege of Bovianum lasted for only a short time and was then lifted.[1] Not so the siege of Luceria. The Roman and Apulian forces there had been too far away to help Latium immediately after Lautulae, and accordingly had pressed home their assault on the strategic bastion. It fell in 315 and in the next year, when the situation in the west had been brought under control, the Romans sent a Latin Colony there.[2]

The Roman victory at Tarracina brought immediate results. The victorious consuls promptly attacked the insurgent Aurunci and made them pay dearly for their revolt: it was the Romans, now in 314, when Sulpicius Longus and Poetelius were consuls, rather than the Sidicini over twenty years earlier (337), when Sulpicius Longus and Aelius Paetus were consuls, who were responsible for the massacres and other harsh measures that put an end to the existence of the Aurunci as a separate, identifiable nation.[3]

In the next year (313), the dictator Q. Fabius Rullianus, operating in familiar territory, regained Fregellae for Rome and *may* have been rewarded with a triumph; and it was either he or C. Junius Brutus, the consul for 313, who must have recovered Teanum Sidicinum and Cales.[4] Junius Brutus certainly seems to have been the one who scored the successes in Campania: Capua hurriedly returned to allegiance; Calatia and Atella were also recovered (presumably they had revolted along with Capua), and Saticula

[1] Livy 9. 28. 1. It was probably the Younger Annalists who so emphasized the role of Bovianum. They were probably impressed by the important part it played in the Social War.

[2] Livy is very confused in what he says about Luceria, but seems to have no doubt that its colonization belongs to 314 (9. 26). Diod. 19. 72. 8 records its capture in 315 and says that its colonization ensued.

[3] Livy 9. 25. 9.

[4] Fabius Rullianus had served in the Liris probably in 325 and 322 and certainly in 313 (for Roman successes there that year, see Livy 9. 28. 3 and Diod. 19. 101. 3, who, however, confuses Fregellae with Sora). Auct. *de vir. ill.* 32, but not the Triumph. Fasti, registers a triumph for Rullianus. The recovery of Teanum Sidicinum and Cales is nowhere recorded; but then the record of their surrender to the Samnites had also been suppressed.

and Nola were captured.[1] Northern Campania had thus been won back, and, to maintain firm communications with it and thus provide security for the restored Ager Romanus, the Romans resuscitated the colonies at Fregellae and Cales and established new ones at Suessa on ex-Auruncan territory and at Saticula on ex-Samnite. Even the communications by sea were safeguarded, by the despatch of a Latin Colony to the island of Pontia (313).[2]

The following year (312) the Romans made sure of their hold on the valley of the middle Liris. Sora and presumably other Volscian towns were recovered by the consul M. Valerius Maximus and a Latin Colony was planted lower down the river at Interamna on its left bank, near its junction with the Rapido (or Gari as it is here called). Meanwhile severe punishment had been meted out to Satricum for its defection: Livy does not go into details about it, but he does reveal that it set the pattern of penalty for rebellious Capua in 211. By a prodigious effort the Romans had restored the damage which Caudium and Lautulae had done. Indeed in the Liris valley and in Campania they were now in an even stronger position than they had occupied when the war began.[3]

[1] For Roman successes in Campania, see Livy 9. 28. 5 f. (emending *Atina* to *Atella*: Atina remained Samnite until the Third War (Livy 10. 39. 5)) and Diod. 19. 101. 3 (emending Κελίαν to Καλατίαν). Despite Mommsen (*CIL*, x, p. 359) and Beloch (*Röm. Gesch.* p. 407) it must have been Calatia and not Caiatia that the Romans took: the defences of Caiatia were massive enough to defy Hannibal and the accounts of later Samnite raiding of the Campus Stellatis suggest that the town must have remained a Samnite stronghold right down to the last days of the Third War. Calatia on the other hand, like Atella, was a member of Capua's League; and the Romans must certainly have re-established control over Capua's League before they could go on to win Saticula and Nola. Saticula was captured, but Nola may have joined Rome voluntarily once the high ground to its north-east (San Francesco) or south-east (Cicala) was firmly garrisoned by Roman troops to shield it from Samnite attack; Diodorus says that it was precisely the *arx* (= anc. *Hyria*?) that the Romans took in 313. A voluntary alliance with Rome would account for the very favourable treaty that Nola enjoyed: the town later was allowed to issue its own silver coins and it resisted Hannibal most determinedly (Livy 26. 33. 10). The Roman commander who was so successful in Campania could not have been the dictator Poetelius, since he was appointed *clavi figendi causa*; and even Livy refuses to believe that it was Fabius Rullianus (9. 28. 2–6). Presumably therefore it was Junius Brutus.

[2] For these colonies, see E. T. Salmon in *Class. Phil.* LVIII (1963), 235–8. Suessa controlled the gap between the Mons Massicus and the Rocca Monfina, Saticula the route via the River Isclero into the Caudine country.

[3] For the Liris valley operations, see Triumph. Fasti *ad an.* 312; Livy 9. 24. 3 (who gives 314 as the date, and Sulpicius Longus as the captor of Sora, probably through confusion with 345 when Sulpicius Rufus originally captured it; Livy also embroiders his account with details from Opimius' capture of Fregellae in 125); and Auct. *de vir. ill.* 27. 1 (who implies that P. Decius took Sora). Interamna was on the left bank of the Liris on territory that had once belonged to the Volsci but more recently to the Samnites (Livy 10. 36. 16; 10. 39. 1; Sil. Ital. 8. 402). It ensured communications with Cales and Campania (Strabo 5. 3. 9, p. 237) and counterbalanced Samnite-held Casinum.

Now that the most pressing sense of urgency was past, a reappraisal of policy was possible. Evidently the patricio-plebeian nobility was now seriously split on the merits of a forward policy in the south which involved wide dispersal of Roman strength and possibly other disadvantages as well. In the eyes of some of them the disasters at Caudium and Lautulae had brought the state to the brink of catastrophe and the policy that had led to these disasters was gravely compromised. As early as 314 they launched violent attacks on its advocates, one of whom is identified by Livy as C. Maenius. They apparently succeeded in saddling Publilius Philo with responsibility for the Lautulae fiasco: he ended his career in disgrace and is never heard of again.[1] Appius Claudius Caecus, another of the advocates of southern expansion, succeeded in saving his political skin by carrying his case directly to the people, whose favour he had prudently cultivated by the construction of an aqueduct: he survived politically to become censor (312) and to carry out his project for linking Rome to Capua by a coastal road, which was to immortalize his name (312–310).[2] Undoubtedly, however, the policy of expansion in the south was to some extent discredited. The influence was rising of those nobles who sponsored other programmes, such as vigorous activity in Central Italy perhaps or in Northern Italy.[3] It may have been this prospect that stirred the Etruscans, or they may have been alarmed by the implications of the rapid Roman recovery after Lautulae for the future balance of power within peninsular Italy. At any rate they chose this moment to intervene in the war.

Hitherto the Etruscans, who after what had happened to them at Sabellian hands in days gone by in Campania had no historical love for Samnites, had resisted the diplomatic pressure of the latter and made no move: they may have been unconvinced of the need to bestir themselves, or they may have been unable to agree among themselves, or they may have been nervous of Carthage, at this time in treaty relationship with Rome.[4] By 312 it was clear that the

[1] See Livy 9. 26, 33, 34; Diod. 19. 76. 3–5. The critics of the southern policy evidently included Ti. Numicius, L. Livius and Q. Maelius, who had been plebeian tribunes in 320 (Livy 9. 8. 14; cf. Cic. *de off.* 3. 109).

[2] For Ap. Claudius Caecus, see Livy 9. 29, 33, 34; Diod. 20. 36.

[3] The Fabii seem to have had an Etruscan policy (M. Sordi, *I Rapporti Romano-Ceriti*, pp. 75 f.).

[4] The treaty of 306 (Livy 9. 43. 26; cf. Polyb. 3. 26) indicates that at about this time Rome was friendly with Carthage, whereas the Etruscans were friendly with Carthage's enemy, Agathocles: Etruscan troops helped Agathocles (Diod. 20. 62. 2) and Tarquinii was cooperating with Syracuse against Carthage (Diod. 20. 16. 6).

Romans had weathered the effects of Lautulae. But by then it was also clear that the Romans were spread very thin: they had to maintain their consular armies, they had to raise emergency forces to support allies on both sides of Italy, and they had to provide the bulk of the garrisons for the new Latin Colonies. Intervention at this stage might not be dangerous for the Etruscans and might well be deadly for the Romans; at the very least it would prevent them from developing any plans they might be meditating for Central or Northern Italy.

The Etruscans began their preparations for active participation in 312 or earlier, but it is not easy to decide which Etruscans were involved. Livy's assertion that it was all of them except Arretium is belied by his own version of the events. Some Etruscan cities had treaties with Rome and evidently respected them.[1] Others were too far north to be much concerned. It must have been the Southern Etruscans, those for whom the sanctuary of Voltumna was a cult centre, who entered the war against Rome, Volsinii probably taking the lead.

The Romans, alert to the possibility of Etruscan intervention, had sought to guard against it by strengthening their position in Central Italy, where, especially after Caudium and Lautulae, pro-Samnite factions were only too likely to emerge among the Sabellic peoples and make physical cooperation between Samnites and Etruscans possible. In 312 when reports of Etruscan preparations were rife, C. Sulpicius Longus, the hero of Tarracina, was named dictator and he appointed C. Junius Brutus as his master of the horse. Forces were at once raised and sent into the country of the Marrucini in Central Italy, presumably under the command of Junius Brutus, who may have been very familiar with the region as a result of operations against the Vestini there five years earlier. Apparently he scored some successes.[2]

[1] Falerii, which had signed a treaty of alliance with Rome in 343, evidently sided with Volsinii (see Livy 9. 29–41). Tarquinii had signed a forty-year treaty with Rome in 348 (Livy 7. 22. 5) and renewed it in 308 (Livy 9. 41. 5; Diod. 20. 44. 8): hence it is unlikely to have been hostile between 311 and 308. Arretium, Perusia and Cortona are described as signing thirty-year treaties in 310 (Livy 9. 37. 12; Diod. 20. 35. 5), but this looks like anticipation of 295 when Arretium, Perusia and Volsinii signed forty-year treaties (Livy 10. 37. 5).

[2] Diod. 19. 105. 5 says that the Romans assaulted Pollitium: which unknown town might be the mod. Pollutri, could we be but sure that its site in antiquity was *in Marrucinis*, and not *in Frentanis* as its proximity to Histonium (mod. Vasto) would seem to indicate. The only known town of the Marrucini is Teate, but the Itineraries record a *vicus* called Interpromium, and Pollitium could have been another. The Triumph. Fasti do not allude to the Marrucine operation; yet the Marrucini were at one time hostile to Rome (App. *B.C.* 1. 39. 175).

In the next year (311) the Etruscans made their move, and now, if not before, the Romans made each consul's army two legions instead of one. Trustworthy details are scarce, since Livy confuses Etruscan activities in the Second Samnite War with those in the Third, in which Fabius Rullianus was likewise prominent.[1] Even the date of the Etruscan intervention is doubtful, since Diodorus seems to place it one year later.[2] But there is no doubt where it occurred. The focus of operations was Sutrium, the Latin Colony that controlled the road (the later Via Cassia) running from Rome to Etruria through the gap between the Ciminian and Sabatinian Mountains. In 311 a strong Etruscan force assaulted the place. It did not fall, but was still under severe pressure at year's end: there is the revealing item that the principal battle for it had been interrupted by darkness. The next year (310) was the crucial one, and involved the Romans very heavily in Southern Etruria. Diodorus' statement that both consuls were operating there may not indeed be accurate, but undoubtedly there was bitter fighting around Sutrium. This remained indecisive, until the consul Q. Fabius Rullianus suddenly threatened the enemy's rear by making his celebrated march through the thickly wooded Ciminian Mountains, presumably north-eastwards along the line of the later Via Amerina, since that way support might be available from Nepet, the other Latin Colony in Southern Etruria. He was taking a calculated risk in thus uncovering the road to Rome, but the gamble paid off. He induced the Etruscans to concentrate their phalanx against him somewhere

[1] The temptation to assign Rullianus' exploits such as his victory near Perusia (Livy 9. 37. 1; 9. 40. 18; Diod. 20. 35. 4) to this stage in his career was strong, since 310 was the year of his celebrated march. The exaggerations are probably an effort to compensate for earlier Fabian failure in Etruria: e.g. Fabius Ambustus, *cos.* 358, had been defeated by Tarquinii (Livy 7. 15. 9; 7. 16. 2). Some of the more flamboyant details in Livy's account (e.g. 9. 41. 18) may derive from the poetry of Ennius (E. Woelfflin in *Rhein. Mus.* L (1895), 152).

[2] Livy (9. 31. 1) and the Triumph. Fasti *ad an.* make the Etruscan operations begin in 311; Diod. (20. 35. 1) first mentions them under 310 when he reports two consular armies (meaning probably two legions) near the colony of Sutrium (Livy also localizes the fighting here in 310 (9. 36), as well as in 311 when he called it an ally (9. 32. 2): on which see M. Sordi, *I Rapporti Romano-Ceriti*, pp. 133–8). The heavy fighting around Sutrium in these years may have given rise to the proverb 'To go to Sutrium', meaning 'to take up arms and go off to fight at a moment's notice' (Plautus, *Cas.* 523; Festus, p. 306 L. (who, however, says that a *tumultus Gallicus* was responsible for it)). Rullianus' exploit in the Ciminian Forest has been greatly exaggerated: Livy later suggests as much (10. 24); and at 9. 36. 1 he admits that his description has been inspired by what he had heard of the forests of Germany in his own day. Diodorus (20. 35. 2) fails to name the Ciminian Forest. For the Via Amerina, see J. B. Ward-Perkins in *J.R.S.* XLVII (1957), 142 f.

north-east of Sutrium, and there defeated it with his more open and mobile manipular tactics.

This blunted the Etruscan threat, and during the next two years (309–308) Roman forces proceeded systematically to pacify Southern Etruria. Details are vague, but it is clear that Volsinii sought and obtained an armistice in 308 after the consul for that year, P. Decius Mus, had overrun a number of its strong-points.[1] Simultaneously Rome was taking the added precaution of signing alliances with some of the Umbrian cities: with Camerinum in 310 and with Ocriculum in 308.[2] By the latter year the Etruscan episode was over.

Although comparatively short-lived, it had not been without effect. There is no telling whether in 311 the Romans would have had sufficient strength left to follow up their remarkable efforts of the preceding three years with a knock-out blow against Samnium itself. In the upshot the Etruscans prevented them from even attempting one. Nor was this the only way that the Samnites profited from the Etruscan intervention. Since Roman forces were tied down in Etruria in 311–308, they had been able to score successes in the deep south.[3]

The Second Samnite War thereby entered on its final phase. Border warfare once again became the rule: 'There were frequent raids throughout the land, sieges of towns, and bivouacs in the field.'[4] In this kind of horseplay it was undoubtedly the operations in the west that were of greatest importance: Roman attempts to knock out Samnium by way of Apulia were not going to be any more successful than Samnite attempts to knock out Rome by way of Etruria, whereas the blows struck in the Samnium–Latium–Campania border region ultimately proved decisive.

Even so, the operations were by no means confined to the western

[1] Some of these are named for us: Caprium (or Caerium) (Diod. 20. 44. 9); Castella Volsiniensium (Livy 9. 41. 6: these, rather than Carsulae, Clusium or Faesulae, are the Kastola of Diod. 20. 35. 5. Castellum Amerinum near Lake Vadimon might be one); Aecalum (Steph. Byz. s.v., quoting Dion. Hal. Bk. 16. Or does this mean Aeclanum *in Hirpinis*?). The violent battle which Livy 9. 39. 5–11 assigns to 309 (one of the four dictator years of the Varronian chronology) can be dismissed as a mere anticipation of the victory at Lake Vadimon in 283: even the language in which it is described is similar (see Polyb. 2. 30. 3). But, despite Beloch, *Röm. Gesch.* p. 415, the Triumph. Fasti are probably right in recording a triumph for Fabius Rullianus in 309. For the truce in 308, see Livy 9. 41. 5–7; Diod. 20. 44. 9.

[2] Livy 9. 36. 7 f.; 9. 41. 8, 17–20; Diod. 20. 44. 8; Auct. *de vir. ill.* 27; cf. *CIL*, XI, 5631; Cic. *pro Balbo*, 46; Val. Max. 5. 2. 8; Plut. *Mar.* 28. The agreement, however, with Mevania (Livy 9. 41. 33) must belong to 295.

[3] Livy 9. 29. 1; 9. 38. 4; Diod. 20. 35. 2.

[4] Diod. 19. 101. 1.

frontiers of Samnium. Also the operations were far from one-sided, although the surviving accounts naturally stress grandiose Roman victories. Damaging admissions, however, are let slip, rarely of Samnite successes it is true, but sometimes of Roman failures to win, due of course to circumstances beyond the Romans' control, such as unfavourable terrain or the coming of nightfall. Clearly the war had become one of attrition in which the Romans had lost some of their earlier dynamic drive now that the forward policy in the south had fallen into some disfavour.

In 311, when the Etruscans were beginning to move, the Romans had had forces seeking to keep Samnites and Etruscans apart, in the vicinity of Cluviae, so Livy's text seems to say: in other words, on the north-eastern borders of Samnium. They were commanded by the consul C. Junius Brutus and were probably the same troops, as well as the same general, as had operated in the nearby Marrucine territory the year before. On this occasion Junius Brutus was campaigning in the kind of mountain terrain in which the Samnites were most at home and was only moderately successful. The sum total of his achievement apparently was to sack some otherwise unknown hamlets, Talium, Cataracta and Ceraunilia.[1] Livy says that he also managed to capture Bovianum Pentrorum, but this is wildly improbable: if Cluviae was where Tacitus locates it, Junius Brutus was nowhere near the territory of the Pentri. Livy is merely reflecting the determination of Junian historians to claim a victory for their *gens* at Bovianum, the great Samnite stronghold. As a matter of fact, Livy is obliged to admit that Junius Brutus sustained some setbacks in 311, one near Cluviae itself and another in a trackless mountain glen, which is no doubt so described in order to excuse the Roman defeat.[2]

[1] These villages (Diod. 20. 26. 3f.) cannot be very far away from Cluviae (near Anxanum: *ILS*, 6526; see above, p. 43, n. 3). Hence they are not in Apulia. Talium may be mere dittography with *Italian* earlier in the sentence: it can hardly be Marrucine Teanum. Cataracta presumably is the name of a village near a waterfall: it might be Civitaluparella, whence the Luparello Cascade tumbles down to join the Sangro near Quadri (= anc. *Trebula*, *CIL*, IX, 2823). Ceraunilia, a name applied to lightning-scarred mountains, would suit a number of places in this part of Italy: e.g. Pizzoferrato due west of Quadri, or Fallo to the north-east of it. The Fasti register a triumph for Junius Brutus in 311, but Diod. *loc. cit.* admits that nightfall terminated one of his engagements.

[2] The Junii Bruti were evidently determined to claim a victory at Bovianum for their *gens*: according to Livy, C. Junius Brutus besieged it in 313 (see above, p. 237) and captured it in 311 (9. 31. 2. Or has Livy here mistaken Iuvanum, which was near Cluviae, for Bovianum?). The ἱερὸς λόφος of Diod. 20. 26. 3 is probably the same as the trackless mountain glen of Livy 9. 31. 7, which Zon. 8. 1 calls 'birdless', probably through a

By the next year (310) the Romans, as we have seen, were heavily involved in Southern Etruria and this may explain why it was not a particularly successful one for them against the Samnites. Their attempt to stage a sea-borne assault on Nuceria Alfaterna with a newly organized naval arm failed. Nor was this all. The Samnites launched a heavy offensive against Apulia, and to divert their pressure from there the consul C. Marcius Rutilus staged a raid on Western Samnium. He is said to have taken Allifae; but, as it was still in Samnite hands three years later, scepticism is justified. In fact Marcius Rutilus got into difficulties: even Livy admits that he was wounded and managed to get himself cut off from his base. Indeed the situation was so serious that the trusty, if venerable, L. Papirius Cursor had to be named dictator to rescue him. Papirius Cursor may have managed to do so, although the statement that nightfall came before he could join battle with the Samnites may mean that he achieved nothing very noteworthy.[1]

In border raiding the Samnites enjoyed the advantage of operating on inner lines. They could move forces swiftly from point to point by sending them straight across Samnium. The Romans, on the other hand, were obliged to send their marauding parties around the circumference of a circle to the various points of assault. Under such circumstances many Roman raids could have been little more than pinpricks.

How damaging the counter-raids of the Samnites were we are seldom told. In 310, when they seized the chance presented by Roman preoccupation with the Etruscans to launch a heavy attack on Roman allies in Apulia, they do not seem to have been able to loosen the Roman grip on Luceria. Perhaps Marcius Rutilus' diversionary effort at Allifae had some effect after all.[2]

The crushing victory which the dictator L. Papirius Cursor is said to have scored in the next year (309), and which is reflected

misinterpretation of Livy's expression *in saltum avium* and through confused comparison of the *vallis Amsanctus* with Lake Avernus. Junius Brutus celebrated his escape from a worse defeat by dedicating a Temple to Salus on the Quirinal (Livy 9. 31. 10; 9. 43. 25; 10. 1. 9), whose walls were adorned with paintings by Fabius Pictor (Val. Max. 8. 14. 6; Pliny, *N.H.* 35. 19; K. Jex-Blake and E. Sellers, *The Elder Pliny's Chapters on the History of Art*, p. 88).

[1] See Livy 9. 30. 3; 9. 38; Diod. 20. 35. 2. Cursor is described as operating near Longula, otherwise unknown (it is not to be confused with the Longula near Ardea, for which see Livy 2. 33; Dion. Hal. 6. 91; Pliny, *N.H.* 5. 69).

[2] Diod. 20. 35. 1. The performance of Marcius Rutilus is reminiscent of that of the other great plebeian hero, Publilius Philo.

in the Triumphal Fasti, is recognized even by Livy to contain features borrowed from his son's victory sixteen years later in the Third Samnite War. Livy does not say where the great achievement took place, but he does name no fewer than four of the most renowned generals of the Roman Republic as participating in it: M. Valerius Corvus, P. Decius Mus, the dictator L. Papirius Cursor and his master of the horse C. Junius Brutus; and the suspicions that this tale arouses are not allayed by the revelation that Livy's main reason for mentioning the engagement at all is to account for certain Roman ritual practices. The victory, if not entirely fictitious, was at most merely some local success that helped maintain Roman diversionary pressure on the western borders of Samnium.[1]

Even so, it did not prevent the Samnites from striking at Central Italy in the following year (308). There they succeeded in galvanizing pro-Samnite factions among the Marsi, the Paeligni and, if Livy is to be believed, the Aequi into revolt against Rome. The consul for that year, Q. Fabius Rullianus, hurriedly moved across to the Sabellic region from Etruria, where after two years' successful campaigning little remained for him to do. He somehow managed to restore the situation, and two years later the Romans were consolidating their hold on Central Italy by building a military highway, the Via Valeria, through it.[2] Livy adds that Rullianus also managed to capture Nuceria Alfaterna in Southern Campania in this year; but this makes no topographical sense and is almost certainly one of those Fabian falsifications of history against which Livy elsewhere complains.[3]

In 307 the Samnites again raided Apulia, and evidently with considerable success. Probably operating out of Venusia they swept

[1] The site of Cursor's alleged victory is left vague (see Livy 9. 40; 10. 38. 1; Auct. *de vir. ill.* 31). Livy's motive in recording the victory is clear. A Papirius Cursor vowed a temple to Jupiter Quirinus, but it was not the younger Cursor (Livy 10. 46. 7). Therefore it must have been the elder Cursor, presumably on the occasion of a victory. Junius Brutus is listed as participating since he had replaced the disgraced Publilius Philo as the usual plebeian partner for Cursor (they were consuls together in 313).

[2] Livy 9. 41. 4; 9. 43. 15; 9. 45. 5. Both Marsi and Paeligni had pro-Roman factions as well (Diod. 20. 44. 8; 20. 90. 3).

[3] It is more likely that whenever Nuceria went over to Rome it did so voluntarily, since its treaty was quite a favourable one (Cic. *pro Balbo*, 11. 28). The Fabii claimed a victory there partly in order to score off their arch-rivals the Cornelii, who had failed in a sea-borne operation there in 310, and partly to account for their connexion with Nuceria (a Fabius Maximus went into exile there: Cic. *loc. cit.*). Almost certainly, too, there is some confusion with Rullianus' later operations near another Nuceria, the town in Umbria. See below, p. 268.

right across the country to the borders of Sallentine territory, where they captured the town of Silvium. The Roman consul, L. Volumnius Flamma, hastened towards the heel of Italy with an army, but at least one Roman chronicler made the damaging admission that Volumnius achieved nothing worth mentioning. Livy credits him with some vague successes; but the most that he could have done was prevent the Samnites from making still further headway, since they were still in possession of Silvium in the following year. As in 310, the Romans tried to take the pressure off Apulia by raiding Western Samnium, Allifae being once again their target. Q. Fabius Rullianus, now proconsul, is said to have successfully engaged the Samnites there in this year, but, as darkness ended the action, one may wonder whether he scored much of a victory, the more so in view of Livy's admission that the Samnites had managed to enlist, and even conscript, Hernici into their army. If they could do this, it is certain that their army was not contained at Allifae.[1]

Clearly, mutual border-raiding was the pattern of operations in 307, and the Romans do not seem to have had the better of it. Their election of Ap. Claudius Caecus, an advocate of strong moves in the south, to one of the consulships for 307 confirms Livy's statement that they wanted to force an end to the war; but 307 contributed little to that end.[2]

The Romans may by now have been beginning to feel the need of really capable commanders. Q. Publilius Philo, C. Sulpicius Longus, and L. Papirius Cursor, if not dead or disgraced, were now past their prime.T his may even have been true also of C. Junius Brutus. Of the great names, only Q. Fabius Rullianus and the relative newcomer P. Decius Mus were active in the field at this time; and the absence of iterated consulships from the Fasti for the last five years of the war suggests that capable newcomers had not appeared. Meanwhile the Samnites had found a commander of

[1] Calpurnius Piso knew nothing of Roman successes near Silvium (for which see Strabo 6. 3. 8, p. 283) in 307 (Livy 9. 44. 3) and neither does Diodorus. In fact Volumnius Flamma's alleged operations there in 307/306 read uncommonly like his operations in Campania in 296/295 (Livy 10. 15. 3; 10. 17. 12). Rullianus' activities around Allifae (Livy 9. 42) are equally suspect. Fabian historiographers were not going to allow Rullianus to be outdone by Marcius (his colleague in 310) either at Allifae or anywhere else: and details about Rullianus' exploit could be easily obtained by appropriating some that had been told of his great rival Papirius Cursor around Luceria (see Livy 9. 15).

[2] Livy 9. 43. 9. This is not to say that Fabian calumnies about the Claudii should be taken at their face value.

exceptional ability in the person of Statius (or Gavius) Gellius.[1] He proceeded in the following year to exploit Samnite inner lines very skilfully.

The deep Samnite penetration of Apulia in 307 tied down for five months the substantial force which Volumnius Flamma had taken to the distant south-east. This means presumably that Flamma's army spent the winter months of 307/306 in Apulia. It did manage to recover Silvium in 306 and drive the Samnites out of Apulia, but this was at the cost of dangerously weakening Roman strength in the west.[2] In that year a Samnite force suddenly burst into Central Campania and captured Calatia (and presumably Nola as well, since otherwise it could not have penetrated into Central Campania). Another Samnite force crossed the Liris and seized Sora. All of this looked like an ominous repetition of 315, and it proved too much for some of the Hernici. Two of their towns, Anagnia and Frusino, which had become restless, doubtless at the prodding of Statius Gellius, the year before, now joined the Samnites. Three other Hernican towns, Aletrium, Verulae and Ferentinum, did not follow their example, but the proximity of Anagnia, less than forty miles from Rome, made the situation sufficiently alarming, especially as there were simultaneous pro-Samnite stirrings among Rome's ancient enemies, the Aequi.[3] Even Livy's naïve insistence on Samnite weakness is shaken: he concedes that there was near panic in Rome in 306. The consul Q. Marcius Tremulus hurriedly rushed to the Trerus valley to deal with the pro-Samnite elements there, while his colleague P. Cornelius Arvina sought to restore the situation in Campania. Marcius' success was sufficient to win him a triumph *de Anagnineis Herniceisque*, but to judge from what happened in the next year Cornelius Arvina was not more than moderately successful in the border country between Campania and Samnium, even though he is said to have slaughtered the usual 30,000 Samnites.

[1] For the name see Livy 9. 44. 13. Diod. 20. 90. 4 calls him Gellius Gaius.

[2] Diod. 20. 80. 2.

[3] The relevant texts are Livy 9. 42. 11; 9. 43. 1; 9. 45. 5; Diod. 20. 80. 1 (emending καὶ ἀτίαν); Pliny, *N.H.* 34. 23; Festus, p. 155 L., 262 L. Frusino has sometimes been regarded as Volscian rather than Hernican. But, as it led the revolt of 306 (Livy 9. 42.11; Diod. 20. 80. 4) and as Marcius did not triumph *de Volscis*, it was almost certainly Hernican. The last previous recorded hostility of the Aequi was in 388 (Livy 6. 4. 8). Aletrium and Ferentinum remained *civitates foederatae* right down to the Social War. Marcius' success was exaggerated to include two victories over Samnites; even so, it was substantial enough to win him a triumph and an equestrian statue of himself in the Roman forum in front of the Temple of Castor (Cic. *Phil.* 6. 5. 13; Pliny, *N.H.* 34. 23).

He evidently managed to avoid another Lautulae and presumably he recovered Calatia, but he was still in the field at year's end.[1]

The absence of both consuls from Rome meant that a dictator had to be appointed to conduct the elections for the following year, which turned out to be the year of decision.[2]

In 305 the Samnites tried to repeat their success of the previous year by assaulting the Campus Stellatis, the most easterly section of the Falernian district of Northern Campania.[3] This time, however, the Romans were ready for them. Both of the newly elected consuls, L. Postumius Megellus[4] and T. Minucius Augurinus, took the field and drove them back, doubtless with the aid of the neighbouring Latin Colonies of Saticula, Suessa Aurunca, Cales and perhaps Interamna Lirenas. The riposte of the consuls was then to attack Western Samnium, evidently in force, seeing that both of them participated in the operation. Both Livy and Diodorus record the Roman assault. Livy gives in addition the information that the consuls advanced on the Montagna del Matese from two directions. This probably does not mean that they tried to go around both the southern and the northern end of that bastion, since so dangerous a dispersal of Roman strength seems unlikely. Nor is it probable that they both made for the southern end, which was difficult of access, deep inside Samnium and well guarded by the fortress of Saepinum. The same, it is true, might also be said of the northern end of the Montagna del Matese, where the fortress of Aesernia stood guard. Nevertheless the situation there was rather different. At the northern end of the massif the Romans could count on diversions to distract the enemy, while their own assaulting consular forces remained well concentrated. Therefore it is probable that the two-pronged Roman approach was made in that direction. In other words, the Romans advanced from the Campus Stellatis towards the gap around the northern part of the Montagna del Matese in two columns, respectively on either side of the Rocca Monfina,

[1] The activities recorded for Cornelius Arvina (Livy 9. 43; Diod. 20. 90. 3) suspiciously resemble those attributed to an earlier Cornelius in 343.

[2] The year 306 also saw the signing of a treaty between Rome and Carthage (Livy 9. 43. 26; Serv. *ad Aen.* 4. 628; cf. Polyb. 3. 26). As Agathocles, the enemy of Carthage, recruited his army from Sabellians, Carthaginian interest in the Samnite War is understandable.

[3] For the routes they could use from their bases in the Monti Trebulani, see Livy 22. 13. 6.

[4] He was the first Postumius to reach the consulship since the Caudine Forks, and it is to be noted that he is not a Postumius Albinus.

Postumius taking the eastern column by way of Cales and Teanum Sidicinum, while Minucius led the other through Suessa Aurunca further to the west.[1] Postumius' force encountered stiff enemy opposition before it linked up again with Minucius', presumably from the Samnite settlements on the Monti Trebulani, although Livy seems to say that it was not until it reached the Montagna del Matese itself that the enemy appeared. After the two columns effected their junction, perhaps somewhere near Rufrae, the resistance must have become fiercer still, since the Samnites would muster all available forces from Venafrum, Aquilonia and Aesernia to oppose Roman passage around the northern end of the Matese massif towards the valley of the Tifernus, where lay the main strength of the Pentri. According to a version known to Livy, it cost the life of the consul Minucius; but the Romans succeeded in overcoming the resistance, took the Samnite general Gellius prisoner, then pressed on into the valley of the Pentri and at long last captured their 'capital' Bovianum. Most of this is confirmed by Diodorus, and it is in any event plausible in itself, since the Samnite defenders had not been able to give their undivided attention to containing the thrust. At the very moment that the consuls were coming up from the Campus Stellatis other Roman forces, operating out of the subdued Hernici country, won back Sora, crossed the Liris into Samnite territory, 'recovered' (*sic*) Arpinum and Cesennia, wherever that was, and thus threatened Venafrum, Aquilonia and Aesernia from another direction.[2]

The combined consular armies, then, rounded the northern end of the Montagna del Matese and at once moved down the east side of that massif. Their speedy ensuing capture of Bovianum has been questioned by some critics, but it seems the logical consequence. Roman braggadocio, as we have already seen, records a capture

[1] Elsewhere (10. 31. 2, = 295) Livy describes precisely these two routes, but in the reverse direction. See above, Map 2, p. 188.

[2] The relevant texts are Livy 9. 44; Diod. 20. 90. 4, but they are not free from reproach. Livy, perhaps with Umbrian Tifernum in mind, evidently regards Tifernus as a town instead of a river or mountain; also he appears to duplicate a report about enemy standards being captured; Diodorus names Bola rather than Bovianum as the town the Romans captured. Neither author actually names Venafrum, Aesernia or Aquilonia in the operation, but they can hardly have failed to play a role. The sites of the first two are beyond doubt. Aquilonia, however, has never been certainly identified: it probably is to be identified with Montaquila (see below, p. 271, n. 3). Cesennia, or as Diodorus calls it Serennia, is quite unknown, but none of the proposed emendations (Casinum, Aesernia, Cerfennia, Cisauna) carries conviction. Could the Templum Cereris Helvinae be meant?

of Bovianum on several occasions (in 311, 305 and 298) and for good measure a temporary siege of the place in addition (313). The kernel of truth here is that the town did fall on one occasion; and as the notices for 313, 311 and 298 are all quite certainly false (since the Roman commanders allegedly involved were not even near Bovianum in those years), the one occasion must have been 305. A capture of the town in that year is by no means impossible on strategic grounds, and it seems very probable as the last major operation of the war.[1] There is no recorded fighting against the Samnites after this, and in the next year they sought and obtained peace. They were more probably induced to do so by a substantial setback such as the loss of Bovianum than by the prospect of a continuance of the stalemate. The conqueror of the town was probably M. Fulvius Curvus Paetinus, who had replaced the deceased Minucius and (according to the Fasti Triumphales) was the only Roman commander to be awarded a triumph in 305. Confusion between him and Cn. Fulvius Maximus, the consul for 298, may account for the tale that Bovianum fell again in the latter year.[2]

The loss of their skilful commander and of the Pentrian capital were very damaging blows, but they did not necessarily mean that the Samnites had been brought to their knees. Their inner lines could still be exploited. The Romans had not yet mortally wounded their hydra-headed enemy,[3] as indeed they must have realized at the end of this very year (305), when they found themselves facing diversionary pressure athwart their Central Italian lifeline: pro-Samnite factions amongst the Paeligni and the Aequi were resisting the construction of the Via Valeria, sword in hand, undoubtedly at Samnite urging and presumably with Samnite support. Thus, the Romans could not impose a peace. On the other hand they had no reason to fear one. They might not be able to defeat the Samnites in their mountains; they might not even be able to pen them up there all of the time. But by now they did know how to deal

[1] The notices about Bovianum are Livy 9. 28. 2; 9. 31. 4f.; 9. 44. 14; 10. 12. 9. There is no sure proof that Bovianum Pentrorum rather than Bovianum Vetus is meant in every instance, although it seems certain. F. E. Adcock, in *Cambr. Anc. Hist.* VII, 606, doubts that the town fell even in 305.

[2] Livy 9. 44. 14 records triumphs for Postumius and Minucius. Front. *Strat.* 1. 1. 2; 1. 6. 1 f. mistakes Fulvius Curvus for Fulvius Nobilior.

[3] King Pyrrhus applied this description to the Romans (App. *Samn.* 10. 3; Dio, fr. 40. 27 B; Zon. 8. 4).

with them in open country and they had consolidated their own Ager Romanus into some semblance of a monolithic block, which the Latin Colonies made reasonably safe against any sudden Samnite assault, especially at its vulnerable narrow waist. Accordingly the Romans were not unwilling to listen to any peace proposals that the Samnites might be disposed to make.[1]

And by now the Samnites were disposed to make some. They were weary of the war,[2] they were discouraged by the loss of Gellius and of Bovianum, and they were more than a little anxious about the south, where the arrival of yet another Greek mercenary captain in the pay of Tarentum, Cleonymus of Sparta, posed a renewed Italiote threat. Final, complete and unconditional victory was at the moment obviously beyond their grasp. It had tantalizingly eluded them at Caudium, at Lautulae, at Sutrium, and most recently of all at Anagnia: by now it had completely disappeared over their horizon. Even though they might manage to stave off defeat indefinitely, they clearly were not going to bend the Romans to their will. On the other hand they might hope to negotiate a peace on an *uti possidetis* basis and with otherwise no surrenders of territory.

Evidently it was on these terms that peace was arranged.[3] Livy represents the Samnites as humbly begging for the peace and the Romans as condescendingly granting it after the consul for 304, P. Sempronius Sophus, had paraded on a victory campaign through Samnium and assured himself of Samnite tractability. This last item is no doubt to be regarded as Roman boasting.[4] Roman troops no more moved at their own sweet will through Samnium in 304 than in 341, and it was not in the Roman interest to push the Samnites to a desperate last-ditch resistance at this stage. Possibly continued Roman raiding did help the Samnites to make up their mind to put out peace feelers, but, if so, that must have been the sum total of Roman operations after the fall of Bovianum.

[1] The Samnites probably stirred up the Sabellic peoples to distract Roman attention away from themselves.

[2] The Romans were likewise willing to entertain proposals, since they could not have been wholly free of anxiety concerning the Gauls in the north and the Italiotes in the south. Cf., too, Livy 10. 11. 7: *multis invicem cladibus haud immerito terribile erat*; Diod. 20. 26. 4.

[3] Livy 9. 45. 1–4; Diod. 20. 101. 5.

[4] No other source confirms the Triumph. Fasti in according him a triumph; and Oros. 3. 8. 2 implies that it was not until the Pyrrhic War that the issue between Romans and Samnites was decided.

The Samnites' action in initiating peace negotiations meant that they were resigned to the loss of Saticula, Luceria and Teanum Sidicinum, even though they might still harbour some aspirations to Northern and, more probably, Central Campania.[1] No longer would they control a territory and a population larger than what Rome dominated.

What must have seemed even more grievous to them was the requirement that they give up the crucial Liris valley. Its strategic significance can be gauged from the fact that by the close of the fourth century the Romans had established no fewer than three Latin Colonies there (Fregellae, Interamna and Sora) with two more nearby (Cales and Suessa Aurunca). The Romans were now firmly established on the left bank of the river, at Arpinum[2] as well as at Fregellae and Interamna: indeed the Roman sphere of interest by now extended well beyond the river. Atina on its hill overlooking the River Melfa, it is true, continued to be Samnite and presumably continued to exploit the metal resources of Mt Meta; but neither from it nor from any other town in the Liris basin would the Samnites henceforth be able seriously to threaten Latium.

On the other hand their own mountain fastnesses were still essentially inviolate, even Bovianum, since the Romans were not planning on its retention. They might no longer control more land and people than Rome, but they also did not control much less. There was no question of the Samnites at this stage becoming second-class members of the Roman state in the manner of the Aurunci, the Campani and some of the Southern Etruscans, Volsci and Hernici; they would not even be dependants of the Romans in the manner of such 'allies' as the Apuli and the Sabellic peoples.[3] It was true that they had probably lost the ability to shatter the Ager Romanus, but they could argue that their own block of territory was just as firmly consolidated as the Roman. If Northwestern Samnium could be menaced from the Liris valley, Northwestern Campania in its turn could be threatened from the Monti

[1] If so, their hopes were far from fully realized, since, even though developments in the Third War suggest that the Samnites had kept some kind of foothold in Central Campania, all the evidence indicates that Nola and Nuceria Alfaterna remained staunch as well as favoured allies of Rome.

[2] Arpinum was annexed *sine suffragio* in 303 (Livy 10. 1. 3; cf. 38. 36; Festus, p. 262 L.).

[3] In 298 their spokesmen could claim that they had not made peace on the understanding that Rome should select their friends and enemies for them (Dion. Hal. 17/18, 2; cf. Livy 9. 45. 4).

Trebulani.[1] It must have been with mixed feelings of frustration, foreboding and calculation that the Samnites made peace in 304 and became once more the 'friends' of the Romans. As Livy puts it, the treaty of 354 was restored to them.

The Romans lost no time in converting the border lands between Latium and Samnium, which they were occupying at the end of hostilities, into 'allied' territories. In this way, Teanum Sidicinum certainly and Aquinum probably were brought within the Roman orbit as *civitates foederatae*. These communities were intended to collaborate closely with one another and with the nearby Latin Colonies, and that they did so is shown by the coins they issued later, some time in the third century. The bronze coins of Aquinum, Teanum Sidicinum, Cales and Suessa Aurunca all display the same types.[2] Some of them, to judge from the moneyer's mark, even came from the same mint. Evidently the mutual relations of these 'allies' and Latin Colonies were of the closest: they were a cohesive monetary league. They formed, so to speak, a collective buffer zone between Roman territory and Samnite, and they effectively shielded the inland route to Campania, the route followed by the Via Latina: the middle section of the Ager Romanus was no longer exposed and vulnerable. Whether the Samnites realized it or not, this meant that they had lost for ever whatever chance they may have had for winning the primacy of peninsular Italy.

[1] In fact Northern Campania was frequently assaulted by the Samnites in the Third War.

[2] Obv.: head of war-goddess; rev.: cock and eight-point star. The coins are all of the same weight and the ethnics in their legends are regularly written with the Latinian -NO- suffix. The 'allied' status of Teanum is further proved by its despatch of auxiliaries to Rome's 'Campanian Legion' in the Pyrrhic War (Dion. Hal. 20. 4. 2). Aquinum is not mentioned in literature until the Second Punic War (Livy 26. 9. 3; Sil. Ital. 8. 403).

CHAPTER 7

THE THIRD SAMNITE WAR

Both Romans and Samnites may have hoped, but could hardly take the chance of assuming, that the peace would endure. In fact it lasted only a little longer than the Caudine Peace, a third test of strength being precipitated when each side tried to guarantee its own security by seeking alliances.

For the Samnites it was imperative to find associates in the north who, in any eventual renewal of the conflict, might help them to deliver a decisive blow by forcing the Romans to dissipate their strength. The Roman strategic aim was to deny to the Samnites any possibility of combined operations with peoples to the north and simultaneously to find fighting associates themselves on the other side of the Samnites. It is beside the point to inquire which side began the manœuvring, since activities of this kind are normal to all states. By the Romans' own account, which is the only one that has survived, they themselves were more than a little responsible for the resumption of hostilities that occurred in 298.

They moved at once after 304 to secure control of Central Italy. Even before the end of the Second Samnite War, they had begun building their great military highway (the Via Valeria), across the peninsula, and in the very year of the peace (304) they converted their ententes with the Sabellic Marsi, Paeligni and Marrucini and the Sabellian Frentani into definitive alliances, and two years later the Vestini also became the friends and allies of the Roman people, at their own insistence, according to Livy.[1] This represented a formidable addition to Roman strength: the four peoples making up the Sabellic League, despite Livy,[2] were not collectively as strong as the Samnites, but they were among the toughest fighting men in all Italy, and besides them there were the Frentani.[3]

The day of reckoning had now come for the Aequi. These old

[1] Livy 10. 3. 1.

[2] See Livy 8. 29. 4: his estimate may have been influenced by the performance of the Sabellic peoples, and especially the Marsi, in the Social War.

[3] Polyb. 2. 24 counts the Frentani with the Sabellic League (less the Paeligni) in 225. Together they could muster 20,000 infantry and 4,000 cavalry, as against the Samnites' 70,000 infantry and 7,000 cavalry.

enemies of Rome were accused of joining the fight against her in the closing stages of the Second Samnite War and were now to receive condign punishment. From a Latin Colony established at Sora in 303 Roman forces could advance up the Liris and attack them from the south, while other forces from Latium were assaulting them from the west. Those of them that dwelt in the Upper Anio region were overwhelmed in short order and their settlement of Trebula Suffenas was annexed to Rome with *civitas sine suffragio* (303).[1] Those dwelling immediately north and west of the Fucine Lake lasted hardly any longer. C. Junius Brutus, appointed dictator for the occasion, presumably because of his intimate knowledge of the region, overwhelmed them, in less than a week according to one version. Their territory was largely taken away from them and the Romans established two Latin Colonies on it: Alba Fucens (303) and Carseoli (298). The Aequi as a separate people disappeared.[2]

The creation in 299 of a new citizen tribe (Aniensis)[3], for the Romans settled in the valley of the Anio, consolidated the firm control of the western end of the Roman corridor across Central Italy. Roman control of its middle and eastern sections was not similarly secure, but at least there were the two new Latin Colonies there *in Aequis* to add strong backing to the new alliances with the Sabellic tribes.[4]

The next step was to roll back any danger that might be apprehended from the north. After staging military demonstrations in Etruria in 302/301,[5] in an effort to cow the Etruscan cities, the Romans sought to supplement whatever degree of security their

[1] For the site of Trebula Suffenas, see L. R. Taylor in *Mem. Amer. Acad. Rome*, XXIV (1956), 9–30: it, not Trebula Balliensis, must be the town in question.

[2] Livy 10. 1. 8 f. says that the Aequi were conquered in a week; but in another passage (9. 45. 17) he agrees with Diod. 20. 101. 5 that it took fifty days to subdue them. Livy similarly reports the colonization of Carseoli twice: in 302 as well as in 298 (10. 3. 2; 10. 13. 1). If this is not mere careless reduplication, it may mean that the decision to send the colony was taken in 302, while the *III viri coloniae deducendae* did not complete their task until 298.

[3] Simultaneously the tribe Teretina was created to accommodate Roman settlers established on former Auruncan lands (Livy 10. 9. 14).

[4] These colonies blocked the only two serviceable north–south routes west of the main Apennine watershed, and they effectively separated the Samnites from their potential allies in the north. Carseoli even provided some control over the route that came up from the Middle Liris by way of the Hernici country or the Anio valley. See J. B. Ward-Perkins, *Landscape and History in Central Italy* (Myres Memorial Lecture, Oxford, 1964), p. 18.

[5] Triumph. Fasti *ad an.* 301; Livy 10. 3–4 (rejecting, however, 10. 4. 5, the assault on Rusellae, which is an anticipation of 294 (10. 37. 3)).

existing treaties with Umbrian states provided by provoking a quarrel with the South Umbrian town of Nequinum: they took it by treachery and converted it into the Latin Colony of Narnia (299).[1] Livy bluntly admits that Roman troops were sent into Umbria merely to keep them from going stale, just as he admits that, even though Roman troops attacked the Etruscans and devastated their lands, the latter made no move; which, however, does not prevent him from also depicting them as the aggressors.[2]

The Gallic menace may account for this Roman behaviour.[3] Indeed, according to Polybius,[4] the Celts raided Roman territory in 299 (and, perhaps not surprisingly, found some Etruscans willing to cooperate with them). Perhaps it was at their hands that the consul for 299, T. Manlius Torquatus, met his death, rather than by falling off his horse, as Livy reports.[5] The Celtic threat also explains the treaty which Rome signed in this same year with the hardy Picentes.[6]

The Celtic and associated Etruscan moves may have been not unrelated to Samnite diplomatic activity.[7] The coalition of Italian peoples that was to fight Rome less than five years later did not simply materialize overnight. The diplomatic preparations for it must have been going on for some time previously. From this point of view Roman actions in Etruria and Umbria between 302 and 299 might not unfairly be regarded as preventive.

Their preoccupation with Central and Northern Italy did not cause the Romans to ignore the south. In 302 they 'protected' the Sallentini against Tarentum's latest soldier of fortune, the Spartan prince Cleonymus. This ranged them on the same side as Cleonymus' principal targets, the Lucani, who in this context are quite clearly the inhabitants of Lucania. In 299, when Cleonymus had betaken himself elsewhere, the Lucani are said by Livy to have been attacked by the Samnites, whereupon they sought the protection of their comrades in arms of three years earlier: the Romans granted it, and this involved them in war with the Samnites.[8] The latter were

[1] Livy 10. 9 and 10. The Triumph. Fasti *ad an.* 299 make M. Fulvius (*cos.* 299) triumph *de Samnitibus* as well as *de Nequinatibus*. This must be due to confusion with Cn. Fulvius (*cos.* 298) who did triumph *de Samnitibus*.

[2] Livy 10. 10.

[3] The Celts, of course, were a threat to the Etruscans as well as to the Romans (Livy 10. 10. 12).

[4] Polyb. 2. 19. 1.

[5] Livy 10. 11. 1.

[6] Livy 10. 10. 12.

[7] Cf. Livy 10. 18. 1.

[8] Dion. Hal. 17. 3 states categorically that the war was caused by the Lucanian alliance. Neither side was prepared to tolerate the addition of Lucanian strength to the other.

prepared to challenge a Rome that already had the Gauls to contend with.

There is some resemblance here to the antecedents of the Second Samnite War, since there was both a pro-Samnite and a pro-Roman party amongst the Lucani, just as there had been at Naples in 327. But the similarity to the events leading up to the First Samnite War is even more striking, that is, if Livy's account is reliable. And of this, of course, we cannot be sure. Livy himself supplies reasons for scepticism. Up to this point, so he insists,[1] the Samnites had been satisfied with the peace settlement of 304 and had not been preparing for war. He now, however, roundly accuses them of plotting war, apparently for doing what the Romans had done: viz. seek allies in North Italy.[2]

It is impossible to say whether the Romans, realizing that peninsular primacy was now within their grasp, were resolved to humble the Samnites for good and all, or whether the Samnites thought that, with a Gallic foray diverting Roman attention in the north, it was a propitious moment for them to strengthen their position in the south. What does seem certain is that in 299 the Romans, for the first time, signed a treaty with the inhabitants of Lucania and by doing so brought about the Third Samnite War. Presumably the group of patricio-plebeian 'nobles' who fostered the policy of southward expansion led Roman sentiment for the treaty. But, if there was a growing general awareness that boldness at this stage might make Rome mistress of the entire Italian pensinsula, they would not lack for followers. There were risks of course. Samnites, Gauls and Etruscans might combine to prevent the emergence of a Roman colossus, and Umbrians and Sabines might join them;[3] and collectively these peoples controlled more territory and perhaps more population than did Rome and her allies. Experience, however, had shown that of these peoples only the Samnites and Gauls were really formidable, and they were separated from each other by the Roman corridor across Central Italy.

The Third Samnite War is in the full light of history to an even

[1] Livy 10. 6. 2; 10. 13. 3.

[2] They undoubtedly sought an alliance with the Picentes, who rebuffed them and informed the Romans (Livy 10. 11. 7). There must have been protracted diplomatic activity before the Sentinum coalition was forged. Zon. 8. 7 mentions a Samnite who went to Volsinii, evidently on a political mission, later in the third century.

[3] The Romans no doubt got wind of the attempts to form such a combination (see Livy 10. 16. 6).

greater extent than is the Second. The chronology is more secure, there being no 'dictator years' to muddle it, and geographical indications appear more frequently. Details generally are more reliable: e.g. 30,000 Samnites killed no longer appears as the standard price of a Roman victory.[1] Even a contemporary reference to the war has survived.[2] All of this, however, is offset by the fragmentary nature of the literary evidence. Diodorus' text is not extant except in fragments, and Livy's continuous narrative does not extend beyond 293. Furthermore, the topographical details, while relatively plentiful, are more often mysterious than enlightening; and, to cap it all, Livy's sources could not agree on the spheres of operations or the exploits of individual Roman commanders.[3] As a result, it is not easy to obtain a clear idea of what the war was like or how and where it was fought.

This uncertainty is reflected in the work of modern scholars, some of whom have even denied that the Samnites had any great part in the war.[4] According to them, the Romans called both Sabines and Samnites by the same name at the beginning of the third century and the account in Livy is really describing a Sabine rather than a Third Samnite War. This theory not only is unlikely in that it invests the Sabines with a palpably improbable role, but also has little to recommend it on philological grounds. Even, however, if we firmly refuse to allow it to make the picture yet more murky, the records of the Third Samnite War are still confused enough to baffle certainty.

According to Livy, hostilities began in 298 and some Etruscans were involved from the outset.[5] The probabilities are that both parties resumed the strategy which they had been using in the Second War. The Samnites exploited their inner lines and the Romans raided them on two fronts, from Apulia in the east and from the Middle Liris and Northern Campanian regions in the west. Besides this, each side tried to vary such stereotyped activity along

[1] This, however, is no guarantee that the figures Livy gives for Samnite losses (10. 14. 21; 10. 15. 6; 10. 37. 3; 10. 39. 3; 10. 42. 5; 10. 43. 8) are accurate.

[2] Duris of Samos *ap.* Diod. 21. 6. 1. The Megacles who reported Samnite attempts to bribe M'. Curius Dentatus (Athen. 10, p. 419 a) probably was not a contemporary.

[3] Evidently the original record merely stated that such and such a place was taken without identifying its captor (B. Niese, *de annalibus Romanis* (Marburg, 1886), p. iv).

[4] B. Bruno, *La Terza Guerra Sannitica*, *passim*; K. J. Beloch, *Röm. Gesch.* pp. 424 f.

[5] According to the Triumph. Fasti *ad an.* 298 Cn. Fulvius Centumalus triumphed *de Samnitibus Etrusceisque.*

lines with which it had experimented in the previous conflict. The Samnites sought to join their allies in the north, and the Romans endeavoured to keep the route across Central Italy open at all times. The absence, however, of any entries in the Fasti Triumphales for 297 and 296 shows that no truly memorable actions occurred in the opening years of the war. The Romans may have committed the bulk of their forces to the watch on Central Italy and have used comparatively small bodies of men for raiding Samnium. The Samnites were busy planning a big surprise.

In 298, according to Livy, the consul L. Cornelius Scipio Barbatus went to Etruria and won a victory at Volaterrae, but otherwise achieved nothing very notable: he discreetly avoided the Etruscan cities.[1] The inscribed sarcophagus of this same Scipio Barbatus has survived and it tells a very different story. Undoubtedly the *elogium* was carved long after Barbatus' death[2] and erasures on the stone may mean that the original inscription was subsequently amended to make his achievements more impressive. Even so, this document is an incomparably older and probably safer authority than Livy. It does not even mention Etruria. In truth, Livy's battle of Volaterrae is a topographical absurdity and it is to be noted that Livy makes nightfall end it.[3] Any other activities in Etruria attributed to Barbatus in 298 probably belong to 295, when he was undoubtedly serving there.[4] The *elogium* implies that in 298 he was in the far south of Italy.[5] In other words, he was the Roman commander who attacked Samnium from the east. Evidently he marched across Central Italy, turned south and reached Apulia. Probably basing himself on Luceria, he raided Samnium, capturing and presumably plundering Cisauna and Taurasia. The site of Cisauna is quite unknown. Taurasia must have lain in the territory known, later at any rate, as the Ager Taurasinus. This is quite securely located between Luceria and Beneventum, so that Taurasia must have been situated somewhere in the vicinity of the modern San Bartolomeo

[1] Livy 10. 12. 8, who may however here be relying on later Scipionic historians. The latter would naturally be anxious to have a member of their *gens* emulate or surpass the Etruscan exploits of Rullianus, a member of the arch-rival Fabian *gens*.

[2] V. Scamuzzi in *Riv. di Studi Classici*, v (1957), 9–12.

[3] Livy 10. 12. 5: has he written Volaterrae in mistake for Volsinii?

[4] But his achievements in 295 were not very notable (see below, p. 266).

[5] *subigit omne Loucanam opsidesque abdoucit* (*ILS*, 1). Presumably his 'subjugation' of all Lucania resembled Augustus' 'subjugation' of the Parthians. At any rate his exploit is not reflected in the Triumph. Fasti. Perhaps it was only a plundering raid.

in Galdo. While in the south Barbatus took the occasion to nip in the bud a movement among the Lucani to end their alliance with Rome: he suppressed the pro-Samnite faction and collected the hostages which, according to Livy, the other Lucani offered as a guarantee of Lucanian good behaviour.[1]

Meanwhile the other consul for 298, Cn. Fulvius Maximus, who was raiding Samnium in the west, may have scored something of a surprise. The story that he took Bovianum, as we have seen, is fictitious and is due to confusion with the earlier exploit of another Fulvius in 305:[2] Bovianum was still in the hands of the Samnites five years later, when it provided asylum for their refugees from the battle of Aquilonia. On the other hand, the story that Fulvius sacked Aufidena may very well be true. He could have reached it via the Paeligni. While the Samnites were expecting a raid around the northern end of the Montagna del Matese in the usual way, he may have threaded his way through the mountains immediately east of the Fucine Lake and moved up the valley of the Sagrus to Aufidena.[3] After plundering the place he could then have withdrawn by the same route.

What the Samnites did in 298 is not revealed. Clearly nothing of exceptional moment occurred in that year.

The Romans, eager perhaps for a quick decision, elected their best generals as consuls for 297, Q. Fabius Rullianus and P. Decius Mus. Livy attributes a glorious victory to Fabius Rullianus somewhere near the Montagna del Matese, but the Fasti Triumphales know nothing of it and the details of the battle really belong to the action at Aquilonia four years later.[4] Evidently 297 witnessed in this region little more than a continuation of the previous year's hit-and-run border warfare. Furthermore Livy's tale that Fabius Rullianus operated from the Middle Liris and Decius Mus from Teanum Sidicinum (Northern Campania) is probably mere supposition based on the usual pattern of western operations. He himself

[1] Livy 10. 11. 13. (Neither Cisauna nor Taurasia can be identified. Taurasia is not the mod. Taurasi (H. Philipp in *R.E.* IV A (1932), s.v. 'Taurasia', col. 2535) nor Taurania in Campania (the town that had disappeared by the time of Pliny (*N.H.* 3. 70).) Taurasinus is, however, the ethnic formed from it (Steph. Byz. s.v. 'Taurasia').

[2] For that matter Livy 10. 12. 9 does not say positively that he captured Bovianum in 298. As might have been expected, Front. *Strat.* 1. 6. 1 f., 1. 11. 2, confuses him with Fulvius Nobilior.

[3] This seems more probable than an approach past Aesernia from the Middle Liris.

[4] Livy 10. 14. 18–21, with which compare Livy 10. 41. 5–9 and Front. *Strat.* 2. 4. 4.

says that the consuls harried Samnium *diversis partibus* and he actually describes Decius as having dealings with the Apuli.[1] This last item is the revealing one.[2] It indicates that one consul (Decius), based on Teanum Apulum rather than Teanum Sidicinum, raided Samnium from the south-east, while Fabius Rullianus operated in and near the Liris valley, a region with which he was very familiar from his earlier career and which was close enough to Rome to permit him to return there for the consular elections: Rullianus is credited with capturing Cimetra and this place, although otherwise unknown, has a Volscian-type name that might well fit the Middle Liris region.[3] According to Livy, the consuls spent no less than five months (the winter months, seemingly) avoiding Samnite strong-points but ravaging the Samnite countryside, Rullianus shifting camp eighty-six times and Decius forty-five times.[4] There may be some duplication here with Volumnius Flamma's activities either in 307/306 or in 296/295,[5] but it is probable enough that *faute de mieux* the Romans would have sought to disrupt Samnite agriculture and to keep Samnite herdsmen away from their drovers' trails and regular pastures. Samnite activities are again for this year unrecorded. Obviously there were no large-scale battles, much less victories, in 297.

By now there was growing impatience on the Roman side at the failure to achieve successes. The Apuli seem to have become dissatisfied;[6] and amongst the Romans themselves Appius Claudius Caecus stirred up agitation for a return in 296 to the ancient system of two patrician consuls, presumably in the hope of speedier and more tangible results.[7] The two patrician consuls did not materialize, but evidently a decision was taken to attempt a major blow in 296, and Fabius Rullianus and Decius Mus were retained as proconsuls in their commands to help deliver it. Decius stayed where he was in

[1] Livy 10. 15. 3. Livy probably mistook Teanum Sidicinum for Teanum Apulum.

[2] Livy *loc. cit.* says that the enemy Apuli met him at Beneventum. Presumably there were anti-Roman factions in some Apulian towns, but we hear nowhere else of Apulian hostility to Rome in the Third Samnite War.

[3] Livy 10. 15. 6. A name such as Cimetra suggests such Volscian names as Ecetra and Velitrae. But a name of its type could also occur elsewhere in Italy: there was, for instance, an Ager Caletranus near Saturnia in Central Etruria (Livy 39. 55. 9; Pliny, *N.H.* 3. 52).

[4] Livy 10. 17. 2. Decius shifted camp less often since he had taken longer to get to his theatre of operations.

[5] See above, p. 248; below, pp. 264, 268.

[6] Livy 10. 15. 7–12.

[7] Livy 10. 18. 8.

Apulia, and Fabius presumably remained in the Liris valley.[1] Both may have received reinforcements. One of the consuls, Appius Claudius Caecus, was assigned to Southern Etruria with two legions, to engage in holding operations and to safeguard the route across Central Italy. The other consul, L. Volumnius Flamma, also with two legions,[2] was apparently sent to Northern Campania. These dispositions show that the major blow was intended in the west, but, as the Samnites soon demonstrated, they represented a dangerous dispersal of Roman strength. In the upshot, the only force for which the Roman tradition could find any successes in 296 was the one under Decius Mus in Apulia, probably because that was the region which the Samnites could most safely denude of troops: Rome's Apulian and Lucanian allies were none too reliable and Decius' own relatively small force was operating at the end of extended lines of communication and hence unlikely to do any really serious damage. The silence of the Fasti Triumphales makes it evident that in fact it did not do so, although its activity in the south may have helped to prevent a repudiation by the Lucani of their alliance with Rome. Apparently Decius did raid and plunder several localities: Murgantia, Ferentinum and Romulea.[3] Romulea can reasonably be identified with the Sub Romula (mod. Bisaccia) of the Itineraries, a station on the Via Appia immediately west of Venusia; Livy's Ferentinum, to judge from a statement in Dionysius of Halicarnassus, is a mistake for Forentum (mod. Forenza), immediately south of Venusia; Murgantia is mentioned nowhere else, but its name seems to survive in the tableland district immediately east of Venusia, which is still known as Le Murghe and contains a number of localities called Murgia.[4] Evidently Decius was operating in the general vicinity of Venusia.

But if the Romans had been preparing a *coup de maître* for 296, so had the Samnites. Their commander now was Gellius Egnatius, a kinsman perhaps of the great captain of ten years earlier. He had formed the bold design of breaking through the Roman encirclement and joining the Etruscans, Gauls and Umbrians in the north: a

[1] Livy 10. 16. 2 (but Livy 10. 17 and 18 is very vague about the activity of Fabius Rullianus).

[2] This is the first recorded occasion when legions get numbers. Volumnius Flamma had II and III, Claudius Caecus I and IV.

[3] Livy 10. 17.

[4] For Forentum, see Dion. Hal. *ap.* Steph. Byz. s.v. 'Ferentinos'. Some sources said that Volumnius Flamma rather than Decius achieved the successes around Venusia (Livy 10. 17. 12). There may be some confusion here with the Apulian operations recorded for Flamma in 307/306 (see above, p. 248).

combination of all their forces might deliver a blow that was mortal. Skilfully exploiting the dispersal of the Roman forces, and possibly the dissensions of the Roman consuls, he burst out of Samnium across Central Italy and into Etruria.[1] His route is not recorded, but it may have been via the town of Milionia in the Marsic country and if so was a very daring escapade.[2] Nor is the site of his rendezvous with his Etruscan allies recorded, nor even the names of the Etruscan cities involved. The latter can, however, to some extent be identified from Livy's account of the Etruscan episode in the Second Samnite War which, as we saw, is embroidered with details that really belong to this one. It was probably now that 'all of the Etruscans except Arretium' made their move and threw in their lot with the Samnites.[3] Gellius' Egnatius meeting with his northern allies may have taken place in the valley of the Upper Tiber, perhaps somewhere near Clusium or Perusia.

Gellius' achievement produced a near panic at Rome. Livy graphically describes the furore and the frantic efforts of the praetor, P. Sempronius Sophus, to set the city's defences in order by proclaiming a levy *en masse* and even enrolling freedmen. To reinforce Ap. Claudius Caecus in Etruria, Northern Campania was hurriedly stripped of some of its troops, whereupon another Samnite force, which had probably been waiting for the Romans to take just this action, swooped down there. Operating with a powerful marauding force obviously out of the Monti Trebulani, Minatius Staius promptly overran and plundered the Falernian and Auruncan districts. Somehow Fabius Rullianus in the Liris valley and Volumnius Flamma in Northern Campania, the former repeating the part he had played after Lautulae in 315 and the latter the role he had discharged in Samnium in 307/306, managed to get the situation under control. The invaders were forced back, and Citizen Colonies were at once authorized for Sinuessa and Minturnae to help contain future incursions of this kind.[4]

[1] Livy 10. 16. 3; 10. 18 and 19; 10. 22. 5; Dio, fr. 36. 28; Zon. 8. 1.

[2] Milionia had been hostile to Rome shortly before (Livy 10. 3. 5) and was certainly in Samnite hands in 294 (Livy 10. 34). The route via it was the one the Samnites had thought of using during the Etruscan interlude in the Second Samnite War: *protinus inde Etruriam per Marsos ac Sabinos petituri* (Livy 9. 38. 7). Livy 10. 16. 2 naïvely says that it was Decius' successes in the deep south that caused Gellius to leave Samnium in 295.

[3] Livy 9. 32. 1 (of the Etruscans alleged to have moved against Rome in the Second War). In the Third War he says (10. 18. 2): *Tusci fere omnes consciverant bellum.*

[4] Livy 10. 21. 8. The Colonies were actually established in 295 (Vell. Pat. 1. 12. 6).

Year's end found both sides grimly girding themselves for the stern trial ahead. 295 was obviously going to be the year of decision. The Romans prepared for it by keeping forces in the field all winter, by once again electing their best generals, Q. Fabius Rullianus and P. Decius Mus, to the consulship, and by using any other experienced men available: L. Volumnius Flamma and Ap. Claudius Caecus, consuls for 296, served in 295 as proconsul and praetor respectively; and no fewer than three other ex-consuls were used in 295 as propraetors: L. Cornelius Scipio Barbatus (*cos.* 298), Cn. Fulvius Maximus Centumalus (*cos.* 298), and L. Postumius Megellus (*cos.* 305). At least six of the legions which the Romans mobilized for 295 can be identified and to these must be added the contingents supplied by their allies. In all, the Romans may have had as many as 100,000 men under arms, that corresponding to the number of the enemy which they slew during the campaign, according to a Greek contemporary:[1] this Greek historian could have arrived at his figure by estimating that on the average each soldier on the Roman side accounted for one on the enemy.

The beginning of 295 found Samnite forces somewhere east of Perusia. They and their Etruscan allies had moved north-eastwards to threaten Camerinum, an obvious centre of pro-Roman sentiment, their object being to win over anti-Roman Umbrians, and to join forces with the Senonese Gauls. Some Sabines, also, may have joined the anti-Roman coalition: there is no record of Sabine resistance to the passage of Samnite and Etruscan forces over their territory, and a few years later a Roman general was sent (on a punitive mission?) against the Sabines. The writer of the *De Viris Illustribus* also includes Marsi amongst the enemies of Rome in 295. The Picentes did not join the coalition, presumably owing to the presence of their perennial enemies, the Gauls. Even so, it is clear enough that the Romans were facing the direst kind of threat.[2]

Even before the end of winter Fabius Rullianus, consul for 295,

[1] See Diod. 21. 6. 1.

[2] The relevant texts are Polyb. 2. 19. 5; Livy 10. 25, 26; Auct. *de vir. ill.* 32, 34; *CIL*, 1^2, p. 192 (the *elogium* of Claudius Caecus, which indicates that he fought Sabines, presumably in 295). Only Livy (10. 9. 8; 10. 18. 2; 10. 21. 12; 10. 26. 12) records Umbrian hostility to Rome, and even he seems doubtful of it (10. 30. 8). Fulginium, later an unfavoured Roman *praefectura* (Cic. *pro Vareno*, fr. 4), may well have opposed Rome. The Gauls involved were the Senones (Polyb. 2. 19. 5; Livy 10. 26. 7). Later Roman measures against the Praetuttii, Vestini and Aequiculi make one wonder whether they too were not ranged against Rome in 295 (A. Afzelius, *Röm. Eroberung Italiens*, p. 180).

leaving his colleague Decius Mus to cover the city, had left Rome and proceeded northward with a picked body of men. He reached Aharna, which may have lain just across the Tiber from Perusia, and, at a point a few miles beyond, took over command of the two legions which had spent the winter in the field. He then made a number of long marches, according to Livy in order to train and toughen his troops. Probably he was also feeling out the enemy and trying to discover his intentions for the coming campaigning season. After crossing the Apennines to the vicinity of Camerinum, Fabius reported that enemy strength was more than a match for his own, an estimate that received almost immediate confirmation when a group of Senones inflicted a sharp reverse on that part of his army which the propraetor Cornelius Scipio Barbatus commanded.[1] Decius Mus and the two legions covering Rome were at once ordered north, and it may have been this move that prevented Gellius Egnatius from following up the Camerinum success more vigorously; or it may be that the mobilization and deployment of his northern allies had not been completed; or it may simply be that the anti-Roman coalition missed its opportunity owing to its having a divided command. When Decius Mus moved north, the propraetors Cn. Fulvius and L. Postumius replaced him as the defenders of Rome, stationed respectively at Falerii and on the right bank of the Tiber at the city itself.[2]

Decius Mus with legions V and VI, after crossing the Apennines, presumably by the Scheggia pass, effected a junction with Fabius Rullianus' legions I and III somewhere near Camerinum, and then the two consuls moved along the valley of the River Aesis (mod. Esino) to the vicinity of Sentinum, whose ruins are to be seen not far from Sassoferrato.[3] It was here that they encountered the enemy and fought one of the most crucial battles in Roman history. The

[1] The topographical details are neither clear nor certain. Fabius Rullianus after leaving Rome reached Aharna, a town recorded nowhere else, although the Arnates recorded by Pliny, *N.H.* 3. 113; Sil. Ital. 8. 456 and Ptol. 3. 1. 54 presumably came from it. (Their town has been identified with Civitella d'Arno, six miles east of Perugia.) To get across the Apennines from here Rullianus would presumably use either the Sella di Fossato (2,400 feet), leading to Fabriano and the valley of the Esino, or the Piano di Colfiorito (2,400 feet), leading to Camerinum. Further uncertainty arises from the confusion between Camertes and Camartes, respectively the ethnics for Camerinum and Clusium (which has caused the latter town to be dragged into the narrative), and from the rivalry between the Fabii and Cornelii Scipiones (which has produced the absurd story that the commander Fabius Rullianus was in Rome when his army was in contact with the enemy in Umbria). [2] Livy 10. 16. 15. [3] See A. Pagnani, *Sentinum*, pp. 2–5.

Etruscans and Umbrians, perhaps as a result of the lack of a unified command, were not present on the historic field. They had doubled back, either to defend Clusium and its neighbourhood against the depredations of Fulvius and Postumius (who had ventured northward), or possibly to stage a diversion nearer Rome, while the Samnites and Senones were dealing with the four consular legions at Sentinum. Whatever the reason for their absence from the battle, it proved fatal to their cause. Even as it was, Sentinum, like Waterloo, was 'the nearest run thing'. Had the Etruscans and Umbrians been present it would almost certainly have gone the other way.[1]

Decius Mus on the Roman left faced the Gauls and their dreaded chariots; Fabius Rullianus on the Roman right was opposed by the Samnites under Gellius Egnatius; and the deaths of both Decius and Gellius in the action clearly illustrate the course of the battle as well as the determination with which it was waged. The Senones dealt roughly with the Roman left, but the Roman right wore down the Samnites and then went on to shatter the Senones. It was to the tactical genius and tenacity of Fabius Rullianus that Rome owed her victory, and he appears to deserve Livy's description of him as *haud dubie tum primus omnium ductor*.[2] At Rome, however, the popular hero of the battle was the fallen Decius Mus, whose death was portrayed as a deliberate act of *devotio*, which ensured that the enemy were sacrificed to the gods below along with himself. Casualties were heavy on both sides. Livy admits that the Romans lost almost 9,000 men killed. The Samnite and Senonese losses must have been still higher, even though less than Livy's figure of 25,000 killed and 8,000 captured.[3] After the battle the Gauls scattered northwards. The defeated Samnites fled home to their mountains, not by the way they had probably come, but by way of the Paeligni, who inflicted heavy additional casualties on them as they passed through.[4]

[1] The relevant texts are Polyb. 2. 19. 6; Livy 10. 27–9; Front. *Strat.* 1. 8. 3; Oros. 3. 21. 3. For a recent study see P. Sommella, *Antichi Campi di Battaglia in Italia* (Rome, 1967), pp. 35–47: he seeks the battlefield immediately north of Sassoferrato. Fulvius dealt with the Etruscans and Umbrians, according to Livy 10. 30. 1. But the notice that brings them to Clusium may well be an error due to the above-mentioned confusion between the ethnics Camartes and Camertes. A Fulvius and Postumius were consuls in 305 as well as proconsuls in 295. The coincidence is suspicious. The day after Waterloo Wellington described it as 'a damned nice thing—the nearest run thing you ever saw in your life' (*The Creevey Papers*).

[2] Livy 10. 21. 15.

[3] Livy 10. 29. 17–18.

[4] Livy 10. 39. 3. We are not told what happened to the defeated Senones. Very probably they were mulcted of territory: at any rate Livy (*Epit.* 11) says that a Citizen Colony was established at Sena on what had been their territory a few years later (290/289).

For Rome Sentinum was the crowning mercy in the Third Samnite War just as Tarracina had been in the Second. The fame of the battle quickly spread,[1] and it made a profound impression on the contemporary Greek world: Duris of Samos, whose *floruit* coincides almost exactly with it, reported that in winning the campaign the Romans had slain no fewer than 100,000 of their enemies.[2] This 'battle of the nations', as it has been called, settled the destiny of peninsular Italy. Years of hard fighting still lay ahead for Rome, but henceforth she could deal with her enemies one by one and she was more than a match for them singly. This indeed was demonstrated immediately: even before 295 was out Fabius Rullianus had already begun the job of completing the subjugation of the Etruscans and of receiving the submission of the Umbri: it was now, rather than in 310, that he won his victory near Perusia, and likewise it was probably now that Mevania and Umbrian Nuceria were brought within the Roman orbit.[3]

During the Sentinum campaign each side had tried to distract the other's attention by staging inconclusive raids in the south. The only forces Rome could spare in 295 for such activities were the two legions (II and IV) with the proconsul, L. Volumnius Flamma, who had apparently remained in the Latium–Campania–Samnium border region from the previous year. His attempt on Samnium around the northern end of the Matese massif appears to have had more nuisance value than success. The countermove of the Samnites was along the lines of their foray of the year before; indeed some of the details recorded for it are probably mere duplications of episodes in the earlier operation or in the operations of 305. In 295 the Samnites are said to have plundered the Falernian and Auruncan districts as far as Formiae. Perhaps the Citizen Colonies at Sinuessa and Minturnae were not yet ready to offer any opposition. The Samnites were stopped only when Ap. Claudius Caecus, now

[1] A body of legend grew up around it, such as the tale that it had been foretold by a soothsayer (Dio, fr. 36. 28; Zon. 8. 1). Giannelli–Mazzarino (*Trattato di Storia Romana*, I, 193) aptly style it 'the battle of the nations'.

[2] Duris, *homo in historia diligens* (Cic. *ad Att.* 6. 1. 18), says that 100,000 of Rome's enemies fell, if not at Sentinum itself, then during Fabius Rullianus' consulship (Diod. 21. 6. 1). Even Livy 10. 30. 5 pours scorn on this kind of exaggeration.

[3] Livy 10. 31. 3; 10. 37. 5; Diod. 20. 35. 4; Zon. 8. 1; Triumph. Fasti *ad an.* 295. In 308 the capture of Nuceria Alfaterna, a topographical absurdity, was attributed to Rullianus (see above, p. 246). Perhaps Fabian historians retrojected his success at Nuceria Camellaria in 295 to the year 308 and made it apply to Nuceria Alfaterna.

praetor, brought a force down to help Volumnius drive them back to their own borders.[1]

In 294 Roman activity against the Samnites was largely in the nature of a holding operation. Perhaps the Romans needed to recuperate from their prodigious effort of the year before, or from the effects of a plague that had been raging in the city. More probably, however, it was because they had decided first to conclude operations against the Etruscans and dissident Umbrians, if any, before giving their undivided attention to the Samnites.

The first step was to go to Marsic territory and plug the gap through which, apparently, the Samnites had poured on their journey north two years earlier. Milionia, an otherwise unknown Feritrum and some unnamed hamlets were taken by the Romans and the position in Central Italy was firmly restored. The Roman troops that carried out this mission then moved into Etruria. There the territory of Volsinii was devastated, the town of Rusellae captured, and Etruria as a whole eliminated from the war. Cortona, Perusia and Arretium signed forty-year treaties with Rome.[2] Except for a few minor mopping-up operations in 293/292 Etruria plays no further rôle in the hostilities. Neither do the Umbri, although no details are recorded of what measures, if any, were taken against them.

While this was going on, the Samnites sought desperately to avail themselves of what was probably their last forlorn chance of victory against Rome, and they provided their enemy with some anxious moments in 294. A Roman force was badly knocked about near Luceria in Apulia: nightfall interrupted the engagement, according to Livy. The Roman force in the Liris basin seems to have had an equally awkward time of it, the Roman quaestor being slain in his own tent: here it was fog that intervened. Owing, however, to the tenacity of troops from the nearby Latin Colony of Suessa Aurunca and from Volscian Luca and to the armed proximity of two other

[1] Suspicious circumstances surrounding the operations recorded for 295 are the following: Volumnius Flamma passes the winter of 296/295 in the field (Livy 10. 27. 11); he is reported to have done precisely this in 307/306 (see above, p. 248); besides similarity of details in the Samnite invasions of Northern Campania in 295 and in 305, it is worth noting that in 305 a Fulvius and Postumius were consuls; in 295 a Fulvius and Postumius were proconsuls.

[2] For 294, see Livy 10. 31. 8; 10. 34; 10. 37; Dion. Hal. 17 *ap.* Steph. Byz. v.s. 'Milonia'; Triumph. Fasti *ad an.* According to Livy 10. 37. 4 Volsinii rather than Cortona was one of the three Etruscan cities to sign a forty-year treaty with Rome. Against this, see Livy 9. 32. 12; Diod. 20. 35. 5 (= 310); Livy, *Epit.* 11 (Volsinii still in arms in 292/291).

Latin Colonies, Sora and Interamna Lirenas, the Samnites could not achieve a break-through.[1] In fact they were now enclosed more tightly than ever within a Roman iron ring. For them the outlook was ominous.

Realizing that the supreme test was at hand the Samnites prepared for it by mobilizing every man capable of bearing arms and by outfitting a *corps d'élite*, the Linen Legion. With it they were to make a desperate throw in 293. Livy's account of it is brilliant writing, even if indifferent history.[2]

The critical encounter took place, as might have been expected, on the north-western borders of Samnium, the only region where either side could hope for a victory that would be really decisive.

For this campaigning season the Romans committed both the consular armies to the Latium–Campania–Samnium border zone: they could not have had more than holding forces elsewhere in Italy in 293. As the strategy of previous years would lead one to expect and as the strategy of this particular year makes abundantly clear, one army operated out of the Middle Liris valley, its jumping-off point being Interamna Lirenas, and the other out of Northern Campania: its starting point is not recorded, but may well have been Teanum Sidicinum.[3] The opposing Samnite forces were based respectively on the fortresses of Cominium and Aquilonia in north-western Samnium.

The consul, Sp. Carvilius Maximus, moving north out of Interamna Lirenas up the River Rapido past Casinum, stormed and plundered a Samnite town named Amiternum,[4] ravaged the

[1] Livy (10. 36. 14) endeavours to make the setback in Apulia look less like a defeat by claiming that the Romans captured exactly the same number of the enemy as they themselves lost: viz. 7,800. That Volscian Luca was involved in the Liris operations is revealed by the mention of a *cohors Lucana* (Livy 10. 33. 1). Perhaps Livy mistook this cohort for Lucani from the south: this might account for his remark that Roman forces returning from Apulia engaged the Samnites at Interamna Lirenas (which is topographically impossible). [2] See above, pp. 182–6: Appendix to Chapter 4 (*g*).

[3] The starting points of the two Roman forces must have been selected with an eye to their respective axes of advance. See above, p. 188, Map 2.

[4] Livy 10. 39. 1. It has been argued that Amiternum can only be the Sabine town of that name (mod. San Vittorino) since Varro (*L.L.* 5. 28) connects the name with that of the River Aternus, and there was no River Aternus near Casinum. This reasoning is far from cogent. Cambridge is named after the River Cam in England, but that does not prevent there being a Cambridge in the state of Massachusetts (which has no River Cam). Amiternum must be sought roughly midway between Interamna Lirenas and Atina (Livy 10. 39. 5), the sites of both of which are certain. It is probably the modern San Elia Fiume Rapido, an ancient site with still existing polygonal remains (C. Mancini, *Giorn. di Scavi di Pompeii*, IV, 40 f.).

territory of Atina, and brought his forces to a halt at Cominium.[1] Simultaneously his colleague, L. Papirius Cursor, son of the great hero of the Second War, was advancing from Northern Campania towards the gap around the northern end of the Montagna del Matese. His march must have taken him past Rufrae and Venafrum, but the only place positively named as on his route is the otherwise unknown Duronia,[2] which he captured and plundered: his forces came to a halt at Aquilonia.[3] After thus carefully synchronizing their movements the two consuls were now some twenty miles apart and were close enough to keep in touch with one another by messenger. They decided that they would both attack on the same day.

At Aquilonia the Samnites' crack Linen Legion valiantly engaged Papirius Cursor's forces, and at the same moment the Samnite troops at Cominium were tied down by the assault of Carvilius Maximus. After a stern struggle the Linen Legion was cut to pieces: some of

[1] For the site of Cominium near modern Alvito, see above, p. 190.

[2] See Livy 10. 39. 4; and cf. 10. 46. 9. In 1875 the name Duronia was given to a village previously known as Terra Vecchia not far from Boiano. There is now general agreement that the identification was completely mistaken. H. Nissen, *Ital. Landesk.* II, 679, and others have sought Duronia just west of Casinum at Roccasecca, a place proved to be ancient by some surviving polygonal masonry. This, however, cannot be correct, since it would mean that Papirius Cursor's axis of advance cut right across Carvilius'. Duronia must have lain somewhere between modern Venafro and Montaquila (for which see next note), most probably at Cerasuolo, an important road junction (in antiquity roads radiated from there to Montaquila, Isernia, and Venafro (G. Verrecchia in *Samnium*, XXX (1957), 185). It is the merest coincidence that the name of a woman involved in the Bacchanalian 'conspiracy' of 186 should be Duronia (Livy 39. 9. 2).

[3] Many scholars have argued that Aquilonia must be the town far to the south *in Hirpinis* (near mod. Lacedonia), and they even assign to this distant town the bronze coins bearing the legend 'Akudunniad'. Topographically this makes no sense at all, not even on the assumption that Cominium Ocritum was where most maps show it (see below, p. 275, n. 4) and was the Cominium mentioned in this campaign. How could refugees from Lacedonia have made their way to an asylum at Bovianum (whether this be Boiano or Pietrabbondante)? And why should bronze coins issued at Lacedonia turn up only in Northern Samnium (at Pietrabbondante and Agnone)? Aquilonia must be sought where Livy (10. 39. 7) places it: viz. some twenty Roman miles from Cominium (near mod. Alvito). The suggestively named Montaquila meets this requirement exactly. Nor has this name been devised for the town by modern scholarship. The name has come down in this form right through the Middle Ages: it occurs in a document of 778 (G. Colasanti, *Cercatori de Ferro*, p. 72, n. 1) and in others of 1321 and earlier (G. V. Ciarlanti, *Memorie Historiche del Sannio* (Isernia, 1644), p. 390). In antiquity the name Aquilonia might have been expected in this part of Italy: not very far away from Montaquila were springs known as Acidulae (Pliny, *N.H.* 31. 9). Montaquila itself is the kind of hill site that Samnite settlements normally occupied; and the natural asylum for refugees from it would inevitably be Boiano (Bovianum Pentrorum) down the valley to the south-east. In antiquity it must have been a site of great importance since it controlled the route between the valleys of the Rivers Rapido and Volturno (a route that indubitably was in use then, since remains of the bridge 'Ponte Latrone' by which it crossed the Volturno have been found near the modern 'Ponte a 25 Archi').

its remnants fled to Bovianum, while Papirius Cursor's victorious soldiers entered and sacked Aquilonia. Carvilius' men no less successfully carried Cominium by storm to make the Roman triumph complete.[1]

It was a famous victory and won for the conquering consuls such lasting glory that among future generations Papirius Cursor and Carvilius Maximus were names to conjure with in somewhat the same way as Fabius Rullianus and Decius Mus.[2] They abundantly earned the triumphs which they celebrated at Rome later in the year. Papirius Cursor received the greater share of the credit, no doubt rightly, and features from his exploit were even borrowed to embellish the already fabulous career of his father.[3] The amount of booty and captured enemy equipment was so enormous that Carvilius was able to have a bronze statue of Jupiter made from it of such huge proportions that when set up on the Capitol it was visible even as far away as the Alban Hills.[4]

It was a decisive, as well as a celebrated, success. The defences of the most critical of all the borders of Samnium had been smashed, and the consuls decided to exploit the break-through at once. Papirius Cursor's troops pushed into the valley of the Pentri and found a Samnite garrison massing for its defence at Saepinum. They attacked and stormed the stronghold in a particularly bloody action.[5] Meanwhile Carvilius' troops were going to work methodically to mop up in Northern Samnium, where they captured places listed as

[1] Livy 10. 38–43; Dio, fr. 36, 29; Zon. 8. 1. The details told of the action at Aquilonia are very suspect: the keeper of the Roman sacred chickens was killed in the front line (Livy 10. 40. 13); a raven intervened to help Rome (Livy 10. 40. 14); the Samnites lost 20,000 men (Livy 10. 42. 5); and at the height of the action Papirius Cursor bragged that he could outdrink Jupiter (Livy 10. 42. 7; Pliny, *N.H.* 14. 91). On the other hand, one must accept the item that a large body of Samnites were midway between Aquilonia and Cominium at the critical moment and did not get into action (Livy 10. 40. 6; 10. 43. 9).

[2] The Papirii were favourably placed to publicize the glories of their clan (see above, p.5), and the Carvilii did not lack family historians: the Spurius Carvilius who modified the Roman alphabet later in the third century B.C. (Plut. *Qu. Rom.* 54) was obviously interested in writing.

[3] Livy 9. 40.

[4] Pliny, *N.H.* 34. 43 (Livy 10. 46. 7 says that the booty was used to adorn the Temple of Quirinus, probably because he got his statues mixed up. He thought that it was the Second War not the Third that was celebrated with a colossal statue and that it was a statue of Hercules: 9. 44. 16. It was, however, Fabius Verrucosus who dedicated the statue to Hercules on the Capitol and he did this in 209: Strabo 6. 3. 1, p. 278; Pliny, *N.H.* 34. 40; Plutarch, *Fabius*, 22. 8).

[5] For Samnite, as distinct from Roman Saepinum, see above, p. 13. The casualties recorded at its fall (7,400 killed, 3,000 captured) seem credible (Livy 10. 44–5).

Velia, Herculaneum and Palumbinum. The identity of the first two of these names with those of the famous towns on the west coast of Southern Italy has aroused the scepticism of modern scholars. It is no doubt possible that these names have been taken from a later chapter in Carvilius' career and transposed to the year of his most glorious achievement. But it is also possible that the names genuinely belong to Samnite settlements in the vicinity of Aesernia and Aufidena: at least two of them, the two in fact to which exception is generally taken, closely resemble the names of *pagi* elsewhere in Samnium, and the name of the third may be preserved by a mountain near Aufidena.[1] Clearly, all three places might be examples of Samnite strong-points, making, like many others, a single evanescent appearance in history. Carvilius' campaign must have injured the Caraceni beyond recuperation.

By now winter had set in in Samnium, and the campaigning season for 293 was almost at an end. Carvilius betook himself to Etruria to still some unrest that had broken out at Falerii, at an otherwise unknown Troilum and at five other, unnamed places; he continued his watchdog role in Etruria in the following year, when he was proconsul. Papirius Cursor for his part returned to Northern Campania to secure the Auruncan territory against the standing menace of Samnite raids (from the Monti Trebulani), which had made it their target for so long and so often.[2]

The first decade of Livy comes to an end with the Battle of Aquilonia and his second decade has been lost, the result being

[1] For a *pagus Veianus* and a *pagus Herculaneus* at Beneventum see *ILS*, 6509; *CIL*, IX, p. 132, and for the celebrated *pagus Herculaneus* at Capua *ILS*, 6302. (In view of Samnite devotion to Hercules such toponymy is not surprising.) The River Velinus is very near to Northern Samnium, where indeed a town called S. Pietro Avellana is to be found in the valley of the River Vandra. Monte Palombo lies due north of the Val di Cómino, near the sources of the River Sangro. Furthermore anyone who has watched the turtle doves rising from the meadows beside the Sangro will not be surprised to learn that there was once a town called Palumbinum in that vicinity.

It must be admitted that chronology was not the strong point of the archivists of the *gens Carvilia*: several different dates are recorded for the divorce of Sp. Carvilius in the late third century (Dion. Hal. 2. 25; Val. Max. 2. 1. 4; Aul. Gell. 4. 3; 17. 21, 44; Plut. *Comp. Lyc. and Rom.* 3). So that it is conceivable that these archivists have referred Carvilius' activities around Herculaneum and Velia on the Tyrrhenian coast in 272 to the year 293 and his exploits in Northern Samnium (F. E. Adcock in *Camb. Anc. Hist.* VII, 614). But the famous Velia (Elea) on the Tyrrhenian coast later seems to have been a favoured *civitas foederata* (Cic. *pro Balbo*, 55), which it hardly would have been had it been carried by assault.

[2] Livy 10. 45, 46: his account of Carvilius' exploits in Etruria suggests a success almost as spectacular as Aquilonia (see especially 10. 46. 13). Troilum might be Trossulum, nine miles south of Volsinii (Pliny, *N.H.* 33. 35). For Falerii, see Front. *Strat.* 2. 5. 9.

that we lack any detailed and continuous narrative for what was left of the Third Samnite War. Fortunately its general character cannot be in much doubt. Aquilonia was the Gettysburg of the war. After it, Samnium was no longer capable of a formidable and concentrated effort, even though an individual section of the country might still give a stout-hearted account of itself. The summary information, which is all that has survived, indicates that the Romans now proceeded systematically to reduce Samnium piecemeal. If it took them over two years to do the job, the length of time is to be ascribed, in part anyway, to the plague at Rome. It had been raging in the city intermittently ever since 295 and seems to have been particularly severe in 292/291. This must have impaired the efficiency of the Roman legions.[1]

The Caraceni had been virtually knocked out of the war already in 293. Accordingly in 292, while one consul, D. Junius Brutus, with the help of the proconsul Carvilius Maximus, policed Etruria, the other, Q. Fabius Gurges, moved against the Caudini. He did not have matters all his own way. Whether through overconfidence or incompetence, he suffered a serious setback in Campania, evidently somewhere near the storied Caudine Forks. He is said to have been extricated from his difficulties only when his father, the veteran Rullianus, who was his *legatus*, helped him to restore the situation and then go on to overwhelm the Samnites, capturing the famed Gavius Pontius in the process, who was taken to Rome, led in Gurges' triumph and then beheaded.[2] This account of Gurges' activities in 292 is highly unconvincing. The picture of father and son respectively playing the roles of consul and *legatus* provides a convenient model for, and doubtless a fictitious anticipation of, the similar partnership of Q. Fabius Maximus and his father Fabius Cunctator in 213.[3] If so, Gurges' setback may have been exaggerated in order to make the tale of Rullianus' serving as his son's *legatus* more plausible. Since Gurges was appointed proconsul for the follow-

[1] The plague at Rome (Livy 10. 31. 8; 10. 47. 6–7; *Epit.* 11; Zon. 8. 1; Oros. 3. 22. 6) was so virulent that to help combat it the Romans imported a statue of Aesculapius from Epidaurus (Ovid, *Metam.* 15. 622 f.; Val. Max. 1. 8. 2; Plut. *Qu. Rom.* 94; Lactantius, *Divin. Inst.* 2. 7).

[2] For the year 292, see Livy, *Epit.* 11; Val. Max. 5. 7. 1; Dio, fr. 36, 30; Zon. 8. 1; Eutrop. 2. 9. 3; Oros. 3. 22. 6; 'Suda' s.v. 'Fabius'. Perhaps Ps. Plut. *Parall. Min.* 37 intended his apocryphal anecdote about Fabius Fabricianus (*sic*) looting a statue of Aphrodite Nicephorus (from Aequum Tuticum?) to refer to this occasion.

[3] Livy 24. 44. 9 f.; Val. Max. 2. 2. 4; Plut. *Fabius*, 24; Aul. Gell. 2. 2.

ing year and in 276 during the crisis of the Pyrrhic War was again elected consul, it is improbable that his consulship in 292 could have been altogether disastrous.[1] And, if his defeat in 292 has been exaggerated, so probably has his recovery. His smashing victory over the Samnites sounds like the immediate expedition of revenge that was always invented to offset any Roman setback in the Samnite Wars. What probably happened in 292 is that Gurges did run into difficulties,[2] since Roman writers might invent victories, but never defeats, for their generals. Nevertheless he managed to defeat the Caudini: that is the kernel of truth in the apocryphal tale of the capture and execution of the Caudine hero, Gavius Pontius.

In 291[3] it was the turn of the Pentri and the Hirpini. As on so many previous occasions, two Roman armies converged on Samnium, and this time there was no stopping them. The proconsul, Fabius Gurges, eliminated the Pentri by making his way through the gap at the southern end of the Matese massif, where the fortress of Saepinum was no longer an obstacle, to capture the stronghold of Cominium Ocritum. The consul, L. Postumius Megellus, operating out of Apulia, was equally successful against the Hirpini. Besides 'very many other places', he even took the populous and important stronghold of Venusia, where the largest Latin Colony ever recorded was immediately established.[4] Evidently the Romans were determined to put an end to Samnite Wars. Gurges and Postumius are said to have quarrelled violently; Dionysius of Halicarnassus even avers that the consul relieved Gurges of his command when he was about to take Cominium Ocritum, and himself took the credit for its capture.[5] Topography makes nonsense of this story, which was doubtless invented to illustrate Postumius' arrogance. That Gurges captured Cominium is proved by his triumph in this year.[6]

[1] Florus 1. 11. 7–11 ranks Gurges with Rullianus and the Papirii as one of the great heroes of the Samnite Wars (admittedly Florus is referring chiefly to his performance in the Pyrrhic War and is not a very reliable witness in any event).

[2] He lost 3,000 men (Eutrop. 2. 9. 3; 'Suda' s.v. 'Fabius').

[3] Triumph. Fasti *ad an.* 291; Oros. 3. 22. 10; Dio, fr. 36, 22; 'Suda' s.v. 'Postumius Consul'. The assault on the Pentri had begun already in 292 (Dion. Hal. 17/18. 4. 4 f.).

[4] Cominium Ocritum (see above, p. 271, n. 3) is traditionally identified with the mod. Cerreto Sannita, but the only basis for this is the variant reading *Cominium Cerritum* at Livy 25. 14. 14.

Venusia was a densely populated Samnite town, according to Dion. Hal. 17/18. 5. 1. For its capture and colonization, see Dion. Hal. 17/18. 4. 5 (whose figure for the number of colonists, 20,000, seems impossibly high). From it Rome could dominate Lucani and Apuli as well as Samnites (Hor. *Sat.* 2. 1. 34 f.).

[5] Dion. Hal. 17/18. 5.

[6] The year of his triumph is 291, not 290 (see A. Degrassi, *Inscript. Italiae*, XIII, 1, 73, 544).

Postumius is said to have behaved with outrageous insolence throughout his consulship; but his achievements in 305 and 294 make it likely that he was also a competent soldier in this year. Undoubtedly he helped to restore some lustre to the escutcheon of his *gens*, which had become badly tarnished at Caudium.[1]

Details of the operations in 290 are lacking. The meagre surviving information suggests that the consuls, the illustrious M.' Curius Dentatus and Sulla's ancestor, P. Cornelius Rufinus, used their four legions to mop up pockets of resistance wherever they were still to be found in Samnium. According to Eutropius and pseudo-Aurelius Victor, this involved them in some large-scale fighting, which may be to magnify their exploits. In any case, their performance was such as to win them triumphs at Rome. Evidently their pacification of Samnium was complete well before the end of the year, since Curius Dentatus moved north from there to crush the Sabines in a short campaign, perhaps for the part they had played or failed to play in the events of 296/295. There is no record of neighbouring Umbri coming to the support of the Sabines. The latter were at once incorporated into the Roman state as *cives sine suffragio* and as a result of Rome's largest territorial acquisition since the Latin War the Ager Romanus was made to stretch right across Italy to the Adriatic Sea.[2]

The Third Samnite War was thus brought to its close in 290;[3] and, says Livy, for the fourth time the Samnites signed a treaty with Rome.[4]

For the Samnites it must have been a grim, as well as a humiliating, experience. The terrorization practised by Curius Dentatus and

[1] Postumius did not belong to the same branch of the *gens* as the unfortunate consul of 321. He was evidently a figure of controversy. He suffered from a bad press (Livy 10. 36. 15; 10. 37. 8 f.; Dion. Hal. 17/18. 4); on the other hand he must have received his full due in the history which A. Postumius Albinus compiled *c.* 150. It is probable that he triumphed in 291 (A. Degrassi, *Inscript. Ital.* 13. 1. 544; Val. Max. 5. 7. 1; Plut. *Fabius*, 24; 'Suda' s.v. 'Fabius').

[2] According to Livy, *Epit.* 11, the Sabines had rebelled in 290.

[3] For the year 290, see Livy, *Epit.* 11; Dio, fr. 37; Eutrop. 2. 9. 3; Auct. *de vir. ill.* 33. 1. B. Bruno (*Terza Guerra Sannitica*, 107) and K. J. Beloch (*Röm. Gesch.* pp. 428, 450) argue that the war against the Samnites ended in 291 and that the hostilities in 290 were exclusively against Sabini. But they attach undue importance to a garbled notice in Oros. 3. 22. 10 f. Livy evidently said that the Samnite Wars lasted forty-nine years (i.e. 343–290, omitting the four dictator years which Livy ignored). M'. Curius Dentatus is said to have triumphed twice, over the Samnites and Sabines respectively (Livy, *loc. cit.*; Auct. *de vir. ill.*, *loc. cit.*; Pliny, *N.H.* 18. 18; Triumph. Fasti *ad an.* 290; cf. Cic. *Cato Maior*, 16. 55; Apul. *Apol.* 17).

[4] *foedus quarto renovatum est* (Livy, *Epit.* 11).

Cornelius Rufinus as they overran Samnium in the final campaign is not described for us, but some idea of it can be formed from the amount of loot and prisoners they took. Their sales of booty and of captives netted over three million pounds of bronze, and it was this windfall that enabled the Roman state to start issuing coins of its own (the famous series of *aes grave*) and to found a system of currency which was swiftly adopted by, if not actually imposed upon, all of Central Italy.[1] Nor was pillage on the wholesale scale the end of the tale of woe. It can be safely inferred that the Samnites were made also to provide clothing and rations for Roman troops, since at this time the Romans regularly made such requisitioning the price for a cessation of hostilities.

The terms of the Samnites' fourth treaty with Rome are nowhere recorded, but Livy's expression *renovatum est* cannot be taken to mean that the instrument was simply renewed on the same terms as before. Livy uses exactly the same language in the case of Rome's treaties with Carthage, which we know differed one from another.[2] After all, the Samnites had been hammered into submission; they had not negotiated a surrender. Under these circumstances it is inconceivable that their relations with Rome were not drastically altered for the worse.

Undoubtedly Samnium was mulcted of territory, much of it the best agricultural land. A large region south of the River Aufidus was seized to provide land for Rome's new Latin Colony at Venusia, the Samnite inhabitants of the town being forcibly dispossessed.[3] In addition, the Samnites must also have had to cede land west of the River Volturnus in the north. It must have been now that the valley of the Upper and Middle Volturnus[4] replaced the Liris as the dividing line between Rome and Samnium. In other words, the Samnite League lost Cominium, Atina, Aquilonia, Casinum,

[1] See R. Thomsen, *Early Roman Coinage*, III, 259 f.; R. Knapowski, *Der Staatshaushalt der röm. Republik*, pp. 9 f., 51 f. The head of Janus, a very Roman deity, on the obverse advertised the supremacy that Rome had achieved. Some idea of the quantity of bronze Rome acquired from the war can be gained from Livy 10. 30. 10 (each soldier received 82 bronze *asses*); 10. 31. 3 (1,740 Perusines were ransomed at 310 *asses* a head, for a total of 539,400 *asses*); 10. 37. 4 (Volsinii (a mistake for Cortona?), Perusia and Arretium pay fines amounting to 1,500,000 *asses*); 10. 46. 5 (at Cursor's triumph 2,533,000 pounds of bronze were displayed); 10. 46. 14 (Carvilius lodged 380,000 pounds of bronze with the treasury).

[2] Polyb. 3. 22–4; Livy, *Epit.* 13.

[3] Hor. *Sat.* 2. 1. 36.

[4] This would be the stretch of river from its source in the Mainarde mountains to the borders of Sidicine territory just south of Rufrae.

Venafrum and Rufrae. Of these towns, Cominium and Rufrae play no further part in recorded history. Atina, Casinum and Venafrum demonstrably became Roman *praefecturae*.[1] There is no evidence to show when they obtained this latter status, but it seems altogether probable that they at least ceased to be 'Samnite' from 290 on. Venafrum certainly could no longer have been part of Samnium, if certain third-century coins with Oscan legends have been correctly ascribed to it. These coins, however, equally mean that it was then an 'independent' state and not yet a Roman *praefectura*.[2] In other words it helped Aquinum, Teanum and the Latin Colonies (Cales, Fregellae, Suessa Aurunca and Interamna) to form the buffer zone between Roman territory and Samnite. There is numismatic evidence also for Aquilonia. Its few surviving coins suggest that it, too, had become a separate civic entity and was no longer part of a Samnite tribal state;[3] and this probably happened in the third century, since the warrior goddess on the obverse of the coins resembles the figure on the contemporary issues of Cales and Teanum. Possibly it was after the Pyrrhic War that Venafrum and Aquilonia became 'Roman'.[4]

The rest of Samnium, so far as we know, was left intact after the Third Samnite War, and the Samnite League presumably remained in being.[5] But, if it did, it could not have 'renewed' the treaty with Rome as an equal. Samnium was no longer equal: by now it was distinctly smaller, both in size and in population, than the area controlled by Rome. Moreover, as noted above, the peace at the end of the Third War was not negotiated, but imposed. Consequently it is certain that henceforth the Samnites were the 'allies' and not just the 'friends' of Rome.[6] When they again took to arms at the time

[1] Atina: Cic. *pro Plancio*, 19; Pliny, *N.H.* 2. 6. 1; Casinum: *CIL*, x, 5193, 5194; Venafrum: Festus, p. 262 L. These towns became part of Teretina, the Roman tribe nearest to them in place and in time (Teretina was created just before the outbreak of the Third Samnite War: above, p. 256, n. 3).

[2] Reject the notion (of W. Giesecke, *Italia Numismatica*, p. 118) that the coins were struck in order to pay the troops serving against Pyrrhus.

[3] Bantia may be an analogy: it may have been taken away from the Lucani and made 'independent' after the Pyrrhic War.

[4] Festus, p. 262 L., suggests that Venafrum, along with Allifae, Arpinum *aliaque complura*, belonged to a less favoured category of *praefecturae*. This is what might have been expected if after receiving 'independence' from Rome they had stayed neutral against, or actually joined, Pyrrhus.

[5] Livy 7. 29. 2 clearly implies as much. The League may have been left in being since it would be the most convenient channel for getting a supply of Samnite troops.

[6] They were certainly 'allies' in 225: Polyb. 2. 24.

of the Pyrrhic War, the expression used by Livy is *Samnites defecerunt*.[1] One cannot, of course, press the meaning of words in a Livian *Epitome*, but there can be very little doubt that, from the Roman point of view, the Samnites did rebel on that occasion. The 'allies' to whom Fabricius was sent in 284 in a fruitless attempt to keep them from siding with Tarentum and other enemies of Rome were clearly the Samnites.[2]

By becoming 'allies' of Rome the Samnites were obliged henceforth to accept the foreign policy imposed by her, to supply troops on demand,[3] and to abstain from acts of violence against their neighbours. They could perhaps find some consolation in the reflexion that their territory, although diminished, was at any rate not divided, and that therefore their League could continue to exist. Even this meagre comfort, however, was tempered by the knowledge that Latin Colonies had been established on Samnite soil, dominated at least three of its frontiers and had put an end for ever to their days of expansion. In fact, the days of a truly independent Samnium were over.

[1] Livy, *Epit.* 12.

[2] Dio, fr. 39. 1; Zon. 8. 2.

[3] The troops may have been supplied by the League as a whole together with their own Samnite commander (cf. above, p. 278, n. 5). This seems to have been the case with the Sabellic League: Plut. *Aem. Paul.* 20 records a Salvius who commanded both Paeligni and Marrucini, and presumably Vestini and Marsi as well.

CHAPTER 8

THE PYRRHIC WAR

The Samnites, sullen and resentful, were grimly determined to rid themselves of their new status the moment an opportunity presented itself; and this happened sooner than they had perhaps dared to hope. Within five years the Romans were actively engaged with enemies in the north and in the south of Italy at the same time. To the Samnites it must have seemed that Gellius Egnatius' anti-Roman coalition had risen phoenix-like from its ashes and on an even grander scale: it now had Lucanian and Bruttian members as well as Etruscan and Celtic, and there were indications that yet other peoples might be added, such as Messapii and Italiotes. It is true that the consolidation of Central Italy, which Rome had effected, and in particular the annexation of the Sabine territory, eliminated the likelihood of her northern and southern foes joining forces in the way that they had done at Sentinum; her Sabellic allies stood firmly by her and indeed occasionally gave her splendid service in battle.[1] Nevertheless it was a fact that the Romans had succeeded in conjuring up enemies against themselves over much of Italy.[2]

Immediately after M'. Curius Dentatus' subjugation of the Sabini, so Livy implies,[3] the Romans found themselves at war with the Senones, either because they were determined to end that particular menace for ever or because the Gauls, alarmed by Roman expansion northward, took up arms again. Some of the Etruscan cities (Volsinii is specifically mentioned)[4] saw this as an opportunity for ridding themselves of Roman influence and made common cause with the

[1] The Frentani distinguished themselves greatly in the Battle of Heraclea, 280 (Florus 1. 13. 7; Plut. *Pyrr.* 16. 8–10). Umbri and Volsci also proved useful allies (Dion. Hal. 20. 1. 2–3).

[2] It is uncertain whether armed hostilities broke out first in the north or in the south. Polyb. 2. 19. 7 suggests the former, by reporting Senonese hostility already in 285. The later Roman tradition, however, insisted that the Sabellians incited the Gauls, and Etruscans too (App. *Samn.* 6; *Celt.* 11; cf. Florus 1. 8; Dio, fr. 39. 2). Anti-Samnite prejudice may have been at work here: Eutrop. 2. 10. 1 even goes so far as to say that the Samnites were present at Vadimon (this is certainly false: the Samnites never came north again after 295).

[3] Livy, *Epit.* 11 and 12.

[4] Livy, *Epit.* 11. An entry in the Triumph. Fasti *ad an.* 280 and the subsequent colonization of Cosa (273) prove that Vulci was also hostile.

Gauls: indeed the Etruscan hostility to Rome may have preceded the Gallic.[1]

Simultaneously the Italiote communities in the far south, most of which were now in decline, found themselves under increasing pressure from their Sabellian neighbours, the Lucani and the Bruttii. Tarentum was the one city of Magna Graecia that might have afforded the Greek cities protection, but they were distrustful of her: if she herself would not abuse her position as the protecting power, almost certainly the mercenary *condottieri* whom it was her habit to employ were bound to do so. Thurii preferred to follow the Neapolitan example and *c.* 286 sought a treaty with Rome. By complying with the request Rome accepted the risk of war with the Lucani and Bruttii and, as she soon discovered, with Tarentum and the Messapii as well.[2]

Presumably some influential group in Roman public life was responsible for adventures in Magna Graecia at a time when many other Romans must have regarded the attitude of Gauls and Etruscans in the north as imposing a policy of caution.[3] It has been suggested that the dynamic and sanguine element that thus rather recklessly involved Rome in two-front war were the leaders of the plebeians.[4] The last years of the Third Samnite War had seen a revival of political strife between patricians and plebeians,[5] which had resulted not merely in the plebeian right to one of the two consulships being rigorously confirmed, but also in the transfer of power to the plebeian assembly (*concilium plebis*): in 287/286 the Lex Hortensia granted the plebeian assembly full legislative authority.[6] One of the first uses to which that assembly is said to have put its newly acquired, law-making discretion was to respond to the

[1] But some Etruscans, the Arretini for instance (Polyb. 2. 19. 7–8), stood by their treaties with Rome.

[2] Tarentine hostility to Rome had long been smouldering. In the Second Samnite War Tarentum is described as a pro-Samnite non-belligerent rather than a genuine neutral (Livy 8. 27. 2; 9. 14. 1); there had been short-lived hostilities between Rome and Tarentum *c.* 303 (Diod. 20. 104. 1); and Tarentum was bound to regard the Latin Colony at Venusia as a threat against herself.

[3] Many Romans advocated a peaceful policy in the south (Plut. *Pyrrh.* 18. 4); and the Romans displayed moderation in the face of Tarentine insults (Dion. Hal. 19. 6. 4).

[4] T. Frank in *Cambr. Anc. Hist.* VII, 641; F. E. Adcock, *Roman Political Ideas and Practice*, p. 33.

[5] In 297 an attempt was made to elect two patricians as consuls (Livy 10. 15. 7–12; Auct. *de vir. ill.* 34. 4).

[6] The People had established their right to make the ultimate decisions concerning peace and war at least as early as the period of the Caudine Peace (see *Cambr. Anc. Hist.* VII, 671).

urging of a plebeian tribune named C. Aelius and vote *c.* 286 to protect Thurii against the encroachment of Lucani commanded by Sthenius Statilius.[1] When war with the Lucani and Bruttii resulted it was largely directed and fought by plebeian generals: the 280s and 270s are the age of the great plebeian worthies.

Whether all this be true or not, it does not necessarily prove that the policy of southern expansion at this time was a plebeian policy.[2] Plebeian generals, who fought well and valiantly in the south, whether against Samnites, Lucani and Bruttii or against Pyrrhus, Italiotes and Messapii, may not have been convinced advocates of the policies that had brought them against those peoples. M'. Curius Dentatus, C. Fabricius Luscinus, Ti. Coruncanius, P. Decius Mus and C. Junius Brutus may merely have been doing their duty as soldiers. Some of these great plebeian heroes seem to have been more interested in expansion north-eastward than south-eastward. This was particularly true of Curius Dentatus, the conqueror of the Sabines, who did not fail to advertise the extent, and direction, of his conquests.[3] Others of them do not seem to have had their hearts really in the war in the south: Fabricius Luscinus was obviously a peacemonger as far as that region was concerned.

Actually it is possible to identify with some degree of assurance the leaders of what might be called the southern lobby, and they are not all plebeians. They included the patrician Appius Claudius Caecus, the builder of the Via Appia,[4] who was determined on war *à outrance* with Pyrrhus and whose blind eye made the Roman Senate turn a deaf ear to the Epirote king's peace proposals.[5] Another seems to have been Sulla's ancestor, the patrician P. Cornelius Rufinus, who was expelled from the senate in 275 by the censors Fabricius Luscinus and Aemilius Papus,[6] allegedly for in-

[1] Pliny, *N.H.* 34. 32 (who gives the name as Sthenius Stallius); cf. Livy, *Epit.* 11; Val. Max. 1. 8. 6; App. *Samn.* 7. 1; L. Pareti, *Storia di Roma*, I, 776. It seems very unlikely that it was the Tribal Assembly, rather than the Centuriate, that voted to assist Thurii. Furthermore it seems probable that Pliny *loc. cit.* is wrong in calling C. Aelius a plebeian tribune; the consul for 286 surely must be the person meant.

[2] F. Cassola, *I Gruppi Politici Romani*, pp. 159–71.

[3] Justin 18. 2. 6; App. *Samn.* 12; Dio, fr. 39. 1; Zon. 8. 7; Auct. *de vir. ill.* 33. 1; Oros. 3. 22. 11; G. Forni in *Athenaeum*, XXXI (1953), 234.

[4] Claudius Caecus has been aptly called 'the Roman Chatham' (J. G. Droysen, *Hist. de Rome*, III, 150).

[5] It was probably the treaty signed with Carthage rather than the eloquence of Claudius Caecus that decided the Romans to reject the proposals brought by Cineas.

[6] It was actually Fabricius who expelled Rufinus from the senate (Livy, *Epit.* 14) but he was the *familiaris* of his patrician colleague (Cic. *Laelius*, 39; cf. Val. Max. 4. 4. 3).

fringing a sumptuary law, but more probably because of political differences with opponents of southern expansionism. Other members of the southern faction seem to have been P. Valerius Laevinus,[1] over whom the Epirote king scored the first of his Pyrrhic victories, at Heraclea in 280, and possibly L. Papirius Cursor, whose father had annexed Campanian Acerrae in 332. They, too, were patricians.

This is not to say that the policy was exclusively a patrician one,[2] but it does mean that it was not specifically or even principally a plebeian one either. The plebeian rank and file may have been more favourably disposed to it now than they had been in an earlier day. During the earlier southern wars the ordinary plebeian may have felt that he was merely fighting for glory and for speculative outlets for his betters. This time there might be something in it for him personally. Victory this time would mean large confiscations of land from the defeated, and, even though these would be chiefly exploited by the 'nobility', there might be some viritane allotments or colonies for indigent plebeians. Even so, the discontent of the ordinary plebeian with the southern operations was very manifest before the war was over: there was resistance to the levy in 275.[3]

On the whole one should conjecture that, as before, it was a faction among the patricio-plebeian nobility that sponsored the policy of carrying expansion in the south to its logical conclusion: the C. Aelius who moved that help be sent to Thurii in 286/285 was obviously a member of the faction and, whoever he was, whether the consul of 286 or an unknown tribune of 285, he was certainly plebeian. It was a risky policy, since it meant that Roman resources had to be divided and spread rather thinly between north and south.

Owing to the fragmentary and at times contradictory nature of our sources, chronological and other details are uncertain, and it is not easy to distinguish cause from effect.[4] But it does seem certain that by 284 Rome had large forces committed in both the north and

[1] For Laevinus' intransigence towards Pyrrhus, see Dion. Hal. 19. 9–10; Plut. *Pyrrh.* 16. 4.; 18. 1.

[2] As argued by A. Passerini in *Athenaeum*, XXI (1943), 92–112, and P. Lévêque, *Pyrrhos*, p. 309.

[3] Livy, *Epit.* 14; Val. Max. 6. 3. 6; cf. Varro, *Sat. Men.* 140 Riese. Perhaps the plebeians discovered that the south was already overpopulated and had comparatively little good agricultural land anyway.

[4] The primary source for the Pyrrhic War was Timaeus (A. D. Momigliano in *Riv. Stor. Ital.* LXXI (1959), 532 f.), but as he is not extant we have to depend on Plutarch's *Life of Pyrrhus* and various epitomes.

the south.[1] This dispersal, dangerous in any case, was rendered doubly so by the inexperience of the commander in the north, L. Caecilius Metellus, one of the consuls for 284. In that year, or possibly in the next, he was overwhelmed in a crushing defeat.[2] In a great battle near Arretium the Senones inflicted upon him and his army what was probably the worst disaster Rome had ever suffered.[3] Indeed it may well be argued that, had it not been for the great victory which P. Cornelius Dolabella managed to win over the Etruscans and Gauls at Lake Vadimon in 283,[4] the whole course of history might have been very different. Even as it was, the consequences of Arretium were serious and protracted.

The news of the destruction of Caecilius Metellus and his army meant for the Samnites that the moment they had been waiting for had come. They at once raised the standard of revolt, and for the next twelve years, down to and including the year 272, they were fighting Rome in what was to all intents and purposes a Fourth Samnite War.[5] Curiously enough, although a longer struggle than the First or Third War or than the pre-Caudine phase of the Second,[6] it is not known to history as a Samnite War.[7] It became merged with and recorded as the Pyrrhic War, in which the chief and most dreaded adversary of Rome, the *caput belli* to use the Roman jargon,[8] was for the first time an enemy from overseas, Pyrrhus of Epirus.[9] Yet the Samnites were in the field fighting before Tarentum ever invited King Pyrrhus to come to Italy, and they remained in arms long after he had tired of the struggle and gone back to Greece.[10] Indeed it is altogether probable that it was only their being in arms that emboldened the Tarentines to transmute into active hostility the

[1] Perhaps war with the Lucani had already begun the year before (Livy, *Epit.* 13).

[2] For the date, see E. T. Salmon in *Class. Phil.* xxx (1935), 23–31; Broughton, *MRR*, I, 188 f.

[3] It will be remembered that Arretium had signed a treaty with Rome in 294 (see above, p. 269). K. J. Beloch, *Röm. Gesch.* p. 454, correctly stresses the magnitude of the Roman defeat.

[4] Where, however, the Gauls concerned were Boii, not Senones (Polyb. 2. 20. 1).

[5] As Livy 31. 31. 10 implies and Oros. 3. 8. 1 positively states.

[6] Even the post-Caudine phase of the Second War was no longer.

[7] The Romans seem to have regarded the three previous wars as one long struggle interrupted by several truces, whereas the present war was a revolt of the conquered against their overlords.

[8] Livy 26. 7. 3; Florus 1. 13. 1.

[9] Pausanias 1. 12. 1; Eutrop. 2. 11. 1; Dio, fr. 39. 2; Zon. 8. 2.

[10] Dion. Hal. 19. 9. 2; Pliny, *N.H.* 34. 22; App. *Samn.* 7. 3; Dio, fr. 39. 2; Zon. 8. 3. Livy, *Epit.* 12, however, seems to say that the Samnites 'revolted' only after the formal declaration of war between Rome and Tarentum (cf. Oros. 3. 22. 12).

resentment they had long been nursing at the spread of Roman power. The fact that Pyrrhus and, besides him, other peoples such as the Lucani, Bruttii, Messapii, and Italiotes were also fighting Rome in this part of Italy at this time presumably explains why this war never became known as the Fourth Samnite. From the Roman point of view it was more than a Samnite War.

The literary sources, such as they are, suggest that all the Samnites were involved in it; the Fasti Triumphales confirm this and register triumphs over Samnites, not over individual Samnite tribes. As a matter of fact two of the individual tribes, the Caudini and the Hirpini, are explicitly recorded as belligerents by Livy,[1] and the immediate aftermath of the struggle suggests that the Caraceni must have been in it too. The Pentri are not separately named, but it is inconceivable that they did not participate.

The fighting against the Samnites took place in the south. Details are almost completely lacking, although something can be inferred from entries in the Fasti Triumphales[2] and from incidents which, although recounted of other wars, more probably belong to this one.[3] That fighting went on for thirteen years, from 284 to 272, may seem surprising in view of the fact that Samnium was now truncated and strategically much more vulnerable and the Samnites were by no means as powerful a nation as they had been in the earlier struggles. The explanation no doubt lies in the division of Roman forces between north and south, the heavy casualties they repeatedly sustained during these years (at Arretium, Heraclea, Ausculum, Beneventum, even in the city itself, where a plague was raging),[4] and the scattered nature of the fighting (and garrisoning) over widely separated portions of Southern Italy. We have no means of following its course in detail. It is clear enough that this time Roman armies entered, crossed and left Samnium almost at will,[5] and one suspects that there was a good deal of guerrilla fighting. At this the Samnites were adepts, especially in the mountain glens, and on at least one occasion (in 277) they inflicted a sharp reverse on the Romans, in the Cranite Mountains, wherever they were.[6]

[1] Livy 23. 42. 2.

[2] The Fasti list triumphs *de Samnitibus* in 282, 280, 278, 276, 275, 273, 272.

[3] See above, p. 231.

[4] Oros. 4. 2. 2 (= 276).

[5] In 280/279 they actually wintered in the heart of Samnium near Saepinum (Front. *Strat.* 4. 1. 18–24, emending *Serinum*).

[6] All that we know of the Cranite Mountains is that they were difficult of access and covered with cornel trees and shrubbery (Zon. 8. 6).

When Tarentum, encouraged by the amount of trouble Rome had on her hands, decided to join the ranks of her enemies and invited Pyrrhus to come and conduct her war effort, the Epirote king responded with alacrity, and almost automatically the Samnites became his allies. Mutual recriminations prove that it was not a particularly happy partnership and, if Livy is to be believed,[1] the Samnites years later retained unfavourable memories of Pyrrhus. In 280 they were not on hand to join their forces to his on his arrival in Italy, nor were they present at the battle of Heraclea in that year.[2] Pyrrhus did not share the booty from that battle with them, and he may well have taken little or no trouble to safeguard their interests in the peace negotiations that he conducted with Rome after the battle and that came within an ace of succeeding.[3] It is true that they accompanied him on his march into Latium in the following year, probably with some relish since it gave them the chance to settle an overdue account with the colonists at Fregellae, but his retreat from Latium greatly disappointed them.[4] Nevertheless they seem to have remained at his side and to have shared his victory at Ausculum (279), where, according to Dionysius of Halicarnassus, they made up his left wing and supplied much of his cavalry.[5] His departure for Sicily (278) must have angered them, and it certainly left them at

1 Livy 23. 42. 6. The story that the Samnites joined the Tarentines in inviting him to Italy (Justin 18. 1. 1) is probably due to confusion with their appeal to him in 276 to return from Sicily to Italy (Plut. *Pyrrh.* 23, 25. 1–5; Zon. 8. 6; Justin 23. 3. 5). Pyrrhus may have been disappointed with the Samnites from the outset since their strength was less than he had been led to expect. The Tarentines had told him that he would find 350,000 infantry and 20,000 cavalry waiting to fight on his side (Plut. *Pyrrh.* 13. 8—K. J. Beloch, *Bevölk. Gr. Röm. Welt*, I, 356, tries vainly to justify these figures). The Samnites for their part resented the fact that, before ever he arrived, they had lost as many of their own men in captured as he lost at Heraclea (Plut. *Pyrrh.* 21. 4).

2 Dio, fr. 40, 22 and 27. They are not mentioned on the dedication Pyrrhus made at Dodona to celebrate Heraclea (Dittenberger, *SIG*, I, p. 627, no. 392). It is possible that Laevinus' deep penetration into the south prevented them from joining him.

3 The date of the peace negotiations is disputed (see Mary R. Lefkowitz in *Harv. Stud. Class. Phil.* LXIV (1959), 147–77). Pyrrhus proposed that the Romans offer 'friendship' to himself and 'immunity' to the Tarentines (Plut. *Pyrrh.* 18. 4; cf. Florus 1. 13; Zon. 8. 4); there is no trustworthy evidence that he demanded more than this. It is not surprising that the Romans should reject the proposal. They had so far lost only one battle, and that was no novelty for a people that had recovered from the disasters at the Allia, the Caudine Forks, Lautulae and, still more recently, Arretium. Moreover they were probably counting on Carthaginian help.

4 Florus 1. 13. 24; Eutrop. 2. 12. 1; Dio, fr. 40. 27.

5 Plutarch, *Pyrrh.* 21. 5–9, reflecting the king's own memoirs, does not mention them at Ausculum. Dion. Hal. 20. 1 f. does, however; cf., too, Polyb. 18. 28. 10; Front. *Strat.* 2. 3. 21 (who says the Samnites were on the right flank: perhaps he is confusing the Samnites' infantry with their cavalry (Dion. Hal. 20. 2. 3)). As in earlier Samnite Wars, the interruption of nightfall is recorded in connexion with a Roman defeat (Dion. Hal. 20. 3. 7).

the mercy of the reprisals of the Romans, once these latter had recovered from their losses at Ausculum.[1] In fact, the Samnites felt the fury of Rome far more than Tarentum did, and they obviously had a very rough time of it in 277 and 276, even though their victory in the Cranite Mountains (277) showed that on familiar terrain they could still give a good account of themselves.[2] They had little option but to rejoin Pyrrhus on his return from Sicily in 275,[3] but by now they were so worn down that they could not give him much help for his last and unsuccessful battle with the Romans near Beneventum.[4] They could not even prevent the 'capital' of the Caudini from falling into Roman hands in that same year.[5]

Pyrrhus' departure from Italy shortly after the Battle of Beneventum must have enraged the Samnites: they could have had no illusions about the uselessness to their cause of the garrison he left behind in Tarentum under the command of his deputy Milo. Thereafter it was only a matter of time. Adopting the same methodical strategy as in the closing stages of the Third Samnite War, the Romans crushed the Samnite tribes one by one. It took some time, since in unurbanized Samnium there were few major targets or critical nerve centres at which to strike. Finally, however, they appointed the generals whose simultaneous victories at Aquilonia and Cominium had really decided the earlier struggle, L. Papirius Cursor and Sp. Carvilius Maximus. Elected consuls for 272, these men brought the hostilities to a close and terminated the long list of triumphs over Samnites.[6]

[1] From autumn 279 to autumn 278 the Romans must have pursued a 'Fabian' policy. But during his absence they used their most experienced commanders (Fabricius Luscinus, Junius Brutus Bubulcus, Fabius Gurges) in order to crush his allies in Italy.

[2] It is to be noted that the Fasti do not list a triumph *de Samnitibus* in 277, although they do record the triumph of Junius Brutus Bubulcus *de Lucaneis et Bruttieis*.

[3] They strongly urged him to return: see above, p. 286, n. 1.

[4] The exact site of the battle, the Arusini Campi (Oros. 4. 2. 3), is unknown. So is its outcome. Justin 23. 3. 12 says that Pyrrhus was heavily defeated, which is quite certainly an exaggeration. Polyb. 8. 11. 10 records the battle as drawn. Livy 38. 4. 5 admits that the Romans lost it. See, too, Plut. *Pyrrh.* 25. 1–5; Dio, fr. 40, 48. It seems unlikely that both consuls were at Beneventum (despite Beloch, *Röm. Gesch.* p. 467). As Pyrrhus felt it necessary to leave Italy soon afterwards, the battle was obviously unsuccessful for him.

[5] A Samnite city was captured by the consul L. Cornelius Lentulus, who rewarded his *legatus* Ser. Cornelius Merenda with a golden crown for his role in the operation (Pliny, *N.H.* 33. 38). The cognomen which the consul received, Caudinus, shows that Caudium must have been the city concerned.

[6] The amount of space on the stone indicates that both the consuls celebrated triumphs (*CIL*, I^2, p. 245; XIV, 4547; G. Calza in *Not. d. Scavi* (1921), p. 255). Papirius Cursor marked the event by dedicating a temple to Consus (Festus, p. 228 L.); but it was his colleague Carvilius who was chiefly responsible for the subjugation of the Samnites, Papirius being mainly active against the Lucani and Bruttii (Zon. 8. 6).

There was a short-lived, violent aftermath. In 269 one of the Caraceni who had been taken as a hostage to Rome, a certain Lollius,[1] managed to escape to his native mountains, where he fomented an uprising and established himself in a stronghold[2] from which to carry on guerrilla warfare against the Romans. It required the efforts of both the consuls for 269, Q. Ogulnius Gallus and C. Fabius Pictor, to suppress the movement;[3] but the Caraceni paid dearly. The leaders of the rebellion were executed, the rank and file were sold into slavery and the Caraceni reduced to a pitiful remnant.

For the Samnites the peace terms were much more severe than for the Lucani, the Tarentines, or the Bruttii (who at least retained their league).[4] Not only did they have to surrender territory once more, but in addition they had to dissolve their League; and this time they were no longer left undivided. Hitherto the Roman policy had been to encircle them: now it was to dismember them.

The Hirpini were obliged to cede a wide strip of land extending right across Samnium from Campania to Apulia; as a result they were henceforth physically separated from the Pentri. To enclose the Hirpini completely and to end for ever the possibility of Samnites and Alfaterni making common cause, the Romans settled a compact mass of Picentes on their western borders. When the inhabitants of Picenum rebelled against Roman authority in 269, the consuls for 268 quickly suppressed the insubordination and prevented any repetition of it by a forcible transfer of the Picentine population to

[1] Dion. Hal. 20. 17. 1–2; Dio, fr. 42; Zon. 8. 7. Whether Lollius is a distant ancestor of Augustus' famous general M. Lollius it is impossible to say. The origin of the latter is unknown, although he seems to have had some connexion with Ferentinum, which is not a great distance from Caracenan territory (*ILS*, 5342–5).

[2] The stronghold may have been Castel di Sangro (L. Mariani in *Mon. Antichi*, x (1901), 417) or possibly Carovilli (which town, it has been suggested, preserves the name of Carvilius, the Roman conqueror of Samnites: A. Carano in *Samnium*, xxxiii (1960), 58–85).

[3] If two consuls were involved, it could not have been as minor an affair as K. J. Beloch (*Röm. Gesch.* p. 474) suggests. Lollius was not merely a bandit (rebels are usually so described). The absence of a triumph is due to the fact that the consuls were not adding to, but recovering, Roman power. Cf. what Val. Max. 2. 8. 4 says to explain Opimius' failure to get a triumph for his success against Fregellae in 125: *cautum erat ut pro aucto imperio non pro reciperatis quae populi Romani fuissent triumphus decerneretur.*

[4] The Lucani had to cede land for the Latin Colony at Paestum (273) and may have lost Bantia (which later appears as an independent civic commonwealth, but may have become such after the Second Punic War rather than now). Tarentum remained technically independent, but an ally of Rome (and its status was so favourable that it could be mentioned in the same sentence with that of Naples: Cic. *pro Arch.* 3. 5). For the continuing existence of the Bruttian League, see Livy 25. 1. 1. The Samnites had to give hostages (Zon. 8. 7), but otherwise the terms imposed on them are not described in ancient literature.

the border country between Hirpini, Alfaterni and Lucani, a district henceforth known as the Ager Picentinus. At about the same time a Latin Colony was established at Paestum (273).[1] The Hirpini were thus effectively isolated and from now on, instead of being referred to as Samnites, they are usually called by their tribal name; and years later, when Augustus subdivided Italy, they were not assigned to 'Samnium' (Region IV), but to 'Apulia' (Region II). The eastern portion of the strip of land annexed from them at the end of the Pyrrhic War, the district known as the Ager Taurasinus, remained Roman state domain (*ager publicus*) for many years and was leased out as grazing land. The western portion of the strip contained Malventum, the Hirpinian 'capital', and it was transformed in 268 into a Latin Colony with the better-omened name of Beneventum,[2] one of whose principal tasks was to maintain surveillance over the Hirpini. Compsa probably replaced Malventum as the Hirpinian administrative centre.[3]

The tribal state of the Caudini seems to have been broken up into fragments. Telesia and the towns on and about the Monti Trebulani (Caiatia, Cubulteria, Trebula Balliensis) became separate 'allies' of Rome.[4] Caiatia and Cubulteria and possibly Telesia as well, being now nominally 'independent' states, issued bronze coins of their own in the third century. In type these coins closely resemble those of Aquinum, Venafrum, Teanum Sidicinum, Cales and Suessa Aurunca, and indicate clearly that these Samnite towns were encouraged, if not directed, to turn their backs on Samnium and form a close monetary league with the neighbouring civic commonwealths in Western Italy. Coins from Trebula Balliensis are not known, but its later municipal institutions suggest that it too could have become a community 'allied' to Rome. Caudium itself did not issue any coins.

[1] For the population transfers, see Triumph. Fasti *ad an.* 268; Strabo 5. 4. 13, p. 251; Pliny, *N.H.* 3. 70; Front. *Strat.* 1. 12. 3; Eutrop. 2. 16 (cf. Livy, *Epit.* 15); Florus 1. 14. 1–2; Oros. 4. 4. 5–7.

[2] The campaign of 275 demonstrated its strategic importance. The annexation of the Ager Taurasinus and the colonization of Beneventum meant that Roman access to Apulia was now much more secure.

[3] Livy 23. 1. 2. Mommsen, in *CIL*, IX, p. 98, suggests that Aeclanum replaced Beneventum as 'capital', but Aeclanum may have attained importance only later (H. Nissen, *Ital. Landesk.* II, 817). Steph. Byz. s.v. 'Aikalon' may not refer to it.

[4] A. Afzelius, *Röm. Eroberung Italiens*, p. 59, thinks that this happened only after the Second Punic War. But the references to the Caudine towns during that war suggest that it had already happened. A unique bronze coin, with the legend *Tedis* or *Telis* (Vetter, p. 136), may belong to 'independent' Telesia. Caiatia and Cubulteria certainly issued bronze coins and therefore enjoyed 'independence' for a time.

In fact it disappears from history until the age of Augustus, unlike the other Caudine towns not even being mentioned in the Second Punic War. Presumably it was now (*c.* 270) annexed by Rome with *civitas sine suffragio*.[1] From this time on the Caudini, like the Hirpini, are rarely referred to under the general name of Samnites; but, unlike the Hirpini, they are also not often called by their tribal name either. It becomes the rule for each Caudine community to be called after the name of its town, and in the later Augustan subdivision of Italy all of these towns belonged to 'Latium and Campania' (Region I), not 'Samnium' (Region IV). The Romans were evidently determined not only to smash the tribal state of the Caudini but also to eradicate for ever their sense of tribal solidarity with their kinsmen further east.

The Pentri were obliged to cede territory on their western frontier. Allifae became a Roman *praefectura* and simultaneously perhaps Venafrum and Aquilonia were also annexed with the same status. Aesernia, assuming it to have been Pentrian and not Caracenan, became a Latin Colony (263).[2]

The Caraceni, for their part, lost Aufidena, which was annexed by Rome.[3] This, on top of their past tribulations, may have brought the separate political existence of the Caraceni to an end;[4] they never appear again as even nominally independent or autonomous. Some of them may have been annexed by the Frentani (at any rate 'Caretini' appear among the latter in Augustus' day).[5] Many of them that were left, however, seem to have merged with the Pentri. Certain it is that from now on whenever the term Samnites is used in the sense of 'dwellers in Samnium' it normally means the Pentri. It was they, not the Hirpini or Caudini, who were later included in Region IV, the region unofficially known as 'Samnium' in the Augustan subdivision of Italy. The colonization of Aesernia and annexation of Aufidena severed them from Sabellic Central Italy. They were now almost completely isolated.

[1] K. J. Beloch, *Röm. Gesch.* p. 472, argues that its quattuorviral type of constitution indicates that it remained a *civitas foederata* down to the Social War. This is not necessarily so: see A. Degrassi in *Mem. dei Lincei*, ser. 8, II (1949), 281–344.

[2] Allifae and Venafrum: Festus, p. 262 L. Both towns belonged to the tribe Teretina. About Aquilonia there is no information.

[3] Archaeological evidence shows that the Samnite character of Aufidena ended in the third century (L. Mariani in *Mon. Antichi*, X (1901), 403 f.). Under the Roman Republic the town was a *praefectura* (*CIL*, IX, 2802, which is earlier than Sulla).

[4] See Dion. Hal. 20. 17.

[5] Pliny, *N.H.* 3. 106. Caracenan Cluviae (Tac. *Hist.* 4. 5) likewise is in Arnensis, the tribe of the Frentani, not in Voltinia, the tribe of the Samnites (*ILS*, 993).

As an additional precaution against any future attempt by the Samnites to renew hostilities the Romans probably also obliged them to dismantle fortifications in various parts of Samnium and to transfer to less defensible sites some of the 'hilly positions accessible only via long trails, that are not even used by men, but are mere goat-tracks through the woods and crags'.[1] Telesia seems to have been unwalled in Hannibal's day;[2] the later Roman town had certainly descended from the Monte Acero. Aeclanum of the Hirpini had only wooden palisades at the time of the Social War.[3] In Roman days Saepinum was on much lower ground, and Bovianum too had come down from its eyrie. These developments may not have been due entirely to orders from Rome. Later in Gaul some settlements left the hilltops of their own accord when the *pax Romana* made it safe for them to do so.[4] This may have been equally true of Samnium. Settled conditions rather than Roman fiat may have brought Allifae down from the Monte Cila or induced Venafrum to descend to a lower level. Yet it is certain that some thirty years after the Pyrrhic War Roman force was needed to make the Falisci leave their elevated site and settle in the plain.[5] *Dirue Maurorum attegias, castella Brigantum*, as Juvenal later was to say.[6] Hence it is quite likely that the Romans may have enforced some changes of this kind in Samnium *c.* 270.[7]

After the Pyrrhic War the Samnite League clearly ceased to exist. Hirpini, Pentri and the individual Caudine towns were sundered from one another and they now became 'allies' of Rome and separate members of her so-called confederacy in Italy. They accepted their role unwillingly, but they had no choice. The great Samnite Wars were over, and further resistance was futile. It has been calculated that Samnium had lost more than half the territory with which it had begun the struggle with Rome about three-quarters of a century

[1] Dion. Hal. 20. 11. 1.

[2] Livy 22. 13. 1. In the corresponding passage, Polyb. 3. 90. 8 mentions 'wall-less Venusia'; which has been plausibly emended to Telesia. Reject the suggestion of H. Nissen, *Ital. Landesk.* II, 802, that Polyb. is referring to an otherwise unknown Venusia near Telesia.

[3] App. *B.C.* 1. 51. 222.

[4] See *ILS*, 6092 (a Spanish town that requested permission to move to the plain); and cf. N. J. De Witt, *Urbanization and the Franchise in Roman Gaul*, pp. 18 f. When disturbed conditions developed in medieval times, the towns showed a disposition to return to the heights (A. von Hofmann, *Land Italien und seine Geschichte*, pp. 331 f.).

[5] The Falisci moved from Civita Castellana to S. Maria di Falleri. For other examples, see Appian, *Hisp.* 44; Florus 1. 19. 4 f.; 2. 33. 59; and above all Livy 40. 38. 4; 40. 53. 3.

[6] Juvenal 14. 196.

[7] The original site often bears the name Civita in present-day Italy.

earlier.[1] Now no longer an Italian great power, it had been broken up into a number of isolated states, which in size and strength were not significantly different from the other 'allies' of Rome. Moreover Beneventum and Aesernia, the two most important communication centres in all Samnium, had been added to the number of Latin Colonies cribbing and confining the Samnites. Henceforth the Samnites might dream of their lost liberty, they might hate Rome,[2] and many of them, late in the third century, might join Hannibal. But it would be all to no avail. Along with the other peoples of peninsular Italy they were to remain browbeaten and dominated until the Social War.

[1] Cf. Livy 31. 10. 10 and see the calculations of G. De Sanctis, *Stor. dei Rom.* II, 421, and A. Afzelius, *Röm. Eroberung Italiens*, pp. 186 f.: the latter relies heavily on Beloch, whose calculations are little better than guesses.

[2] They had good reason to hate a Rome that had broken the treaty of 354, had repeatedly devastated their homeland, had confiscated much of their territory (including much good agricultural land) and had dissolved their League.

CHAPTER 9

ROMAN DOMINATION

Between 270 and 220 Roman leadership in Italy was not seriously challenged, the revolts of the Caraceni (269) and Falisci (242) being isolated, short-lived and abortive. This was the period when the Romans consolidated their hegemony, accustomed even the most recalcitrant of their Italian Allies to their domination, and through their victory in the First Punic War became a leading power in the Central Mediterranean. It was also the period during which, as we are specifically told,[1] the Samnites lived at peace.

How the Romans comported themselves inside Italy during this half century is not described in detail in the surviving ancient texts, although it is evident that they had recourse to pro-Roman local regimes of a distinctly oligarchical flavour. They established cliques at Nola, at Croton, in fact everywhere (*omnes Italiae civitates*). Even among the Samnites they must have seen to it that so far as possible the power-wielding aristocracies in the various tribes were from their point of view reliable. At any rate, at Compsa, the probable 'capital' of the Hirpini, the house of Statius Trebius had ceased by 216 to be the most prominent clan, having been outstripped by the Mopsii, *familia per gratiam Romanorum potens*, calculating opportunists of the type of the unsavoury Pacuvius Calavius at Capua.[2]

Local time-servers, however, were not the only instrument that the Romans employed for maintaining their supremacy. Enforcement of law and order throughout the peninsula also played a part. By putting an end to intertribal wars they brought Italy to a state of

[1] Polyb. 3. 90. 7 and Livy 23. 42. 3, both of whom are referring to conditions inside Italy. The extent of Samnite involvement outside Italy (viz. in the First Punic War) is not recorded. Zon. 8. 11 says that a large number of Samnites intended for service with the fleet in 259 plotted the destruction of Rome with some captives. 'Samnites' here means 'Sabellians': their commander Herius Potilius, a pro-Roman and presumably an aristocrat, bears a distinctly Oscan name. The men referred to could not have come from land-locked Samnium but from coastal Campania, Nuceria perhaps. Oros. 4. 7. 12, in fact, identifies them as 4,000 *socii navales*.

[2] Livy 23. 1. 2; 23. 2. 2 f.; 23. 14. 7; 24. 13. 8. At Volsinii in 265 the Romans nipped in the bud a 'popular' movement that had some Samnite support (Zon. 8. 7: on this see now R. Enking in *R.E.* IX A (1961), s.v. 'Volsinii', col. 843). Diod. 26. 10 calls the pro-Roman nominee at Capua Pancylus Paucus.

material well-being such as it had never known and thereby diminished restiveness among its inhabitants. Even the Samnites were enjoying unparalleled prosperity when Hannibal arrived in their midst late in the third century.[1]

To what extent the Romans succeeded in creating a pan-Italian patriotism cannot be decided. There was evidently some,[2] since the hostility of the Italians towards invaders of the peninsula seems to have transcended their resentment of the supremacy of the Romans. When the Gallic menace assumed sudden and alarming proportions in 225 the Romans were able successfully to muster various peoples of the peninsula for its defence. The forces at their disposal on that occasion, quickly mobilizable if not in actual being, were carefully surveyed by the censors and are listed by the father of Roman history Fabius Pictor, who probably obtained the figures from the state archives and certainly bequeathed them to Polybius.[3] These figures, if accurate,[4] are of the greatest interest. They reveal that in the last quarter of the third century the Samnites collectively were easily the strongest non-Latin allies which the Romans had in Italy. In fact their military potential was almost identical with that of all the then-existing Latin Colonies put together: 70,000 infantry and 7,000 cavalry, as against 80,000 infantry and 5,000 cavalry.[5]

If such was Samnite strength in 225, by which time they had lost at least half the territory and a correspondingly large proportion of the population which they had had in 343, it is not surprising that they were so redoubtable in their heyday.

Much more surprising is the inclusion of the Samnites, proverbial for their readiness to rebel against Roman authority,[6] in the list of Allies upon whom Rome could rely in 225. Their hatred of the alien

[1] *Felixne populus cuius nulla historia?*

[2] See such passages as Livy 23. 5. 11; 24. 47. 5.

[3] Polyb. 2. 24; Livy, *Epit.* 20; Diod. 25. 13; Pliny, *N.H.* 3. 138; Eutrop. 3. 5; Oros. 4. 13.

[4] Fabius Pictor may, of course, have deliberately inflated the figures, and the degree of Italian solidarity, in order to impress the Greek-reading public he was aiming at.

[5] Polybius' roster is not a complete one. It contains no mention of the north Italian cavalry, the Picentes, the Paeligni, the Bruttii, or the Italiotes (the latter being *socii navales* would be out of place in an army list). The roster is not a list of states, but of peoples: Etruscan and Sabine communities are not individually listed, nor are the separate Samnite tribal states. Hence his total for the Samnites in 225 covers all the tribes of Samnium, including the Hirpini, whom later in his History (beginning at 3. 91. 9) he is inclined to regard as a distinct people. K. J. Beloch (*Ital. Bund*, p. 98), however, can hardly be right in arguing that Polybius also includes Sidicini and Southern Campanians in his total for the Samnites.

[6] See, for instance, Livy 31. 7. 12.

Celtic intruders in Italy hardly accounts for this, since they had enthusiastically welcomed the *tumultus Gallicus* of 299 and had not hesitated at that time to range themselves alongside the Gauls in the fight against Rome.[1] For that matter they do not seem actually to have fielded forces against the Gauls in 225. Their presence at Telamon is not attested (it was north Italians who were at the Romans' side there).[2] In fact they were able entirely to escape war inside Italy in the period between Pyrrhus and Hannibal. If the Samnites did not ally themselves with the Gauls in 225, it was probably not so much out of pan-Italian patriotism as out of doubt about the outcome. The year 269 had revealed the dangers in any isolated defiance of Rome, and, unless the Boii, Insubres, Gaesati and Taurini penetrated into Southern Italy in 225, it was the course of prudence for the Samnites to make no anti-Roman move. Telamon justified their wariness.

When, shortly after 225, another alien invader appeared in Italy, the Samnites again displayed a careful, if not altogether characteristic, caution. They did not rush to join Hannibal as they had rushed to join Pyrrhus.

The great Carthaginian, however, counted on getting their support. His planned strategy was not to make a frontal assault on, or siege of, Rome itself, since that stronghold was impregnable to the means at his disposal. He intended to reduce Rome to impotence by inducing the Italians to renounce their alliances with her:[3] once isolated and alone, Rome would be forced to make peace on his terms. Accordingly Hannibal treated as gently as he could the 40,000 infantry and 4,000 cavalry which the Italians, including presumably the Samnites, had supplied to Rome's northern armies in 218 and 217.[4]

After his early victories at the Ticinus, Trebia and Trasimene, Hannibal at once headed for those parts of the peninsula where prospects seemed best for raising opposition to Rome, the Oscan-speaking districts. His route took him from Lake Trasimene to the Via Flaminia and thence eastwards through the Apennines to the

[1] They had also jumped at the opportunity which the Gauls presented for challenging Roman power in 284. According to Livy (23. 42. 6), they did not regard the Gauls as intruders: he makes their spokesmen say that Pyrrhus was the only *external* ally they had ever had until Hannibal.

[2] See F. W. Walbank, *Commentary on Polybius*, I, 197 f.

[3] And many Italians found the Roman hegemony burdensome (Livy 23. 43. 11).

[4] Livy 21. 17. 3.

Adriatic coast. After resting his men and replenishing his supplies in Picenum he made his way through the peoples living on the Adriatic (the Praetuttii, the Latin Colonists at Hadria, the Marrucini and the Frentani), and reached northern Apulia.[1] Undoubtedly his hope was to provoke defections from Rome either by his mere presence or by spreading alarm and despondency. In this he signally failed: not a single Italian community threw in its lot with him.[2] They may not have had much love for Rome, but they found it hard to believe that an utterly alien invader from overseas was going to redress their grievances. Some of them, whose defences were inadequate, may even have obeyed the instruction of the Roman senate to 'scorch the earth' and transfer their populations elsewhere.[3] There is no record of Samnite communities taking this desperate step, although many of them, thanks to Rome, must at this time have had very makeshift defences indeed. It is equally true that there is no record of Samnite communities going over to Hannibal at this time.

Samnium, however, was a region of which Hannibal had high hopes, and he now put it to the test. He moved from the vicinity of Arpi into the territory of the Hirpini.[4] He plundered and lived off the country as he went, but once amongst the Hirpini he sought to win their favour by ravaging the territory of Beneventum, the Latin Colony in their midst.[5] He failed, however, to win them over; so he headed for other Sabellian districts by way of the valleys of the Calor and Volturnus.[6] At Allifae, by now almost certainly a Roman *praefectura*, two possibilities lay open to him: he could advance into the Pentri or into the Campani. His choice of the latter almost proved fatal. After moving westward past the Caudine settlements

[1] Polyb. 3. 86–8. The account in Livy 22. 9 is very confusing. Hannibal assaults Spoletium without success (cf. Zon. 8. 25), then goes (on 'a curiously zig-zag route': Walbank, *Commentary on Polyb.* I, 423) to Picenum, the Praetuttii, Hadria, the Marsi, the Marrucini, the Paeligni. How he reached Northern Apulia from the Paeligni Livy does not say: evidently not by Eastern Samnium (Polyb. 3. 90. 7).

[2] Polyb. 3. 90. 13.

[3] Livy 22. 11. 4 f. Livy's statement (22. 18. 7) that Gerunium, situated somewhere in Northern Apulia, did so is disproved by Polyb. 3. 100.

[4] Livy 22. 13. 1 (emending *Hirpinis* to *Arpinis*: G. Grasso, *Studi di Geografia Classica e di Topografia Storica*, pp. 1 f.).

[5] Polyb. 3. 90. 7; Pliny, *N.H.* 3. 105.

[6] Polyb. 3. 90. 8 brings him from Beneventane territory to 'unwalled Venusia': Livy 22. 13. 1 corrects this to 'Telesia' and may well be right (A. Klotz in *Rhein. Mus.* LXXXV (1936), 103): this could be a lower, but still Samnite (Livy 24. 20. 3 f.) Telesia brought down to somewhere near the site of the later Roman Telesia.

on the Monti Trebulani he swung south-westward and reached the Campus Stellatis at the eastern end of the Ager Falernus. Here the Roman dictator Q. Fabius Maximus, the famed Cunctator, almost trapped him. Hannibal saved himself only by resort to the famous ruse of driving into the encircling gloom a herd of 2,000 oxen with burning faggots attached to their horns that both bewildered and frightened the Romans.

So far Hannibal had clearly not succeeded in winning the peninsular peoples over to his side. This was true of the speakers of Oscan no less than of the speakers of Latin. In fact it was from bases in Samnium that the Romans had mounted part of the operation that came within an ace of succeeding in the Campus Stellatis.[1]

Hannibal now made for Northern Apulia, his plan being to store his booty and pass the winter in Gerunium.[2] His route took him straight across Samnium by way of the Vinchiaturo Gap and Campobasso, and the passage of his army must have been a singularly unpleasant experience for the Pentri.[3]

Thus, during 217, the Samnite tribes felt the weight of Hannibal's mailed fist more than once, perhaps because he wished to convince them that Rome was abandoning them to his none too tender mercies. But, even though put to so severe a test, their alliances with Rome still stood the strain[4] and it was precisely they, late in the year, who inflicted the first military setback upon the Carthaginian. The opportune appearance near Gerunium of 8,000 Samnite infantry and 500 cavalry under the Pentrian Numerius Decimius of Bovianum rescued Fabius' obstreperous master of the horse, M. Minucius Rufus, from disaster. On this occasion Hannibal was forced to withdraw with some loss. The major role of Numerius Decimius in this episode was not recognized in some of the sources known to Livy,[5] but can be accepted as certain. Pro-Roman writers were seldom willing to give credit where credit was due to Samnites. Polybius records the incident, but not very surprisingly suppresses all mention

[1] Livy 22. 16. 4.

[2] Gerunium was not far from modern Casacalenda.

[3] See Polyb. 3. 100. 2 with Walbank's comments: his Λίβυρνον ὄρος must be the Mons Tifernus. Livy 22. 18. 6 f. sends Hannibal on a long detour via the Paeligni; but his words (*tum per Samnium Romam se petere simulans*) show that he is confusing Hannibal's march in 217 with his march in 211 when he did go through the Paeligni (Livy 26. 11. 11).

[4] *nec tamen is terror cum omnia bello flagrarent fide socios amovit* (Livy 22. 13. 11).

[5] Livy 22. 24. 11 f.

of the Samnites' part.[1] Livy, more generously, was willing to admit, and even to boast with some emphasis, that down to 216 the loyalty of the Italian Allies was unshakable.[2]

It was the fatal field of Cannae that caused Italians, whole communities as well as individuals, to desert Rome for Hannibal.[3] Capua, of course, is the most notorious rebel, but Capua was not alone. Some Italians had anticipated the Campani in repudiating their alliances with Rome; others followed the Campanian example. Samnites, Lucani, Bruttii, Apuli and Italiotes all seceded, although not simultaneously. To what extent they actually gave service to Hannibal is a moot point. The terms of the agreement between Capua and Hannibal suggest that their support was minimal. That agreement stipulated that no Carthaginian official, military or civil, should have any authority over any Capuan, that no Capuan should serve as a soldier or in any other capacity against his will, and that Capua should have its own constitution.[4] This sounds more like pro-Carthaginian non-belligerency than a genuine fighting alliance. Nor is there any reason to think that Hannibal obtained better terms from other Italians than he did from Capua: he dared not attempt to constrain them, and, even if he had dared, the Bruttii and possibly the Lucani were the only ones completely at his mercy.[5] Thus, even though Hannibal could expect comfort from those who rebelled against Rome, he could expect very little else. They were not anxious to rid themselves of one overlord in order to submit to another, and an utterly alien one at that. It was with mixed feelings that they availed themselves of his help to get rid of their Roman masters, but they were content to let him undertake the task of eliminating the Roman threat once and for all. And, ominously for

[1] Polyb. 3. 105. 5 f. Polybius was never disposed to say much about Italian contributions to Roman war efforts. Note, however, his admission (3. 106. 10 f.) that he has omitted many details about the encounters with the Carthaginians in 217.

[2] *fides sociorum, quae ad eam diem firma steterat, tum labare coepit, nulla profecto alia de re quam quod desperaverant de imperio* (Livy 22. 61. 10).

[3] The Samnite role at Cannae is not recorded in the ancient sources, which merely reveal that the Italian troops that fought at the side of Rome in the battle included Sabellians (Livy 22. 45. 7; 23. 15–16; Plut. *Marc.* 10. 2; cf. Sil. Ital. 9. 270; 10. 314).

[4] Livy 23. 7. 1 f. The Campani after 343 would be particularly aware that external aid did not necessarily mean the preservation of local liberty. The Campanians who sided with Capua were Atella, Calatia and the Sabatini (Livy 26. 16. 5; 26. 33. 12). The town of the latter may have been Velecha, whose coins at this period were similar in all respects to those of Capua, Atella and Calatia. (The site of Velecha is unknown. It may have been the same town as Volcei: R. Thomsen, *Early Roman Coinage*, II, 120 f.)

[5] Livy 24. 15. 2 makes this clear.

him, there were some who would not go even that far: the total elimination of Rome might expose the peninsula to other dangers, possibly Carthaginian in origin.

The Samnites who rebelled were the Hirpini and Caudini.[1] The Pentri did not;[2] and even amongst the Caudini there were those who stood by Rome: the town of Caiatia did not join Hannibal. Other inhabitants of Southern Italy also remained loyal: unidentified factions among the Lucani, Petelia and Consentia among the Bruttii, Canusium among the Apuli, Rhegium, Naples and other places among the Italiotes.[3] In Campania Hannibal found little support outside the League of Capua.

Perhaps these peoples were sceptical that a semi-oriental and uninvited visitor from another continent was going to settle their accounts with the Romans for them; or they may have been influenced by a shrewd appraisal of the military situation. Rome had lost a battle, in fact several battles, but she had not yet lost the war; the surviving consul did not despair of the Republic. She still had control of the seas, and no stream of supplies and reinforcements was going to reach Hannibal with any degree of regularity. In Italy he could not be everywhere at once, whereas the Romans seemingly could be: there were tracts of Ager Romanus, or *municipia*, or Citizen Colonies, or Latin Colonies, or non-rebellious Italian allies everywhere. Even if the Italians who defected from Rome had been eager to supply Hannibal with additional forces, they could hardly dare to do so: all had to nurse their military strength against the day when Rome would try to compel them to return to alliances. Hannibal, for his part, could scarcely demand reinforcements from them, since that would alienate all prospective adherents to his cause in Italy. All he could do was protect them, if possible, from Roman reprisals.

Many Italians appreciated the situation correctly and refused to

[1] See Livy 22. 61. 10. A. J. Toynbee, *Hannibal's Legacy*, II, 21 f., 32, argues that the Caudini were not wantonly secessionist, but were obliged to join Hannibal through sheer inability to resist.

[2] As noted above (p. 290), the Caraceni had probably been absorbed by either the Pentri or the Frentani, both of which tribes stood by Rome. There is no evidence referring unmistakably to Caraceni in the Second Punic War. The Sabellian town Fugifulae that joined Hannibal (Livy 24. 20. 5) can hardly have been Fagifulae, but rather an otherwise unknown *oppidum* of or near the Lucani. Fagifulae, securely located at S. Maria a Faifoli just west of Montagano (H. Nissen, *Ital. Landesk.* II, 792), seems to have been *in Pentris*.

[3] Livy 22. 52–4; 23. 14. 13; 23. 20. 4; 25. 16. 6. Polyb. 7. 1. 3 describes how Petelia held out against Hannibal until reduced to starvation, whereupon Rome authorized its surrender. Consentia also proved unable to hold out against Hannibal indefinitely (Livy 23. 30. 5).

desert Rome, even after Cannae. Not that their continued support received much recognition in later Roman literature. The loyalty of the Pentri is mentioned by Livy in only the briefest and most casual fashion, and is otherwise left unnoticed. Silius Italicus stigmatizes all the Samnites indiscriminately as enthusiastic rebels after Cannae. Even today the Pentrian action is generally overlooked.[1] Yet it must have been of crucial importance.

During the rest of the Second Punic War the Samnites suffered grievously. The Pentri were liable to be attacked by Hannibal. The others were liable to be attacked by both sides, since the Romans were bent upon punishing all rebels and forcing them back to obedience, while Hannibal finally adopted the policy of destroying towns that he could no longer defend.[2]

The Romans began to move against the rebels as early as 215 when the praetor *peregrinus* M. Valerius Laevinus recovered two obscure hamlets, Vescellium and Sicilinum, from the Hirpini.[3] In the same year the consul *suffectus*, Q. Fabius Maximus, is said to have recovered Cubulteria, Trebula and Austicula from the Caudini.[4] Perhaps the imaginative genius of Fabian historiographers has been at work here to ensure that in that year the consul Fabius should not be outdone by the praetor Valerius. Unlike the latter, Fabius is credited with capturing, not obscure hamlets but relatively well-known towns. Since, however, the evidence suggests that the Roman recovery of Cubulteria belongs to 214 and not to 215, the probability is that its near neighbour Trebula also did not fall until then. This would leave only the otherwise unknown Austicula as the sum total of Fabius's achievements in 215.

The proconsul M. Claudius Marcellus, the successful defender of Nola, also wreaked havoc and destruction on the Samnite rebels in

[1] Livy 22. 61. 10; Sil. Ital. 11. 8. B. L. Hallward in *Cambr. Anc. Hist.* VIII, 55; F. W. Walbank, *Commentary on Polybius*, I, 746, number the Pentri among the defectors from Rome.

[2] See Diod. 27. 9; cf. Polyb. 9. 26. 4. Hannibal himself bragged that he had destroyed 400 Italian towns (App. *Libyca*, 63; cf. 134; *Syriaca*, 10).

[3] Livy 23. 37. 12 says that the praetor recovered three towns, Vercellium, Vescellium and Sicilinum. These names occur nowhere else, unless Pliny, *N.H.* 3. 105, is alluding to Vescellium. It and Vercellium look like mere doublets of one another. Valerius Antias may be responsible for this account of Valerius Laevinus' exploits.

[4] Livy 23. 39. 6 (emending *Trebianum*). Austicula is otherwise unknown. It probably is not a misprint for Saticula. This type of name is not unparalleled in this part of Italy (cf. Mons Callicula). Perhaps Austicula was a village on the territory of Trebula (so H. Nissen, *Ital. Landesk.* II, 801): it could be Castellone, which is certainly both a very strong and a very ancient site.

215. The account of his exploits almost certainly contains much exaggeration, although there is no need to doubt Livy's assertion that when he recovered a town he punished it severely.[1]

In the next year Marcellus and Fabius were consuls, and the Carthaginian hold on Campania was permanently broken. The stage was set for the recovery of the still rebellious parts of Samnium and eventually of Capua as well. Caudine Cubulteria and Telesia were both recovered, so was Hirpinian Compsa, and along with these towns the otherwise unknown *oppidum* Orbitanium and a town called Fugifulae. The latter two may have been Lucanian rather than Samnite.[2]

No operations against Samnites are recorded for 213, but it must have been in that year that the mopping-up of the Caudine towns was successfully completed. For in the following year the Romans were able to mount the operation for the recovery of Capua, which they did by crossing Caudine territory, apparently unresisted, from an assembly area near Bovianum Pentrorum.[3] Throughout 212 the Romans concentrated troops in Campania and drew their siege lines tighter around Capua, without Hannibal being able effectively to intervene. By year's end the city was closely invested.

In 211 Hannibal made his famous attempt to relieve the pressure on Capua by marching on Rome. His route is a matter of dispute but he certainly passed through the Pentri, destroying and devastating as he went.[4] On his withdrawal from Rome he must once again have tramped over some part of Pentrian territory. His manœuvre failed in its object, and before the end of the year Capua had capitulated to the Romans. Its dependencies, Atella and Calatia, quickly followed suit.[5]

It was now the turn of the Hirpini. Those who dwelt in the valley of the River Sabatus south of Beneventum had surrendered at about the same time as Capua.[6] The subjugation of the rest was methodically undertaken in 210 by M. Claudius Marcellus, now consul for the fourth time. Near the border of Apulia he captured two obscure Samnite *oppida*, Marmoreae and Meles, which Hannibal had converted into provisions dumps, and to do so had to penetrate deep into Hirpinian territory. He ravaged and destroyed as he went.[7] In

[1] See G. De Sanctis, *Stor. dei Romani*, III, 2, 235 n. 47; Livy 23. 37. 12.

[2] Livy 24. 20. 5: he places Orbitanium in Lucania (and probably Fugifulae also), and he obviously believes that the reconquest of Lucania began in that year.

[3] Livy 25. 13. 8.

[4] E. T. Salmon in *Phoenix*, XI (1957), 153–63.

[5] Livy 26. 16. 5.

[6] Livy 26. 33. 12; 26. 34. 6.

[7] Livy 27. 1. 15; 27. 2. 4; Plut. *Marc.* 24. 3.

the next year the Hirpini surrendered to the consul Q. Fulvius Flaccus, the recoverer of Capua, treacherously betraying to him the garrisons that Hannibal had left in their midst. The Lucani behaved similarly and ultimately so did the Bruttii.

Thus the Samnite rebels had been forced back into the Roman camp and thenceforth disappear from the annals of the Second Punic War. Not that Samnium now found peace. Samnite (i.e. Pentrian) troops continued to see action.[1] We know that in 207 Quintus Claudius, the Roman propraetor commanding at Tarentum, entrusted two troops of their cavalry with the task of conducting to the consul C. Claudius Nero near Canusium the messengers who had been sent by Hasdrubal but had been captured before they could reach Hannibal.[2] Samnites were selected for this escort duty since the route to Claudius Nero's headquarters ran through Oscan-speaking country. This incident closes the surviving record of the Samnites in the Second Punic War.[3]

The restoration of peace brought its reckoning with it. The Romans meted out punishment to those Italians who had sided with Hannibal, and Livy suggests that a regular reign of terror ensued, in which persons accused of collaboration with Hannibal were ruthlessly liquidated. Undoubtedly any Samnites who had given aid and comfort to the Carthaginian invader were made to pay dearly. A decemviral board appointed by the praetor for 201 came into their midst and they were deprived of territory, or had wartime seizures of their territory confirmed, to make provision for veterans who had fought against Hannibal, especially Scipio's.[4]

The Hirpini, a large and populous tribe, even after such deprivations of territory still managed to maintain some kind of separate, tribal existence. But they lost some important areas: Gracchan terminal stones have been found near Abellinum on what was once Hirpinian territory and indicate that Rome had acquired valuable *ager publicus* there.[5]

[1] The ex-rebels among them were probably used in menial capacities, as were the Bruttii and Lucani (Strabo 5. 4. 13, p. 251).

[2] Livy 27. 43. 5.

[3] Samnites are not listed amongst those who contributed men or materials to Scipio's North African expeditionary force (Livy 28. 45. 13 f.).

[4] Livy 30. 24. 4; 31. 4. 1 f.; 31. 8. 11. Each veteran received two *iugera* for every year of service (Livy 31. 49. 5).

[5] Degrassi, *ILLRP*, I, 473; Cic. *de lege agr.* 3. 8, 9 suggests the same thing.

The Caudini were in much worse case. Their tribal state had been broken up long before and replaced by a number of separate boroughs. These now seem to have lost whatever autonomy had still remained to them. They were annexed, so it would seem, and turned into Roman *praefecturae*, and the proximity of Roman colonists led to their rapid romanization.[1]

Nothing is anywhere recorded about favours to the Pentri for their loyalty. They remained a tribal state, technically independent and allied to Rome. Rome expected obedience from her Allies; she did not reward it.

The new order of things in Samnium meant that contacts between Pentri and Hirpini now became more difficult than ever. Ever since 268, when the intrusive Latin Colony at Beneventum split the two tribes apart, communication between them had been impeded. Henceforth the obstructions were even greater. Nevertheless subsequent events were to prove that the two tribes still maintained community of feeling and outlook, so that they must have found ways and means for keeping in contact with one another. In particular, they evidently shared to the full one another's dislike for Rome and her masterful ways.

Both Pentri and Hirpini were *socii* of Rome: that is, they were members of a military alliance, usually but inaccurately called a confederacy, which the mistress of peninsular Italy had organized. It is uncertain whether actual treaties of alliance between them and Rome had been formally drawn up and committed to writing. If they had been, they could scarcely have been described officially as *foedera iniqua*, since such a term seems too derogatory for public use. This, however, does not disguise the fact that, relative to Rome, the Samnites were in a position of marked inferiority.[2]

[1] Perhaps it was now that Telesia (and the other Caudine towns) became 'Roman'. Certainly it obtained a colony later, if not in Gracchan times (K. J. Beloch, *Röm. Gesch.* pp. 493–6) then under Sulla or the Triumvirs. *CIL*, IX, 2277, from *Roman* Telesia, is sometimes adduced as evidence that the place remained peregrine down to the Social War, since it seems to reveal a chief magistrate of Telesia, whose filiation lacks his father's *praenomen*. But a Roman filiation did not invariably show the father's *praenomen*: see, for example, Cic. *Brutus*, 72 (*C. Claudius Caeci f.*). Caiatia was certainly 'Roman' in the second century (*ILS*, 5742), but its status may not be conclusive for other Caudine towns, since it had not revolted to Hannibal.

[2] The treaty with Aetolia of 189 (Polyb. 21. 32. 2 f.; Livy 38. 11. 2 f.) may be a typical *foedus iniquum*, although neither it nor any other alliance is so described in ancient literature. E. Badian, *For. Client.* p. 26, must be right in thinking that treaties would not be so described in official documents. *In dicione populi Romani*, the expression used of the Apulian Teates much earlier by Livy (9. 20. 8, = 317), was another way of putting it.

Owing to the exigencies of the Second Punic War Rome, as the directing power in that struggle, had gradually acquired the position of the acknowledged leader whose slightest wish was a command. More than ever before Rome made the decisions that affected peninsular Italy: Polybius, indeed, avers that she could even interfere directly in the private life of an individual anywhere in Italy.[1] In effect, no matter what the legal theory might be about sovereign Italian states independent of Rome, Rome ruled Italy; and this was palpably clear to contemporaries.[2] During the Second Punic War her assumption of the right to do what she thought best anywhere in the peninsula could scarcely be challenged owing to the presence and pressure of the Carthaginian invader on Italian soil. After the war Rome simply continued to give orders. It is quite likely that the nature of her relations with the various Italian states made such an assumption of power on her part very easy. Italy, after all, was not really organized as a confederacy: there was no confederate council to decide on policy.[3] The so-called Roman Confederacy was a system of bilateral agreements between Rome and individual Italian states. Italy resembled a conglomerate much more than a confederacy. The agreements seem to have clearly specified Rome's right to demand troops of each ally. But it is by no means certain that her rights against each ally in other respects were always clearly defined or everywhere the same. If such vagueness existed, then in the second century it could not have been easy to decide whether Rome was or was not, on any given occasion, exceeding her legal powers; and, where there was any doubt, her decision on the point in question had to be accepted as that of the stronger partner. Whatever the explanation, Rome did rule Italy. The most that she allowed

[1] Polyb. 6. 13. 5.

[2] Note the casual way that Apulia is called *terra nostra* by Plautus, *Casina*, 72. See, too, such passages as Livy 30. 30. 6 f. (= 202), and 33. 40. 2 (= 196); both are unhistorical but are accurate enough in depicting the state of affairs. Rome's refusal to let Italian states mint silver once she herself had started to do so is conclusive.

[3] The lack of a confederate diet could not have been due to oversight, since there had been proposals on at least two occasions before 200 for the enrolment of non-Romans into the Roman senate (Livy 8. 5. 5, = 350; 23. 22. 5, = 216). Italy was not even organized into a League of the type found in the Greek and Sabellian worlds. J. A. O. Larsen, *Representative Government*, p. 159, points out that there were no representative institutions in the Roman 'confederacy' and that Rome permitted her Allies less freedom than Athens and Sparta had allowed theirs. See, too, M. Gelzer in *Gnomon*, XVII (1941), 147. P. Fraccaro, *Opuscula*, I, 111 f., aptly describes second-century Italy as a *stato unitario, pseudo-federativo.*

her allies was administrative autonomy.[1] And once she had assumed such power, she was not proof against its corruptions. After 200 she behaved with an arrogance that she took less and less trouble to conceal. She issued the orders in Italy, and did so without much reference to her Italian Allies, least of all to the Samnites among them.

The Italian Allies had the duty of supplying troops, *ex formula togatorum*, to serve alongside those of Rome in any operation which Rome might see fit to undertake. This, in fact, was their chief duty as Allies; and Polybius leaves one with the impression that in Roman eyes the principal, if not indeed the only, value of the Allies was the military contribution they could make.[2] In practice this meant that Samnites and others had the privilege of fighting, and dying, in wars not of their own choosing and not necessarily in or even near Italy or on its behalf, although the Romans no doubt were always ready to claim that the campaigns were in defence of the peninsula. Indeed very soon after the Second Punic War, in 193 to be precise, Rome, unilaterally so far as we know, altered the formula which up till then had prescribed what quotas of troops her Italian Allies should supply. Henceforth each Italian state, instead of supplying a fixed number of troops, was to contribute soldiers according to the number of its men that were of military age. This has been interpreted as a concession to reality by Rome: the Italian states had lost population and therefore would be unable to supply the fixed totals hitherto prescribed for them.[3] In other words we are invited to believe that the purpose of the change was to permit the Allies to reduce the number of troops they supplied.

The sad truth would appear to be exactly the opposite. The new arrangement was merely a device for regularizing the larger numbers which Rome had been imposing for some years.[4] Henceforth the

[1] There was no 'confederate procedure' (A. H. McDonald in *Camb. Hist. Journ.* VI (1939), 145; *J.R.S.* XXXIV (1944), 11). The most that Rome allowed her allies was some administrative autonomy, and it is problematic how real this was. It is significant that Cumae thought it necessary in 180 to get Roman permission to change its official language to Latin (Livy 40. 42. 13).

[2] Polyb. 6. 21. 4; 26. 5–7; 31. 9. The expression *ex formula togatorum* was applied only to Italians (Lex Agraria of 111): it has an antique flavour but its exact meaning is uncertain.

[3] Livy 34. 56. 5 f. See T. Frank in *Camb. Anc. Hist.* VIII, 355; A. H. McDonald in *Camb. Hist. Journ.* VI (1939), 126; A. J. Toynbee, *Hannibal's Legacy*, II, 130, n. 2 (who thinks that it was an 'emergency measure' carried out on a single occasion by a Roman official trying to put Rome on to an 'equitable course').

[4] Livy 41. 8. 8 f. makes it clear that for Paeligni and Samnites a dwindled population meant no alleviation of military burdens.

demands for men were dictated by what Rome alleged her needs to be. In effect, Rome was extending to all her Allies the treatment she had meted out to the twelve recusant Latin colonies of 209. This is stated with brutal frankness by Polybius: 'The consuls are empowered to make what demands they choose on the allies.'[1] The demands were far from moderate. Whereas in the third century the Allies supplied about 60 per cent of the effectives of the whole army, after 200 they were only too likely to supply 65 per cent or more, and meanwhile their share of the peninsula had shrunk.[2] The evidence is supplied by Livy, who is unlikely to exaggerate the Allied war effort. In 200, when war was declared on Macedon, the four praetorian armies were each composed of non-Romans, exclusively so far as our evidence goes. In 198, when reinforcements were sent to Macedon, they included 5,500 Allies and only 3,300 Romans, while other forces, in Sicily and Sardinia, were made up exclusively of non-Romans. In 197 each of the two armies in Spain, a particularly tough and unpleasant sphere of operations, was reinforced by 8,400 Allies. It became normal for Allies to outnumber Romans in the forces by two or more to one, and they were likely to be assigned to tasks that Roman soldiers found either too distasteful or too dangerous.[3]

This picture of the situation is confirmed by the well-documented reluctance, and even refusal, of Roman citizens to serve. We read of citizen resistance to military orders, including conscription, throughout the second century. Livy supplies abundant evidence for the first half of the century, and, if we are not equally well informed about the second half, it is because Livy is not extant beyond 167. Such evidence as there is, however, indicates that it was precisely in the second half of the century that citizen resistance to the levy became most obstinate. The citizens were supported, and protected, in their insubordination by the plebeian tribunes, who were prepared, if necessary, to place the consuls under arrest in order to prevent them from enrolling Romans. The evidence is clear that many citizens managed to escape service altogether; others had

[1] See Livy 27. 10. 1 and 9; Polyb. 6. 12. 6.

[2] For the respective military burdens before 200, see Polyb. 2. 24; Livy, *Epit.* 20; Diod. 25. 13.

[3] Livy 31. 8. 7; 32. 8. 2; 32. 28. 11; 37. 2. 3; 40. 18. 5; 42. 31. 3; Velleius 2. 15. 2. Moreover Allies (and not merely *socii navales*) were likely to be called upon for naval personnel as well (Livy 42. 27. 3; 42. 31. 7; 43. 12. 9).

their period of service drastically limited (to six years); all had their conditions of service greatly improved by the Leges Porciae of 195 and 184, which prevented Roman citizens in the field from being executed or even heavily flogged without the right of appeal. Allied soldiers were not similarly protected, and the surviving evidence indicates that Roman commanders showed both alacrity and ferocity when dealing with them, flogging them with cudgels instead of with vine twigs and sometimes sentencing them to death. Even the Latins among them were not immune and could be executed without appeal. It is obvious that the Roman senate was freeing Roman citizens of military burdens by assigning an increasingly heavy share to the Allies.[1]

Nor was this all. The statistics collated by Afzelius reveal that in many engagements the Allied casualties were far heavier than the Roman.[2] Of course, as Allied soldiers outnumbered the Roman, their losses were bound to be greater anyhow; but they seem to have been even larger than the Allied proportion of the army would have led one to expect. Evidently the Italians were given the dirty and dangerous tasks, to enable the Roman generals of the Republic to anticipate the Roman generals of the Empire in boasting of victories won without the shedding of Roman blood.[3] The Romans were prepared to fight to the last Italian. *Periculum facere in corpore vili* was their motto.

The Italians became, in fact, the sacrifice troops with which a Mediterranean empire was won in the second century, and it is inconceivable that they relished their role. Badian may be right in suggesting that in the third century 'the members of the alliance were welded together in sentiment by a series of wars felt to be defensive'.[4] But they could hardly have felt this about the wars of the second century. No doubt the Romans insisted that these latter wars, too, were being fought to keep prospective aggressors far away from Italian shores; but it may well be doubted whether the Italians

[1] The evidence for the avoidance of military duties by *cives Romani* is copious enough and well enough known that it need not be documented here. For maltreatment of Latins see Polyb. 6. 29; Sall. *Iug.* 69. 4; App. *Num.* fr. 3. The dates of the Leges Porciae are uncertain (G. Bloch–J. Carcopino, *Hist. Romaine*³, II, 152): there was a third one, belonging to the period 150–135 (Livy, *Epit.* 57; A. H. McDonald in *J.R.S.* XXXIV (1944), 19 f.). See, too, J. Bleicken, *Das Tribunat der klassischen Republik*, pp. 102–5, and L. R. Taylor in *J.R.S.* LII (1962), 21, 26 f.

[2] *Röm. Kriegsmacht 200–167*, pp. 74 f.

[3] Tac. *Agr.* 35.

[4] *Foreign Clientelae*, p. 30.

viewed them in this light. They must have regarded them as Roman imperialist wars of conquest. And there is not the slightest doubt that Roman monopolization of the fruits of victory offended them and strained their patience to the utmost. Rome alone gained territory from the wars[1] and collected tribute from the territory thus acquired; Rome alone was embellished from the spoils of war[2] and, so far as we know, regaled with spectacles and entertainments on the occasions of victory. It may also be suspected that only Rome harvested huge booties and war indemnities:[3] certainly it is quite improbable that the Samnite states made such profits out of conquests in the Eastern Mediterranean as to be able to pay back 25½ years of basic taxes to their citizens, in the manner that Rome did for hers from the war booty brought home by Manlius Vulso in 187.[4] Twenty years later Rome was able to abolish *tributum* entirely for her citizens.

Nor could any Latin or Italian town provide its burghers with cheap or free grain in the manner that Rome could do for her citizens towards the end of the second century.

Above all only Roman citizens could exploit their military talents to carve glittering careers for themselves in the political life of the Roman state. A Roman notable who distinguished himself on the field of battle could, and did, expect to become a person of consequence in the state. An equally distinguished Italian notable could nurse no such prospect. And the discrimination was all the more marked since the Roman state had now become so large: it was the only Italian state to gain territory as a result of the Second Punic War. To be a person of consequence in such a state was distinction indeed. No doubt it was necessary to conserve the majesty of the Roman people, since the defence of Italy was in its keeping. But this surely was to conserve it with a vengeance.[5]

[1] Unless the Pentri and Frentani were rewarded for their loyalty with Caracenan land.

[2] 'Sabine' towns were (*ILS*, 20, 21 'tituli Mummiani'): but 'Sabine' towns were 'Roman'. If the Roman censors saw to it that buildings were constructed 'throughout Italy' (Polyb. 6. 17. 2; cf. Auct. *de vir. ill.* 60), Roman Italy must be meant. E. Badian, *For. Client.* p. 151, can find no evidence for thinking that Scipio Aemilianus may have adorned Italian cities.

[3] Allies may have been given some share. We hear, for instance, of *aes Martium* at Cora (*ILS*, 6131). The amounts Rome harvested were enormous: see Pliny, *N.H.* 33.14; 33. 56; Sall. *Iug.* 62. 5; Plut. *Aem. Paullus*, 38. 1; *Marius*, 12. 4; cf. Cic. *de off.* 2. 76.

[4] Livy 39. 7. 5.

[5] For the expression *maiestatem populi Romani comiter conservare* see Cic. *pro Balbo*, 16. 35 and Mommsen, *Röm. St. R.* III, 664 f. It is positively attested only for treaties with extra-

Romans moreover profited individually as well as collectively. Roman notables, by virtue of being officers commanding, were able to plunder overseas areas of their works of art and become snappers-up of assorted other unconsidered trifles.[1] The same opportunities were not open to Allied notables. Roman citizens in the ranks got larger shares of military largesse. It is true that Allied soldiers might profit from the division of war-booty or from the distribution of donatives in lieu of it, and on one quite exceptional occasion Latins (but apparently not Italians) participated, unequally however, in a viritane distribution of land.[2] In general the share of the non-Roman in any kind of booty was rare and only too likely to be smaller than that of his Roman comrade-in-arms. Equal shares may have been distributed in the first quarter of the second century,[3] but they had become only half shares or less from 177 on; and even though Latins did occasionally thereafter share and share alike with Romans, in 167 for instance, it would be rash to assume that Italians in general and much less Samnites in particular did so.[4]

Despite the discrimination under which they laboured the Allies supplied the troops demanded of them, even though they found it difficult to field the numbers required[5] and even though they had virtually no say in the policies which made the use of them necessary. Possibly soldiering was the only employment that many of them could find in the economically disordered second century. It would, however, be straining credulity greatly to imagine that they often did so willingly or with a good grace. The Samnites, it is true, rarely receive separate recognition in the Roman wars of conquest in the second century, whereas the surviving accounts of these wars do

Italian states (Aetolia, Gades, and possibly Mitylene and Chios): E. Täubler, *Imperium Romanum*, I, 62, 450. But Italian states hardly needed it in their treaties: they were presumed to accept it without question. This incidentally meant that they had to keep abreast of changing Roman definitions of *maiestas* (H. S. Jones in *J.R.S.* XVI (1926), 171, n. 3). The decree of the senate concerning Tibur (*ILS*, 19) reads like the reply to a state that had sought to defend itself against the charge of having failed to conserve the majesty of the Roman people.

[1] A few examples will suffice: Sulpicius Galba (App. *Iber.* 60); Marius (Plut. *Marius*, 34. 2; 45. 7); Lucullus and Pompey (App. *Iber.* 51; Pliny, *N.H.* 37. 16). Roman bigwigs also enjoyed widespread opportunities for fleecing provinces and accepting bribes.

[2] In 173: Livy 42. 4. 4. On that occasion Latins got 3 *iugera* each and Romans 10.

[3] See, for instance, Livy 34. 52. 11 (= 194); 37. 59. 6 (= 189); 39. 5. 17 (= 187); 39. 7. 2 (= 187); 40. 43. 7 (= 180).

[4] Livy 41. 13. 7; 45. 40 and 43.

[5] Livy 41. 8. 6 f. Possibly some Allies volunteered (cf. Livy 28. 45. 19; 37. 4. 3; 42. 32. 6), soldiering being the only employment they knew. But it is clear that some alleged 'volunteers' were in fact unhappy conscripts (Livy 31. 8. 6 and 32. 3. 4).

allude occasionally to the roles of some of the other Italian Allies, Paelignians for instance. This should not be taken to mean that the Romans relied exclusively on these other peoples and failed to avail themselves, to the full extent that they dared, of Samnite martial skill. Livy suggests that they took from Samnium all the soldiers they could.[1] The Sabellian and Sabellic peoples, in fact, seem to have been the real core of the Roman 'Confederacy', far more so than effete Etruscans or submissive Umbrians.[2] Undoubtedly Pentri and Hirpini served, no matter how reluctantly, in Roman campaigns by the thousand.[3] But their services have gone largely unrecorded. The Romans were not apt to advertise that they were beholden in any way to the Samnites. On the contrary they were much more prone to accuse them of nursing designs of treachery.[4]

By participating in Roman warfaring, the Allies must have contributed to their own romanization; and there were also many other factors helping to promote this. Her populousness, her political superiority, her favourable geographical position half-way down the west side of the peninsula, and above all the use of her language as the only possible *lingua franca* helped Rome gradually to impress her own character upon Italy. Not that this made the Romans any readier to treat the Italians as equals; and naturally the more romanized the Italians became the more they must have resented their own inferior status.

A very influential factor in shaping Italy into a Roman mould was the Roman practice of scrambling the population of Italy, in an effort, it is true, not so much to foster romanization as to eliminate foci of anti-Roman sentiment. Forced transfers of whole peoples from one section of Italy to another started early and Samnium was affected more than any other area. Just as in 268 the Picentes,[5] so in 180 the Apuani were forcibly transferred thither from Northern Italy. Altogether 47,000 of them were established on the Ager

[1] Livy 41. 8. 8. For Roman reluctance to admit that Allies had helped, see F. Münzer in *R.E.* IV (1901), s.v. 'Decimius', col. 2274.

[2] Cf. Livy 9. 37. 6: [*Fabius Rullianus*] *Samnitium bella extollit, elevat Etruscos*; 27. 27. 5 (Etruscan flight proved fatal for the great Marcellus).

[3] Even though they had been depopulated by emigration they contributed their full quota to Roman armies (Livy 41. 8. 8). Samnite cavalry is casually mentioned as present at the Battle of Pydna in 168 (Livy 44. 40. 5), along with Marrucini and Paeligni (Plut. *Aem. Paullus*, 20). Greater notice is taken of the distinguished services of Gnaeus Petreius of Atina against the Cimbri in 102 (Pliny, *N.H.* 22. 11); but Atina could hardly have been still regarded as Samnite at that late date.

[4] See, for example, Livy 31. 7. 11 (= 200).

[5] Strabo 5. 4. 13, p. 251.

Taurasinus, where they formed two communities, the Ligures Baebiani and the Ligures Corneliani.[1]

In addition to such forced mass transfers of population, there was also the voluntary migration of individuals or groups in search of wider opportunities and a more prosperous life. Their numbers were large, since the wars of the second century resulted in a great influx of wealth into Italy, whether in the form of tribute, loot or anything else. This wealth, of course, went chiefly and in the first instance to Rome, but its effects manifested themselves elsewhere. An influx of Italians into Rome to avail themselves of the economic opportunities there meant that the places they vacated might be filled by immigrants from other districts. Between 204 and 187 at least 12,000 Latins migrated to Rome, and Livy hints broadly that they were not the only newcomers.[2] The peoples of Italy in the second century seem, in fact, to have been very mobile. When Latins left Fregellae, Paeligni poured in; so did Samnites, by the thousand. Samnites were quite ready to leave Samnium and its scanty resources in order to make their living elsewhere, and large numbers of them did so.

Large-scale migration, whether forced by Roman policy or induced by Roman prosperity, must have helped to spread the use of Latin as a *lingua franca*.

In certain other respects, also, Roman behaviour was well calculated to encourage the adoption of Rome's language and Rome's ways, and simultaneously to depress the status of Rome's Allies.

The cool claim of the Roman senate to exercise jurisdiction in the case of any crime committed anywhere in Italy, if it was of a sort to 'require public investigation',[3] was bound to result in gross infringement of Italian rights and autonomy, and also in the spread of Roman customs. The suppression of any crimes with certain or probable inter-state ramifications was obviously in the interests of all the inhabitants of Italy. And such crimes were only too likely to occur. Brigandage on a large scale, for instance, was an almost inevitable consequence of the wholesale importation of slaves from the wars of conquest and their employment as herdsmen on large, absentee-owned ranches.

When necessity arose, the Roman authorities did not hesitate to issue orders, even detailed orders, for ensuring the maintenance of

[1] Livy 40. 38 and 41. The ruins of the urban centre of the Ligures Baebiani lie in the woodland about two miles from mod. Circello.

[2] Livy 39. 3. 5 f.; and cf. 41. 8. 11 (= 177).

[3] Polyb. 6. 13. 4.

law and order throughout peninsular Italy. But, seeing that it was the Roman authorities themselves who decided when action ought to be taken, it is clear that the practice could easily lead to abuse.

The earliest recorded instance of Roman activity of this kind was in 196 when the *praetor peregrinus*, M'. Acilius Glabrio, intervened in Etruria to suppress an uprising of serfs. But the most celebrated instance occurred ten years later, when the senate issued minute and detailed instructions for the suppression of Bacchanalian rites throughout Italy, on the ground that they were contributing to delinquency and even conspiracy. As some of the chief agents in fostering the cult seem to have been speakers of Oscan, this Roman measure affected the Samnites directly.[1] Both of these examples leave very little doubt that it was fatally easy for Rome to make public security a pretext for interference in the internal affairs of her Italian Allies, and it is hard to believe that those Allies did not resent such documents as the *senatus consultum* to Tibur of *c.* 159.[2] Measures against alleged conspiracy (*coniuratio*) were one way of ensuring pro-Roman regimes. Rome could make the Italian world safe for oligarchy by suppressing in the name of law and order all attempts to eject a pro-Roman minority of time-servers from local office or to bring about changes in the existing social order. One can be justifiably suspicious of the occasions when Roman help in maintaining order is said to have been solicited, as for example at Patavium in 174. (On that occasion the Romans saw to it that the nobles kept the commons in their place. Patavium, of course, was technically outside Italy: but its case was essentially no different from that of communities immediately to the south.)[3]

One aspect of the maintenance of law and order was the Roman practice of arbitrating whenever disputes arose between Italian states.[4] Sometimes perhaps Roman judgement on the point at issue was genuinely sought; on others it was imposed, whether the dis-

[1] Livy 39. 8 f.; *ILS*, 18; and see A. H. McDonald in *J.R.S.* XXXIV (1944), 28 f. The instruction of the Senate is couched in the form of a recommendation to the Allies rather than a positive order (D. Daube, *Forms of Roman Legislation*, pp. 37–49, who exaggerates the non-minatory aspect). Nevertheless its tone was so threatening that non-compliance was effectively discouraged (A. Dihle in *Hermes*, XC (1962), 376–9.)

[2] *ILS*, 19. A. H. McDonald, *C.H.J.* VI (1939), 131, suggests that whenever Rome took such measures she sought and obtained Allied approval with the result that 'concurrence in policy did not allow any encroachment upon autonomous rights'. In my view this certainly was not the case.

[3] Livy 41. 27. 3.

[4] Cf. Livy 45. 13. 10–11. (There are numerous examples, outside Italy as well as within.)

putants wanted it or not. Under either arrangement it could be exploited to the advantage of Rome. When, early in the second century, Nola and Naples quarrelled over some territory, the Roman arbitrator, Q. Fabius Labeo (praetor 189, consul 183), outrageously pronounced that the land belonged to neither, but to Rome. According to Cicero, this was 'swindling, not arbitration'. But neither Nola nor Naples obtained redress,[1] and there is evidence to suggest that such things happened on other occasions.[2]

Less objectionable to the Allies would be Roman initiative in coping with natural disasters of a magnitude that taxed and perhaps transcended the powers of any single Italian state to deal with them. Earthquakes obviously were bound to affect more than one community, and the concerted measures of a number of states might be needed to relieve the ensuing distress. This, incidentally, was something that vitally concerned the Samnites, since theirs was, and still is, a land where seismic disturbances are common. In a way the organization by Rome of relief for Italian states, sorely striken by fevers, famines, floods, fires, and the like, was simply one aspect of the defence of the Italian peninsula and the promotion of order and good government therein. But the Romans were doubtless able to prostitute this also for their own ends. Polybius' statement, that 'if any individual or community in Italy is in need of arbitration, or indeed claims damages or requires succour or protection, the senate attends to all such matters', is neither as innocent nor as benevolent as it sounds.[3] It is, however, probably safe to conjecture that it was something that was productive of far less resentment among the Allies, and at the same time it must have had considerable effect in familiarizing them with things Roman.

The extension of the Roman road system in Italy, which became very marked in the second century, must also have played some part in helping to remove the cultural and linguistic barriers to closer intercourse. It was in the second century that the road system, which has already been described,[4] began to be organized. By transmitting

[1] Cic. *de off.* I. 33; Val. Max. 7. 3. 4. [2] Note the implication of Livy 3. 71.

[3] Polyb. 6. 13. 5.

[4] There is no ancient evidence of the date for the Via Minucia or for the prolongation of the Via Appia. But H. Nissen, *Ital. Landesk.* II, 805, must be right in thinking that the latter at least was extended as Roman arms were successful and Latin Colonies established. In other words the development of the road system of Samnium, to which allusion has already been made (above, pp. 21–3), got well under way in the second century. Certainly the volume of traffic to the east could not have been small then.

Roman ideas and practices the roads must have done something towards making Samnium less exclusively Sabellian.

The most effective romanizing agent of all, however, was the ubiquity of Romans. Citizens of the Republic by the Tiber were to be found, and in significant numbers, quite literally everywhere. The Ager Romanus, by the second century, was no longer confined to the area near Rome or even to the solid, unbroken bloc of territory which stretched across Central Italy from the mouth of the Tiber to the mouth of the Aesis. There existed enclaves of Roman territory separate from this central core. And, as the area of Roman land grew, the degree of interpenetration of Romans with Italians inevitably increased. Italians were bound to find themselves more and more mixed up with Romans. Trading and commercial contacts must have been everyday occurrences, and social intercourse was also not lacking.

We have Livy's word for it that there were numerous marriages between Romans and Italians and there is no need to disbelieve him: Italians, as well as Latins, seem to have enjoyed *conubium* with Rome.[1] Such mixed marriages must have contributed to the growing romanization of peninsular Italy. Yet one wonders to what degree Samnite blood had mingled with Roman by 100. According to Aulus Gellius, some of the Marsi, a people just as accessible as the Samnites and much more amenable to latinization, had maintained themselves pure and uncontaminated by wedlock with 'foreigners' right down to the end of the Roman Republic and later.[2] The same must have been generally true also of the Samnites, especially those of them who lived in the remote and mountainous interior. The famous case of the Otacilii can hardly be cited as typical of Roman–Samnite marital relations, since the Otacilii were nobles, and aristocracies have always and everywhere been prepared to marry outside their own nation. The same can be said about the marriage, presumably well before 100, of a Papius from Hirpinian Compsa with a woman from Lanuvium (this was the pair that became grandparents of the notorious T. Annius Milo). But only in such Samnite communities as Venafrum and Allifae, which had been annexed and whose inhabitants were technically Roman, could mixed marriages have been relatively common.

[1] See, for example, Diod. 37. 15. 2. Such intermarriage is also implied by the Lex Minicia (of 91?).

[2] Aul. Gell. 16. 11. 2.

From Livy we learn how instrumental business dealings were in getting Italians very much involved with Romans. Latins, for instance, between 187 and 177, could 'sell' their sons to Romans, who in turn would manumit them: as freedmen, the liberated sons were thenceforth technically Roman citizens. The implication is that, in the early second century, Latins enjoyed the Roman right of *commercium*. That Italians also enjoyed it is shown by the case of the Roman moneylenders in 193, who in order to circumvent the stringent Roman laws of usury employed Italian agents, from states that did not frown excessively upon high rates of interest. On this occasion the Roman authorities stepped in brusquely to stop the practice: in effect, they put severe limitations on the Allied right of *commercium* (and it is to be noted that they did so quite unilaterally and arbitrarily).[1]

The 'right of exile' was another avenue leading to increased intercourse of Romans and Italians. Polybius reveals how Roman fugitives from their own law might find asylum and honourable exile in Naples, Praeneste, Tibur and certain other Allied communities.[2] The Allies may or may not have been content with this relationship (although it is hard to believe that they could have relished the role of custodians of Roman state prisoners which Rome forced upon them).[3] Clearly the existence of a multiplicity of states in Italy provided various opportunities for the unscrupulous or the unfortunate, somewhat as it does in the U.S.A. today. But it was a symbiosis in which the influence of the stronger and more populous partner inevitably imposed itself. In the long run Roman speech and Roman customs were bound to prevail.

It is true that mutual antipathy probably militated against the growth of any really great degree of intimacy between Romans and Samnites, so that the latter managed to preserve their national identity with less adulteration than did most of the other peninsular

[1] Livy 35. 7. 2 f.

[2] These latter also included Nuceria and Tarquinii (Cic. *pro Balbo*, 27–9; Livy 26. 3. 12).

[3] Prisoners such as Syphax, Perseus, Bituitus, Carthaginian and Achaean hostages. Towns specifically recorded as places of confinement were Alba Fucens, Norba and Signia (which were Latin Colonies) and Ferentinum and Tibur (which were not). A Latin Colony might successfully protest against being used for this purpose (as Spoletium did, when King Gentius of Illyricum and his family were assigned to it), but an Italian community evidently could not (Iguvium had to take Gentius). See Livy 45. 43. 9 (and Iguvium was one of the more favoured Allies: Cic. *pro Balbo*, 47).

peoples. Nevertheless even the Samnites and especially the Caudine towns must have shown some of the effects of exposure to Roman influence.

Samnium, in fact, like all other areas of Italy, could not entirely escape the romanization that was making ever greater headway throughout the peninsula.[1] If the evidence survived we should undoubtedly be able to trace this in various aspects of Samnite life. Roman influence on the Samnite religion can certainly be detected, and the Oscan language, especially after what had happened to Capua its chief metropolitan centre in 211, was also affected. This is shown by the long inscription from Bantia, a small community in Lucania, in the very heart of Southern Italy. The inscription, which belongs to the late second or early first century, is the longest surviving document in the Oscan language: but the Latinisms in it are both notable and numerous. Evidently by 100 romanization had made much headway, even in the remote south, and in the Caudine districts it must have been quite marked.

Exaggeration, however, should be avoided. The Samnites were a conservative people and tenacious of their ancestral customs;[2] by 100 they had not completely discarded Oscan for Latin by any means nor had they refashioned their political institutions along Roman lines. Lucanian Bantia, near-neighbour of the Latin Colony at Venusia, was in an area of mixed Latin and Oscan speech, whereas towns and villages in the interior of Samnium were less exposed to the encroachment of Latin. In fact from them some counter-influence flowed back to the Latin Colonies. There are grounds for believing that Venusia itself, like its fellow Latin Colony at Luceria, was more than a little oscanized by 100. The same is true also of Fregellae (down to 125), Saticula, Aesernia and Beneventum.[3]

[1] On the romanization of Italy, see G. Devoto, *Scripta Minora*, I, 287 ff.

[2] Cicero mentions no Samnites in his chapters on Latin-speaking Italians (*Brutus*, 169–72).

[3] All of these places, except Venusia and Fregellae, have yielded inscriptions of one sort or another showing Oscan influence (Vetter, pp. 97, 98, 99, 102, 136, 137, 164). Venusia had received a fresh infusion of colonists immediately after the Second Punic War (Livy 31. 49. 6), which is hardly surprising in view of its isolation in the region dominated by Hannibal. But its colonists lived in the countryside rather than in the town proper (the Colony had plebeian tribunes specifically in order that the interests of its scattered inhabitants should not be overlooked): how could such countryside dwellers be expected to escape assimilation by the Sabellians all around them? Republican inscriptions from there contain many Sabellian names (A. Degrassi, *ILLRP*, II, 690–2). For the case of Fregellae see below, p. 318.

It is one of the commonplaces of history that the country districts of Italy languished as a result of the trend of events in the second century. All students of the Gracchi will be aware of the drift of the small farmer class to Rome, of the widespread growth of slave-operated *latifundia*, and of the problems that these developments imposed upon the Roman state. All of this, however, has reference in the first instance to Roman Italy.

Non-Roman Italy was similarly affected since it did not escape the social and economic effects of the Hannibalic and succeeding wars. The Bacchanalian excesses of *c.* 190 are symptomatic of widespread unrest. Although many small farmers emigrated to the cities, the peasant class of course did not disappear from second-century Italy. Nor did every region see the growth of industries. The Sabellian highlands retained their agrarian character. Cato *c.* 170 names more than a few towns in Southern Italy which had small industrial establishments, but none of them were in Samnium.[1] Its inhabitants still lived on and off the land. It was a life of 'penury, taxes and military service' and for many of them made precarious by the uncertainty of the tenure of their holdings. Appian describes how soil, that was technically Roman *ager publicus*, might be left for the nonce in native hands;[2] such land, however, might be put to very different use should the Roman authorities ever decide to exploit it to the full.[3] Appian must be thinking particularly of Samnite soil since by the second century many of the traditional grazing lands of the Samnites had become Roman *ager publicus*.

In Samnium, as in other parts of Italy, the peasant farmer was tending to be forced off the land. One cause for this was population pressure: after all the Roman seizures, there probably was not enough really good land to go round. Another cause was the monopolization of much land for large estates. Some such estates were formed, more or less precariously, out of *ager publicus*; others, however, consisted of land legally belonging to individuals. The great profiteers from the wars of the second century were for the most part at Rome, and many of them invested their wealth in land. This, however, did not

[1] Unless we include Venafrum in second-century Samnium. T. R. S. Broughton points out to me that Cato may have limited his lists to towns where he had property or with which he was familiar (his great-grandson had estates in Lucania (Plut. *Cato Minor*, 20. 1)).

[2] App. *B.C.* 1. 7. 27 f. For *ager publicus* left in native hands, see Livy 41. 27. 5; 42. 1. 6; 42. 8. 4; 42. 9. 7; 42. 19. 1.

[3] For herdsmen being prevented from using *ager publicus* see Livy 33. 42. 10 (= 196); 35. 10. 11 (= 193).

necessarily have to be Roman land. Presumably they could acquire title to soil in any Italian community which enjoyed *commercium* with Rome; and there were many such. Moreover besides the Roman capitalists who created large absentee-owned estates in non-Roman Italy, there were some of their Italian counterparts doing so. For assuredly capitalists were not confined to the ranks of the Romans. Shrewd individuals from non-Roman Italy also succeeded in amassing respectable fortunes.[1] Many South Italian business men went out to the Roman provinces to trade and reaped tidy profits, and some of these profits were undoubtedly invested in South Italian land. There were Italian, as well as Roman, proprietors of *latifundia*.[2]

The Oscan-speaking peasants of Samnium, unlike the peasants from the Roman and Latin parts of Italy, did not go to Rome in any numbers when they forsook the land. Other parts of Italy and the Roman provinces overseas were the destinations for which they headed. The clearest evidence for this comes from Fregellae, which probably lost much of its own indigenous population through emigration of its sons to Rome. Their places were taken by Samnites and Paeligni. According to Livy, the immigrants by 177 amounted to 4,000 families, although he does not say how many of these were Samnites.[3] That Fregellae became very largely oscanized in the process can hardly be doubted.

Fregellae was not unique.[4] Other Latin Colonies also received an influx of Sabellian immigrants. Inscriptions or coins demonstrate their presence at Luceria, Saticula, Venusia, Aesernia, and Beneventum.[5] In all of these places, it is safe to assume, the Samnites were accepted into the body of burghers and allowed to acquire the local citizenship (in other words, to exercise Latin rights). Apparently the Latin city-states were not permitted to exchange citizenship rights with one another, but there is no record of a similar embargo being imposed on the Italians; nor do we hear that it was impossible for 'Latin' states to exchange citizenships with 'Italian' states.[6] If

[1] Diod. 34. 2. 27–34.

[2] *Accessit ager quem privatim habent Gallicus, Samnitis, Apulus, Bruttius* (Cato, fr. 230 M.).

[3] Livy 41. 8. 8.

[4] Sentinum (like Fregellae a scene of earlier Samnite frustration) received Samnites: *CIL*, XI, 5778. The Romans, of course, were content to let emigration weaken Samnium.

[5] See above, p. 316, n. 3.

[6] See Livy 8. 14 and A. N. Sherwin-White, *Roman Citizenship*, p. 120. Italians migrated to Latin Narnia and *usurped* its citizenship (Livy 32. 2. 6 f.): but there is no reason to believe that Narnia was forbidden to extend its citizenship to them. Intermarriage of a Latin colonist with an Italian woman was possible: a man of Brundisium married Ennius' sister.

Samnites did not migrate to Rome on the same generous scale as they did to Fregellae, it should perhaps be attributed to the difficulty that they would have had in making their way owing to their Oscan speech; and after 177 they would have encountered legal barriers as well, since after that year the Romans not only refused to grant their citizenship any longer to Italians, but also periodically expelled those Italians who nevertheless ventured to migrate to the city.

Emigration reached beyond Italy. Italians who fought in Rome's wars of Mediterranean conquest sometimes remained in the countries where they had served, married native women and failed to return home. Furthermore, of the soldiers who did return, many left off-spring behind them who were thus at least half Italian. Carteia, in Spain, is the best-known example of a provincial community which could claim this sort of Italian origin.[1] But there were others, and apart altogether from whole communities there must have been many individual Italians in the provinces. These, of course, were not all Samnites by any means, but some of them were.

Admittedly the existence of a town called Osca (mod. Huesca) in Spain may not have been due to Sabellian settlers: in fact, Osca was peopled, not with Samnites, but with Ilergetes.[2] But many Oscan names have been found elsewhere in Spain, and even though we do not know when their bearers first reached the Iberian peninsula, many of them undoubtedly did so before 100, in the days when the Samnites were still technically independent.

Cisalpine Gaul is another place where the presence of settlers with Oscan-type names is securely documented, and it has been suggested that Samnites started migrating thither immediately after the Second Punic War, forsaking the scene of devastation and destruction that Hannibal had left behind him in Samnium. Whether this conjecture be true or not, it would seem to be indisputable that many a Sabellian was ultimately settled near the River Po.[3]

One type of emigrant from Italy to the provinces deserves special

[1] Livy 43. 3. 1 f. (= 171).

[2] Ptol. 2. 6. 57; cf. Strabo 3. 4. 10, p. 161. But Osca, the town where Perperna assassinated Sertorius in 72, also contained many speakers of Greek and Latin (Plut. *Sert.* 14. 2). Despite R. Menéndez Pidal, *Origenes del Español*[3], p. 303, and W. J. Entwistle, *The Spanish Language*, pp. 63, 74, the name Osca does not derive from a Sabellian settlement there. Its silver coins (*oscenses*) were famous: see, for example, Livy 34. 10.

[3] E. Pais in *Atti Accad. Napoli*, N.S., VI (1918), 453 f.; D. O. Robson in *Class. Journ.* XXIX (1934), 599–608. Cisalpine Gaul was of course the goal of many dispossessed Italian peasants in the second century (A. J. Toynbee, *Hannibal's Legacy*, II, 184 f.).

mention: namely the traders and businessmen who proceeded overseas to make or to improve their fortunes. Their numbers ran into the thousands. The ancient writers often refer to them simply as Italians; indeed Greek-using authors fail to distinguish between the various types of Italian and frequently call them all alike indiscriminately 'Romans'. When Mithridates' invasion of Asia was imminent these 'Romans' hastily doffed the toga which they had recently taken to wearing (possibly as a result of the Lex Julia of 90) and assumed Greek garb in the hope that they would not be taken for real Romans. This may imply that many of them were Italiote Greeks. Whether that was so or not, the epigraphic evidence leaves very little doubt that, in pre-Gracchan times at any rate, the overwhelming majority of them came frcm Southern Italy.[1]

It is clear that only Rome acquired territory and tribute as a result of the Mediterranean Wars which were fought by the armies of the Roman 'Confederacy'. One must assume, further, that only Romans were eligible for the official posts in the adminstration of the provinces. Yet manifestly non-Romans were not physically excluded from the provinces. They were freely permitted to go there in an unofficial capacity to seek their fame and fortune. About 100 the Roman assembly, after listening to a delegation from Rhodes, ordered all allied states to exclude pirates from their harbours in order that 'Roman citizens and their Latin Allies from Italy might carry on business on the seas in safety';[2] and in at least one instance, Ambracia, Rome stipulated that Latins should have free and unfettered access.[3] Evidently large numbers of Italians availed themselves of provincial opportunities, especially after Delos was declared a free

[1] Poseidonius *ap.* Athen. 5. 213 and T. Frank, *Econ. Survey*, I, 274–82. See, too, O. Hirschfeld, *Kleine Schriften*, pp. 30 f.; T. Frank in *Amer. Hist. Rev.* XVIII (1913), 241–7; J. Hatzfeld, *Les trafiquants italiens, passim*; M. Holleaux, *Rome, la Grèce et les monarchies hellénistiques*, 85 f.; F. Münzer in *R.E.* VI A (1937), s.v. 'Trebius', col. 2270; E. Gabba in *Athenaeum*, XXXII (1954), 297; E. Badian, *Foreign Clientelae*, p. 152. South Italians were still prominent in post-Gracchan times too, to judge from the third Augustan edict from Cyrene.

[2] *SEG*, III, p. 79, no. 378. See H. A. Ormerod, *Piracy in the Ancient World*, pp. 242–7, for the date of this *lex de piratis persequendis*. It is usually thought that the formula 'Latin allies from Italy' is also meant to include the Italians (J. Göhler, *Rom und Italien*, pp. 193 f.), but this may not be the case: as M. Cary points out (in *Class. Rev.* XXXVIII (1924), 60, 162), *socii Italici* are in fact not mentioned.

[3] Livy 38. 44. 4 (= 187), where *socii nominis Latini* is often regarded as including Italians (Mommsen, *Röm St. R.* III, 660). This proviso in the Ambraciote treaty is exceptional according to M. Holleaux in *Camb. Anc. Hist.* VIII, 238; but it may be exceptional only in being laid down in writing (F. Cassola, *I Gruppi Politici*, p. 63).

port in 167.[1] In Narbonese Gaul they ultimately controlled an intricate network of operations.[2]

The south Italians, who thus flocked into the Roman provinces to exploit business opportunities to the full, are shown by the evidence from Delos and elsewhere to have included many speakers of Oscan as well as of Greek. Trebius Loesius, who *c.* 162 traded all the way from Delos to Drepanum and whose name has turned up on a wine jar found at Carthage, is the most renowned;[3] but he was far from unique. These Oscan-speaking *negotiatores* must have been pre-eminently urbanized Sabellians, in other words Campanians, since these latter would not only be the most naturally alert to opportunities of this kind, but would also have the great experience and the necessary capital to invest in such trading ventures. In the second century Campania was industrialized and wealthy; and it is conceivable that the Houses of the Faun, of Pansa and of Sallustius and some of the nearby country villas at Pompeii, which were built at this time, belonged to Sabellians who had made money in the provinces. Nevertheless Sabellians from Samnium proper must also have participated in the lucrative pursuit. They would, of course, be middle or upper class speculators rather than peasant farmers, and the name of at least one of them (from the first century) is known, Verres' miserable victim, Publius Gavius of Hirpinian Compsa. One wonders how many of them were among the 80,000 'Romans' who are said to have lost their lives in Mithridates' 'Asiatic vespers' in 88.[4]

If the emigration of the second century B.C. had merely relieved Samnium of excess population, it might have been a welcome solution to a pressing need. But this was not all that it did. It also advertised, even if it did not cure, the serious social problem caused by the protracted war-caused interruptions to peasant activities and by the growth of large estates; and, so far as Samnium was concerned, no real remedy was devised, much less attempted, for this problem. In fact no solution could have been effectively applied either in Samnium or anywhere else in non-Roman Italy independently of Rome, for the affairs of Rome and of non-Roman Italy had

[1] Polyb. 30. 20. 7; 30. 31. 10.

[2] Cicero, *pro Fonteio*, 11.

[3] *CIL*, x, 8051; xii, 425–8, 22637.

[4] Val. Max. 9. 1. 3 calls them 'Roman citizens', and it is of course true that by then the Lex Julia had already been passed. Italians were certainly numbered amongst the victims (App. *Mith.* 22; Memnon, in F. Jacoby, *Frag. griech. Hist.* iiiB, 434, 22. 9).

by now become so intertwined that action taken anywhere in the peninsula was bound to have repercussions elsewhere.

It was this entanglement of non-Roman activities with Roman that caused Italians to take so lively an interest in Roman political life. They knew that political squabbles at Rome would probably be fought at their expense; and legislation passed at Rome would inevitably affect them, 'foreigners' though they technically were. Accordingly they sought ways and means for intervening at Rome, and the Roman system of *clientela* could be exploited to this end. By becoming *clientes* of the appropriate *patronus* at Rome, individual Italians may have been able to exert some slight influence on the course of Roman politics, since they could usually find some support from a Roman *patronus* eager to have a large following of retainers which would bolster his own prestige and help him obtain very material and concrete advantages.[1]

The Samnites, however, probably did not make much of an impact through *patroni* on the political life of Rome in the second century. The idea of becoming *clientes* was probably repugnant to them, and in any case they were not the type of people that Roman nobles wished to have as *clientes*, since they were too refractory and could not be controlled as successfully as Latins or others. Their only recorded *patroni* are the Fabricii, and we hear of them only vaguely and probably inaccurately.[2] There is, in fact, no record or hint of Samnite influence on Roman policy; and there is likewise no evidence of much concern being wasted by the Romans, or by anyone else for that matter, on the plight of the peasants in Southern Italy. The

[1] Even purely personal and petty squabbles among Roman notables, such as a quarrel over the auction of a ring, might affect the Allies disastrously (see Pliny, *N.H.* 33. 20). For Italians influencing Roman politics, see Sall. *Iug.* 40. 2. Some Italians 'passed' as Roman citizens: one even got himself elected to the consulship before he was unmasked (M. Perperna in 130: Val. Max. 3. 4. 5). For the Roman patron's desire to have *clientes*, see Sall. *Iug.* 42. 1; Dion. Hal. 2. 10. 4; App. *B.C.* 1. 19. 78. One thinks of Ap. Claudius, the censor of 312, who *Italiam per clientelas occupare temptavit* (Suet. *Tib.* 2. 2). The client paid dearly for the patron's services (E. Badian, *For. Clientelae,* 161): the father of the Gracchi, for instance, fleeced his *clientes*, Italian and provincial alike, unmercifully (Livy 40. 44. 12).

[2] Val. Max. 4. 3. 6; see G. Forni in *Athenaeum*, XXXI (1953), 177 f. Even if the relationship between Fabricii and Samnites were fact and not fiction, it would not imply much indirect Samnite participation in Roman affairs; for the Fabricii did not produce a single illustrious figure after the Pyrrhic War. After 218, it is true, a victorious Roman general often became the *patronus*, even if not a particularly beneficent one, of the people he conquered (see Cic. *de Off.* 1. 35 and E. Badian, *For. Clientelae*, p. 156). But there is no evidence that Claudius Marcellus or Fabius Maximus became patrons of Hirpini or Caudini.

Roman peasants finally found champions of a sort in the Gracchi.[1] But no one thought of providing much relief for the Samnite peasants, least of all the Gracchi, unless one regards Gaius Gracchus' abortive citizenship proposal as a form of relief. On the contrary, the Gracchan programme must have exacerbated the situation in Samnium still further, since any Roman *ager publicus* there which Samnites had been exploiting was now only too likely to be reclaimed by the Gracchan land commission and distributed *viritim* in small (30 *iugera*?) allotments—but to Romans, not to Samnites.[2] That this actually happened is demonstrated by the surviving Gracchan stone boundary markers of 132–130, which, with one exception, all come from Samnium or other parts of Southern Italy. They prove that the Gracchan commissioners had resumed in the name of the Roman state land which they had decided, whether justly or unjustly, to be 'Roman'. We get a glimpse of what this meant in practice from an inscription of *c.* 132, which records the activity of a road-building Roman praetor, who made presumably native herdsmen give way to immigrant Roman farmers in Lucania: *primus fecei ut de agro poplico aratoribus cederent paastores.*[3] It is also worth noting that there were Gracchan colonies as well as viritane assignations in Samnium.[4] Fraccaro has shown that only Romans could be recipients of the land allotted in small parcels to individuals, and the Lex Appuleia of Saturninus (in 103?) suggests that there was a similar rule for the land collectively allotted to a colony.[5] The Gracchan agrarian 'reform' must have contributed to the decision of the Sabellian peoples of the south to join the Sabellic peoples of the centre against Rome in the Social War.

It was not only in land distributions that Italians fared badly. Roman haughtiness and insensitivity to Italian sentiment manifested themselves in various other ways as well.

As early as 173 Roman aristocrats expected to be received with obsequious deference if they visited Italian towns even in a private

[1] Cic. *de leg. agr.* 2. 81: *duo Gracchi qui de plebis Romanae commodis plurimum cogitaverunt.* See G. Bloch–J. Carcopino, *Hist. romaine*³, II, 173, for the period preceding the Gracchi.

[2] There undoubtedly were encroachments on the *ager publicus.* See, for example, Livy 42. 1. 6: *senatui placuit L. Postumium consulem ad agrum publicum a privato terminandum in Campaniam ire cuius ingentem modum possidere privatos paulatim proferendo fines constabat.*

[3] See A. Degrassi, *ILLRP*, I, 454, 467–75 (rejecting, however, the view that the first inscription belongs to P. Popillius Laenas).

[4] Abellinum, Allifae, Telesia according to K. J. Beloch, *Röm. Gesch.* p. 493.

[5] Cic. *pro Balbo*, 21. 48.

capacity, and, when they visited them arrayed in the trappings of office, their behaviour was likely to be quite insufferable. L. Postumius Albinus, the Roman consul, acted with outrageous insolence at Praeneste in 173: he demanded that Praeneste should pay for his lodging, entertainment and transport when he passed through the town and that its local office-holders should wait upon him. Yet Praeneste had displayed the stoutest-hearted loyalty to Rome in the dark days of the Second Punic War and its wealthier burghers had been offered Roman citizenship as a reward for their behaviour. Postumius, like other notable Romans, may have felt a special antipathy for Praenestines; or possibly his spleen was due to the temerity of the Praenestines in rejecting the citizenship offer.[1] It was likewise in 173 that another Roman magistrate plundered a famous Italian temple without the local Italian officials daring to say him nay;[2] while yet another Roman office-holder assaulted, apparently with impunity, an unoffending Ligurian tribe distinguished for its loyalty and sold many of its members into slavery.[3]

Before the second century was over, Roman officials would not only be descending on 'independent' Italian towns and demanding entertainment; they would even be forcing a local official to commit suicide or publicly scourging the leading man of an Allied town who could not clear the men's baths in short order for use by a Roman consul's wife.[4] In no less arrogant a fashion the Romans prescribed how Italians should worship, what they should eat and how much they should pay for it; they even extorted from them contributions for the gladiatorial shows at Rome.[5] The Italian Allies, in fact, were treated like the provincials (who, incidentally, were also called allies), but with this difference: the provincials provided Rome with tribute in cash, the Allies in kind, and human kind at that, and when they supplied bodies in the shape of soldiers they had to pay the

[1] Livy 42. 1. 6 f. For Praenestine behaviour in the Second Punic War, see Livy 23. 20. 3. The antipathy existing between the Roman nobility and Praeneste is shown by various incidents: in 319 Papirius Cursor bullied and terrified a 'praetor' of Praeneste (Livy 9. 16. 17 f.); in 280/279 some Praenestines tried to revolt to Pyrrhus (Zon. 8. 1; 8. 3); in 242 the senate forbade the victor in the First Punic War to consult the Temple of Fortune in 'foreign Praeneste' (Val. Max. 1. 3. 1); in 82 Sulla treated the Praenestines, but not other Italians, like Samnites and massacred them (App. *B.C.* 1. 94. 438).

[2] Livy 42. 3.

[3] Livy 42. 7. 7 f., 21 f. Liguria technically was outside Italy; but the episode illustrates the Roman attitude.

[4] Aul. Gell. 10. 3. 3: he is quoting Gaius Gracchus.

[5] Livy 39. 22. 8; 40. 19. 5; 40. 44. 12; Pliny, *N.H.* 10. 139; Macrob. 3. 17. 6 (the latter two passages referring to the Leges Didia and Fannia).

costs of their maintenance (except for their rations when on an actual campaign).[1]

Apologists for Rome argue that these developments were late and gradual in coming,[2] a view that the dates of some of the incidents hardly confirm.[3] It is also argued that Roman acts of arrogance were the exception rather than the rule,[4] an assertion that the fragmentary nature of the surviving evidence hardly warrants: on the contrary, to some students the startling thing is that, although comparatively little information survives concerning the second century, that little nevertheless furnishes numerous and varied instances of Roman abuse of power. The words of Polybius are very revealing: 'one can estimate the fear (τὴν κατάπληξιν) and the respect (καταξίωσιν) of the Allies for the Roman administration (πολιτεύματος)'.[5]

The modern apologists may have been misled by a passage in Livy: 'The silent acquiescence of the Praenestines (to Postumius' brutal arrogance), whether due to moderation or to fear, established the Roman magistrates' right, as if by endorsed precedent, to make such demands, which became daily ever more grievous.'[6] Possibly, too, they have been unduly impressed by Sallust's rhetorical commonplace[7] that it was only after the capture of Carthage in 146 that the Romans began to be corrupted by their own power.[8] Other Romans were of the opinion that moral decay had begun before 184, when Cato tried to stop it.[9]

Roman misbehaviour, in fact, started very early. Any appearance of a creeping encroachment on Allied rights is due to that lack of clear definition in the bilateral treaties with Rome which has been

[1] Cf. A. J. Toynbee, *Hannibal's Legacy*, II, 113. Clearly there was no *modestia apud socios* (to use the expression of Tacitus, *Ann.* 1. 9) or any conception of the moral duty of the rulers towards the ruled.

[2] See, for example, E. Pais, *Storia di Roma*³, V, 449.

[3] Acts of Roman high-handedness before 202 (e.g. those of Plemmius at Locri in 205: Livy 29. 8. 6 f.) are normal to warfare in any age. But ever since 280 the Romans thought of all Italy as theirs (Polyb. 1. 6. 6), and after 200 regarded themselves as masters of the world (Polyb. 15. 10. 2; 21. 16. 8; 21. 23. 4; Velleius 1. 6. 6; F. Cassola, *I Gruppi Politici*, p. 65; K. E. Petzold in *Historia*, IX (1960), 251 f.).

[4] J. Göhler, *Rom und Italien*, p. 60.

[5] Polyb. 3. 90. 14.

[6] Livy 42. 1. 12.

[7] The historian L. Calpurnius Piso Frugi, for whom the moral decline of the Romans began in 154 (Pliny, *N.H.* 17. 244), put forward the same view (K. Latte in *S. B. Berlin* (1960), no. 7, 3 f.): but Sallust got the notion from Polybius rather than from Piso.

[8] Already in 164 the senate contemptuously overrode the expressed wishes and policy of Athens in the matter of Serapis worship (*SIG*, II, 664), and Athens was a particularly favoured 'free state'.

[9] Plut. *Cato Maior*, 19. 3.

postulated above. The Romans nakedly paraded their authority first in one matter, then in another. This gave them the appearance of usurping power gradually, but in fact the iron fist rather than the velvet glove was always there.[1] It is true that, even so, individual Allied states still retained a large measure of local autonomy; but this was chiefly due to the lack of a Roman civil service and bureaucracy. It is also doubtless true that Roman officials or, what is worse, Roman private citizens were not continuously and uninterruptedly bullying Italian communities and individuals: after all, a Roman consul's time and even a Roman private citizen's time was usually taken up with other things than visits to Allied towns. It may even be true, wildly improbable though it seems, that the many instances of outrage were all quite abnormal and do not reflect the usual state of affairs at all. One can also concede that it was not always the policy of the Romans to maltreat the Allies; they were merely so indifferent to the rights and well-being of others that they nonchalantly rode roughshod over their Italian associates. Even so, the fact that Roman misbehaviour was possible and did frequently occur is securely documented, and it is a fact of cardinal importance.

As far as the speakers of Oscan are concerned one wonders whether it was not only common, but not also quite deliberate. When the Romans in 125 obliterated Fregellae, which, like Praeneste, had been conspicuously loyal in the Second Punic War,[2] it was probably because the town had become much oscanized through large-scale Samnite and Paelignian immigration and was therefore anathema to Rome (and possibly also to its fellow Latin Colonies, none of which made any move to help it in its hour of agony).[3] The place whose leading citizen was flogged over the bath incident was likewise Sabellian: Teanum Sidicinum. At about the same time a young Roman, of no official position, had a peasant of Venusia flogged to death for suggesting that his litter might contain a corpse:[4] the murdered man presumably belonged to the Oscan-speaking element in Venusia, since it is inconceivable that the Roman would

[1] They established local oligarchs of their own choosing in Lucania as early as 296 (Livy 10. 18. 8).

[2] Livy 27. 9. 3; 27. 27. 6.

[3] Asculum Picenum, an Italian town (of Sabellian origin?), is said to have bestirred itself on behalf of Fregellae; but the evidence (Auct. *de vir. ill.* 62. 2) is more than a little dubious.

[4] The exact date of this incident is unknown: 'within the last few years', according to Gaius Gracchus *ap.* Aul. Gell. 10. 3. 5.

have dared to despatch a Latin-speaking member of that colony. If, later, in 72 Verres, the governor of Sicily, had the hardihood to crucify someone who was technically a Roman citizen, it was probably because the victim, who bore the unmistakably Sabellian name of P. Gavius, was a native of Compsa in Samnium and therefore a safe and suitable subject for persecution.[1]

Admittedly these incidents belong to the period after 146, when, as Sallust insists,[2] the old Roman virtues began to degenerate into selfishness and worse. But the Roman attitude did not sprout overnight; there must have been similar outrages earlier.[3] These affairs graphically illustrate the Roman opinion of Samnites and abundantly justify the famous Samnite denunciation of the Romans as *raptores Italicae libertatis*.[4]

If the submissiveness of the Italians to their treatment at Roman hands seems surprising, it is to be attributed to the skilful way in which the Romans exploited a policy of *divide et impera*. The system of separate and non-uniform bilateral treaties reduced the Allies to helplessness. Had Rome, no doubt for her own self-defence or in order amiably to conserve the majesty of the Roman people, felt it necessary to take disciplinary measures against one Ally, she could immediately have invoked the aid of the other Allies, and under the terms of their individual treaties with her they would have been bound to supply it. Thus the so-called Confederacy could be exploited by Rome to make the Allies help to police the recalcitrants amongst their own numbers. Under these circumstances no single Italian people could afford to challenge Rome by itself, no matter how great the injustice under which it was labouring or how unconscionable the interference in its internal affairs.

Among the most favoured states were those of Umbria, places like Camerinum;[5] among the least favoured we can safely reckon

[1] Cic. *II Verr.* 5. 160–4. It is possible that Gavius did not come from Compsa but from the mysterious town where Milo died (Caes. *B.C.* 3. 22), *Cosa in agro Thurino* (mod. Cassano? See E. Aletti, *Sibari*, p. 29). In any event he was a Sabellian.

[2] Sall. *Cat.* 10. 1 f.; *Jug.* 41. 2 f.; *Hist.* 1, fr. 11 M.; D. C. Earl, *Political Thought of Sallust*, pp. 13 f.

[3] Italian restiveness also began earlier. The Bacchanalian disturbances in various parts of Italy *c.* 190 were to some extent anti-Roman protest movements (D. W. L. van Son, *Livius' Behandeling van de Bacchanalia*, pp. 164–9).

[4] Velleius 2. 27. 2 (Pontius Telesinus' alleged description of the Romans at the battle of the Colline Gate).

[5] *Camertinum foedus omnium foederum sanctissimum atque aequissimum* (Cic. *pro Balbo*, 20. 46; cf. Livy 9. 36. 8; 28. 45. 20; Val. Max. 5. 2. 8; Plut. *Marius*, 28. 2).

those of Samnium. States with higher privileges would not have been inclined to make common cause with those worse off than themselves; and in any event it would have been difficult for the tribal states of the Samnites to reach agreement on concerted action with the city-states of the Umbrians.

Moreover there were not only differences of privilege, and of disability, between one Italian state and another: there were gradations of favour even inside the body of a single state. The Roman practice of supporting a particular class rendered interstate resistance still more difficult. The well-to-do group, the local aristocrats, the squires of the Italian communities, were favoured, especially in the states organized as boroughs. The Romans saw to it that members of this class, the so-called *principes*, were safely and securely installed in positions of authority in their own states (and, if those states were urban commonwealths, it was even easier for the Romans to exercise control).[1] They also seem to have permitted all Italian men of substance, whether from urban or from tribal communities, to participate to some extent in the profits of empire. The Italian bourgeoisie was allowed some share in the exploitation of the Roman *ager publicus* in Italy and in the profitable trading opportunities in the provinces. Crumbs for Lazarus. One may wonder whether such patronizing condescension really satisfied either the pride or the cupidity of the Italian gentry.[2] It did, however, suffice to keep them quiescent.

It kept them from coming forward as the natural leaders of anti-Roman movements among their own peoples. Until the isolated uprising at Fregellae in 125, no armed revolt by free men against Roman authority is recorded in Italy in the second century;[3] nor would any revolt have stood the least chance of success without the most thoroughgoing preparation. Only a purposeful minority could have organized it, and such organization was not forthcoming. The small handful of upper-class families was the only minority with the

[1] Compsa, Volsinii and many other examples can be cited. Even without Roman support, the local aristocrats would have been very powerful. They controlled local Italian politics (Cic. *pro Rosc. Am.* 15; *pro Sulla*, 25; *pro Mur.* 47; Livy 29. 36.11; 30. 26. 12; *Epit.* 71; R. Syme, *Rom. Revolution*, pp. 82 f.). Presumably not every local aristocrat was an unabashed partisan of Rome: there were divergent interests within the ranks of the gentry.

[2] They must have resented the fact that their provincial enterprises were subject to the judgement—and inappellable judgement—of the Roman governors.

[3] Slave uprisings are recorded (Livy 32. 26. 4; 33. 36. 1; 39. 29. 8; 39. 41. 6; Obsequens 27, 27b; Oros. 5. 9. 4), even in Rome (Diod. 34. 11).

experience and the prestige necessary for harnessing and directing the activities of any community.[1] But the well-to-do oligarchies in the Italian states, especially the city-states, usually preferred to play safe and cooperate with Rome than to live dangerously. Thanks to the speculative outlets their Roman masters obligingly allowed, they were probably better off economically than they had ever been; and, besides this, they could and did become the *clientes* of prominent and powerful Roman families. They interchanged *hospitium* with their Roman patrons;[2] occasionally they even intermarried with the great Roman houses.[3] It was not a heroic existence,[4] but it had its compensations.

A Roman *patronus* was traditionally bound to display *fides* towards his dependant. Consequently a member of a Roman senatorial family might use his influence to defend or promote the well-being of individual Italians whom he had accepted as his *clientes*. This meant that individual Italian aristocrats, if they had Roman patrons, could normally count on their personal interests being safeguarded. This accounts for certain of the actions which were taken by Roman statesmen at various times.

It would nevertheless be rash to assume from this that the Roman noble and his senatorial faction were pursuing a pro-Allied policy. As a class the Allies were regarded with a lordly indifference bordering on contempt.[5] The best indication of this is Polybius' discussion of the causes of Rome's greatness in his sixth book. From it one infers that the Allies as a group were quite incidental so far as the activities of the Roman state were concerned. To us it is very evident that the mastery of the Mediterranean world, which the Romans had achieved by 135, was largely won by the military services of the Italians. Yet Polybius, reflecting the prejudices and viewpoint of the aristocratic Roman circle in which he moved, consistently minimizes the Italian contribution. For him the cause of Rome's greatness was

[1] It is probably true to say, also, that Roman control of Italy had kept the peace in the peninsula for a century and more: this must have reconciled many Italians to it.

[2] *Privata hospitia habebant* (Livy 42. 1. 10). Vettius Scato and Pompeius Strabo provide an instance of intimacy between an 'Italian' and a 'Roman' notable (Cic. *Phil.* 12. 27; cf. *pro Rosc. Am.* 15; *pro Cluentio*, 165, 176, 177, 198).

[3] Cf. Livy 26. 33. 3; 31. 31. 10; 38. 36. 5; Diod. 37. 15. 2; Dion. Hal. 6. 1.

[4] Even when an Italian obtained the Roman citizenship and took up residence in Rome he was sneeringly referred to as a *civis inquilinus urbis Romae* (Sall. *Cat.* 31. 7).

[5] No second-century aristocrat would have bothered to anticipate the specious claim of Petilius Cerealis that the same rights were accorded to the conquered as to their Roman conquerors (Tac. *Hist.* 4. 74).

the 'mixed constitution'. True, the 'mixed constitution' had to have an instrument of power to carry out its policies, and for that reason Polybius deals at some length with the Roman army; and in that connexion one might have expected him to dilate on the Allied role in Roman military operations. In fact, however, he barely recognizes the Italians' services. He finds it impossible to ignore them altogether, but he can and does belittle their war efforts. He actually represents the Allied contribution as smaller than it was, by insisting more than once[1] that the Roman infantrymen usually numbered as many as those of the Allies, an assertion that may have been true at the time of Cannae (the period he is purporting to describe), but was demonstrably false for his own day (the period which in all other respects he is in fact describing in his sixth book).[2] Polybius' attitude suggests that senatorial circles in Rome took little account of the Allies and evinced little concern for them as a class, even though individual Roman nobles might be prepared on occasion to make some exertions on behalf of their own clients.[3]

In matters economic Roman indifference to the welfare and well-being of the Allies had varying effects. The Roman decision to import grain from the provinces instead of from Italian growers who had helped her to win them must have dislocated earlier marketing arrangements for a time. Livy has a revealing item for the year 202: 'supplies from Sicily and Sardinia caused the price of grain to fall so low that the trader left the grain to the sailors as payment for the freight charges'.[4] Evidently the short-term effects were disastrous for certain individuals, even if Frank is right in thinking that Italian grain growers as a class were not permanently ruined (since Italy could consume all its home-grown wheat).[5]

Nor was grain the only object of trade affected. The Roman senate, some time in the second century, banned mining operations in Italy, we do not know for how long. This, too, need not have had permanent adverse conequences since even in antiquity, when the mineral resources of Italy were much larger than they are today, a good case could be made out for husbanding them. But the immediate effect must have been catastrophic for those engaged in mining

[1] Polyb. 6. 26. 7; 6. 30. 2; cf. 3. 107. 12.

[2] The sixth book was published *c.* 150 (C. O. Brink in *Class. Quart.* IV (1954), 97–122. See F. W. Walbank, *Commentary on Polybius*, I, 200, 636, 709).

[3] See, for example, Livy 39. 17. 4.

[4] Livy 30. 38. 5.

[5] T. Frank, *Econ. Survey of Anc. Rome*, I, 160.

enterprises in Italy. And, despite the Elder Pliny's virtuous claim that the intention of the decree was to conserve the resources of the peninsula, the Italians would suspect, probably with reason in view of the Roman action in shutting down the mines of pre-provincial Macedonia for a decade, that its real purpose was to eliminate any possible competition with the metal supplies now coming in from the newly acquired provinces, such as the daily 25,000 *denarii* from the Iberian peninsula.[1]

The Roman senate, in fact, coolly and arrogantly decided what should be imported into or exported out of Roman and non-Roman Italy alike.[2] The Allies must have resented such behaviour, even if the Romans had been invariably scrupulous about consulting Italian interests in these matters; and it would be very rash to assume that the Romans ever consulted them.

Ultimately it was Roman unconcern for Allied economic welfare that was chiefly responsible for bringing Roman–Italian relations to the breaking point. As we have seen, no Ally was likely to rebel unless its prominent native sons mobilized its anti-Roman discontent; and, as it was the Italian masses who were chiefly under grave disabilities at Roman hands, while the gentry obtained material advantages from the Roman connexion, the local aristocrats were for long not disposed to give a lead. In any case revolt was foredoomed to failure unless a considerable number of Allies acted in unison. The probability of governing minorities in a number of states all seizing on exactly the same moment to organize anti-Roman movements was remote, unless some sudden development occurred that gravely affected many or all of them simultaneously. What Cicero calls the *ferocitas Gracchorum*[3] precipitated precisely such a situation.

Amongst the Romans, it was the landed aristocracy through their large-scale exploitation of the *ager publicus* who were chiefly affected by the agrarian programme of the Gracchi and consequently became its bitterest opponents. The same must have been broadly

[1] See Livy 45. 18. 3; 45. 29. 11; Diod. 31. 8. 6; Strabo 3. 2. 10, p. 148; Pliny, *N.H.* 3. 138; 33. 78; 37. 202. According to A. J. Toynbee in *John Rylands Bull.* XXXVII (1954/55), 283, the ban on Macedonian mining operations was intended to foil greedy Roman contractors; this is very unconvincing.

[2] See Cic. *de re pub.* 3. 9. 16; Livy 43. 5. 8. *C.* 145 or 125 the senate forbade vine and olive growing in Southern Gaul to keep Gallic wine and oil out of Italy (Cic. *loc. cit.*; M. Rostovtzeff, *Soc. Econ. Hist. Rom. Emp.* p. 548, n. 17).

[3] Cic. *in Vat.* 23.

true also in the case of the Allies. According to Cicero,[1] Tiberius Gracchus, when plebeian tribune, showed a blind disregard for the treaty rights of Italians and Latins. His law of 133 that the Roman state should resume its surplus state domain and re-allot it to Roman smallholders bore heavily on the Allies, many of whom were actually occupying it. The Gracchan land commission, whose task it was to decide precisely what land should be repossessed, evidently ejected many of these Allied holders and they, not being Roman citizens, were then ineligible to share in the redistribution. The upper class in the Allied states began to grumble ominously, and their motives may not have been exclusively selfish. It is not unreasonable to conjecture that the land commission would direct its attention first to the state domain held by Allies rather than to those sections of it occupied by Romans. Moreover the commission was probably quite arbitrary in specifying which land was Roman *ager publicus* and which was privately owned Allied soil. An Italian land-holder might find himself ejected, summarily and without appeal, unless his claim to title was so well established and obvious (or sustained by such heavy bribery) as to be indisputable.[2]

The outcries from the Allies against the activities of the commission were so widespread, loud and vigorous that in 129 the senate at Scipio Aemilianus' urging instructed it in effect to leave Italians in undisturbed possession;[3] and the surviving Lex Agraria of 111 seems to confirm that Italians did obtain some security of tenure.[4] But one may wonder whether there was not discrimination in practice against the areas where Oscan was the language. The nine surviving Gracchan terminal stones from Italy are some indication of the scene of the activities of the land commission. No fewer than eight of these nine come from Southern Italy: two from Campania, four from Lucania, and two from Samnium.[5] Undoubtedly the bulk of the state domain was in the south; and, since most of Campania was specifically excluded from the Gracchan agrarian reform, it was inevitable that the land commission would be more active in Sabellian areas than anywhere else.[6] Admittedly it did not operate

[1] Cic. *de re pub.* 3. 29. 41; cf. 1. 19. 31.

[2] Cic. *pro Flacco*, 76–80, shows how difficult it could be for a non-Roman to establish title to his property.

[3] Schol. Bob. p. 118 Stangl; App. *B.C.* 1. 19. 78f.

[4] See lines 29–30. Cf. Cic. *de orat.* 2. 284.

[5] A. Degrassi, *ILLRP*, 1, 269–74.

[6] This is also indicated by the *libri regionum*: see E. Pais, *Storia della Colonizzazione di Roma Antica*, p. 1, *passim*.

only in them. After all it was the derelict countryside of Etruria which had especially aroused Ti. Gracchus' reforming zeal.[1] The Ager Gallicus also witnessed the activity of the land commission since a Gracchan stone, or more accurately a first-century copy of one, from there survives. But it was the south that chiefly received the unwelcome attentions of the commission, and it is possible that there the Senate did not insist that its instruction to leave the Allies alone be carried out.[2] Whether this was so or not, it was obvious that the best safeguard against high-handed treatment from such a commission was possession of the Roman citizenship or, at the very least, the Roman right of appeal. And, significantly, it was precisely at this juncture that the demand for Roman citizenship or, failing that, for the Roman right of appeal began to be raised by the Italians, for the first time.[3] Levantine Greeks and others who had reached Rome as slaves could hope for citizenship on manumission and become founders of 'Roman' families. Indeed by Gracchan times not a few freedmen had risen to prominence at Rome.[4] Were men of servile status to be preferred to Rome's fellow inhabitants of Italy? *Non Italicus provinciali potior est?* as the Emperor Claudius was later to ask.[5]

There was, however, no disposition at Rome to accede to the Italian request. The Italians, kinsmen and neighbours of the Romans, must resign themselves to permanent exclusion. After admitting Arpinum, Formiae and Fundi in 188, the Romans ceased granting their citizenship to Italian towns.[6] Roman citizenship by now had acquired such value that those who possessed it were unwilling to share it with others, even with people so closely related to them, geographically, culturally and ethnically, as the Italians; and for the time being they managed to avoid sharing it, on any large scale at least. There was even a proposal in 126 to expel *peregrini* (=Italians) from Rome.[7]

[1] Plut. *Tib. Gracch.* 8. 7.

[2] It must be remembered, however, that the stones antedate the instruction of the senate.

[3] App. *B.C.* 1. 34. 152; cf. 1. 21. 86; Val. Max. 9. 5. 1; *F.I.R.A.* 1, no. 7, 76 f. But the *ius provocationis* did not provide sure protection against a magistrate determined to ignore it (see P. A. Brunt in *J.R.S.* LV (1965), 105).

[4] T. Frank, *Econ. Survey*, 1, 292.

[5] *ILS*, 212, col. II, l. 6.

[6] The citizenship might be conferred upon individuals: on the priestess from Velia, for instance, who obtained it *c.* 98 in order that the rites of Ceres might be administered by a Roman citizen (Cic. *pro Balbo*, 24. 55). But Arpinum, Formiae and Fundi in 188 were the last communities to receive it.

[7] The law of Pennus, 126, which Gaius Gracchus is said to have opposed (Cic. *de off.* 3. 11. 47; *Brutus*, 28. 109; Plut. *Gaius Gracchus*, 3. 1; 12. 1).

The upper classes among the Latins were won over by adoption of the rule, probably in 125 or thereabouts, that office-holders in Latin communities should automatically become Roman citizens.[1] The upper class in Italian communities was mollified, in some instances at any rate, by the instruction to the Gracchan land commission to confine its activities to *ager publicus* occupied by Romans. The lower orders everywhere, lacking a lead from their own local squires, could be bullied into a continuing state of passivity. To that end Rome made an object-lesson of Fregellae when it showed signs of restiveness. The choice was shrewd. Fregellae was technically Latin, but actually Italian, Sabellian largely. Its Latin element, we may suspect, was chiefly confined to the bourgeoisie, and this class was firmly on the side of Rome.[2] Hence it was safe to take drastic measures against the town; and it would probably be salutary too, since Fregellae in earlier days, before being swamped by Oscan-speaking immigrants, had rendered distinguished service to Rome.[3] To destroy a Latin town, and above all one with such a record, would demonstrate that the Romans were not going to show any favouritism but would deal with insubordination firmly, no matter where it occurred. Accordingly in 125 the Romans sent an army to Fregellae and wiped it off the map.[4]

Agitation amongst the Allies seems to have died down; in other words, the various measures had the desired effect. Perhaps indeed they were too successful in that they made the Romans completely overweening: a few years later the Romans were encouraged to spurn with contempt Gaius Gracchus' proposal to extend the Roman citizenship. The exact scope of Gaius' proposal will presumably never be known;[5] at the very least it must have aimed at conferring upon the Italian gentry the privilege already enjoyed by their Latin counterparts. Whatever his proposal, the Romans, nobles and commons alike, with arrogant over-confidence repudiated it (122), and events were launched upon their fatal course.

[1] G. Tibiletti in *Rend. Ist. Lomb.* LXXXVI (1953), 45–63.

[2] It included elegant speakers of Latin (for instance, L. Papirius: Cic. *Brutus*, 170), and one of its members, Q. Numitorius Pullus, betrayed the town to the Romans in 125 (Cic. *de inv.* 2. 34; *de leg. agr.* 2. 33. 90; Livy, *Epit.* 60; Velleius 2. 6. 4).

[3] See Livy 27. 10. 3; 27. 27. 6; Plut. *Marc.* 29. 7 f.

[4] Carthage, Corinth and Numantia served as the models for the obliteration: Auct. *ad Herenn.* 4. 37: *populus Romanus Numantiam delevit, Karthaginem sustulit, Corinthum disiecit, Fregellas evortit.*

[5] See Val. Max. 9. 5. 1. Livius Drusus' counter-proposal included *ius provocationis* for the Latins (Plut. *Gaius Grac.* 9): in fact they do not seem to have obtained it (Cic. *ad Att.* 5. 11. 2; Diod. 37. 12. 3).

The crisis did not come to a head immediately. A quarter of a century and more was to elapse before the logic of events brought about such a combination of circumstances that the leaders of a large number of Allied communities simultaneously reached the conclusion that conditions were intolerable and at long last decided to act as one. This was in the nineties when there had been recent heavy demands for Italian troops for the operations against Jugurtha, the Cimbri and the Teutoni. The Allies had contributed notably to the Roman victories in these wars and had been rewarded by having it made clear that they were to remain second-class inhabitants of Italy and not become Roman citizens.[1] In addition Italian economic activities were increasingly liable to interference. By his judiciary law, which established the Roman *equites* as an organized and none too scrupulous class, Gaius Gracchus in his own words had thrown daggers into the Roman forum.[2] But he had in fact done more than that. He had set up a group that would embark on jealous rivalry not only with the senate, but also with the Italian gentry. The Roman equestrian class would have no hesitation about encroaching on the business ventures of the Italians in the provinces and of rigging the situation there in their own favour by trying to maintain control over the court for provincial extortion (*quaestio repetundarum*), a control which, as Appian rightly stresses,[3] enabled them to lord it over the Italians. Nor were the Italians going to get much opportunity to protest, since the Romans now passed an alien exclusion act expelling from the city any Italians who posed as Roman citizens. This was the notorious Lex Licinia Mucia of 95. It does not seem to have been as drastic as some other Roman expulsion acts;[4] but owing largely to its psychological impact its effects were far more serious. It goaded the leaders of some Allied states into activity: they began to stir up and direct anti-Roman activity.[5] And this happened at a moment when a lull in the external wars

[1] If Italians distinguished themselves in action, they could expect very little recognition from Rome. When Marius rewarded soldiers of the Marrucini and from highly favoured Camerinum for their bravery against the Cimbri with the Roman citizenship, he was reproved by the senate (Plut. *Marius*, 28. 2; Val. Max. 5. 2. 8; Cic. *pro Balbo*, 46).

[2] Cic. *de leg.* 3. 20; App. *B.C.* 1. 22. 93.

[3] App. *B.C.* 1. 22. 94.

[4] See, for example, App. *B.C.* 1. 23. 100; Plut. *Gaius Grac.* 12. 1 f. The law was aimed at Italians who had somehow contrived to masquerade as Roman citizens (Ascon. p. 68 Cl.). It was useless and harmful to the state (Cic. *ap.* Ascon. p. 67 Cl.) and all Italians hated it (Sallust, *Hist.* 1. 20 M.).

[5] Ascon. p. 68 Cl.; Livy, *Epit.* 71.

left a lot of trained Italian soldiers temporarily, and dangerously, unemployed.

The initiative seems to have been taken among the Marsi,[1] where Q. Poppaedius Silo, a local notable who was intimate with noble Roman houses,[2] emerged as the leader.[3] From the Marsi agitation quickly spread to other Italic peoples. The Samnites needed little urging. Their rank and file certainly had no love for the Romans, and there is no reason to think that their upper class had either. In the second century when the Samnite squires had not led their tribes into rebellion against Rome, their restraint was not due to any love for Rome or to contentment with their own lot. We have already seen that there was little disposition on their part to seek out Roman patrons. They had been deterred by the knowledge that for them to move alone was futile. What they had been unable to achieve in the fourth century was more than ever beyond their capacity in the second, when the relative strengths of Rome and Samnium had changed so drastically to the disadvantage of the latter. At the beginning of the fourth century Roman territory amounted to only one-twentieth (or less) of the area of peninsular Italy; by 100 it was at least one-third; and meanwhile Samnite territory had shrunk considerably.[4] It was hopeless to think of moving alone against such overwhelming odds. But now, in the nineties, when other Italian states were minded to organize an anti-Roman movement, it must have seemed as though something similar to Gellius Egnatius' great scheme of 296 had again materialized. Accordingly the Samnite leaders listened with receptive ears and proceeded to mobilize the hatred which all their countrymen felt for Rome. Some of these leaders can be identified. Foremost among them was Gaius Papius Mutilus of the Pentri.[5] Others were Marius Egnatius, a certain Statius, Numerius Lucilius and Minius or Minatius Iegius, although

[1] The Marsi had bared their teeth as early as 103, according to Plutarch (*Sulla*, 4. 1), who, however, either has made a mistake or else is alluding to the tribe in Germany (Tac. *Germ.* 2; *Ann.* 1. 20; Strabo 7. 1. 3, p. 290).

[2] Poppaedius Silo was the friend of Drusus and Marius (Plut. *Cato Minor*, 2; Diod. 37. 15. 3; Val. Max. 3. 1. 2; Auct. *de vir. ill.* 80. 1).

[3] Poppaedius, not Pompaedius, is the correct form of his name (H. Nesselhauf in *R.E.* XXII (1953) s.v. 'Poppaedius', col. 78). He is called Q. Silo on the one coin of his that survives (A. Sambon, *Les monnaies antiques de l'Italie*, I, 105). He was indefatigable in organizing anti-Roman resistance everywhere (Florus 2. 6. 10).

[4] See the calculations of K. J. Beloch, *Röm. Gesch.* 621; T. Frank, *Econ. Survey of Anc. Rome*, I, 37–56.

[5] Epigraphic evidence (Vetter, no. 160) proves that he came from Bovianum.

it is a matter of conjecture which of these were Pentrian and which Hirpinian.[1] The first two display the same *gentilicia* as Samnite leaders of the fourth and third centuries and might belong to the same families.

Pontius Telesinus, who claimed to belong to the same Caudine family as the Second Samnite War hero, is also listed by Velleius Paterculus and Florus as one of the Samnite leaders at this time.[2] But the Caudini were not secessionist in the Social War and there is no record of Pontius' actual participation in any event before the Civil War of the late eighties, so that it was probably only then that he came to the fore. As one who was very likely already a Roman citizen in 100, he could hardly have been directly concerned with the struggle for the citizenship in the nineties.

Even now it proved impossible for all the Allied peoples of Italy to act as one. The grievances of some states were much less acute than those of others, and in many regions the local aristocrats, content with the money-making pursuits which the Romans allowed them to practise, did not relish the risks which a rebellion against Roman authority entailed. It was chiefly the peoples who lived under a tribal rather than a municipal organization (for the most part in the poorer districts of Italy) and who were the most important reservoir from which the Roman 'Confederacy' drew its soldiers, that agreed to take matters into their own hands: in a word, the Sabellian and Sabellic peoples.

Naturally it was impossible for a widespread anti-Roman movement to be organized among the Allied states in Italy without the Roman authorities getting wind of it, and they accordingly sent commissioners, invested apparently with the *imperium*, to investigate the areas chiefly affected. The names of some of these commissioners are known: Q. Servilius among the Picentes, Domitius (Ahenobarbus?) among the Marsi, L. Postumius among the Campanians, Ser. Sulpicius Galba among the Lucani, and L. Scipio and L. Acilius among the Samnites.[3]

It seems unlikely that the despatch of such inspectors could have

[1] A Numerius Statius was *meddix tuticus* at Bovianum at about the time the war broke out (Vetter, no. 160) and might well be the Statius to whom App. *B.C.* 4. 25. 102 alludes. Iegius was almost certainly Pentrian, since the Hirpini were already out of the war by the time he came to prominence in it.

[2] Velleius 2. 16. 1; Florus 2. 6. 6.

[3] App. *B.C.* 1. 38. 173; Diod. 37. 13. 1; Livy, *Epit.* 73; Livy, *Epit.* 72; App. *B.C.* 1. 41. 182. There is no certainty about the identity of the Domitius among the Marsi.

succeeded in preventing the explosion. Indeed it was an inflammatory, not a conciliatory gesture.

The crisis was quickly brought to a head by the activities of the egregious M. Livius Drusus in 91. Various views of the character and aims of this turbulent plebeian tribune[1] have been put forward.[2] All that need be said here is that his programme was a singularly ill-judged one at this juncture. He proposed, and apparently passed, an agrarian law and a judiciary law; then, to quieten the furore which such laws were only too well calculated to raise amongst the Italians, he proposed that the latter should be granted the Roman citizenship. It is said that this last proposal made Drusus so popular with the Italians that they swore a solemn oath (the so-called Oath of Philippus) to have the same friends and enemies as he. That the Italians did bind themselves together by an oath is implied by the designs of some of the coins that they issued. But the surviving text of the oath is almost certainly a forgery.[3] Nevertheless the tale shows that the Italians welcomed Drusus' citizenship proposal, whatever they may have thought about his other laws. Far otherwise was it with the Romans. The idea of giving their citizenship to the Italians was just as repugnant to them in 91 as it had been a third of a century earlier, and it encountered bitter opposition among all classes.[4] The senate, hoping perhaps that serious trouble might even yet be avoided if Drusus' agrarian and judiciary laws were repealed, pronounced them, as well as his citizenship proposal, null and void.

This seems to have mollified the Etruscans and the Umbrians; but it did not satisfy the more discontented among the Italians. The Sabellic and Sabellian peoples had come to the conclusion that only the Roman citizenship would safeguard them. It was no longer sufficient to seek protection against land commissioners and their arbitrary misuse of the *imperium* through the right of appeal.

[1] Cf. Cic. *in Vat.* 23: *in colluvione Drusi.*

[2] See, for example, A. Bernardi in *Nuova Rivista Storica*, XXVIII/XXIX (1944/45), 83.

[3] For the text see Diod. 37. 11. It cannot be an Oath to Philippus, since he was the enemy of the Italians, who indeed planned to murder him at the Latin festival: probably Ὅρκος Φιλίππου is a mistake for Ὅρκος Φιλίας (O. Hirschfeld, *Kleine Schriften*, pp. 288 f.). H. J. Rose (in *Harvard Theol. Rev.* XXX (1937), 165–81) describes the non-Roman features in the oath. A. von Premerstein, *Vom Werden und Wesen des Prinzipats*, pp. 27 f., regards the non-Roman features as Greek and attributes them to Diodorus' source. The oath is, however, accepted as genuine by L. R. Taylor, *Roman Politics*, pp. 46, 174. See above, p. 176, n. 1.

[4] The Lex Minicia, passed probably in this very year, is indicative of the temper of the Romans: it stipulated that children of marriages between Romans and non-Romans should be regarded as non-Roman.

The *ius provocationis* by itself was inadequate.[1] The one way of ensuring that Roman policies would not adversely affect their interests was to help to frame them. The one certain way of participating in the benefits available to Romans was to acquire *consortium imperii* by becoming part of the Roman citizen body. Accordingly nothing but the citizenship would satisfy them. To extort it a body of 10,000 Marsi actually began to march on Rome along the Via Valeria, but they turned back on being assured that their demand would be considered.[2] When the citizenship was still nevertheless denied to them, they set in motion the plan that they had evidently already formulated[3] and proceeded to organize their own confederacy, a genuine confederacy, in Italy. With it they proposed to go their own way independently of Rome.

Such defiance rendered violence inevitable. In the autumn of 91[4] an unknown assassin struck down Livius Drusus. Amongst the Allies this was interpreted as the Roman reply to the suggestion that they be granted the Roman citizenship.[5] Shortly afterwards Q. Servilius, the commissioner whom the senate had sent to Asculum in Picenum,[6] was murdered in his turn: this was the Italian response. The inhabitants of Asculum had risen in rebellion in a frenzy of rage and slaughtered not only Servilius and his deputy Fonteius,[7] but also every Roman citizen they could lay their hands on. It was with this outburst of insensate fury that hostilities began in the Social War.[8] The Italian bull had challenged the Roman wolf.[9] *Libertas ad honesta coegerat arma.*[10]

1 On the *ius provocationis* as an alternative to the full citizenship, see Val. Max. 9. 5. 1.

2 Diod. 37. 13. 1. For the expression *consortium imperii* see Justin 38. 4. 13.

3 Livy, *Epit.* 71.

4 Drusus was still alive in mid-September (Cic. *de or.* 1. 24).

5 *Mors Drusi iam pridem tumescens bellum excitavit Italicum* (Velleius 2. 15. 1); *vota pro illo per Italiam publice suscepta* (Auct. *de vir. ill.* 66. 12).

6 The town alleged to have risen with Fregellae in 125 (Auct. *de vir. ill.* 65. 2).

7 Title and *praenomen* of Servilius are alike uncertain: he may have been an ex-praetor rather than a praetor, and he may have been Gaius rather than Quintus (R. Syme in *Hermes*, XCII (1964), 410). His deputy Fonteius was the father of the client of Cicero (*pro Font.* 41).

8 Contrary to what is usually asserted, the expression Social War is not a coinage of Livy's: Cicero uses it (*pro Font.* 41). It was often called Bellum Marsicum because of the outstanding role of the Marsi in it. The best name for it is the one preferred by Cicero, Bellum Italicum.

9 The rebels called themselves *Itali* (cf. *vitulus* 'a steer') and the Romans referred to them collectively as *taurus* (*CIL*, I², 848, 877; IX, 6086). Some of their coins, issued perhaps after their successful operations of 90, show a bull goring a wolf: evidently they were unaware that, according to the Argive legend, the wolf ultimately conquers the bull (Plut. *Pyrrhus*, 32. 4 f.; Pausanias 2. 19. 3).

10 Ovid, *Amores*, 3. 15. 9.

CHAPTER 10

THE END OF THE SAMNITES

When the rebellion broke out in 91 not all of the non-Roman peoples of peninsular Italy joined it.[1] The policy of *divide et impera* served Rome well in the crisis. Throughout the peninsula the Latin communities, with the notable exception of Venusia, remained loyal to Rome.[2] The Umbrians and Etruscans in the north also failed to make common cause with the insurgents. The great insurrection was in fact a movement of peoples and tribes in Southern Italy, the northern limit of rebel territory being the line of the Liris from the mouth of that river to its source and continuing on in the same general direction until the Adriatic coast was reached somewhat south of Ancona.[3] But even below this line there were communities that did not rise. The Greek settlements on the coast and the Messapii in the heel of the peninsula did not move against Rome, and the Bruttii in the toe could hardly do so, since most of their territory by now was included within the Ager Romanus.

The organization of the rebels and the military dispositions of the Romans in the first full year of hostilities both suggest that the rebels were twelve in number, and Appian names them for us. Partial lists in Livy and his epitomators and in Diodorus confirm Appian.[4] From this it emerges that the following peoples were arrayed against Rome (the order is Appian's):

(i) Marsi. Named first by Appian presumably as the eponymous instigators of the war.

(ii) Paeligni, (iii) Vestini, (iv) Marrucini: These three presumably are named next because of their long and uncommonly close association with the Marsi in the Sabellic League.

[1] Livy, *Epit.* 72, Diod. 37. 3, Obsequens 54 and Pliny, *N.H.* 33. 55, make it clear that the war began in 91. The year 90 of Velleius (2. 15. 1), like his description of the rebels as *universa Italia*, is an inaccuracy. Moreover the secessionist peoples did not all rise as one. See below, p. 345, n. 1.

[2] The statement of Orosius (5. 18. 2) that the Latins were stirred to arms is a gross error: Venusia was the only town of Latin status to move (App. *B.C.* 1. 39. 188).

[3] This is pointed out by Appian, *B.C.* 1. 39. 175. He also distinguishes Etruscans and Umbrians from the insurgents (*B.C.* 1. 36. 163).

[4] App. *B.C.* 1. 39. 175; Livy, *Epit.* 72; Eutrop. 5. 3. 1.; Oros 5. 18. 8; Diod. 37. 2. 5.

(v) Asculani. Appian calls them Picentini; Diodorus and Livy both give the name Asculani, although Diodorus for good measure also lists the Picentini separately. The Triumphal Fasti make it clear that only one people is meant, the Picentes Asculani, who in fact seem to have been the only Picentes to join the rebels.[1]

(vi) Frentani.

(vii) Hirpini.

(viii) Pompeiani. Diodorus calls them Nolani, presumably because Nola was the place in Campania which, more than any other, became identified with the rebel cause.

(ix) Venusini.

(x) Iapygii. The practice of other Greek writers shows that this means Apuli.[2]

(xi) Lucani.

(xii) Samnites. Named last by Appian presumably for climactic effect, since they proved to be the most durable of all the insurgents.

For most of these peoples there is no problem of identification. Uncertainty arises only in the case of the Pompeiani, Iapygii and Samnites.

The Pompeiani are ostensibly those who lived at Pompeii, and there is independent evidence that they joined the insurgent cause. Appian's Pompeiani, however, probably includes more than the inhabitants of Pompeii. This might be suspected from the fact that Pompeii was, or at one time had been, merely one part of a league headed by Nuceria Alfaterna; and it is supported by Diodorus' variant Nolani. Presumably insurgent Campanians in general are to be understood under Appian's Pompeiani: he calls them by the latter name since Pompeii was the original nucleus of insurrection in Campania.

Appian's Iapygii must be a blanket term for all rebel Apuli, who ultimately included the inhabitants of Canusium, Salapia, Cannae, Ausculum and Larinum (if it can be reckoned North Apulian).[3] Appian does not single out one town to represent insurgent Apulia, as he does Pompeii in the case of Campania, probably because there no single town took the initiative. The revolt spread to Apulia when insurgents from elsewhere went thither and 'persuaded' certain Apuli to join their ranks.

[1] As there had been a mass exodus of Picentes to Southern Italy in the third century (see above, p. 288), Picenum had been left very largely 'Roman' by the first century.

[2] See, for example, Polyb. 2. 24. 11; cf., too, App. *Hann.* 45.

[3] App. *B.C.* 1. 52. 277 f.

Map 4. The Social War insurgents.

By Samnites Appian obviously means the Pentri and any still surviving Caraceni. The Hirpini are excluded and almost certainly so are the Caudini. By 91 the latter were normally no longer called Samnites; indeed they were rarely referred to even by their tribal name of Caudini. Usually each Caudine community was individually named, after its own town (Telesini, Combulterni, etc.), since they had long before been broken up into separate boroughs. Many, perhaps all, of these latter had been incorporated as *municipia* into the Roman state and therefore had no need to join an insurrectionary movement to obtain Roman citizenship. In fact there is no evidence for Caudine participation in the Social War. It is true that two passages, in Florus and Velleius respectively,[1] which are couched in purely general (and in the case of Florus wildly inaccurate) terms, list Pontius Telesinus (that is, from Caudine Telesia) as one of the insurgent generals. But it is impossible to find any occasion in the Social War when he was present: he comes in later, in the Civil War.

Eight of Appian's insurgent twelve were tribal states. The Iapygii (Apuli) apparently were not, to judge from their coinage issues; and Venusia, a Latin Colony, certainly had a municipal form of constitution. The same seems true of Pompeii and Asculum. The other eight, however, were not boroughs at this time, a fact which confirms what has already been suggested: namely that the Romans were most successful in controlling communities that were urbanized.

It is to be noted further that the first four peoples on Appian's list, and probably the Asculani as well, had all at one time used dialects closely resembling Oscan; as for the Frentani, they actually spoke Oscan. Thus five of these peoples can be reckoned Sabellic and the sixth Sabellian. All six of them were largely latinized.

Of the remaining six, five used Oscan as their language. Venusia officially used Latin; but its population included a big Oscan-speaking element. By 91 latinization had also made considerable headway amongst these peoples, but their general character was still Sabellian.

The insurgents fall naturally into these two categories of a Sabellic group in the north-central area and a Sabellian group in the south. Such a division is unmistakably implied by Appian's order of listing them and it is explicitly emphasized by Diodorus,

[1] Velleius 2. 16. 1; Florus 2. 6. 6.

who points out that the one group, sometimes collectively styled 'Marsic' apparently, was separated from the other, the so-called 'Samnite' group, by 'the Cercolae as they are called'.[1]

The arrangement is neatly schematic, the only people apparently misplaced, linguistically anyhow, being the Frentani. From quite early times they had always cooperated very closely with the Marsi, Marrucini, Paeligni and Vestini:[2] so that it was natural for them now to form part of the Sabellic wing of the rebels.[3] This had the advantage of ensuring that the two insurgent groups were evenly balanced, with six peoples apiece.

This twofold division was reflected in the political arrangements for the grand alliance; but, although divided into two groups, the rebels nevertheless possessed a certain degree of ethnic community. They all belonged, or at one time had belonged, to the same linguistic family and both Q. Poppaedius Silo, the 'Marsic' leader, and C. Papius Mutilus, his 'Samnite' counterpart, bear unmistakably Sabellian names. Thus the war was not without its nationalist aspect.[4]

Nevertheless, despite the apparent Oscan solidarity, there were pro-Roman elements even in the insurgent districts, especially among the propertied classes and particularly in urban areas. Pompeius Strabo raised a considerable force for Rome, perhaps as much as two legions, among the Picentes.[5] Amongst the Vestini the town of Pinna stood firmly by Rome.[6] In Samnite country Minatus Magius raised a volunteer 'free corps' of Hirpini to fight on Rome's behalf.[7] Nuceria sided with Rome in Southern Campania,[8] and both in the latter region and in Apulia rebel coercion was needed to induce some towns to join the rebel cause. For that matter

[1] Diod. 37. 2. 7. H. Nissen, *Ital. Landesk.* II, 790, seeks the Cercolae in the Serra Carracino which forms part of the Maiella massif. J. Carcopino, *Hist. Rom.*[3], II, 370, with at least equal plausibility, suggests somewhere near the Monte della Meta.

[2] The Frentani are grouped with the Sabellic League, for instance, in the roster for 225 (Polyb. 2. 24. 12).

[3] Cic. *pro Cluentio*, 21 makes it clear that the Frentani were part of the 'Marsic' group in the Social War.

[4] This is stressed, with some exaggeration, by W. Schur in *Klio*, Beiheft 46, 115. Perhaps it was the ethnic aspect of the war that caused Roman antiquarians to coin the word *Sabellus* at about this time (see above, p. 32).

[5] One of his legions, to judge from the epigraphic evidence, seems to have been largely made up of Picentes (E. Gabba in *Athenaeum*, XXIX (1951), 190).

[6] Diod. 37. 19; Auct. *ad Herennium*, 2. 45. But there was an insurgent faction in the town (Val. Max. 5. 4. 7).

[7] Velleius 2. 16. 2.

[8] Presumably at the urging of P. Sittius (Cic. *pro Sulla*, 58).

even the insurgent twelve did not all rise as one.[1] The Marsi, who took the initiative, were quickly joined by their Sabellic associates and the Sabellian Frentani. The Asculani, as the strikers of the first blow, were obviously in the movement from the start. Nor need one believe that the Samnites with their long-standing grudge against the Romans lagged far behind.[2]

In throwing down the gauntlet thus to Rome the Italic peoples, as the insurgents may appropriately be called,[3] were embarking on an extremely hazardous venture. Rome had the great geographical advantage of possessing a solid bloc of territory which included the Sabine land and ran right across the peninsula, effectively separating the insurgents from direct physical contact with the Umbrians and Etruscans. Besides this Rome could in time mobilize very large resources, much larger than the Italici could ever hope to do. The rebel areas were among the poorest in Italy, whereas Rome even after their defection still controlled the best, wealthiest and most fertile regions. The strongest element on the insurgent side was undoubtedly the Samnites: it was they who held out longest and Diodorus shows what he thought of them by placing them first on his list of rebels. Yet they could be easily outmatched by the Latins alone. Moreover Rome could also count on Cisalpine Gaul and the provinces beyond the sea. Throughout, her maritime supremacy was never challenged by the insurgents, so that she was never cut off from provincial sources of manpower and materials. At the same time she could effectively prevent any overseas help from reaching the rebels.[4]

The odds against the insurgents were thus formidable indeed,

[1] App. *Mithr.* 22; Velleius 2. 15. 1; Auct. *ad Herenn.* 4. 13 and Oros. 5. 18. 8 imply the same thing. The seven peoples listed by Livy, *Epit.* 72, were those who were in the movement from the outset (cf. Oros. 5. 18. 8); they include the Samnites. The Apuli and the secessionist Campanians were the laggards.

[2] Cf. Sil. Ital. 11. 8: *odium renovare ferox in tempore Samnis.*

[3] Their sling bullets and their coins show that they called themselves *Itali*.

[4] Rome could count on help from the Latins and the provinces from the outset (Livy, *Epit.* 72). Campania sent supplies uninterruptedly (Cic. *de leg. agr.* 2. 80). Sicily contributed clothing and other things (Cic. *II Verr.* 2. 2. 5; 5. 4. 8). Asia also helped Rome (Memnon, frag. XXIV in Müller's *Frag. Hist. Graec.* III, p. 540). The importance to Rome of her control of the sea is graphically illustrated by *CIL*, I², 203 (= Bruns, pp. 176–80), the *senatus consultum de Asclepiade* honouring three Greek captains for their services in the war. One of the Otacilii held a naval command (Sisenna, fr. 38 P.), thereby repeating the role of a third-century ancestor. According to Livy, *Epit.* 75, A. Postumius Albinus was in charge of naval operations when he lost his life at Pompeii in 89. The Italici may have attempted operations by sea: they certainly used the services of a Cilician pirate named Agamemnon (Diod. 37. 3. 1; Oros. 5. 18. 10).

and in the long run Rome was almost sure to defeat them. Consequently, if the Italic peoples nevertheless challenged her, it must have been because they counted on there not being a long run. They hoped to force a decision in short order, their confidence being bolstered by the fact that their actual forces in being were stronger than those at the disposal of Rome. For the moment that was vital and crucial: the advantage would lie with them.

In fact Roman chickens now came home to roost. For years Rome had obliged the Allies to produce soldiers in order that her own citizens might avoid military service. As a result by the end of the first century it is safe to say that the Allies possessed a far bigger pool of trained manpower than Rome, and at that particular juncture it became an unemployed pool also, since the wars which ever since 115 had been causing Rome to make inordinate military demands of her Allies had come to a temporary standstill.[1] The Allies saw their chance: they could use these troops of theirs, which for the moment were not involved in Rome's wars, against Rome herself. It is to be noted that the Allies who revolted were precisely the chief suppliers of soldiers to the army of the Roman 'Confederacy', and it is difficult to resist the conclusion that they chose this moment to fight because they knew that the forces they had ready and in being were more than a match for those at the disposal of Rome.[2] With these forces they hoped to settle the issue in short order. Unfortunately for them winter followed hard on the violent doings at Asculum and imposed a delay of some weeks on active warfaring, a delay which the Romans put to very good use. Even so, the fighting during the first few months of the Social War went so heavily in favour of the insurgents that their appreciation of the situation seems realistic enough.

But the breathing spell which Rome providentially obtained during the winter of 91/90 proved to be the margin between survival and complete disaster. She was able to muster sufficient resources to survive the opening months. Thereafter she gradually got stronger and prospects for an insurgent victory steadily receded. After some striking early victories the reverses of the rebels became increasingly frequent and increasingly serious, until by 88 they were reduced to

[1] Eutrop. 5. 3. 1; cf. E. Gabba in *Athenaeum*, XXIX (1951), 190.

[2] Their officers, too, had seen service with the Roman armies. For example, Ti. Cleppius of the Lucani had distinguished himself in the operations in Sicily in 101 (Diod. 36. 8. 1; 37. 2. 11).

desperate straits. Nevertheless the initial advantage possessed by the Italici enabled them to make the conflict a singularly hard and bloody one. The ancient writers agree on its sanguinary character, and the many casualties among the high-ranking officers on both sides make it certain that they are not exaggerating. For Diodorus it was the greatest war, and Florus avers that neither Pyrrhus nor Hannibal caused as much devastation.[1]

The fate of Servilius and his aide at Asculum caused the other inspecting commissioners who had been sent out from Rome to remove themselves to less dangerous places. Ser. Sulpicius Galba was spirited to safety from the Lucani by a woman.[2] L. Postumius found refuge from the southern Campanians temporarily in Nola, and L. Acilius and L. Scipio from the Samnites equally temporarily in Aesernia;[3] but the situation of the three last-named was precarious, since both Nola and Aesernia were destined to fall into insurgent hands. If the Domitius who had been amongst the Marsi also needed to seek safety, he probably found it at the Latin Colony at Alba Fucens, which turned out to be a safe asylum.[4]

As the uprising at Asculum had occurred late in 91, there was not much time left for any serious campaigning in that year. But there was some. Both insurgent groups moved at once in an effort to remove the obstacles that barred their respective roads to Rome. Alba Fucens was assaulted in the 'Marsic' area and Aesernia in the 'Samnite'. Neither town fell at this time. Had the secessionists captured these Latin Colonies in 91 they might have been able to threaten Rome itself, although it must always remain doubtful whether they would ever have been able to carry that stronghold by assault.

If there were any other military operations in 91 no details concerning them have survived.

Both sides passed the winter of 91/90 making preparations, and

[1] Diod. 37. 2. 15; Florus 2. 6. 11. We hear of men resorting to self-mutilation to escape service in it (Val. Max. 6. 3. 3). Eutrop. 5. 3. 1 lists some of the high-ranking officers who fell: the Romans Rutilius, Caepio and Porcius Cato; the Italici Vettius Scato, Herius Asinius, Herennius and Cluentius.

[2] Livy, *Epit.* 72. He reappears almost immediately as a Roman commander: he must be the Ser. Sulpicius Galba who served with Pompeius Strabo at Firmum in 90; and he may be the *-cius C.f. Ani(ensi)* who was on Strabo's staff in 89 (*ILS*, 8888): see C. Cichorius, *Röm. Studien*, pp. 137–41.

[3] Livy, *Epit.* 73; App. *B.C.* 1. 41. 182.

[4] This seems to have been Cn. Domitius Ahenobarbus. But see F. Münzer in *R.E.* v (1905), s.v. 'Domitius, 21', col. 1327.

the interval proved crucial. It would have been better for the Italic cause if the Asculani had held their hand in 91. For, if it is true that they took the Romans by surprise in that year, they also provided them with the breathing spell of the winter, as we have seen; and the Romans used it to good advantage. Every Roman of good family, even if like the youthful Cicero he could not boast of any real military experience, was pressed into service as an officer. As ordinary soldiers not only did they enrol Roman citizens, even including freedmen, but they also got troops from the Latin Colonies and the provinces during this winter.[1] The campaigning season of 90 found the Romans with no fewer than fourteen legions in some sort of shape to put in the field.[2] The sequel was to show that these were made up in large part of men with little military training: but they staved off irreparable disaster. Before 90 was over each legion with its auxiliaries, who might include Spaniards, Africans and Gauls, had been built up into a formation of 10,000 men.[3]

The Italici for their part used the winter months not only to get troops in readiness, but also to set up their organization. It is described by Diodorus, who for this part of his history was probably relying on the good authority of Poseidonius. Some other ancient writers also allude to it. Nevertheless its precise character baffles us. Many modern scholars say that the insurgents banded themselves together into a federal union. There are, however, some doubts about this. This is what Diodorus says:[4]

'The Italici had as their capital city[5] Corfinium, which was very large and remarkable and had only recently been completed. They provided it with everything calculated to strengthen a large city and administration, with a spacious forum and council-chamber and lavishly with everything else for a war effort, including a wealth of money and an abundant supply of provisions. They also set up there a common senate of 500 members, from whom those best fitted to administer the state and competent to deliberate for the common safety would be the ones to take the initiative. They entrusted the direction of the war to these latter, although it was the senate-members who were

[1] Livy, *Epit.* 72 (*saga populus sumpsit*); App. *B.C.* 1. 49. 212; Macrob. 1. 11. 32; cf. Livy, *Epit.* 74. [2] App. *B.C.* 1. 40. 179; Cic. *pro Font.* 43.

[3] App. *B.C.* 1. 41. 183. The expense of the war effort caused debasement of the coinage. Hoards of plated Roman *denarii* belonging to this period have been unearthed.

[4] Diod. 37. 2. 4 f. See Mommsen, *Röm. Gesch.* II, 221 f.

[5] Diodorus' expression, κοινὴ πόλις, is also used by Strabo 5. 4. 2, p. 241.

invested with sovereign authority. The senate-members[1] decreed that two consuls and twelve praetors should be chosen every year. As consuls there were chosen:[2] Quintus Pompaedius Silo, Marsic by birth and the leading man of his tribe, and as the other Gaius Aponius (*sic*) Mutilus, a Samnite by birth, he too foremost among his own people in reputation and exploits. Dividing all Italy into two zones, they created consular commands and subordinate commands as follows: To Pompaedius they entrusted the territory from the so-called Cercolae [Kerkoles?] to the Adriatic Sea, the areas facing west and north. And they assigned him six praetors. To Gaius Mutilus they entrusted the rest of Italy, the areas facing east and south, assigning him too six praetors. Thus did they arrange their administration in all respects cleverly and, to put it bluntly, in imitation of the ancestral Roman constitution; but in everything else, namely the hostilities that immediately ensued, they were quite violent. They called their common capital Italia.'

From this it clearly emerges that the insurgents decided to make Corfinium their war headquarters, and this town now makes its first appearance in history. Situated on Paelignian territory near the point where the Rivers Gizio and Aternus come together, it was excellently placed to become the rebel capital since it lay in the midst of the 'Marsic' group, but was also close to the 'Samnite' group via a short and direct, if not exactly easy, route through Sulmo. Diodorus' remarks about the monumental aspect it acquired from the rebels can be dismissed as rhetorical exaggeration: Corfinium lasted as the capital much too short a time to give them any real chance to embellish the place. But that it did in fact serve as their capital is confirmed by Strabo and Velleius.[3] The problem is to decide what was the precise nature of the political organization that was established there.

Much light would be thrown on this if we could accept as accurate Diodorus' assertion that the insurgents copied Roman constitutional arrangements. Unfortunately this statement is only superficially approximate. No doubt the insurgent 'senate' and the insurgent

[1] Diodorus does not make it fully clear whether it was the inner committee or the full senate that decided on the two consuls and twelve praetors.

[2] Diodorus does not say how the 'consuls' were chosen. Strabo 5. 4. 2, p. 241, says that they were voted into office (by a primary assembly?).

[3] Strabo 5. 4. 2, p. 241; Velleius 2. 16. 4. They give the name as Italica; but 'Italia' is found on the insurgent coins.

'consuls' with their subordinate 'praetors' suggested the comparison to Diodorus. But the analogies between them and their alleged Roman counterparts are far from exact. In 91 the Roman senate did not number 500 or the Roman praetors 12. The Roman consuls were indeed two in number, but the competence of each was not confined to only one half of the Ager Romanus. The probability is, of course, that the two consuls at Corfinium were due, not so much to imitation of Rome, as to the fact that the insurgents were in two groups and had to have a head for each. No doubt the number of praetors, twelve, was similarly determined by the number of insurgent peoples.

The name Italia may be much more significant for throwing light on the kind of arrangements that the insurgents set up. Strabo not only confirms that Italia was the name of the Italic capital but adds that it was intended to replace Rome. The implication is that, whereas Rome was of and for the Romans only, Corfinium was to be somehow representative of all the rebel areas, the administrative centre for some kind of federal organization. This emphasizes clearly the distinction between the Roman and the Sabellian political outlook.

After the American Civil War, however, it is hardly necessary to point out that federal organizations are not all alike. Exactly how close the federal bonds of the Italici were there is no means of knowing. Presumably all the rebel peoples were represented in the senate of 500 members; but the number of senators from each people, their tenure of office and the composition of the smaller war committee are nowhere revealed. Strabo's statement that the Italici elected their 'consuls' and 'praetors' suggests that there was a primary assembly, presumably of the arms-bearing males of the constituent peoples.[1] Perhaps this assembly elected the senate as well, but Strabo does not say so: in fact he does not mention the senate. On the whole it may be conjectured that the senate was intended to be some sort of representative government which, once appointed, could exercise sovereign authority entrusted to it by the assembly.

The temptation to argue that the rebel organization in 90 must have resembled the old Samnite League or the Sabellic League is strong; but we do not have enough information about these to

[1] H. D. Meyer in *Historia*, VII (1958), 77–9.

speak with confidence. Furthermore it may be that the constitutional arrangements of the Italici, even though not copied (as Diodorus says) from those of Rome, nevertheless do owe something to Roman practice.[1] Our information about the government at Corfinium, meagre though it is, indicates that it was strikingly similar to that of the Thessalian League which Flamininus established in 196 and which lasted virtually unchanged for centuries.[2] The senate (*synedrion*) at Larisa was composed of representatives from the various Thessalian cities, and served as the centre of administration for the Thessalians. It became the standard government for any league under the domination of Rome. That the Italici should organize themselves along the lines with which Roman usages had made them familiar is likely enough; so that the constitution at Corfinium may well have been very much like the one at Larisa. If this was so, it might help to explain why it evoked so little surprise in antiquity. Livy evidently did not think it sufficiently unusual to call for any special comment; at any rate the Periochae of Books 72 to 76 inclusive fail to mention it. Diodorus and Strabo did regard it as a notable enough phenomenon to deserve disproportionate space in their texts. Yet they do not comment on its novelty; they may have merely been uncritical, but that is hardly true of their presumptive source, Poseidonius. The argument from silence is risky, of course; but it does imply that the insurgent organization did not impress those who were presumably familiar with its details as something unparalleled.

The two 'consuls' clearly were the commanders-in-chief of the two groups, Poppaedius Silo of the 'Marsic' and Papius Mutilus of the 'Samnite'.[3] Each of them was in overall command of an assigned region, 'the so-called Cercolae' being the boundary between their respective spheres. In conformity with this Papius Mutilus is actually styled *embratur* (= the oscanized form of *imperator*) on surviving insurgent coins. The six 'praetors' (or, in the 'Samnite' sphere, 'meddices') which each commander-in-chief had under him were the generals of the six peoples that composed the group

[1] The coinage issues of the insurgents prove how ready they were to imitate things Roman.

[2] See Livy 33. 32. 5; 34. 51. 4; 36. 8. 2; 42. 38. 6; *I.G.* 9. 2. 89 (= the *senatus consultum* concerning Narthacium).

[3] This emerges from all the literary texts and is implied by the coins even though only one survives with Poppaedius' name on it. Papius' name occurs on a tile from Bovianum (*Not. d. Scavi* (1913), pp. 480–4; *Klio*, XXIV (1924), 237, 239).

in his region. To match these twelve separate rebel forces, the Romans also had twelve forces, six for each area.[1]

With the opening of the campaigning season for 90 the Italici immediately took the field. Their aim essentially was the same as Hannibal's: they proposed to render Rome impotent by isolating her and depriving her of all her Allies in Italy. To this end, the 'Marsic' group in the north-central area sought to open up a broad and unimpeded corridor of communication, if not to Rome, then at least to the Umbrians and Etruscans, who might thereby be induced to participate in the insurrection. For this purpose it was not enough for the rebels merely to retain Asculum: they needed to get control as well of other strongholds that barred the way to an effective junction with their potential allies to the north. Accordingly, besides Asculum, such key places as Pinna, Firmum and the two Latin Colonies on the Via Valeria, Alba Fucens and Carseoli, quickly became the centres of heavy fighting.[2]

To foil this strategy the Roman consuls for 90 assigned seven of the fourteen legions they had mobilized to the north-central zone.[3] The consul there had two legions, and under him he had five *legati*, each commanding one legion. In other words, the Romans had six armies facing the 'Marsic' group.

The development of the operations suggests that for the campaign of 90 the consul advanced along either the Via Salaria or the Via Valeria and disposed his legions roughly in an arc stretching from north to south. Furthest north was Cn. Pompeius Strabo with Legion XI near Asculum; Q. Servilius Caepio with Legion XII took up position near Reate; while Gaius Perperna with Legion XIII near Trebula Mutuesca may have been immediately north of Gaius Marius with Legion XIV. The consul himself, Rutilius Lupus, had his headquarters with Legions III and IV higher up the Tolenus near Carseoli, while M. (or M'.) Valerius Messalla had his Legion XV west of the Fucine Lake.[4]

[1] App. *B.C.* I. 40.

[2] In the 'Samnite' theatre, too, the Latin Colonies were heavily assaulted. For Aesernia, see Livy, *Epit.* 72, 73; Oros. 5. 18. 11, 14; App. *B.C.* I. 41. 182; for Luceria, see Diod. 19. 72. 9 (who might, however, be referring to the Civil War between Caesar and Pompey; Luceria played a prominent role in it: see, for example, Cic. *ad Att.* 7. 20; 8. 1; 8. 11a); for Beneventum, see Cic. *Verr.* I. 38, and the schol. thereon p. 169 Or.

[3] To find commanders the Romans called out practically all members of the *nobilitas* who had had military experience (App. *B.C.* I. 40).

[4] P. Rutilius Lupus was a parvenu whose lack of experience soon proved costly. For his military dispositions in 90 see *CIL*, IX, 6086, no. XXI; Oros. 5. 18. 10; App. *B.C.* I. 41. 83 and A. von Domaszewski in *S. B. Akad. Wien* (1924), pp. 21 f.

Roman dispositions in the 'Samnite' theatre are much more difficult to establish.[1] Undoubtedly there was a consul there too with two legions, and under him five *legati*, each with one legion. Furthermore it is clear that, just as Pompeius Strabo operated almost in isolation in the most northerly part of the 'Marsic' theatre, so did P. Licinius Crassus in the most southerly part of the 'Samnite'.[2] The bulk of Rome's southern forces, however, were nowhere near that far afield. The consul facing the 'Samnite' group was L. Julius Caesar,[3] and he was evidently mindful of the strategy in the Samnite Wars of old: he kept his own two legions and his other four *legati* in the border regions of Western and North-western Samnium. The Liris valley and Campania were once again to feel the scourge of war in the manner of two centuries earlier. Teanum Sidicinum may have been the principal base for the consul and his two legions (I and II), and the *legati* were within reasonable distance of this stronghold.[4]

The 'Marsic' insurgents, even though we cannot always decide precisely which insurgent, quickly won some striking successes in 90. The Picentes, aided no doubt by the Vestini and possibly others, repulsed Pompeius Strabo's attempt to capture Asculum, inflicting heavy losses on him and obliging him to retreat northwards to the Latin Colony of Firmum.[5] There he was put under heavy siege by T. Lafrenius, whose nationality, like that of the troops under his command, is not recorded, but was presumably Vestinian. No doubt it was likewise insurgent Vestini who invested Pinna, itself a Vestinian town but with a pro-Roman faction;[6] ultimately they captured it. Meanwhile the Paeligni, commanded perhaps by P. Praesentius,[7] seem to have pressed the attack on Alba Fucens, and,

[1] On these the suggestions of Domaszewski, *loc. cit.*, are much more conjectural and unconvincing.

[2] This is the father of the later so-called 'triumvir', who as a mere stripling may have been serving with him. As Crassus was driven into Grumentum (App. *B.C.* I. 41. 184), he must have been serving in the far south.

[3] Appian, *B.C.* I, *passim*, regularly calls him Sex. Julius Caesar, thereby confusing him with the consul of 91 (who also served in 90, but as a proconsul). Appian was careless with names: he calls Memmius Mummius (I. 37. 167) and Pontidius Pontilius (I. 40. 181).

[4] The course of the fighting proves that there was a heavy concentration of troops in this historic region. Some Roman troops were undoubtedly based on Capua (Cic. *de leg. agr.* 2. 90). The other four *legati* of L. Julius Caesar were: L. Cornelius Sulla, the future dictator, T. Didius, P. Cornelius Lentulus, M. Claudius Marcellus (see Broughton, *M.R.R.* II, 28–31).

[5] The Φάλερνον ὄρος of App. *B.C.* I. 47. 204 must be Falerio, north-west of Asculum.

[6] Diod. 37. 19. Val. Max. 5. 4. 7 shows that the town also had a secessionist faction; cf. Auct. *ad Herenn.* 2. 45. Pinna lay to the east of the Apennine watershed.

[7] App. *B.C.* I. 41. 183 records Praesentius' success, but not his nationality.

even though they failed to capture that Latin Colony,[1] they knocked Legion XIII about so badly that the consul Rutilius transferred the command of it from Gaius Perperna to another *legatus*, the famed Gaius Marius.

The greatest successes of all, however, were won by the Marsi. Their general, P. Vettius Scato,[2] led them southward from their own country presumably down the valley of the Upper Liris (the so-called Val Roveto), in order to effect a junction with their Oscan-speaking comrades-in-arms; and they at once scored a startling victory.[3] They worsted the consul L. Julius Caesar, evidently somewhere near Atina, and forced him to fall back towards Teanum Sidicinum. This enabled the southern insurgents, who in this context can only be the Pentri, to put Aesernia under close siege.[4] Vettius Scato and his victorious Marsi then hastened back to their own country, once again by way of the Liris valley. They encountered Valerius Messalla with Legion XV somewhere south of Carseoli and handled him so roughly that the consul Rutilius was again obliged to make a change: he transferred Messalla's command to the proconsul Sex. Julius Caesar.[5] But Rutilius' own turn was not long in coming. Vettius Scato and the Marsi met him in a set battle-piece on 11 June on the banks of the Tolenus close to Carseoli, and the consul went down in shattering defeat.[6] He himself died of a head wound received in the battle, and the Latin Colony seems to have been plundered.[7]

There was near panic in Rome when the bodies of Rutilius Lupus and other notables were brought there for burial.[8] Rutilius' *imperium* and the remnants of his forces were entrusted to two of his *legati* jointly: his elderly kinsman Gaius Marius and the previous year's praetor Q. Servilius Caepio.[9] This arrangement, however,

[1] The garrison was reinforced with *milites Africani* (*CIL*, IX, 3907).

[2] Cic. *Phil.* 12. 27 identifies him as Marsic and refers to a Vettius Scato of his own time who was born *in Marsis* and was in straitened circumstances (Cic. *de domo*, 116; *ad Att.* 4. 5. 2; 6. 1. 15). The praenomen of the general was Publius (Cic. *Phil.* 12. 27): he is called Titus by Eutrop. 5. 3. 3 and Gaius by Seneca, *de benef.* 3. 23. 5.

[3] Livy, *Epit.* 73; App. *B.C.* 1. 41. 182.

[4] See below, p. 358.

[5] Sextus Julius quickly won a success against the Paeligni (Livy, *Epit.* 73, emending *Sex. Sul.*).

[6] Ovid, *Fasti*, 6. 563–6; App. *B.C.* 1. 43. 192. Rutilius committed his men before they were fully trained and lost 8,000 of them (Oros. 5. 18. 12). Florus (2. 6. 12) identifies the losing consul in error as L. Julius Caesar.

[7] Florus 2. 6. 11 says that Carseoli was plundered: but he is not a reliable witness.

[8] App. *B.C.* 1. 43. 194 f.

[9] App. *B.C.* 1. 44. 195.

did not long endure, since Caepio in his turn was soon enticed into an ambush by Poppaedius Silo and slain somewhere near Amiternum by a combined force of Vestini and Marsi.[1]

That the latter people should have provided the name by which the war came to be known, Bellum Marsicum, is not surprising. Their leader Q. Poppaedius Silo was its heart and soul, and ten thousand of them had marched on Rome before ever the fighting started. Now in the first full year of hostilities their general Vettius Scato achieved the astonishing feat of defeating separately each of the Roman consuls, and Poppaedius Silo slew the successor of one of them. Probably it was now that the proverb 'No triumph over, and no triumph without, the Marsi' gained currency at Rome, if indeed it was not coined at this time.[2] Further point was to be given to it in the following year when the Marsi defeated and killed yet another Roman consul.

By the late summer of 90 Marius was left as commander-in-chief against the Central Italian insurgents: and to avoid any further catastrophes he resorted to a grim holding operation. Realizing that the Roman defeats were largely due to the greenness of the troops,[3] he refused to risk large-scale engagements, but preferred to drill and discipline his men. Fortunately for him the harvesting season brought about a lull in the fighting,[4] giving him the respite he needed and even permitting some fraternization between his troops and their opponents.[5]

That Marius needed, or received, the help of Sulla in holding his own seems improbable. Appian tells a story of thousands of Marsi being caught between Marius and Sulla in a vineyard somewhere in the Liris valley, where thanks exclusively to Sulla more than 6,000 of them lost their lives, while an even greater number lost their weapons.[6] This tale undoubtedly derives from the *Memoirs* of Sulla, who, anxious to magnify his own achievements and belittle those of his hated rival, was bent on saddling Marius with a reputation for incompetence in the Social War. The truth was probably very different. The insurgents undoubtedly did spread some alarm and

[1] *CIL*, i², 708; *ILS*, 29, 2488; App. *B.C.* 1. 44. 197; Oros. 5. 18. 14.

[2] Vettius later paid for this achievement with his life in the war and with the impoverishment of his family after it (Cic. *de domo*, 16). The proverb is quoted by App. *B.C.* 1. 46. 203 and alluded to by Strabo 5. 4. 2, p. 241.

[3] Oros. 5. 18. 11; Plut. *Marius*, 33. 2.

[4] Diod. 37. 25.

[5] Diod. 37. 15. Some fraternization also occurred in 89: Cic. *Phil.* 12. 27.

[6] App. *B.C.* 1. 46. 201.

despondency in the Liris valley. A force of them commanded by a certain T. Herennius (from Campania?) managed to reach the vicinity of Sora.[1] Whether they came from the 'Samnite' or the 'Marsic' theatre, they had evidently evaded Sulla, the Roman commander in the Aesernia region, to penetrate this far, and they seem to have been finally dealt with by Marius.[2] Sulla, however, to make sure that he would never be blamed for letting them outwit him, boldly reversed the roles of himself and Marius in the episode: it was Marius' fault that they got all the way to Sora and it was his (Sulla's) skill that had repaired the situation; and, to add verisimilitude to this cool claim, he boldly borrowed some details from a battle fought at Faventia in the Civil War some years later by his lieutenant Metellus Pius.[3]

The fact is that it was Marius who got the situation in Central Italy under some sort of control. The Marrucini lost their general Herius Asinius,[4] grandfather of the celebrated Asinius Pollio, and Marius engaged the Marsi, avoiding defeats[5] and on at least one occasion sharply defeating them.[6] Moreover, before the year's end Pompeius Strabo at Firmum was rescued by his subordinate Servius Sulpicius Galba and won a victory over the Picentes, while Sextus Julius Caesar, after replacing Valerius Messalla as commander of Legion XV, inflicted a sharp defeat on the Paeligni and then led his troops to join Strabo's.[7] Taking command of the joint forces as proconsul he renewed the assault on Asculum, and was still engaged on that task when 90 came to an end.

For the present study the operations in the north-central zone in 90 are of less immediate relevance than those in the southern area. There the concern of the consul L. Julius Caesar was to prevent any insurgent breakthrough into Latium or even into Northern

[1] Serv. *ad Aen.* 9. 587. For Herennius see also Eutrop. 5. 3. 2. F. Münzer (in *R.E.* VIII (1913), s.v. 'Herennius (15)', col. 665) regards him as Picentine; and this is accepted by R. Syme, *Rom. Revolution*, p. 92. But it is not easy to see what a Picentine would be doing in the Liris valley. The name Herennius was common in Oscan-speaking Campania (Vetter, no. 115; cf., too, the *praenomen* of Pontius *père* in 321). It was also found amongst the Marsi (*ILS*, 4022). Obsequens 55 seems to refer to the insurgent success near Sora (*ubique in Latio clades accepta*).

[2] Plut. *Marius*, 33. 2; Oros. 5. 8. 15 (the casualty figures show that they are alluding to this incident).

[3] App. *B.C.* 1. 9. 418–19.

[4] Livy, *Epit.* 73. Herius Asinius may have been replaced by Obsidius (Oros. 5. 18. 25).

[5] Livy, *Epit.* 74.

[6] Livy, *Epit.* 73.

[7] Livy, *Epit.* 74; cf. Oros. 5. 18. 17. For Sex. Julius Caesar's victory over the Paeligni see Livy, *Epit.* 73 (emending *Sex. Sul.*) and cf. App. *B.C.* 1. 48. 210. See, too, A. von Domaszewski, *op. cit.*, pp. 25 f.

Campania. At the start of the campaigning season he sought to divert the attention and to split the forces of the 'Samnite' rebels by ordering his *legatus* P. Licinius Crassus to overrun Lucania. But Crassus was at a disadvantage in the mountainous terrain, and Marcus Lamponius, *meddix* of the Lucani,[1] promptly defeated him and forced him to seek refuge in Grumentum.[2]

Meanwhile the revolt had spread. In Apulia, and as we shall see in Southern Campania as well, towns were induced to join the insurgents: Canusium, Salapia, Cannae, Larinum, Ausculum. Appian says that it was Gaius Vidacilius, praetor of the Asculani Picentes, who helped thus to extend the rebellion. But Appian is misled by a similarity of names. Vidacilius must have operated against the forces of Sex. Julius Caesar at Picentine Asculum, not against those of L. Julius Caesar at Apulian Ausculum.[3] The person chiefly responsible for rebel success in Apulia was more likely a certain Trebatius, who is recorded as an insurgent leader, praetor of the Venusini perhaps, in the 'Samnite' theatre in the next year.[4]

Even more important, however, in the south than the Apulian centres were the Latin Colonies. Heavily oscanized Venusia joined the insurgents. But Luceria stood firmly by Rome and played a significant but undefined role in the hostilities. Beneventum also remained under Roman control throughout.[5] About Saticula information is completely lacking.[6] Aesernia, on the other hand, figures prominently in the annals of the war. As the gateway from Samnium to Latium and Northern Campania it had come under insurgent attack from the very outset, and in 90 the consul L. Julius Caesar sought to relieve it with two legions (I and II), while calling upon his *legatus* M. Claudius Marcellus to aid him with another

[1] App. *B.C.* I. 41. 184.

[2] App. *B.C.* I. 41. 184. What ultimately happened to Crassus and his force is not revealed.

[3] App. *B.C.* I. 42. 190. (Appian regularly calls Ausculum Asculum.) Oros. 5. 18. 21 confirms that Vidacilius was the commander of the Picentes. See, too. H. Gundel in *R.E.* VIII A (1958), s.v. 'Vidacilius', cols. 2094 f.

[4] App. *B.C.* I. 52. 228 f. Because of Appian's cavalier manner with names (see above, p. 353, n. 3) it has often been suggested that he has mistakenly written Trebatius for Egnatius. This is improbable, however, since he records Egnatius separately (*B.C.* I. 40. 181; I. 45. 199). Could Trebatius be a relative of the famed jurist, the friend of Cicero and the Sabellian Horace?

[5] See above, p. 352, n. 2.

[6] As a Latin Colony it presumably remained loyal. So did the neighbouring Caudine towns, so far as our evidence goes.

(Legion XX?). As noted above, however, Vettius Scato and the Marsi came down to defeat Caesar somewhere near Atina and drove him away. As he fell back towards Teanum Sidicinum he was heavily defeated by a force of insurgents (Hirpini?) commanded by Marius Egnatius, who then went on to capture Venafrum and slaughter its garrison.[1]

Aesernia was now put under close siege, presumably by the Pentri (under Numerius Lucilius?), and its ordeal is reflected in the cognomen *Aeserninus* bestowed upon the son, born at about this time, of Claudius Marcellus who had assumed command of the beleaguered garrison.

Meanwhile C. Papius Mutilus, generalissimo of the 'Samnite' group, noting that much of Roman strength was concentrated in the region of the Montagna del Matese, promptly invaded Southern Campania, forced Surrentum, Stabiae and the Picentini who were attributed to Salernum to join the rebel cause, ravaged the territory of Nuceria, consolidated the insurgent hold on Pompeii, and then did what Hannibal had been unable to do: he captured Nola.[2] His action in starving to death L. Postumius and the other officers there for refusing to join the rebel side is in keeping with the tales regularly told of Sabellian behaviour at the capture of cities. After this dark deed Papius Mutilus made Nola into a great rebel stronghold, and such it remained until the end of the war.

Meanwhile the consul Lucius Caesar, after his setback near Aesernia, hastened south-eastwards from Teanum to stop Papius Mutilus' further advance. Mutilus had got as far as Acerrae and was besieging that town when Lucius Caesar met him. In the protracted engagement that followed both sides suffered heavy losses. Finally Papius Mutilus was driven back to Nola. This was the first real success for Rome in the war and was celebrated at Rome by the doffing of the military cloaks which all males had assumed at its

[1] App. *B.C.* 1. 45. 199; Oros. 5. 18. 11. Livy, *Epit.* 75, calls Egnatius a 'Samnite', which by now normally means a Pentrian. Yet the identity of the Pentrian commander in 90 is not beyond the reach of conjecture (see below, p. 359, n. 5) and Egnatius in 89 seems to have a Hirpinian command. We have no means of knowing whether he was related to the hero of Sentinum (in any case, the tribal affiliation of the latter is unknown). His massacre of the garrison at Venafrum may have been a reprisal or an attempt to commit the insurgents irrevocably.

[2] App. *B.C.* 1. 42. 185 f. As Salernum was a Citizen Colony it was not likely to join the rebel cause. But Papius Mutilus captured it; the Picentini who were 'attributed' to it (their town was Picentia: Pliny, *N.H.* 3. 70) then joined the insurgents (Florus 2. 6. 11).

outbreak.[1] But the price for the deliverance of Acerrae was the fall of Aesernia.

When Lucius Caesar left Teanum, one of his *legati*, L. Cornelius Sulla, made strenuous efforts to relieve M. Claudius Marcellus and the garrison in the beleaguered Latin Colony,[2] possibly in an effort to make a prophecy pronounced there by a soothsayer, when a chasm opened in the earth and belched forth flame, apply to himself.[3] But Sulla failed to save Aesernia. Indeed, as we have seen, he almost lost Sora as well.

According to what is obviously Sulla's own account, he did manage to extricate the garrison at Aesernia. But even this may well be doubted. Appian knows nothing of the alleged rescue, although he does report that L. Acilius and L. Scipio, the two Roman commissioners who had sought refuge in Aesernia, managed to get away by disguising themselves as slaves.[4] In any case, whether the garrison was saved or not, Aesernia certainly was not. It fell to its besiegers, who seem to have been the Pentri commanded by Numerius Lucilius.[5] Like Nola it was converted into a powerful insurgent bastion, and such it remained throughout the war.[6]

The fall of Aesernia does not seem to have been followed by an insurgent foray into Latium or Northern Campania, so that it may be conjectured that Sulla managed to contain the rebels and prevented them either from threatening Rome itself or from attacking Lucius Caesar's rear as he faced Papius Mutilus at Acerrae.[7]

Clearly in both the southern and the north-central zone the Romans had a bad year in 90. But it was not a fatal year. What

[1] Livy, *Epit.* 73; App. *B.C.* 1. 45. 200.

[2] Sulla used twenty-four cohorts, according to Oros. 5. 18. 16.

[3] The omen occurred *in Samnitibus*, according to Oros. 5. 18. 5, near Aesernia (Plut. *Sulla*, 6. 6, emending his Λαβέρνην; Obsequens 54, emending his *Aenariae*). Natural phenomena of this sort were not uncommon near the north-west frontier of Samnium, to judge from Sil. Ital. 12. 529 (*et quae fumantem texere Giganta Fregellae*) and Oros. 4. 4. 3 (a flame bursting from the ground at Cales).

[4] For the fall of Aesernia see App. *B.C.* 1. 41. 182; Strabo 5. 3. 10, p. 238, who says with some exaggeration that the town was destroyed: it certainly must have suffered extensive damage.

[5] Front. *Strat.* 1. 5. 17 calls him Duilius, certainly in error (F. Münzer in *R.E.* v (1905), s.v. 'Duilius (1)', col. 1777). A coin issued by the insurgents proves that the name was Lucilius.

[6] Livy *Epit.* 72, 73; Oros. 5. 18. 14 f.; Sisenna, fr. 6. 16 P; App. *B.C.* 1. 42. 185; 1. 50. 220; Diod. 37. 11. Nola remained a Sabellian stronghold until 80 (see below, p. 387).

[7] See note 1, above. This exploit probably is the basis for Sulla's claim to have slaughtered over 6,000 Marsi in a vineyard.

Florus calls the *magna populi Romani fortuna*[1] enabled them to survive; and, when the secessionists failed to impose a definitive decision in the opening phases of the war, they lost their chance of ever doing so. In the 'Marsic' theatre besides Herius Asinius, another of their praetors, Titus Lafrenius, had perished;[2] and in the second half of the year the Romans had begun ominously to score victories. In the 'Samnite' zone the operations had revealed something of the military talents of Sulla, and year's end found the rebels firmly held at Acerrae. As the Romans were bound to use the winter respite for a massive build-up, the outlook for the Italici had become cloudy.

Nevertheless insurgent successes in 90 had been sufficiently striking and Roman setbacks sufficiently serious to affect other peoples in Italy.[3] Late in the year the Etruscans and Umbrians,[4] realizing that the opportunity might never recur, demanded Roman citizenship; and they backed up their claim by putting men purposefully in the field. The Romans hastily mobilized additional forces, which included freedmen, under the command of the propraetor L. Porcius Cato, the consul elect. Cato himself engaged the Etruscans, perhaps at Faesulae, while a *legatus*, A. Plotius, met the Umbrians, apparently at Ocriculum, which was uncomfortably close to Rome.[5]

Concession of the original point at issue, however, nipped the Etruscan–Umbrian movement in the bud still more effectively. During the year 90 the surviving consul L. Julius Caesar had proposed and carried a law which bears his name. This Lex Julia offered Roman citizenship to any Latin or Italian people that was not actually in arms or that laid down its arms promptly. It also authorized commanders in the field, with the concurrence of their council of staff officers, to grant Roman citizenship to non-Romans serving under them; and it was quickly supplemented by additional acts, the Lex Calpurnia (90/89) and the Lex Plautia Papiria (89), which were designed to make provision against any loopholes over-

[1] Florus 2. 6. 13.

[2] App. *B.C.* 1. 47. 206.

[3] It was probably now that the insurgents struck the coins with a laurelled head on the obverse, the so-called 'victory' issues. On the reverse some show a (Samnite?) bull goring a lion, others a female figure (Italia?) seated on shields and being crowned by a wingless victory. See E. A. Sydenham, *Roman Republican Coinage*², pp. 627, 628, 630, 639.

[4] And others, too, according to Appian, *B.C.* 1. 49. 211. Oros. 5. 18. 7 exaggerates the size of the Etrusco-Umbrian movement.

[5] Livy, *Epit.* 74; App. *B.C.* 1. 49. 211; Macrob. 1. 11. 32; and Florus 2. 6. 6 (untrustworthy as usual).

looked by the Lex Julia itself.[1] As a result of this legislation the Etruscans and Umbrians became citizens immediately; and this added to the pool of Roman manpower available for use against the insurgents.

The action of the Romans in deciding thus to extend their citizenship after all was the biggest single factor in enabling Rome to escape defeat in the Social War. Not only did it prevent the rebellion from spreading still further, but it also must have sapped the morale of those already in rebellion by infecting them with the nagging notion that from now on they were fighting needlessly. Defeatism amongst the insurgents was henceforth predictable; that there was some is shown by the necessity that the Picentine praetor C. Vidacilius was under of executing many Picentes in Asculum for failure to obey orders.[2] In 89 the Italici were going to be at a psychological, as well as a military, disadvantage.

That they nevertheless continued the struggle was due partly to their conviction that the Lex Julia could hardly apply to peoples as deeply compromised as themselves and partly to their suspicion that, even if it did, it might never be equitably implemented. Their suspicion on this latter point was quickly corroborated.

Appian reveals that the Romans, instead of enrolling the new citizens in the existing thirty-five tribes, put them in new ones which voted after all the others, by which time the issue normally had already been decided.[3] The number of these new tribes, which endured for only three years at most, is quite uncertain. Presumably, in accordance with historic Roman practice, and in order that the total of the tribes might be kept at an odd number, thereby making tie votes impossible, they were created two at a time; and since Appian reveals that meetings of the Assembly took place at which new tribes were present, at least one pair of them must have been brought into being.[4] How many others also came into their short-lived existence it is impossible to say. But Appian and Velleius make

[1] *ILS*, 8888; Cic. *pro Balbo*, 19. The Lex Julia was passed after Rutilius' death, but how late in the year is uncertain. The Lex Calpurnia presumably was named after the plebeian tribune for 89, L. Calpurnius Piso, a huge war profiteer (Cic. *in Pis.* 87). Simultaneously Pompeius Strabo was authorized to confer Latin rights on the towns of Gallia Transpadana; but this has little bearing on the Social War.

[2] App. *B.C.* 1. 48. 209.

[3] App. *B.C.* 1. 49. 214.

[4] See Sisenna, fr. 17 P. App. *B.C.* 1. 49. 214 has been interpreted as meaning that, in all, ten new tribes were created (but this interpretation requires an unparalleled meaning for the word δεκατεύοντες and ignores the later statement of Appian, *B.C.* 1. 53. 231, that

it clear that the new citizens were enrolled in so few tribes that they could never outvote the citizens voting in the 35 old tribes.[1] Nor is it difficult to see why the Romans might hope that their sharp practice in confining the new citizens to only a few tribes, and new tribes at that, would be accepted. They could speciously claim that they were simply following their ancestral practice. Down to 241 it had been their normal procedure to create new tribes whenever Italians were enfranchised, and incidentally the Italians of an earlier day seem to have preferred this to being enrolled in the old tribes. They could also adduce a precedent for restricting the number of tribes in which the newcomers might vote. Ever since the Second Punic War, if not earlier, Latins present in Rome at the time of a Tribal Assembly had been permitted to vote in one of the tribes chosen by lot.[2] What was now being proposed for the Italians was essentially similar.

The Italians, however, were not content to let Roman trickery masquerade as tradition. Perhaps the ordinary Italians, the rank and file who were seldom likely to come to Rome to vote, either did not notice or did not care that their vote had been nullified.[3] With the Italian leaders it was different. They quite possibly would attend the Assembly, and in any event they were not prepared to tolerate anything less than absolute equality with the Romans. As a result, the question of the fair and equitable distribution of the new citizens in the Roman citizen body was a fierce and contentious issue for the next three years: it ended with the Italians gaining their point.

The Lex Julia and the inevitable Roman build-up in the winter

the Allies admitted to citizenship after 89 were enrolled in additional new tribes of their own 'just like those who had been granted the citizenship earlier'). Velleius 2. 20. 2 says that the new citizens were to be enrolled in eight tribes, but he does not say eight *new* tribes: he probably has in mind the ultimate destination of those new citizens who had been secessionist (E. T. Salmon in *T.A.P.A.* LXXXIX (1958), 179–84). The number eight was chosen for them since this ensured that they could never be a majority, not even in Assemblies with a restricted electorate, for example those where only seventeen tribes voted (so, plausibly, G. Niccolini in *Rend. dei Lincei*, ser. 8, I (1946), 123).

[1] This means meetings of the Tribal Assembly for legislative or judicial purposes. In elective assemblies simultaneous voting was the usual rule. It is to be noted that the enfranchisement of the Italians had little effect on the consular *fasti*. For that matter the Centuriate Assembly hardly comes into the picture: the classes to which the new citizens ought to be assigned are never mentioned, and certainly the censors of 89 did not assign any (Cic. *pro Arch.* 89). Registration with the urban praetor probably sufficed to enable one to vote in the Tribal Assembly (L. R. Taylor, *Voting Districts*, p. 106).

[2] Livy 25. 3. 16.

[3] According to Appian, *B.C.* 1. 50. 215, this was the case.

of 90/89 quite unmistakably boded ill for the Italici. Accordingly they made a desperate effort to score a crippling success before the effects of these developments could be felt. They gambled on a winter campaign.

A strong force of 'Marsic' insurgents sought to thread their way through the Apennine passes to the Umbrians and Etruscans in the hope of greatly extending the area of rebellion. But the attempt ended in a repetition of the Sentinum disaster of two centuries earlier. Pompeius Strabo defeated the Italici with heavy losses and sealed off the passes. Thousands more of the expedition perished in the snow trying to make their way back to rebel-held territory over the snow-clad heights of the Gran Sasso.[1] This was but a foretaste of worse to follow.

The campaigning season of 89 soon revealed that the balance of advantage had shifted decisively to the Romans. Their strategy now was to roll up the 'Marsic' group one by one, while conducting an aggressive-defensive campaign in the 'Samnite' theatre. To that end the new consuls for 89, Cn. Pompeius Strabo and L. Porcius Cato, campaigned in the region where they had both operated the year before, the north-central zone. Marius, however, was not there, and in view of his performance in the year before it is surprising to find him without a command in this. Plutarch suggests that he retired voluntarily because of his age and physical infirmities,[2] which, it might be noted, did not deter him one year later from seeking the command in the war against Mithridates. No doubt domestic politics were more than a little responsible for his retirement in 89. Perhaps as an Arpinate, instead of a dyed-in-the-wool Roman, he was suspected of pro-Italian sympathies; both he and his men had fraternized with the enemy on at least one occasion in 90. Perhaps, too, he himself was not very eager to continue serving in a war where the appointment of Caepio to joint command with himself the previous year had demonstrated that under no circumstances was he going to be allowed to monopolize the glory. Whatever the reason, Marius played no recorded part in the Social War in 89.[3]

[1] Livy, *Epit.* 74; Oros. 5. 18. 17–20, who says that the wretches who perished were refugees from Asculum.

[2] Plut. *Marius*, 33. 3.

[3] Marius' record of duplicity and of intolerance of his military peers must have made every commander reluctant to have him for a *legatus*. For the fraternization of the troops see Diod. 37. 15. The story that Marius discussed with Poppaedius Silo the possibility of extending the citizenship to Italians is unconvincing (E. Badian, *Foreign Clientelae*, p. 234, n. 5).

On the other hand, Marius' great rival, Sulla, was to play a very prominent role in that year. Like Pompeius Strabo and Porcius Cato, he was retained in the zone where he had served in the previous year, in his case the south. Indeed, it is sometimes assumed that, since both consuls served in the 'Marsic' zone in 89, Sulla was in charge in the 'Samnite', presumably with a proconsular *imperium*; and the ancient accounts, which depend heavily on Sulla's *Memoirs*, manage to convey the impression that this was so. Thus, Livy avers that Sulla in 89 achieved successes of a magnitude rarely equalled by anyone who had not been consul. Valerius Maximus and Orosius go further and describe him as consul in this year, while Eutropius singles him out as the foremost Roman general in 89.[1] Yet even the ancient accounts let the truth slip out: Sulla was a *legatus* in 89, apparently of the consul Porcius Cato. For that matter it would have indeed been surprising if he had held higher rank than the two consulars serving in the south, A. Postumius Albinus and T. Didius, of whom the latter at least had had important military experience.[2] Whatever the situation at the end of 89, its beginning found Sulla in a subordinate position.

In the north-central region the year 89 started badly for the Romans. Once again the Marsi demonstrated their prowess: the consul L. Porcius Cato, after several encounters with them, met his end while attempting to storm one of their camps, presumably somewhere near the Fucine Lake. This happened even before the winter was entirely at an end, and Cato's own troops may have been, in part at least, responsible: rowdy and undisciplined, they are said to have been stirred up by a certain C. Titius or Titinius.[3]

Despite this setback the Romans were soon scoring success after success in the 'Marsic' theatre. When the Picentine praetor Gaius Vidacilius attempted to rescue invested Asculum, the Roman response was to draw the siege lines tighter than ever around the

[1] See Livy, *Epit.* 75 (who styles the consular Postumius a *legatus*); Val. Max. 1. 6. 4; Eutrop. 5. 3. 3; Oros. 5. 18. 22 (who makes Postumius the *legatus* of Sulla).

[2] Diod. 37. 8; Livy, *Epit.* 75, admits that Sulla, as well as Postumius, was a *legatus*. Cf., too, Pliny, *N.H.* 3. 70. Postumius was more probably a promagistrate (Broughton, *Supplt. to M.R.R.* p. 50), and he may have been sent to Campania to avenge the massacre of his namesake (or relative?) in Nola the year before. Didius was a man *non litteris ad rei militaris scientiam sed rebus gestis ac victoriis eruditus* (Cic. *pro Font.* 43).

[3] *ILS*, 2489; Livy, *Epit.* 75; App. *B.C.* 1. 50. 217; Sisenna, fr. 52 P.; Cass. Dio, fr. 100; Eutrop. 5. 3. 2. Oros. 5. 18. 24 depicts the Younger Marius as Cato's slayer: if true, this is a measure of the Younger Marius' resentment of Cato's usurping a command that seemed more rightly to belong to his adoptive father.

town, and Vidacilius killed himself in despair.[1] It is true that the Romans also lost their own commander at Asculum, Sextus Julius Caesar. But he died of illness, not at the hands of the enemy. Nor did his death bring the Asculani any relief, for the consul Pompeius Strabo, fresh from a shattering victory over the Vestini, gave Gaius Baebius, Sextus Caesar's successor, every help in pressing the siege.[2]

Pompeius Strabo's *legatus*, Ser. Sulpicius Galba, completed the discomfiture of the Vestini and defeated the Marrucini; while another *legatus*, L. Cornelius Cinna, cooperated with the praetor, Q. Caecilius Metellus Pius, to worst the Marsi.[3] By now the situation on the 'Marsic' front had deteriorated so badly that the insurgents transferred their capital to Bovianum, and a short-lived period of glory came to an end for Corfinium–Italia.[4] On 17 November Pompeius Strabo, whose army included the youthful Cicero and the youthful Pompey, scored the crowning achievement on the 'Marsic' front by capturing Asculum. The fall of this, the town which had first resorted to violence, made a vivid impression at Rome, and on 25 December Strabo celebrated the only triumph recorded for the Social War—*de Asculaneis Picentibus*. The insurgents captured in the town were sold into slavery. Not that the Roman treasury profited, since Strabo lived up to his reputation as a money-grubber and failed to hand any of his war-booty over to it.[5]

Operations on the 'Samnite' front in 89 are hard to trace in accurate detail amid the propaganda surrounding the name of Sulla. In the surviving accounts that worthy looms large, inevitably so in view of his subsequent undisputed mastery of the Roman world and its propaganda. His *Memoirs* ensured that his exploits in 89

[1] App. *B.C.* 1. 49. 209. According to Oros. 5. 18. 18 a certain Fraucus of the 'Marsi' had tried to relieve Asculum.

[2] App. *B.C.* 1. 49. 210.

[3] Oros. 5. 18. 25 says that the Marrucini were defeated at the River Teanum (otherwise unknown) and lost their commander Obsidius in the action. If this is not mere confusion with the defeat and death of Poppaedius (at Teanum Apulum?) in 88, it must mean the town of Teanum, the principal settlement of the Marrucini. The *legatus* L. Cornelius Cinna was the ex-praetor and future consul (see below, p. 373): cf. Cic. *pro Font.* 43. His exploits with Metellus Pius probably belong to early 88 (Livy, *Epit.* 76, refers to that year, and in 89 Metellus was a *praetor*, not a *legatus*).

[4] App. *B.C.* 1. 51. 224. Poppaedius Silo accompanied the insurgent capital to Samnium.

[5] Livy, *Epit.* 76; Oros. 5. 18. 26; Cic. *pro Cluentio*, 21. The Social War must have caused many Italians to be enslaved.

eclipsed those of any other commander. There is not much doubt that they have been greatly exaggerated.

Actually in the 'Samnite' zone as in the 'Marsic' the year 89 started off none too auspiciously for the Romans. Before Gaius Cosconius managed to get the situation in Apulia under some sort of control with the help of a certain Lucanus, he ran into serious difficulties: on one occasion he had to seek refuge in Cannae. Ultimately indeed he slew Marius Egnatius (of the Hirpini?), defeated Trebatius (of Venusia?) and subjugated the Poediculi (= Peucetii?). But he could not recover any of the important towns: the most that he could do was ravage the territories of Larinum, Asculum (Ausculum), and Venusia.[1] The *legatus* Aulus Gabinius, operating against the Lucani, stormed many of their strongholds, but was finally killed in action. Florus, an untrustworthy recorder, makes Carbo replace him, meaning presumably the famous Cn. Papirius Carbo, later the fellow consul and associate of Cinna; but even Florus does not credit Carbo with any successes.[2]

No similar reticence enshrouds Sulla's activities in 89. The start of the campaigning season found him in Campania, where insurgent Pompeii was under siege. The tenacity of the Pompeian resistance, however, made the Roman troops suspect their commander, A. Postumius Albinus, of treachery, so they lynched him. Sulla did not punish the mutineers: he simply took over Postumius' command, and one wonders whether he may not himself have instigated the murder for that very purpose.[3] Soon afterwards Sulla heavily engaged Lucius Cluentius, the south Campanian *meddix*, when the latter sought to relieve beleagured Pompeii. After some indecisive skirmishes Sulla defeated and slew Cluentius near Nola. The figures of 23,000 Italic and 1 Roman dead are obviously Sulla's, but not

[1] Cosconius was probably a *legatus* (Broughton, *M.R.R.* II, 39, n. 21). Lucanus might be a pro-Roman Venusine; the name must be a *gentilicium* and is probably an error for Lucanius, who served on Pompeius Strabo's staff (C. Cichorius, *Röm. Studien*, p. 131) and was a member of Horatia, the tribe to which Roman citizens in Venusia belonged.

[2] For Gabinius see E. Badian in *Philologus*, CIII (1959), 86 f. Oros. 5. 18. 25 calls him Gaius, and Florus 2. 6. 13 says that he fell against the Marsi. (Florus probably made this mistake by confusing Gabinius' successor Carbo with Cinna: Cinna did fight against the Marsi (see above, p. 365, n. 3).)

[3] Livy, *Epit.* 75; Plut. *Sulla*, 6. 9; Oros. 5. 18. 22. It is safe to infer that Sulla's *Memoirs* stressed Postumius' suspected treachery, and that some at least of the Postumii hated Sulla. An Albinus (= A. Postumius Albinus?) fought against him at the Colline Gate (see below, p. 385, n. 5). Treachery was only too likely to be suspected in the Social War (see Cass. Dio, fr. 98. 1).

even he dared claim that Nola fell. He did, however, recapture Stabiae, destroying it in the process on 29 April.[1]

Meanwhile Minatus Magius, an ancestor of the historian Velleius Paterculus, had raised a strong force amongst the Hirpini. Exactly when he did this is not clear, but one can be reasonably sure that in the main these were volunteers who had been settled on *ager publicus* that had once been Hirpinian land. With this force Magius penetrated into Campania, effected a junction with the Roman commander T. Didius and helped him to recover Herculaneum. Providentially for Sulla, Didius fell on 11 June, the anniversary of the disaster on the River Tolenus in the preceding year, and this enabled Sulla to add yet another consular's forces to those he already commanded. He obtained Magius' 'free corps' as well, for the two men now proceeded jointly to storm Pompeii.[2]

Ignoring the threat to his rear from rebel-held Nola, Sulla took the bold risk of invading enemy territory proper. With Magius to guide him he advanced into the country of the Hirpini, captured and sacked Compsa and Aeclanum, and before summer was over had forced the surrender of the whole tribe.[3] This left him free to attack the Pentri. Moving north-westwards from the Beneventum area, he took Papius Mutilus by surprise, perhaps somewhere near Saepinum, and then went on to capture Papius' native town, Bovianum.[4] Papius himself, who was wounded, found refuge in Aesernia. It was to Aesernia, too, that the insurgents transferred their capital from fallen Bovianum.[5]

[1] The figures for casualties are given by App. *B.C.* 1. 50. 221; Eutrop. 5. 3. 3; Oros. 5. 18. 23 (who calls the Italic general Juventius and says he lost 18,000 men). Pliny, *N.H.* 3. 70, expresses some doubt as to the truth of Sulla's claim to have been awarded a grass crown by his troops at Nola. A snake suddenly appearing at an altar where Sulla was sacrificing foretold his success against an enemy encampment near Nola (Cic. *de divin.* 1. 72; 2. 65. Cf. Val. Max. 1. 6. 4 (who calls Sulla consul)); but to paraphrase Sil. Ital. 8. 534: *Sullae non pervia Nola.*

[2] Velleius 2. 16. 2; Ovid, *Fasti*, 6. 567.

[3] Aeclanum had its wooden stockade burned, and was then pillaged and plundered (App. *B.C.* 1. 51. 223; Plut. *Sulla*, 6. 8 f.; cf. Sall. *Cat.* 11). Its walls were rebuilt shortly after the war (*CIL*, 1^2, 1722).

[4] It has often been suggested that this must be Bovanium Vetus (e.g. by A. von Domaszewski, *op. cit.* p. 30). Appian, *B.C.* 1. 51. 225, says that the town had three citadels, and undoubtedly this could describe Pietrabbondante very well. But many towns in the Abruzzi fit the same description. That is shown by the heraldic arms of the country: 'an eagle argent crowned, standing upon three mounts or, in a field of azure'. Boiano is no exception, and it suits the topography of Sulla's campaign excellently. An Oscan inscription shows that Papius came from there (Vetter, no. 160). Poppaedius briefly recovered the town in 88 (Obsequens 116). See Plate 2.

[5] Diod. 37. 9.

Sulla's successes in 89 were important enough to win him the consulship for 88, but in the extant record they are grossly exaggerated. If an insurgent account of 89 had survived, it is more than likely that the year would seem much less one-sided. Even the extant records reveal that the year had cost the Romans a consul in the 'Marsic' theatre and three *legati*, including two ex-consuls, in the 'Samnite', and they had not been able to retake either Nola or Aesernia.

By now, however, the situation in Italy was much less critical for Rome. The citizenship legislation had been successful in keeping other Italian peoples from joining the revolt and had also extracted much of the tenacity from the resistance of the rebels themselves. The recovery of Asculum had ended organized opposition on the most northerly front, and some ancient writers even go so far as to finish the war on the day when Pompeius Strabo celebrated his triumph over the people that began it.[1] Other ancient authors, however, noting that large-scale operations still continued in the central and southern regions in 88, are inclined to end the war with the death, late in this latter year, of Q. Poppaedius Silo.[2] Both these dates for the war's end, however, are inexact; and they were probably put forward to give the conflict a neatly schematic appearance. The war outlasted 89 and even 88.

During the winter of 89/88 the rebels at their new capital of Aesernia reorganized their war establishment. They appointed Poppaedius Silo as supreme commander-in-chief and under him four generals. It has been suggested that the latter were the *meddices* of the four Samnite tribes.[3] But this could not have been the case. The Samnite tribes no longer numbered four; and, besides this, the Lucani as one of the rebel peoples still carrying on the war must have had some say in its higher direction. The arrangement adopted at Aesernia must have provided for the four posts under Poppaedius to be equally shared between Samnites and Lucani. As a matter of fact Diodorus identifies the Lucanian pair: Marcus Lamponius and Tiberius Cleppius. He also names one of the two Samnite

[1] Flor. 2. 6. 14; Oros. 5. 18. 26.

[2] Livy, *Epit.* 76; Diod. 37. 2. 10; cf. Strabo 5. 4. 2, p. 241; Eutrop. 5. 3. 3. Poppaedius was *dux et auctor belli* (Florus 2. 6. 10), the one who had the greatest authority and power (Plut. *Marius*, 33. 2). But his death only *seemed* to be the end of the war (Plut. *Sulla*, 6. 9).

[3] A. von Domaszewski, *op. cit.* p. 14; G. Devoto, *Gli Antichi Italici*², p. 338.

generals: Papius Mutilus.[1] The other is not identified, but he may not be beyond the reach of conjecture. He could be Minius Iegius, who is proved by numismatic evidence to have been one of the Oscan-speaking leaders at about this time.[2]

This reorganization must have taken place early in 88 but it failed to halt the string of Roman successes. What was left of rebel resistance in Central Italy collapsed when Pompeius Strabo, now proconsul, moved southwards from Picenum, reduced to subjection the few Vestini still resisting, and then overwhelmed the Paeligni. Simultaneously, the Marsi lost their great commander Vettius Scato, who was killed by his own slave when about to fall into Roman hands.[3] Strabo after his exploits seems to have been content to remain in Picenum, ostensibly to prevent any renewal of hostilities in the north. But his fellow proconsul, Q. Caecilius Metellus Pius, who had defeated the Marsi while Strabo was dealing with the Vestini and Paeligni, moved south into Apulia, took over the command from Gaius Cosconius, and rapidly scored some striking successes, one of which cost the rebels the life of Poppaedius Silo.

The rebels fought back desperately, appointing Papius Mutilus at once to succeed the fallen Poppaedius as insurgent commander-in-chief. Metellus Pius, however, followed up his victory by recapturing Venusia; and he gave every indication of being able to finish off the Social War.[4]

The Lucani, faced with the ominous implications of the fall of Venusia, fell back late in 88 or early in 87 into Bruttium, a region admirably suited for guerrilla operations. Their intention was to spread alarm and despondency throughout Roman territory there and if possible invade Sicily. They were foiled in the latter plan when C. Norbanus, the governor of Sicily, prevented them from capturing Rhegium, the springboard for any attempt on the island.

[1] Diod. 37. 13 (emending Pompeius).

[2] The name appears on a single golden coin (see below, p. 370). It is usually given as Iegius, which is certainly Italic (*CIL*, IV, 208; IX, 4166, 4477). On the coin the name is carefully written as Ieiius (R. S. Conway, *Italic Dialects*, I, 217); but this is the form one would expect for Iegius in Oscan (Vetter, p. 139). Some very crude and legendless insurgent *denarii* were probably issued at almost exactly the same time as this gold coin.

[3] Metellus Pius had been praetor in 89. For the death of Vettius Scato see Seneca, *de ben.* 3. 23. 5. Livy, *Epit.* 76, names Mamercus Aemilius Lepidus as the one who defeated and slew Poppaedius: but Aemilius could have been Metellus' legate.

[4] Diod. 37. 10. The rebels captured there and sold into slavery may have included Horace's father.

Sicily was thus kept out of the Social War. The Lucani were no more successful in an attempt to capture Tisia in Bruttium.[1]

By the end of 88 the insurgents still remaining in arms had undoubtedly been reduced to desperate straits. Their numbers by now were greatly reduced, but still by no means negligible, for in addition to the Samnites and Lucani there were the diehard elements who had escaped from the other war theatres, and also, so it is said, a mass of fugitive slaves. They retained their hold on Aesernia, and Papius Mutilus remained in control of Nola even though hard-pressed by Sulla, who by now was consul and in command of an army of four legions.[2] This was not a great deal of territory; nor was it a compact and undivided bloc. But developments had occurred elsewhere which encouraged them to go on fighting.

Already in 89 the situation at the eastern end of the Mediterranean had assumed an ugly aspect for Rome. The aggressive behaviour of Nicomedes of Bithynia, who enjoyed Roman backing, had obliged Mithridates VI, King of Pontus, to mobilize. In 88 hostilities between Rome and the Pontic king flared up in very deadly earnest when Mithridates' troops overran the province of Asia and in the process brought about the massacre, so it is said, of 80,000 Italians who were resident there.[3] This stamped him as no friend of Italians. He was, however, the active enemy of Rome and, as such, provided some cheer and comfort for the Italic insurgents. They began *pourparlers* with him, one evidence of this being the surviving gold coin with an Oscan legend which was struck (in 88?) in the name of Minius Iegius and which, to flatter the monarch, imitates the coin types of Amisus, the principal city in Mithridates' kingdom. According to Diodorus, the rebels exhorted the king to bring his troops to Italy; and, even though they could have had few illusions about his ability to do so, they were right in thinking that his activities would help to pull their chestnuts out of the fire.[4] In fact the rebels obtained

[1] Diod. 37. 14 (emending 'Ασίας). For Bruttium as guerrilla country see T. P. Wiseman in *P.B.S.R.* XXXII (1964), 34 f.

[2] Oros. 5. 19. 4. According to Diod. 37. 10, they had 30,000 infantry, 20,000 runaway slaves and 1,000 cavalry when they carried out their reorganization at Aesernia (at the beginning of 88?). He adds that they lost over 6,000 of these almost immediately in Apulia; and they lost 3,000 more at Venusia.

[3] App. *Mithr.* 22; Memnon, *F.g.H.* III B, 434, 22. 9; Val. Max. 9. 2. 3. Plut. *Sulla*, 24. 4, gives the figure 150,000, an exaggeration probably obtained from Sulla's *Memoirs*.

[4] Diod. 37. 11. Besides the gold coin another may reveal insurgent attempts to woo Mithridates: it shows a warrior just disembarked from a ship and offering his hand to another warrior who meets him; the coin bears no legend. Some Italici may have fled to Mithridates: see Front. *Strat.* 2. 3. 17.

greater relief than even they themselves could have hoped for, since the Mithridatic War brought about a ruinous rivalry for the command in it and a state of veritable civil war in Rome: above all, it took Sulla, their principal scourge, away from their front.

Sulla was the general upon whom the lot had fallen for the command against Mithridates, but much happened before he took up the assignment.[1]

On 10 December 89, P. Sulpicius Rufus had become tribune of the *plebs* at Rome. He was a patrician turned plebeian and had been a friend of Livius Drusus. He was also, according to Cicero, one of the greatest orators of the age. Early in 88, Sulpicius, as tribune, introduced a bill, presumably in the *concilium plebis*, which proposed to distribute and register the new Roman citizens, together with the freedmen, in all of the old thirty-five tribes and thereby put an end to the existing discrimination which confined them to a handful of new ones. Sulpicius' motive will never be certainly known. Perhaps he genuinely sympathized with the Italians, although it is to be noted that in 89, before becoming tribune, he had fought with distinction against them. In any case, whatever his motive, his proposal quickly provoked disorder. The two consuls and apparently the senate and many other elements in the Roman state were opposed to it.

To prevent the bill from coming to the vote in the Assembly, Sulla and his fellow consul Q. Pompeius Rufus, who had hitherto been Sulpicius' friend but now evidently shared Sulla's views, announced a suspension of all public business. Whether they were within their constitutional rights in proclaiming such a *iustitium* may well be doubted, but in any event Sulpicius refused to be burked. He not only threatened, but actually resorted to violence. Both the consuls managed to escape with their lives, Sulla owing his,

[1] The so-called revolution of Sulpicius Rufus is so well known that detailed documentation for its principal episodes need not be given here. Cicero, *Brutus*, 304, and *Laelius*, 2, are relevant for Sulpicius' earlier behaviour. For a recent discussion of his motives see E. Badian in *Durham University Journal* (1964), p. 152. Perhaps he thought that the recent death of the senatorial stalwart M. Aemilius Scaurus opened up the way for him to become the leading figure in Roman political life, provided only that he came forward with a bold programme. C. Cichorius, *Röm. Studien*, pp. 137–41, shows that the Sulpicius who served on Pompeius Strabo's staff was Sulpicius Galba rather than Sulpicius Rufus. E. Gabba, *Ann. Scuola Normale di Pisa*, ser. 2, XXXIII (1964), 4 f., suggests that Sulpicius Rufus (and also Pompeius Rufus and Sulla) had been close to Livius Drusus, initially at least. Although both Sulla and Pompeius Rufus saved their skins, Rufus' son, who was also Sulla's son-in-law, was less fortunate.

so it is said, to providential asylum opportunely provided by the house of Marius. Sulla then called off the moratorium and betook himself to the army which he had been commanding against the Samnites in Campania. Before he could lead it off to the east, however, Sulpicius carried his bill for the fair registration of the Italians, and then promptly proposed another: to transfer the Mithridatic command from Sulla to Marius. This was a repetition of the procedure which had brought about the supersession of Q. Caecilius Metellus Numidicus by Marius in the Jugurthine command some twenty years earlier. But Sulla had obviously learnt a great deal from his Metellan connexions: he did not propose to accept such treatment as tamely as Metellus had done. The two military tribunes who arrived to take over his army in the name of Marius found to their cost that Sulla had already secured the allegiance of the rank and file and were stoned to death. To contain the Samnites at Nola Sulla left one legion under the command of a matrimonial connexion of his, Appius Claudius Pulcher, who had been praetor in 89, and then marched on Rome. Such an action by a Roman general was without precedent[1] and Sulpicius, Marius and their supporters were quite unprepared for it. Sulla took possession of the city with comparative ease, killed those leaders of the opposing faction that he could get his hands on (including Sulpicius, who was betrayed by one of his own slaves)[2] and drove others of them into exile (including Marius, who fled to Africa). Sulpicius' legislation was then annulled as unconstitutional, and Sulla proceeded to pass measures of his own, which were intended to promote a stability favourable to himself.

Elections for the consulship of 87 were also held, Gnaeus Octavius and Lucius Cornelius Cinna being the successful candidates. Sulla then went down to Capua, where his expeditionary force was assembling. Before the end of 88 he had led it out of Italy to settle accounts with Mithridates.

Sulla was hoping that his fellow consul Pompeius Rufus would protect his interests while he was gone; and, to get the armed backing that would be necessary for this role, Rufus proceeded to

[1] R. Syme, *Rom. Revolution*, p. 47. Only one of Sulla's officers supported him: this was probably L. Licinius Lucullus (T. F. Carney, *Biography of Gaius Marius*, pp. 33, n. 165).

[2] Sulla ordered the slave to be executed for his treachery towards his master (Livy, *Epit.* 77; see, too, Velleius 2. 19. 1; Val. Max. 6. 5. 7; Plut. *Sulla*, 10. 2; App. *B.C.* 1. 57–60).

Picenum with the intention of taking over as consul the army of the proconsul Pompeius Strabo. But the proposed change of commanders was not to the liking of Strabo's troops; they lynched the new arrival. Strabo connived at, if he did not actively instigate, this act of violence.

Happenings such as these inevitably relieved the military pressure on the Italic insurgents. It is true that Strabo, who was technically a proconsul, still had an army which might be used against them: but that calculating schemer, rather than march against still-resisting rebels, preferred to police pacified Picenum, and even there he kept watch with only one eye and fixed the other on developments in Rome, where he hoped to win a second consulship. He was not named Strabo for nothing.[1] There was also the other proconsul with an army in Italy, Metellus Pius. He, undoubtedly, was prepared to use it against any rebels who were still actively resisting, and, as we have seen, he had been strikingly successful in Apulia in 88. The year 87 may have found him trying to restore order against the Lucani in Bruttium. But the disorders in Rome had drawn Roman troops away from Campania; and the year 87 was not far advanced before Metellus was obliged to take his forces thither in order to help contain Papius Mutilus and the Samnites at Nola, now that Sulla had left Italy.

Despite the arrival of Metellus Pius' troops, the Roman position in Campania continued to deteriorate. For the consuls of 87 began to quarrel the moment that Sulla departed for the East. Octavius was a stalwart supporter of Sulla, whereas Cinna favoured the programme of Sulpicius, even though, like the latter, he had served as one of the legates fighting the Italici in 89.[2] Cinna, in fact, proposed to re-enact Sulpicius' measure for distributing the new citizens and freedmen fairly over the thirty-five old tribes, and to that end proceeded to import Italians into Rome and to resort to force. This encountered answering force from Octavius, and Cinna, who does not seem to have found much support inside Rome, was obliged to flee from the city together with Quintus Sertorius and other supporters. Thereupon his consulship was pronounced vacant by the senate, and the Flamen Dialis, L. Cornelius Merula, was appointed in his place.

[1] On the role of Pompeius Strabo at this time, see M. Gelzer, *Vom römischen Staat*, II, 77 f.

[2] Cinna had probably been a *legatus* to Pompeius Strabo (Livy, *Epit.* 76, emending *Pnina* to *Cinna*).

Octavius' day was short lived. Cinna promptly took a leaf out of Sulla's book and hastened to the army which Sulla had left under Appius Claudius Pulcher in Campania to watch the Samnites at Nola. He did not hesitate to bribe it. Moreover he was a proved soldier, a genuine noble, a patrician no less, and a legitimately elected consul.[1] The upshot was that he was able to persuade the army to accept him as its commander. With it he proposed to march on Rome.

In this emergency the senate called upon the sinister Pompeius Strabo to help the consul Octavius to defend the capital: but Strabo, after bringing his troops down to the outskirts of Rome, bestirred himself but little.[2] Cinna meanwhile, like Sulla before him, was marching on Rome. Besides getting Claudius Pulcher's troops, he had secured the support of Gaius Marius, who now returned from his exile in Africa, landed in Etruria and quickly raised a force.

Cinna's action in removing still more Roman troops from Campania placed the Samnites there in a strong position; possibly it was at this stage that the men from Nola set fire to Abella.[3] Moreover, operating out of Nola they were able to plunder even beyond the boundaries of Campania.[4] It became necessary to negotiate with them. The senate at Rome, distrusting with reason Pompeius Strabo's ambiguous temporizing,[5] decided that additional forces would be needed to keep the city out of the hands of Cinna and Marius and had therefore instructed Metellus to negotiate a truce speedily with the Samnites in Campania and bring his army to Rome. Simultaneously the senate had granted the Roman citizenship unconditionally to all of the surrendered insurgent peoples, no doubt in the hope that this gesture would facilitate Metellus' efforts to reach an accommodation with the Samnites. The latter, however, could now play off one Roman faction against the other and, understandably but perhaps unwisely, responded to his overtures with demands that he regarded as too humiliating for acceptance. On referring the matter to the senate he was advised to

[1] In each of these respects he resembled Sulla, as no doubt the soldiers noted (see Velleius 2. 20. 4; App. *B.C.* 1. 65. 208 f.).

[2] Possibly Pompeius Strabo could not rely on his officers: a surprisingly large number of them were subsequently found on the side opposed to Sulla (see C. Cichorius, *Röm. Studien*, pp. 130–85).

[3] Granius Licinianus, p. 20. 8 Fl.

[4] Dio, fr. 102. 7: τὴν Καμπανίαν καὶ τὴν ἐπέκεινα αὐτῆς ἐκακούργουν.

[5] Strabo evidently kept some contact with Cinna and his supporters to judge from the help given later to his son (Cic. *Brut.* 230; Val. Max. 6. 2. 8).

leave a small force facing the Samnites and bring the rest to Rome as quickly as possible. He did as he was told, entrusting the impossible task of containing the Samnites with a totally inadequate force to a legate named Plautius, probably the experienced soldier A. Plotius, who had served as *legatus* in the winter of 90/89 (see above, p. 360).

Cinna and Marius, meanwhile, whether out of firmness of conviction or lack of scruple, were not disposed to haggle with the Samnites, but through an agent, C. Flavius Fimbria, agreed to give them what Metellus had refused. The terms are preserved for us by Cassius Dio, who receives some confirmation from Granius Licinianus.[1] The Samnites demanded: (1) Roman citizenship for themselves and for all who had joined them (this would cover the Lucani); (2) retention of any booty they had taken; (3) return of all the captives and deserters from their own ranks. According to Dio, it was not the citizenship demand that Metellus Pius had found so unpalatable: it was the other items. And the Samnites would have been more astute not to insist on their pound of flesh, since a day of reckoning at the hands of the departed Sulla could conceivably dawn. As it was, their demands were granted, and the Social War came to its end leaving the Sabellian element in control not only in Nola but also in Aesernia, from where there was an easy approach to Rome.[2]

Clearly, however, the agreement was likely to remain a dead letter unless Cinna and Marius managed to obtain power in Rome and implement it. The Samnites at once tried to ensure that they did. They (but, so far as we know, not the Lucani) took up arms again, made short work of the small army Metellus Pius had left in Campania, killing its unfortunate commander Plautius, and then made common cause with Cinna and Marius. In the event, the latter pair do not seem to have needed, or used, the Samnite soldiers for their assault on Rome. They closed in on the capital simultaneously from several sides and the Bellum Octavianum was soon over. Late in the year 87 Cinna entered the city and resumed his interrupted consulship. Marius followed hard on his heels. The two men then made themselves masters of the state. They promptly procured the deaths of a number of notables, including the consuls Octavius and

[1] Cass. Dio, fr. 102. 7; Gran. Licin. p. 20 Fl.; App. *B.C.* 1. 68. 309 f.

[2] The inhabitants of both towns now obtained Roman citizenship; but local administration was firmly in the hands of the Sabellian elements.

Merula, and they also re-enacted Sulpicius' measure concerning the new citizens.

So far as the surviving evidence goes, all this took place in 87, so that the formal end of the Social War is to be dated to that year. That the Samnites were admitted into the Roman state as full-fledged citizens (*cives optimo iure*) admits of no doubt. Not only was the full citizenship stipulated in the peace terms accepted by Flavius Fimbria and carried into law by the re-enactment of Sulpicius' legislation, and, according to Livy, actually conferred in 87, but it is also implied by the circumstance that, when C. Papius Mutilus finally met his end at Nola in 80, it was as a full Roman citizen. Indeed there is a clear indication in Appian that Nola, the stronghold controlled by the Samnites, obtained the full Roman citizenship along with Tibur and Praeneste in 87.[1]

The 'Samnites' were assigned to the tribe Voltinia and the Hirpini, apart from Aeclanum, to Galeria.[2] (Aeclanum became part of Cornelia.) What decided this choice of tribes we can only guess. In Etruria, an area favoured by Marius, there was a wide distribution of tribes.[3] The absence of a similar distribution in Samnium may mean that it was not particularly favoured by Marius; but it is more probably to be attributed to the lack of municipally organized communities there and the consequent desirability of keeping a tribal people with strong ethnic feelings together in one tribe.[4] Voltinia may have been selected for the 'Samnites' since it was the tribe to which Aufidena already belonged, and the Hirpini may have gone to Galeria for some similar reason. Aeclanum, exceptionally, may have been assigned to Cornelia as a mark of favour: it had raised Magius' free corps to fight on the side of Rome and was rewarded by being placed in Marius' own tribe.[5]

Presumably some registration in the tribes occurred in 86 when Roman citizen numbers increased by some 70,000. The censors were L. Marcius Philippus and M. Perperna, of whom the former at least had been the bitter opponent of M. Livius Drusus and,

[1] Technically only the *populus* could extend the citizenship (Livy 38. 36. 7 f.); in practice this meant that the 'people' ratified a decision of the senate to extend the citizenship (Cic. *pro Balbo*, 55): and they were called upon to do so in 87 (Livy, *Epit.* 80: *Italicis populis a senatu civitas data est*; cf. App. *B.C.* 1. 53. 231). That Sabellian Nola now became 'Roman' is shown by Livy, *Epit.* 89; Gran. Licin. p. 32 Fl.; App. *B.C.* 1. 65. 294.

[2] On the tribal affiliations see especially L. R. Taylor, *Voting Districts of the Roman Republic*, p. 111.

[3] Taylor, *op. cit.* p. 117. [4] Taylor, *op. cit.* p. 157. [5] Taylor, *op. cit.* p. 310.

unless induced in special instances by the Marian faction,[1] was hardly likely to show much favour to the Italians. The smallness of the increase in citizen numbers indicates that these censors were not very energetic in listing the Italians. But whatever principles they followed in registering the new citizens their decisions seem to have been ratified by the senate in 84; and subsequently there does not seem to have been any agitation for a re-registration.[2]

Thus it was in 87 or shortly afterwards that the Samnite soldiers were demobilized. This is not the general view. Modern scholarship will have it that the Social War instead of coming to an end simply faded away like the old soldier and became merged with the Civil War that broke out in 83 after Sulla's return from the East. In the words of Heitland: 'We need not try to define exactly at what point the war with the Allies as such ends and the civil war begins. The one is the continuation of the other.'[3] In other words the Samnites remained for a number of years on an active war footing waiting for Sulla to return, even though they had no idea when that would be or whether, whenever it happened, he would come back in the role of an invader.[4]

The ancient evidence suggests something very different. Cicero, who was in early manhood during the three years in question (86–84), describes them as a *triennium* during which *fuit urbs sine armis*: the *res publica* may have been *sine iure* and *sine ulla dignitate*,

[1] Neither of the censors in 86 was pro-Marian: in fact, they both joined Sulla when he returned to Italy. 'Marianist regions...were favoured by registration in small wards' (T. F. Carney, *Biography of Gaius Marius*, p. 70). As the Samnites were not so registered, Marius presumably did not view them with particular favour. His entourage, so far as is known, was not Samnite (E. Gabba in *Athen.* XXIX (1951), 256–61).

[2] Presumably the Italian local aristocrats were registered in the Roman tribes reasonably quickly. But the Marian faction did not show much interest in registering the rank and file of the new citizens until 84 (Livy, *Epit.* 84). They did bestir themselves then, obviously with the hope of getting the new citizens' support against Sulla, whose homecoming was now imminent. Nevertheless it may not have been until 70 that many Italians got on to the censors' lists: in that year the number registered was about double what it had been sixteen years earlier: *c.* 450,000 in 86 (Hier. *Ol.* 173, 4) as against some 900,000 in 70 (Phlegon, *Ol.* 177, 3; Livy, *Epit.* 98).

[3] W. E. Heitland, *Roman Republic*, II, 428, 460; R. Syme, *Roman Revolution*, p. 17; *Sallust*, p. 21. Cf., too, G. Bloch–J. Carcopino, *Hist. romaine*³, II, 400; L. Pareti, *Storia di Roma*, III, 602; A. Heuss, *Röm. Gesch.* p. 169. Most recently of all, A. J. Toynbee, *Hannibal's Legacy*, I, 163, states categorically: 'The Samnites remained under arms after the rest of the Italian Confederates had accepted Rome's terms.'

[4] On the situation in Italy during Sulla's absence, see E. Badian in *J.R.S.* LII (1962), 47–61. Even on the assumption that Sulla was bound to return, there was no certainty about his intentions. Sulla himself does not seem to have made up his mind to return sword in hand until 84 at the earliest (C. R. Bulst in *Historia*, XIII (1964), 329); even then he hoped to avoid the necessity of having to fight a civil war.

but Cicero does not mention it as being still at war with any of the Italic peoples.[1] Appian, whose account of the period may be uneven but is at least continuous, undoubtedly distinguishes the two conflicts; and the surviving epitomes show that Livy did so too.[2]

Modern scholars have been misled, partly by their assumption that the insurgents of the Social War were inevitably Marian partisans in the Civil: and certainly by the fact that in the final stages of the Civil War, as of the Social, it was Samnites who fought to the bitter end, even after others had quit.[3] The rebels of the Social War, however, cannot be automatically regarded as Sulla's enemies in the Civil. Admittedly Sulla had been their implacable foe: even after they laid down their arms, he had been quite uncompromising towards them and had opposed their unconditional admission into the Roman citizen body.[4] But the Italians must have noted that the Marian leaders also and not least Cinna himself had equally been their enemies in the Social War. Of course the Marians had subsequently agreed to their becoming citizens. But this was true also of Sulla. When it really came to the point, he too had been prepared to accept the Italians, no matter how grudgingly, as full fellow citizens. In 88 it was not Sulpicius' attempt to enfranchise them, but his attempt to deprive Sulla of his Mithridatic command that had caused the latter to march on Rome. Furthermore Sulla in 85 had proclaimed from the East that on his return to Italy, whatever else he might do, he would fully respect the newly acquired status of

[1] Cicero, *Brutus*, 308 and 227.

[2] By inserting a chapter on internal affairs after his account of the Social War, Appian (*B.C.* 1. 54) shows that he distinguishes it from its successor: in fact he pinpoints the beginning of the latter to 83 (*B.C.* 1. 84. 380). Livy's *Periochae* show that he ended his account of the Social War with Book 80 and did not begin his account of the Civil War until Book 83. His epitomators also make it quite clear that he sharply separated the two conflicts: see Florus 2. 9. 6, 18; Eutrop. 5. 3, 4; Oros. 5. 18, 19, 20 (who actually names them and calls them *duo bella funestissima*: 5. 22. 1). Val. Max. 8. 6. 4 also sharply separates the Civil War from the Social.

[3] *Samnitibus qui soli ex Italicis populis nondum arma posuerant* (Livy, *Epit.* 88).

[4] One of Sulla's objects in abolishing the censorship, when he got the chance, may have been to prevent the Italians from being registered. But between 87 and 82 the Italians may not have seen much difference between him and the Marians. Many of the latter, such as Cinna, Carbo, Damasippus, the younger Marius, had fought for Rome in the Social War. Moreover the Marians had done to death the author of the Lex Julia, and they had shown little interest in getting ordinary Italians registered until they thought that they badly needed their help (see above, p. 377, n. 2). Sulla may have been one of Livius Drusus' circle in 91: Pompeius Rufus, his friend and colleague in the consulship in 88, had been (E. Gabba, *Annali Scuola Normale di Pisa*, ser. 2, XXXIII (1964), 5). Parties, or more accurately factions, at Rome were much more fluid than political parties in modern states; so were men's attitudes towards them.

the Italians.[1] Some of the latter, including ex-rebels, evidently believed him. On his return forces were raised on his behalf in formerly insurgent districts: by Crassus among the Marsi, and by Pompey among the Picentes.[2] Those who later deserted from the Marian to Sulla's side also included ex-rebels, a legion of Lucani for instance.[3] Of others the reverse may have been true: Abella, whose destruction by Samnites operating out of Nola indicates that it was loyal to Rome in the Social War, is shown by the colony it received *c.* 80 to have opposed Sulla in the Civil.[4]

As far as the Samnites are concerned, it is clear that those who fought Rome from 91 to 87 were by no means identical with those who fought Sulla in 82. The insurgents against Rome in the Social War were the Pentri and, separately listed, the Hirpini: the Caudini were not involved. In the Civil War the Samnites who opposed Sulla unquestionably included Pentri and doubtless Hirpini as well. But they were not confined to these two peoples. Caudini fought against Sulla, and so did Sabellians from Capua and from Messana.[5] What was true of whole peoples was also true of individuals. Papius Mutilus, the Pentrian hero of the Social War, played no known part in the Civil: he seems to have retired to private life at Nola.[6] Statius, a Samnite leader in the Social War, seems to have thrown in his lot with Sulla soon after the latter's return to Italy.[7] Some of the Magii, the family that had been so pro-Roman in the Social War, may have opposed Sulla in 83/82.[8] Neither Pontius Telesinus nor his younger brother played any role in the Social War: yet they were the leaders of the Samnites in the war against Sulla.[9]

[1] App. *B.C.* 1. 77. 352; cf. Livy, *Epit.* 85.

[2] Plut. *Crass.* 6. 2; App. *B.C.* 1. 80. 366 f.

[3] App. *B.C.* 1. 91. 420.

[4] *CIL*, x, 1210; K. J. Beloch. *Röm. Gesch.* p. 511.

[5] Plut. *Pomp.* 10. 2; App. *B.C.* 1. 90. 416. Capua had supported Rome in the Social War (Cic. *de leg. agr.* 2. 80, 90).

[6] Livy, *Epit.* 89; Gran. Licin. p. 32 Fl.

[7] App. *B.C.* 4. 25. 102; R. Syme in *P.B.S.R.* XIV (1938), 23; E. Gabba in *Athen.* XXIX (1951), 264. He probably came from Bovianum (Vetter, no. 160).

[8] E. Gabba in *Athen.* XXXII (1954), 101; C. R. Bulst in *Historia*, XIII (1964), 312.

[9] Pontius Telesinus (almost certainly a Caudine: above, p. 225, n. 2) is named by Velleius (2. 16. 1) as one of the *Italicorum celeberrimi duces*, and Florus (2. 6. 6), no very reliable witness, regards him as a Social War general: cf., too, F. Münzer in *R.E.* XXII (1953), s.v. 'Pontius, 21', cols. 36–8. Yet there is no evidence for his actual participation in any action of the Social War (the Pompeius of Diod. 37. 13 must be emended to Papius, not to Pontius: above, p. 369, n. 1). For his role in the Civil War see Cic. *pro Caec.* 87; Velleius 2. 16. 2, 27; Val. Max. 6. 8. 2; App. *B.C.* 1. 90. 416; 1. 92. 431; Florus 2. 9. 22. Oros. 5. 21. 8 confuses Pontius Telesinus with his brother.

As a matter of fact changing of sides in the two wars was sufficiently common to bring to mind Messalla's biting phrase *desultor bellorum civilium*.[1]

The measures taken by Sulla's opponents indicate that the Samnites who had fought Rome in the Social War had not remained in arms. When in 84 Cinna and Carbo began making military preparations against Sulla's homecoming, now clearly imminent, they had no pool of military manpower armed and ready: they had to traverse the whole of Italy in a search for recruits.[2] They directed their appeals especially to the new citizens, who were not necessarily ex-rebels, on the assumption that these would be grateful to the Marian faction for having legislated their fair distribution in the Roman tribes. But the Marians had not proceeded energetically with the registration of the new citizens, and in any case in politics gratitude is a lively sense of favours to come. What determined the alignment of any Italian community in the Civil War was not its role in, or its profit from, the earlier struggle, but a cool and realistic appraisal of its own immediate and future interests. Every Italian community, whether newly enfranchised or not, was asking itself whether the programme of the Marians or the policy of Sulla, so far as it was then known, was likely to suit it better. Many communities had little confidence in the Marians, and Cinna and Carbo had considerable difficulty in raising a force. Cinna's efforts to recruit one led to his own assassination early in 84, while Carbo thought that the only way he could assure himself of Italian, including presumably ex-rebel, support was to seize hostages from the Italian towns. His lack of success, however, is indicated by his proposal, intended for Sulla's consumption and enacted into law by the senate in 84, that all armies everywhere should be disbanded.[3] This obviously was the clumsy expedient of one who had himself not much of an army to disband.

Sulla's enemies somehow succeeded in raising a force. But, even though it ultimately contained Samnites and Lucani amongst others, there is nothing to show that its nucleus was a Samnite army that had remained in being and on a war footing ever since 87. On the contrary, the evidence suggests that, at first anyway, the core of the

[1] Seneca, *Suas.* I. 7; cf. L. R. Taylor, *Voting Districts*, p. 119.
[2] App. *B.C.* I. 76–8.
[3] Livy, *Epit.* 84.

Marian army was composed of 'those in the city' and of Etruscans.[1] In other words the strongest Marian support was initially found in districts that had not been truly insurgent in the Social War at all.

There is, then, no need to assume that the Samnites, or the Lucani either for that matter, were continuously and uninterruptedly on a war footing from the uprising at Asculum in 91 until the battle at the Colline Gate in 82. From Cinna in 87 they had obtained, in the words of Appian,[2] what they wanted, and after that they had no more need than any other Italic people to maintain an attitude of armed hostility towards the Roman state of which they now formed part.

Exactly what the Samnites did during Sulla's absence from Italy we are nowhere told. Syme and Badian suggest that they were then virtually independent of Rome.[3] But this may mean no more than that they lived very much to themselves, devoting their efforts almost exclusively to the attempt to restore some kind of order, well-being and prosperity to their shattered homeland. Certainly, in this period of alleged independence, they did not continue minting coins to demonstrate their sovereignty: their issues came to an end with the Social War.

One thing at any rate is certain. When Sulla did return from the East he could not have found a Sabellian army awaiting him. The ancient evidence insists that his force was small enough for its landing at Brundisium to have been resisted without undue difficulty. Yet he landed at Brundisium with no opposition at all.[4] He then marched, as if through a friendly country, along the Via Appia

[1] App. *B.C.* I. 82. 373 says that the force comprised 200 cohorts (= some 100,000 men) to begin with and later was larger than this. Sulla's own figure makes the Marian army number 450 cohorts from the start (Plut. *Sulla*, 27. 3), a gross exaggeration. Its enrolment from the city mob (App. *loc. cit.*) accounts for its poor quality (P. A. Brunt in *J.R.S.* LII (1962), 74).

[2] App. *B.C.* I. 53. 231.

[3] R. Syme, *Rom. Revolution*, p. 87; E. Badian, *Foreign Clientelae*, p. 240. For a contrary view see C. R. Bulst in *Historia*, XIII (1964), 326.

[4] The ancient evidence derives from Sulla and undoubtedly minimizes the size of his own force and exaggerates that at the disposal of his enemies: he says that his army amounted to five legions, while that of his enemies was the equivalent of forty-five. Sulla ultimately had twenty-three legions (App. *B.C.* I. 100. 470: Livy, *Epit.* 89, gives the figure forty-seven), and even making allowance for the fact that his army grew as the campaign progressed it may be doubted that it was initially as small as he said it was. What is not to be doubted is the lack of opposition when it landed at Brundisium (App. *B.C.* I. 79. 364): the privileges that Brundisium won as a result of this endured long after his day.

right across Southern Italy, in other words, the heart of Samnium, without encountering any resistance.[1] So far as the record goes, Sulla up to this stage encountered only one Samnite, and a friendly one at that. This was Pontius' servant (runaway slave?) who met Sulla's army at Silvium, not far from Venusia, and resorting to the divinatory practices so popular among his countrymen prudently foretold not only Sulla's certain victory, but also the burning of the Capitol (which duly occurred later in 83).[2] Manifestly Sulla, on his arrival in Italy, did not need to concern himself unduly about Samnite hostility. The principal threat to him came from much further north. It was in Etruria that the main Marian strength lay, and accordingly he headed for there as fast as he could. Not until he reached Campania was he obliged to fight. There, somewhere near Capua, he defeated the army of one of the consuls for 83, Norbanus; and shortly afterwards, near Teanum, he enticed over to his own side the army of the other, Scipio Asiagenus.[3] The army of neither consul is described as containing many, or indeed any, Samnites.

During the winter of 83/82, which Sulla passed in the vicinity of Teanum, he bargained for support in various parts of Italy. To that end he signed a treaty with 'Italic peoples', ratifying the citizenship status they had acquired in 87.[4] Precisely which 'Italic peoples' these were is not specified, but there is every reason for believing that

[1] Velleius 2. 25. 1: *tanta cum quiete exercitum...perduxit in Campaniam.* App. *B.C.* 1. 84. 382 says that the Marians engaged Sulla at Canusium. But this is an obvious error for Casilinum. That the battle occurred near Capua is proved not only by the explicit assertion of Florus (2. 9. 21) but by Sulla's votive offerings there (Velleius 2. 25. 4).

[2] Plut. *Sulla*, 27. 6. Sulla was not above using a prophecy *post eventum* in an effort to find scapegoats for the burning of the Capitol, and Sabellians seemed suitable since they had long been saddled with the reputation of would-be burners of Rome (Livy 26. 27. 7 f.). Appian is unable to assign responsibility for the conflagration (*B.C.* 1. 83. 378); according to Tacitus (*Hist.* 3. 72) it was caused *fraude privata.*

[3] This was the Scipio who had escaped from the Samnites at Aesernia in 90 by disguising himself as a slave (above, p. 359) and had replaced M. Aemilius Scaurus as *pontifex maximus.* Sulla's seduction of his soldiers was aided by the foolish action of Sertorius in seizing Suessa Aurunca during a truce (App. *B.C.* 1. 85; Plut. *Sulla*, 28; Florus 2. 9. 19; Sall. *Hist.* 1. 91 M.). Indeed, if it had not been for Sertorius' move, full-scale civil war might even at that late stage have been avoided. E. Gabba, in *Ann. Scuola Norm. di Pisa*, ser. 2, XXXIII (1964), 13, suggests that Sulla was hoping for some kind of peaceful settlement right down to this point. He himself later dated the irrevocable rupture to the moment when Sertorius ended all possibility of a truce (App. *B.C.* 1. 95. 441). It was then that Sulla sought support among the *populi Italici* and signed an agreement with them.

[4] Livy, *Epit.* 86. Once convinced that civil war was inevitable, he naturally sought support—and a slogan calculated to make the widest appeal.

they did not include the Samnites. The ancient sources insist on the implacable hatred he felt for this people,[1] and as the ancient sources derive from Sulla's own *Memoirs* they can hardly be mistaken on the point. He had various reasons for detesting Sabellians. Within his own family there may have been a violently anti-Sabellian tradition. The last of his ancestors to anticipate him in reaching the consulship had been P. Cornelius Rufinus, *cos.* 290, 277, in the Third Samnite War and the Pyrrhic War, and he had been a bitter and unregenerate foe of Oscan-speaking Italy.[2] But, even if Sulla's own family had not inculcated hatred of Samnites into him, he could easily have conceived the most virulent antipathy for them during his operations against them in the Social War. And he must have hated them even more when they managed virtually to dictate their own terms in 87. We know what indignation this had provoked in Metellus Pius, and Metellus Pius was a scion of the house which had promoted Sulla's political fortunes and with which he was still intimately associated in 83/82.[3] Metellus Pius joined Sulla shortly after his arrival in Italy and undoubtedly gave him a full account of his abortive negotiations with the Samnites in 87; Sulla listened with mounting indignation. Above all, however, hatred of the Samnites, real or pretended, could be exploited to serve his own ends. When he returned to Italy he was an object of deep suspicion: the Romans had not forgotten that he was the first Roman ever to march on Rome and capture it as if it were an enemy city. There were not many men prominent in Roman public life at his side when his forces landed at Brundisium in the spring

[1] Plut. *Sulla*, 29. 4. For the exclusion of the Samnites from the treaty see A. Degrassi, *Scritti Vari di Antichità*, I, 188. Even if Sulla had not hated the Samnites to begin with, he would be offended because they had not offered him help when he returned: he himself tells us, through Plutarch (*Sulla*, 29. 1), that they had chosen to remain neutral, malevolently so according to him. Those that were not for him were against him: already in the Social War he had not hesitated to assault and plunder a Samnite town for not promptly committing itself (Aeclanum: App. *B.C.* 1. 51. 221 f.). The Samnites presumably did not proffer their aid to Sulla in the Civil War since they mistrusted his intentions. According to Tacitus (*Ann.* 13. 60. 3), who receives some corroboration from Cicero (*pro Font.* 6), a principal point at issue between Sulla and the Marians was the control of the law courts. As Appian remarks (*B.C.* 1. 22. 94), whoever controlled the courts controlled the people; and the Samnites may have been fearful that a victorious Sulla would use the law courts as drumhead courts-martial; which in fact is what he did (App. *B.C.* 1. 96. 446).

[2] He had good cause to hate the Samnites: their defeat of him in the Cranite Mts seems to have led to his eviction from the senate (above, pp. 282, 285), and perhaps to the political eclipse of his family for almost 200 years.

[3] In these years his wife (his fourth) was Metella: she profited handsomely from his murders (Pliny, *N.H.* 36. 116).

of 83.[1] In 83 he still had to win over public opinion. A convenient means to this end was the Samnite bogey. The Samnites were the traditional enemies of the Romans; he, Sulla, was the paladin who would save Rome and the Romans from this age-long menace. He would fight a Samnite War to end all Samnite Wars. As Strabo tells us, Sulla let it be known that in his view no Roman was safe so long as an organized Samnite community existed.[2] To get Roman public opinion solidly behind him he proceeded to convert his faction fight into an anti-Samnite crusade.

When, late in 83, somewhere between Cales and Teanum, he met the consul Scipio, himself no friend of Samnites, he entered into discussions *de auctoritate senatus, de suffragiis populi, de iure civitatis*.[3] These talks broke down, whereupon Sulla negotiated about these matters with Italic leaders. The result was the treaty already alluded to, with unquestionably a pointed exclusion of Sabellians.

The Samnites, according to Plutarch, who must have got the item from Sulla's own *Memoirs*, up to this time had observed neutrality in the war between Sulla and the Marians.[4] But their exclusion from Sulla's treaty with the Italic peoples showed that their days of neutrality were over. Nor were they going to be allowed to work their passage home. Other Italic peoples might arrive at some *modus vivendi* with Sulla: the Samnites would never be given the chance to do so. They were among the many persons who, in Appian's words, 'well knew that Sulla was not merely planning punishment, correction and alarm for them, but destruction, death, confiscation and wholesale extermination'.[5] Faced with this prospect they had no option but to fight, and before the winter was out they had mobilized.

At the beginning of the campaigning season for 82 Sulla set out from Teanum to continue his journey north-westward along the Via Latina.[6] Thereupon the Samnites sent troops (presumably via

[1] This has been demonstrated by E. Badian, *J.R.S.* LII (1962), 54 f. It was after he signed his treaty with the Italic peoples that 'the most prominent and excellent citizens' left their homes and hastened from all quarters to his camp as to a haven of refuge (Plut. *Pomp.* 6. 1); see C. Lanzani, *Mario e Silla*, p. 281, n. 1.

[2] Strabo 5. 4. 11, p. 249; cf. Plut. *Sulla*, 29. 4 (from Sulla's *Memoirs*?).

[3] Cic. *Phil.* 12. 27; cf., too, App. *B.C.* 1. 77. 352; 1. 85. 383. Note above all, App. *B.C.* 1. 95. 441, a passage which makes it certain that those who were not included in the *foedus* of the winter of 83/82 were marked down for destruction.

[4] See above, p. 383, n. 1.

[5] App. *B.C.* 1. 82. 375.

[6] Velleius 2. 26. 1; App. *B.C.* 1. 87. 394; cf. Livy, *Epit.* 86.

Aesernia, effectively a Samnite city ever since the Social War, and the storied region of the Middle Liris) to join the Younger Marius, one of the consuls for 82, who proposed to dispute Sulla's advance somewhere in the valley of the River Trerus in Latium. The Samnite force was commanded by a Caudine, the brother of Pontius Telesinus, who claimed to be a member of the same family as the hero of the Caudine Forks.[1] Battle was joined near Signia at a spot called Sacriportus, close to, if not on, the site of modern Colleferro. Many of the Marian troops, but not the Samnites so far as is known, deserted to Sulla and the day was lost. The Younger Marius and the Samnite commander escaped with the remnants of their army to Praeneste, there to be placed under siege by a *desultor civilium bellorum*, the Marian renegade Lucretius Ofella, whose *cognomen* and ultimate fate suggest that he was a Sabellian.[2] Sulla's forces had taken many prisoners in the battle, and Sulla ordered that all the Samnites among them should be slaughtered in cold blood:[3] the lives of the other prisoners were apparently spared. After getting his anti-Sabellian crusade off to this bloodthirsty start, Sulla resumed his advance on Etruria, the Marian stronghold. En route, he made himself master of, but did not linger long in, Rome.

It was after the atrocity at Sacriportus that the Samnites, much too late, made their really determined effort under Pontius Telesinus in the Civil War. The Lucani did likewise, under Marcus Lamponius,[4] who had proved his mettle as a general both before and during the Social War. Other Sabellians, presumably because they felt that they too would be the object of Sullan persecution, joined their kinsmen, led by a certain Gutta of Capua.[5]

The action of these peoples can well be described as desperate,

[1] Epigraphic evidence (*ILS*, 6510) confirms the theory that the brother was called Telesinus since Telesia of the Caudini was the town to which the Pontii belonged. The Caudini had long had Roman citizenship so that it is not surprising that they were not amongst the insurgents in the Social War.

[2] Sulla had him publicly executed for contumacy (App. *B.C.* 1. 101. 471), an action he would take with some relish against a Sabellian.

[3] According to Sulla himself, the prisoners numbered 8,000 in all (in addition his troops had killed 20,000 of the enemy in action); his own losses were 23 (Plut. *Sulla*, 28. 8).

[4] Oros. 5. 20. 9 calls him Camponius and makes him a Samnite.

[5] App. *B.C.* 1. 90. 416. Gutta is otherwise unknown. It is unlikely that he is the Albinus who fell at the Colline Gate (App. *B.C.* 1. 93. 431): the latter is probably the moneyer of 89, A. Postumius Albinus (but see F. Münzer in *R.E.* XXII (1953), s.v. 'Postumius, 36', col. 910). A Tiberius Gutta is stigmatized as a venal juror by Cicero, *pro Cluentio*, 71, 75, 78, 98, 103, 127; but he belonged to Larinum.

but Sulla's revealed attitude to Sabellians left them with very little choice but to fight on to the last. Moreover they may have hoped that the outbreak of the Second Mithridatic War in 83 would bring about a repetition of the miracle of 87.

The Sabellian forces, discovering that all attempts to relieve Marius at Praeneste were vain, made a sudden dash for Rome and came within an ace of capturing it. But Sulla rushed back from Etruria in the very nick of time and met them in the decisive Battle of the Colline Gate (1 November 82). This bitter battle, unlike those of the Samnite Wars of old, did not end when the sun went down, but lasted well into the night. Had darkness separated the combatants, the Sabellians may or may not have lived to fight another day. As it was, after gaining the upper hand over Sulla himself on the Roman left wing, they went down to defeat at the hands of Crassus and his troops on the Roman right. Crassus routed the force ranged opposite him and chased it to Antemnae, on the hillock where the Anio joins the Tiber. This clinched Sulla's victory. The Battle of the Colline Gate was over. The Samnites had fought, and lost, their last great battle.[1]

There ensued a grisly aftermath. Once again Sulla had all the prisoners collected. The Samnites amongst them were herded into the Villa Publica in the Campus Martius and there massacred to the last man. They numbered not less than three and possibly as many as eight thousand men.[2] Nor was this all. Taking the corpses of prominent Marian leaders (such as C. Carrinas, L. Junius Damasippus, C. Marcius Censorinus and Pontius Telesinus), who had either fallen in the battle or been murdered after it, he lopped off the heads and then had these displayed to the defenders of Praeneste. The gruesome exhibits were not without effect. The Marians at Praeneste realized that all was over. The younger Marius and the brother of Telesinus thereupon committed suicide and the rest of the garrison surrendered. The grim story then repeated itself. The Samnites among the garrison, together with the native Praenestines, were segregated from their Roman fellow

[1] Livy, *Epit.* 88; Velleius 2. 27; App. *B.C.* 1. 93; Plut. *Sulla*, 29, 30.

[2] Strabo 5. 4. 11, p. 249, says 3,000–4,000. Livy, *Epit.* 88 and App. *B.C.* 1. 93. 432 put the figure at 8,000. Possibly they have confused the Colline Gate prisoners with those from Sacriportus, who also are said to have numbered 8,000 (above, p. 385, n. 3). But the figure may be accurate, since Sulla himself admitted that he slaughtered 6,000 (Plut. *Sulla*, 30. 6).

prisoners and put to the sword.[1] This bloodthirsty brutality may have steeled the Sabellians at Aesernia and Nola to hold out much longer than they otherwise would have done: at any rate, these places do not seem to have fallen to Sulla until 80.[2] Even before then, however, so it would appear, the vindictive Sulla, like 'Butcher' Cumberland after Culloden, had sent his soldiers into the highlands on a mission of extirpation and expulsion, his justification for such savagery being that the Romans would never know peace so long as a cohesive Samnite nation survived.[3] Thousands must have perished or been scattered in this pogrom. Strabo indeed insists that Sulla's massacre left the Samnium of his own day a mere collection of hamlets; and Florus goes even further, insisting that the conqueror hardly left one stone upon another, so that even inside Samnium it was almost impossible to discover Samnium.[4] Such descriptions are exaggerations:[5] even before Sulla, Samnium had not been a region of large towns. Nevertheless the merciless and deadly nature of Sulla's vengeance need not be questioned: he did make some kind of a desert and call it peace in Samnium. It is significant that Samnium, unlike Etruria, was unable to rise in support of Lepidus in 78. Sulla's effort to obliterate the Samnites did not of course succeed. As the Turks discovered in Armenia in World War I and the Germans against European Jews in World War II, genocide is easier to plan than to perpetrate. It was a physical impossibility quite literally to erase a population that was both large and scattered. There were relatively few big centres and the highlands provided refuges and hiding-places. The Samnites must have contrived in various ways to evade the Sullan slaughter.

Certain it is that Samnium continued to be peopled by many persons of Samnite stock, all of them presumably nursing bitter feelings for years towards their conquerors. Lepidus, it is true, does not seem to have sought help from Samnium in his effort to undo Sulla's work in 78, even though his programme was to restore the

[1] The town surrendered to Lucretius Ofella (App. *B.C.* 1. 94. 434; 1. 101. 471), not to Catiline as an inconclusive fragment of Sallust (*Hist.* 1. 46 M.) has led some scholars to believe: see C. Cichorius, *Röm. Studien*, p. 172.

[2] Livy, *Epit.* 89; Gran. Licin. p. 32 Fl. It is this that enables Appian (*B.C.* 1. 84. 380) to say with assurance that the Civil War lasted three years: 83–80.

[3] Strabo 5. 4. 11, p. 249. A passage in Appian (*B.C.* 1. 95. 440) alludes indirectly to the destruction of Samnium.

[4] Florus 1. 11. 8.

[5] J. Heurgon, *Capoue préromaine*, p. 95; E. Gabbia, *Appiano e la Storia delle Guerre Civili*, p. 94.

lands that Sulla had confiscated: perhaps he realized that Samnium was too exhausted to give any. But Spartacus in 71, Catiline in 63 and Caelius Rufus in 48 all proposed to make their last-ditch stand against constituted Roman authority in Samnium, as the place where rebels against Rome would be most likely to find a welcome.[1] In fact Oscan names persisted in Samnium into imperial times, and bearers of them reached local offices of one kind or another in the region during the first centuries B.C. and A.D.[2]

Many non-Samnite names, however, also occur there, their proportion not being significantly lower in Samnium than in other parts of Italy. In other words the savagery of Sulla had greatly changed the face of Samnium and deprived it of its Sabellian character. Strabo, writing in the age of Augustus, insists that there was no longer anything typically Samnite about it.[3]

This is also suggested by the way the Samnites were dispersed. Samnite names occur not infrequently in other parts of the Roman Empire. Their bearers may have been descendants of those who had fled from the Sullan terror; or they may have been emigrants from a land that held out little promise of well-being for them. Gaul, both the Cisalpine and the Transalpine portions, contained not a few of them. Onomastic investigation of the *CIL* shows that Sabellian-type names were almost as numerous in the Cisalpina as in Samnium itself. One wonders whether the N. Magius of Cremona who is mentioned by Caesar,[4] and the Magia of Mantua who had the poet Vergil for a son, may not have been of Samnite stock.

Evidently Sulla had found it impossible to wipe the Samnites entirely off the face of the earth. Indeed it is one of the ironies of history that his own daughter, the lascivious Fausta Cornelia, took a second generation Samnite for her second husband: the dead dictator must have turned in his grave.

Nevertheless it is no exaggeration to say that the Battle of the Colline Gate and its terrible sequel did complete the ruin of Samnium and did mean the end of the Samnites as a separate, identifiable nation. Never again were they to play collectively a role in history. The Social War had made the assimilation of the various races and

[1] App. *B.C.* I. 119. 552; Cic. *pro Sestio*, 5. 12; Caes. *B.C.* 3. 21; Livy, *Epit.* III.

[2] E. Pais, *Ricerche sulla Storia e sul Diritto Pubblico di Roma*, IV, 295.

[3] Strabo 6. I. 2, p. 254.

[4] Caes. *B.C.* I. 25. 4.

peoples of Italy certain in any event: in obtaining what they asked for, they had ensured the disappearance of their own separate identities. Hence the Samnites would not have remained distinct from other Italians for very much longer in any event. But the evidence suggests that, in the new all-Roman Italy that emerged in the first century B.C. from the fires of the Social and Civil Wars, their role was disproportionately small.

In the years between Sulla and the so-called First Triumvirate Samnites were anything but prominent in the Roman state. Even those Romans who opposed Sulla's policies and actions hardly concerned themselves with the sufferings of his Samnite victims and the discrimination under which they laboured. In other words, the doors that had been closed to them were allowed to remain shut. In any case, even if there had been no deliberate policy of keeping the Samnites as mere hewers of wood and drawers of water, so to speak, the wastage brought about by war and massacre had deprived Samnium of a whole generation of its sons, so that there could have been but few outstanding ones left to make their mark in the public life of Rome. Most of the Samnite gentry had joined the Samnite lower orders in determined opposition, first to Rome in the Social War and then to Sulla in the Civil.[1] Therein they differed markedly from their counterparts in other regions of Italy, who, as often as not, in cool calculation had either sided with or early submitted to Sulla and thereby ensured the future participation of their families in the affairs of the Roman Republic in its last years.[2] C. Asinius Pollio, for instance, grandson of the leader of the insurgent Marrucini in the Social War, became one of the most powerful personages in the Roman world in the forties. Even the clan of the great Marsian, Poppaedius Silo, did not fare too badly: one of its scions, himself named Poppaedius Silo, was no insignificant figure in the retinue of Mark Antony in 39.[3] But few Samnite families similarly came to the fore in Rome.

On the contrary, instead of Samnites flocking to the capital to make their fame and fortune, the reverse seems to have been the case. The defeated south, in Roman Italy as in post-bellum USA, became a mecca for carpet-baggers. Sulla may not have planted any

[1] Sulla significantly had sought to exterminate above all the leading men in Samnium (Strabo 5. 4. 11, p. 249).

[2] For the progress of insurgent progeny at Rome, see R. Syme, *Roman Revolution*, p. 91.

[3] Cass. Dio 48. 41. 1.

military colonies in Samnium proper, except possibly at Abellinum.[1] But of the veterans from more than a score of legions that he is said to have settled on 'captured' areas[2] many must have been placed in that tristful land. Large tracts of territory were simply confiscated and distributed *viritim* to his minions. *Villae rusticae* began to dot the landscape. Samnite renegades no doubt got some of the loot, but in the main it went to Romans, *Septimii, Turranii ceterique Sullanarum adsignationum possessores*.[3] The *beati possidentes* of the *Sullani agri* included Quinctius Valgus (father-in-law to P. Servilius Rullus, *trib. pl.* in 63), probably the *gens* Fulvia, and perhaps also Cicero's *bête noire* Verres and his nonpareil Rabirius.[4] One wonders, too, how the family of Cocceius Nerva, who came from Narnia, managed to acquire the *plenissima villa quae super est Caudi cauponas*.[5] The confiscated lands that were not assigned to individuals became Roman *ager publicus* and were occupied by graziers, so that in the last days of the Roman Republic some parts of Samnium must have presented an appearance of desolation.

As soon as enough time had elapsed for the grievous losses of the eighties to be repaired, the Samnites might have been expected to become rather more conspicuous in Roman affairs. Yet they failed to be so. This is surprising, since the violence of that period placed a high value on military talent, and the young men of so martial a people ought to have been prominent above most others.[6] Such, however, does not appear to have been the case. Recent

[1] Mommsen, *Gesammelte Schriften*, V, 245 f. For Sulla's *coloniae* and *assignationes* see E. Gabba in *Athenaeum*, XXIX (1951), 270 f.

[2] Twenty-three legions, according to App. *B.C.* I. 100. 470 (cf. I. 96. 448). Livy, *Epit.* 89, gives the impossible number of forty-seven legions.

[3] For Sullan *coloni* and their behaviour see Sall. *Cat.* 16. 4; 28. 4; Cic. *Mur.* 49; *Cat.* 2. 20; *de leg. agr.* 3. 3. One of the Septimii may have paid for the ill-gotten gains with his life: the Second Triumvirate proscribed him (App. *B.C.* 4. 23). The Turranii were large-scale pastoral operators (Varro, *R.R.* 2. praef. 6).

[4] See Cic. *de leg. agr.* 3. 3; 3. 8; *CIL*, I², 825; Cic. *II Verr.* 2. 1. 38; *ILS*, 9445; H. Dessau in *Hermes*, XLVI (1911), 613; XLVII (1912), 320. Rullus' *gens*, the *Servilia*, was strongly pro-Sullan: two Servilii were victorious for him at Clusium in 82. To judge from what Cicero says, Rullus was trying to restore his fortune, and, if it is true that his father-in-law owned practically all of the Hirpinian territory, he evidently succeeded. The names of Roman senators and knights that turn up on South Italian pottery of the last century (A. Oxé in *Germania*, VIII (1924), 80 f.) may also belong to exploiters of conquered Samnium.

[5] Hor. *Sat.* I. 5. 50 f. Remains of the villa may have been found (P. Cavuoto in *Samnium*, XXXIV (1961), 182–91).

[6] Consider the implications of such an expression as *militiae turbine factus eques* (Ovid, *Amores*, 3. 15. 6). Octavian in 44 evidently had hopes of finding soldiers in Samnium (Cic. *ad Att.* 16. 11. 6).

investigations have revealed very few Samnites among the junior officers of the Roman army between 80 and 30. The four centurions named Papius from Pietrabbondante were a very unusual phenomenon and they belonged to an ephemeral legion.[1] Even in the entourages of Catiline and Caesar, both of whom seem to have rallied to their side many malcontents from areas that had suffered in the Social War or from Sulla's persecution, Samnites were usually conspicuous by their absence: Catiline found support among the Paeligni, Caesar among the Picentes.[2]

The absence of Samnites could hardly be due any longer to the loss of the generation in the eighties.[3] Perhaps the lack of urban centres accounts for it. It was the *municipia* of Italy that supplied the Roman armies of the last century B.C. with their military tribunes, prefects and centurions,[4] and Samnium, even after the urbanization brought about by the Social War, had few such towns.

If the Samnites provided few junior officers, they supplied even fewer men of higher rank. It has been suggested that one of Julius Caesar's generals may have been a Samnite, L. Staius Murcus,[5] *legatus* in 48. There was also L. Decidius Saxa, whom Caesar made a plebeian tribune in 44 and who became governor of Syria and died defending it against the Parthians in 40. He bears the same *gentilicium* as the Samnite Cn. Decidius, who when proscribed was possibly defended by Caesar: perhaps the two men were related. Decidius Saxa, it is true, came from Spain, but he could have been

[1] *ILS*, 2234: the legion is XXXII. Some of Caesar's junior officers bore Abruzzi-type names: the *aquilifer* L. Petrosidius (*B.G.* 5. 37. 5) and the *eques* T. Terrasidius (*B.G.* 3. 7. 4), of whom the former has a name that is found in Picenum (*CIL*, VI, 24052; *ILS*, 6132 b). But there is no evidence that they came from Samnium. P. A. Brunt's table of the recruitment areas of Roman armies in the last century B.C. (in *J.R.S.* LII (1962), 85) shows no troops from Samnium before 44 and very few after then. According to J. Suolahti, *The Junior Officers of the Roman Army*, p. 169, 'after the Social War the officers were recruited also from the roadless mountain regions. The great Armies of the Second Civil War had officers from all over Italy'. This bold statement contradicts the evidence which he himself has assembled: neither his tables (pp. 307–408) nor his map (facing p. 403) show any coming from Samnium.

[2] Oros. 6. 6. 7; Caes. *B.C.* 1. 12. Catiline did have at least one Sabellian among his followers, P. Sittius (Sall. *Cat.* 21). He also had a plan for seizing the drovers' trails in the south and if he had succeeded in doing so 'he would never have been overthrown except at great cost in bloodshed and dreadful desolation' (Cic. *pro Sestio*, 8. 12).

[3] Also their unpopularity had waned: see, for instance, Cic. *pro Cluentio*, 197.

[4] See Suolahti, Brunt (in the works cited in note 1 above).

[5] Murcus may have come from Bovanium Vetus (L. R. Taylor, *Voting Districts*, p. 255).

a Samnite of the Sullan dispersion.[1] If he was, he with Staius Murcus may be the exception to prove the rule that Samnites did not become persons of consequence in the last century B.C.

The political sphere reveals the same state of affairs as the military, which is hardly surprising in view of the way that the two were inextricably intertwined at Rome. There was a plebeian tribune named Papius in 65, but there is no sign that he was related to the Social War leader.

The disordered times of the so-called First Triumvirate and later were prolific of men who rose from obscure origins to hold office and to sit in the senate at Rome. The First and Second Triumvirates especially provided opportunities for lucky or time-serving adventurers of low birth. Yet among those whose careerist determination made good in the latter part of the first century there were but few Samnites.[2] After 60, and even more markedly after 42, the Roman state saw many a *hominem novum parvumque senatorem*, dim characters with fantastic names.[3] They came from Etruria, from Umbria, from Picenum, and even from such Sabellian peoples as the Lucani and the Frentani. Yet very few came from the highlands of Samnium.[4]

Only the merest handful of Roman senators in the closing years of the Roman Republic can be certainly identified as Samnites. T. Annius Milo, notorious as the hot-blooded slayer of Clodius, had a Samnite father. He himself was born at Lanuvium, but his background was Hirpinian Compsa. He reached the high office of praetor and even got so far as to be considered a possible candidate for the consulship. More authentic Samnites who gained admission into the Roman *curia* were Statius, who had given a good account of himself against Rome in the Social War, and the two Magii

[1] Cic. *pro Cluentio*, 161; Tac. *Dial.* 21. 6 (who calls him Decius). Cicero, *Phil.* 11. 12, with heavy-handed humour calls Decidius Saxa a 'primitive Celtiberian'. See R. Syme in *J.R.S.* XXVII (1937), 132.

[2] Cn. Plancius, Cicero's client, hardly counts as one: he came from Atina, which had ceased to be Samnite long before 90. Safinius Atella (Cic. *pro Cluentio*, 68, 99) has a very Sabellian name, but he seems somewhat disreputable and in any case belonged to Larinum.

[3] *Bellum Africanum*, 57. 4; cf. R. Syme, *Roman Revolution*, p. 91. According to Sallust, *Jug.* 4. 8, it was possible for any nonentity to become praetor or consul: yet Samnites did not.

[4] Their exclusion seems to outlast the ban that was automatically placed on all Marians. The Emperor Claudius may have said that all of Italy provided members for the republican Senate (Tac. *Ann.* 11. 24: not confirmed in the extant parts of the speech (*ILS*, 212)): but Samnium did so only exceptionally.

brothers, who had sided with Rome in that struggle. The latter pair got into the Roman senate (and indeed into the office of praetor) as a result of their choice of sides in 90. Statius probably entered the august body because of the speed with which he supported Sulla in 83: Sulla, it will be remembered, more than doubled the size of the senate. None of the three owed their preferment to the second set of triumvirs. On the contrary, the triumvirs of 42 proscribed and slaughtered Statius for his wealth in his old age.[1]

If Samnites had difficulty in getting into the Roman senate, they had still more difficulty in getting into the Roman consulship. Years were to elapse before any member of their nation succeeded in reaching that lofty pinnacle.[2] Even Larinum, a town much more likely to produce criminals than consuls, got two of its sons into the high post before Samnium did.

Moreover, of the very few men of distinction in the last years of the Republic who could claim Samnium as their birthplace, how many were genuine Samnites? The original territory of Samnium had been progressively whittled away. Roman seizure and settlement of Samnite land (and good land at that) had begun already in the fourth century. After the Pyrrhic and Second Punic Wars Samnium had been reduced in size, and for good measure many of the winter pastures of the Samnites had become Roman *ager publicus.* The confiscations of Sulla merely continued a process that had begun centuries earlier. By the first century, and more particularly after the Sullan terror, a large proportion of the population of Samnium must have been other than Samnite. Extermination, dispossession and pauperization had done their work. Accordingly when, in the closing decades of the first century, eminence is occasionally attained by a man from Samnium, M. Nonius Gallus of Aesernia for example,[3] it would be rash to regard him as Samnite in nationality and still more in sentiment.[4]

[1] App. *B.C.* 4. 25. 102.

[2] M. Lollius, Augustus' marshal (see Dio 54. 20. 3), who became consul in 21, belonged to Voltinia, the Roman tribe in which the Samnites were enrolled (*Anneé Epigr.* (1938), p. 85); and his name occurs among the Caraceni in the third century (Zon. 8. 7) and at Telesia in imperial times (*CIL*, IX, 2230); but there is no indication that he was in fact a Samnite.

[3] The last man not of the imperial family to erect a triumphal monument (it still survives at Isernia): C. Picard in *Rev. Etudes Latines*, XXXVII (1960), 254.

[4] 'Most of the great landowners in Samnium now were not of Samnite stock' (R. Syme, *Rom. Revolution*, p. 91). Cf. Strabo 6. 1. 2, p. 254: 'The degeneration of the Samnites is so complete that it is difficult even to distinguish their settlements. The reason is that there

The unimportance of the Samnites in the Roman state after 82 is indicated by the fact that the Romans did not feel it necessary to conciliate them in any way. Latin literature is generally hostile in its allusion to them, and their defeat at the Colline Gate in 82 was celebrated by the Romans for hundreds of years as a national triumph rather than as an incident in a civil war. Other Italians might fight the Romans and, once safely defeated, be transformed into friends: the Latins, for instance, or the Sabini. But not the Samnites: they are conspicuously missing from Cicero's list of Italian peoples who had been incorporated to form the Roman state.[1] After their harsh repression when no further danger was apprehended from them, they were relegated to obscurity and largely ignored. With lordly indifference the Romans let assimilation do its work amongst them.

By the beginning of the first century A.D. sufficient time had elapsed for the wounds to have healed; and no doubt when Augustus took pains to have *omnem florem ubique coloniarum et municipiorum, bonorum scilicet virorum et locupletium* in the senate, the proportion of Samnites in that body rose somewhat. Velleius Paterculus, an authentic Hirpinian, qualified for admission in A.D. 7, by becoming quaestor,[2] and in A.D. 9 a Samnite, and one from a historic family, actually became *consul suffectus*. This was M. Papius Mutilus, obviously a relation of the Samnite Social War hero. While consul he made himself famous as one of the sponsors for Augustus' morality programme. His sycophantic character, however, was not in keeping with his name. Moreover, it is obvious that he was thoroughly romanized.[3] Indeed by A.D. 9 there had been time not only for an entirely new generation of Samnites to emerge but also for the romanization of Samnium to make great progress. Augustus himself was probably more than a little responsible for it. After the Battle of Philippi in 42 he had settled numbers of his veterans on land seized from Beneventum and Venusia and had thereby

is no longer any common organization in any of the individual tribes, and their characteristic differences in language, armour, dress and the like have completely vanished. Furthermore their settlements, both severally and partially, are utterly lacking in distinction.' Note, too, Strabo's insistence (*loc. cit.*) that the Lucani, 'Samnites by race', have become 'Romans' by his day.

[1] Livy 7. 24. 4; Cic. *pro Balbo*, 13. 31.

[2] Velleius 2. 111. 2.

[3] Note how a few years later in company with another descendant of a notable Italic family, Asinius Gallus, he carried flattery of Tiberius to a servile extreme: he proposed that the day on which the 'conspirator' Scribonius Libo Drusus committed suicide should be kept as a public festival (Tac. *Ann.* 2. 32).

strengthened the non-Oscan element in and around those former Latin colonies.[1] We are not specifically told that Samnium was also among the areas that after the Battle of Actium in 31 were accused of having favoured Antony and were therefore forced to provide lands for veterans;[2] but it may well have been one.[3] If this was the case, then it must have contributed to the denationalization of Samnium. Had Augustus not been convinced that Samnite national feeling was dead, he would hardly have permitted his stepson to rehabilitate the town of Saepinum *c.* A.D. 2.[4]

Once they obtained the Roman citizenship, the Samnites did not make much of a distinctively Sabellian contribution to the life of the Roman state. It is true that in the troubled year A.D. 69 they felt for a fleeting moment some stirring of their old fighting instincts,[5] but in the event they were scarcely distinguishable from the Romans and the Italians generally in the haste with which they sought the Flavian victor's favour.

Already by Augustus' day there were persons almost certainly of Samnite stock who on rising to positions of some importance seemed more like Romans than authentic Samnites. The poet Horace from Venusia, *Lucanus an Apulus anceps*, resembles the consul of A.D. 9: he was not only a spokesman for Augustus, but also a self-proclaimed Roman patriot.[6] The sadist P. Vedius Pollio, who seems to have come from Beneventum or its vicinity, may have been pandering to an atavistic streak of Sabellian barbarity when he fed his wretched slaves to his lampreys, but he was typically Roman in his fondness for fishponds.[7] Whether another eminent son of Beneventum, the famous schoolmaster *plagosus* Orbilius, who insisted on not sparing the rod for fear of spoiling the child, was more genuinely Samnite is a moot point.[8]

The Oscan language continued to have some vogue in the Augustan age. The scholiasts believed that the *bilingues Canusini* of

[1] Appian, *B.C.* 4. 3.

[2] Cass. Dio 51. 4. 6. Many of the dispossessed were sent to Macedonia.

[3] With the very dubious possible exception of M. Lollius, Samnium had no powerful native son to shield it from indignities in the way that Lucania had Statilius Taurus, who could conceivably be a descendant of the third-century Lucanian hero, Statius Statilius (Val. Max. 1. 8. 6; Pliny, *N.H.* 34. 32, calls him Sthenius Stallius).

[4] *CIL*, IX, 2483.

[5] Tac. *Hist.* 3. 59. 1.

[6] *Clarum genus Osci* (*Sat.* 1. 5. 54) is a barely disguised sneer, *clarum genus* and *Osci* being a contradiction in terms.

[7] Cic. *ad Att.* 1. 18. 6; 2. 9. 1; Cass. Dio 54. 23.

[8] Hor. *Sat.* 1. 6. 76 f.; Suet. *de gramm.* 9.

Horace,[1] like the Brutii, spoke Oscan and Greek. There is also Strabo's surprising statement that dramatic performances were still given in Oscan, even in Rome, in his own day (although it may be surmised that such plays, or parts of plays, were curiosities rather than regular spectacles, since elsewhere Strabo insists that Oscan had 'disappeared').[2] In the remoter districts it must have lingered on for many years, and in fact it was the last of the non-Latin languages of Italy other than Greek to die out. Even in so sophisticated and romanized a community as Pompeii it had still not become entirely extinct by A.D. 79. But, in view of Quintilian's assertion that by his day (*c.* A.D. 90) Latin was the language of all Italy,[3] it is safe to say that even in Samnium Oscan had declined by A.D. 79 to the status of a peasants' patois; and soon it gave place completely to Latin, so completely indeed that today few traces of Oscan can be positively identified in the dialects or even in the speech habits of that part of Italy.[4] The increased municipalization which the Social War brought about in Italy undoubtedly helped to promote this spread of Latin; and by the first century A.D. Samnium had acquired a few municipalities. Besides the Latin Colonies of an earlier day (Aesernia, Beneventum, Luceria, Saticula and Venusia), Pliny lists, in Northern and Central Samnium, Aufidena, Bovianum, Bovianum Vetus, Fagifulae, Saepinum and Ter(e)ventum.[5] In the region of the Hirpini there were Abellinum, Aeclanum, Aquilonia, Caudium and the town near modern Circello which served the Ligures Baebiani as their administrative centre.[6] To these may be added the places which by the time of Strabo, Pliny and Ptolemy had long formed part of Campania: Allifae, Caiatia, Telesia, Trebula and Venafrum. All of these places seem to

[1] Hor. *Sat.* I. 10. 30.

[2] Strabo 5. 3. 6, p. 233; 6. 1. 2, p. 254.

[3] Quint. I. 5. 56. Cf., too, Pliny, *N.H.* 3. 39: *numine deum electa quae...tot populorum discordes ferasque linguas sermonis commercio contraheret.*

[4] H. Nissen, *Ital. Landesk.* I, 523; G. Rohlfs in *Germ. röm. Mon.* XVIII (1930), 37–56; E. Vetter in *R.E.* XVIII (1942), s.v. 'Osci', col. 1567. The softening of *c* before *i* and *e* and the tendency to drop final *s* in the modern Romance Languages may be due to Osco-Umbrian influence on Latin (G. Devoto, *Lingua di Roma*, pp. 281 f.); and perhaps the quality of the stem vowel in such Italian words as *ebbi* and *seppi* is a residual Oscan speech habit (M. G. Delfino, *Serta Eusebiana*, pp. 44, 72). But in general Oscan has disappeared almost without a trace.

[5] Pliny, *N.H.* 3. 107, also lists a Ficolea in Samnium, probably in error: Ficolea was in Latium (H. Dessau in *CIL*, XIV, p. 447).

[6] Perhaps Aequum Tuticum should be listed, even though Pliny omits it. A recently published inscription suggests that it enjoyed municipal autonomy after the Social War (D. Petroccia in *Samnium*, XXXVI (1963), 83).

have been municipally organized, at least from the time of Augustus on. That does not necessarily mean that they were all big places: Roman Saepinum was even smaller than Samnite Saepinum, its town walls extending no more than 1,400 yards. Not that we need accept the statements of Strabo and Florus about the utter insignificance of the towns of Samnium.[1] Actually Beneventum and to a lesser extent Venusia were places of consequence, as even Strabo himself admits;[2] and some of the other places also may have attained respectable dimensions. It was from these towns that a knowledge of Latin was spread over the surrounding countryside.

There cannot be any reasonable doubt that in the early Empire Latin must have been the mother tongue of such natives of Samnium as rose to positions of prominence. There were such individuals, even though the literature of the period identifies but few of them. C. Petronius Pontius Nigrinus, *consul ordinarius* in the year when Tiberius died, from his name looks like a Sabellian, although the name Pontius is not confined to Samnium or to Samnites. Annius Vinicianus, the son-in-law of Corbulo who plotted against Nero, may have come from Beneventum, which however is no proof that his blood was Samnite.[3] Helvidius Priscus, another opponent of Nero, is described by Tacitus as coming from Caracenan Cluviae.[4] The two illustrious brothers, L. Neratius Priscus and L. Neratius Marcellus, who became consuls and famed jurists under Trajan and Hadrian, were authentic sons of Saepinum and members of an old local family which Vespasian had made 'patrician'.[5] Nevertheless the Saepinum from which they came was a Roman town founded *c.* A.D. 2. It had Oscan-speaking inhabitants, at first at any rate,[6] but it was not the old Samnite town that had played its part in the Samnite Wars; and the Neratii were so completely assimilated that one of them could be envisaged as a possible successor to Trajan.[7]

Epigraphy reveals rather more names of Samnites who made some kind of a mark in the Roman Empire. The clan of the Pontii, for instance, seems to have remained prominent in the Caudine area: a Pontia from Telesia, a relative presumably of Pontius Telesinus, married into the illustrious family of the Minucii Thermi.[8]

[1] See above, p. 387, ns. 3, 4. [2] Strabo 5. 4. 11, p. 250. [3] Suet. *Nero*, 36. 1.
[4] Tac. *Hist.* 4. 5. [5] *Année Epigr.* (1927), 118.
[6] Oscan graffiti have been found there (V. Cianfarani, *Guida delle Antichità di Sepino*, p. 45). [7] S. H. A. *Hadr.* 4. 8. [8] *ILS*, 6510.

At Fagifulae even the storied name of Gavius Pontius turns up. Bovianum produced Arruntius Atticus and Arruntius Iustus, patrons of towns both in and out of Samnium. From Caiatia came L. Pacideius Carpianus, who served as patron of Saepinum and other places and must have been a native of Samnium.[1]

Some Samnites served as junior officers in the army: L. Eggius of Aeclanum in A.D. 9, M. Allius Rufus of Abellinum in A.D. 15, L. Laetilius Domitianus of Beneventum *c.* A.D. 15, M. Vecilius Campanus of Luceria *c.* A.D. 15.[2] But there is no reason to regard any of these as unassimilated Sabellians: on the contrary they can safely be reckoned indistinguishable from Romans in general.

Some other notables may have been Samnites. His name and his picaresque novel imply that Petronius, Nero's famed arbiter of elegance, was at home in Sabellian Italy. Papinius Statius, the most outstanding non-provincial Latin poet between the reigns of Nero and Hadrian, was clearly of Sabellian origin; but he came from Naples[3] and was almost certainly a Campanian, not a Samnite highlander. Another person with a Sabellian, and indeed a Samnite, name is Pontius Pilate,[4] the most famous (or notorious) of all provincial governors, prefect of Judaea from A.D. 26 to 36.

But even if all these more or less eminent personalities of the Roman Empire were of Samnite stock, they would not form an extensive company; and it is unlikely that their Sabellian origin was a matter of any real or abiding consequence either to themselves or to their contemporaries. From the offices they held, from the cities they patronized, from the flavour of their writing and from their activities generally, one would infer that their Samnite birth was more or less incidental. The notion of Samnite descent was not without its romantic and sentimental aspect. But, just as today a Piedmontese is first and foremost an Italian no matter how wistful and nostalgic his memories of the Kingdom of Sardinia, so a Pentrian in the first and second centuries A.D. must have been much more conscious of being a citizen of Rome than a son of Samnium.

The completeness of the assimilation is shown by the very few

[1] *ILS*, 5547a; 5524; 5017; 5014.

[2] *CIL*, v, 1986; x, 1032; xii, 1793; *Année Epigr.* (1938), 110.

[3] *Silvae*, 3. 5. 81.

[4] Even his *cognomen* seems Sabellian: *ehpeilatas* (= Latin *expilatae*) occurs on an Oscan inscription from Capua (Vetter, no. 81). But the name Pontius is by no means confined to Sabellian Italy.

occasions on which there is separate mention of Samnium and the Samnites in the great days of the Roman Empire. Not that the names were ever entirely forgotten.[1] 'Samnium' occurs as a geographical expression in the Diocletianic reorganization of the Roman world and in documents of the fourth and fifth centuries; and even a casual reading of Procopius shows that it was still being used in the sixth.[2] Indeed for long thereafter the Lombard princes of the Duchy of Beneventum proudly assumed the title *Dux Samnitium.*[3]

[1] They are ignored, however, in the *Liber Coloniarum* I.

[2] Procop. 5. 15. 1; 5. 20. 1; 6. 5. 2; 7. 61.

[3] T. Hodgkin, *Italy and her Invaders*, VI, 68.

CHAPTER II

CONCLUSION

Steadfast valour and an unflagging will to be free make the story of the Samnites one of stirring interest. Even their Roman opponents found this to be so, and their historians used incidents from the Samnite Wars to embellish and magnify episodes from other periods of their history. The tale of a Fabius, for instance, taking four thousand retainers with him to the Cremera in 477 derives from the action of a later Fabius who selected that number to accompany him to Sentinum in 295.[1] Roman poets likewise found material for story and song in the Samnite saga. The rosters of the Italic peoples in Vergil and Silius Italicus owe more than a little to the record of the Samnite Wars.[2]

Even greater was the impact which the Samnites made on Roman life. Apart from any usages and institutions which can be traced to them, the Samnites were the unwitting cause of some of the major developments in Roman history. In a sense they had affected it before it can be said even to have properly begun. Their expansion over Southern Italy interrupted the stream of ideas and influences which early Rome had been receiving from archaic Greece through the Italiotes and the Etruscans. The oft-noted isolation of Rome from Hellenic culture during the fifth and fourth centuries was chiefly due to the consolidation in Samnium and Campania of the Sabellian tribes which were slow to depart from their traditional ways. They formed an obstacle to any continuing and easy contact between Rome and the hellenized South. The Romans in course of time removed the barrier, and the intercourse was resumed. But the inevitable consequence of the interruption had been to keep the national character of the Romans true to itself. The climate in which the Romans came of age was Italic. They developed their own forms of government and civil institutions and they perfected their military organization in the face of the hard challenge of a virile and valiant opponent.

[1] Dion. Hal. 9. 15. 3; Livy 10. 25. 2.

[2] Verg. *Aen.* 7. 641 f.; Sil. Ital. 8. 356 f. (who may go back, through Varro, to Cato: J. Nicol, *Hist. and Geogr. Sources Used by Sil. Italicus*, pp. 166–9).

The effect of the Samnites on the Romans was for a long and crucial time constant, immediate and inescapable; they roused and sped them on the road to empire. Before the Samnite Wars the vision of the Romans had hardly stretched beyond Latium and the Trerus valley: as a result of those great struggles the Roman horizon widened to embrace all Italy.

If at one time the Samnites had also looked afar, they did not have the same capacity as the Romans for making the best use of their opportunities. In helping Rome to defeat the Latins they were guilty of a grave error of political judgement. And more than once they showed that they did not know how to exploit their victories. In this regard their own skill in arms may have been a handicap to them: it lulled them into complacency and failure to press an advantage with all due intransigence and it caused other Italians to fear rather than support them, even after the balance of power had tilted towards Rome. Indeed it would hardly be an exaggeration to say that, by diverting Italian qualms away from Rome and towards themselves, they provided a shield for Roman expansion.

Moreover, once the Samnites got away from their native mountains, separatism tended to get the better of their federative instincts. This would have frustrated any attempt on their part to create a far-flung empire.

Far otherwise was it with the Romans. It was the effort needed to subdue the Samnites that cemented the Roman citizen body together. Gavius Pontius, like Hannibal, could fairly be described as one of the creators of Roman greatness, even though he and the great Carthaginian would certainly have hated the title.

Whether or not the initial urge amongst the Romans for southward expansion had its origin within a group of their own patricians, it was largely thanks to the Samnite Wars that the plebeian victory in the Struggle between the Orders came when it did. The plebeians exploited the First War to extort the concession that one of the consuls and one of the censors must always come from them.[1] In the Second War the power of the senate was firmly established[2] and a patricio-plebeian nobility created and consolidated; and, for weal

[1] It was in 340, according to Livy (8. 12. 16), that it was stipulated that one of the two censors must be a plebeian.

[2] The debate on the Caudine Peace must have greatly helped to transform the senate into something more than an advisory council. See, further, F. Cassola, *I Gruppi Politici*, p. 197.

or woe, both the senate and the nobility were to play roles of consequence in the days to come.[1] In the Third War the plebeian triumph was brought to fulfilment: the Lex Hortensia was passed a bare three years after hostilities ceased.

It was the Samnite Wars likewise that first obliged the Romans to resort to *prorogatio imperii* with all its implications for the future constitutional development of the state;[2] just as it was in the heat and trials of the same conflicts that the Romans forged the military machine that was to humble Carthage. The campaigns against Samnium first taught the Romans how to recuperate from defeat, how to mount operations far away from home, and how to master grave logistical difficulties.[3] Assuredly, too, it was not the fortuitous stranding of a Punic warship on an Italian beach that led to Roman victory in the war at sea, but the creation of a fledgling navy almost half a century earlier to raid the territories controlled by Samnites.

Hardly less striking was the influence of the Samnites during a much later phase of the Roman story. It was Sabellian stamina and dogged determination in the Social War that forced the Romans to convert their civic commonwealth into a large geographical state and depart from their original plan to keep the surrendered Italic insurgents in lasting inferiority.

Not so immediately obvious is the precise effect which the Samnites may have had on Roman political thought and practice. If they helped Rome to be great, it is arguable that they also helped to make her arrogant. She emerged from the hard-fought struggles with them infinitely stronger, more able to impose her will and less inclined to compromise or even to consult.[4] And ultimately it was this arrogance, embodied in Sulla, that the Samnites fought until their nation perished. It may be difficult to decide to what extent it was due to their example that the Romans took note of, and became reconciled to, the notion that Roman and Italian were not incompatible terms; but it will be admitted that it was chiefly due to their exertions that the Romans were obliged, finally, to accept something resembling a

[1] G. Forni in *Athenaeum*, XXXI (1953), 228–39.

[2] Livy 8. 23. 11–12; Triumph. Fasti *ad an.* 326.

[3] It also introduced the Romans to certain Greek technological achievements. The first sundial ever to reach Rome was brought there from the south by Papirius Cursor towards the end of the Third Samnite War (Pliny, *N.H.* 7. 213; Censorinus 23. 6).

[4] It was only after the defeat of the Samnites that the Romans ceased to regard the Italians as equals and began to ride roughshod over them and to interfere with their autonomy (A. N. Sherwin-White, *Roman Citizenship*, p. 44).

federal system for Italy. If Rome ultimately emerged as the *communis patria* of all Italians, it was paradoxically due in large part to the recalcitrance of the Samnites.

The religious life of the Roman Republic was intensified during the Samnite Wars. The stresses and strains which they imposed led to the introduction into Rome of foreign gods[1] and to an outburst of temple-building.[2]

The penurious Samnites could hardly have improved Rome's economy with huge spoils, but it was during the long struggle with them that a trading class, typified perhaps by Ap. Claudius Caecus, the celebrated censor, grew up and burgeoned at Rome. And it will be remembered that the first coins ever issued by the Roman state (the *aes grave*) were a direct outcome of the Third Samnite War.

It can, of course, be argued that all of these developments would have taken place in any case and that the only contribution of the Samnites was to make them happen when they did. This in itself, however, is enough to give them relevance. For, even if it were true that the Samnites merely expedited the inevitable, the world is a vastly different place for their having come to prominence precisely when they did. Who can say what future there would have been in store for Italy, for Europe and the world, had they not accelerated the tempo of the strife between the patricians and plebeians of Rome and immeasurably increased the pace of social and economic change?

The Romans did not admit and may not have realized the importance of the Samnites in their development. They felt a hostility for them that never abated. The emperor Claudius later insisted that the true secret of successful imperialism lay in a willingness to accept the defeated.[3] But the Romans of the Republic showed a marked reluctance to make the Samnites one with themselves. They preferred to decimate, disperse and depress them, not welcoming, but overwhelming them. With other Italians they were willing to

[1] Aesculapius was imported from Greece in 292 (Livy, *Epit.* 11; Val. Max. 1. 8. 2; Auct. *de vir. ill.* 22. 1).

[2] Many Roman generals felt it necessary to invoke divine aid during the Samnite Wars. In the short space of twenty years temples were vowed, built and dedicated to Salus, Bellona, Victoria, Jupiter Victor, Jupiter Stator, Quirinus. See Livy 9. 31. 10; 10. 19. 17 f.; 10. 29. 14; 10. 33. 9; 10. 37. 15; 10. 46. 7; cf. Pliny, *N.H.* 7. 213.

[3] *Quid aliud exitio Lacedaemoniis et Atheniensibus fuit, quamquam armis pollerent, nisi quod victos pro alienigenis arcebant* (Tac. *Ann.* 11. 34).

let bygones be bygones:[1] to the Samnites they never really opened their ranks. The latter might be an Italic people—indeed they were the most Italic of all the peoples in the peninsula—but they were not fit for inclusion within the Roman pale. They were on a par with Spaniards, Numidians and Parthians.[2] Their defeat at the Colline Gate, where they had been but one element on the losing side of a civil war, was celebrated for centuries by the Romans as a triumph over external enemies rather than as the last act of an internecine conflict.

Not but that the Samnites extorted a measure of respect from their conquerors. The latter were prone to devise phrases of tolerant contempt for other Italians: *obesus Etruscus*, *parcus Umber*, *Lanuvinus ater atque dentatus*.[3] For the Samnites they reserved a sterner title: *belliger Samnis*.[4] Livy calls them stubborn, enduring and brave: even when the fortunes of war were against them they faced the Romans 'with more courage than hope' and 'only death could conquer their resolution'.[5]

It was the way of Rome, the poet said, to spare the conquered. Yet the Samnites were not spared. They were made to disappear, scattered and absorbed by the enveloping Latin flood. As a result the tongue they spoke has long been silent and their way of life has vanished almost beyond our ken.

We may regret the defeat of the last champions of local liberties in Italy, or we may approve the suppression of an obstinate and dangerous regionalism; and no doubt it must be conceded that independence for them meant nuisance for their neighbours. Yet admiration for human courage and constancy abides, and nowhere is it more eloquently expressed than in the words of the most patriotic of Rome's historians: 'They shrank not from war and so far were they from wearying of even an unsuccessful defence of their freedom that they preferred to be conquered rather than make not the effort to win.'[6]

[1] *Romulus... docuit etiam hostibus recipiendis augeri hanc civitatem oportere* (Cic. *pro Balbo*, 13. 31; cf. Livy 7. 24. 4).

[2] See Tac. *Ann.* 15. 13; Eutrop. 10. 17. 2; Rutil. Namat. 1. 125 f.; cf. Velleius 2. 27. 6; *CIL*, 1, p. 333.

[3] Catullus 39. 11–12; cf. Verg. *Aen.* 11. 732–40; Diod. 5. 40. 3; Dion. Hal. 2. 38. 3.

[4] Sil. Ital. 10. 314.

[5] Livy 7. 33. 12 f.; 10. 14. 8; 10. 31. 12.

[6] *Bello non abstinebant: adeo ne infeliciter quidem defensae libertatis taedebat et vinci quam non temptare victoriam malebant* (10. 31. 14).

BIBLIOGRAPHY

The following bibliography does not claim to be exhaustive. It mentions only works of a specialized nature that were found to be particularly useful by the author of this book. Books and articles of a general kind or that can fairly claim to be well-known or standard works are not included. Moreover, the notes in the text allude to many publications not listed here.

ADCOCK, F. E. *Cambridge Ancient History*, VII (1928), 581–616.

—— 'Consular tribunes and their successors', *Journal of Roman Studies*, XLVII (1957), 9–14.

AFZELIUS, A. *Die römische Eroberung Italiens, 340–264 v. Chr.* Copenhagen, 1942.

—— *Die römische Kriegsmacht.* Copenhagen, 1944.

ALBIZZATI, C. 'Saggio di esegesi sperimentale sulle pitture funerarie dei vasi italo-greci', *Dissertazioni della Pontificia Accademia*, ser. 2, XIV (1920), 149–220.

ALFÖLDI, A. *Early Rome and the Latins.* Ann Arbor, 1965.

ALTHEIM, F. *Terra Mater.* Giessen, 1931.

—— *A History of Roman Religion.* London, 1938.

—— *Lex Sacrata.* Amsterdam, 1940.

—— *Geschichte der lateinischen Sprache.* Frankfurt a/M., 1951.

—— 'Der Rhotazismus in den italischen Sprachen', *Studies Presented to D. M. Robinson*, II (1953), 459–68.

ALVISI, G. 'Problemi di viabilità nell'Apulia settentrionale', *Archeologia Classica*, X (1962), 148–61.

ALY, W. *Strabon von Amaseia.* Bonn, 1957.

AMBROSETTI, G. 'Testimonianze preaugustee da Sepino-Altilia', *Archeologia Classica*, X (1958), 14–20.

ARIAS, P. E. (and others). *La Ricerca Archeologica nell'Italia Meridionale.* Naples, 1960.

ARNIM, H. VON. 'Ineditum Vaticanum', *Hermes*, XXVII (1892), 118–30.

ASHBY, T. *The Roman Campagna in Classical Times.* London, 1927.

—— *Some Italian Scenes and Festivals.* London, 1929.

ASHBY, T. (with GARDNER, R.). 'The Via Traiana', *Papers of the British School at Rome*, VIII (1917), 104f.

AURIGEMMA, S. *Configurazione Stradale della Regione Sorana nell' Epoca Romana.* Perugia, 1911.

BADIAN, E. *Foreign Clientelae.* Oxford, 1958.

—— 'Waiting for Sulla', *Journal of Roman Studies*, LII (1962), 47–61.

BAILEY, C. *Cambridge Ancient History*, VIII (1930), 423–65.

BALZANO, V. *Aufidena Caracenorum.* Rome, 1923.

BALZANO, V. *Notizie degli Scavi* (1932), pp. 128–9.
BANTI, LUISA. *Il Mondo degli Etruschi.* Rome [1961 ?].
BARRECA, F. 'Il ricordo di una via antica in una epigrafe dell'Amiternino', *Bulletino del Museo della Civiltà Romana,* XVIII (1956), 15–20 (= Supp. to *Bulletino Comunale,* LXXV (1956)).
BASANOFF, V. 'Gaius Caedicius, legatus à Aquilonia', *Latomus,* IX (1950), 265–72.
BAYET, J. *Les origines de l'Hercule romain.* Paris, 1926.
—— 'Etrusques et italiques: position de quelques problèmes', *Studi Etruschi,* XXIV (1955/56), 3–17.
—— *Histoire politique et psychologique de la religion romaine.* Paris, 1957.
BEELER, M. S. 'The Relation of Latin and Osco-Umbrian', *Language,* XXVIII (1952), 435–43.
BELOCH, K. J. *Der römische Bund.* Leipzig, 1880.
—— 'Le fonti di Strabone nella descrizione della Campania', *Atti dei Lincei: Memorie,* ser. 3, X (1882), 429–48.
—— *Campanien,* 2nd ed. Breslau, 1890.
—— *Römische Geschichte bis zum Beginn der punischen Kriege.* Leipzig and Berlin, 1926.
BERNARDI, A. 'Roma e Capua nella seconda metà del quarto secolo avanti C.', *Athenaeum,* XX (1942), 86–103; XXI (1943), 21–31.
—— 'La guerra sociale e le lotte dei partiti in Roma', *Nuova Rivista Storica,* XXVIII/XXIX (1944/45), 60–99.
BIEBER, MARGARETE. *History of the Greek and Roman Theater.* Princeton, 1939.
BIENKOWSKI, P. *Les celtes dans les arts mineurs.* Cracow, 1928.
BINNEBOESSEL, P. *Untersuchungen über Quellen und Geschichte des zweiten Samniterkrieges von Caudium bis zum Frieden 405 u. c.* Diss.: Halle, 1893.
BISCARDI, A. 'La questione italica e le tribù soprannumerarie', *Parola del Passato,* VI (1951), 241–56.
BLAKE, MARION E. *Ancient Roman Construction in Italy,* vol. I. Washington, D.C., 1947.
BLUMENTHAL, A. VON. 'Volkstum und Schicksal der Samniten', *Die Welt als Geschichte,* II (1936), 12–32.
—— 'Zu einigen oskischen Götternamen', *Rheinisches Museum,* LXXXV (1936), 64–7.
BONFANTE, G. 'The origin of the Latin name-system', *Mélanges Marouzeau,* pp. 41–59.
BOTTIGLIONI, G. *Manuale dei Dialetti Italici.* Bologna, 1954.
BOURNE, F. C. Review of E. Valgiglio's *Silla e la crisi repubblicana* (Firenze, 1956) in *American Journal of Philology,* LXXIX (1958), 214–16.
BRANDENSTEIN, W. *R.E.* XX (1941), s.v. 'Picenum', cols. 1186–97.
BRUNO, BIANCA. *La Terza Guerra Sannitica.* Rome, 1906.
BRUNO, MARIA GRAZIA. 'I Sabini e la loro lingua', *Rendiconti Istituto Lombardo,* XCV (1961), 501–41; XCVI (1962), 413–42, 565–640.

BRUNT, P. A. 'Italian aims at the time of the Social War', *Journal of Roman Studies*, LV (1965), 90–110.

BÜCHNER, K. and HOFMANN, J. B. *Lateinische Literatur und Sprache in der Forschung seit 1937*. Bern, 1951.

BUCK, C. D. *Grammar of Oscan and Umbrian*². Boston, 1928.

BULST, C. R. ' "Cinnanum Tempus" ', *Historia*, XIII (1964), 307–37.

BURGER, C. P. *De Bello cum Samnitibus Secundo*. Harlem, 1884.

—— *Neue Forschungen zur ältern Geschichte Roms*, 2 vols. Amsterdam, 1894, 1895.

—— *Der Kampf zwischen Rom und Samnium*. Amsterdam, 1898.

CALABI, I. 'I commentarii di Silla come fonte storica', *Atti dei Lincei: Memorie*, ser. 8, III (1950/51), 247–302.

CAMPOREALE, G. 'La terminologia magistratuale nelle lingue osco-umbre', *Atti dell' Accademia Toscana di Scienze e Lettere* (1956), pp. 33–108.

—— 'Note sul bronzo di Agnone', *Archivio Glottologico Italiano*, XLII (1963), 161–5.

CANTER, H. V. 'Venusia and the Native Country of Horace', *Classical Journal*, XXVI (1930), 439–56.

CAPOZZI, F. C. 'The Horatian Pilgrimage and Apulia', *Classical Journal*, XXX (1935), 225–32.

CARCOPINO, J. 'Les lois agraires des Gracques et la guerre sociale', *Bulletin de l'association Guillaume Budé* (1929), pp. 3–23.

CASSOLA, F. *I Gruppi Politici Romani nel III Secolo a. C.* Trieste, 1962.

CAVUOTO, P. 'Ricerche archeologiche Caudine', *Samnium*, XXXIV (1961), 182–91.

CHANTRAINE, H. *Untersuchungen zur römischen Geschichte am Ende des zweiten Jahrhunderts v. Chr.* Kallmünz, 1959.

CIANFARANI, V. 'Touta Marouca', *Studi in Onore di A. Calderini e R. Paribeni*, III (Milano, 1956), 311–27.

—— *Guida delle Antichità di Sepino*. Milan [1958?].

CICHORIUS, C. *Römische Studien*. Leipzig–Berlin, 1922.

COLASANTI, G. *Fregellae*. Rome, 1906.

—— *I Cercatori di Ferro*. Rome, 1928.

—— *Come Livio Scrive che non Erra*. Lanciano, 1931.

COLONNA, G. 'Pallanum', *Archeologia Classica*, VII (1955), 164–78.

—— 'Sul sacerdozio Peligno di Cerere e Venere', *Archeologia Classica*, VIII (1956), 216–17.

—— 'Sul ritratto detto da Pietrabbondante', *Studi Etruschi*, XXV (1957), 567.

—— 'Saepinum', *Archeologia Classica*, XIV (1962), 80–107.

CONWAY, R. S. *The Italic Dialects*, 2 vols. Cambridge, 1897.

—— 'The K-folk, the Q-folk, and the P-folk', *Contemporary Review*, LXXVII (1900), 266–76.

—— *Cambridge Ancient History*, IV (1930), 433–68.

CONWAY, R. S. *Ancient Italy and Modern Religion.* Cambridge, 1933.

CORNELIUS, F. *Untersuchungen zur frühen römischen Geschichte.* Munich, 1940.

COSTANZI, V. 'Osservazioni sulla terza guerra sannitica', *Rivista di Filologia*, XLVII (1919), 161–215.

COUISSIN, P. *Les armes romaines.* Paris, 1926.

—— 'Guerriers et gladiateurs samnites', *Revue Archéologique*, ser. 5, XXXII (1930), 235–79.

D'AMICO, V. *La Religione e Lingua dei Sanniti nella Tavola di Bronzo di Agnone.* Campobasso, 1952.

—— 'Cercemaggiore', *Samnium*, XXX (1957), 27–36.

DEGRASSI, A. *Scritti Vari di Antichità*, 2 vols. Rome, 1962.

DELFINO, MARIA GIOVANNA. 'Il problema dei rapporti linguistici tra l'osco e il latino', *Serta Eusebiana, Miscellanea Philologica* (Istituto di filologia classica Università di Genova, 1958), pp. 27–86.

DE PETRA, G. 'Aufidena: scavi e topografia', *Archivio Storico per le Province Napoletane*, XXVI (1901), 325–42.

DETLEFSEN, D. *Die Beschreibung Italiens in der Naturalis Historia des Plinius und ihre Quellen.* Leipzig, 1901.

—— *Die Anordnung der geographischen Bücher des Plinius und ihre Quellen.* Berlin, 1909.

DEVOTO, G. Articles on 'Oschi', 'Sanniti' in *Enciclopedia Italiana* (1935–6).

—— *Gli Antichi Italici*, 2nd ed. Florence, 1951.

—— 'La romanisation de l'Italie médiane', *Cahiers d'histoire mondiale*, III (1956/7), 443–62.

—— *Scritti Minori.* Florence, 1958.

—— 'Per la storia delle regioni d'Italia', *Rivista Storica Italiana*, LXXII (1960), 221–33.

DIHLE, A. 'Zum s.c. de Bacchanalibus', *Hermes*, XC (1962), 376–9.

DOMASZEWSKI, A. VON. 'Bellum Marsicum', *S.B. Akad. Wiss. Wien* (Philol.-hist. Kl.), CCI (1924).

DUCATI, P. *L'Italia Antica.* Milan [1936?].

DUDLEY, D. R. 'Blossius of Cumae', *Journal of Roman Studies*, XXXI (1941), 94–9.

DUHN, F. VON. *Italische Gräberkunde*, vol. I. Heidelberg, 1924.

DURANTE, M. 'Osco Hirpo: "Lupo" o "Capro"?', *Parola del Passato*, XIII (1958), 412–17.

EISENHUT, W. *R.E.* XV A (1955), s.v. 'Picenum', cols. 911–23.

EVANS, E. C. *The Cults of the Sabine Territory.* Rome, 1939.

FISCHER, T. *La Penisola Italiana.* Naples, Rome, Milan, 1902.

FOGOLARI, G. 'Bronzetti etruschi e italici nei musei italiani e stranieri', *Studi Etruschi*, XXI (1950/51), 343–400; XXII (1952/53), 287–304; XXIII (1954), 383–96.

FORNI, G. 'Manio Curio Dentato uomo democratico', *Athenaeum*, XXXI (1953), 170–240.

FOWLER, W. WARDE. *The Religious Experience of the Roman People*. London, 1911.

FRACCARO, P. *Opuscula*, 3 vols. Pavia, 1956–7.

FRANK, T. *Economic History of Rome*². London, 1927.

—— *Roman Imperialism*. New York, 1929.

—— *Cambridge Ancient History*, VIII (1930), 326–87.

—— 'On Suetonius' Life of Terence', *American Journal of Philology*, LIV (1933), 268–73.

—— *Economic Survey of Ancient Rome*, 5 vols. Baltimore, 1933–40.

FRASSINETTI, P. *Fabula Atellana*. Pavia, 1959.

FREDERIKSEN, M. W. 'Republican Capua: a Social and Economic Study', *Papers of British School at Rome*, XIV (1959), 80–130.

FRIEDLANDER, J. *Die oskischen Münzen*. Leipzig, 1850.

FRITZ, K. VON. '"Leges Sacratae" and "plebei scita"', *Studies Presented to D. M. Robinson*, II (1953), 893–905.

—— *The Theory of the Mixed Constitution in Antiquity*. New York, 1954.

GABBA, E. 'Ricerche sull'esercito professionale romano da Mario a Silla', *Athenaeum*, XXIX (1951), 171–272.

—— 'Le origini della guerra sociale', *Athenaeum*, XXXII (1954), 41–114; 293–345.

—— *Appiano e la Storia delle Guerre Civili*. Florence, 1956.

—— 'M. Livio Druso e le riforme di Silla', *Annali della Scuola Normale Superiore di Pisa*, ser. 2, XXXIII (1964), 1–15.

GAGÉ, J. 'Pyrrhus et l'influence religieuse de Dodone dans l'Italie primitive', *Revue de l'histoire des religions*, CXLV (1954), 137–67; CXLVI (1954), 18–50; 129–39; CXLVII (1955), 1–31.

GARDNER, R. 'The Siege of Praeneste', *Journal of Philology*, XXXV (1919), 1 f.

—— *Cambridge Ancient History*, IX (1932), 185–200.

GARDNER, R. (with ASHBY, T.). 'The Via Traiana', *Papers of the British School at Rome*, VIII (1917), 104 f.

GAROFALO, F. P. 'Sui "meddices"', *Rendiconti dei Lincei*, ser. 5, XII (1903), 61–79.

GARZETTI, A. 'Appio Claudio Cieco nella storia politica del suo tempo', *Athenaeum*, XXV (1947), 175–224.

GELZER, M. *Kleine Schriften*, 3 vols. Wiesbaden, 1962–4.

GIACOMELLI, G. 'Forme parallele a *sancio* e *sanctus* nei dialetti italici', *Studi Etruschi*, XXIV (1955/56), 337–42.

GIANNELLI, G. and MAZZARINO, S. *Trattato di Storia Romana*, vol. I. Rome, 1953.

GIESECKE, W. *Italia Numismatica*. Leipzig, 1928.

GIGLIOLI, G. Q. 'Bronzetti italici ed etruschi di arte popolare', *Archeologia Classica*, IV (1952), 174–95.

GÖHLER, J. *Rom und Italien*. Breslau, 1939.

GOIDANICH, P. G. 'I rapporti culturali e linguistici tra Roma e gli Italici', *Historia*, v (1931), 535–54.

GRENIER, A. 'La transhumance des troupeaux en Italie et son rôle dans l'histoire romaine', *Mélanges d'archéologie et d'histoire*, XXV (1905), 293–328.

HALLWARD, B. L. *Cambridge Ancient History*, VIII (1930), 25–115.

HANELL, F. 'Zur Problematik der älteren römischen Geschichtsschreibung', *Histoire et historiens dans l'antiquité* (= Entretiens sur l'antiquité classique: vol. IV), 149–84. Geneva, 1956.

HATZFELD, J. *Les trafiquants italiens dans l'orient hellénique*. Paris, 1919.

HAUG, I. 'Der römische Bundesgenossenkrieg, 91–88 v. Chr. bei Titus Livius', *Würzburger Jahrbücher für die Altertumswissenschaft* (1947), pp. 100–39, 201–58.

HERBIG, R. 'Die italische Wurzel der römischen Bildniskunst', *Das neue Bild der Antike*, II (1942), 85–99.

HERMANSEN, G. *Studien über den italischen und den römischen Mars*. Copenhagen, 1940.

HEURGON, J. *Capoue préromaine*. Paris, 1942.

—— *Etude sur les inscriptions osques de Capoue dites Iúvilas*. Paris, 1942.

—— 'D'Apollon Sminthius à P. Decius Mus', *Nouvelle Clio*, III (1951), 105–9.

—— 'Trois études sur le "ver sacrum"', *Latomus*, XXVI (1957), 5–51.

HOFMANN, A. VON. *Das Land Italien und seine Geschichte*. Berlin and Stuttgart, 1921.

HOFMANN, J. B. 'Altitalische Sprachdenkmäler', *Bursians Jahresberichte über die Fortschritte der klassischen Altertums-Wissenschaft*, CCLXX (1940), 1–122.

HOFMANN, M. *R.E.* XVIII (1942), s.v. 'Paeligni', cols. 2227–71.

HOLLAND, L. A. 'The purpose of the Warrior Image from Capestrano', *American Journal of Archaeology*, LX (1956), 243–7.

HUNRATH, G. *Die Quellen Strabos im sechsten Buche*. Diss.: Marburg, 1879.

JACOBELLI, M. 'Dov'era la "Cominium" distrutta nel 293 av. C. dai Romani?', *Bullettino della Commissione Archeologica Comunale di Roma*, LXXI (1943/45), Appendice 9–19.

JOHNSON, A. C.; COLEMAN-NORTON, P. R.; BOURNE, F. C. *Ancient Roman Statutes* (Austin, 1961).

JUNG, J. *Grundriss der Geographie von Italien*[2]. Munich, 1897.

KAERST, J. 'Kritische Untersuchungen zur Geschichte des zweiten Samniter Krieges', *Jahrbücher für classische Philologie*, Supplementband XIII (1884), 725–69.

KAISER, B. *Untersuchungen zur Geschichte der Samniten*, vol. I (all publ.). Programm, Pforta, 1907.

KAJANTO, I. *The Latin Cognomina*. Helsinki, 1965.

KLOTZ, A. 'Diodors römische Annalen', *Rheinisches Museum*, LXXXVI (1937), 206–24.

KLOTZ, A. 'Livius' Darstellung des zweiten Samniterkrieges', *Mnemosyne*, ser. 3, VI (1938), 83–102.

—— *Livius und seine Vorgänger*. Amsterdam, 1964.

KORNEMANN, E. 'Polis und Urbs', *Klio*, V (1905), 72–92.

—— Articles on 'Oppidum', 'Pagus' in Pauly–Wissowa–Kroll, *Real-encyclopädie der Altertums-Wissenschaft*.

KRAHE, H. 'Zum oskischen Dialekt von Bantia', *Glotta*, XIX (1931), 148–50.

—— 'Zwei Flussnamen aus dem alten Italien', *Indogermanische Forschungen*, LX (1949/52), 292–301.

KROMAYER, J. 'Die wirtschaftliche Entwicklung Italiens in II. and I. Jahrhundert vor Chr.', *Neue Jahrbücher für das klassische Altertum*, XXIII/XXIV (1914), 145–69.

LAKE, AGNES K.: *see under* MICHELS.

LARSEN, J. A. O. *Representative Government in Greek and Roman History*. Univ. of California, 1955.

LATTE, K. 'Zwei Exkurse zum römischen Staatsrecht', *Göttinger Gelehrte Nachrichten* (Fachgruppe Altertumswissenschaft), I (1934), 59–77.

—— *Römische Religionsgeschichte*. Munich, 1961.

LE BONNIEC, H. *Le culte de Cérès à Rome*. Paris, 1958.

LEJEUNE, M. 'Vénus romaine et Vénus osque', *Hommages à Jean Bayet*. Collection Latomus, Brussels, 1964.

LÉVÈQUE, P. *Pyrrhos*. Paris, 1957.

LUDOVICO, D. *Dove Italia Nacque*. Rome, 1961.

LUGLI, G. *La Tecnica Edilizia Romana*, 2 vols. Rome, 1957.

MAGALDI, E. *Lucania Romana*, vol. I. Rome, 1947.

MAIURI, A. *Notizie degli Scavi* (1926), pp. 244–51; (1927), pp. 450–60; (1929), pp. 33–8; (1930), pp. 214–28.

—— *Passeggiate Campane*. Florence, 1957.

MARIANI, L. 'Aufidena', *Monumenti Antichi*, X (1901), 225–638 + plates VI–XV.

MARROCCO, D. *L'Antica Alife*. Piedimonte d'Alife, 1951.

MARZULLO, A. *Le Origini Italiche e lo Sviluppo Letterario delle Atellane*. Modena, 1956.

MATTINGLY, H. 'A coinage of the Revolt of Fregellae?', *Centennial Publication of the American Numismatic Society* (New York, 1958), pp. 451–7.

MAULE, Q. F. and SMITH, H. R. W. *Votive Religion at Caere: Prolegomena*. California, 1959.

MCDONALD, A. H. 'The history of Rome and Italy in the Second Century B.C.', *Cambridge Historical Journal*, VI (1939), 124–46.

—— 'Rome and the Italian Confederation (200–186 B.C.)', *Journal of Roman Studies*, XXXIV (1944), 11–33.

MEYER, E. *Kleine Schriften*, 2 vols. Halle, 1924.

MEYER, H. D. 'Die Organisation der Italiker im Bundesgenossenkrieg', *Historia*, VII (1958), 74–9.

MICHELS, AGNES K. 'The archaeological evidence for the "Tuscan Temple"', *Memoirs of American Academy in Rome*, XII (1935), 89–150.

—— 'Early Roman religion 1945–1952', *Classical Weekly*, XLVIII (1955), 25–35, 41–5.

MILONE, F. *L'Italia nell'Economia delle Sue Regioni.* Turin, 1955.

MINGAZZINI, P. *Corpus Vasorum Antiquorum*: Italia, fasc. XI: Museo Campano. Vol. I (1935).

MIRONE, S. 'La statue d'Athéna en terre cuite de Rocca d'Aspromonte', *Aréthuse*, I (1923/24), 141–50 + plates XXII, XXIII.

MOMIGLIANO, A. 'Sul "dies natalis" del santuario federale di Diana sull'Aventino', *Rend. Accad. Lincei*, ser. 8, XVII (1962), 387–92.

—— 'An interim report on the origins of Rome', *Journal of Roman Studies*, LIII (1963), 95–121.

MOMMSEN, T. *Die unteritalischen Dialekte.* Leipzig, 1850.

—— 'Die italischen Regionen', *Gesammelte Schriften*, V (1908), 268–85.

—— 'Die römische Tribuseintheilung nach den marsischen Krieg', *Gesammelte Schriften*, V (1908), 262–7.

—— 'Über die Unteritalien betreffenden Abschnitte der ravennatischen Kosmographie', *Gesammelte Schriften*, V (1908), 286–319.

MÜNZER, F. *Beiträge zur Quellenkritik der Naturgeschichte des Plinius.* Berlin, 1897.

—— *Römische Adelsparteien und Adelsfamilien.* Stuttgart, 1920.

—— Articles on Roman *gentes* in Pauly–Wissowa–Kroll, *Realencyclopädie der Altertumswissenschaft.*

—— 'Atticus als Geschichtschreiber', *Hermes*, XL (1905), 50–100.

MUSTILLI, D. *Il Museo Mussolini.* Rome, 1939.

NAPOLI, M. A. 'Testa di divinità sannitica da Triflisco', *Parola del Passato*, XI (1956), 386–91.

NEAPOLIS (Naples). Articles in *Parola del Passato*, VII (1952), 241–369.

NICCOLINI, G. 'Le "leges sacratae"', *Historia*, II (1928), 1–19.

—— 'Le leggi "de civitate romana" durante la guerra sociale', *Rendiconti dei Lincei*, ser. 8, I (1946), 110–24.

NICOL, J. *The Historical and Geographical Sources used by Silius Italicus.* Oxford, 1936.

NOCK, A. D. 'A feature of Roman religion', *Harvard Theol. Rev.* XXXII (1939), 83–96.

—— 'The Cult of Heroes', *Harv. Theol. Rev.* XXXVII (1944), 141–74.

—— 'Hellenistic mysteries and Christian sacraments', *Mnemosyne*, ser. 4, V (1952), 177–213.

—— Rev. of J. Leipoldt and S. Morenz' *Heilige Schriften* in *Gnomon*, XXVI (1954), 420–3.

OGILVIE, R. M. 'Livy, Licinius Macer and the "Libri Lintei"', *Journal of Roman Studies*, XLVIII (1958), 40–6.

ONORATO, G. O. 'La sistemazione stradale del quartiere del foro triangolare di Pompei', *Rend. Accad. Lincei*, ser. 8, VI (1951), 250–64.

—— 'L'iscrizione osco-greca di Atena Lucana', *Rendiconti della Accad. Napoletana*, N.S., XXVIII (1953), 335–45.

—— *La Ricerca Archeologica in Irpinia*. Avellino, 1960.

PAGANI, A. 'Le monete della Guerra Sociale', *Rivista Italiana di Numismatica*, ser. 4, IV (1944–7), 9–34.

PAGNANI, A. *Sentinum*. Sassoferrato, 1954.

PAIS, E. 'Gli elementi italioti, sannitici e campani nella più antica civiltà romana', *Memorie dell'Accademia di Archeologia, Lettere e Belle Arti di Napoli*, XXI (1900), 3–55.

—— 'La persistenza delle stirpi sannitiche nell'età romana', *Atti della reale Accademia di Napoli*, N.S., VI (1918), 417–58.

—— *Storia Critica di Roma*, 4 vols. Rome, 1921.

—— *Storia dell'Italia Antica*. Rome, 1925.

PALLOTTINO, M. *Etruscologia*[3]. Milan, 1955.

—— 'Le origini storiche dei popoli italici', *Relazioni del Congresso Internazionale di Scienze Storiche in Roma* (1955).

—— *The Etruscans*. Harmondsworth, 1955.

PARLANGELI, O. *Storia Linguistica e Storia Politica nell'Italia Meridionale*. Florence, 1960.

PASSERINI, A. 'Sulle trattative dei Romani con Pirro', *Athenaeum*, XXI (1943), 92–112.

PERGOLA, A. and R. *Irpinia: Piccola Guida della Provincia di Avellino*. Avellino, 1932.

PERL, G. *Diodors römische Jahrzählung*. Berlin, 1957.

PETERSEN, H. 'The numeral "Praenomina" of the Romans', *Transactions of American Philological Association*, XCIII (1962), 347–54.

PETERSON, R. M. *The Cults of Campania*. Rome, 1919.

PETROCCIA, D. 'Origini e rovine di Aequum Tuticum', *Samnium*, XXXV (1962) and succeeding numbers.

PHILIPP, H. *R.E.* I A (1920), s.v. 'Samnites', cols. 2138–58; I A (1920), s.v. 'Sabini', cols. 1570–84; XII (1925), s.v. 'Larinum', col. 839.

PICARD, G. C. 'Chronique de la sculpture romaine', *Rev. Etudes Latines*, XXXVII (1960), 253–4.

PISANI, V. *Le Lingue dell'Italia Antica oltre il Latino*. Turin, 1953.

—— 'Zur lateinischen Wortgeschichte', *Rhein. Mus.* C (1958), 105–6.

PLANTA, R. VON. *Grammatik der oskisch-umbrischen Dialekte*, 2 vols. Strassburg, 1892, 1897.

POLIGNANO, M. 'A proposito dell'incorporazione di Capua nello stato romano', *Rendiconti dei Lincei*, ser. 8, I (1946), 330–41.

POULTNEY, J. W. 'Observations on the Italic dialects and Latin', *Classical World*, LII (1958), 33–7.

—— *The Bronze Tables of Iguvium*. Amer. Philol. Assn., 1959.

Pugliese-Carratelli, G. 'Sul segno indicante F nelle epigrafi osche in alfabeto greco', *Parola del Passato*, xv (1960), 60.

Puglisi, S. *La Civiltà Appenninica*. Firenze, 1959.

Pulgram, E. *The Tongues of Italy*. Harvard University Press, 1958.

Radke, G. *R.E.* viii A (1958), s.v. 'Vestini', cols. 1779–88.

Reitler, R. 'Ein frühitalisches Portrait eines tonsurierten Mannes', *Museum Helveticum*, xvii (1960), 106–10.

Ribezzo, F. *Enciclopedia Italiana*, xix (1933), s.v. 'Italici', 1053–6.

Richter, G. M. A. *Ancient Italy*. Ann Arbor, 1955.

Rix, H. 'Picentes-Picenum', *Beiträge zur Namensforschung*, ii (1951), 237–47.

—— 'Bruttii, Brundisium und das illyrische Wort für "Hirsch"', *Beiträge zur Namenforschung*, v (1954), 115–29.

—— 'Zwei Völkernamen aus den alten Italien', *Beiträge zur Namenforschung*, vi (1955), 14–26.

Robson, D. O. 'The Samnites in the Po Valley', *Classical Journal*, xxix (1933/4), 599–608.

—— 'The nationality of the poet Caecilius Statius', *Amer. Journ. Philol.* lix (1938), 301–8.

Romanelli, P. *Enciclopedia Italiana*, s.v. 'Sannio' (1936), 740–1.

Romano, D. *Atellana Fabula*. Palermo, 1953.

Rose, H. J. 'The Cult of Volkanus at Rome', *Journal of Roman Studies*, xxiii (1933), 46–63.

—— 'The Oath of Philippus and the Di Indigetes', *Harvard Theol. Review*, xxx (1937), 165–81.

Rosenberg, A. *Der Staat der alten Italiker*. Berlin, 1913.

Rotili, M. *L'Arte nel Sannio*. Benevento, 1952.

Rudolph, H. *Stadt und Staat im romischen Italien*. Leipzig, 1935.

Ruggiero, M. *Scavi di Antichità nelle Province di Terraferma dal 1743 al 1876*. Naples, 1888.

Säflund, G. 'Ancient Latin cities of the hills and plains', *Opuscula Archaeologica*, i (1934), 64–86.

Sartori, F. *Problemi di Storia Costituzionale Italiota*. Rome, 1953.

—— 'Libertà italiota e civitas romana', *Rivista Storica Italiana*, lxxii (1960), 5–19.

Scerrato, U. 'Bronzetto bifronte del museo di Lucera', *Archeologia Classica*, vii (1955), 192–4 + plate lxxix.

Schilling, R. *La religion romaine de Venus*. Paris, 1954.

Schmitz, P. *Die Agrarlandschaft der italischen Halbinsel*. Berlin, 1938.

Schönbauer, E. *Anzeiger oesterr. Akad. der Wissenschaften*, no. 10 (1955).

Schulten, A. 'Die Landgemeinden im römischen Reich', *Philologus*, liii (1894), 629–86.

—— 'Italische Namen und Stämme', *Klio*, ii (1902), 167–93, 440–65; and iii (1903), 235–67.

Schulze, W. *Zur Geschichte lateinischer Eigennamen*. Berlin, 1904.

Schur, W. 'Fremder Adel im römischen Staat der Samniterkriege', *Hermes*, LIX (1924), 450–73.
—— 'Das Zeitalter des Marius und Sulla', *Klio*, Beiheft XLVI (1942).
Schwyzer, E. 'Zur Bronze von Agnone', *Rhein. Museum*, LXXXIV (1935), 97–119.
Sestieri, P. C. *Illust. London News* for 22 Sept. 1956, p. 464.
—— 'Tombe dipinte di Paestum', *Riv. dell'Istituto Nazionale d'Archeologia e Storia dell'Arte*, N.S., V/VI (1956/7).
Sherwin-White, A. N. *The Roman Citizenship*. Oxford, 1939.
Siena, E. 'La politica democratica di Quinto Publilio Filone', *Studi Romani*, IV (1956), 509–22.
Sirago, V. 'Lucanus an Apulus?', *L'Antiquité Classique*, XXVII (1958), 13–30.
Sogliano, A. 'Sanniti ed Oschi', *Rend. dei Lincei*, ser. 5, XXI (1912), 206–16.
—— *Enc. Italiana*, V (1930), 379, s.v. 'Aurunci'.
Solari, A. 'La espansione sannita in Silvium Apula e in Nola Campana', *Rend. dei Lincei*, ser. 8, V (1950), 371–5.
Son, D. W. L. van. *Livius' Behandeling van de Bacchanalia*. Amsterdam, 1960.
Sonnenschein, E. A. '"Sabellus": Sabine or Samnite?', *Class. Rev.* XI (1897), 339–40.
—— 'The Nationality of Horace', *Class. Rev.* XII (1898), 305.
Sordi, M. *I Rapporti Romano-Ceriti e l'Origine della Civitas sine Suffragio*. Rome, 1960.
Spaeth, J. W. *Causes of Rome's Wars, 343–265 B.C.* Diss.: Princeton, 1926.
Stazio, A. 'L'apporto della monete ad un problema di archeologia: il santuario di Mefiti nella valle d'Ansanto', *Annali di Numismatica*, I (1954), 25–38.
—— 'Un ripostiglio monetale da Cales e la monetazione campano-sannitica de IV. secolo A.C.', *Parola del Passato*, XV (1960), 225–8.
Steinbrück, O. *Die Quellen des Strabo im fünften Buche seiner Erdbeschreibung*. Diss.: Halle, 1909.
Strong, Eugénie. *Cambridge Ancient History*, IX (1932), 803–29.
—— 'Terra Mater or Italia?', *Journal of Roman Studies*, XXVII (1937), 114–26.
Suolahti, J. *The Junior Officers of the Roman Army*. Helsinki, 1955.
—— *The Roman Censors*. Helsinki, 1963.
Täubler, E. 'Die umbrisch-sabellischen und die römischen Tribus', *S.B. der Heidelberger Akad. der Wissenschaften* (Phil.-Hist. Kl.), 1929/30, no. 4.
Taylor, Lily Ross. *The Voting Districts of the Roman Republic*. Rome, 1960.
Thomsen, R. 'Das Jahr 91 v. Chr. und seine Voraussetzungen', *Classica et Mediaevalia*, V (1942/3), 13–47.
—— *The Italic Regions*. Copenhagen, 1947.
—— *Early Roman Coinage*, 3 vols. Copenhagen, 1957–61.

Tibiletti, G. 'Il possesso dell' "Ager Publicus"', *Athenaeum*, XXVI (1948), 173–236 and XXVII (1949), 3–41.

—— 'La politica delle colonie e città latine nella Guerra Sociale', *Rendiconti Istituto Lombardo*, XXXVI (1953), 45–63.

Toynbee, A. J. 'Economic and Social Consequences of the Hannibalic War', *Bulletin of the John Rylands Library*, XXXVII (1954/55), 271–87.

—— *Hannibal's Legacy*, 2 vols. Oxford, 1965.

Trendall, A. D. *Paestan Pottery*. Brit. Sch. at Rome, 1936.

Verrecchia, G. 'Le Tre Guerre Sannitiche narrate da Tito Livio', *Samnium*, XXV–XXIX (1952–6).

—— 'Pagine non chiare di Tito Livio nelle Guerre Sannitiche', *Samnium*, XXX–XXXII (1957–9).

—— 'Isernia Etrusca', *Samnium*, XXXIII (1960), 35–97.

Vetter, E. *R.E.* XVIII (1942), s.v. 'Osci', cols. 1543–67.

—— *Handbuch der italischen Dialekte*, I. Heidelberg, 1953.

—— 'Pentri Samnites', *Beiträge zur Namenforschung*, VI (1955), 243–4.

Veyne, P. 'La Table des Ligures Baebiani et l'institution alimentaire de Trajan', *Mélanges d'archéologie et d'histoire*, LXIX (1957), 81–135.

Walker, D. S. *A Geography of Italy*. London, 1958.

Ward-Perkins, J. B. 'Etruscan & Roman Roads in S. Etruria', *Journal of Roman Studies*, XLVII (1957), 139–43.

—— *Landscape and History in Central Italy*. Myres Memorial Lecture, Oxford, 1964.

Weege, F. 'Abruzzenkunst', *Mitt. des deut. arch. Inst.: Röm. Abteilung*, XXIII (1908), 26–32.

—— 'Oskische Grabmalerei', *J.B. des deutschen arch. Inst.* XXIV (1909), 99–141.

—— 'Bewaffnung und Tracht der Osker', *J.B. des deutschen arch. Inst.* XXIV (1909), 141–62 + plates VII–XII.

Weinstock, S. *R.E.* XV (1931), s.v. 'Meddix'.

—— 'Zur oskischen Magistratur', *Klio*, XXIV (1931), 235–46.

—— 'Victor and Invictus', *Harvard Theological Review*, L (1957), 211–47.

Whatmough, J. *Classical Quarterly*, XVI (1922), 185 f.

—— *Language*, III (1927), 106 f.

—— 'The calendar in ancient Italy outside Rome' in *Harv. Stud. in Class. Phil.* XLII (1931), 157–79.

—— *The Foundations of Roman Italy*. London, 1937.

Wikén, E. *Die Kunde der Hellenen von dem Lande und den Völkern der Apenninen-Halbinsel bis 300 v. Chr.* (Lund, 1937).

Wissowa, G. *Religion und Kultus der Römer*^{2}. Munich, 1923.

Wuilleumier, P. *Tarente*. Paris, 1939.

Zancan, P. *Floro e Livio*. Padua, 1942.

Zazo, A. 'Gli antichi sepolcreti Saticulani e Caudini in una relazione del XVIII secolo', *Samnium*, VII (1934), 231–48.

1. Venafrum and the Valley of the Volturnus (see p. 16).

2. The Country of the Pentri: Bovianum (*Boiano*) with its three citadels (see pp. 237, 272, 367 and cf. Appian, *Bellum Civile* 1. 51. 225).

3. The Country of the Caudini: the celebrated Caudine Forks (see p. 226 and Map 3).

(*a*) Aerial photograph of the defile.

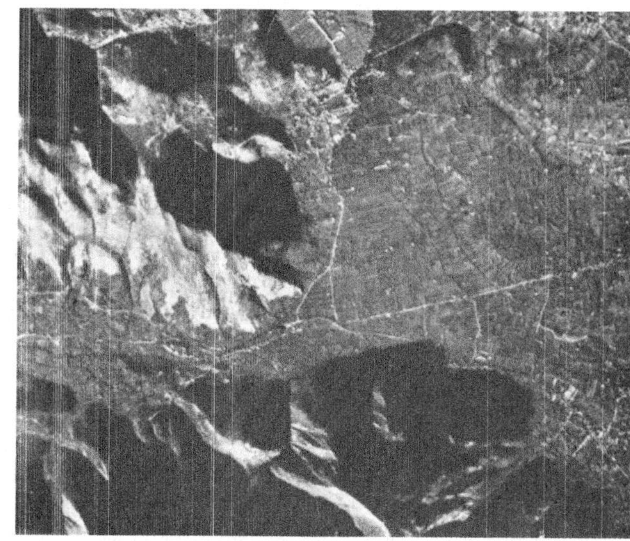

•) The forks proper: the *ıltus artior* at the eastern ıd.

(*a*)

(*b*)

4. The Country of the Hirpini. (*a*) Agricultural country near Aeclanum (see p. 66)
(*b*) The *vallis Amsanctus* (see p. 150).

5. (*a*) Saepinum (*Terravecchia*): Samnite polygonal masonry (see p. 133).

(*b*) Saepinum (*Terravecchia*): the south-western postern gate (see p. 135).

7. (*a*) Pietrabbondante: the south *parodos* of the theatre (see p. 139).

(*b*) Pietrabbondante: *podium* of large temple (see. p. 137) with theatre in the background.

(*a*)

(*b*)

8. (*a*) Pietrabbondante: Campanian-type *podium* of small temple (see p. 137).
(*b*) Aesernia (*Isernia*): Latin-type *podium* of temple (see p. 137).

9. (*a*) Terracotta head from Triflisco (see p. 127).

(*b*) Limestone head from Pietrabbondante (see p. 129).

10. (*a*) Bronze head, probably from San Giovanni Lipioni near Trivento (see p. 130).

(*b*) Fresco of a mounted warrior, formerly at Capua (see p. 142).

11. (*a*) Bronze statuette of a Samnite warrior (see p. 130).

(*b*) Bronze statuette of Hercules (see pp. 132, 170, 181). This specimen, probably from Venafrum, is unusual in that the head is bare. Note the crudely scratched Oscan inscription.

12. (*a*). The tablet from Agnone, back (see pp. 157–64).

(*b*) The tablet from Agnone, front. (For the right to left writing see p. 117.)

INDEX

Roman names are listed by *gentilicium*, except when they are those of authors: in such cases they are listed by the names most familiar to English readers. (Cicero, for example, is not listed under Tullii.)

INDEX

INDEX

Made in the USA
Coppell, TX
28 December 2021